CASSEROLES

Favorite Recipes of Home Economic Teachers

Too good to be forgotten...

2,000 Favorite Recipes

CASSEROLES

Favorite Recipes of Home Economic Teachers

Copyright © 2009 by

(|||) Favorite Recipes® Press

an imprint of

FRP.INC

a wholly owned subsidiary of Southwestern/Great American, Inc.
P.O. Box 305142
Nashville, Tennessee 37230
1-800-358-0560

ISBN: 978-0-87197-842-4

Cover and chapter opener design by Rikki Ogden Campbell/pixiedesign, llc

Printed in the United States of America

Other books in this series:

DESSERTS

MEATS

SALADS

VEGETABLES

Originally published in 1965. This book has gone through numerous revisions throughout the years and this printing is taken from the last known edition.

TABLE OF CONTENTS

Abbreviations, Measuring, Substitutions 4

Cooking Terms and Definitions 5

It's A Matter Of Measurement 6

Each Ingredient To Its Own Measurement 7

Calorie Chart 9

An Introduction To Carefree Cookery 12

Containing A Casserole 13

Making A Main Dish Casserole 15

Guides To Meat Care 16

Ground Beef 17

Main Dish Freezer Fare 18

Meat Casseroles 19

Ground Beef and Hamburger Favorites 39

Poultry Casseroles 59

Combination Meat Casseroles 87

Variety Meat Casseroles 97

Seafood Casseroles 113

Meat-Vegetable Casseroles 151

Vegetable Casseroles 185

Skillet Meals 217

Cereal, Pasta, Egg and Cheese Dishes 235

Convenience Casseroles 269

Casseroles With A Foreign Flavor 299

Breads 325

Quick Breads 333

Yeast Breads 353

Breads From Foreign Lands 367

Index 379

Abbreviations Used In This Book

Cup	c.	Medium	med.
Tablespoon	T.	Large	lge.
Teaspoon	t.	Package	pkg.
Pound	lb.	Quart	qt.
Ounce	oz.	Dozen	doz.
Gallon	gal.	Pint	pt.
Small	sm.	Square	sq.

In Measuring, Remember . . .

3 t.	=	1 T.	4 c.	=	1 qt.
2 T.	=	⅛ c.	2 pt.	=	1 qt.
4 T.	=	¼ c.	½ c. + 2 T.	=	⅝ c.
5 T. + 1 t.	=	⅓ c.	¾ c. + 2 T.	=	⅞ c.
8 T.	=	½ c.	1 oz.	=	2 T. fat or liquid
10 T. + 2 t.	=	⅔ c.	4 oz.	=	½ c.
12 T.	=	¾ c.	8 oz.	=	1 c.
16 T.	=	1 c.	16 oz.	=	1 lb.
2 c.	=	1 pt.			

Substitutions

1 T. cornstarch (for thickening) = 2 T. flour (about)

1 c. sifted all-purpose flour = 1 c. plus 2 T. sifted cake flour

1 c. sifted cake flour = 1 c. minus 2 T. sifted all-purpose flour

1 t. baking powder = ¼ t. baking soda plus ½ t. cream of tartar

1 c. bottled milk = ½ c. evaporated milk plus ½ c. water

1 c. sour milk = 1 c. sweet milk into which 1 T. vinegar or lemon juice has been stirred; or 1 c. buttermilk

1 c. sweet milk = 1 c. sour milk or buttermilk plus ½ t. baking soda

1 c. sour, heavy cream = ⅓ c. butter and ⅔ c. milk in any sour milk recipe

1 c. sour, thin cream = 3 T. butter and ¾ c. milk in sour milk recipe

1 c. molasses = 1 c. honey

1 c. honey = ¾ c. sugar plus ¼ c. liquid

1 c. canned tomatoes = about ⅓ c. cut up fresh tomatoes, simmered 10 minutes

¾ c. cracker crumbs = 1 c. bread crumbs

Cooking Terms And Definitions

Bake	To cook foods in the oven.
Baste	To brush or pour water, melted fat or other liquid over food.
Beat	To make a mixture smooth or to introduce air by using a brisk, regular motion that lifts the mixture over and over.
Beat Lightly	To beat lightly with a fork to mix. This process usually applies to just mixing the whites and or yolks of eggs.
Bind	To hold foods together with a sauce.
Blanch	To parboil in water for a minute, or to pour boiling water over food and then drain it almost immediately.
Blend	To thoroughly mix two or more ingredients.
Boil	To cook in boiling water.
Bread	To roll in crumbs. Often the food is dipped first into beaten egg and then rolled in the crumbs.
Brush	To brush food with melted fat or liquid to coat it.
Chop	To cut into pieces with a sharp knife.
Cream	To work one or more foods until mixture is soft and creamy or fluffy.
Cube	To cut into small equal squares.
Dice	To cut into cubes.
Disjoint	To cut poultry into pieces at the joints.
Dissolve	To completely mix dry ingredients with liquid until in solution.
Dot	To scatter small pieces of butter or other fat over food before cooking.
Dust	To sprinkle food lightly with a dry ingredient such as paprika.
Fillet	To cut a piece of meat or fish into desired shape, removing all bones.
Flake	To break into small pieces with a fork.
Fold	To combine by using two motions, cutting vertically through the mixture and turning over and over by sliding the implement across the bottom of the mixing bowl with each turn.
Garnish	To decorate foods, usually with other foods.
Grate	To cut food into minute particles by rubbing on a grater.
Grind	To cut food into tiny particles by running through a grinder.
Julienne	To cut foods into match-thin strips.
Knead	To fold, turn and press down on dough with the hands until it becomes smooth and elastic.
Mince	To cut or chop into very small pieces.
Mix	To combine ingredients in any way that evenly distributes them.
Parboil	To partially cook food in boiling water before completely cooking in another way.
Pare	To cut off the outside covering.
Peel	To strip off the outside covering.
Scald	To heat milk to just below the boiling point.
Scallop	To bake food in layers with a sauce.
Shred	To cut finely with a knife or sharp instrument.
Sift	To put dry ingredients through a sifter or sieve.
Sliver	To slice into long, thin strips.
Stew	To cook long and slow in a liquid.
Stir	To mix foods with a circular motion for the purpose of blending or securing uniform consistency.
Tear	To break or tear into bite-size pieces.
Whip	To beat rapidly to produce expansion due to the incorporation of air as applied to cream, egg and gelatin dishes.

It's A Matter Of Measurement

No matter if the cook is a beginner or one with long experience, neither wants a failure when she prepares a dish. In many cases, "flops" can be avoided by taking just a little time to follow these simple rules of cooking.

READ THE RECIPE

Make sure that you understand every step of the recipe. Look up any unfamiliar terms. Check to see if you have all of the needed ingredients.

GATHER INGREDIENTS

Save precious time and energy by assembling all of the ingredients that you will need before you start cooking. Saves steps back and forth across the kitchen.

ROUND UP UTENSILS

Whether it be measuring spoons, spatula or mixing bowl — cooking is easier and more fun if everything is handy and within reach.

MEASURE METICULOUSLY

Measure all ingredients carefully and as accurately as possible. Only the most experienced cook who has tried a recipe many times is able to use the "pinch of this and speck of that" method successfully.

FOLLOW DIRECTIONS

A recipe is your guide to a perfect finished product. Follow it step by step.

MEASURING MUSTS

Always use standardized measuring cups and spoons. Never use coffee cups, glasses or serving spoons for measuring. Unless the recipe states otherwise, all measurements should be level.

MEASURING CUPS

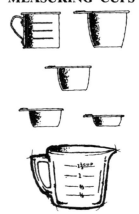

There are two kinds of measuring cups — dry and liquid. Dry measuring cups are made straight across the top so that ingredients can be "leveled off" with the straight edge of a spatula or knife. These measuring cups may be purchased in a set of graduated sizes which includes ¼-cup, ⅓-cup, ½-cup and 1-cup measures.

Liquid measuring cups are usually glass or clear plastic. They have a rim that extends above the top measurement mark. This rim prevents liquids from spilling while being measured. Liquid measuring cups also have an extended lip which makes pouring easier. They can usually be found in 1-cup, 2-cup and 1-quart sizes.

MEASURING SPOONS

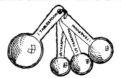

They come in sets with ¼-teaspoon, ½-teaspoon, 1-teaspoon and 1-tablespoon sizes. They are used when a recipe calls for less than ¼ cup of any ingredient.

Each Ingredient To Its Own Measurement

All ingredients are not measured alike. Follow these suggestions for perfect measurements every time.

WHITE GRANULATED SUGAR

It needs sifting only if it has lumps. Lift sugar lightly into a dry measuring cup and level off with the straight edge of a spatula or knife.

CONFECTIONER'S SUGAR

It's best to always sift before measuring. Stubborn lumps that won't sift out may be removed by pressing through a sieve. Unless the recipe calls for packed confectioner's sugar, it should be spooned lightly into a dry measuring cup and leveled off.

BROWN SUGAR

If it is lumpy, sift before measuring. Big lumps may be removed by crushing with a rolling pin. Unless the recipe specifies otherwise, brown sugar should be firmly packed into a measuring cup and leveled off. If it is packed firmly, sugar will "hold its shape" when turned out.

FLOUR

Handle flour gently. Sift before measuring, but do not sift directly into the measuring cup. Instead, lift lightly with a spoon and place in cup. Do not shake or pack down. Fill the cup to overflowing and then gently level off.

SPICES, SALT, BAKING POWDER, ETC.

Dip measuring spoon down into the container holding the ingredients; level off.

SOLID SHORTENING

Firmly pack room temperature shortening into a dry measuring cup. Level off. If less than ¼ cup is needed, pack into measuring spoon in same manner. Remove with rubber spatula.

WATER REPLACEMENT METHOD

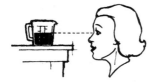

Solid shortening may also be measured by this method. Use a liquid measuring cup. Subtract the amount of shortening the recipe calls for from 1 cup. Put that amount of water in the cup. For example. If you need ¼ cup shortening, fill a cup with water up to the ¾ cup level. Then add the solid shortening until the water reaches the 1-cup mark. Be sure the shortening is completely covered with water. Drain off the water and remove the fat.

BUTTER OR MARGARINE

Measure as for solid shortening. If stick margarine or butter is used, measurement may be made by the following estimates:

¼ stick = 2 T.
½ stick = 4 T. or ¼ c.
1 stick = ¼ lb. or ½ c.
4 sticks = 1 lb. or 2 c.

MELTED FAT

Measure before or after the fat is melted — it doesn't matter because the amount will be the same. Fat is easier to measure after it has been melted, however. Measure salad oil just as you would any other liquid.

MOLASSES

Measure in a graduated dry measuring cup. The molasses will "round up" so it must be leveled off with the straight edge of a spatula or knife. Remove from cup with a spatula.

MILK OR WATER

Use a liquid measuring cup. Place the cup on a level surface. Slowly pour the liquid into the cup while bending so the measuring line will be at eye level.

GRATED CHEESE

If a recipe calls for ½ lb. cheese, grated, weigh or estimate the weight of the cheese and then grate it. Pack loosely into a measuring cup until level with the top.

Calorie Chart

MILK, CREAM, CHEESE AND RELATED PRODUCTS

	Amount	Calories
Milk, cow's:		
Fluid, whole	1 c.	165
Fluid, nonfat (skim)	1 c.	90
Buttermilk, cultured, from skim milk	1 c.	90
Evaporated, unsweetened, undiluted	1 c.	345
Condensed, sweetened, undiluted	1 c.	985
Dry, whole	1 c.	515
Dry, nonfat	1 c.	290
Cream:		
Half and half (milk and cream)	1 c.	330
Light, table or coffee	1 c.	525
Whipping, unwhipped (volume whipped):		
Medium	1 c.	745
	1 T.	45
Heavy	1 c.	860
	1 T.	55
Cheese:		
Blue mold (Roquefort type)	1 oz.	105
Cheddar or American:		
Ungrated	1 in. cube	70
Grated	1 c.	455
Cheddar, process	1 oz.	105
Cheese foods, Cheddar	1 oz.	95
Cottage cheese, from skim milk:		
Creamed	1 c.	240
Uncreamed	1 c.	195
Cream cheese	1 T.	55
Swiss	1 oz.	105

EGGS

	Amount	Calories
Large, 24 ounces per dozen		
Raw, whole, without shell	1 egg	80
White of egg, raw	1 white	15
Yolk of egg, raw	1 yolk	60
Boiled, shell removed	2 eggs	160

MEAT, POULTRY, FISH, SHELLFISH AND RELATED PRODUCTS

	Amount	Calories
Bacon, broiled or fried crisp	2 slices	95
Beef and vegetable stew	½ c.	90
Beef pot pie, baked, 4½ in. diameter	1 pie	460
Chicken, cooked:		
Breast, fried	½ breast	215
Thigh and drumstick, fried		245
Canned, boneless	3 oz.	170
Corned beef, canned	3 oz.	180
Dried beef, chipped	2 oz.	115
Crab meat, canned or cooked	3 oz.	90
Clams, canned, solids and liquids	3 oz.	45
Ham, smoked, cooked, lean and fat	3 oz.	290
Heart, beef, trimmed of fat, braised	3 oz.	160
Hamburger pattie:		
Regular ground beef	3 oz.	245
Lean ground round	3 oz.	185
Meat Loaf	2 oz.	115
Luncheon meat, cooked ham, sliced	2 oz.	170
Oysters, meat only, raw 13-19 med. selects	1 c.	160
Oyster stew, 1 part oysters to 3 parts milk: 3-4 oysters	1 c.	200
Salmon, pink, canned	3 oz.	120
Shrimp, canned, meat only	3 oz.	110
Tuna, canned in oil, drained, solids	3 oz.	120

(Continued on Next Page)

Calorie Chart

MATURE DRY BEANS AND PEAS, NUTS AND RELATED PRODUCTS

	Amount	Calories
Almonds, shelled	1 c.	850
Beans, dry:		
Red	1 c.	230
White with tomato or molasses	1 c.	330
Limas, cooked	1 c.	260
Cowpeas or blackeye peas, dry, cooked	1 c.	190
Peanuts, roasted, shelled, chopped	1 T.	50
Peas, split, dry, cooked	1 c.	290
Pecans:		
Halves	1 c.	740
Chopped	1 T.	50
Walnuts, shelled:		
Black or native, chopped	1 c.	790
English or Persian, chopped	1 T.	50

VEGETABLES AND VEGETABLE PRODUCTS

	Amount	Calories
Asparagus:		
Cooked, cut spears	1 c.	35
Canned spears, medium, green or bleached	6 spears	20
Beans:		
Limas, immature, cooked	1 c.	150
Snap, green cooked	1 c.	25
Beets, cooked, diced	1 c.	70
Broccoli spears, cooked	1 c.	45
Brussels sprouts, cooked	1 c.	60
Cabbage, cooked	1 c.	40
Carrots, cooked, diced	1 c.	45
Cauliflower, cooked, flowerbuds	1 c.	30
Corn, sweet, canned, solids and liquids	1 c.	170
Cowpeas, cooked, immature seeds	1 c.	150
Mushrooms, canned, solids and liquids	1 c.	30
Onions, mature cooked	1 c.	80
Parsnips, cooked	1 c.	95
Peas, green, cooked	1 c.	110
Canned, solids and liquids	1 c.	170
Potatoes, medium, about 3 per pound		
Boiled:		
Peeled before boiling	1 potato	90
Peeled after boiling	1 potato	105
Mashed:		
Milk added	1 c.	145
Milk and butter added	1 c.	230
Spinach, cooked	1 c.	45
Squash:		
Summer, diced, cooked	1 c.	35
Winter, baked, mashed	1 c.	95
Sweet potatoes:		
Boiled, peeled after boiling	1 potato	170
Canned	1 c.	235
Tomatoes, canned or cooked	1 c.	45
Tomato catsup	1 T.	15

GRAIN PRODUCTS

	Amount	Calories
Biscuits, baking powder with enriched flour	1 biscuit, 2½ in. dia.	130
Breads:		
Boston brown bread, made with degermed cornmeal	1 slice (3x¾ in.)	100
French or Vienna Bread	1 loaf	1,315
Italian Bread	1 loaf	1,250

(Continued on Next Page)

Calorie Chart

	Amount	Calories
Raisin bread	1 slice	60
Rye bread	1 slice	55
Pumpernickel, 1 pound	1 loaf	1,115
White bread, enriched	1 slice	60
Whole wheat, 20 slices per loaf	1 slice	55
Breadcrumbs, dry, grated	1 c.	345
Cornflakes, plain	1 oz.	110
Corn meal, white or yellow, dry:		
Whole ground	1 c.	420
Degermed, enriched	1 c.	525
Corn muffins, made with enriched meal	1 muffin, 2¾ in. dia.	155
Doughnuts, cake type	1 doughnut	135
Macaroni:		
Enriched, cooked 8-10 minutes	1 c.	190
Cooked until tender	1 c.	155
Macaroni and cheese, baked	1 c.	475
Muffins, with enriched white flour	1 muffin, 2¾ in. dia.	135
Noodles (egg noodles), cooked	1 c.	200
Oatmeal or rolled oats, cooked	1 c.	150
Pancakes, 4-in. diameter	1 cake	60
Buckwheat (pancake mix)	1 cake	45
Rice, cooked:		
Parboiled	1 c.	205
White	1 c.	200
Rolls		
Plain, 12 per pound	1 roll	115
Hard, round; 12 per 22 ounces	1 roll	160
Sweet, pan; 12 per 18 ounces	1 roll	135
Spaghetti, cooked until tender	1 c.	155
Spaghetti, with meat sauce	1 c.	285
Spaghetti in tomato sauce with cheese	1 c.	210
Waffles, ½ x 4½ x 5½ in.	1 waffle	240
Wheat flour:		
Whole wheat	1 c.	400
All purpose	1 c.	400
Self rising	1 c.	385

FATS AND OILS

	Amount	Calories
Butter	1 c.	1,605
	1 T.	100
Lard	1 T.	135
Vegetable fats	1 T.	110
Margarine	1 c.	1,615
	1 T.	100

MISCELLANEOUS ITEMS

	Amount	Calories
Soups, canned, ready to serve		
Bean	1 c.	190
Beef	1 c.	100
Bouillon, broth, consomme	1 c.	10
Chicken	1 c.	75
Cream soup (asparagus, celery, mushroom)	1 c.	200
Noodle, rice, barley	1 c.	115
Tomato	1 c.	90
Vegetable	1 c.	80
Vinegar	1 T.	2
White sauce, medium	1 c.	430
Yeast:		
Baker's compressed	1 oz.	25
Baker's dry active	1 oz.	80

An Introduction To Carefree Cookery

The day of the casserole is here. No longer is the casserole confined to a hurried, last-minute family meal. The casserole, in any of its many decorative serving dishes, now graces the most formal table.

Casserole cookery goes farther back into history than most people realize. The first method of cooking was probably nothing more complicated than burying meat in live coals. As man became more civilized over the centuries, he invented woven reed baskets in which to cook his food.

The first one-dish meal was probably prepared by cooking meat and wild vegetables or roots together in a skin or reed basket. The American Indians of the Southwest still make waterproof baskets of this kind.

Later the hunter's spoils were tossed into a big pot on the fire to simmer into edibility. The word "casserole" means "little pot."

The French pot au-feu is traditional. It bubbles constantly on the back of the French homemaker's stove and is made with all sorts of leftovers, pieces of meat, odd vegetables and sauce. Now practically every country has developed its own casserole recipes, some of which have achieved national or regional renown.

Casseroles probably came into being because a thrifty cook couldn't bear to throw away a bone with pieces of meat still clinging to it or a lone vegetable.

The virtues of the casserole are many. Some require long hours of cooking but require little attention during the process. Many can be made one day, refrigerated or frozen and served later.

A casserole cooking in the kitchen makes it easier for the homemaker to plan and prepare her meals. A mix-in-one-bowl main dish can be stirred up in the greased casserole in which it is to be cooked. This saves an extra bowl to wash.

Serving is easier too, for most casseroles can be mixed, baked and served in the same dish. The worry of being a hostess is gone, too, for the food stays hot, looks and tastes appetizing as it should.

Containing A Casserole

Glazed pottery, earthenware, glass, metal . . . take your pick. All can be used for casseroles. Many of these casserole containers come in bright colors and pleasing designs to contrast or complement your kitchen decor or tableware. The variety and selection is almost unlimited.

The type of container you use really makes very little difference, as long as it is heatproof. Some of the earliest casseroles were made of earthenware and were glazed inside. They had covers and were similar to those that are still used today in France.

Certain baking dishes are essential, however, for a basic casserole wardrobe. Casseroles range from the large size for crowds to individual serving sizes.

Shallow rectangular glass baking dishes are the backbone of casserole cookery. Following closely behind are covered baking dishes. Some of the common sizes in shallow rectangular baking dishes are 1½-,2-, and 3-quart sizes. They can also be found with dividers in the middle for baking a main dish and vegetable at the same time. Select family-sized ones or larger ones for company meals.

Covered baking dishes are most often round, but can be found in rectangular. oval and square shapes. The most common are the 1-,1½-, and 2-quart capacities. These baking dishes have handles and come in attractive colors and designs.

Perhaps the most feminine and graceful among the casserole containers is the shallow round baking dish with its aluminum, stainless steel or silver plated holder. The main dish can be cooked in the glass dish, wisked out of the oven and placed in its serving rack.

Souffle dishes are especially designed to help your souffle climb to magnificent heights. A souffle dish has straight sides. Ramekins are good for serving individual casseroles.

Individual casseroles add a personal touch to a meal. If you are in doubt about how much an individual casserole will hold, simply fill it with water and then measure the water. If, for example, your individual casseroles will hold 1 cup of water each, a recipe which calls for a 1-quart casserole will fill four 1-cup individuals.

Skillets come in a wide variety of materials, sizes and shapes. Some are of cast iron and are especially good for dishes that call for top-of-the-stove cooking and then a transfer to the oven for final cooking. You'll find porcelain enameled cast iron skillets in bright colors, too.

The new ceramic skillets can go directly from oven to freezer and back to the oven. These skillets have detachable handles so they can go directly to the table from the oven.

Another skillet that looks as at home on the table as it does on the range is the china skillet. Most of these skillets match ovenproof dinnerware.

If you like to cook as you eat, the electric skillet is for you. As long as you have a convenient electric outlet, the electric skillet can fill a multitude of purposes such as serving as a chafing dish.

A Little Care . . .

is all that most baking dishes require to keep them lasting, new looking and serviceable through the years.

ALUMINUM	Wash with soap and water. Scour to remove any stubborn spots. Dry thoroughly.
CHROME	Wash with soap and water. Polish to a soft luster with a dry soft cloth.
ENAMEL	Treat the same way as glassware.
GLASS	Glass made especially for cooking needs little attention except for washing in warm, soapy water. Use scouring pads or a fine cleansing powder for removing any stubborn spots.
IRON	Do not scour if possible, but wash in warm soapy water. Dry thoroughly to prevent rusting.
STEEL	Scour lightly to remove spots and wash with soap and water. Dry thoroughly.

Casserole baking dishes will last indefinitely if they are treated with proper care. Breakable materials, except the new ceramic containers, should never be taken from a hot oven and placed on a damp spot. The sudden change in temperature will cause them to break.

Other things to avoid are placing an empty casserole dish on heat or putting cold ingredients into a hot casserole. Never pick up a hot casserole with a wet cloth. It might break and the damp cloth will cause steam which will burn your hand.

Making A Main Dish Masterpiece

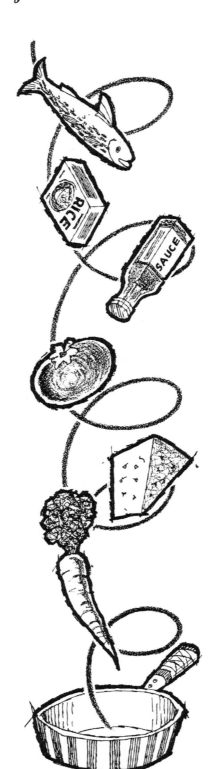

BEGIN WITH:

CHEESE

POULTRY

SEAFOOD

MEAT

COMBINE WITH:

VEGETABLES

RICE

ROLLED OATS

EGGS

BIND WITH:

EGGS

SAUCE

CRUMBS

SOUP

GELATIN

GRAVY

FINISH WITH:

BISCUITS

CRUMBS

PASTRY

BEGIN WITH:

NOODLES

MACARONI

RICE

SPAGHETTI

BEANS

CORN MEAL

COMBINE WITH:

CHEESE

MEAT

SOUR CREAM

SAUCES

VEGETABLES

SOUPS

BIND WITH:

SOUP

EGGS

GELATIN

CRUMBS

SAUCE

GRAVY

Meaty Main Dishes

When a casserole that contains meat is served, the nutritional value of the meal is increased. Meats and vegetables that are combined to make a delicious main dish need only a salad, bread and beverage to make a complete nourishing meal. If a pastry crust is added to the casserole, or if a crisp crusty pastry shell is filled with casserole mixture, additional food value is added and bread may be omitted from the meal.

Meat is a relatively expensive item in the food budget. The homemaker must recognize the need to buy meat wisely, care for it properly and prepare it to retain the nutrients and develop the flavor.

Guides To Meat Care

FRESH MEAT

Place fresh meat in the coldest part of the refrigerator or in the meat compartment. The temperature should be as low as possible without actually freezing the meat.

Unless meat is to be used on the same day it is purchased, it should be removed from the market wrapping paper and stored unwrapped or loosely wrapped in waxed paper or aluminum foil.

If fresh meat is to be kept for three or more days, it should be frozen. To freeze fresh meat, wrap it in special freezing wrap or bags but not in ordinary waxed paper. To insure easy separation before thawing, separate individual cuts or meat such as chops, steaks and ground patties. Two pieces of freezer paper make a satisfactory separation. Wrap together the desired number of servings into larger packages.

Remember that fresh meat that is frozen for longer storage should be frozen and stored at 0 degrees F. or lower. The frozen food storage or ice cube section of most household refrigerators is not designed for rapid freezing and will not substitute for a home freezer when the meat is to be frozen and stored for longer than one week.

PROCESSED MEAT

Store cured and ready-to-serve meats in the coldest part of the refrigerator. Store in the original wrapper. Keep ready-to-serve meats no longer than one week. Keep cured meats not longer than one to two weeks (hams, picnics, loin).

It is not advisable to freeze cured meats and ready-to-serve meats because the salt in the meat favors the development of rancidity when the meat is frozen. The texture of some cured meats, such as frankfurters, is affected by freezing. When freezing is absolutely necessary, wrap properly and limit the storage time to not more than sixty days.

Canned hams should not be frozen. Store unopened in the refrigerator until ready to use.

FROZEN MEAT

Meats which have been properly wrapped and promptly frozen under recommended freezing conditions should be stored at 0 degrees F. or lower for periods not to exceed those in the following table:

Meat	Maximum Storage Time*
	Months
Beef	6 to 12
Lamb and Veal	6 to 9
Fresh Pork	3 to 6
Ground Beef and Lamb	3 to 4
Ground Pork	1 to 3

*This range in maximum storage time reflects differences in recommendations of various authorities using meat from different sources.

COOKED MEAT

Cooked meat should be chilled rapidly, then covered and stored in the coldest part of the refrigerator.

Ground Beef Or Hamburger

is an all-time American favorite. It can be prepared in various ways for numerous delicious dishes. Ground beef becomes extra special when combined with other ingredients to become a flavorful casserole fit for a king.

The appeal for ground beef is based upon the fact that it is relatively inexpensive, nutritious and almost everyone likes the flavor.

Buying Ground Beef

Ground beef should be bright red in color. Never buy ground beef that is not freshly ground. Ground beef can be purchased in two styles—regular ground and lean ground. Both styles are ground twice but contain different amounts of fat. Regular ground beef should not contain more than 25 per cent fat and is likely to be less expensive than lean ground which should contain not more than 12 per cent fat.

Ground beef or hamburger can be purchased pre-packaged. However, some homemakers prefer to buy beef and have it ground to their order. For more economical, flavorful, juicier ground beef, buy boned chuck and then have it ground. If you buy round, be sure to have two ounces suet ground with each pound round. Ground beef becomes more compact the more grinding it gets. This is fine for meat balls, loaves, etc. For ground beef that is to be used for juicy tender patties, have it coarsely ground only once.

Usually one pound of ground beef will make four good servings. When extenders such as rice, spaghetti or vegetables are to be added, a pound of ground beef may yield five servings. A meat loaf made with two pounds of hamburger will probably serve four people for two meals.

Storing Ground Beef

If you plan to use ground beef the day you purchase it or on the following day, wrap the meat loosely in waxed paper and refrigerate immediately. Be sure to use within two days.

If the meat is to be used within a week, shape it into patties and stack them between squares of waxed paper. Wrap tightly in double thickness of waxed paper or foil. Store in freezer compartment or ice cube compartment of refrigerator. Be sure to use within one week.

If the ground beef is to be frozen for a longer period of time, wrap patties in freezer wrapping material and store in home freezer. Be sure to use within two or three months.

The Lowly Leftover . . .

can be transformed into a delectable mouth-watering casserole with just a little imagination.

Gravies or sauces add flavor to left-over meat dishes. All busy homemakers know the value of canned creamed soups which are convenient and add zest to most casseroles.

Cheese sprinkled over the top of almost any casserole adds color and nutritional value when the cheese seasons the dish but does not dominate it.

Hot cereals and pastes—cooked rice, spaghetti, noodles or macroni—are economical extenders and make leftovers go further. Use equal amounts of ground, slivered or diced meat with these starchy extenders to stretch your casserole. Perk up the flavors of these combinations with plenty of seasonings.

Speaking of seasonings . . . it's great fun to experiment with different seasonings. Parsley, mashed garlic, chili sauce, mustard, tomato paste, meat sauce or lemon juice . . . all give a delightful, different flavor.

Almost any cooked left-over vegetable can be successfully combined with left-over meats to make an excellent casserole.

One word of warning in making casseroles of leftovers. Never make too large a leftover dish. Nothing is so monotonous as eating a left-over leftover for several consecutive meals.

Main-Dish Freezer Fare

Casserole cookery can mean carefree cookery when the dish can be used for more than one meal.

When preparing a casserole, make additional batches to freeze. Then, when there isn't time to plan a meal or when unexpected guests appear, simply take the casserole from the freezer and pop it into the oven.

Freezing casseroles also means economy. Take advantage of less expensive vegetables when they are at the peak of their season and meats while they are most plentiful. Buy large amounts for casserole mixtures and then freeze in family- or guest-size portions.

For successful freezer casseroles, follow these general rules.

Casserole mixtures that are to be frozen are better if they are under-salted or under-seasoned. Some flavors tend to fade while others become stronger. It's better to add more seasonings later if necessary.

Never overcook foods that are to be frozen. Foods will finish cooking while being heated.

Cool casserole mixtures quickly before packaging. Place the pan of cooked food in a container of ice and water. Cool to room temperature. Immediately transfer food to freezer containers and freeze. Or, if you prefer, pour hot mixture into foil-lined ice cube trays and chill until firm. Remove package and wrap properly. Transfer to freezer to complete freezing.

Label each container with the contents and the date it was put into the freezer. Store at 0° F. Always use frozen cooked foods within one to two months.

Don't refreeze cooked thawed foods.

Heat frozen dishes without thawing. Empty contents into a shallow casserole or pan. Heat in double boiler over hot water or in a moderate oven. Stir gently to avoid breaking up foods. Allow a little extra time for heating.

Do's and Don'ts For Casserole Freezing

DO cook enough seasoned stew meat for several stews. Freeze. Add different vegetables later for other stews, meat pies, etc.

DO roast a large turkey because it usually costs less per pound than a small one. Remove large portions of meat from the breast. Freeze white and dark meat together or separately for casseroles. Use within one or two months.

DO avoid freezing a large recipe of casserole mixture until you try freezing a small amount. Some flavors tend to change during freezing.

DO freeze left-over stuffing and left-over gravy in separate packages rather than with the cooked poultry.

DON'T freeze spaghetti, macaroni or noodle mixtures. These tend to lose texture and become too soft when reheated. Freeze the meat sauce to be heated when needed. Cook spaghetti or noodles while sauce is heating.

DON'T freeze potatoes. Green pepper may change the flavor in frozen casseroles. Clove, garlic and pepper flavors get stronger when they are frozen while sage, onion and salt get milder or fade out.

DON'T put hot foods in waxed cartons.

DON'T freeze boiled or fried poultry or meats. They lose their crispness and dry out if heated long enough to crisp.

DON'T freeze cooked egg white. It becomes tough.

DON'T refreeze thawed meats and poultry. Use thawed meat or poultry within 24 hours. Don't refreeze unless absolutely necessary. If refreezing is necessary, use the meat or poultry as soon as possible.

Meat Casseroles

BAKED LASAGNA

1 lb. ground round steak
1 med. onion, cooked
½ lb. lasagna noodles, cooked
1 lb. Velveeta cheese, sliced
6 T. Parmesan cheese
1 No. 2½ can tomatoes
Butter

Brown meat and onions. Place a layer of noodles in a greased 8 x 12-inch pan. Cover with meat; add a layer of cheeses and tomatoes. Repeat layers. Dot with butter; sprinkle with additional grated cheese. Bake at 350°F. for 45 minutes. Yield: 10 servings.

Frances M. Watson, Lake H.S.
Millbury, Ohio

BEEF STROGANOFF CASSEROLE

1 lb. round steak, cubed
1 lge. onion, cut in rings
Salt and pepper
1 can mushroom soup
1 c. sour cream
1 8-oz. pkg. macaroni, cooked
Olives (opt.)
Green pepper (opt.)

Brown meat and onions; add seasonings and green pepper if desired. Add mushroom soup; simmer for 10 minutes. Remove from heat; mix in sour cream and sliced olives if desired. Combine meat mixture with macaroni; bake in a greased casserole for 45 minutes at 350°F.

Mrs. Constance Cebulla, Staples H. S.
Staples, Minnesota

BRAND NEW MEAT BALL CASSEROLE

2 lb. ground chuck
1 t. salt
¼ t. pepper
½ c. onion, chopped
⅓ c. stuffed olives, chopped
2 eggs, slightly beaten
¼ c. butter
2 T. flour
½ c. water
1 t. lemon juice
½ t. Worcestershire sauce
¼ t. paprika
½ t. salt
1 c. sour cream
1 T. chopped parsley

Mix together beef, salt, pepper, onion, olives and eggs; shape into 24 meat balls. Melt butter; brown meat balls and place in shallow casserole. Pour off excess fat reserving 2 tablespoons; blend in flour. Add water, lemon juice, Worcestershire sauce, paprika and salt; cook until thickened. Remove from heat; blend in sour cream. Pour over meat balls; bake 10-15 minutes at 350°F. Garnish with chopped parsley. Yield: 8 servings.

Mrs. Melba D. Stoffers, Hermiston Sr. H.S.
Hermiston, Oregon

MEAL-IN-ONE CASSEROLE

1 lb. round steak, cut ¼-inch thick
1 t. salt
1 t. paprika
2½ T. flour
2 T. fat
1½ onion, sliced
3 potatoes, thinly sliced
1 c. canned tomatoes
½ t. sugar
1 t. salt
1 T. catsup

Cut steak into 4 pieces. Combine salt, paprika and flour in a paper bag; dust meat in mixture. Brown meat in hot fat. Put meat in casserole; arrange onions and potatoes over meat. Stir remaining ingredients together; pour over casserole. Bake covered at 350°F. for 1 hour and 30 minutes. If casserole becomes dry, add a small amount of water or red wine. Yield: 4 servings.

Mrs. Sandra Williams, Spanger Jr. H.S.
Wilmington, Delaware

MY ORIGINAL BEEF-MACARONI CASSEROLE

2 T. butter
1 med. onion, diced
1 stalk of celery, chopped
2 c. cooked beef, cubed
1 c. macaroni, cooked
1 can tomato soup
2 T. cheese, grated
½-1 t. salt

Cook onion and celery in melted butter for 5 minutes; add beef and brown. Add macaroni, tomato soup and salt to taste. Top with cheese; heat thoroughly at 350°F. Yield: 4 servings.

Mrs. Nadine Elder, Union H.S.
Warsaw, Ohio

SPICY BAKED STEAK

¼ c. flour
1 t. salt
¼ t. pepper
3 T. shortening
2 lbs. round steak, ½-inch thick
1 c. catsup
½ c. water
1 med. onion, sliced
1 lemon, thinly sliced
1 green pepper, sliced
5 whole cloves

Combine flour, salt and pepper; pound into steak. Melt shortening in skillet and brown steak. Place steak in baking dish. Blend catsup with water; pour over steak. Add remaining ingredients. Cover and bake 1 hour at 350°F. on lower oven shelf. Yield: 6 servings.

Dorothy E. Brevoort, Former State Supervisor,
Home Economics, New Jersey Department
Education
Beach Haven, New Jersey

ROUND STEAK HOT DISH

1½ lb. round steak, cubed
1 lge. onion, diced
½ c. celery, diced
½ c. instant rice
1 can chicken and rice soup
1 can cream of mushroom soup
1 4-oz. can whole mushrooms (opt.)
1 soup can water

Brown steak, onion and celery in small amount of fat. Pour into 2-quart casserole. Add rice, soups, mushrooms and water. Blend ingredients; bake at 350°F. for 1 hour to 1 hour and 30 minutes. Yield: 6 servings.

This recipe submitted by the following teachers:
Valerie Vinje, Page H.S.
Page, North Dakota
Mrs. Mildred Anderson, East Sr. H.S.
Moorhead, Minnesota

ROUND STEAK CASSEROLE

1½ lb. round steak, cut ½-inch pieces
3 T. butter or margarine
1 med. onion, chopped
6 sm. potatoes, sliced
3 carrots, sliced (opt.)
Salt and pepper to taste
Dash of garlic salt
2 c. beef bouillon

Brown steak in butter; remove from pan. Saute onion in drippings until lightly browned. In a shallow baking dish layer half of meat, onion, potatoes and carrots. Season with salt, pepper and garlic salt. Repeat layers. Pour bouillon over all. Bake covered at 300°F. for 2 hours. Add more bouillon if necessary. Yield: 4-6 servings.

Mrs. Doris Gruber, Walsh H.S.
Walsh, Colorado

STEAK-RICE CASSEROLE

2 lbs. flank steak
2 T. salad oil
1 clove garlic, minced
1 sm. lemon, thinly sliced
4 whole cloves
2 beef bouillon cubes
1 c. water
2⅔ c. instant rice
½ c. stuffed olives
2 lge. peeled tomatoes, thickly sliced

Score steak in diamonds; brown on both sides in oil in a Dutch oven. Add garlic, lemon slices, cloves, bouillon cubes and water. Cover and simmer 1-2 hours. Strain liquid; add water to make 3 cups. Bring to a boil and stir in rice. Cover and remove from heat; let stand 13 minutes. Pour into a 3-quart casserole. Toss with olives. Tuck steak into rice; top with tomato slices. Cover and refrigerate. Bake 45 minutes at 350°F.; season to taste. Yield: 6 servings.

Mrs. Mary Weaver, Schwenksville Union
Schwenksville, Pennsylvania

STEAK CASSEROLE

1 lb. ground steak
2 T. butter
½ t. salt
1½ c. celery, chopped
⅓ c. rice
1 c. tomato soup

Brown steak in butter; add remaining ingredients. Pour into baking dish; bake at 350°F. for 2 hours.

June Houchins, Tuslaw H.S.
Massillon, Ohio

SURPRISE CASSEROLE

1 2-lb. sirloin tip or round steak, cubed
2 T. onion, minced
1 c. butter or margarine
1 3-oz. can whole mushrooms
1 bay leaf
1 t. Worcestershire sauce
2 c. cooked wide noodles
½ c. evaporated milk
½ c. water
1 t. salt
¼ c. Cheddar cheese
1 c. croutons
2 T. pimento strips

Saute meat and onion in 1 tablespoon butter until lightly browned. Add liquid from mushrooms, bay leaf and Worcestershire sauce. Cover and simmer gently 30 minutes or until meat is tender. Remove bay leaf. In a greased 1½-quart casserole, combine meat with pan juice, mushrooms, noodles, remaining butter, milk, water and salt. Sprinkle with grated cheese and croutons. Bake at 325°F. for 1 hour. Garnish with pimento strips. Yield: 4-6 servings.

Dorothy G. Scothorn, Kennedy Public Schools
Kennedy, Minnesota

SWISS STEAK CASSEROLE WITH BUTTER CRUMB DUMPLINGS

2 lbs. round steak
⅓ c. flour
¼ c. shortening
1 can cream of chicken soup
1 can water
½ t. salt
⅛ t. pepper

Cut meat into 6 portions; dredge in flour. Lightly brown meat in large skillet; transfer to 2-quart baking dish. Combine in skillet soup diluted with water, salt and pepper. Heat until boiling; pour over meat in baking dish. Bake at 350°F. for 30 minutes or until meat is tender. Remove from oven; increase oven temperature to 425°F.

BUTTER CRUMB DUMPLINGS:

1 c. fine dry bread crumbs
½ c. melted butter
2 c. flour
3 t. baking powder
1 t. poultry seasoning
½ teaspoon salt
1 c. milk

(Continued on Next Page)

Mix bread crumbs and ¼ cup butter. Combine flour, baking powder, poultry seasoning and salt. Pour in milk and remaining butter; stir until dry ingredients are moistened. Mixture will not be smooth. Drop by rounded spoonsful into buttered crumbs; roll until coated with crumbs. Place on top of meat; bake 20-30 minutes. Yield: 6 servings.

Mrs. Eleanor Miller, Center H.S.
Selma, Indiana

WEEKEND CASSEROLE

1 lb. beef chuck or stewing beef, cut in chunks
½ c. Burgundy or other red dinner wine
1 can condensed consomme
¾ t. salt
⅛ t. pepper
1 med. onion, sliced
¼ c. flour
¼ c. fine dry bread crumbs

Combine beef, wine, consomme, salt, pepper and onion in casserole. Mix flour with bread crumbs; stir into casserole mixture. Cover; bake at 300°F. for 3 hours or until beef is tender. Serve over rice, noodles or mashed potatoes. Yield: 4 servings.

Mrs. Mary A. Lambert, Lemoore Union H.S.
Lemoore, California

PORK CHOP CASSEROLES

APPLE-PORK CHOP CASSEROLE

4-6 pork loin chops
1 No. 2½ can sauerkraut, undrained
2 T. brown sugar
1 med. apple, chopped

Fry pork chops until well done. Place chops in bottom of casserole dish. Spread kraut and liquid over chops. Sprinkle with brown sugar and apple cover. Bake at 350°F. for 1 hour and 30 minutes. Add ¼ cup water at a time during baking if needed. Yield: 4-6 servings.

Mrs. Beverly Boyer, North Plainfield H.S.
North Plainfield, New Jersey

BAKED PORK CHOPS

4 pork chops
1 can cream of mushroom soup
1 T. vinegar
1 T. sugar
1 c. water

Brown pork chops in small amount of fat. Combine soup, vinegar, sugar and water in a casserole dish. Top with pork chops. Cover with lid of foil. Bake at 350°F. for 1 hour. Yield: 4 servings.

Mrs. Ruth Huber, Northampton Area Sr. H.S.
Northampton, Pennsylvania

BAKED PORK CHOPS NORMANDE

4-6 loin pork chops
Dash of salt and pepper
3 lge. apples, thinly sliced
2 t. sugar
2 t. cinnamon
1 T. butter
1 lge. bay leaf
2 T. onion, grated
3 whole cloves
½ c. cider or bouillon

Trim fat from chops; season with salt and pepper. Arrange in a buttered baking dish; cover with thin slices of cored, pared apples. Sprinkle mixture with sugar, cinnamon and butter. Add remaining ingredients. Cover and bake at 400°F. for 1 hour and 30 minutes. Remove cover and cook 10-15 minutes longer. Yield: 4-6 servings.

Jane Ann Sloan, Covina H.S.
Covina, California

BAKED PORK CHOPS WITH RICE

4 pork chops
1 onion
½ t. salt
½ c. rice
1 can cream of tomato soup
1 soup can water

Brown chops. Place a slice of onion on each chop; sprinkle salt and rice over top. Pour soup and water over chops. Cover; bake 1 hour and 30 minutes at 350°F. Yield: 4 servings.

Anna Mae Strickler, H.S.
Chino, California

BREAD DRESSING AND PORK CHOPS

6 slices bread
½ c. milk
1 sm. onion, chopped
1 egg
½ t. sage
½ t. salt
Pepper
4 pork chops

Break bread into bowl; pour milk, onion, egg, sage, salt and pepper over bread and mix. Add more milk if needed to moisten bread. Brown pork chops. Place 2 chops in bottom of greased casserole; add dressing and put 2 chops on top. Add a small amount of water to grease from chops; pour over top of casserole. Bake covered, for 1 hour at 350°F. Yield: 4 servings.

Mrs. Joyce Powers, Shiocton H.S.
Shiocton, Wisconsin

BROWN RICE-PORK CHOP CASSEROLE

1 c. brown rice
2 T. butter
2 c. boiling water
2 beef bouillon cubes
4 pork chops
Salt and pepper to taste

Brown rice in butter, stirring constantly. Add bouillion cubes to boiling water; stir until dissolved. Pour over browned rice. Pour rice mixture into casserole. Bake covered at 300°F. for 20 minutes. Brown seasoned pork chops in frying pan used for rice. Place browned pork chops on top of rice; continue baking for 20 minutes. Yield: 4 servings.

Mary Jane Bertrand, Blackfoot H.S.
Blackfoot, Idaho

CHOPS AND STUFFING LOAF

4 pork chops, ½-inch thick
Salt and pepper
1½ c. bread crumbs
1 t. poultry seasoning
¾ c. unpared apples, chopped
¼ c. seedless raisins
¼ c. celery, chopped
1 c. onion, chopped

Trim fat from chops; salt and pepper chops. Combine remaining ingredients, adding just enough water to moisten. Stand chops on edge, fat side up, in center of foil. Run skewer through chops, spacing them ½-inch apart. Spoon stuffing loosely between chops. Fold foil over and seal. Bake at 450°F. for 1 hour and 30 minutes. Yield: 4 servings.

Mrs. Jeanette Bogue, Clara City Public School
Clara City, Minnesota

FAVORITE PORK CHOP CASSEROLE

6 pork chops
¾ c. rice
1 lge. onion, sliced
2 lge. tomatoes or 2 c. tomatoes, sliced
1 green pepper, cut in rings
Salt and pepper to taste
1 can beef bouillon or tomato juice
¼ t. thyme
¼ t. marjoram

Brown pork chops; place chops on top of rice in bottom of deep casserole. Add pork chop drippings. Place a thick slice of onion, tomato and green pepper ring on each chop. Salt and pepper to taste. Pour in bouillon; add thyme and marjoram. Cover and bake at 350°F. for 1 hour or until chops are tender. Yield: 6 servings.

This recipe submitted by the following teachers:
Roselyn Skarsten, Maryvale H.S.
Phoenix, Arizona

Karen Pylman, Douglas School System
Ellsworth Air Force Base, South Dakota

DEVILED PORK CHOPS

6 loin chops, ⅔-inch thick
⅓ c. flour
½ t. salt
¼ t. paprika
4 T. onion, chopped
4 T. catsup
⅓ c. boiling water

Roll chops in flour; sprinkle with salt and paprika. Place in a baking dish; add remaining ingredients. Cover and bake at 350°F. for 1 hour. Yield: 6 servings.

Hazel E. Schaad, Fulton Community H.S.
Fulton, Illinois

PORK CHOP CASSEROLE

4 pork chops
6 T. rice
1 lge. onion
2 ripe tomatoes
½ green pepper
Salt and pepper
1 can consomme
Marjoram
Thyme

Brown pork chops. Place chops on top of rice in bottom of deep casserole; add drippings. Put a thick slice of onion, tomato and ring of pepper on each chop. Salt and pepper each layer. Pour in consomme and sprinkle with marjoram and thyme. Bake at 350°F. for 1 hour. Yield: 4 servings.

This recipe submitted by the following teachers:
Mrs. Madge Shaw, Borger H.S.
Borger, Texas

Mrs. Sharon McCormack, Madelia H.S.
Madelia, Minnesota

ONE-DISH PORK CHOP DINNER

6 pork chops
1 T. shortening
Salt to taste
½ t. pepper
1 T. Worcestershire sauce
½ t. monosodium glutamate (opt.)
2 T. onion, grated
1 can condensed tomato soup
½ c. water
4 c. cooked noodles

Brown chops in hot shortening. Place noodles in greased casserole. Combine all remaining ingredients except chops; pour over noodles. Overlap chops over noodles around edge of casserole. Cover and bake for 1 hour at 350°F. Yield: 4-6 servings.

This recipe submitted by the following teachers:
Mattie Finney, Vashon H.S.
Burton, Washington

Mrs. Shirley Gulbronson, Flandreau Indian H.S.
Flandreau, South Dakota

FRUITED PORK CHOPS IN CASSEROLE

4 pork chops
2 T. shortening
1 onion, sliced
1½ c. dried prunes
2 T. lemon juice
½ t. dry mustard
1 t. Worcestershire sauce
3 whole cloves
1 t. salt
¾ c. hot water
Paprika

Brown chops in shortening; Pour off drippings. Place chops in casserole and cover with sliced onion. Arrange dried prunes around chops. Combine lemon juice, mustard, Worcestershire sauce, cloves, salt and hot water; pour over chops. Sprinkle with paprika. Cover and bake for 1 hour at 325°F. Yield: 4 servings.

Muriel W. Corliss, St. Johnsbury Jr. H.S.
St. Johnsbury, Vermont

ONION-PORK CHOP CASSEROLE

6-8 pork chops
Salt and pepper to taste
2 T. fat
¾-1 c. raw rice
1-2 cans onion soup
1-2 soup cans water

Dredge chops in seasoned flour. Brown in fat; drain excess drippings. Sprinkle rice in bottom of 2-quart casserole. Add soup, water and chops. Cover and bake at 375°F. for 45 minutes or until rice is tender. Remove cover during last 10 minutes to brown. Yield: 6-8 servings.

This recipe submitted by the following teachers:
Mrs. Roberta Null, Hosterman Jr. H.S.
Minneapolis, Minnesota
Mrs. Alice Applegate, Knoxville Sr. H.S.
Knoxville, Iowa

PORK STEAK SUPREME

4 thick pork steaks
¾ c. rice
1 yellow onion, sliced
1 bell pepper, cut in rings
1 ripe tomato or 1 No. 303 can tomatoes
4 stalks of celery, sliced
Salt and pepper to taste
2 c. tomato juice

Brown pork steaks. Leave in fry pan if it has lid or move to casserole with lid. Place 3 tablespoons rice, 1 slice of peeled onion, 1 ring of bell pepper, 1 slice of peeled tomato or 2 tablespoons canned tomato, 1 sliced stalk of celery and seasonings to taste on steaks in order listed. Gently pour in tomato juice; do not dislodge rice. Cover and bake 45 minutes at 350°F. If rice is not moist, add 1 cup hot liquid and bake 30 minutes. Yield: 4 servings.

Mrs. Betty Lou Davis, Washington Jr. H.S.
Dinuba, California

CHICKEN-PORK CHOP CASSEROLE

4 pork chops
Salt and pepper
Flour
1 can chicken noodle soup

Season pork chops with salt and pepper; roll in flour. Brown on both sides in hot fat. Place in shallow casserole so that there is only one layer. Pour undiluted soup over chops, arranging noodles on top of chops. Cover dish with aluminum foil, making a tight seal to permit steaming inside. Bake at 350°F. for 45-60 minutes or until chops are tender. Yield: 4 servings.

Sue Baylor, Georgetown H.S.
Georgetown, Indiana

HIDDEN TREASURE

6 lean pork chops
Salt and pepper
2 c. chopped onions
1 c. raw rice
1 can tomatoes
½ c. sugar

Lay chops flat in a roasting pan. Sprinkle with salt, pepper and 1 cup onion. Spread rice over chops; cover with tomatoes, remaining onion, sugar, pepper and salt. Cover tightly. Bake for 1 hour and 30 minutes at 350°F. Yield: 6 servings.

Mrs. Sally Cheney, Pioneer Jr. H.S.
Wenatchee, Washington

KRAUT A LA CHOPS

6 pork chops
3 T. flour
3 c. water
¼ c. vinegar
½ c. brown sugar
1 can sauerkraut

Fry chops until golden brown; remove chops. Pour off excess fat; make gravy by adding flour to 3 tablespoons fat in frying pan. Remove from heat; add water gradually, stirring until smooth. Cook until thickened. Add vinegar and sugar; stir in kraut. Put in casserole; top with chops. Bake at 350°F. for 45 minutes. Yield: 6 servings.

Sister Alice Veronica, Academy of Holy Angels
Minneapolis, Minnesota

PORK AND TOMATO CASSEROLE

1 lb. pork steak or chops
1 med. onion, thinly sliced
1 t. salt
¼ t. pepper
1 t. celery salt
6 T. rice
¾ c. water
1 No. 303 can tomatoes

Brown meat; pour off excess fat. Add remaining ingredients. Bake at 350°F. for 1 hour. NOTE: May be cooked on top of stove or in an electric skillet. Yield: 4-6 servings.

Mrs. Petrena Forsythe, Fredonia Sr. H.S.
Fredonia, Kansas

PORK CHOPS WITH CURRY STUFFING

3 T. fat
1¼ c. apple, chopped
⅓ c. onion, diced
½ c. celery, chopped
6 slices whole wheat bread, crumbled
⅓ c. milk
¾ t. curry powder
½ t. salt
6 1-inch pork chops
¼ c. flour
¼ t. pepper

Melt 1 tablespoon fat in frying pan; add apple, onion and celery. Cook over low heat until golden browned. Mix bread crumbs and milk; fold in cooked apple mixture. Sprinkle ½ teaspoon curry powder and ¼ teaspoon salt over mixture; toss lightly. Cut pockets in pork chops; stuff chops with mixture. Combine flour, ¼ teaspoon salt, ¼ teaspoon curry powder and pepper. Dredge chops in mixture and brown in 2 tablespoons fat. Arrange chops in a 3-quart casserole. Cover and bake 1 hour at 350°F. Yield: 6 servings.

Shelba W. Barnes, Rossville H.S.
Rossville, Indiana

PORK CHOPS WITH LEMON SLICES

4-6 pork chops
2 c. brown sugar
¼ cup catsup
4-6 slices of lemon

Place pork chops in casserole; cover with brown sugar. Pour catsup over sugar. Place lemon slices on top. Cover and bake 1 hour to 1 hour and 30 minutes at 350°F. VARIATIONS: Omit catsup and lemon slices. Add ¼ cup apple cider or orange juice. Ham can be used instead of pork chops and ground cloves can be sprinkled over ham. Yield: 4-6 servings.

Mrs. Kay Schneider, Ponus Ridge Jr. H.S.
Norwalk, Connecticut

PORK CHOP AND POTATO SCALLOP

4 pork chops
1 can cream of mushroom soup
½ c. sour cream
¼ c. water
2 T. parsley, chopped
4 c. potatoes, thinly sliced
Salt and pepper to taste

Brown chops. Blend soup, sour cream, water and parsley. In a 2-quart casserole alternate layers of potatoes sprinkled with salt and pepper and sauce. Top with chops. Cover; bake at 375°F. for 1 hour and 15 minutes. Yield: 4 servings.

Mrs. Diane Feys, Shelby Jr. H.S.
Utica, Michigan

PORK AND RICE CASSEROLE

6 pork chops or 4 pork steaks
1 med. onion, sliced
1 c. uncooked rice
1 qt. tomatoes
Salt and pepper

Arrange chops or steaks in bottom of cake pan. Sprinkle rice evenly over meat; top with onions. Pour tomatoes over rice; season. Bake at 350°F. for 1 hour. At the end of 45 minutes, lift meat to surface for browning. Yield: 4 servings.

Mrs. Jan Odmark, Charlevoix H.S.
Charlevoix, Michigan

PORK CHOP SCALLOP

6 pork chops
5 T. butter
4 med. potatoes
1 sm. onion, chopped
2 T. flour
1 t. salt
¼ t. pepper
2 c. milk
1 t. soy sauce (opt.)
½ c. sliced water chestnuts

Cook chops in 3 tablespoons butter for 15 minutes; drain. Pare and slice potatoes; cook 5 minutes and drain. Cook onion in remaining butter until tender. Blend in flour, salt and pepper. Gradually stir in milk and soy sauce; cook until smooth and thickened, stirring constantly. Alternate layers of potatoes and water chestnuts in a buttered 2-quart casserole. Pour white sauce over all. Place pork chops on top. Cover and bake at 350°F. for 25-30 minutes. Yield: 6 servings.

This recipe submitted by the following teachers:
Mrs. Eleanor Hatch, Joseph H.S.
Joseph, Oregon
Mrs. Esther H. Collin, Evergreen H.S.
Evergreen, North Carolina

PORK CHOP-VEGETABLE CASSEROLE

4 pork chops
Salt and pepper
1 T. mustard
½ c. chopped celery
¼ c. chopped onion
½ c. chopped carrots
⅓ c. uncooked rice
1 can chicken-rice soup
1 soup can hot water

Season and brown pork chops. Place browned chops in a 2-quart casserole. Spread with mustard. Add celery, onion, carrots and rice. Pour soup and water over chops. Bake at 300°F. for 1 hour. Yield: 4 servings.

Mrs. Rose Pyle, Pateros H.S.
Pateros, Washington

RICE-PORK CHOP BAKE

4 lean pork chops
Salt and pepper
1 med. onion, sliced
8 T. rice
1 No. 2 can tomatoes

Place pork chops in casserole; add salt and pepper. Slice onion and place on top of chops. Spoon rice over chops and onion; add tomatoes and additional salt and pepper. Bake, covered, at 350° F. for 1 hour or until rice is cooked and pork is done. Yield: 4 servings.

Katherine Rude, Randolph H.S.
Randolph, Minnesota

WILD RICE-PORK CHOP CASSEROLE

4 pork chops, 1-2 inch thick
1 green pepper, sliced
1 lge. onion, sliced
1 tomato, sliced
½ c. wild rice, rinsed
1 can consomme
½ c. white wine
Salt and pepper to taste

Brown pork chops; place in a baking dish. Place slices of green pepper, tomato and onion on top of pork chops. Pour 1 cup boiling water over rice; let stand 5-10 minutes. Drain and place in casserole. Combine rice, water and consomme and bring to a boil; remove from heat and add wine. Pour into casserole; cover and bake at 300°F. for 1 hour 30 minutes to 2 hours. Yield: 4 servings.

Mrs. Bernice Ratgen, Bird Island Public School
Bird Island, Minnesota

WILD RICE CASSEROLE WITH PORK CHOPS

1 c. wild rice
1 can beef consomme
1 sm. onion, finely sliced
1 can mushroom pieces
⅓ c. celery, chopped
1 can cream of mushroom soup
4 pork chops, fried

Rinse rice with water. Mix rice and beef consomme; let stand overnight. Saute onion and mushroom pieces in butter. Steam celery in saucepan until tender. Mix onion, mushrooms and celery with rice. Add mushroom soup; put mixture in casserole dish. Top with fried pork chops. Bake 1 hour at 350°F. Yield: 4 servings.

Mary M. Frank, Healy Jr. H.S.
Pierz, Minnesota

HAM CASSEROLES

BAKED HAM AND NOODLES

2 T. butter
2 T. flour
2 c. milk
4 oz. sharp cheese, grated
Salt and pepper
1 7-oz. package fine egg noodles, cooked
½ lb. cooked ham, ground

Make white sauce of butter, flour and milk; add cheese and stir until melted. Season with salt and pepper. Put a layer of noodles in bottom of greased baking dish; sprinkle with ham and cover with sauce. Repeat layers; sprinkle cheese on top. Bake at 350°F. for 25-30 minutes. Yield: 8 servings.

Bertha Keller Benthien,
Clermont Northeastern H.S.
Owensville, Ohio

BAKED HAM SALAD

3 c. diced cooked ham
1 c. diced celery
½ c. chopped stuffed olives
2 hard-cooked eggs
2 t. minced onion
1 T. lemon juice
2 t. mustard
Dash of pepper
¾ c. mayonnaise
1 c. crushed potato chips

Combine all ingredients except potato chips; put mixture into 8 x 8 x 2 baking dish. Sprinkle with chips. Bake at 400°F. for 20-25 minutes. Yield: 6 servings.

Sonja Crummy, Wyoming Community H.S.
Wyoming, Illinois

CANNED HAM HOT DISH

1 c. macaroni
1 can chopped ham
1 T. onion
1 T. green pepper
1 c. grated cheese
1 c. dry bread crumbs
1 c. hot milk
2 eggs, beaten

Grind all ingredients except milk and eggs. Fold in milk and eggs. Spread mixture into an oblong cake pan. Set pan in pan of water. Bake at 350°F. for 1 hour. Serve with cream sauce or soup. Yield: 6 servings.

Patricia M. Brown, Edgewood Jr. H.S.
New Brighton, Minnesota

CAROL'S HAM CASSEROLE

1 8-oz. pkg. noodles
1½ c. cooked ham, chopped
1 c. sharp cheese, grated
1 can cream of chicken soup
½ c. milk
½ t. curry powder
2 T. butter or margarine

Cook noodles as directed on package; drain. Combine ham and ¾ cup cheese. Alternate layers of noodles and ham in greased 1-quart baking dish. Mix soup, milk and curry; pour over noodles. Sprinkle top with remaining cheese; dot with butter. Bake at 375°F. for 20-30 minutes. Yield: 6-8 servings.

Carol Schmorleitz, Bidwell Jr. H.S.
Chico, California

GOLDEN HAM PIE

3 T. onion, chopped
¼ c. green pepper, chopped
¼ c. fat
6 T. flour
2 c. milk
2 c. cooked ham, diced
1 can cream of chicken soup

Saute onions and green pepper in fat; remove from heat. Blend in flour; gradually stir in milk, ham, and soup. Boil 1 minute. Pour into greased casserole. Bake at 450°F. while preparing biscuits.

CHEESE BISCUITS:

1 c. sifted flour
1½ t. baking powder
½ t. salt
2½ t. shortening
¾ c. cheese, grated
1 pimento, chopped
⅓ c. milk

Sift together flour, baking powder and salt. Cut in shortening; stir in remaining ingredients. Roll out and cut. Place biscuits on hot mixture; bake 15-20 minutes. Yield: 4 servings.

Mrs. Joyce Rapes, Sebewaing Public School
Sebewaing, Michigan

HAM CASSEROLE

¼ lb. cheese
½ lb. ham
6 lge. soda crackers
1 c. milk
1 t. Worcestershire sauce
3 eggs
½ t. baking powder

Use finest cutters for grinding cheese, ham and crackers. Add Worcestershire sauce and milk. Beat eggs lightly; add to mixture. Mix and put into greased casserole. Add baking powder after it is mixed by lightly folding it in with fork. Bake at 350°F. for hour or until a knife comes out clean. Yield: 4-6 servings.

Mrs. Layne Storment, Kahlotus H.S.
Kahlotus, Washington

COUNTRY CASSEROLE

2-3 c. diced cooked or canned ham
6 hard-cooked eggs, sliced
1 6-oz. can mushroom crowns, drained
1 can cream of celery soup
½ c. milk
2 c. grated American cheese
2 t. Worcestershire sauce
5-6 drops Tabasco sauce
¾ c. dry med. bread crumbs
3 T. melted butter or margarine

In a 2-quart casserole alternate layers of ham, egg and mushrooms, starting and ending with ham. Combine soup and milk; add cheese, Worcestershire and Tabasco. Heat, stirring until cheese melts; pour over casserole. Mix crumbs and butter; sprinkle over top. Bake at 375°F. for 25 minutes. Yield: 6 servings.

This recipe submitted by the following teachers:
Mrs. Frances Moorman, Sterlington H.S.
Sterlington, Louisiana
Mrs. Bobbye Wooleyhan, Sudlersville H.S.
Sudlersville, Maryland

GOURMET CHEESE AND HAM CASSEROLE

½ c. celery, sliced
¼ c. green pepper, chopped
½ c. boiling water
1 c. milk
1 8-oz. pkg. cream cheese
½ t. salt
½ t. garlic salt
½ c. Parmesan cheese, shredded
2 c. cooked ham, diced
½ lb. pkg. med. noodles, cooked and drained

Cook celery and green pepper in boiling water for 5 minutes; drain. Gradually add milk to cream cheese, blending until smooth. Place over low heat and stir until heated. Add seasonings, half of cheese, ham, celery and green pepper; Mix well. Pour sauce over noodles; toss lightly. Place in a buttered 1½-quart casserole. Sprinkle with remaining cheese. Cover; bake at 350°F. for 30-35 minutes. Yield: 8 servings.

Sister M. Dorothy, I.H.M., Marian H.S.
Birmingham, Michigan

HAM-MACARONI CASSEROLE

¼ lb. uncooked macaroni
2 c. cooked ham, diced
1 can cream of mushroom soup
¾ c. water
1 T. onion, diced
¾ c. Cheddar cheese, grated

Cook and drain macaroni as directed on package. Combine with ham, mushroom soup, water and onion. Arrange in greased 1½-quart casserole. Sprinkle top with cheese. Bake at 400°F. for 30 minutes. Yield: 6 servings.

Jeri Thurow, Hesperia H.S.
Hesperia, Michigan

HAM AND NOODLE CASSEROLE

6 oz. egg noodles
½ c. onion, chopped
½ c. green pepper, chopped
2 T. fat
1 c. cooked ham, chopped
1 can mushroom soup
¼ c. evaporated milk
½ c. cheese cubes
¼ c. buttered bread crumbs

Cook noodles in salt water until tender; drain. Fry onion and green pepper in fat until tender but not brown. Combine all ingredients except bread crumbs. Put mixture into a greased baking dish; top with crumbs. Bake for 20 minutes at 375°F. Yield: 4 servings.

Mrs. Mildred Elliott, Sparks H.S.
Sparks, Nevada

HAM CASSEROLE ORIENTALE

2 c. cooked ham, diced
1 can pineapple tidbits, drained
1 c. celery, thinly sliced
1 T. butter or margarine
1 c. green pepper, thinly sliced
1 pkg. dry cream of leek soup mix
1 c. Chinese noodles

Toss ham with pineapple in a 1½-quart casserole. Saute celery and green pepper in butter until slightly tender but crisp; add to ham mixture. Combine soup mix with 1½ cups water; bring to a boil, stirring constantly. Reduce heat; simmer 3 minutes. Stir into ham mixture, mixing thoroughly. Sprinkle top of casserole with Chinese noodles. Bake at 375°F. for 20 minutes or until sauce is bubbly. Yield: 4-6 servings.

Mrs. Diana Holtz, Escalon Union H.S.
Escalon, California

HAM-SOUR CREAM CASSEROLE

Sliced potatoes
Ham, cooked and sliced
Salt and pepper to taste
Dash of sage
Dash of nutmeg
Dash of marjoram
Dash of thyme
¾ c. mushrooms, thinly sliced
3 hard-cooked eggs, sliced
1¼ c. sour cream
1 bay leaf
1 whole clove
½ c. crumbs
½ c. cheese, grated

Place layer of potatoes in bottom of greased casserole; cover with individual portions of ham. Combine all seasonings except bay leaf and clove; sprinkle over ham. Combine mushrooms and eggs; arrange over ham layer. Pour sour cream over top; add bay leaf and clove. Bake covered at 350°F. for 35 minutes. Uncover; sprinkle with crumbs and cheese and brown. Yield: 4-6 servings.

Joan Daniels Pedro, Evansville H.S.
Evansville, Wisconsin

HAM TETRAZZINI

2 lb. spaghetti, broken into 2-inch pieces
2 cans cream of mushroom soup
2 c. milk
1 T. onion, chopped
2 c. sharp cheese, shredded
½ t. salt
¼ t. pepper
2 t. Worcestershire sauce
¼ c. parsley, chopped
1 c. chopped pimento
3 c. baked ham, cubed
Tomato wedges

Cook and drain spaghetti. Combine soup and milk, stirring until smooth. Add remaining ingredients except ham and tomatoes. Pour soup mixture over spaghetti; toss to coat evenly. Arrange layers of spaghetti and ham in greased 2½-quart casserole. Bake 30 minutes at 350°F. Garnish top with tomato wedges. Yield: 8 servings.

Charleen Dahlgren, Onamia Public School
Onamia, Minnesota

SOUTH SEA CASSEROLE

1 can pork and ham luncheon meat or leftover ham
1 T. cornstarch
1 c. water
⅓ c. pineapple juice
1 T. vinegar
½ t. Worcestershire sauce
1 t. soy sauce
¼ t. mustard
1 9-oz. can pineapple tidbits, drained
1 tomato, cut in sixths
½ green pepper, sliced
½ c. celery, chopped
3 c. cooked rice or half rice and half chow mein noodles

Cut meat into ¾-inch cubes; brown lightly in skillet. Combine cornstarch, liquids and seasonings. Add meat; cook until mixture thickens, stirring constantly. Add remaining ingredients except rice; simmer five minutes. Serve over rice. Yield: 4 servings.

Mrs. Sylvia Michaud, Genesee H.S.
Genesee, Idaho

STUFFED BAKED HAM

4 slices of bacon, diced
¾ c. celery, chopped
¾ c. onion, chopped
¼ c. green pepper, chopped
4 tart apples, chopped
3 c. soft bread crumbs
1 T. chopped parsley
2 slices of center-cut ham

Saute bacon, celery, onion and green pepper; mix with apples, bread crumbs and parsley. Place dressing as a filling between ham slices in casserole. Bake uncovered at 325°F. for 1 hour. Yield: 6-8 servings.

Elizabeth Tullock, East Dubuque H.S.
East Dubuque, Illinois

AFRICAN CHOW MEIN

1 lb. pork steak, cubed
2 med. onions, chopped
1 sm. can mushrooms
2 cans cream of mushroom soup
2 cans condensed chicken and rice soup
¼ lb. cashew nuts or blanched almonds
1 c. rice
2 c. celery, diced
2 c. water
¼ t. salt

Brown meat and chopped onions. Put in flat casserole. Add other ingredients. Bake 1 hour and 30 minutes at 350°F. Yield: 12 servings.

Mrs. Mary M. Lund, Arlington Jr. H.S.
Arlington, Washington

BARBECUED RIBS

4 lb. spareribs
2 T. butter
1 med. onion, finely cut
4 T. lemon juice
2 T. vinegar
2 T. brown sugar
⅛ t. cayenne pepper
1 c. catsup
3 T. Worcestershire sauce
½ T. ground mustard
1 c. water
½ c. celery or 1 T. celery salt
2 T. fat

Brown ribs in fat on both sides in skillet. Place in baking pan. Melt butter; brown onions. Add remaining ingredients and bring to a boil. Pour over spareribs. Roast for 2 hours, basting every half hour. Yield: 5 servings.

Mrs. Patricia Ringenberg, Manchester H.S.
No. Manchester, Indiana

CANADIAN BACON CASSEROLE

4 c. potatoes, sliced
1 No. 2 can French green beans
½ c. onion, chopped
1 roll garlic cheese, cut in slices
8-10 slices Canadian bacon
2 T. flour
½ t. celery seed
½ t. oregano
Salt to taste
¾ c. milk
1 T. catsup
Dash of Tabasco sauce

Arrange potatoes, beans, onion, cheese and bacon in layers. Sprinkle flour mixed with celery seed, oregano and salt over each layer. Combine milk, catsup and Tabasco sauce; pour over all. Bake at 350°F. for 1 hour or until potatoes are done. Bake covered the first part of baking period. Yield: 6 servings.

Mrs. Marjorie Dye, Homer Community School
Homer, Michigan

JIMSETTI

1 sm. pkg. med. wide noodles
1 pork shoulder, ground
1 onion, chopped
½ lb. American cheese, grated
1 can tomato soup
1 can water
Mushrooms

Brown meat and onion. Boil noodles until tender; drain. Combine all ingredients. Bake in greased casserole at 350°F. for 30 minutes. Yield: 4-6 servings.

JoAnn L. Bedore, Grand Blanc H.S.
Grand Blanc, Michigan

OVEN CHOP SUEY

1 lb. pork, cubed
2 T. shortening
1 med. onion, chopped
1 c. celery, diced
2 T. green pepper, chopped
2 T. pimento, diced
½ c. rice
1 can mushroom soup
1 can water
1 can chicken soup or beef broth
1 4-oz. can sliced mushrooms
2 T. soy sauce
½ c. chow mein noodles

Brown meat in shortening; stir in other ingredients except noodles. Pour into greased 1½-quart casserole. Bake at 350°F. for 1 hour. Cover for first 20 minutes. Sprinkle chow mein noodles on top for last 20 minutes of baking. Yield: 4 servings.

Jo Anne Kelsey, Kimball H.S.
Royal Oak, Michigan

PORK AND MACARONI BAKE

1 lb. ground pork
½ c. onion, chopped
2 T. fat
1 8-oz. can tomato sauce
1 6-oz. can tomato paste
1 can mushrooms
½ t. salt
⅛ t. pepper
1 7-oz. pkg. macaroni, cooked
2 c. sharp cheese, grated

Cook pork and onion in fat until onion is golden; add tomato sauce and paste, mushrooms and seasonings. Simmer 15 minutes. Alternate layers of macaroni, cheese and meat in a greased 2-quart casserole, ending with cheese. Bake at 350°F. for 45 minutes. Yield: 8 servings.

Mrs. Margaret Daugherty, Chestnut Ridge H.S.
Fishertown, Pennsylvania

PORK AND NOODLE CASSEROLE

1 med. onion, diced
1 med. green pepper, diced
3 T. butter
2 lb. lean pork shoulder, ground
3 c. strained cooked tomatoes
1 8-oz. pkg. noodles, cooked
¼ lb. American cheese, finely chopped
Salt and pepper to taste

Fry onion and green pepper in butter until onion is yellow. Add ground pork and brown. Add tomatoes, noodles and cheese. Season with salt and pepper. Pour into baking dish. Bake at 350° F. for 1 hour. Yield: 6-8 servings.

Marion Lehigh, Waverly H.S.
Waverly, Nebraska

PORK 'N' RICE CASSEROLE

1-1¼ lb. pork steak, cubed
1 med. onion, chopped
1 c. dry rice
2 cans chicken and rice soup
1 can cream of mushroom soup
½-1 c. water

Saute pork and onions until slightly browned. Put rice, soups and water in casserole; add browned meat and onion. Bake covered at 400°F. until it begins to bubble up. Reduce heat to 300-325°F. for remaining baking time. Stir once or twice. Total baking time is approximately 1 hour. Yield: 6-8 servings.

Patricia Dykstra, Forest Hills H.S.
Grand Rapids, Michigan

SWEET AND SOUR PORK

1½ lb. lean pork, cut in ½ x 2-inch strips
2 T. bacon drippings
¾-1 c. pineapple juice
½ c. water
⅓ c. vinegar
¼ c. brown sugar, firmly packed
2 T. cornstarch
½ t. salt
1 T. soy sauce
½-¾ c. green pepper, thinly sliced
½ c. onion, thinly sliced
1 No. 2 can pineapple chunks, drained

Brown pork in bacon drippings in large skillet. Combine pineapple juice, water, vinegar, brown sugar, cornstarch, salt and soy sauce. Cook until clear and slightly thickened, about 2 minutes. Add sauce to pork. Cook, covered, over low heat for 1 hour or until done. Refrigerate overnight. Reheat over low heat for 30 minutes or until steaming hot. Add green pepper, onion and pineapple chunks. Cook 2 minutes. Serve over hot rice if desired. Yield: 4 servings.

This recipe submitted by the following teachers:
Barbara Gaylor, Consultant, Home Economics and Family Life Education Service, Michigan Department of Public Instruction
Lansing, Michigan
Mrs. Sally Kemp, Grand Ledge H.S.
Grand Ledge, Michigan

PORK STEAK CASSEROLE

⅔ c. rice
⅓ c. water
¾-1 lb. pork steak, cubed
1 c. celery, chopped
1 c. onions, chopped
1 c. mushroom soup
⅓ c. water
2 T. soy sauce

Combine rice and water; soak for 1 hour. Brown steak in fat; place in bottom of casserole. Layer celery and onions over meat. Pour excess water from rice over celery; layer rice over celery. Combine remaining ingredients; pour over casserole. Bake at 375°F. for 45 minutes.

Catherine Hasenmyer, Mt. Carmel H.S.
Mt. Carmel, Illinois

RICE BAKE

1 c. boiling water
½ c. instant rice
1 t. salt
1 lb. chop suey meat
2 T. fat
½ c. sliced celery
1½ c. onion, sliced
½ c. green pepper, sliced
¼ c. pimento
1 can cream of mushroom soup
2 T. soy sauce

Pour boiling water over rice and salt. Brown meat in fat. Combine all ingredients. Bake for 1 hour and 15 minutes at 350°F. Yield: 4-5 servings.

Mrs. Shirley A. Randall, John Edwards H.S.
Port Edwards, Wisconsin

SAUSAGE CASSEROLES

ELENBURG'S SPECIAL

1 lb. sausage
⅓-½ green pepper, chopped
2-3 stalks of celery, chopped
2 pkg. dry chicken soup
2-4 c. water
1 c. uncooked rice
⅓-½ c. slivered almonds, toasted

Brown sausage, pepper and celery. Dissolve soup mix in hot water. Combine all ingredients. Refrigerate 24 hours. Bake 1 hour at 350°F. Yield: 6-8 servings.

This recipe submitted by the following teachers:
Mrs. Marvel Washnok, Waubay H.S.
Waubay, South Dakota
Clara Barrows, Groton H.S.
Groton, South Dakota

JOHN MAZETTI

1 lb. pork sausage
1 lge. onion, diced
½ pkg. noodles
1 can tomato soup
¼ lb. American cheese, diced

Brown sausage and onion. Cook noodles in boiling salted water until tender; drain. Combine noodles, sausage and onions, tomato soup and cheese in a casserole. Bake for 1 hour at 350°F. Yield: 6 servings.

Mrs. Sandra Faber,
North Chicago Community H.S.
North Chicago, Illinois

LASAGNA CASSEROLE

1 8-oz. pkg. broad noodles
1 T. salad oil
1 8-oz. pkg. heat and serve sausages
1 1-lb. can tomatoes
1 6-oz. can tomato paste
1 T. instant minced onion
1 t. mixed Italian herbs
1 c. cottage cheese, drained
¼ c. Parmesan cheese, grated
1 6- to 8-oz. pkg. Mozzarella cheese, cut in ½-inch strips

Cook noodles as directed on package and drain. Return to saucepan. Toss with salad oil. Dice sausages and brown, stirring often. Stir in tomatoes, tomato paste, onion and herbs. Heat to boiling and simmer, stirring occasionally, for 5 minutes. Layer half the noodles, cottage cheese, Parmesan cheese, tomato mixture and Mozzarella cheese in greased 2-quart casserole. Repeat, trimming the top with criss-crossed cheese strips. Bake at 350° F. for 30 minutes until bubbling at edges and cheese is browned. Yield: 6 servings.

Judy J. Jeffries, Hoffman H.S
South Amboy, New Jersey

MOCK CHICKEN-ALMOND

2 lb. sausage
2 lge. onions
1 bell pepper
1 bunch of celery
2 c. raw brown rice
9 c. water
2 cans bouillon cubes
½ lb. blanched almonds, chopped

Brown sausage, onions and pepper lightly; add celery and rice. Bring water to boil; add bouillon cubes. Combine all ingredients. Bake for 1 hour at 375°F. in a greased covered casserole. Yield: 16 servings.

Mrs. Ruth Methvin, Fall River H.S.
McArthur, California

MOCK CHICKEN CASSEROLE

1 lb. sausage
2 pkg. dry chicken-noodle soup mix
1 c. rice
5 c. boiling water
1 can cream of mushroom soup
1½ c. celery, diced
¼ c. green pepper, chopped
½ t. salt
Pepper to taste

Brown and drain sausage; add all remaining ingredients. Simmer 40 minutes or until rice and celery are thoroughly cooked. Yield: 8 servings.

Mrs. Herbert Milroy, Belle Center Local
Belle Center, Ohio

PORK-ALMOND CASSEROLE

1 lb. pork sausage
½ lge. onion, chopped
2 c. celery, chopped
1 green pepper, chopped
2¾ c. water
1 c. instant rice
1 pkg. dry chicken-noodle soup
½ c. blanched almonds

Brown sausage; add onions, celery and pepper. When thoroughly cooked, add 2¼ cups water; boil several minutes, stirring often. Add rice; stir well and continue to cook. When in full boil, add soup mixture. Pour mixture into casserole; cover and refrigerate overnight. Add ½ cup of water; sprinkle almonds on top. Heat uncovered at 300°F. until browned. Yield: 6 servings.

Elvira Benne, Columbus Sr. H.S.
Columbus, Nebraska

RICE-PORK CASSEROLE

3 pkg. dry chicken-noodle soup
5 c. hot water
1 c. raw rice
1 stalk of celery, finely chopped
1 sm. onion, finely chopped
1 sm. green pepper, finely chopped
1 lb. ground pork sausage
¼ c. blanched almonds, chopped
1 can cream of mushroom soup
½ c. milk

Combine dry soup and hot water; bring to a boil. Add rice and cook until tender. Add celery, onion and green pepper. Brown sausage; drain off excess fat and add to mixture. Add chopped almonds; stir well. Place in a casserole dish; cover with mushroom soup which has been diluted with milk. Bake at 350°F. for 45 minutes. Yield: 8 servings.

Mildred E. Peterson, Pendleton Sr. H.S.
Pendleton, Oregon

RICE-SAUSAGE AND ALMOND DISH

¾ lb. sausage
⅓ bunch celery, diced
⅓ green pepper, diced
⅓ lge. onion, diced
3 c. boiling water
¾ c. rice
1 pkg. dry chicken-noodle soup mix
½ t. salt
Buttered crumbs
Slivered almonds, toasted

Brown sausage, crumbling with a fork; pour off all fat. Add celery, green pepper and onion to crumbled meat; saute until tender. Combine water, rice and soup mix in a greased casserole; add sausage mixture and salt. Cover and bake for 40 minutes at 350°F. Remove cover; sprinkle with buttered crumbs and toasted slivered almonds and bake 20 minutes, uncovered. Yield: 6 servings.

Mrs. E. J. Bahnsen, Reed City H.S.
Reed City, Michigan

SAUSAGE-NOODLE CASSEROLE

1 lb. sausage
2 T. green pepper, diced
½ c. celery, diced
¾ c. rice
4½ c. water
1 pkg. dry noodle soup mix
½ pkg. slivered almonds

Fry sausage in a small amount of grease. Add green pepper and celery and saute. Pour off grease; add remaining ingredients. Simmer 30 minutes. Bake 20 minutes at 350°F. Yield: 7 servings.

Mrs. Jean Otterson, San Luis Obispo, Jr. H.S.
San Luis Obispo, California

SAUSAGE AND RICE CASSEROLE

1 lb. pork sausage
1 can mushroom soup
2 cans condensed chicken and rice soup
1 c. raw rice
1 c. diced celery
1 green pepper, chopped
½ lb. grated American cheese

Lightly brown sausage and pour off fat. Mix all ingredients together and pour into a 2-quart casserole. Bake covered at 375°F. for 1 hour and 15 minutes. Yield: 8 servings.

Mrs. Hope B. Green, West Jr. H.S.
Rapid City, South Dakota

ROYAL RICE DISH

1½ lb. pork sausage
2 onions, chopped
1 bell pepper, chopped
2 pkg. dry chicken-noodle soup
2 c. uncooked rice
9 c. water
1 c. celery, cut up
1 c. slivered almonds

Brown sausage and remove from skillet. Use same fat to fry onions and bell pepper until limp. Oil a large 9 x 13-inch pan; sprinkle in sausage, onions and bell pepper. Sprinkle in dried soup; top with rice. Pour water over casserole. Bake for 30-45 minutes at 375°F. When rice is done and mixture is thickened, remove from oven and fold in celery and almonds.

Carol Boyer, Davis Sr. H.S.
Davis, California

SAUSAGE WITH RICE

1 lb. pork sausage
3 stalks of celery, diced
½ onion, finely chopped
½ green pepper, chopped
1 pkg. dry chicken-noodle soup
⅝ c. raw instant rice
3 c. water

Lightly brown and separate sausage. Mix all ingredients together and place in a casserole. Bake, uncovered, for 45 minutes at 350°F. NOTE: If desired all ingredients except water may be combined and mixture refrigerated until time to bake. Yield: 4-6 servings.

Mrs. Lillian Englmann, Battle Ground H.S.
Battle Ground, Washington

SAUSAGE-SPAGHETTI HOT DISH

1 10-oz. package thin spaghetti
1 can tomato soup
1 can water
1 pkg. little link sausages
Salt and pepper to taste

Break spaghetti into desired size and cook until tender in salted water; rinse in cold water. Mix with soup and water. Brown sausage; add salt and pepper. Mix with spaghetti. Pour into casserole. Bake 30-35 minutes at 350°F. Yield: 8 servings.

Patricia Irvin, Wells Public School
Wells, Minnesota

BAKED VEAL AND NOODLES

5 lb. veal or pork, cubed
2 lge. green peppers, chopped
6 med. onions, chopped
3 lb. noodles
5 cans tomato soup
1 pt. stuffed olives
2½ c. broth
Salt and pepper to taste
1¼ lb. cheese, grated or thinly sliced

Brown meat; add peppers and onions. Cook for several minutes. Combine remaining ingredients except cheese; add to meat mixture. Put into casserole; top with cheese. Bake at 350°F. until noodles are tender. Yield: 65 servings.

Mrs. Eloise Lotz, Edgar H.S.
Edgar, Wisconsin

BAKED VEAL CHOP SUEY

1 lb. veal, cut in small pieces
2 med. onions, chopped
2 T. fat
1 c. celery, chopped
¾ c. raw rice, washed
2 T. soy sauce
1 can condensed cream of chicken soup
1 can condensed cream of mushroom soup
2 c. water
1 t. salt
⅛ t. pepper

Brown veal and onions in fat; add celery, rice and soy sauce. Add soups, water, salt and pepper. Put into greased casserole; bake 2 hours at 325° F. Stir lightly once when it begins to cook so rice does not settle on bottom. Yield: 6-8 servings.

Mrs. Ruth Lathrope, Wonewoc Center H.S.
Wonewoc, Wisconsin

BEST EVER VEAL CASSEROLE

2 lb. veal, cubed
¼ c. butter
1 t. salt
2 t. curry powder
½ t. pepper
¼ t. paprika
1½ t. sugar
1 10-oz. can condensed beef broth
1¼ c. sour cream
⅓ c. flour
½ c. cold water
½ c. ground parsley
4 oz. noodles
2 T. slivered almonds, toasted
¼ t. poppy seed

Brown veal in butter; sprinkle with salt, curry, powder, pepper, paprika and sugar. Add broth and sour cream. Blend together flour, water and parsley; stir into mixture. Simmer 1 hour. Cook noodles; drain and rinse. Place in casserole dish. Put veal in center. Sprinkle almonds and poppy seeds on top. Bake 15 minutes at 350°F. Yield: 4 servings.

Jean Carolyn Leis, Buhler Rural H.S.
Buhler, Kansas

CALIFORNIA VEAL CASSEROLE

BUTTER CRUMB DUMPLINGS:

2 c. sifted flour
4 t. baking powder
½ t. salt
1 t. poultry seasoning
1 t. celery seed
1 t. dry onion flakes
¼ c. salad oil
1 c. milk
¼ c. melted butter
1 c. bread crumbs

Sift flour, baking powder, salt and poultry seasoning into bowl. Add seeds and onion flakes. Blend in oil and milk, stirring until just moistened. Combine butter and bread crumbs; drop dough by rounded tablespoons into mixture and roll to coat.

⅓ c. flour
1 t. paprika
2 lb. veal round steak
¼ c. shortening
1 1-lb. can sm. cooked onions
2 cans cream of chicken soup
1 can water or onion liquid
1 c. sour cream

Mix flour and paprika; pound into meat. Cut into 2-inch cubes; brown in fat. Put into a 3-quart casserole; add onions. Heat 1 can soup in skillet; blend in liquid. Bring to a boil; pour over meat. Bake at 350°F. for 45 minutes or until meat is tender. Top with 14-16 dumplings. Increase temperature to 425°F.; bake for 20-25 minutes or until browned. Serve with sauce made by heating 1 can soup and sour cream just to boiling. Yield: 8 servings.

This recipe submitted by the following teachers:
Mary Denton Pierce, Clinton County H.S.
Albany, Kentucky
Mrs. Clara O'Neil, North Junior H.S.
Rapid City, South Dakota

CASHMERE CASSEROLE

¾ c. raw rice
2 c. celery, diced
1 c. mushrooms
2 T. fat
2½ c. water
1 can cream of mushroom soup
1 can cream of chicken soup
1¼ lb. veal steak, cubed
1 T. onion, grated
1 c. cashew nuts

Brown rice, celery and mushrooms in fat. Add water and soups. Combine mixture with veal and onions. Put in a casserole. Bake at 350°F. for 1 hour. Add nuts; bake 30 minutes. Yield: 12 servings.

Mrs. Ralph Earhart, Elk City H.S.
Elk City, Kansas

CONTINENTAL VEAL CASSEROLE

1 clove garlic
1 lb. veal, cut in 12 thin slices
2 T. salad oil
1 t. salt
¼ t. pepper
1 4-oz. can mushrooms or 2 3-oz. cans
¼ lb. wide noodles
½ c. sour cream
¼ lb. Swiss cheese, sliced
2 tomatoes, sliced
½ c. water
½ c. Parmesan cheese

Brown garlic and veal in salad oil; sprinkle with half of salt and pepper. Remove garlic; add undrained mushrooms. Simmer covered 15-20 minutes. Cook noodles as directed on package; drain. Toss with sour cream. In a 2-quart casserole, put half of noodles, half of veal, half of Swiss cheese and half of tomatoes. Sprinkle with remaining salt and pepper. Repeat layers. Stir water and Parmesan cheese into drippings in skillet; pour over casserole. Bake at 375°F. for 35-40 minutes. Yield: 6 servings.

Mrs. Bea Myers, Western H.S.
Tulare, California

GREEN NOODLE HOT DISH

1 lb. veal steak or rump
1 c. flour
1 t. salt
1 t. pepper
1 c. hot water
1 pkg. sour cream
4 oz. green noodles
¼ c. butter
2 T. poppy seed
½ c. almonds, toasted
10½ oz. cream or evaporated milk

Cut meat into serving pieces; roll in flour, salt, pepper and paprika. Brown in hot fat; add water. Cover and simmer 1 hour. Just before serving, add sour cream; heat but do not boil. Cook noodles; drain. Add butter, poppy seed and almonds. Layer meat and noodles in a casserole dish. Bake at 350°F. for 30 minutes. Yield: 4-6 servings.

Mrs. Beverly Wruck, Clintonville Sr. H.S.
Clintonville, Wisconsin

PAT'S PARTY CASSEROLE

3 lb. veal, cubed
Flour
Oil
1 bunch of celery, diced
1 med. onion, chopped
1 can mushroom soup
1 4-oz. can mushrooms
10½ oz. cream or evaporated milk
½ c. blanched almonds

1 can chow mein noodles
1½ t. salt
Pepper to taste

Dredge veal in flour; brown in oil. Remove veal; add celery and onions and cook until limp and glazed. Return veal to skillet; add remaining ingredients except almonds and noodles. Simmer 1 hour. Put mixture in buttered casserole; top with noodles and sprinkle with almonds. Bake at 350°F. for 40 minutes. Yield: 10-12 servings.

Mrs. Irene Voorhees, Reading Community H.S.
Reading, Michigan

VEAL A LA KING

2 lb. veal, cut in 1-inch cubes
1 lge. onion, chopped
6 carrots, diced
1 can peas and liquid
1 can mushrooms and liquid
1 green pepper, finely chopped
4 whole cloves
2 bay leaves
6 c. milk

Brown veal in shortening; add onion and brown. Put veal, onion, carrots, peas, mushrooms and green pepper into a casserole. Put cloves and bay leaves into a cheesecloth bag and place in casserole. Bake 2 hours at 250-300°F. Make a thick white sauce using 6 cups milk. Remove spice bag. Add veal mixture to white sauce. Serve on heated chow mein noodles or in patty shells. Yield: 8-10 servings.

Mrs. James H. Witt, Williston Jr. H.S.
Williston, North Dakota

VEAL CASSEROLE

2 T. flour
1 t. salt
¼ t. pepper
2 lb. veal, thinly sliced
6 T. butter, margarine or oil
6 sm. white onions, thinly sliced
1 c. mushrooms, thinly sliced
4 med. potatoes
Paprika
2 c. hot chicken stock or bouillon cubes dissolved in hot water

Pound flour, salt and pepper into veal. Heat electric skillet to 350°F. Melt butter or oil; saute veal on both sides. Add onions, mushrooms and potatoes which have been scooped into balls with melon scoop or cut in chunks. Brown lightly. Sprinkle potato balls with paprika; arrange around edge of skillet. Pour in stock; reduce heat to simmering temperature. Cover and cook 40 minutes or until veal is tender. Add more stock as necessary. Yield: 6 servings.

Clara James, Northwest H.S.
Canal Fulton, Ohio

VEAL DELIGHT

1 lb. thinly sliced veal
2 T. butter or margarine
1 med. onion, thinly sliced
2 T. chopped celery
2 T. chopped green pepper
1 clove garlic, minced
1 bay leaf
1 10¾-oz. can beef gravy
¼ c. sour cream
Buttered cooked noodles

Brown veal in butter. Add onion, celery, green pepper, garlic, bay leaf and gravy. Cook, covered, over low heat about 30 minutes. Stir in sour cream just before serving. Serve with noodles. Yield: 4 servings.

Photograph for this recipe on page 19

VEAL GOULASH IN RICE RING

¼ c. butter
2 c. onion, chopped
3 c. cooked veal
2 beef bouillon cubes
1½ c. hot water
¼ c. chili sauce
4 t. paprika
1 t. caraway seed
½ t. marjoram
Pepper
⅓ c. cold water
2 T. flour

Melt butter in skillet; add onion and cook until almost tender, about 4 minutes. Add veal and cook until lightly browned. Dissolve bouillon cubes in hot water. Add bouillon, chili sauce, paprika, caraway seed, marjoram and pepper to skillet; cover and simmer 10 minutes, stirring occasionally. Blend together cold water and flour; stir into skillet and cook over low heat until thickened, stirring constantly. Serve in rice ring. Yield: 6 servings.

Barbara Spears, Shafter H.S.
Shafter, California

VEAL HOT DISH

1 lb. veal or round steak
1 lge. onion, chopped
1 c. celery, chopped
1 can chicken and rice soup
1 can cream of mushroom soup
½ c. rice
3 T. soy sauce

Cut meat in 2-inch squares. Brown in hot fat. Combine all ingredients with meat. Bake in greased casserole for 3 hours at 350°F. Yield: 6-8 servings.

Mrs. Hilda C. Burt, Las Cruces H.S.
Las Cruces, New Mexico

VEAL MARENGO

2 c. sliced mushrooms
3 T. butter
2 lb. veal cutlets
Flour
Salt
Pepper
4 T. cooking oil
1 sm. onion, chopped
2 T. chopped parsley
2 c. tomato sauce
¾ c. water
1 t. salt
⅛ t. freshly ground pepper
¼ t. basil

Saute mushrooms in butter until tender. Cut veal into serving pieces; roll in flour seasoned with salt and pepper. Brown veal in oil, add onion and parsley and cook until onion is tender. Remove veal from fat; blend in 3 tablespoons flour. Gradually add tomato sauce and water; mix well. Add seasonings; cook over low heat, stirring constantly, until thickened. Add browned veal and mushrooms; spoon sauce over meat. Cover and bake at 350°F. for 1 hour and 30 minutes or until veal is tender. Twenty minutes before serving, remove cover to brown top. Yield: 6 servings.

Mrs. Helen Mason, Cascade H.S.
Clayton, Indiana

VEAL SCALLOPINI AND RISOTTO

1 lb. veal, cut in 1-inch pieces
Flour
Salt and pepper
Butter
½ c. Sherry or red wine
1 3-oz. can mushrooms

Dredge veal in seasoned flour; brown in butter. Add wine and mushrooms; simmer for 10 minutes.

RISOTTO:
½ c. onions, chopped
½ c. butter
1 c. long grain rice
1 can consomme
¼ t. salt
Parmesan cheese, grated

Saute onions in ¼ cup butter; stir in rice and brown lightly. Add enough water to consomme to make 2 cups; pour into saucepan. Add salt; heat to boiling. Stir in rice and onions; cover and simmer 20 minutes. Stir in remaining butter; sprinkle with cheese. Serve over veal. Yield: 6-8 servings.

Mrs. Lavonne Schuetz, Arvin H.S.
Arvin, California

VEAL AND NOODLE CASSEROLE

1 lb. lean veal
1 sm. onion, minced
1 t. salt
2 c. noodles
2 c. milk
3 eggs, slightly beaten
1 2-oz. can sliced mushrooms and juice
2 T. pimento, minced
3 T. butter
½ c. cornflakes, crushed

Cut veal in 1-inch cubes; add onion and salt. Boil in water to cover for 1 hour until tender. Remove meat; boil noodles in broth until tender. Noodles should take up all of the broth. Combine eggs, milk, meat, noodles, mushrooms and pimento. Pour into greased casserole; cover with buttered crumbs. Bake at 350°F. for 1 hour. Yield: 6 servings.

Carolyn Fillmore Fredrick, Brighton H.S.
Brighton, Michigan

VEAL AND RICE CASSEROLE

1½-2 lb. veal steak
2 med. onions, chopped
2 c. diced celery
2 cans cream of mushroom soup
2 cans chicken and rice soup
4 soup cans water
1 lge. can mushrooms, undrained
1 c. uncooked rice
Blanched almonds

Cube veal; brown with onions in fat. Add all remaining ingredients except almonds. Place in large casserole. Sprinkle with almonds. Bake 1½ to 2 hours at 325 to 350°F. Yield: 10-14 servings.

This recipe submitted by the following teachers:
Edith Bacon, Johnson H.S.
St. Paul, Minnesota
Gladys Parry, Two Harbors Jr-Sr. H.S.
Two Harbors, Minnesota

WHITE VEAL STEW

2 lb. boneless veal shoulder, cut in chunks
1 qt. water
1 sm. onion, stuck with 2 cloves
2 stalks of celery, cut up
1 lb. sm. mushrooms
Few drops of lemon juice
2 T. butter
2 T. flour
1 t. salt
1 can onions or 12 sm. onions
2 sprigs of parsley, minced

Combine veal, water, onion and celery. Simmer gently for 1 hour and 30 minutes. Remove onion, celery and veal. Strain stock; simmer mushrooms in it adding a few drops of lemon juice. Melt butter; blend in flour and salt. Add stock; cook until smooth. Add mushrooms and drained onions; pour over veal. Place in casserole; top with minced parsley. Cook at 350°F. for 20 minutes. Yield: 4-6 servings.

Mrs. Anne Milloy, Gibbstown School
Gibbstown, New Jersey

LAMB CASSEROLES

LAMB-APPLE CASSEROLE

1 lb. lamb shoulder, diced
Salt and pepper
1 T. salad oil
2 c. tart apples, sliced
1 t. lemon rind, grated
3 whole cloves
2 T. water
⅓ c. bread crumbs
¼ c. brown sugar

Season meat with salt and pepper. Brown on all sides in hot oil. Transfer meat to shallow casserole. Add apples, lemon rind, cloves and water. Sprinkle with crumbs and brown sugar. Cover and bake at 350°F. for 30 minutes. Uncover and bake 15 minutes longer or until browned. Yield: 4 servings.

Mrs. Carolyn R. Stuckum, Covert H.S.
Covert, Michigan

LAMB COUNTRY STYLE

2 lb. lamb
¾ lb. Cheddar cheese
1½ lb. tomatoes, sliced
Salt and pepper to taste
Oregano (opt.)
Marjoram (opt.)
1-2 T. butter

Cut lamb in pieces as for stew. Line in a baking dish. Cut cheese in small pieces and place on top. Cover with tomatoes. Sprinkle with seasonings; baste with melted butter. Bake at 375°F. for 1 hour and 30 minutes. Yield: 4-6 servings.

Mrs. Sally Rhoads Parks, Audubon H.S.
Audubon, New Jersey

LAMB CURRY

1 T. shortening
1½ lb. lamb shoulder, diced
1 c. onions, sliced
3 T. flour
1 T. mint-flavored apple jelly
2 t. curry powder
¼ t. ginger
1 t. salt
¼ t. pepper
1½ c. stock or bouillon
2 c. cooked rice

Melt shortening; add lamb and onions. Cook over medium heat until lamb is browned. Add flour, jelly, curry powder, ginger, salt, pepper and stock. Cover and cook over medium heat for 1½ hours, stirring occasionally. Serve over rice. Yield: 6 servings.

Mrs. Kelley Storey, Paris H.S.
Paris, Texas

PERSIAN LAMB SKILLET

2½ lb. boned, cubed lamb shoulder
2 T. salad oil
½ t. salt
¼ t. pepper
½ t. tumeric
¼ t. cinnamon
1 1-lb. can sm. whole onions
1 t. white vinegar
1 c. water
2 T. cornstarch
1 1-lb. can kidney beans, drained
Cooked rice
Parsley

Brown lamb in oil over medium heat, stirring occasionally. Mix salt, pepper, tumeric and cinnamon; sprinkle over lamb. Drain onions; reserve liquid. Pour onion liquid, vinegar and ¾ cup water over lamb. Simmer, covered, 50-60 minutes or until tender. Mix remaining water and cornstarch; stir into lamb mixture. Cook, stirring, until thickened. Add onions and kidney beans; cook 5 minutes longer or until heated through. Serve with rice; garnish with parsley. Yield: 6 servings.

Photograph for this recipe on inside front cover

DOVE-WILD RICE CASSEROLE

1 cube chicken bouillon
1 c. hot water
1 c. celery, chopped
1 t. celery salt
1 t. onion salt
⅛ t. pepper
1 T. parsley, minced
1 T. soy sauce
1 c. white rice, cooked
¼ c. wild rice, cooked
2 T. butter
8 doves or 2 pheasants

Dissolve bouillon in hot water; add celery and parboil. Add seasonings, rice and butter. Place skinned birds in a greased casserole; cover with rice. Bake at 350°F. for 3 hours or until tender. Yield: 4-6 servings.

Ann Moore, Bliss H. S.
Bliss, Idaho

PHEASANTS

2 pheasants, cut up
Flour
Salt and pepper to taste
Shortening
2 c. brown rice
1 pkg. dry onion soup mix
1 can mushroom soup
3 c. milk

Flour and season pheasant; brown in shortening. Spread rice in a greased baking dish; mix remaining ingredients until smooth. Pour a third of mixture over rice, moistening well. Evenly arrange pheasant over rice; cover with remaining sauce. Bake at 325-375°F. for 1 hour and 30 minutes or until rice is tender.

Charlotte Rew, Fort Pierre H.S.
Fort Pierre, South Dakota

BAKED PHEASANT

2-3 pheasants, cut in serving pieces
Pancake flour
Shortening
Salt and pepper
2-3 c. beer

Roll pheasant in flour; brown in hot shortening. Season to taste. Place in roaster; pour drippings over meat. Add beer; cover. Bake at 300°F. for 1 hour and 30 minutes. Increase temperature to 350°F. and cook 1 hour and 30 minutes longer, basting every 30 minutes. Yield: 6 servings.

Mrs. Don L. Pack, Waterbury Public School
Waterbury, Nebraska

HUNTER'S SCALLOPED PHEASANT

1 pheasant
1 sm. onion
1 stalk celery
3½ slices dry bread, cubed
2½ c. broth
½ can cream of mushroom soup
2 T. pimento (opt.)
2 eggs, beaten
½ t. salt
¼ t. pepper
Dry bread crumbs

Boil pheasant, onion and celery until tender; strain broth and cool. Cut pheasant into bite size pieces; add cooled broth. Add bread, soup, pimento, eggs and seasonings. Pour into a buttered casserole; sprinkle with bread crumbs. Bake at 350°F. for 45 minutes. NOTE: This freezes well. Yield: 8 servings.

Ella Mae Korthals, Huron H.S.
Huron, South Dakota

PHEASANT CASSEROLE

2 Pheasants
Flour
Salt and pepper
Butter
2 onions, chopped
1 c. celery, chopped
1 green pepper, chopped (opt.)
2 cans mushroom soup
2 soup cans water

Cut pheasants into pieces. Roll in flour, salt and pepper; brown in butter. Remove pheasant from pan; place in casserole. Brown onions, celery and green pepper. Add mushroom soup and water; mix well. Pour mixture over pheasant in casserole. Cook at 250-275°F. for 2-3 hours or until tender. Cooking time will vary according to size and age of birds. Yield: 6 servings.

Mrs. Lois Brichacek, Roosevelt Jr. H.S.
Great Bend, Kansas

PHEASANT LUNCHEON DISH

¼ c. onion, chopped
1 c. celery, chopped
1 can cream of mushroom soup
⅓ c. broth or water
1 T. soy sauce
3 drops Tabasco sauce
Pepper to taste
2 c. cooked pheasant, diced
1 c. chow mein noodles
⅓ c. cashew nuts

Saute onion and celery in butter until transparent. Add soup, broth and seasonings. Add pheasant; simmer for 15 minutes. Place in 1½-quart casserole; sprinkle noodles over top. Bake at 350°F. for 30 minutes. Sprinkle nuts on top; brown 5 minutes longer. Yield: 4 servings.

Mrs. Clarice J. Hubbard, Mitchell Jr. H.S.
Mitchell, South Dakota

PHEASANT-MUSHROOM BAKE

3 cooked pheasants or Cornish hens
1 c. flour
1 t. salt
½ t. pepper
1 onion, chopped
¼ c. butter
2 cans cream of mushroom soup
1 pt. half and half cream
½ t. monosodium glutamate
¼ t. oregano or paprika

Cube cooked pheasant or hens. Dredge cubes with flour, salt and pepper. Saute meat and onion in butter; place in greased casserole. Make mixture of soup, half and half and monosodium glutamate. Pour over cubes; sprinkle with oregano or paprika. Bake at 375°F. for 30-45 minutes. If mixture becomes dry while baking add small amount of milk. Yield: 8-10 servings.

Veau Dell Prochazka, Atwood Community H.S.
Atwood, Kansas

PHEASANT-RICE CASSEROLE

1½ c. pheasant, slivered
½ t. salt
Dash of pepper
⅓ c. butter or margarine
2 c. cooked rice
1 can condensed cream of chicken soup,
¾ celery, diced
1 T. onion, chopped
¼ t. garlic salt
½ t. leaf oregano
1 T. chopped pimento

Thoroughly brown pheasant in butter; season with salt and pepper. Cook rice two-thirds length of time recommended on package instructions. Place pheasant, drippings and rice in 1-quart casserole. Mix in remaining ingredients. Cover; bake at 400° F. for 20 minutes. Remove cover and bake 10 additional minutes. Yield 4-6 servings.

Mrs. Margaret M. Hudson, Mount Marty H.S.
Yankton, South Dakota

SOUTH DAKOTA PHEASANT IN SOUR CREAM

1 pheasant, cut in serving pieces
½ c. flour
1 t. salt
½ t. pepper
Fat
1 green pepper, chopped
1 c. sour cream

Dip pheasant in flour, salt and pepper; brown in hot fat until golden. Cover and cook slowly for 30 minutes. Add green pepper and sour cream; cook over very low heat until cream is just hot. Yield: 4 servings.

Mrs. Vivian Strand, Chester H.S.
Chester, South Dakota

DEER OR ELK STEW

1½ lb. deer or elk meat
1 T. flour
Salt and pepper to taste
2 T. butter
2 onions, cut in lge. pieces
1 c. hot water
1½ c. tomato juice
Juice of 1 lemon or ⅓ c. wine
2 carrots, diced
¼ c. celery, diced
3 lge. potatoes, quartered
1 sm. can peas
1 T. chopped parsley

Parboil meat 2 minutes; wash and dry. Roll in mixture of flour, salt and pepper. Braise in butter with onions; add water, tomato juice, lemon juice or wine, carrots and celery. Cook at 350°F. for 1 hour or until meat is tender. Add potatoes and cook until done; add peas and parsley and cook until thoroughly heated. Yield: 4 servings.

Mrs. Mary Jean Earl, Adams City H.S.
Commerce City, Colorado

HAWAIIAN VENISON

1 lb. boneless elk or deer round steak
¼ c. flour
¼ c. butter or margarine
½ c. boiling water
1 t. salt
2-3 green peppers
½ c. pineapple chunks
2½ T. cornstarch
½ c. pineapple juice
¼ c. vinegar
¼ c. sugar
2½ T. soy sauce

Cut steak into 1-inch cubes; dredge in flour. Brown meat in hot butter. Add water and salt; simmer until meat is tender. Cut green peppers into 1-inch squares; boil 10 minutes and drain. Add peppers and pineapple chunks to meat. Combine remaining ingredients; cook until sauce is clear and thick. Pour sauce over meat mixture; simmer 5 minutes. Serve over Chinese noodles or cooked rice. Garnish with chilled pineapple chunks. Yield: 4 servings.

Mrs. Lenore Whitmore, Cotopaxi H.S.
Cotopaxi, Colorado

Ground Beef & Hamburger Favorites

AMERICAN CHOP SUEY

4 oz. uncooked macaroni
1 lb. hamburger
1 med. onion, chopped
1 c. diced celery
1 can tomato soup
1 soup can hot water
1 t. salt
Dash of pepper
2 T. soy sauce
½ c. American cheese, grated
Buttered bread crumbs

Brown meat slowly; add onions and celery and cook. Combine all ingredients except cheese and bread crumbs. Put in buttered casserole. Cover and cook at 350°F. for 1 hour. Remove cover and stir in cheese. Top with crumbs; continue baking for 15 minutes or until brown. Yield: 6 servings.

Mrs. Alfrieda Jacobson, Granite Falls H.S.
Granite Falls, Minnesota

CHOP SUEY CASSEROLE

6 slices of bacon
1 lb. hamburger
½ c. onion, chopped
⅓ c. green pepper, chopped
1 No. 2 can tomatoes
½ c. catsup
Salt and pepper
Italian seasoning
1 t. sugar
1¼ c. elbow macaroni

Fry bacon and drain. Pour off drippings reserving enough to saute onion and green pepper. Remove vegetables; brown hamburger. Return vegetables to pan with meat. Add tomatoes, catsup, seasonings and small amount of water. Simmer while cooking macaroni in salted boiling water. Drain macaroni and place in greased casserole. Add sauce, stirring into macaroni. Lay strips of bacon on top; refrigerate. Bake at 325°F. until thoroughly heated. Yield: 6 servings.

Mrs. Phebe G. Walker, Lebanon Sr. H.S.
Lebanon, New Hampshire

MACARONI-HAMBURGER CASSEROLE

1 lb. hamburger
2 onions, chopped
1 green pepper, chopped
Salt and pepper to taste
Chili pepper to taste
1 t. sugar
1 qt. tomato juice
3-4 c. cooked macaroni

Brown hamburger; pour off excess grease. Add onions and green pepper; saute until tender. Add salt, pepper, chili pepper and sugar. Add tomato juice. Add cooked macaroni to above mixture. Place in casserole; bake at 350°F. for 30 minutes. Yield: 6 servings.

Patricia Oglesby, Fort Vancouver H.S.
Vancouver, Washington

HAMBURGER HOT DISH

1½-2 lb. hamburger
1 sm. onion, diced
¼ c. green pepper, chopped
1 8-oz. pkg. macaroni
2 cans condensed tomato soup
1 c. American cheese, cubed
Salt to taste

Brown hamburger and onions; drain excess fat. Cook macaroni according to package directions. Combine all ingredients. Cook at 350°F. until cheese melts. Yield: 6-8 servings.

Mrs. Rosalie Orth, Hawkins H.S.
Hawkins, Wisconsin

HEARTY CASSEROLE

1 c. elbow macaroni or noodles
2 med. onions, quartered
2 qt. boiling water
¾-1 lb. ground beef
2 T. butter
1 sm. onion, chopped
¼ t. salt
Dash of pepper
1 c. catsup
1½ t. mustard
½ t. oregano
½ c. grated cheese

Cook macaroni and onions in salted water until tender; drain. Saute beef and chopped onion in butter. Stir in macaroni mixture and remaining ingredients except cheese. Put in a 1-quart casserole; top with cheese. Bake 15 minutes at 375°F. Yield: 4 servings.

Mrs. Madra Fischer, Mendota H.S.
Mendota, Illinois

MOCK RAVIOLI

3 lge. onions, chopped
2 cloves garlic, minced
2 lb. ground beef
⅓ c. plus 3 T. olive oil
1 4-oz. can mushrooms
1 can tomato paste
1 can tomato sauce
1½ c. water
1½ t. Italian herbs
½ c. minced parsley
1 c. soft bread crumbs
1 t. sage
1 t. salt
4 eggs, beaten
1½ c. canned chopped spinach
1 lb. butterfly macaroni, cooked

Saute onions, half of garlic and meat in 3 tablespoons oil; add mushrooms, tomato paste and sauce, water and herbs. Simmer 15 minutes. Combine remaining garlic and oil with parsley, bread crumbs, seasonings, eggs and spinach. Place layers of macaroni, spinach mixture and meat sauce in a casserole. Repeat layers. Bake at 350°F. for 30-40 minutes. Yield: 14-16 servings.

Mrs. Elizabeth Kilburn, Watsonville H.S.
Watsonville, California

BEEF-CHEESE CASSEROLE

1½ lb. ground beef
1 med. onion, chopped
1 t. salt
⅛ t. pepper (opt.)
2 8-oz. cans tomato sauce
1 c. cottage cheese
1 8-oz. pkg. cream cheese
¼ c. sour cream
¼-⅓ c. green pepper, chopped
¼-⅓ c. green onion, chopped
1 8-oz. pkg. noodles, cooked and drained

Brown ground beef and onion in skillet. Add salt, pepper and tomato sauce; simmer slowly while preparing remaining ingredients. Combine cottage cheese, cream cheese, sour cream, green pepper and onion. Place half of cooked noodles in a greased 3-quart casserole. Top with cheese mixture, then remaining noodles. Pour meat mixture over top. Bake at 350°F. for 30 minutes. Yield: 8-10 servings.

This recipe submitted by the following teachers:
Doris Rhodebeck, Highland H.S.
Sparta, Ohio
Mrs. Sue T. Glovier, Old Fort H.S.
Old Fort, North Carolina

BEEF-NOODLE BAKE

1 8-oz. pkg. wide noodles
2 lb. ground beef
2 T. butter
2 t. salt
2 8-oz. cans tomato sauce
2 T. flour
1 t. chili sauce
1 c. sour cream
2 c. sm. curd cottage cheese
½ c. onion, chopped
2 T. green pepper, chopped
¼ c. ripe olives, chopped

Cook noodles according to package directions; drain. Brown meat in butter; drain excess drippings. Stir in 1 teaspoon salt, tomato sauce, flour and chili sauce; simmer 10 minutes. Combine remaining ingredients. Put half of noodles in buttered 3-quart casserole. Layer cottage cheese mixture, remaining noodles and ground beef mixture. Bake at 350°F. for 50 minutes. Let stand 10 minutes before serving. Yield: 12 servings.

Gladys Anderson, Fort Collins H.S.
Fort Collins, Colorado

BEEF-NOODLE RING

8 oz. noodles
1 lb. ground beef
2 T. shortening
1 can tomatoes
1 8-oz. can tomato puree
1 beef bouillon cube
1 T. sugar
1 t. salt
1 c. onion, chopped
2 c. Cheddar cheese, grated

Cook noodles according to package directions. Brown beef in hot shortening. Stir in remaining ingredients. Heat slowly until bouillon cube is dissolved. Stir in noodles. Pour into baking dish; Bake at 350°F. for 1 hour.

Marguerite Noblitt, Rockville H.S.
Rockville, Indiana

CASHEW-BEEF BAKE

1 lb. ground beef
1 c. onions, chopped
1 c. celery, diced
3 T. butter
1 6- or 8-oz. pkg. noodles, cooked and drained
1 can cream of chicken soup
1 can cream of mushroom soup
1 c. milk
1 t. salt
¼ t. pepper
1 c. salted cashew nuts

Brown beef, onions and celery in butter. Arrange beef mixture and noodles in layers in a greased 2-quart casserole. Combine soups, milk and seasonings; pour over beef and noodles. Cover and bake at 325°F. for 1 hour. Uncover; sprinkle with cashew nuts and bake 10 minutes longer. Yield: 8 servings.

This recipe submitted by the following teachers:
Mrs. Mary C. Krysl, Stuart Public School
Stuart, Nebraska
Mrs. Mildred Williams, Cadott H.S.
Cadott, Wisconsin

COMPANY CASSEROLE

1 8-oz. pkg. noodles
1 lb. ground beef
5 T. butter
2 8-oz. cans tomato sauce
1 t. salt
Cayenne or black pepper to taste
1 c. cottage cheese
¼ c. thick sour cream
1 8-oz. pkg. cream cheese
½ c. green onions chopped
1 T. or more green pepper, chopped

Cook noodles in 3-quarts of salted water. Brown ground meat in 3 tablespoons of butter. Stir in tomato sauce, salt and pepper. Remove from heat. Combine cottage cheese, cream cheese, sour cream, onions and green pepper. Spread half of cooked noodles in a greased casserole; cover with cheese mixture. Top with remaining noodles. Pour 2 tablespoons melted butter over noodles. Put meat sauce on top. Bake at 350°F. for 30 minutes. Yield: 6-8 servings.

This recipe submitted by the following teachers:
Connie Easton, Moorestown Jr. H.S.
Moorestown, New Jersey
Mrs. Swanie Smoot, Scott H.S.
Madison, West Virginia
Mrs. Janie B. Mofield, Benton H.S.
Benton, Kentucky
Mrs. Barbara B. Henson, Santa Rosa H.S.
Santa Rosa, Texas

CHINESE-CASHEW CASSEROLE

1½ lb. hamburger
¼ c. onions, finely chopped
1 8-oz. pkg. egg noodles
1 c. stuffed olives
¾ c. milk
1 can mushroom soup
1 6-oz. can mushrooms, undrained
Salt and pepper to taste
1 can pkg. chow mein noodles
1 c. salted cashew nuts

Brown meat and onions. Cook egg noodles and place in a buttered baking dish. Add meat, onion, olives, milk, soup, mushrooms, salt and pepper; mix well. Bake 1 hour at 350°F. Remove from oven; top with noodles and cashews. Bake an additional 15 minutes. Yield: 12 servings.

Mrs. Florence Nelson, Milroy School
Milroy, Minnesota

SOUR CREAM-NOODLE BAKE

1 8-oz. pkg. med. noodles
1 lb. ground beef
2 T. butter or margarine
1 t. salt
⅛ t. pepper
¼ t. garlic salt
1 8-oz. can tomato sauce
1 c. creamed cottage cheese
1 c. sour cream
6 green onions, chopped
¾ c. sharp Cheddar cheese, shredded

Cook noodles according to package directions; rinse and drain. Brown meat in butter. Add salt, pepper, garlic salt and tomato sauce; simmer for 5 minutes. Combine cottage cheese, sour cream, onions and noodles. Alternate layers of noodle mixture and meat mixture in a 2-quart casserole, beginning with noodles and ending with meat. Top with cheese. Bake at 350°F. for 20-25 minutes. Yield: 6-8 servings.

Blanche Weaver, Herrin H.S.
Herrin, Illinois

CRUSTY BEEF CASSEROLE

2 T. vegetable oil
1 med. onion, chopped
2 lb. ground beef
4 cans mushroom sauce
1 t. salt
1 lb. fine noodles, cooked and drained
1 lb. sharp Cheddar cheese, grated
Seasoning salt

Heat oil; add onions and cook until golden. Add meat and brown, stirring occasionally. Add mushroom sauce and salt; heat thoroughly. Layer half of noodles, half of sauce and half of cheese; sprinkle with seasoning salt. Make another layer of noodles, sauce and top with cheese. Bake at 325°F. for 1 hour. Yield: 8-10 servings.

Carol Richards, West Mifflin South H..S
West Mifflin, Pennsylvania

DOUBLE NOODLE CASSEROLE

2 lb. ground beef
1 med. onion, chopped
½ c. stuffed olives, sliced
1 can mushroom soup
1 soup can milk
¾ t. salt
1 8-oz. pkg. narrow noodles, cooked
½ c. sharp cheese, grated
1 c. chow mein noodles
¼ c. salted nuts, chopped

Brown ground beef and onion; add olives, soup, milk and salt. Place layers of meat mixture and cooked noodles in a 2-quart casserole having meat on top; sprinkle with cheese. Bake at 350°F. for 30 minutes. Sprinkle with mixture of chow mein noodles and nuts; cook 10 minutes longer. Yield: 8 servings.

Mrs. Lucile Jacobsen, Manistee H.S.
Manistee, Michigan

GOULASH

1 lb. hamburger
1 c. celery, chopped
1 c. onions, chopped
8-oz. pkg. noodles
2 cans chicken noodle soup
2 cans mushroom soup
½ can tomato soup
1 sm. jar stuffed olives

Brown hamburger, celery and onions. Boil noodles; drain. Combine all ingredients except olives; pour into casserole. Bake at 350°F. for 25 minutes. Add olives and bake 15 minutes longer. Yield: 6-8 servings.

Mrs. David Olerud, Haines Public School
Haines, Alaska

HAMBURGER-CASHEW HOT DISH

½ 10-oz pkg. noodles
1 lb. ground beef
1 med. onion, chopped
2 T. butter
½ t. salt
½ lb. Cheddar cheese, diced
1 4-oz. can mushrooms, drained
1 can cream of mushroom soup
½ c. milk
⅔ c. chow mein noodles
½ c. cashews

Cook noodles and drain. Brown meat and onions in butter; add remaining ingredients except chow mein noodles and cashews. Mix well in a casserole. Bake at 325°F. for 20 minutes. Add chow mein noodles and cashews; bake about 10 minutes. Yield: 7-8 servings.

Barbara Hannon, Bedford Community School
Bedford, Iowa

HOT DISH

1 lb. ground beef
Chopped onion (opt.)
1 can mushroom soup
1 can cream of chicken soup
1 soup can water
1 6-oz. package egg noodles, cooked
1 c. celery, diced
¼ lb. cashew nuts

Brown meat and onions if desired. Pour in soup and water. Mix with cooked noodles, cashew nuts and celery. Bake 35-45 minutes at 350°F. Yield: 6-8 servings.

Ann K. Sethre, Springfield Public School
Springfield, Minnesota

JOHN MARZETTI

1 lb. hamburger
1 sm. onion, chopped
2 sm. stalks celery, chopped
Salt and pepper to taste
1 4-oz. pkg. noodles
½ c. water
1 8-oz. can tomato sauce
4 slices sharp cheese

Brown hamburger, onion and celery; salt and pepper to taste. Cook noodles in salted water following directions on package; drain. Add water to hamburger mixture; add tomato sauce and simmer 5 minutes. Add noodles; place in a greased casserole. Bake at 350°F. for 45 minutes. Top with cheese. Yield: 6 servings.

Phyllis A. Barrett, Seven Mile H.S.
Seven Mile, Ohio

JOHNNY MARZETTI

2 T. margarine
2 lge. onions, chopped
1 clove of garlic, minced
1 lb. ground beef
1 can tomato paste
1½ c. water
2 4-oz. cans sliced mushrooms
1 c. celery, diced
1 green pepper, diced (opt.)
1 t. vinegar
Salt and pepper to taste
½ lb. sharp cheese, grated
1 8-oz. pkg. broad noodles

Melt margarine; add onions and garlic and cook until soft. Add ground beef and cook until well browned. Stir in tomato paste, water, mushrooms with liquid, celery, green pepper, vinegar, salt, pepper and cheese. Simmer 15 minutes to make a rich sauce. Cook noodles until just tender in boiling salted water. Drain and mix with sauce. Cover and cook slowly on top of range or at 350°F. for 1 hour. Yield 6-8 servings.

Mrs. Kathryn Moore, Brazil Sr. H.S.
Brazil, Indiana

MARZETTE

1 T. butter
1 onion, chopped
1 green pepper, chopped
1 lb. ground beef
1 can mushroom soup
1 8-oz. pkg. noodles, cooked
1 can tomato sauce
1 lb. sliced American cheese
1 c. crushed potato chips

Saute onion and green pepper in butter; add ground beef and cook until browned. Season to taste; add mushroom soup and simmer 5 minutes. Pour drained noodles into a buttered casserole; add meat mixture in a layer. Pour tomato sauce over top; cover with sliced cheese. Top with crushed potato chips. Bake at 350°F. for 30 minutes. Yield: 4-6 servings.

Evelyn Ruth, Garnett H.S.
Garnett, Kansas

MEAT BALL-NOODLE CASSEROLE

1 lb. ground beef
½ pkg. noodles
1 can cream of mushroom soup

Form meat balls out of ground beef; brown. Cook noodles; drain. Mix meat balls, noodles and soup in a casserole. Bake at 325°F. for 20 minutes. Yield: 4-6 servings.

Marilee Sellman, Northridge H.S.
Dayton, Ohio

NOODLE MEDLEY

½ c. onions, diced
½ c. green pepper, diced (opt.)
2 T. shortening
1 c. celery, coarsely chopped
½ lb. ground beef
1 can red kidney beans
3 c. tomatoes
1 c. button mushrooms
2 t. seasoning salt
1⅛ t. chili powder
⅛ t. pepper
12 black olives
1 pkg. uncooked noodles

Saute onions and green pepper in shortening; boil celery. Add meat and celery to onions and pepper; stir until lightly browned. Add remaining ingredients except noodles. Put mixture into a covered casserole forming a ring around outside. In center flatten dry noodles pushing them down into juices. Circle noodles with olives. Bake covered at 350°F. for 30 minutes. Yield: 6-8 servings.

Mrs. Ruth F. Smith, Burlington-Edison H.S.
Burlington, Washington

NOODLE STROGANOFF

¼ c. onions, chopped
¼ t. garlic powder
Butter
1 lb. ground chuck
½ c. Sherry
1 t. salt
¼ t. pepper
1 can mushroom soup
1 can onion soup
2 cans water
¼ lb. noodles
1 pt. sour cream

Saute onions and garlic powder in butter; add meat and brown well. Add sherry and seasonings; simmer. Dilute soups with water; add to meat and heat to simmering. Stir in noodles; cover and cook until noodles are tender. Add sour cream; heat quickly, mixing in sour cream. Serve sprinkled with parsley. Yield: 6-8 servings.

Mrs. Nancy A. Quick, Bonita H.S.
La Verne, California

NUTTY CASSEROLE

1 lb. ground beef
1 sm. onion, finely chopped
4 oz. fine noodles
½ can evaporated milk
20 stuffed olives, sliced
¼ lb. cheese, grated
1 can chow mein noodles
Salted nuts, chopped

Cook ground beef and onion until meat is almost cooked. Cook noodles and drain. Combine beef, noodles, milk and olives. Put into a casserole dish; cover with cheese. Bake covered at 350°F. for 30 minutes. Remove from oven; cover with noodles and sprinkle nuts on top. Bake uncovered for 30 minutes longer. Yield: 8 servings.

Nancy Newman, Joliet Township H.S.
Joliet, Illinois

ONE-DISH MEAL

1 8-oz. pkg. noodles
½ t. butter
2 lb. ground beef, browned
1 sm. onion, chopped (opt.)
4-5 slices cheese
1 can mushroom or tomato soup
1 soup can water

Cook noodles with butter in salted water. Brown meat and onion; season to taste. Place layers of noodles, meat and cheese in casserole until all are used. Dilute soup with water; pour over layers. Bake at 350°F. for about 1 hour. Yield: 8-10 servings.

This recipe submitted by the following teachers:
Delores Vondrak, Elk Point H.S.
Elk Point, South Dakota
Mrs. Gingie Hines, Butler County H.S.
Morgantown, Kentucky

PIZZA FLAVOR CASSEROLE

1 lb. ground beef
⅓ c. onion, chopped
1 med. clove garlic, minced
1 t. oregano
½ t. salt
1 can condensed tomato soup
⅓ c. water
2 c. cooked wide noodles
½ c. cheese, shredded

Brown beef with onion, garlic and seasonings, stirring to separate meat. Combine all ingredients except cheese. Sprinkle cheese over top. Bake at 350°F. for 30 minutes. NOTE: If desired ½ teaspoon onion salt and ½ teaspoon garlic salt may be substituted for onion and garlic. An additional ½ cup cheese may also be added to meat mixture. Yield: 4 servings.

This recipe submitted by the following teachers:
Joyce Bales, Lewisville School
Lewisville, Indiana
Kay L. Goodman, Rockbridge H.S.
Fairfield, Virginia

SUPER SUPPER

1-2 c. onion, chopped
1-2 c. celery, chopped
1 lb. ground beef
1 8-oz. pkg. noodles, cooked
1 can cream of mushroom soup
1 can cream of chicken soup
Cracker crumbs (opt.)

Brown onion, celery and ground beef. Add cooked noodles and soups. Mix all ingredients well except crumbs. Place in two 1½-quart casseroles; top with cracker crumbs if desired. Bake for 1 hour at 275°F. Yield: 10-12 servings.

Mrs. Ruth McDonald, Eldora H.S.
Eldora, Iowa

GROUND BEEF-RICE

BAKED CHILI

2 T. fat
2 onions, diced
1 lb. ground beef
1 No. 2½ can tomatoes
1 No. 2 can kidney beans
1 t. salt
½ t. pepper
½ c uncooked rice

Heat fat; add onion and cook slowly until golden brown. Add meat; stir until well done. Add tomatoes, beans and seasonings. Pour into casserole; add uncooked rice. Bake 1 hour and 30 minutes. Yield: 6 servings.

Mrs. Marion Biscup, North Jr. H.S.
Grant Pass, Oregon

BEEF PORCUPINES

1 lb. ground beef
1 c. raw rice
¾ t. salt
⅛ t. pepper
1 med. onion, diced
1 can condensed tomato soup

Combine beef, rice, salt, pepper and onion. Form into 1½-inch balls; place in baking dish. Add tomato soup; cover. Bake at 350°F. for 1 hour or until rice is tender. Yield: 6 servings.

Mrs. Florence Russell, Napoleon H.S.
Napoleon, Ohio

BEEF-RICE-ALMOND CASSEROLE

½ c. boiling water
½ c. instant rice
1 lb. hamburger
½ sm. onion
1 can cream of mushroom soup
1 can cream of chicken soup
½ c. slivered almonds
Buttered crumbs or Special K

Combine water and rice; let stand while you brown meat and onion. Add soups and almonds. Pour mixture into buttered casserole; sprinkle with buttered crumbs. Bake at 350°F. for 1 hour. Yield: 6 servings.

Carolyn Griesse, Auburn H.S.
Auburn, Nebraska

BEEF AND RICE CASSEROLE

1½ c. ground beef
1 c. onion, chopped
1 c. dried celery
1 can cream of mushroom soup
1 can cream of chicken soup
1 sm. can mushrooms
1 c. cooked rice
Soya sauce

Saute meat, onion and celery; simmer 20 minutes. Mix in soups, mushrooms and cooked rice. Season with soya sauce. Bake at 350°F. for 1 hour.

Ann Marie Arend, Durand H.S.
Durand, Michigan

BEEF-RICE HOT DISH

2 c. celery, chopped
1 lge. onion, chopped
3 lb. ground beef
3 c. cooked rice
2-3 cans mushroom soup
3 cans cream of chicken soup
3 soup cans water
Salt and pepper to taste

Brown celery and onion in butter; add meat and brown. Add remaining ingredients. Bake at 350°F. for 2 hours. Yield: 25 servings.

Mrs. Jerry Rodacker, Portland H.S.
Portland, North Dakota

BEEF-WILD RICE CASSEROLE

1 c. wild rice
2 lb. ground beef
1 med. onion, chopped
1 c. celery, chopped
½ t. salt
1 can chicken and rice soup
1 can cream of mushroom soup

Cook wild rice until tender. Brown meat; add onions and celery. Drain excess fat. Add soups; simmer slowly until celery is cooked. Mix with wild rice in a 2-quart casserole. Bake at 325°F. for 45 minutes. Yield: 8-10 servings.

Mrs. Alma Miller, Pillager H.S.
Pillager, Minnesota

CHEROKEE CASSEROLE

1 lb. ground beef
1 T. olive oil
¾ chopped Bermuda onion
1½ t. salt
⅛ t. pepper
⅛ t. garlic powder
⅛ t. ground thyme
½ sm. bay leaf
⅛ t. oregano
2 c. canned tomatoes
1 can condensed cream of mushroom soup
1 c. instant rice
6 stuffed olives, sliced
2-3 slices American cheese, cut in ½-inch strips

Brown meat in olive oil. Add onion; cook over medium heat until tender. Stir in seasonings, tomatoes, soup and rice. Bring to a boil; reduce heat. Add half of olive slices; simmer 5 minutes, stirring occasionally. Spoon into 1½-quart baking dish. Top with cheese strips. Broil until cheese is melted or bake in 425°F. oven for 30 minutes. Garnish with remaining olive slices. Yield: 4-6 servings.

This recipe submitted by the following teachers:
Mrs. Saralu C. Jenkins, Clarkston H.S.
Clarkston, Georgia
Mrs. Evelyn W. Newsom, Mt. Vernon H.S.
Mt. Vernon, Texas
Mrs. Kathryn Schomburg, Oregon H.S.
Oregon, Wisconsin
Mrs. Georgia Day, Hamilton Heights H.S.
Arcadia, Indiana

CHOW MEIN CASSEROLE

1 lb. hamburger
1 med. onion, chopped
1 c. celery, diced
½ c. raw rice, rinsed in hot water
1 can mushroom soup
1 can chicken and rice soup
3 T. soy sauce
Chow mein noodles

Brown hamburger and onion. Put in casserole with celery, rice, soups and soy sauce. Bake 1 hour at 375°F. Sprinkle with chow mein noodles; bake 30 minutes longer. Yield: 4-6 servings.

Louise M. Jasken, Sr. H.S.
St. James, Minnesota

CHINESE HAMBURGER CASSEROLE

1½ lb. hamburger
2 T. salad oil
2 med. onions, finely chopped
1 c. celery, finely chopped
1 can cream of mushroom soup
1 can cream of chicken soup
1 can bean sprouts, drained
1½ c. warm water
½ c. uncooked rice
¼ c. soy sauce
¼ t. pepper
1 can Chinese noodles

Brown meat in oil until crumbly; add onions, celery, soups, bean sprouts and water. Stir in rice, soy sauce and pepper. Turn into greased dish; cover with foil or lid. Bake at 350°F. for 30 minutes. Uncover and bake 30 minutes. Top with noodles; bake 15 minutes. Yield: 8 servings.

Phyllis Williams, Vernonia H.S.
Vernonia, Oregon

CREOLE JUMBO HOT DISH

1 lb. ground beef
2 lge. onions, cut up
2 c. celery, cut up
1 c. rice
1 can mushroom soup
1 can chicken soup
2 c. water
4 T. soy sauce
Salt and pepper to taste
1 can bean sprouts

Brown first three ingredients; transfer to casserole. Add all remaining ingredients except bean sprouts. Bake for 1 hour and 30 minutes at 350° F. Add sprouts; bake 30 minutes longer. Yield: 15 servings.

Verlys Malme, Erskine H.S.
Erskine, Minnesota

GROUND BEEF-RICE HOT DISH

1 lb. ground meat
2 sm. onions, chopped
1 c. uncooked rice
1 can cream of mushroom soup
1 can cream of chicken soup
2 c. celery, diced
2 c. water
1 can mushrooms
¼ lb. cashew nuts

Brown meat and onion. Add the rice, soups, celery and water. Put into a greased casserole. Bake for 1 hour at 350°F., stirring occasionally. Add mushrooms and cashew nuts 10 minutes before end of baking time. Yield: 8-10 servings.

Ann Ring, Cambridge H.S.
Cambridge, Minnesota

FAVORITE HOT DISH

1 lb. hamburger
1 onion, chopped
1 sm. bunch celery, chopped
½ c. rice
1 can cream chicken soup
1 can cream of mushroom soup
2 soup cans milk

Brown meat, onion and celery; add rice, soup and milk. Pour into casserole; bake 2 hours at 350°F.

Mrs. Dorothy Soderlund, Milaca H.S.
Milaca, Minnesota

GROUND BEEF AND WILD RICE CASSEROLE

½ c. wild rice
½ c. regular rice
3 c. boiling water
6 T. onions, chopped
4 T. bacon fat
1½ lb. ground beef
2 cans cream of chicken soup
2 4-oz. cans sliced mushrooms and liquid
2 bouillon cubes dissolved in 1 c. hot water
1 t. celery salt
1 t. onion salt
1 t. pepper
1 t. garlic salt
1 t. paprika
1 bay leaf, crumbled
½ c. chopped parsley, toasted (opt.)
Chopped parsley (opt.)

Pour boiling water over rice. Let stand 15 minutes and drain. Brown onion in fat; add meat and brown. Combine all ingredients. Let stand in casserole overnight. Bake at 325°F. for 1 hour and 30 minutes. Yield: 12 servings.

Mrs. Ronald Havenstein, Regina H.S.
Iowa City, Iowa

HAMBURGER CASSEROLE

1 lb. ground beef
1 med. onion, chopped
1 c. celery, diced
2 T. drippings
½ c. rice
2 c. water
1 can cream of mushroom soup
1 can cream of chicken soup
3 T. soy sauce
2 T. Worcestershire sauce
1 4-oz. can mushrooms
1 3-oz. can Chinese noodles

Brown ground beef, onions and celery in drippings. Combine all ingredients except noodles in a greased casserole. Bake at 350°F. for 45 minutes. Serve over noodles. Yield: 6-8 servings.

Mrs. Janice Stewart, Shabbona H.S.
Shabbona, Illinois

HAMBURGER-RICE CASSEROLE

1 lb. hamburger
1 med. onion, chopped
1 c. celery, chopped
1 can cream of chicken soup
1 can cream of mushroom soup
1 c. water
1 c. rice
Dash of salt and pepper
1 T. soy sauce
1 can Chinese noodles

Brown hamburger, onion and celery. Add soups; rinse cans with water and add. Cook rice in 2 cups water for 20 minutes. Combine all ingredients except noodles. Bake 1 hour at 375°F. When done sprinkle top with noodles. Yield: 6 servings.

Mrs. Marion Clark, Humphrey H.S.
Humphrey, Nebraska

HANDY HOT DISH

1½ lb. ground beef
1 c. rice
1-2 T. onions, minced
2 cans cream of chicken soup
2 cans water
1 t. salt
3 T. pimento, minced
Buttered bread crumbs or potato chips

Brown beef until crumbly; drain fat. Combine meat with rice; add remaining ingredients. Place in a buttered 8 x 12-inch baking dish; bake at 350°F. for 2 hours, stirring several times. Add bread crumbs and brown lightly. NOTE: Three cups cooked chopped chicken or turkey may be substituted for ground beef. Do not brown chicken. Yield: 6 servings.

Rosanne Williams, David City H.S.
David City, Nebraska

MOCK CHOP SUEY

1 c. rice, partially cooked
2 lb. ground beef
2 c. onions, sliced
1 c. celery, chopped
1 green pepper, diced
1 can cream of mushroom soup
1 can chicken and rice soup
½ c. water
¼ c. soy sauce

Cook rice until partially done. Brown beef; add onions, celery and green pepper. Cook together over medium heat for 5 minutes. Add soups, water and soy sauce. Add rice to above mixture; place in a casserole. Bake 1 hour at 350°F. Yield: 8 servings.

Ann L. Walsh, Lathrop H.S.
Fairbanks, Alaska

HAMBURGER-RICE HOT DISH

1 lb. hamburger
2 cans chicken and rice soup
1 soup can water
2 c. celery, chopped
½ c. rice

Brown hamburger. Add soup, water and celery; bring to a boil. Add rice and put in a casserole dish. Bake 1 hour and 15 minutes at 350°F. Yield: 6 servings.

Lois Ann Knutson, Sibley H.S.
West St. Paul, Minnesota

MEAT BALLS WITH BUTTERMILK SAUCE

1½ lb. ground beef
1 sm. onion, finely chopped
⅓ c. celery, sliced
3 T. green pepper, chopped
1 c. cooked rice
1 t. salt
½ t. pepper
1 egg
1 can mushroom soup
1 can buttermilk
1 2-oz. can mushroom stems and pieces

Combine ground beef, onion, green pepper, celery, rice, salt, pepper and egg; work together until well mixed. Divide meat into 12 portions; roll each portion into a ball and place in a greased 2-quart casserole. Combine mushroom soup, buttermilk and liquid from mushrooms; beat until smooth. Add mushrooms; pour over meat balls. Bake at 350°F. for 1 hour. Yield: 6 servings.

Mrs. Geraldine Asell, Thomas Downey H.S.
Modesto, California

MEAT-RICE HOT DISH

1 lb. stew meat, cubed
1 c. celery, chopped
½ c. green pepper, chopped
1 onion, finely cut
1 c. rice
1 can chicken-rice soup or chicken broth
1 can mushroom soup
1 can chicken soup
2 soup cans water
1 t. salt
Black olives, slivered
Potato chips, crushed (opt.)

Brown meat, celery, green pepper and onion each separately in small amount of butter. Put rice in buttered casserole dish; add browned ingredients. Add soups and water. Sprinkle salt on top; mix ingredients together thoroughly. Cut slivers of black olives and sprinkle on top. Bake 1 hour at 375°F. Potato chips may be sprinkled on top for last few minutes of baking time. More water may be added if casserole becomes too dry. Yield: 4-6 servings.

Mrs. Glen Huebner, Centennial Sr. H.S.
Circle Pines, Minnesota

MOCK CHOW MEIN

1 lb. ground beef
2 onions, chopped
1 c. celery, chopped
½ c. water
1 can cream of mushroom soup
1 can chicken gumbo soup
2 soup cans water
2 T. Worcestershire sauce
4 T. soya sauce
½ c. uncooked rice
1 pkg. chow mein noodles

Brown ground beef and onions. Add remaining ingredients except chow mein noodles and mix. Bake at 350°F. for 1 hour and 30 minutes in covered casserole. Remove from oven and sprinkle with chow mein noodles. Return to oven and bake 30 minutes longer. Yield: 10 servings.

Marilyn Peterson, Alexander Ramsey
St. Paul, Minnesota

MORE PLEASE

1 lb. ground beef
2 lge. onions, thinly sliced
1 c. celery, chopped
½ c. instant rice
3 T. soy sauce
1 can cream of mushroom soup
1 can cream of chicken soup
1½ soup cans water
1 lge. can Chinese noodles

Brown ground beef; add onions and celery. Cook until browned. Add remaining ingredients except noodles. Bake at 350°F. for 50 minutes, stirring once or twice during baking period. Sprinkle noodles over top; bake ten minutes longer. Yield: 8 servings.

Mrs. Louella R. Pence, Macon H.S.
Macon, Illinois

MULLIGAN STEW CASSEROLE

1 bunch of celery, chopped
1 med. onion, finely chopped
3 T. butter
1 lb. ground beef
1 t. salt
¼ t. pepper
1 c. canned tomatoes
2 c. cooked rice
1 can condensed tomato soup

Saute celery and onion in butter. Add ground beef, salt and pepper; brown meat. Layer meat mixture, tomatoes and rice in a 2-quart baking dish. Pour tomato soup over top. Bake at 350°F. for 30 minutes. Yield: 6-8 servings.

Mrs. Janet Urbanz, Bear Creek,
Bear Creek, Wisconsin

RICE-HAMBURGER HOT DISH

1 lb. ground beef
1 onion, chopped
3 c. celery, cooked
1 c. uncooked rice
4 T. soy sauce
1 can cream of chicken soup
1 can cream of mushroom soup
2 c. celery water
1 can bean sprouts
1 t. salt
½ t. pepper
1½-oz. chow mein noodles (opt.)

Brown ground beef and onion. Add remaining ingredients except noodles. Bake at 350°F. for 1 hour and 30 minutes. Top with noodles 10 minutes before removing from oven. Yield: 6-8 servings.

Marie Birr, Lester Prairie H.S.
Lester Prairie, Minnesota

SUPER BEEF-RICE CASSEROLE

1 c. rice
1 lb. ground beef
1 lge. onion, chopped
Butter
1 c. celery, chopped
1 can cream of chicken soup
1 can cream of mushroom soup
2 t. soy sauce

Brown ground beef and onion in butter. Cook rice for 15 minutes. Simmer celery until tender. Combine all ingredients. Bake at 275°F. for 1 hour. Yield: 6-8 servings.

Martha Lunday Nornberg, Dr. S. G. Knight School
Randall, Minnesota

TEXAS HASH

3 lge. onions, thinly sliced
1 lge. green pepper, minced
3 T. fat
1 lb. ground beef
2 c. cooked tomatoes
½ c. uncooked rice
1-2 t. chili powder
2 t. salt
⅛ t. pepper

Saute onions and green pepper in fat until tender. Add meat and brown until crumbly. Stir in remaining ingredients. Pour into greased 2-quart baking dish. Cover and bake 45 minutes at 350°F. Remove cover and bake 15 minutes longer. NOTE: If desired mixture may be simmered slowly on top of stove rather than baked. Yield: 6-8 servings.

This recipe submitted by the following teachers:
Mrs. Ann Hoit, Ousley Jr. H.S.
Arlington, Texas
Dianne Tufts, Valley Regional H.S.
Deep River, Connecticut

BARBEQUE BURGERS

1½ lb. ground beef
¾ c. rolled oats
1 c. milk
1½ t. salt
1 sm. onion, chopped
¾ t. pepper
1 c. catsup
½ c. water
3 T. vinegar
2 T. Worcestershire sauce
2 T. sugar

Mix beef, rolled oats, milk, salt, onion and pepper together and form into patties. Brown patties in skillet. Combine remaining ingredients in a casserole; place browned patties into it. Bake at 300°F. for 1 hour and 30 minutes. Yield: 8 servings.

Mrs. Lois Platt, Laurel H.S.
New Castle, Pennsylvania

BEEF CRUST CASSEROLE

1½ lb. ground beef
½ c. onion, chopped
2 t. salt
¼ c. catsup
2 cans cream of mushroom soup
1 pkg. frozen mixed peas and carrots
½ c. raw converted rice
½ c. water
½ t. salt
1 c. chow mein noodles

Combine meat, onion, salt and catsup; line a 2½-quart casserole with mixture. Combine soup, vegetables, rice, water and salt. Mix well; pour into meat shell. Cover and bake at 350°F. for 1 hour and 15 minutes. Top with noodles; bake uncovered 15 minutes. Yield: 6 servings.

Ruth Schmitz, Luxemburg Union H.S.
Luxemburg, Wisconsin

BEEF STROGANOFF

½ c. onion, minced
¼ c. butter
1 lb. ground chuck
1 clove garlic, minced
2 T. flour
1 can cream of mushroom soup
1 t. salt
¼ t. monosodium glutamate
¼ t. pepper
¼ t. paprika
1 c. sour cream
Parsley

Saute onions in butter until golden. Stir in meat, garlic, flour, salt, monsodium glutamate, pepper and paprika; saute for 5 minutes. Add soup; simmer uncovered for 10 minutes. Stir in sour cream; sprinkle with parsley. Serve over rice, noodles, or mashed potatoes. Yield: 4-6 servings.

Barbara Paulson, Portola Jr.-Sr. H.S.
Portola, California

BUDGET MEAT LOAF

1 lb. ground beef
2 eggs
1½ c. bread crumbs
1 sm. can tomato paste
1 sm. can mushrooms
¼ c. green pepper, diced
1 T. mustard
1 t. salt
¼ t. pepper
1 t. celery salt
¼ t. garlic
1 sm. onion, diced
½ t. thyme
½ t. rosemary

Combine meat, eggs, bread crumbs, tomato paste and mushrooms. Add remaining ingredients; thoroughly mix with hands. Place in a loaf casserole or in individual casserole. Bake at 325°F. for 45 minutes to 1 hour or until meat is done. Yield: 6 servings.

Carol O'Connor, Manteno H.S.
Manteno, Illinois

BURGER CHILI AND CHIPS

1 lb. ground beef
½ c. onion, chopped
¼ c. celery, diced
1 t. salt
¼ t. pepper
1 1-lb. can chili with beans
1 c. corn chips
1 c. processed American cheese, diced

Brown meat; add onion and celery and cook until tender but not brown. Season with salt and pepper. Add chili and mix. Place layer of corn chips in greased 1½-quart casserole. Alternate layers of chili mixture, corn chips and cheese, ending with corn chips. Bake at 350°F. for 10 minutes. Yield: 6 servings.

Mrs. Mildred E. Miller, Chico Sr. H.S.
Chico, California

CHICKEN-BEEF BAKE

1½ lb. ground beef
1½ T. shortening
2 sm. onions, finely chopped
6 stalks celery, finely chopped
1 sm. can chow mein noodles
1 can condensed cream of chicken soup
1 can condensed chicken and rice soup
1 soup can water
1 t. salt
½ t. pepper

Brown ground beef in shortening. Add onions and celery; simmer 10 minutes. Add half can chow mein noodles, soups, water, salt and pepper; mix well. Put in a greased casserole; top with remaining noodles. Bake 35 minutes at 325°F. Yield: 6 servings.

Ava Tretsven, Muscoda H.S.
Muscoda, Wisconsin

CHILI CASSEROLE

1½ c. chili beans
½ lb. hamburger
1½ lge. onion, chopped
1 clove garlic, chopped
1 pt. tomato juice
1 T. salt
¼ t. cayenne powder
½ t. chili powder

Soak beans overnight. Cook in fresh water until tender. Brown hamburger, onion and garlic. Add tomato juice, salt, cayenne powder and chile powder. Pour into casserole. Bake at 375°F. for 1 hour and 30 minutes. Yield: 6 servings.

Mrs. Thomas E. Maxwell, Big Sandy Public Schools
Big Sandy, Montana

CHILI-CHEESE CASSEROLE

1 lb. ground beef
2 t. salt
½ t. pepper
¾ c. onion, chopped
1 clove garlic, minced
1 T. chili powder
1 t. paprika
¼ t. oregano
1 8-oz. can tomato sauce
1 1-lb. can pinto or kidney beans
½ c. corn chips, crushed
¾ c. cheese, grated

Brown seasoned beef and onion; put into a medium casserole. Saute ¼ cup of meat mixture with garlic until golden. Combine all ingredients except chips and cheese. Spoon over hamburger; sprinkle chips and cheese over top. Bake at 350°F. for 30 minutes. Yield: 6 servings.

Freda F. Bennett, Elgin Public School
Elgin, Nebraska

CHILI CON CARNE CASSEROLE

1 can cream of mushroom soup
1 can chili con carne
½ c. onion, finely chopped
1 c. cheese, grated
1 pkg. tortillas or 1 pkg. corn chips

Combine soup and chili; mix thoroughly. Add onion and grated cheese to mixture. Lightly grease casserole dish. Line bottom of casserole with tortillas broken into quarters or corn chips. Pour half of soup mixture over tortillas. Put layer of tortillas or corn chips over mixture; cover with remaining soup mixture. Bake at 375°F. for 45 minutes. NOTE: If desired, chopped lettuce and tomatoes may be sprinkled over top of casserole after it is cooked and served as a one dish meal and salad combined. Yield: 6 servings.

Zada Lines, Santa Cruz Valley Union H.S.
Eloy, Arizona

CHINESE GOULASH

1 lb. hamburger
1 med. onion, chopped
1 c. celery, chopped
1 can tomato soup
1 can chicken and rice soup
½ c. water
1 can Chinese noodles

Brown hamburger, onion and celery in hot fat. Add soups and water; cook for 30 minutes. Pour into casserole; bake 10 minutes at 450°F. Add noodles and bake 10 minutes longer. Yield: 4-6 servings.

Mrs. Eileen McCarty, Plentywood H.S.
Plentywood, Montana

CHOP SUEY CASSEROLE

1 med. onion, minced
1½-2 lb. chop suey meat
2 c. celery, chopped
1 can bean sprouts, drained
1 can cream of mushroom soup
1 can cream of chicken soup
1 can chow mein noodles
Salt and pepper to taste

Brown onion in small amount of fat. Add chop suey and cook until meat is tender. Add celery; cook until done. Combine in a 2½-quart casserole with bean sprouts, soups, half of noodles, and seasonings. Mix together and top with other half of noodles. Bake 1 hour at 350°F. Yield: 6 servings.

Barbara Brotherton, Kenowa Hills H.S.
Grand Rapids, Michigan

GROUND BEEF CRUST CASSEROLE

2 lb. ground beef
1 c. evaporated milk
½ t. salt
½ t. pepper
½ t. seasoning salt

Combine beef, milk and seasonings. Pat part of mixture into bottom and sides of a 2-quart casserole.

FILLING:
7-8 slices bread, broken in pieces
½ med. onion, finely chopped
½ c. celery, finely chopped
1 t. seasoning salt
½ t. salt
½ t. pepper
¼ c. butter, melted
2 strips of bacon

Combine all ingredients except bacon. Fill meat center with bread filling; cover with reserved meat mixture. Seal meat edges so filling is completely enclosed. Place slices of bacon on top of meat. Cover with foil that has been punctured with small holes. Set in pan of water. Bake at 350°F. for 30 minutes. Pour off any excess liquid before serving. Yield: 6 servings.

Linda Dee Hart, Lamphere Sr. H.S.
Madison Heights, Michigan

CORN CHIP PIE

1 8-oz. pkg. corn chips
½ lb. Cheddar cheese, grated
1 med. onion, diced
1 lb. lean hamburger
1 green chili or 2 t. chili powder
1 No. 2½ can tomatoes

Alternate layers of all ingredients in casserole except tomatoes. Repeat layers. Pour tomatoes over top. Bake at 350°F. for 1 hour. Yield: 6 servings.

Mrs. P. V. Porter, San Jon Municipal School
San Jon, New Mexico

COUNTRY BEEF PIE

½ c. tomato sauce
½ c. bread crumbs
¼ c. chopped onion
1½ t. salt
⅛ t. pepper
1 lb. ground beef
¼ c. chopped green pepper
⅛ t. oregano

Thoroughly mix all ingredients. Pat mixture into bottom of greased 9-inch pie pan. Pinch 1-inch flutings around edge.

FILLING:
1⅓ c. instant rice
1 c. water
½ t. salt
1½ c. tomato sauce
1 c. grated Cheddar cheese

Combine rice, water, salt, tomato sauce and ¼ cup cheese. Spoon mixture into meat crust. Cover with foil. Bake at 350°F. for 25 minutes. Remove foil; sprinkle with remaining cheese. Bake, uncovered, 10-15 minutes longer. Cut into pie-shaped pieces for serving. Yield: 6-8 servings.

This recipe submitted by the following teachers:
Mrs. Geraldine Jenkins, Emanuel County Institute
Twin City, Georgia
Mrs. Lucille Bradbury, Central H.S.
San Angelo, Texas
Mrs. Rochelle Heider, Menosha, Wisconsin
Mrs. Agnes Wautier, Southern Door H.S.
Brussels, Wisconsin
Mrs. Vivian Nanny, Riviera H.S.
Riviera, Texas

ENCHILADA CASSEROLE

2 lb. ground beef
2 med. onions, chopped
1 lge. can enchilada sauce
1 can cream of mushroom soup
1 sm. can green chili peppers
1 lb. longhorn cheese, grated
2 pkg. corn tortillas

Saute beef and onions. Blend enchilada sauce and soup together. Take seeds and viens from peppers. Layer tortillas, meat, peppers, sauce and cheese. Pierce holes through layers; pour any remaining sauce over top. Bake at 375°F. 35-45 minutes.

Mrs. Barbara Smith, Tolleson Union H.S.
Tolleson, Arizona

HAMBURGER CASSEROLE

1 lb. hamburger
6 slices of bread
4 T. butter or margarine
Salt and pepper
Sage
Onion
1 can mushroom soup

Make small patties with hamburger; brown. Put half of patties in casserole. Combine all remaining ingredients except soup. Put layer of dressing on top of hamburger patties. Add another layer of dressing on top of second layer of hamburger. Pour soup over top. Bake at 350°F. until done.

Janice Bendshadler, Banks H.S.
Banks, Oregon

HAMBURGERS CREOLE

1 lb. ground beef
1 t. Accent
1½ t. salt
⅛ t. pepper
2 T. butter or margarine
1 sm. onion, sliced
½ lb. mushrooms, sliced
¼ c. diced green pepper
¼ c. diced celery
1 1-lb. can tomatoes

Sprinkle beef with Accent, ¾ teaspoon salt and pepper. Toss gently with fork. Shape into four patties. Brown on both sides in melted butter in skillet. Remove meat; add all remaining ingredients except tomatoes, patties and remaining salt. Cook over low heat for 5 minutes. Add tomatoes, salt and patties. Cook slowly for 15 minutes. Yield: 4 servings.

Photograph for this recipe on page 39

HAMBURGER-TOMATO SOUP CASSEROLE

1 lb. hamburger
½ onion, chopped
½ c. celery, chopped
¼ c. green pepper, chopped
4 oz. noodles, cooked
1 can tomato soup

Brown meat, onion, green pepper and celery. Cook noodles; drain. Put in casserole with tomato soup. Bake covered 1 hour at 350°F. Yield: 4-6 servings.

Mrs. Emily Slamar Strahler, Pueblo H.S.
Tucson, Arizona

HAMBURGER GOOP

1 c. onion, chopped
1 c. green pepper, chopped
1 c. celery, chopped
Shortening
1½ lb. ground beef
1 sm. can tomato sauce or
1 can condensed tomato soup
2 T. barbecue sauce
1 t. chili powder
2 t. salt
½ t. pepper

Cook onion, green pepper and celery in small amount of hot shortening until limp. Add ground beef and brown. Pour tomato soup over meat; stir in barbecue sauce, chili powder, salt and pepper. Cover and simmer 30 minutes. Spoon over hot dog or hamburger buns. Yield: 8-10 servings.

Sister M. Raphael, O.S.F., St. Francis Academy
Hankinson, North Dakota

HAMBURGER HOT DISH

1½-2 lb. ground beef
¼- c. onion, finely chopped
½-1 c. celery, chopped
1 sm. can chopped mushrooms (opt.)
1 can cream of mushroom soup
1 can cream of chicken soup
1 t. cracked pepper (opt.)
1-2 cans chow mein noodles

Brown ground beef, onion and celery in fat. Add remaining ingredients except noodles. Mix and put in a greased casserole. Sprinkle chow mein noodles over top. Bake at 350°F. for 25-30 minutes. Yield: 4-6 servings.

This recipe submitted by the following teachers:
Mrs. Thelma Valbracht,
R.O.V.A. Community Unit Schools
Oneida, Illinois
Jean Van Heuvelen, Deadwood H.S.
Deadwood, South Dakota

LAYERED ENCHILADA CASSEROLE

1 lge. can evaporated milk
1 lb. processed cheese, chopped
1 lb. ground beef
1 t. salt
1 t. garlic salt
1 pkg. corn tortillas
Shortening
1 4-oz. can chopped green chili peppers
¾ c. onion, chopped

Melt cheese in milk over low heat. Brown meat; add seasonings. Fry tortillas in ½ inch shortening on each side until soft. Place a layer of tortillas in a 2-quart casserole. Add layers of meat, chili and onions. Repeat layers, pour on cheese sauce. Cover and bake at 350°F. for 25-30 minutes. NOTE: Pinto beans may be added. Yield: 6 servings.

Genevieve Dillon, Rio Grande H.S.
Albuquerque, New Mexico

JUMBO CORNBURGER

1 lb. ground beef
1 egg, slightly beaten
½ c. seasoned tomato sauce
1 T. Worcestershire sauce
1 t. salt
Dash of pepper

Combine beef, egg, sauces and seasonings; spread half of mixture in an 8-inch shallow round dish.

FILLING:
2 c. whole-kernel corn, drained
½ c. med. coarse cracker crumbs
1 egg, slightly beaten
¼ c. green pepper, diced
¼ c. onion, chopped
2 T. pimento, chopped
½ t. salt
¼ t. sage
½ c. sharp process cheese, shredded

Combine all ingredients except cheese; spoon over meat. Cover with remaining meat mixture. Bake at 350°F. for 40 minutes. Sprinkle with cheese during last 5 minutes baking. Garnish with parsley if desired. Yield: 6 servings.

Mrs. Phyllis Greene McAfee
Old Rochester Regional H.S.
Mattapoisett, Massachusetts

LOUISIANA GET-TOGETHER

1 lb. ground beef
1 lge. onion, chopped
1 c. celery, chopped
1 c. rice
1 t. salt
1 can tomato soup or 6 tomatoes
1 lge. green pepper, chopped
1¼ c. water

Brown ground beef; add remaining ingredients. Simmer for 1 hour or until rice is tender. Yield: 6 servings.

Virginia Van Popering, Churchill Jr. H.S.
Muskegon, Michigan

MEAT BALL CASSEROLE

½ lb. hamburger
2 T. celery, chopped
1 slice bread, wet
2 Uneeda biscuits, wet with hot water
1 egg
¼ t. salt
½ green pepper
2 onions
½ can tomato soup
½ soup can water

Combine hamburger, celery, bread, biscuits, egg and salt. Form into 1-inch meat balls. Place sections of green pepper and onions between meat balls in greased casserole. Salt again. Add diluted tomato soup. Bake in covered casserole 1 hour at 375°F. Yield: 4-5 servings.

Mrs. Marion Burtt, Classical H.S.
Lynn, Massachusetts

MEAT BALLS PIQUANT

2 eggs, beaten
1 c. milk
2 c. fine dry bread crumbs
1 lb. ground beef
1 t. onion salt
⅛ t. thyme
½ t. white pepper
2 T. parsley flakes
1 T. green pepper, chopped
1 T. onion flakes
1 T. salt
1 bay leaf
4 T. butter, melted
4 T. flour
1 c. half and half cream
3 c. meat stock
½ c. mayonnaise
1 3-oz. jar capers, undrained
1 t. dry mustard
1 T. Worcestershire sauce

Add milk to eggs; stir in bread crumbs. Add meat, onion salt, thyme, white pepper and 1 tablespoon parsley flakes. Shape into 18-20 meat balls. Simmer remaining seasonings in 6 cups water for 5 minutes; add meat balls and simmer 15 minutes. Combine butter and flour; add cream and stock from meat balls. Cook over medium heat, stirring until thickened. Blend in remaining ingredients. Serve meat dumplings over rice with cream sauce. Yield: 5-6 servings.

Mrs. Mary Westfall, Colusa H.S.
Colusa, California

MEAT-POTATO PIE

1 lb. ground beef
½ c. tomato soup
½ c. fine dry bread crumbs
¼ c. onion, chopped
1¼ t. salt
⅛ t. pepper
1 packet instant potatoes
½ c. cheese, shredded
1 egg, beaten
¼ t. onion salt
¼ c. cheese, grated

Combine beef, soup, bread crumbs, onion, salt and pepper. Line bottom of a pie plate with mixture. Prepare instant potatoes according to package directions; add shredded cheese and cool. Stir in egg and onion salt; spread over meat mixture. Sprinkle with grated cheese. Bake at 350°F. for 30 minutes. Yield: 6 servings.

Patricia Miller, Hicksville H.S.
Hicksville, Ohio

MEAT LOAF-BEAN CASSEROLE

1 lb. ground beef
1 box frozen green beans
½ c. raw instant rice
1 can cream of mushroom soup
¼ c. water
1 sm. can mushrooms
French-fried onions

Prepare meat according to your favorite meat loaf recipe. Form mixture into a border in a 10-inch casserole, leaving the center exposed. Fill the center with a layer of beans; sprinkle the rice over beans. Top with the mixture of soup, water and mushrooms. Sprinkle with onions as desired. Cover and bake at 325°F. for 45 minutes. Yield: 5-6 servings.

Mrs. Roy Hefty, Dakota Community Unit
Dakota, Illinois

NUTTY NOODLE CASSEROLE

2 lb. ground beef
¼ c. onion, diced
2 T. fat
1 t. salt
⅛ t. pepper
1 can cream of mushroom soup
1½ c. milk
¼ lb. American cheese, cubed
1 3½-oz. jar olives, sliced
1 can chow mein noodles
½ c. walnuts, pecans or almonds

Brown meat and onions in fat. Stir soup and milk together in bowl. Spread meat mixture in flat casserole; pour soup mixture over meat. Place cheese and olives over top; scatter nuts over cheese. Bake 20 minutes at 350°F. Cover with noodles and bake for 15-20 minutes more. Yield: 10 servings.

Mrs. Violet Ray, Charlotte H.S.
Charlotte, Michigan

MOCK CHOP SUEY HOT DISH

1 lb. hamburger
1 onion, chopped
2 c. celery, diced
1 can mushroom soup
1 can water
½ can chow mein noodles

Brown hamburger, onions, and celery; add soup and water. Season and simmer 30 minutes. Add noodles; transfer to baking dish. Bake 30 minutes at 350°F. Yield: 6 servings.

Mrs. David Melby, Dover-Eyota H.S.
Eyota, Minnesota

MOCK CHOW MEIN

1½ lb. ground beef
1 c. onion, chopped
1 c. cream of mushroom soup
1 c. chicken soup
3 c. minus 2 T. water
1 can chow mein noodles

Brown hamburger; combine with remaining ingredients. Bake at 350°F. for 1 hour and 30 minutes. Yield: 8 servings.

Carol Machovec, Colby H.S.
Colby, Wisconsin

STUFFED MEAT ROLL

4 T. margarine
2 t. onion
4 c. soft bread crumbs
½ c. celery, finely diced
2 t. dried parsley
1 t. salt
¼ t. seasoned pepper
1 lb. ground beef
¼ c. milk

Melt butter; add onion and cook until tender but not brown. Add bread crumbs, celery, parsley, ½ teaspoon salt and pepper; mix lightly. Combine beef, milk and remaining salt. Into meat mixture, add one cup of stuffing; place meat mixture on waxed paper and pat into a rectangle. Spread remaining stuffing and roll like a jelly roll. Place in shallow pan. Bake for 45 minutes at 350°F. Yield: 4-6 servings.

LaVergne Wilken, Burlington H.S.
Burlington, Colorado

TEXAS HAMBURGERS

3½ lb. hamburger
2 c. chopped onion
2 c. finely diced celery
1 c. chopped green pepper
2 t. monosodium glutamate
1 t. salt
½ t. pepper
3 T. chili powder
1 2-lb. can tomatoes
1 8-oz. can tomato paste
1 8-oz. can tomato sauce
1 can enchilada sauce
2 c. corn chips
Grated cheese

Fry hamburger until well done. Remove meat from pan and saute onion, celery, and pepper in drippings. Add all remaining ingredients except cheese and corn chips and simmer for at least 1 hour. Stir in corn chips; top with cheese. Bake in 350°F. oven until cheese is melted. NOTE: Place sauce, corn chips, grated cheese, and minced onion on a buffet table and allow guests to build their own Texas Hamburgers if desired. Yield: 6-8 servings.

Mrs. Laura E. Sumner, Cobe H.S.
Bayard, New Mexico

THREE-SOUP HOT DISH

1½-2 lb. ground beef or cubed pork
1 lge. onion, chopped
1 can mushroom soup
1 can chicken and rice soup
1 can vegetable - beef soup
1 lge. pkg. or 2 cans chow mein noodles
¾ c. chopped celery (opt.)

Brown meat, onion and celery in small amount of fat; season lightly. Combine undiluted soups and heat. Arrange noodles in large casserole. Pour meat over noodles; top with soups. Bake at 350°F. for 30-40 minutes. NOTE: If desired, soups and noodles may be mixed with browned meat, covered and baked at 250°F. for 1 hour and 30 minutes. Yield: 8 servings.

This recipe submitted by the following teachers:
Mrs. Lalah H. Newman, Pulaski H.S.
Pulaski, Virginia
Lois G. Chrisinger, Taylor H.S.
Taylor, Wisconsin

TORTILLA CASSEROLE

1 lb. hamburger
1 8-oz. can tomato sauce
1 c. water
¼ t. garlic salt
1 t. chili powder
1 pkg. tortillas
1 c. grated cheese
1 sm. can chopped olives
1 sm. onion, chopped

Brown hamburger; add tomato sauce, water, garlic salt and chili powder. Simmer 20 minutes. In buttered 1-quart casserole dish, alternate layers of buttered tortillas, hamburger mixture, cheese, olives, and onion, ending with grated cheese. Bake at 350°F. for 20 minutes. Yield: 6 servings.

Mrs. Bonnie Miller, Princeton Jr-Sr. H.S.
Princeton, California

VEGETABLES IN MEAT SHELL

1½ lb. lean beef, chopped
¾ c. oatmeal, uncooked
1 c. tomato juice or milk
1 egg, slightly beaten
1 sm. onion, minced
2 t. salt
¼ t. pepper
4 drops Tabasco sauce
¼ c. soft margarine
½ c. Cheddar cheese, grated
¼ c. flour
¼ c. parsley, minced
2 c. diced potatoes, cooked
1 c. peas, cooked
½ c. diced carrots, cooked
½ c. sliced celery, cooked
6 tiny onions, cooked

(Continued on Next Page)

Mix beef, oatmeal, tomato juice, onion, egg, salt, pepper and Tabasco sauce. Press evenly into bottom and sides of a 9-inch pie plate. Bake at 350°F. for 15 minutes or until almost firm. Blend margarine, cheese, flour and parsley. Combine with drained, mixed hot vegetables. Pour into meat shell. Garnish with cheese diamonds and sliced cooked carrots. Bake until thoroughly heated. Serve with mushroom sauce. Yield: 6 servings.

Jeanette Rauscher, Aitkin Public School
Aitkin, Minnesota

HAMBURGER-NOODLE PIE

6 oz. lasagna noodles
½ lb. hamburger
¼ c. onion, chopped
Salt and pepper to taste
2 c. flour
¼ c. shortening
¼ t. salt
6 oz. tomato paste
6 oz. Mozzarella cheese, sliced

Cook noodles and drain. Brown seasoned hamburger and onions. Make pastry using flour, shortening, salt and water to moisten. Roll out more than enough to fit casserole. Fit pastry into casserole; alternate layers of hamburger, noodles, tomato paste and cheese. Repeat layers. Fold extra pastry over top. Bake at 350°F. for 30-40 minutes or until crust is done. Yield: 4 servings.

Mrs. Helen Sherwood, Sweet Grass County H.S.
Big Timber, Montana

CHEESEBURGER CASSEROLE

2 T. fat
1 lb. lean ground beef
¼ c. onion, chopped
¾ t. salt
⅛ t. pepper
¼ c. catsup
1 8-oz. can tomato sauce
1 8-oz. pkg. cheese slices
1 can biscuits or sesame seed rolls

Combine fat, beef and onion in skillet; cook until meat is lightly browned. Drain; add salt and pepper. Stir in catsup and tomato sauce; heat thoroughly. Turn into an 8-inch square or 1½-quart casserole. Cut cheese into thin strips and spread over meat. Top with biscuits or rolls. Bake at 425°F. for 20-25 minutes or until biscuits are golden brown. NOTE: Tomato soup may be substituted for tomato sauce if desired. Yield: 4-6 servings.

This recipe submitted by the following teachers:
Myrtis L. McAlhany, Saint George H.S.
Saint George, South Carolina
Sharon Lou Carter, Wheelersburg H.S.
Wheelersburg, Ohio
Mrs. Jean C. Bachman, Muleshoe H.S.
Muleshoe, Texas

HUNGRY BOY'S CASSEROLE

1-1½ lb. ground beef
1 c. celery, sliced
½ c. onion, chopped
½ c. green pepper, chopped
1 clove garlic, minced
¾-1¼ c. water
1 6-oz. can tomato paste
¾-1 t. salt
1 t. paprika
½ t. monosodium glutamate
1 1-lb. can pork and beans
1 1-lb. can chick peas or lima beans, undrained

Saute beef, celery, onion, green pepper and garlic until tender; drain off excess fat. Add water, tomato paste, and seasonings. Simmer for 5 minutes. Remove 1 cup of mixture for biscuits. Add both cans of beans; pour into oblong baking dish.

BISCUIT TOPPING:
1½ c. flour
2 t. baking powder
½ t. salt
¼ c. shortening
½ c. milk
Cooking oil
½ c. stuffed olives
½ c. blanched slivered almonds (opt.)
½ t. paprika
Butter
Yellow food coloring (opt.)

Sift together flour, baking powder and salt; cut in shortening. Add milk to mixture. Knead on lightly floured waxed paper. Roll out to a 12 x 9-inch rectangle. Brush with cooking oil. Combine olives, almonds and paprika with reserved meat mixture. Spread over dough. Roll up and seal edges. Slice into 1-inch pieces. Place on meat mixture. Dot with butter and paprika. Bake at 425°F. for 25 to 30 minutes, or until golden brown. NOTE: For a richer topping, combine 1 egg with the milk to make ½ cup liquid. Food coloring may be added to milk mixture. Yield: 10-12 servings.

This recipe submitted by the following teachers:
Mrs. Luther Taylor, Durant Jr. H.S.
Durant, Oklahoma
Mrs. Dale R. Lewis, Wakpala H.S.
Wakpala, South Dakota

HAMBURGER-BISCUIT BAKE

3 T. onion, chopped
2 T. butter
1 lb. ground beef
1 T. A-1 steak sauce
1 t. salt
2 c. cooked green beans
1 can condensed tomato soup
⅔ c. milk
2 c. dry prepared biscuit mix

Saute onion in butter. Add ground beef, A-1 sauce and salt; brown lightly. Stir in beans and soup. Pour into a 1½-quart casserole. Add milk to biscuit mix and stir to a soft dough. Roll dough

(Continued on Next Page)

around on a pastry cloth. Knead gently 8 to 10 times. Roll to ¾-inch thickness. Cut with a sharp knife into small squares. Arrange the biscuit squares in two rows around the edge of the casserole with one corner of each square inserted into the meat mixture. Bake at 425°F. for 20 minutes. Yield: 6 servings.

Carol L. Weimer, Saltsburg Joint H.S.
Saltsburg, Pennsylvania

HAMBURGER COBBLER

1 sm. onion, sliced
½ clove garlic, minced
1 T. fat
¾ lb. hamburger
1 t. salt
¼ t. pepper
¼ lb. cheese
1 c. tomatoes, drained
2 T. Worcestershire sauce
3 T. catsup
1½ c. sifted flour
1½ t. baking powder
½ c. shortening
½ c. milk
½ t. salt

Saute onion and garlic in fat. Add hamburger and seasonings; brown lightly. Spread mixture in 9-inch square pan. Arrange cheese on meat; top with tomatoes mixed with Worcestershire sauce and catsup. Make a biscuit dough with remaining ingredients; drop on top of casserole. Bake at 450°F. for 20 minutes. Yield: 6 servings.

Delores Kluckman, Montevideo Jr. H.S.
Montevideo, Minnesota

CHILI CORN PONE PIE

2 cups chili
1 No. 2 can ranch style beans, drained
1 No. 2 can whole kernel corn, drained
1 sm. can tomato puree
1 bunch fresh green onions or 1 lge. onion, chopped
1 lge. pod green pepper, chopped

Mix all ingredients in a baking dish. Bake at 350°F. for 20-25 minutes.

CORN BREAD BATTER:
¾ c. corn meal
¼ c. flour
2 t. baking powder
½ t. salt
¼ t. soda
¾-1 c. sour milk
1 egg
2 T. oil

Mix dry ingredients and sift. Stir in milk. Mix egg and oil and fold into batter. Pour batter over top of casserole. Bake at 350-400°F. for 20-30 minutes. Yield: 8 servings.

Mrs. Edna Earle Beck, Anson H.S.
Anson, Texas

FAMILY STYLE MEXICAN TAMALE

3 c. cooked yellow corn meal mush
2 T. fat
⅓ c. onion, chopped
⅓ c. green pepper, chopped
1 lb. ground beef
2 c. tomatoes, chopped
1 t. salt
¼ t. pepper
¼-½ t. chili powder

Line bottom and sides of a 2-quart casserole with mush in a 1-inch layer. Set aside to cool. Saute onion and green pepper in fat. Push to one side and add meat. Brown well, stirring occasionally. Add tomatoes and seasonings, simmer 25-30 minutes. Pour into casserole; top with a layer of corn meal mush. Bake at 350°F. for 30 minutes or until crust is golden brown. Yield: 6 servings.

Mrs. Virginia Boyle, Ashland H.S.
Ashland, Illinois

GROUND BEEF AND VEGETABLE CASSEROLE

1 lb. ground beef
1 med. onion
¼ t. garlic salt
Salt and pepper to taste
1 No. 300 can mixed vegetables
2 c. corn bread mix

Brown beef, onion, garlic salt, salt and pepper; drain off excess liquid. Spoon vegetables over meat. Prepare corn bread mix as directed on package. Spoon batter onto vegetables. Bake at 350°F. for 10-12 minutes or until corn bread is done. Yield: 4 servings.

Patricia Cross, Metamora H.S.
Metamora, Illinois

MEXICAN HAMBURGER CASSEROLE

1 lb. beef hamburger
¼ t. pepper
¼ t. chili powder
½ t. salt
1 sm. onion, chopped
¼ c. green pepper, chopped
¼ c. celery, chopped
1 No. 303 can peas, drained
1 No. 303 can corn, drained
1 pkg. corn muffin mix

Season hamburger with pepper, chili powder and salt. Add the onion, green pepper and celery. Saute until hamburger is grey in color. Place layers of corn, hamburger, peas, and another layer of hamburger in greased casserole. Make the corn muffin mix as directed on package and put it on top of the casserole by spoonfuls. Bake at 345°F. until the top is golden brown. Yield: 6 servings.

Carol Stockburger, Edgerton H.S.
Edgerton, Ohio

HAMBURGER-CORN PONE PIE

1 lb. ground meat
⅓ c. onion, chopped
1 T. shortening
½-¾ t. salt
2 t. chili powder (opt.)
2 t. garlic salt (opt.)
1-2 t. Worcestershire sauce
1 c. canned tomatoes
1 c. cooked pinto or kidney beans
1 c. corn bread batter

Saute meat and onions in hot shortening. Add seasonings and tomatoes; simmer for 15 minutes. Add beans. Place in 1½-quart baking dish and cover with corn bread batter spreading carefully with wet knife. Bake in 425°F. oven 20 minutes or until bread is brown. NOTE: Do not make the layer of batter too thick or it will not cook through before browning on top. Simmering may be omitted. Yield: 8 servings.

This recipe submitted by the following teachers:
> Mrs. Jean Pearson, Robert E. Lee H.S.
> San Antonio, Texas
> Mrs. Ruth Marshall, Borger Sr. H.S.
> Borger, Texas
> Novella Mae Melton, Roswell Sr. H.S.
> Roswell, New Mexico
> Mrs. Emely Sundbeck, Manor H.S.
> Manor, Texas
> Mrs. Glenna A. Starbird, Oxford Hills H.S.
> South Paris, Maine
> Mrs. Marilynn T. Johanson, Hico H.S.
> Hico, Texas

QUICK TAMALE

¾-1 lb. ground beef
¾ c. onion, chopped
Salt to taste
⅛ t. pepper
1-2 t. chili powder
3 T. salad oil
1 12-oz. can whole-kernel corn
1 No. 2 can cooked tomatoes
1 box corn muffin mix

Cook beef, onion and seasonings in hot oil for 8-10 minutes, stirring until crumbly. Add corn and tomatoes; bring to a boil. Pour into 3 x 9 x 2-inch pan. Prepare corn muffin mix according to directions on package. Spoon batter over meat mixture. Bake at 400°F. for 30-40 minutes. Yield: 7-8 servings.

This recipe submitted by the following teachers:
> Mrs. Nola Y. Coates, Union City Area H.S.
> Union City, Pennsylvania
> Mrs. Dorothy Smith, Senior H.S.
> Palacios, Texas

EVERYBODY'S FAVORITE HAMBURGER PIE

1 med. onion, chopped
1 lb. ground beef
1 T. A-1 sauce (opt.)
½ t. monosodium glutamate (opt.)
Salt and pepper
2-2½ c. cooked green beans, drained
1 can tomato soup
5 med. potatoes, cooked
½ c. warm milk
1 egg, beaten
½-1 c. grated Cheddar Cheese (opt.)

Saute onion until golden in small amount of fat. Add meat, sauce, monosodium glutamate, salt and pepper; brown. Mix in beans and soup. Pour into greased 1½-quart casserole. Mash potatoes; add milk, egg and seasonings to taste. Mix well. Spoon mounds of potatoes on meat mixture. Cover with cheese if desired. Bake at 350°F. for 30 minutes. NOTE: Instant mashed potatoes may be used if desired. Yield: 6-8 servings.

This recipe submitted by the following teachers:
> Kathleen S. Johnston, Fairfield H.S.
> Fairfield, Montana
> Mrs. Sam Smith, Piketon H.S.
> Piketon, Ohio
> Mrs. Carolyn K. Hubbard, Bibb County H.S.
> Centreville, Alabama
> Mrs. Beverly S. Hall, Midway H.S.
> Dunn, North Carolina
> Nancy Griffith, Woodbine Community School
> Woodbine, Iowa
> Mary F. Ragsdale, Dumas Sr. H.S.
> Dumas, Texas
> Janice Hancock, Ipswich H.S.
> Ipswich, South Dakota
> Estella Crowell, Whitmore Lake H.S.
> Whitmore Lake, Michigan
> Mrs. Marcene Pederson, Murdock H.S.
> Murdock, Minnesota
> Joyce Profitt, Garrard County H.S.
> Lancaster, Kentucky
> Evelyn Anthony, Gaston School
> Joinerville, Texas
> Arlene Riddle, Commerce H.S.
> Commerce, Texas
> Mrs. Euzelia M. Vollbracht, Burns at Fallston H.S.
> Fallston, North Carolina
> Lois S. Gass, Mahoney Joint H.S.
> Herndon, Pennsylvania
> Mrs. Anna L. Blohm, Central Sr. H.S.
> Helena, Arkansas
> Anita Golter, Genoa Public School
> Genoa, Nebraska
> Ann Robinson, Anthony Wayne-Fallen Timbers Schools
> Whitehouse, Ohio
> Mrs. Dorothy Kennedy, Philip Independent School
> Philip, South Dakota

FULL-MEAL DISH

1 med. onion, sliced
2 T. fat, melted
3 T. flour
1 lb. ground round steak
1 pt. canned tomatoes
½ c. water
1½ t. salt
1½ pt. canned string beans
2 c. mashed potatoes

Saute onions in fat in a heavy skillet. Mix the flour and ground beef and add to the fat and onion. Brown meat well; pour tomatoes over meat. Add water and salt; simmer for 20 minutes. Pour string beans over mixture. Place in a 2-quart casserole and cover with mashed potatoes. Cover and bake at 375°F. for 15 minutes. Remove cover and bake 15 minutes longer. Yield: 4 servings.

Billie Louise Sands, Plainwell Sr. H.S.
Plainwell, Michigan

GROUND BEEF-STRING BEAN CASSEROLE

¾ lb. ground beef
¼ sm. onion, chopped
1 green pepper, chopped
1 can French-style string beans, drained
1 can undiluted tomato soup
Mashed potatoes
Salt and pepper
1 egg

Brown the ground beef, onion and green pepper in a heavy skillet. Add the string beans and tomato soup; mix well. Bake for 40-45 minutes at 350°F. Prepare mashed potatoes; add salt, pepper and egg. Mix well. About 15-20 minutes before the casserole is done; spoon the mashed potatoes on top. Yield: 5 servings.

Karen Hofer, Beresford H.S.
Beresford, South Dakota

GROUND BEEF CASSEROLE

1 lb. ground beef
¼ c. onion, chopped
2 T. shortening
1 pkg. frozen peas, cooked
1 can condensed celery soup
1 t. salt
2 T. mustard
2 c. mashed potatoes
½ c. cheese, grated

Brown beef and onion in shortening; pour off all drippings. Combine with peas, soup, salt and mustard. Spoon into 1½-quart casserole; arrange mashed potatoes around edge. Sprinkle with cheese. Bake 25 to 30 minutes at 350°F. Yield: 4-6 servings.

Mrs. Jacqueline Fanning, Omak Jr.-Sr. H.S.
Omak, Washington

HAMBURGER PIE

1 med. onion, chopped
1 lb. ground beef
1 t. salt
¼ t. pepper
1 T. Worcestershire sauce
¼ t. chili powder
1 1-lb. can green beans, drained
1 can condensed tomato soup
6 T. warm milk
1 egg, beaten
2 c. mashed potatoes
¼ c. sharp cheese, grated

Brown onion and beef; drain fat. In greased 2-quart casserole combine beef mixture, seasonings, beans and soup. Beat milk and egg into potatoes; spoon in ¼-cup mounds over bean mixture. Top with cheese. Bake at 350°F. for 30 minutes or until heated through. Yield: 8 servings.

Mary Lou Traster, Keener Township School
DeMotte, Indiana

HAMBURGER-POTATO PUFFS

1 lb. ground beef
1 onion, chopped
½ green pepper, chopped
1 clove garlic, minced
¼ t. basil
½ t. seasoned salt
½ pt. box mushrooms, sliced
1 6-oz. can tomato sauce
⅓ c. Parmesan cheese, grated
1 T. parsley, chopped
Mashed potatoes

Brown beef, onion, green pepper and garlic in skillet. Add seasonings, mushrooms and tomato sauce. Simmer for 5 minutes. Add Parmesan cheese and parsley to potatoes; place spoonsful around edge of casserole dish on beef mixture. Bake at 400°F. for 10 minutes or until potato puffs are lightly browned. NOTE: If desired, canned mushrooms may be used. Yield: 6 servings.

Vera Engstrom, Howell H.S.
Howell, Michigan

Poultry Casseroles

CHICKEN AND DRESSING

1 4-lb. chicken
1 can cream of chicken soup
½ 8-oz. pkg. seasoned bread stuffing
¼ c. celery, chopped
¼ c. onion, chopped
2 c. chicken broth

Cook chicken in salted water until tender. Remove chicken from bones and cut into small pieces. Place in greased baking dish. Cover with chicken soup. Mix stuffing, celery and onion. Moisten with chicken broth; spread over chicken soup. Cover with foil; bake at 375°F. for 30 minutes. Uncover and bake about 30 minutes or until dressing is browned. Yield: 6-8 servings.

Ramona Chapman, Springport H.S.
Springport, Michigan

CHICKEN AND DRESSING

1 chicken
4 T. chicken fat
6 c. bread crumbs
1 sm. onion, chopped
2 eggs, beaten
Sage
Salt and pepper
3-4 c. chicken broth
Parsley

Boil chicken; break in pieces and place in bottom of pan. Make dressing of fat, bread crumbs, onion, eggs and seasonings. Drop by spoonfuls on top of chicken. Use thickened broth for gravy; pour over top. Bake 30-40 minutes at 350°F. Sprinkle with parsley. Yield: 8 servings.

Ruth Conner, Arnold H.S.
Arnold, Nebraska

CHICKEN AND DRESSING (SCALLOPED)

1½ qt. dry bread cubes
1 T. sage
½ t. salt
⅛ c. sugar
¼ c. onion, minced
¼ c. celery, chopped
½ c. butter, melted
1 3- to 4-lb. chicken, cooked
Chicken broth
Ritz cracker crumbs, buttered.

Combine bread cubes, seasonings, onion and celery; add butter and mix well. Bone chicken, leaving meat in medium sized pieces. Alternate layers of chicken and dressing in a greased baking pan. Slightly thicken and season broth; pour over casserole to moisten. Cover with cracker crumbs; bake at 375°F. for 30 minutes. Yield: 6-8 servings.

Mrs. Vivian Ross, Callaway Public Schools
Callaway, Nebraska

CHICKEN 'N' STUFFING SCALLOP

1 8-oz. pkg. seasoned stuffing
3 c. cooked or canned chicken, cubed
½ c. butter
½ c. flour
¼ t. salt
Dash of pepper
4 c. chicken broth
6 eggs, slightly beaten
1 can cream of mushroom soup
¼ c. milk
1 c. sour cream
¼ c. pimento, chopped

Prepare stuffing. Spread in a baking dish; top with a layer of chicken. Melt butter; blend in flour and seasonings. Add cool broth; cook and stir until mixture thickens. Stir small amount of hot mixture into eggs; return to hot mixture. Pour over chicken. Bake at 325°F. for 40-45 minutes; cut in squares. Combine remaining ingredients; heat, stirring until hot. Serve over squares.

Crystal K. Rowe, Supervisor of Home Economics, Detroit Public Schools
Detroit, Michigan

CHICKEN AND STUFFING WITH MUSHROOM SAUCE

1 8-oz. pkg. prepared stuffing
3 c. cooked chicken, cubed or shredded
½ c. butter or margarine
½ c. flour
¼ t. salt
Dash of pepper
4 c. chicken broth
6 eggs, slightly beaten
1 can cream of mushroom soup
¼ c. milk
1 c. sour cream
¼ c. pimento, chopped

Prepare stuffing according to directions on package for dry stuffing. Spread in 13x9x2-inch baking dish. Top with layer of chicken. In saucepan, melt butter; blend in flour, salt, and pepper. Add cool chicken broth; cook until thickened. Stir small amount of hot mixture into eggs; add to hot mixture. Pour over chicken and bake 50 minutes at 325°F. Mix remaining ingredients; heat. Serve over casserole. Yield: 12 servings.

Mrs. Jean H. Teale, Bentleyville-Ellsworth Area Joint H.S.
Ellsworth, Pennsylvania

CHICKEN-CHIP CASSEROLE

1 c. celery, finely cut
1 t. onion
2 cans or 2 c. chicken
1 can cream of chicken soup
3 hard-cooked eggs, cut up
½ c. mayonnaise
2 c. potato chips, crushed

(Continued on Next Page)

Boil celery and onions until tender. Mix chicken, cream of chicken soup, celery and onion mixture, eggs, mayonnaise and 1 cup potato chips; place in 1½-quart casserole. Sprinkle chips on top. Bake at 350°F. for 45 minutes. Yield: 4 servings.

Jean M. Modreske, Wayland Union School
Wayland, Michigan

EASY CHICKEN CASSEROLE

2 c. chicken
2 c. celery, diced
2 T. onion, chopped
1 c. mayonnaise
Potato chips, crushed

Combine all ingredients except potato chips. Top with chips. Bake 20 minutes at 400°F. Yield: 4 servings.

Joyce L. Wuchle, Galesburg Sr. H.S.
Galesburg, Illinois

HOT CHICKEN SALAD

2 c. cooked chicken breast, cut up
2 c. celery, chopped
1 can cream of chicken soup
1 c. mayonnaise
1 c. water chestnuts, sliced
Salt to taste
1 t. lemon juice
1 t. (heaping) onion, grated
Crushed potato chips

Combine all ingredients except potato chips; place in casserole. Top with potato chips. Cook at 350°F. for 15 minutes or until slightly browned. Yield: 6-8 servings.

Mrs. Marilyn Bushnell, Avonworth School
Pittsburgh, Pennsylvania

HOT CHICKEN SALAD WITH ALMONDS

2 c. chicken
1 sm. onion, chopped
2 t. lemon juice
1 c. mayonnaise
2 c. celery, finely cut
2 c. almonds, toasted
½ c. Romano cheese, grated
1 c. potato chips, crushed

Combine all ingredients except cheese and potato chips; place in casserole. Sprinkle cheese and chips over top. Bake at 350°F. for 45 minutes. Yield: 6 servings.

Sharon Kirkpatrick, Prophetstown H.S.
Prophetstown, Illinois

HOT CHICKEN SALAD

2 c. cooked chicken, cut up
2 c. celery, thinly sliced
½ c. nuts chopped
½ t. salt
2 t. onion, grated
1 c. mayonnaise
2 T. lemon juice
1 c. bread cubes, toasted (opt.)
½ c. grated cheese
1 c. crushed potato chips or bread cubes

Combine all ingredients except cheese and potato chips. Place in baking dish; sprinkle with cheese and potato chips. Bake 10-15 minutes at 450°F. Yield: 6 servings.

This recipe submitted by the following teachers:
Mrs. Kathryn J. Keith, Southern Huntingdon
County H.S.
Orbisonia, Pennsylvania
Kathryn G. Bennett, United School
Hanoverton, Ohio

HOT CHICKEN SALAD WITH EGGS

1 can cream of chicken soup
1 can chicken
1 c. celery, chopped
¼ c. almonds, chopped
¼ c. mayonnaise
2 T. onions, minced
3 hard-cooked eggs
1½ c. corn flakes
½ c. potato chips

Combine all ingredients; Place in a casserole. Cover with foil; bake at 450°F. for 25 minutes. Yield: 6 servings.

Mrs. Doris Waller, Chino H.S.
Chino, California

CHICKEN CASSEROLE

1 c. cooked macaroni
1 c. cream, evaporated milk or mushroom soup
1 c. chicken broth
2 t. butter or chicken fat
3 T. flour
1 c. chicken
1 sm. onion, sauted
1 sm. can mushrooms
¾ c. cheese, grated

Place cooked macaroni in bottom of casserole. Make sauce of cream, broth, butter and flour. Add chicken, onion, mushrooms and half of cheese. Pour over macaroni. Sprinkle remaining cheese over top. Bake at 350°F. until it bubbles. Yield: 3-4 servings.

Mrs. Carolyn Moore, Avon H.S.
Avon, Ohio

CHICKEN CREOLE

1 4- 5-lb. stewing chicken
1 c. cream
2 chopped pimentos
2 egg yolks, beaten
2 c. cooked macaroni
½-¾ c. buttered bread crumbs

Cook chicken until tender. Remove bones and cut up. Cook broth down to 3 cups. Thicken broth and season. Add cream, pimentos and egg yolks. Add chicken and macaroni. Place in greased pan; sprinkle toasted bread crumbs over top. Bake 40 minutes at 375°F. Yield: 12 servings.

Mrs. Edith Solomon, Blair H.S.
Blair, Nebraska

CHICKEN DELICIOUS

1 4- to 5-lb. stewing chicken, cooked and boned
8 hard-cooked eggs, chopped
1 pkg. frozen peas, cooked
1 4-oz. can chopped mushrooms
3 c. cooked macaroni
2 T. melted butter
2 T. flour
1 c. chicken broth
Salt and pepper
½ c. buttered bread crumbs or crushed potato
  chips

Combine chicken, eggs, peas, mushrooms and macaroni. Combine butter and flour in heavy saucepan. Slowly add broth, stirring constantly until sauce is smooth and thick. Season with salt and pepper. Add chicken mixture. Pour into a 3-quart buttered casserole. Sprinkle with bread crumbs or potato chips. Bake at 350°F. for 45 minutes. Yield: 8 servings.

Ghlee Kershner, Montpelier Community Corp.
Montpelier, Indiana

CHICKEN MONTEGO

3 lge. chicken breasts, halved
3 T. flour
1 t. salt
⅛ t. pepper
¼ c. shortening
4 oz. elbow macaroni
1 can mushroom buttons, slightly drained
1 can cream of celery soup
1 t. marjoram
1 pt. sour cream
1 can asparagus
Paprika

Roll chicken breasts in mixture of flour and seasonings. Brown in hot shortening; remove from skillet. Cook macaroni; drain. Put mushrooms in skillet; add soup and marjoram, stirring until smooth. Add sour cream. Put macaroni in casserole; add asparagus and half of soup mixture; mix well. Arrange chicken breasts on top; pour remaining soup over top. Cover and bake 45 minutes at 350°F. Uncover; bake 15 minutes longer. Sprinkle with paprika. Yield: 6 servings.

Mrs. Vesta Glessner, Shanksville H.S.
Shanksville, Pennsylvania

CHICKEN SUPREME

2 c. cooked chicken
2 c. raw macaroni
2 cans cream of mushroom soup
2 c. milk
2 med. onions, chopped
½ t. salt
¼ t. pepper
3 T. butter
1 c. sharp cheese, grated

Combine all ingredients except cheese. Put in casserole; grate cheese over top. Refrigerate overnight. Bake at 350°F. for 1 hour and 30 minutes. Yield: 8 servings.

Dee Meyer, Sac Community H.S.
Sac City, Iowa

CRUMB TOPPED-CHICKEN CASSEROLE

1 8-oz. pkg. uncooked elbow macaroni
2 c. milk
2 cans condensed cream of mushroom soup
3 hard-cooked eggs, chopped
½ c. mild cheese, diced
1 T. onion, minced
1 t. salt
2½ c. cooked chicken, chopped
1 c. corn flakes or potato chips crushed

Combine all ingredients except corn flakes; pour into a greased casserole. Refrigerate overnight or for several hours. Top with crumbs. Bake at 350°F. for 1 hour. Yield: 10 servings.

Gwendolyn Rhodenbaugh, Sherrard Jr. H.S.
Sherrard, Illinois

HUNTINGTON CHICKEN

1 7-oz. pkg. macaroni
1½ c. cooked chicken, cut up
1 T. flour
1 T. butter
1 c. cream
1 c. chicken broth
½ lb. American cheese, grated
1 can pimento
½ t. salt

Cook macaroni. Make a cream sauce with flour, butter, cream and chicken broth. In it melt cheese. Stir in the cooked macaroni, cut up chicken, pimento and salt. Bake at 325°F. for 1 hour. Yield: 4-6 servings.

Mrs. Alice Requa Smith, Central Jr. H.S.
White Bear Lake, Minnesota

HUNTINGTON CHICKEN

1 stewing chicken
2 c. macaroni
4 c. chicken broth
8 T. flour
½ lb. cream cheese
4 c. buttered bread crumbs
4 T. butter

Stew chicken; cut into bite size pieces. Cook macaroni in salted water; drain. Combine chicken broth and flour. Add chicken, cheese and macaroni. Spread mixture into pan; top with buttered bread crumbs and butter. Bake at 350°F. for 45 minutes. Yield: 15-20 servings.

Charlene Swanson, Wilber H.S.
Wilber, Nebraska

BAKED CHICKEN-NOODLE CASSEROLE

1 8-oz. pkg. noodles
3 c. chicken, chopped
1 c. corn flakes
2 c. milk or chicken broth
2 T. flour
2 T. butter
2 T. green pepper, chopped
1 T. onion, chopped
1 T. celery, chopped
1 can mushroom soup
Crushed potato chips or bread crumbs

Cook noodles in boiling water for 20 minutes; drain. Add chicken and corn flakes; mix well. Make a gravy of milk or broth, flour and butter. Add pepper, onion, celery and mushroom soup. Combine noodles, chicken and gravy; pour into greased pan. Sprinkle with potato chips or bread crumbs. Bake 45 minutes at 350°F. Yield: 15 servings.

Mrs. Beverly Soden, Wisner H.S.
Wisner, Nebraska

ALMOND-CHICKEN CASSEROLE

1 8-oz. pkg. noodles
2 T. butter
1 c. celery, thinly sliced
2 T. flour
¼ t. dry mustard
1¼ t. salt
Pepper
2½ c. milk
2 t. Worcestershire sauce
1 c. American cheese, grated
2 c. cooked chicken or turkey, diced
¼ c. pimento, diced
¼ c. green pepper, diced
1 c. toasted almonds, diced
½ c. buttered soft bread crumbs

Cook noodles. Melt butter; add celery. Cover and cook over low heat for 10 minutes. Blend in flour, mustard, salt and pepper. Add milk and Worcestershire sauce; cook until thickened. Stir in cheese, chicken, pimento, green pepper, noodles and half of almonds. Put into shallow baking dish; sprinkle with crumbs and remaining almonds. Bake at 425-450°F. for 15-20 minutes. Yield: 8-10 servings.

Marilyn Gies, Olympia H.S.
Olympia, Washington

CHICKEN A LA KING AND NOODLE RING

NOODLE RING:
1 lb. noodles, cooked
3 eggs, well beaten
1½ c. milk
1 t. salt
¼ t. pepper
1 t. minced parsley

Combine all ingredients; pour into a buttered ring mold. Sit in a pan of hot water; bake at 350°F. for 45 minutes.

CHICKEN:
1½ c. mushrooms
½ c. butter
4 T. flour
2½ c. light cream
½ c. chicken stock
2 egg yolks
1 t. salt
1 T. minced parsley
1 4 to 5-lb. cooked chicken, diced
½ c. pimento, cut in strips
⅛ t. paprika

Saute mushrooms in butter; blend in flour. Add cream and chicken stock; cook until thickened. Add a small amount of cream to egg yolks; add to remaining cream. Season; add chicken and pimento. Pour into noodle ring; garnish with paprika. Yield: 8 servings.

Mrs. Judith Boeck, Amherst H.S.
Amherst, Wisconsin

CHICKEN CASSEROLE

6 T. butter
6 T. flour
1 t. salt
¼ t. pepper
2 c. milk, scalded
2 c. chicken broth
1 c. cheese, grated
2 sm. onions, minced
1 green pepper, diced
1 c. celery, sliced
1 c. noodles, cooked and drained
2 c. cooked chicken, cubed

Melt 4 tablespoons butter; blend in flour and seasonings. Add milk and 1 cup broth; cook until thick and smooth. Stir in cheese. Saute onion, green pepper and celery in remaining butter. Add 1 cup broth; simmer for 5 minutes. Add to sauce with noodles and chicken. Turn into a casserole dish. Bake at 350°F. for 30 minutes. Yield: 8 servings.

Trudy Jan Groothuis, Assumption H.S.
Assumption, Illinois

CHICKEN-CHEDDAR CASSEROLE

1 can Cheddar cheese soup
½ c. milk
1 c. cooked chicken, diced
2 c. cooked noodles
2 T. pimento, diced
1 T. chopped parsley

In a 1½-quart casserole blend cheese soup until smooth; gradually add milk. Mix in remaining ingredients. Bake at 350°F. for 30 minutes. Yield: 4 servings.

Mrs. Gloria Lorenz, Prospect H.S.
Mt. Prospect, Illinois

CHICKEN AND GRAVY CASSEROLE

1 12-oz. pkg. wide egg noodles
1 can cream of chicken soup
1-1¼ c. canned chicken gravy
2 chicken bouillon cubes
1 c. boiling water
1 2-oz. jar chopped pimento
1 green pepper, finely chopped
1 T. dried onion flakes or ¼ c. onion, finely
  chopped
2 c. cooked chicken, coarsely diced
½ c. sharp Cheddar cheese, grated

Cook noodles according to directions on package; drain thoroughly. Combine chicken soup and chicken gravy. Dissolve bouillon cubes in water and add to soup and gravy. Add pimento, green pepper, onion and chicken; heat thoroughly. Grease 3-quart casserole. Layer chicken mixture and noodles. Put a layer of noodles on top. Sprinkle cheese over top of casserole. Bake at 350°F. for 1 hour. Yield: 6-8 servings.

Mrs. Pearl M. Delaney
Reading, Massachusetts

CHICKEN FINALE

2 c. med. noodles
¼ c. green pepper, chopped
¼ c. onion, minced
2 T. butter or margarine
1 c. sour cream
¼ c. milk
1 can cream of chicken soup
½ t. salt
¼-⅓ c. ripe olives, sliced
¼ t. pepper
1½ c. cooked chicken, diced
¼ c. blanched almonds, quartered
1 T. parsley, minced (opt.)

Cook noodles according to directions on package. Saute green pepper and onions in butter until tender. Add sour cream, milk, soup, salt, olives, pepper and chicken. Stir in noodles. Turn into greased 1½-quart casserole; sprinkle top with almonds and parsley. Bake 35-40 minutes at 350°F. NOTE: Almonds may be mixed in casserole. Yield: 6 servings.

This recipe submitted by the following teachers:
Mrs. Gail Kelly, Clearfield H.S.
Clearfield, Pennsylvania
Mrs. Margaret Jones, United Joint H.S.
New Florence, Pennsylvania
Mrs. Alza Dunn, Addison Community Schools
Addison, Michigan

CHICKEN-NOODLE CASSEROLE

1 3-lb. hen
1 lge. pkg. noodles
¼ loaf bread, finely cut
¼ lb. butter
Salt and pepper
½ c. sour cream

Cook chicken until tender in salted water. Remove meat from bones. Cook noodles in salted water; drain. Melt butter; mix with bread. Alternate layers of bread, noodles and chicken in casserole. Season to taste. Pour sour cream over all. Top with 1 cup of buttered crumbs. Bake for 30 minutes at 450°F. Yield: 10 servings.

Mrs. Gladys Fry, Brown County H.S.
Mt. Sterling, Illinois

CHICKEN SUPREME

1 stewing hen
½ 8-oz. pkg. noodles
1 can cream of mushroom soup
Buttered bread crumbs
½ c. green pepper, chopped (opt.)

Stew hen until tender; cut into pieces. Remove 1 cup broth. Cook noodles in remaining broth. Put a layer of noodles and a layer of chicken in a greased casserole. Cover with sauce made of 1 cup broth and soup. Top with crumbs and sprinkle with green pepper. Yield: 10-12 servings.

Mrs. Frank Clark, Elmwood Community H.S.
Elmwood, Illinois

CHICKEN NOODLE TETRAZZINI

4 c. water
1 t. salt
1 c. noodles
1 can mushroom soup
1 c. milk
3 T. butter
1 can or left-over boned chicken
Bread crumbs

Bring water to a boil; gradually add noodles so that water continues to boil. Cook 8-10 minutes; drain noodles and put back into saucepan. Mix soup and milk together in a bowl until blended. Put soup and chicken with noodles and mix; put into buttered casserole. Melt butter; mix in crumbs and spread over casserole. Bake 15 minutes at 375°F. Yield: 4-5 servings.

Karen M. Shuster, Seneca Valley H.S.
Harmony, Pennsylvania

CREAMED CHICKEN CASSEROLE

3 c. boiled noodles
2 c. boiled chicken, chopped
¼ c. celery, finely chopped
1 sm. can mushroom pieces
1 c. thick white sauce
½ c. thick chicken broth
¾ c. bread crumbs
4 T. butter
Salt and pepper to taste

Combine noodles, chicken, celery and mushrooms. Mix white sauce and chicken broth until smooth. Add white sauce mixture to noodle mixture; blend thoroughly. Put in casserole. Saute bread crumbs in butter; spread over top. Bake 35 minutes at 350°F. Yield: 8 servings.

Mrs. Wanda Hollingsworth, Hawthorne Jr. H.S.
Pocatello, Idaho

PENNSYLVANIA CHICKEN CHOW MEIN

1 lb. noodles
Chicken broth
2 c. celery, diced
¾ c. onion, diced
½ c. green pepper, diced
1 5- to 6-lb. cooked chicken, chopped
1 t. seasoned salt
½ t. pepper
1 c. buttered bread crumbs

Cook noodles in chicken broth until tender. Cook celery, onion and pepper in a small amount of water until tender; add chicken, noodles and seasonings. Mix well; pour into baking dishes. Top with bread crumbs; bake 30 minutes at 350°F. Yield: 12-15 servings.

Mrs. Dorothy Jones, Big Spring H.S.
Newville, Pennsylvania

MARGERY'S CHICKEN-NOODLE CASSEROLE

2 lge. chicken breasts, split
1 onion, sliced
8 stalks celery, chopped
Salt and pepper to taste
¾ c. chicken fat
¾ c. flour
1 c. milk
1 sm. green pepper, finely diced
1 6-oz. pkg. egg noodles, cooked
1 4-oz. jar pimentos, sliced
1 8-oz. can mushrooms
½ c. toasted almonds

Cook chicken breasts with sliced onion and celery until tender. Season to taste; strain broth and cool. Bone meat and cut into 1-inch cubes. Simmer bones, onion and celery in 2 cups cold water for 1 hour; strain and add to broth. Refrigerate chicken and broth. Melt fat; add flour, mixing well. Add broth and milk. Heat to a rolling boil, stirring constantly; add green pepper and cool. Combine all ingredients in a large baking pan; mix well. Cover with buttered crumbs if desired. Bake at 350°F. for 45 minutes. Yield: 12 servings.

Mrs. Margery Might, Columbia City Joint H.S.
Columbia City, Indiana

ALMOND, CHICKEN AND RICE

3 c. cooked rice
1 4-oz. can pimentoes, chopped
1½ c. cooked chicken, diced
¼-½ c. canned mushrooms
½ c. blanched almonds
1¾ c. chicken broth
Salt and pepper
1½ T. flour

Combine rice and pimento. Place one-third of rice mixture in greased casserole. Alternate layers of remaining rice, chicken, mushrooms and almonds. Combine chicken broth, salt, pepper and flour. Pour over casserole. Bake at 350°F. for 1 hour.

Manona Brewer, Orestimba Union H.S.
Newman, California

ALMOND, CHICKEN-RICE CASSEROLE

1 c. cooked chicken, chopped
1 c. celery, diced
2 t. onions, chopped
1 c. slivered almonds
1½ c. cooked rice
Dash of pepper
⅔ c. mayonnaise
4 hard-cooked eggs, sliced
2 c. potato chips

Combine all ingredients except potato chips. Put in casserole; top with potato chips. Bake at 450°F. for 20-25 minutes. Yield: 8 servings.

A. Dorothea Nevramon, Steele H.S.
Steele, North Dakota

BAKED CHICKEN AND RICE

1 sm. box instant rice
1 can cream of celery soup
1 can cream of mushroom soup
½ c. milk
1 envelope dry onion soup mix
1 fryer, cut up

Place rice in greased baking dish. Heat soups with milk. Blend mixture and pour over rice. Place chicken on top of rice. Pour dry onion mix over top. Cover; bake at 325°F. for 2 hours. Yield: 4-6 servings.

Mrs. Cleone Ness, Menahga H.S.
Menahga, Minnesota

CHICKEN CASSEROLE

1 c. rice
2 c. water
1 bouillon cube
1 pkg. onion soup
1 pkg. sl. almonds
1 can mushroom soup
1 chicken, cut up
Salt and pepper

Place rice, water, bouillon cube, onion soup, sliced almonds and mushroom soup in a large baking dish. Spread chicken over mixture; season to taste. Spoon mushroom soup over chicken. Bake covered at 300°F. for 2 hours. Yield: 6 servings.

Mrs. Kay Elder, Fairhaven Jr. H.S.
Bellingham, Washington

CONE'S CHICKEN CASSEROLE

3 cooked chicken breasts or 2-3 c. cooked chicken
4 T. instant rice
¼ c. celery, diced
¼ t. salt and pepper
1½ c. mushroom soup
¼ c. water
¼ c. buttered crumbs
¼ c. stuffed olives, sliced

Place cooked chicken in casserole; sprinkle with rice, celery and seasonings. Add soup and water evenly over mixture. Sprinkle with buttered crumbs and dot with olives. Bake 30 minutes at 350°F. Yield: 4 servings.

Beryl Cone, The Plains H.S.
The Plains, Ohio

CHICKEN CASSEROLE

1 4 to 4½-lb. stewing chicken
9 sl. day old bread
3 c. chicken broth
½ c. rice
½ c. parsley, chopped
½ c. pimento, chopped
2 t. salt
4 eggs, well beaten

Cook chicken until tender; cool and cut into cubes. Soak bread in broth for several minutes. Add all ingredients. Bake at 325°F. for 1 hour or until firm. Serve with mushroom sauce. Yield: 10 servings.

Mrs. Grace Kukuk, Negaunee H.S.
Negaunee, Michigan

CHICKEN CASSEROLE

1 c. rice, cooked
1 sm. onion, thinly sliced
2 T. pimento, chopped
1 can mushrooms, chopped
4 chicken breasts
1 can cream of celery soup
1 can cream of chicken soup
1 c. water

Put cooked rice in bottom of greased casserole. Mix onion, pimento and mushrooms with liquid; pour over rice. Brown chicken in fat; place on top of rice. Dilute soups with water; pour over casserole. Bake at 350°F. for 30 minutes or until chicken is tender. Yield: 4 servings.

Katharine Lee Hoover, Hyre Jr. H.S.
Akron, Ohio

CHICKEN-CHOW MEIN NOODLE CASSEROLE

7 c. cooked chicken, cut up
1½ sm. cans evaporated milk
2 cans mushroom soup
2 cans chicken-rice soup or 1 c. cooked rice
1½ c. chicken broth
2 cans chow mein noodles
1 c. celery, finely cut
¼ lb. slivered blanched almonds
1 sm. can mushrooms

Combine all ingredients; let stand 30 minutes to 1 hour. Bake at 350°F. for 1 hour. NOTE: All ingredients except noodles can be combined the day before needed. Yield: 12 servings.

Mrs. Margaret Hostetler, Eel-River Perry
Consolidated Schools
Huntertown, Indiana

CHICKEN CURRY

3 lb. chicken, cut up
Flour
1/3 c. butter
2 onions, sliced
1 T. curry powder
2 t. salt
1 t. vinegar
Boiled rice

Flour chicken; brown in butter for 10 minutes. Add liver and gizzards and cook 10 minutes longer. Add onion, curry powder, salt and vinegar. Add boiling water to cover. Simmer until chicken is tender. Add more water if necessary. Serve with boiled rice. Yield: 6 servings.

Mrs. Ruth Marie Skaggs, Mapletown H.S.
Greensboro, Pennsylvania

CURRIED CHICKEN CASSEROLE

1/2 c. onions, chopped
1/2 c. celery, chopped
1/2 stick butter
2 c. chicken, diced
1 can cream of mushroom soup
1 can cream of chicken soup
1 can chicken stock
1 c. milk
1 t. curry powder
Salt to taste
3/4 c. instant rice

Saute onions and celery in butter. Combine all ingredients in casserole. Bake at 350°F. for 1 hour and 30 minutes. Yield: 6 servings.

Betty Watts, Benzie Central H.S.
Benzonia, Michigan

CHICKEN-RICE CASSEROLE

2 c. celery, chopped
1/3 c. green pepper, chopped
2 T. onion, chopped
2 T. pimento, chopped
2 c. cooked chicken, chopped
1 c. cooked rice
1/2 t. salt
3/4 c. mayonnaise
1/2 c. slivered blanched almonds
Grated cheese

Cook celery, green pepper and onion until soft. Combine all ingredients except cheese; top with grated cheese. Bake 25 minutes at 350°F. Yield: 6 servings.

Mrs. Violet Rhodes, Odin Community H.S.
Odin, Illinois

CHICKEN AND RICE BAKE

1/4 c. onion, chopped
1/2 c. celery, diced
Butter
1 c. raw rice
1 can consomme
1 can chicken-gumbo soup
1 lge. cooked chicken breast, diced
1 T. pimento, diced

Sauce onion and celery in butter until tender. Combine all ingredients and place in a buttered casserole; stir lightly. Bake 1 hour at 350°F., stirring twice. Add chicken broth if additional liquid is needed. Yield: 4 servings.

Mrs. Geraldine Branstetter, Helix H.S.
LaMesa, California

CHICKEN-RICE CASSEROLE

1 4-lb. cooking chicken, cut up
2 c. soft bread crumbs
1 c. cooked rice
1 T. salt
3 eggs, well beaten
3 c. stock
1 can mushroom soup

Combine all ingredients except soup. Pour into cake pan or dish. Bake 1 hour and 30 minutes at 325°F. During last part of baking time pour can of soup over top.

Mrs. Carol Groth, Walker School
Walker, Minnesota

CHICKEN-RICE CASSEROLE

1 chicken, cut up
1 c. rice
1 pkg. dry onion soup
1 can cream of mushroom soup
1 can cream of chicken soup
Salt to taste

Place chicken in bottom of greased casserole; salt lightly. Add rice and onion soup. Pour cream soups evenly over rice. Cover and bake at 350°F. for 1 hour and 30 minutes. Yield: 4-6 servings.

Mrs. Beth Scholin, Franklin Jr. H.S.
Thief River Falls, Minnesota

CHICKEN AND RICE CASSEROLE

1 4 to 5-lb. hen
3 c. chicken broth
2 c. bread crumbs
4 eggs
1 c. instant rice, cooked
1 can cream of mushroom soup or chicken broth
Yellow food coloring

Cook chicken and remove from bones. Cut up skin and add to chicken. Mix with other ingredients. Bake 1 hour at 325°F. Yield: 12 servings.

Mrs. Charles Kingon, Adrain H.S.
Adrian, Michigan

CHICKEN AND RICE MILANESE

1 4½ to 5-lb. chicken
1 c. rice
2 T. butter
2 c. chicken broth
2 cloves garlic
2 t. salt
3½ c. canned tomatoes
2½ c. canned spaghetti sauce
1 c. onion, chopped
1 green pepper, chopped
1 can mushroom soup
⅛ t. oregano
⅛ t. basil
⅛ t. pepper

Cook chicken until tender; remove meat from bones. Brown rice until golden brown in butter, stirring constantly. Add chicken broth; simmer over low heat. Gradually add remaining ingredients one at a time. Mix well; pour into a large casserole. Bake 1 hour at 400°F. Add additional spaghetti sauce if casserole becomes dry.

Mrs. Bobbie K. Troutman,
Rosiclare Community Unit #1 H.S.
Rosiclare, Illinois

CHICKEN AND RICE WITH MUSHROOMS

1 fryer, cut up
1¼ c. uncooked rice
1 can mushroom soup
1 soup can water
1 pkg. dry onion soup
1 6-oz. can mushrooms

Place rice in bottom of casserole. Cover with mushrooms; add mushroom soup diluted with water. Place uncooked chicken on top of rice; sprinkle with whole package of onion soup. Cover tightly with foil or lid. Bake 1 hour and 15 minutes at 350°F. Yield: 4-6 servings.

Joyce L. Miller, Campbell H.S.
Campbell, California

CHICKEN-RICE ORIENTAL

1 sm. clove of garlic, minced
3 T. salad oil
1 c. cooked chicken, diced
2 c. hot water
⅛ t. pepper
1⅓ c. instant rice
1½ c. lettuce, shredded
2 T. soy sauce

Saute garlic in oil until golden brown. Mix in chicken, water, pepper and rice. Bring quickly to a boil. Cover; remove from heat and let stand 5 minutes. Just before serving, add lettuce and soy sauce; toss lightly. Yield: 5 servings.

Mrs. Carole Fisher, Jackson School
Westport, Indiana

CHICKEN SCALLOP

1 4 to 5-lb cooked chicken, cut up
1½ c. broth
1½ c. milk
1 c. cooked rice
¼ c. pimento, diced
¼ c. butter
2 c. fresh soft bread crumbs
4 eggs, beaten

Combine all ingredients except eggs. Add eggs; pour in casserole. Bake 1 hour at 325°F.

Mrs. Lyla David, Benkelman H.S.
Benkelman, Nebraska

CHICKEN SUPREME

2 c. cooked rice
2⅔ c. chicken broth
4 c. cooked chicken, chopped
1 lge. can mushrooms
2 T. butter
1 sm. can pimentos, finely chopped
1 c. blanched almonds, halved
½ c. flour
Buttered crumbs

Combine rice and ⅔ cup broth; mix well. Add chicken and place in a casserole. Saute mushrooms in butter. Place half of mushrooms, half of pimento and half of almonds on chicken mixture. Combine remaining broth and flour; heat until thickened. Pour half of sauce over casserole. Repeat layers; top with crumbs. Bake at 350°F. for 45 minutes. Yield: 8-10 servings.

Evelyn Hackney, Iola Sr. H.S.
Iola, Kansas

CLUB CHICKEN CASSEROLE

¼ c. butter or margarine, melted
¼ c. flour
1 c. chicken broth
1⅔ c. evaporated milk
½ c. water (opt.)
1½ t. salt
½ c. blanched almonds, slivered and toasted
3 c. cooked rice
2½ c. cooked chicken, diced
1 3-oz. can sl. mushrooms, drained
¼ c. pimento, chopped
⅓ c. green pepper, chopped

Blend butter and flour; add broth, milk and water. Cook over low heat until thickened, stirring constantly. Stir in salt, rice, chicken and vegetables. Pour into a greased baking dish; bake at 350°F. for 30 minutes. Top with almonds. NOTE: Canned chicken consomme or 1 to 2 chicken bouillon cubes dissolved in 1 cup hot water may be substituted for broth. Yield: 8-10 servings.

This recipe submitted by the following teachers:
Mrs. Ruby Z. Doughty, Kentwood H.S.
Kentwood, Louisiana
Mrs. Mildred Wilson, Kennard Dale H.S.
Fawn Grove, Pennsylvania

CHOW MEIN BAKE

1 c. rice
2½ c. boiling water
1 med. onion, diced
2 T. brown sugar
2 c. boned chicken
2 c. celery, diced
1 can mushroom soup
3 T. soy sauce

Cook rice in boiling water until tender. Brown onions in small amount of fat. Add brown sugar. Combine all ingredients with drained rice. If dry add milk to desired moistness. Bake at 350°F. for 50 minutes. Yield: 8 servings.

Mrs. Roberta Schroeder, Long Prairie Jr. H.S.
Long Prairie, Minnesota

EASY CHICKEN CASSEROLE

1 c. uncooked rice
1 can mushroom soup
1 pkg. dry onion soup
1½ soup cans of milk
1 lge. fryer, cut up
Salt and pepper to taste

Mix together rice, soups and milk. Place in large casserole. Put chicken on top, skin side down. Add salt and pepper to taste. Cook at 250°F. for 3 hours. Turn chicken over once. Yield: 4 servings.

Mrs. Susan W. Breidenbach, Washington Jr. H.S.
Olympia, Washington

FAVORITE CHICKEN CASSEROLE

1 c. cooked chicken, diced
1 can cream of chicken soup
1 c. celery, chopped
2 T. onion, chopped
½ c. walnuts, chopped
1½ c. cooked rice
¼ t. pepper
½ t. salt
1 T. lemon juice
½ c. mayonnaise
¼ c. water
3 hard-cooked eggs

Combine chicken, soup, vegetables, nuts, rice and seasonings; blend well. Stir in lemon juice, mayonnaise and water. Chop 2 eggs; add to mixture. Place in a greased casserole; bake at 400°F. for 15 minutes or until bubbly. Let stand 15 minutes before serving. Garnish with remaining sliced egg. Yield: 4 servings.

Pat McKevitt, Morro Bay H.S.
Morro Bay, California

COUNTRY CAPTAIN

4 lb. chicken breasts
Seasoned flour
½ c. shortening
2 onions, finely chopped
2 green peppers, chopped
1 clove garlic, minced
¾ t. curry powder
1½ t. salt
½ t. white pepper
½ t. thyme
2 cans tomatoes
1 t. parsley, chopped
6 c. cooked rice
¼ c. currants
¼ lb. toasted almonds
Parsley sprigs

Skin chicken and dust with seasoned flour; fry in shortening until browned. Remove chicken; keep warm. Cook onions, peppers and garlic in remaining fat until tender; stir in seasonings. Mix well; add tomatoes and parsley. Heat thoroughly. Place breasts in a large casserole; cover with sauce. Cover and bake 45 minutes at 350°F. or until tender. Arrange chicken in center of platter; place rice in mounds around chicken. Sprinkle currants into sauce; pour over rice. Sprinkle almonds over chicken, garnish with parsley sprigs. Yield: 8 servings.

Mary Lou Mosele, Ganesha H.S.
Pomona, California

DELICIOUS CHICKEN CASSEROLE

1 c. cooked cubed chicken
1 c. chopped celery (opt.)
1 T. chopped onion
½ c. chopped walnuts or almonds (opt.)
1½ c. cooked regular or wild rice
1 can cream of chicken soup
½ t. salt
½ c. sl. green olives (opt.)
½ t. pepper
1 T. lemon juice
½-1 c. mayonnaise
2½ T. water
3 hard-cooked eggs, diced
2 c. crushed potato chips

Combine all ingredients except ½ cup potato chips. Place mixture in casserole. Top with reserved crushed potato chips. Bake in 325-350°F. oven for about 30 minutes or until heated through. NOTE: Corn flake crumbs may be used for topping. Yield: 6-8 servings.

This recipe submitted by the following teachers:
Mrs. Lorna Waltz, Murray Jr. H.S.
Pendleton, Oregon
Mrs. Marlys Herstad, Ulen H.S.
Ulen, Minnesota
Marianne Heller, Dwight H.S.
Dwight, Illinois

FLAVORFUL CHICKEN-RICE CASSEROLE

1 chicken, cut up
Salt and pepper
Garlic salt
Paprika
Lemon juice
1 can chicken soup
1 can mushroom soup
1 can celery soup
1 c. uncooked long grain rice
½ c. chicken broth

Season chicken with salt, pepper, garlic salt, paprika and lemon juice. Combine rice and soups; place in bottom of casserole. Place chicken on top of rice mixture; pour chicken broth over top. Cook at 325°F. for 2 hours. Add more broth if needed. Yield: 4 servings.

Beryl Giddings, Harbor Springs H.S.
Harbor Springs, Michigan

CHICKEN PARISIAN

1 fryer, cut up
1 pt. sour cream
1 sm. onion, diced
¼ c. instant rice
1 t. salt
Paprika
1 can cream of mushroom soup

Arrange chicken in a deep casserole. Combine all other ingredients. Pour over chicken. Sprinkle with paprika. Bake 1 hour and 15 minutes. at 350°F. Yield: 4 servings.

Betty Otteson, Pearl City H.S.
Pearl City, Illinois

JAMBALYA

1½ c. cooked chicken, diced
1 c. cooked rice
2 c. canned tomatoes
1 lge. onion, chopped
½ green pepper, chopped
2 stalks of celery, chopped
4 T. butter
Salt and pepper to taste
½ c. buttered bread crumbs

Mix chicken, rice and tomatoes; cook for 10 minutes. Saute onion, green pepper and celery in butter; add to chicken mixture. Season to taste. Pour into a buttered 1½-quart casserole; cover with buttered crumbs. Bake, uncovered, at 350°F. 1 hour. NOTE: Ham or veal may be substituted for chicken. Yield: 6-8 servings.

Janet White, Washington H.S.
Vinton, Iowa

JEANNE'S CHICKEN-RICE CASSEROLE

2 c. uncooked rice
1 chicken, cut up
1 pkg. dried onion soup
1 can cream of celery soup
1 can cream of mushroom soup
2 soup cans water

Sprinkle rice in bottom of cake pan. Lay raw chicken on bed of rice, skin-side up. Sprinkle dried soup over chicken; pour on both cans of soup and water. Cover tightly with foil; bake at 400°F. for 2 hours to 2 hours and 30 minutes. Yield: 4 servings.

Jeanne West, Carrington H.S.
Carrington, North Dakota

PIQUANT CHICKEN CASSEROLE

2 cans cream of chicken soup
¼ c. onions, finely diced
2 t. salt
⅛ t. pepper
1 t. parsley flakes
1 t. celery flakes
¼ t. thyme
2⅔ c. water
2 c. instant rice
1-2 c. chicken, diced
½ t. paprika

Combine soup, onions and seasonings, mixing well; gradually add water, stirring constantly. Bring to a boil over medium heat, stirring occasionally. Pour half of soup mixture into a 2½-quart casserole; add rice and chicken. Top with remaining soup; mix well, being sure to moisten all rice. Cover and bake at 375°F. for 10 minutes. Stir well and bake 5-10 minutes. Sprinkle with paprika. Yield: 8 servings.

Florence Wood, Fairmount H.S.
Fairmount, Indiana

QUICKEST-EVER CHICKEN CASSEROLE

1 c. rice
1 can cream of chicken soup
1 can cream of mushroom soup
1 can cream of celery soup
1½ c. water or milk
2½-3 lb. chicken thighs

Combine all ingredients except chicken in greased casserole. Place thighs on top of mixture. Bake, covered, for 1 hour and 15 minutes at 350°F.; uncover and bake 30 minutes longer. Yield: 4-6 servings.

Mrs. Katherine Lyle, Los Gatos H.S.
Los Gatos, California

SCALLOPED CHICKEN WITH MUSHROOM SAUCE

1 med. cooked chicken, diced
2 c. soft bread crumbs
1 c. cooked rice
½ c. pimento. diced
4 eggs, beaten
1 t. salt
½ c. melted butter or chicken fat
3 c. chicken stock

Combine all ingredients; pour into a ring mold. Bake 1 hour and 15 minutes at 325°F. Let stand 10 minutes; turn out on round platter.

MUSHROOM SAUCE:

4 T. fat
5 T. flour
2 c. chicken stock
Salt and pepper to taste
1 T. parsley, chopped
1 t. lemon juice
½ lb. mushrooms, sauted
2 egg yolks, beaten
¼ c. heavy cream

Combine all ingredients; cook in top of double boiler until thickened. Fill center of mold. Yield: 8 servings.

Mrs. Earl Soderquist, Patrick Henry H.S.
Minneapolis, Minnesota

SHOREHAM CHICKEN

1 c. rice
1 pkg. dry onion soup mix
1 chicken, cut up
1 can mushroom soup
1½ c. milk
Paprika

Place rice in a greased casserole; sprinkle with soup mix. Arrange chicken over rice. Combine mushroom soup and milk; pour over chicken. Sprinkle with paprika. Cover and bake at 325°F. for 1 hour; uncover and bake 45 minutes. NOTE: Frozen peas may be added during 45 minute baking period. Yield: 6 servings.

Mrs. Lois Lovas, Mayville H.S.
Mayville, North Dakota

SIMPLE CHICKEN

1 c. instant rice
1 chicken, cut up
1 can cream of chicken soup
1 can cream of mushroom soup
1 can cream of celery soup

Put rice in bottom of greased casserole. Arrange chicken on rice. Combine soups; pour over chicken. Bake at 225°F. for 2 hours and 30 minutes to 3 hours. Cover after chicken is browned. Yield: 4-6 servings.

Mrs. Carol Arnold, Cascade H.S.
Cascade, Idaho

SEASONED CHICKEN CASSEROLE

3 to 4-lb. chicken pieces
⅓ c. seasoned flour
¼ c. butter
1 can cream of chicken soup
2½ T. onion, grated
1 T. chopped parsley
1 t. salt
⅛ t. thyme
½ t. celery flakes
1⅓ c. water
1⅓ c. instant rice
½ t. paprika

Roll chicken in flour. Saute in butter until golden brown. Mix soup, onion and seasonings in saucepan. Gradually stir in water. Bring to a boil, stirring constantly. Pour rice into a shallow 2-quart casserole. Stir all except ⅓ cup soup mixture into rice. Top with chicken; pour remaining soup mixture over top. Bake 30 minutes at 375°F. or until chicken is tender. Sprinkle with paprika. Yield: 4 servings.

Margaret McIntire, Mitchell H.S.
Mitchell, Indiana

SOUR CREAM-CHICKEN CASSEROLE

¼ c. onion, diced
¼ c. celery, diced
2 T. butter
½ c. sour cream
1 can cream of celery soup
2 c. long grain rice, steamed
1 c. chicken
¼ c. toasted almonds (opt.)

Saute onions and celery in butter until tender. Mix sour cream and soup until smooth. Layer rice, chicken, vegetables and soup mixture. Sprinkle with toasted almonds. Bake at 325°F. for 20 minutes. Yield: 6-7 servings.

Mrs. Janet L. Allen, Eddyville H.S.
Eddyville, Oregon

WHOLE CHICKEN CASSEROLE

1½ c. uncooked rice
1 can mushroom soup
1 can celery soup
2 cans water
2 onions, diced
1 c. celery, coarsely chopped
1 t. salt
½ t. pepper
Mushrooms (opt.)
1 chicken, quartered

Combine all ingredients except chicken in large casserole. Salt and pepper chicken quarters; place on top of casserole. Cover and bake 1 hour at 325°F. Remove cover and bake 1 hour longer. Yield: 4 servings.

Karen O. Nitz, Edgewood Jr. H.S.
New Brighton, Minnesota

WOODBURY CHICKEN LOAF

1 4-lb. cooked chicken, diced
2 c. fresh bread crumbs
1 c. cooked rice
1½ t. salt
⅛ c. chopped pimento
3 c. milk or chicken stock
4 eggs, well beaten

Mix all ingredients, adding eggs last. Bake at 325°F. for 40 minutes.

SAUCE:

Butter
¼ lb. fresh mushrooms or ½ lb. canned mushrooms
¼ c. flour
1 pt. chicken broth
¼ c. cream
⅛ t. paprika
½ t. chopped parsley
½ t. lemon juice
Salt to taste

Melt butter; add mushrooms. Cook 5 minutes. Add flour and mix well. Add broth slowly, stirring constantly until thickened. Add remaining ingredients. Serve over chicken loaf. Yield: 12 servings.

Mrs. Marjorie G. Stevens, Southbury H.S.
Southbury, Connecticut

CHICKEN CASSEROLE WITH WILD RICE

1 c. wild rice
1 pkg. onion soup
1 can cream of chicken soup, diluted
1 chicken, cut up

Put half of rice, onion soup and cream of chicken soup in casserole. Add remaining rice and onion soup. Put chicken on top of mixture and pour remaining chicken soup over top. Bake at 350°F. for 1 hour and 15 minutes. Yield: 4 servings.

Sandra J. Jacobson, Mahnomen H.S.
Mahnomen, Minnesota

CHICKEN AND WILD RICE

1 c. wild rice
1 lb. hamburger
1 c. celery
1 can cream of chicken soup
1 can cream of mushroom soup
1 can evaporated milk
2 cooked chicken breasts or 1 sm. chicken, chopped

Follow directions on package for cooking rice. Brown hamburger and celery. Combine all ingredients in a greased casserole. Bake at 325-350°F. for 1 hour. Yield: 8 servings.

Mary Hassman, Caro Community H.S.
Caro, Michigan

CHICKEN-WILD RICE CASSEROLE

¼ c. chicken fat or butter
5 T. flour
1½ t. salt
⅛ t. pepper
1 c. chicken broth
1½ c. milk
1½ c. cooked wild rice
¾ c. sliced mushrooms (opt.)
2 c. cooked chicken, cut up
⅓ c. green pepper, chopped
¼ c. slivered almonds

Melt fat in saucepan; blend in flour, salt and pepper. Cook over low heat until smooth and bubbly; remove from heat. Stir in chicken broth and milk. Bring to a boil and boil 1 minute, stirring constantly. Mix sauce with remaining ingredients. Pour into greased oblong baking dish. Bake 40-45 minutes at 350°F. Yield: 8 servings.

This recipe submitted by the following teachers:
Ellen Y. Davidson, Union Local H.S.
Belmont, Ohio
Mrs. Jane C. Roberts, Quincy H.S.
Quincy, Michigan
Josephine Tupy, Belle Plaine H.S.
Belle Plaine, Minnesota

CREAMY CHICKEN-WILD RICE CASSEROLE

1 c. wild rice
½ c. onion, chopped
½ c. butter
¼ c. flour
1 6-oz. can broiled sliced mushrooms
Chicken broth
1½ c. light cream
3 c. cooked chicken, diced
¼ c. pimento, diced
2 T. parsley, snipped
1½ t. salt
¼ t. pepper
½ c. slivered blanched almonds

Prepare wild rice according to package directions. Cook onions in butter until tender but not brown. Remove from heat and stir in flour. Drain mushrooms and reserve liquid. Add enough chicken broth to mushroom liquid to make 1½ cups. Stir liquid into flour mixture. Add cream and cook until thickened, stirring constantly. Add all remaining ingredients except almonds. Place in 2-quart casserole. Sprinkle with almonds. Bake at 350°F. for 25-30 minutes. Yield: 8-10 servings.

This recipe submitted by the following teachers:
Mrs. Mary Nestande, Fairfax Public School
Fairfax, Minnesota
Mrs. Ila Vaughn, Sequoyah H.S.
Tahlequah, Oklahoma

CHICKEN-WILD RICE CASSEROLE

1 c. wild rice or 1 box wild rice mix, cooked
½ c. onion, chopped
1 can cream of chicken soup
1 6-oz. can sliced mushrooms
3 c. cooked chicken, diced
¼ c. pimento, diced
2 T. parsley, minced
1 t. salt
¼ t. pepper
½ c. slivered almonds

Spread by alternating layers in a 2-quart casserole. Sprinkle top with almonds. Bake at 350°F. for 25-30 minutes. Yield: 8 servings.

Dianne Peterson, Wauconda H.S.
Wauconda, Illinois

CASSEROLE CHICKEN SPAGHETTI

1 5-lb. hen cooked
3 c. chicken stock
2 c. tomato juice
1 c. celery, chopped
1 lge. green pepper, chopped
1 7-oz. pkg. spaghetti
1 sm. can mushrooms
1 sm. can pimento, chopped
18 stuffed olives
1 T. Worcestershire sauce
Salt to taste
Celery salt to taste
Onion powder to taste
¾ lb. cheese
1 c. chow mein noodles

Combine all ingredients except cheese and noodles. Blend well and pour into a flat baking dish; slice cheese over top and cover with noodles. Bake at 300°F. for 30 minutes. Yield: 15 servings.

Emma Catherine Lawson, Carrizozo H.S.
Carrizozo, New Mexico

CHEDDAR CHICKEN SPAGHETTI

1 8-oz. pkg. spaghetti
¾ t. garlic salt
1 med. onion, chopped
1 T. butter
1 lge. pimento, chopped
1 can cream of chicken soup
1 c. Cheddar cheese, grated
1-2 cans chicken
Salt to taste
Grated cheese
Cracker crumbs

Cook spaghetti in boiling salted water with garlic salt; rinse with hot water. Saute onion in butter until brown. Mix all ingredients except cheese and crumbs. Sprinkle with cheese and cracker crumbs. Bake 25 minutes at 350°F. Yield: 5-6 servings.

Anita Darnell, Greenville H.S.
Greenville, Texas

CHICKEN CASSEROLE WITH MUSHROOMS

1 stewed chicken, diced
1 qt. chicken broth
1 bunch celery, diced
1 can mushrooms
1 lb. cheese, grated
1 No. 2½ can or 1 qt. tomatoes
1 onion, diced
1 pimento
1 c. cream
1 pkg. long spaghetti

Put chicken and broth into a large baking dish. Add remaining ingredients with uncooked spaghetti on top. Cover tightly and cook at 350°F. for 1 hour and 30 minutes. Do not stir. Yield: 12 servings.

Mrs. Ada Lindsey, Jr. H.S.
Mitchell, South Dakota

CHICKEN SPAGHETTI WITH OLIVES

1 6-oz. pkg. spaghetti
1 4 to 5-lb. hen
1 onion
1 can cream of mushroom soup
1 can tomatoes
1 c. olives
Grated cheese

Cook spaghetti until tender; drain well. Cook hen and whole onion until very tender. Combine all ingredients except cheese in casserole. Sprinkle cheese over top. Bake at 300°F. for 1 hour and 30 minutes. Yield: 10 servings.

Mrs. Mary George Elliott, Walnut School Center
Walnut, Mississippi

CHICKEN TETRAZZINI

1 5-lb. hen, cooked
1 box spaghetti
Chicken broth
Milk
¼ lb. butter
⅔ c. flour
½ lb. Old English cheese, grated
½ lb. American cheese, grated
1 lge. onion, diced
1 green pepper, diced
1 lge. can mushrooms
Mushroom liquid
Bread crumbs

Bone chicken and dice meat. Cook spaghetti; season with a small amount of broth. Add milk to remaining broth make 1 quart; add butter and flour. Heat until thickened, stirring constantly. Saute onion, pepper and mushrooms in mushroom liquid. Thoroughly blend all ingredients except crumbs in a buttered casserole; top with crumbs. Bake at 350°F. for 30 minutes. Yield: 15 servings.

Mrs. Evelyn A. Kee, Stell Jr. H.S.
Brownsville, Texas

CHICKEN TETRAZZINI

1 whole chicken
1 qt. chicken broth
1 12-oz. pkg. spaghetti
1 lge. onion
1 lge. bell pepper
1 stick margarine
1 2-oz. can mushrooms
1 can mushroom soup
1 soup can milk
1 lb. Cheddar cheese, grated
Salt and pepper to taste

Boil chicken and take all meat off bone and cut in cubes. Cook spaghetti in broth until tender. Saute onion and pepper in margarine. Mix all ingredients together leaving enough cheese to sprinkle on top. Bake at 350°F. about 20 minutes. Yield: 15 servings.

Mrs. Patsy Davina, Mesa Jr. H.S.
Roswell, New Mexico

ALMOND-CHICKEN SUPREME CASSEROLE

3 lb. chicken legs and thighs
¾ c. flour
½ t. salt
¼ t. pepper
¼ c. salad oil
½ c. onions, chopped
1 qt. chicken broth or bouillon
1 can tomato sauce
¾ c. almonds, blanched
1 c. mushroom buttons
1 T. parsley flakes
8 slices American cheese
Parsley (garnish)

Combine ¼ cup flour, salt and pepper; roll chicken in mixture to coat well. Brown in salad oil; place chicken in a large casserole. Saute oniors in drippings, add ½ cup flour, tomato sauce and water. Add almonds, mushrooms and parsley to chicken; cover with sauce. Bake 1 hour at 350°F. Top with cheese slices and garnish with parsley. Serve over rice. Yield: 8-10 servings.

Katherine Rigby, Thomas Ewing H.S.
Lancaster, Ohio

BAKED CHICKEN

2 2 to 2½-lb. chickens, cut up
1 c. flour
1⅓ T. salt
2 T. paprika
½ t. pepper
¾ c. butter
1 7-oz. jar pitted ripe olives
1 c. orange juice
1 T. brown sugar
½ t. thyme
1 med. onion, sliced in rings

Combine flour, 1 tablespoon salt, 1 teaspoon paprika and pepper in paper bag. Put chicken in bag and shake enough to coat each piece with mixture. Brown in ½ cup butter. Place browned chicken in a large flat casserole. Combine ¼ cup butter, olives, orange juice, brown sugar, 1 teaspoon salt, thyme and onion rings; simmer 4 minutes. Pour sauce over chicken. Sprinkle top of chicken with paprika. Bake 1 hour and 30 minutes to 1 hour and 45 minutes at 375°F. or until tender. Baste 4-5 times during baking. Serve with hot rice. Yield: 4-6 servings.

Mrs. Kathleen H. Stuart, Roosevelt H.S.
Minneapolis, Minnesota

BARBECUED CHICKEN CASSEROLE

6-8 lge. pieces chicken
Salt and pepper
Paprika
Flour
½ c. oil or shortening
½ c. tomato catsup
1 can bouillon
¼ c. water
1 T. lemon juice
1 T. onion, grated
1 T. Worcestershire sauce
1 t. mustard
1 clove of garlic, finely crushed
2 T. parsley, chopped

Season chicken with salt, pepper and paprika; dredge in flour. Brown to rich golden color in hot oil. While chicken is browning, combine remaining ingredients and bring to a boil. Arrange chicken in large casserole; pour hot sauce over top. Cover pan with foil. Bake covered at 375°F. for 25 minutes. Remove cover and continue baking 20-30 minutes. Baste frequently with sauce while baking. Yield: 4 servings.

Mrs. Lenora Lang, Abraham Lincoln H.S.
San Jose, California

BREAST OF CHICKEN ALMONDINE

3 whole chicken breasts, cooked
1 can cream of chicken soup
1 c. celery, diced
2 t. onion, minced
½ c. slivered almonds
½ t. salt
¼ t. pepper
1 T. lemon juice
¾ c. mayonnaise
Bread crumbs or crushed potato chips

Remove chicken from bones. Mix all ingredients gently. Place in buttered casserole; top with bread crumbs or potato chips. Bake at 375°F. for 30 minutes. Serve over cooked rice. Yield: 4-6 servings.

Mrs. Deanna Egge, Forest Lake H.S.
Forest Lake, Minnesota

CHICKEN-N-QUE

1 t. salt
1 t. monosodium glutamate
1 t. black pepper
1 t. red pepper
1 t. chili powder
1 t. paprika
¼ t. curry powder
1 can tomato sauce
½ c. catsup
½ c. water
3 T. lemon juice
3 T. vinegar
2 T. prepared mustard
2 T. Worcestershire sauce
¼ lb. butter or margarine
4 chickens, split or quartered

Mix all ingredients for sauce; heat slowly until butter is melted. Soak chicken in sauce for 1 hour before cooking. Place chicken in casserole and cover with extra sauce. Cover; bake 15 minutes at 500°F. Reduce heat to 250°F. and bake for 2 hours. Yield: 8 servings.

Mrs. Laura C. Webb, Imperial Jr. H.S
Ontario, California

CHICKEN A LA CHEESE CUPS

¼ c. green pepper, chopped
1 c. sl. mushrooms
¼ c. plus 2 T. butter
2 T. flour
¾ t. salt
2 c. half and half cream
3 c. cooked chicken, diced
1 t. onion juice
1 T. lemon juice
2 T. cooking Sherry
3 egg yolks
½ t. paprika
¼ c. pimento, chopped

Saute green pepper and mushrooms in 2 tablespoons butter; blend in flour and salt. Add cream; stir until thickened. Add chicken, onion and lemon juice and cooking Sherry. Heat until bubbling. Blend egg yolks, paprika and remaining butter; add to chicken mixture. Blend well and heat thoroughly.

CHEESE CUPS:
1 1-lb. sandwich loaf, unsliced
½ c. butter, melted
1 egg, beaten
2 c. American cheese, grated
½ c. cream

Freeze bread and trim crust; cut into 6 or 8 slices. Cut a square pocket out of each slice; brush inside and outside with butter. Combine egg, cheese and cream; fill cups half full. Bake on an ungreased cookie sheet for 15-20 minutes at 350°F. Pour hot chicken mixture into cups and serve.

Mrs. Marlene Gottschald, Stowe Jr. H.S.
Duluth, Minnesota

CAN-CAN CASSEROLE

1 sm. can evaporated milk
1 can chicken and rice soup
1 can cream of chicken soup
1 sm. can boned chicken
1 No. 303 can chow mein noodles
1 sm. can mushrooms
Corn flakes, crushed
American cheese, grated

Combine milk and soups. Fold in chicken and noodles. Pour into a buttered casserole. Top with corn flakes and cheese. Bake 1 hour at 350°F. Yield: 6 servings.

Mrs. Opal Pruitt, Western Community Unit H.S.
Buda, Illinois

CHICKEN-APPLE SCALLOP

2 c. cooked chicken, cubed
1 T. mustard
2 c. sl. apples, cooked
1 T. lemon juice
½ t. salt
1 can cream of mushroom soup
⅓ c. light cream
½ c. soft bread crumbs
2 T. butter or margarine, melted

Combine chicken and mustard; spread in a 1-quart buttered baking dish. Top with apple slices; sprinkle with lemon juice and salt. Combine soup and cream; and pour over apples. Top with crumbs and butter. Bake at 350°F. for twenty minutes, or until crumbs are brown. NOTE: Tuna may be substituted for chicken. Yield: 4 servings.

Kate Strachan, Elsinore Union H.S.
Elsinore, California

CHICKEN BREASTS (BAKED)

8 chicken breasts
Butter
Salt
1 can cream of celery soup
½ c. dry Sherry
½ pt. sour cream
Slivered almonds

Remove skin from chicken; brown in butter and salt. Place in baking dish. Combine soup, Sherry and sour cream; pour over chicken. Sprinkle with slivered almonds. Bake at 350°F. for 1 hour and 30 minutes. Yield: 8 servings.

Mrs. Evelyn Moss, Jr. H.S.
Palisades Park, New Jersey

CHICKEN BREASTS IN WINE

4 to 5 whole chicken breasts, split in half
3 T. lemon juice
Salt
Freshly ground black pepper
Thyme
3 T. olive oil
½ lb. mushrooms, sliced
3 T. butter
4 T. flour
2 c. chicken stock
½ c. dry white wine
1 bay leaf

Sprinkle dry chicken breasts with lemon juice, salt, pepper and thyme. Cover and refrigerate. Pat breasts dry; saute in hot olive oil until deep golden brown. Transfer to deep casserole. Saute mushrooms in butter. Blend in flour. Add chicken stock and wine, a little at a time. Cook, stirring constantly, until thickened. Add bay leaf and pour sauce over chicken breasts. Cover and bake at 325°F. for about 1 hour or until tender. Sauce will thin to proper consistency as chicken simmers. NOTE: 3 chicken bouillon cubes dissolved in 2 cups boiling water may be substituted for stock. Yield: 6 servings.

Mrs. Mary Prideaux Blackman, Blacklick Township School Twin Rocks, Pennsylvania

CHICKEN CASSEROLE

3 c. cooked chicken, diced
1 can condensed mushroom soup
1 can condensed cream of chicken soup
1 13-oz. can evaporated milk
1 6-oz. can mushrooms, drained
1 3-oz. can chow mein noodles
½ c. sl. almonds
1 c. corn flakes, crushed

Combine chicken, soups, milk, mushrooms and noodles. Place in 2-quart baking dish. Sprinkle with almonds and crushed corn flakes. Bake 1 hour at 350°F. Yield: 6 servings.

Mrs. Pauline Kirby, Marcellus .HS. Marcellus, Michigan

CHICKEN CASSEROLE

1 can cream of mushroom soup
1 can cream of chicken soup
1 15-oz. can evaporated milk
1 can Chinese noodles
1 7-oz. can chicken
Crushed cereal flakes or potato chips

Combine soups and milk. Spread noodles and flaked chicken in bottom of a greased baking dish. Cover with soup mixture. Bake at 325°F. for 45 minutes. Cover top with crushed cereal flakes or poato chips. Bake 15 more minutes. Yield: 8 servings.

Mrs. Henrietta Matz, Attica Local School Attica, Ohio

CHICKEN CASSEROLE MEDLEY

¼ c. butter
1 sm. onion, chopped
1 stalk celery with top, chopped
Parsley
½ loaf day-old bread, crumbled
1 t. salt
Dash of pepper
1 t. poultry seasonings
4 c. plus 6 T. chicken broth
½ c. milk
½ c. chicken fat, melted
½ c. flour
2 eggs, slightly beaten
1 3-lb. chicken, cooked

Melt butter; add onion, celery and parsley. Cook 6 minutes. Add to bread crumbs; add seasonings and 6 tablespoons broth. Heat remaining broth and milk; do not boil. Blend flour into fat; stir into milk. Cook, stirring constantly, until thickened. Add eggs. Place dressing in a greased 13x9x2-inch pan; add half of sauce and cut up chicken. Cover with remaining sauce. Bake at 350°F. for 45 minutes. Yield: 6 servings.

Mrs. Ann Siebenaler, Tongue River School Dayton, Wyoming

CHICKEN-CHEESE CASSEROLE

2 c. chicken broth
Flour
½ c. celery, thinly sliced
2 cans mushroom buttons
½ c. onions, thinly sliced
1 5-oz. can water chestnuts, thinly sliced
½ can pimento strips
2 c. cooked chicken, diced
1 c. buttered bread crumbs
1 c. Cheddar cheese, diced

Strain broth; add flour to thicken to consistency of white sauce Combine vegetables and chicken; place in a shallow casserole. Pour sauce over mixture; sprinkle with buttered crumbs and cheese. Bake at 350°F. for 30 minutes. Yield: 6 servings.

Mrs. Harold K. Wood, Rockford Sr. H.S. Rockford, Michigan

CHICKEN CRUNCH

¼ c. chicken broth
2 10-oz. cans cream of mushroom soup
3 c. cooked chicken, diced
¼ c. onion, minced
1 c. celery, diced
1 5-oz. pkg. water chestnuts, sliced
1 3-oz. pkg. chow mein noodles
⅓ c. toasted almonds, sliced

Blend broth into soup and mix well. Combine chicken, onion, celery, chestnuts and noodles. Place in greased baking dish. Pour soup mixture over top. Cook at 325°F. for 40 minutes. When partially browned, sprinkle almonds over top. Yield: 8 servings.

Mrs. Anne Teter, Pike H.S. Indianapolis, Indiana

CHICKEN CASSEROLE WITH PIMENTO

¼ lb. sl. fresh mushrooms or 1 4-oz. can mushrooms
1 T. butter
3 c. cooked chicken, cut up
3 c. soft bread crumbs
1 c. milk
1 c. chicken broth
¼ c. pimento, finely chopped
2 eggs, beaten
2 T. onion, minced
Salt and pepper
Celery salt
Paprika

Saute mushrooms in butter. Mix with remaining
ingredients. Pour into greased 2-quart baking dish;
set in pan of water. Bake for 1 hour and 30
minutes at 350°F. Yield: 6 servings.

This recipe submitted by the following teachers:
Mrs. LaVaughn Larson
Bertrand Community School
Bertrand, Nebraska
De Wayne Law, Valley H.S.
Hot Springs, Virginia

CHICKEN AND DRESSING SUPREME

1 loaf stale bread, crumbled
2 T. onion, minced
½ t. salt
½ t. pepper
½ t. celery seed
½ t. sage
2 hens, cooked and diced
½ c. butter
¾ c. flour
6 eggs, beaten
6 c. chicken broth

Combine bread, onions and seasonings; place in
a 9x13x2-inch pan. Spread chicken over dressing.
Melt butter; blend in flour until smooth. Add
broth; stir well. Add eggs; cook until thickened.
Pour sauce over chicken and dressing. Sprinkle
lightly with bread crumbs. Bake at 300°F. for
45 minutes. Yield: 15-20 servings.

Mrs. Mary Hilda Parrish, Calapooya Jr. H.S.
Albany, Oregon

CHICKEN HOT DISH

1 egg, beaten
1 can mushroom soup
1 can chicken-noodle soup
3 slices day-old bread, cubed
2 chicken breasts or 1 can of boned chicken
Cracker crumbs or crushed corn flakes
½ stick butter, melted

Beat egg; blend in soups. Add bread cubes and
chicken. Pour into buttered casserole. Top with
cracker crumbs which have been stirred in melted
butter. Bake 1 hour at 350°F. Yield: 6 servings.

Mrs. Ethelyn Richman, Wawaka H.S.
Wawaka, Indiana

CHICKEN HOT DISH

2 c. cooked chicken, diced
1 sm. can button mushrooms
1 sm. can pimentos, chopped
½ green pepper, diced
1 can mushroom soup
1 can cream of chicken soup
1 sm. can evaporated milk
1 c. diced celery, cooked
2 c. chow mein noodles
¼ c. blanched almonds

Combine all ingredients except almonds. Bake in
a greased casserole at 350°F. for 1 hour. Sprinkle
with almonds during last 10 minutes of baking.
Yield: 6 servings.

Ethelwyn Weir, Technical H.S.
St. Cloud, Minnesota

CHICKEN HOT DISH

8 c. bread crumbs
1-2 stalks of celery, chopped
1 med. onion, chopped
½ c. fat
2 eggs, beaten
½ t. baking powder
Salt and pepper
Sage to taste
2 c. milk
1 cooked chicken, cut up
1 can mushroom soup
1 c. chicken broth

Combine all ingredients except chicken, soup and
broth. Alternate layers of chicken and dressing.
Pour soup and broth over top. Bake at 350°F.
for 30 minutes to 1 hour. Yield: 8 servings.

Mrs. Donna A. Emmert, Hoffman H.S.
Hoffman, Minnesota

CHICKEN ON A CLOUD

1 c. flour
1 t. baking powder
1 t. salt
3 eggs, well beaten
1½ c. milk
¼ c. butter, melted
¼ c. parsley, chopped
1 2½ to 3-lb. fryer, cut up

Sift flour, baking powder and salt. Combine remaining ingredients except chicken; add to dry
ingredients. Stir until smooth. Pour mixture over
chicken that has been placed in baking dish.
Bake at 350°F. for 1 hour. Yield: 4-6 servings.

Alice M. Dill, New England Public H.S.
New England, North Dakota

CHICKEN SCALLOPED

1 lge. hen
2 med. onions, chopped
1 med. carrot, chopped
5 t. salt
2 stalks of celery, chopped
¾ c. butter
1 loaf day-old bread, crumbled
Pepper
1 t. poultry seasoning
Chicken broth
½ c. flour
4 eggs, slightly beaten
1 c. bread crumbs

Cook hen with 1 onion, carrot and 2 teaspoons salt in 2 quarts water. Cook remaining onion and celery in ½ cup butter for 5 minutes. Mix with crumbs; add 1 teaspoon salt, pepper and poultry seasoning. Add 6 tablespoons chicken broth. Skim fat from chicken broth and add enough melted butter to make 1 cup. Put in saucepan; stir in flour. Add broth and enough milk to make a total of 5 cups. Add 2 teaspoons salt; cook until thick. Stir in eggs; cook 3 minutes. Put crumb mixture into buttered casserole. Pour half of sauce over mixture. Cut up chicken; layer on top of sauce. Add remaining sauce. Sprinkle bread crumbs mixed with ¼ cup butter over top. Bake at 375°F. for 45 minutes. Yield: 12-15 servings.

Mrs. Michael Center, Owatonna H.S.
Owatonna, Minnesota

CHICKEN STRATA

16 sl. bread
4 c. cooked chicken, diced
1 lge. onion, chopped
1 c. celery, finely chopped
1 lge. green pepper, chopped
1 c. mayonnaise
½ T. salt
⅛ t. pepper
3 eggs, slightly beaten
3 c. milk
2 cans mushroom soup
1 c. sharp cheese, grated

Butter 4 slices of bread; cut into ½-inch cubes and set aside. Cut remaining bread into 1-inch cubes; place half in a 13x9x2-inch baking pan. Combine chicken, vegetables, mayonnaise and seasonings; pour over bread cubes in casserole. Top with remaining bread cubes. Combine eggs and milk; pour over bread. Cover and chill 1 hour or overnight. Spread soup on top; cover with buttered bread cubes. Bake at 325°F. 50-60 minutes; sprinkle with cheese during final 15 minutes of baking. Yield: 12 servings.

Nellie P. Millar, Beaver Dam Sr. H.S.
Beaver Dam, Wisconsin

CHICKEN-SOUP CASSEROLE

1 egg, beaten
1 can mushroom soup
1 can chicken-noodle soup
3 sl. day-old bread, cubed
2 cooked chicken breasts, cut up
½ stick butter, melted
Cracker crumbs or crushed corn flakes

Blend egg and undiluted soups; add bread and chicken. Pour into buttered casserole; top with crumbs which have been mixed with butter. Bake at 350°F. for 1 hour. Yield: 6 servings.

Nelle Alspaugh, Jefferson Township School
Upland, Indiana

CHICKEN TIMBALES

1 T. butter
¼ c. dry bread crumbs
⅔ c. milk
1 c. chopped chicken or tuna
1 T. parsley, chopped
2 eggs, slightly beaten
Salt and pepper to taste

Melt butter; add bread cubes and milk. Cook 2 minutes, stirring constantly. Remove from heat; add chicken, parsley and eggs and season to taste. Pour into individual molds, filling two-thirds full. Set molds in a pan of water; cover with waxed paper and bake at 400°F. for 45 minutes.

BECHAMEL SAUCE:

½ c. chicken stock
1 onion, sliced
1 bay leaf
1 carrot, sliced
Sprig of parsley
1 T. butter
1 T. flour
½ c. milk
¼ t. salt

Cook stock with onion, carrot, bay leaf and parsley for 10 minutes; strain. Melt butter; gradually add flour, stock and milk. Season to taste. Bring to boiling point. Serve hot sauce over timbales. Yield: 4-5 servings.

Vivian Johnson, Willmar Jr. H.S.
Willmar, Minnesota

CHICKEN SPOONBREAD

1½ c. corn meal
2⅔ T. tapioca
1 T. salt
2 qt. chicken broth
½ c. butter or margarine
⅔ c. egg yolks
1½ qt. cooked chicken, chopped
1 c. egg whites

Combine corn meal, tapioca, salt and broth in top of double boiler. Cook until thickened, stirring occasionally. Stir in fat. Remove from heat; cool slightly. Beat egg yolks and blend into cornmeal mixture. Add chopped chicken. Beat egg white until stiff; fold into chicken mixture. Place in four casseroles. Bake at 375°F. for 45 minutes. Yield: 25 servings.

Sister Mary St. Therese, PBVM
Dubuque, Iowa

CHICKEN AND TINY BISCUITS

BISCUITS:
1 c. sifted flour
1½ t. baking powder
⅛ t. soda
⅛ t. salt
3 T. shortening
6 T. sour milk

Sift dry ingredients together; cut in shortening. Add milk; lightly mix. Knead gently for 30 seconds. Roll out to ½ inch thick; cut with a tiny biscuit cutter.

1½ T. butter
2 T. flour
1 c. broth
¼ c. milk
Salt and pepper to taste
1½ c. cooked chicken
½ c. rice, cooked

Melt butter; blend in flour. Gradually add broth and milk; cook until thickened. Season to taste. Place chicken and rice in a casserole; add sauce. Cover with biscuits. Bake at 400°F. for 25-30 minutes. Yield: 4 servings.

Caryl Nelson, Osakis H.S.
Osakis, Minnesota

CREAMED CHICKEN CASSEROLE

1 3 to 4-lb. broiler, cut up
½ c. flour
1 t. salt
½ t. pepper
¼ lb. butter
3 c. milk

Dust chicken with mixture of flour, salt and pepper. Brown in butter; place in casserole. Cover chicken with milk. Bake at 300°F. for 2 hours. Garnish with paprika and parsley sprigs. Yield: 6 servings.

Mrs. Thomas P. Loose, Cornwall Joint School
Cornwall, Pennsylvania

CHICKEN WITH WINE EN CASSEROLE

⅔ c. Sauterne
2 cans condensed mushroom soup
2 c. cooked or canned chicken, cut into pieces
2 c. potato chips, slightly broken
4 hard-cooked eggs, chopped
1 lb. mushrooms, sliced and sauted
Celery salt
Freshly ground pepper
Grated Parmesan cheese
1 c. slivered almonds

Blend wine into soup; fold in chicken, potato chips, eggs, and mushrooms. Season to taste with dash of celery salt and pepper. Turn into a greased large casserole. Cover top with grated cheese; sprinkle with almonds. Bake at 375°F. for 25 minutes. Yield: 8 servings.

Mrs. Jane M. Wulf, Mother of Sorrows H.S.
Blue Island, Illinois

GLORIFIED CHICKEN

DRESSING:
⅔ c. butter or chicken fat
⅓ c. onion, minced
¾ c. celery, chopped
1 can water chestnuts
2 t. salt
½ t. pepper
1 t. sage
½ t. thyme
8 c. dry bread cubes
3 eggs, beaten
Cooked giblets, chopped
Ground chicken skin

Saute onion, celery and chestnuts in butter over low heat until onions are clear. Combine all ingredients, blending well. Add milk or chicken broth to moisten if necessary.

1 5 to 6-lb. hen
1 c. chicken fat
4 egg yolks, beaten
1 c. flour
1½ qt. milk or part broth
1 can mushroom soup
2 qt. dressing
½ c. butter, melted
2 c. crushed crackers

Cook hen until tender; bone and cut meat into bite-size pieces. Blend chicken fat with egg yolks until smooth. Add flour and blend well. Stir in milk to make a sauce; add soup. Place a layer of dressing in an oblong pan; cover with half of the sauce. Add chopped chicken and remaining sauce. Top with buttered cracked crumbs. Bake at 350°F. for 35-40 minutes. Yield: 18-20 servings.

Lythene Lambert, Cherokee Co. Rural H.S.
Columbus, Kansas

INDIAN CHICKEN CURRY

½ c. butter
2 lge. onions, sliced
3 whole cardamon (opt.)
1 1-inch piece stick cinnamon
2 garlic cloves, minced
1 t. ginger
1 T. ground cumin seed (opt.)
1 T. curry powder
1½ t. ground coriander seed (opt.)
1 t. tumeric powder (opt.)
½ t. Tabasco
¾ c. warm water
2 tomatoes, peeled and cut
3½ to 4-lb. roasting chicken, cut up

Melt butter in deep saucepan Add onions, card-amon and cinnaman; cook until onion is tender and lightly browned. Combine garlic, ginger, cum-in, curry powder, coriander, tumeric, Tabasco and ¼ cup water; stir to a paste. Stir into butter mixture. Add tomatoes. Simmer, covered, 20 minutes. Add chicken and remaining water. Cook over low heat for 1½ to 2 hours, or until chicken is tender. Add more warm water and salt if necessary. Serve with hot cooked rice. Yield: 6 servings.

(Photograph for this recipe on page 59)

FIVE-CAN CHICKEN CASSEROLE

1 can chicken soup
1 can mushroom soup
1 can noodles
1 sm. can evaporated milk
1-2 cans chicken
Buttered bread crumbs

Mix all ingredients except crumbs; put in baking dish. Sprinkle with buttered bread crumbs. Bake 30-40 minutes at 350°F. Yield: 6 servings.

Bonnie Dickinson, Fort Sumner H.S.
Fort Sumner, New Mexico

HONEY-CHICKEN CASSEROLE

1 frying chicken, cut up
½ c. milk
1½ c. seasoned flour
½ c. shortening
½ c. honey
1½ c. fresh orange juice

Dip pieces of chicken into milk and coat with seasoned flour. Cook chicken in fat on both sides until golden brown. Place chicken in a cas-serole dish. Combine honey and orange juice; pour mixture over chicken. Cover and bake at 325°F. for 40-50 minutes or until chicken is ten-der. Yield: 4-6 servings

Mrs. Mary Kolischak, Chatham Sr. H.S.
Chatham, New Jersey

FRIED CHICKEN HAWAIIAN

1 chicken, cut up
1 can crushed pineapple
1 can shredded coconut

Fry chicken until golden brown. Place in deep baking dish and top with pineapple. Brown in 375°F. oven. Cover with coconut and brown lightly.

Leah Jane Powell, Wheelersburg H.S.
Wheelersburg, Ohio

CHICKEN SOUFFLE

8 sl. bread, cubed
1 4-lb. cooked stewing chicken, cut up
1 c. celery, finely cut
½ c. mayonnaise
4 eggs, beaten
1 c. broth
2 c. milk
1 can mushroom soup
½ t. salt
Grated cheese
Paprika

Place half of bread cubes in bottom of 9x13-inch pan. Mix chicken with celery and mayonnaise; cover with remaining bread. Combine eggs, liq-uid and salt. Pour over chicken and bread mix-ture; refrigerate overnight. Cook at 350°F. for 15 minutes. Pour in mushroom soup; bake for 1 hour. Add cheese and paprika last 10 minutes of baking. Yield: 16 servings.

Mrs. Phyllis McFarland, North Salem H.S.
Salem, Oregon

CHICKEN CASSEROLE

8 sl. bread
2 c. chicken, diced
1 lge. onion, diced
1 sm. green pepper, diced
1 c. celery, diced
½ c. mayonnaise
4 eggs
3¼ c. milk
1 can cream of mushroom soup
1½ c. grated cheese
Paprika

Remove crust from bread; dice 4 slices of bread and put in bottom of oiled pan. Combine chicken, onion, green pepper, celery and mayonnaise. Pour over bread; top with remaining slices of bread. Combine eggs and 3 cups milk; pour over mix-ture. Refrigerate overnight. Bake at 325°F. for 15 minutes. Remove from oven; add soup diluted with ¼ cup milk. Sprinkle with cheese and pap-rika. Bake for 1 hour. Yield: 12-15 servings.

Mrs. Darlene LaBorde, Carmichael Jr. H.S.
Richland, Washington

MILDRED'S SCALLOPED CHICKEN

1 lb. soda crackers, crushed very fine
4 T. butter, melted
2 T. flour
2 t. salt
3 c. chicken broth
1 4 to 5-lb. cooked chicken, diced

Stir butter into half of cracker crumbs. Add flour and salt to broth; stir well. Arrange ingredients in a buttered casserole in layers of chicken, gravy, unbuttered crumbs, chicken, gravy and buttered crumbs. Bake for 1 hour at 350°F. Yield: 15 servings.

Mildred Burris, Delta School
Delta, Ohio

SARAH'S CHICKEN CASSEROLE

1 chicken, cubed
½ c. butter
6 sprigs parsley
2 stalks celery
1 onion
1 c. fat
4 c. broth
1 c. milk
1 c. flour
4 eggs, slightly beaten
1 t. salt
⅛ t. pepper
1 t. poultry seasoning
1½ loaves bread, finely crumbled

Cook chicken and cut in cubes. Cook butter, parsley, celery and onion until tender. Heat fat, broth and milk; thicken with flour. Add eggs and seasonings; cook 3 minutes. Layer bread crumbs, chicken and sauce, ending with another layer of bread crumbs. Bake 20 minutes at 250°F. Yield: 8 servings.

Sarah M. Westerberg, Eastside School District
Preston, Idaho

MRS. SULLIVAN'S CHICKEN CASSEROLE

1 5-lb. hen
2 c. bread crumbs
2½ c. broth
2 T. parsley
6 eggs, separated
Salt and pepper to taste

Cook hen in 2-quarts boiling salted water; cool. Bone and chop into 1-inch cubes. Put skin through food chopper; add to meat. Add crumbs, broth, parsley, beaten egg yolks and seasonings. Fold in beaten egg whites. Shape into firm loaf in greased casserole. Set in pan of water. Bake at 375°F. for 1 hour. Serve with giblet gravy. Yield: 6 servings.

Mrs. Marcella Sullivan, Loveland H.S.
Loveland, Colorado

ORANGE GLAZED CHICKEN CASSEROLE

1½ c. flour
1 t. oregano
1 t. basil
1 t. savory
½ t. nutmeg
½ t. rosemary
1 3½-lb. fryer, boned
2 t. salt
¼ t. pepper
¼ c. olive oil

Combine flour, oregano, basil, savory, nutmeg and rosemary in a bag. Rub chicken with salt and pepper. Shake chicken in flour mixture. Fry in olive oil until brown.

SAUCE:
2½ lb. mushrooms, sliced
6 onions, sliced
½ c. olive oil
2-3 t. salt
2 cloves of garlic, crushed
1½ c. orange juice
½ c. white wine
½ t. basil
¼ t. pepper
2 bay leaves
½ t. savory
¼ t. nutmeg
Cooked rice

Saute mushrooms and onions in olive oil. Add remaining ingredients. Pour over chicken; simmer for 5 minutes. Pour chicken and sauce over bed of cooked rice in casserole. Bake at 300°F. for 1 hour and 30 minutes. Yield: 15 servings.

Joanne Hooey, Clarissa Public School
Clarissa, Minnesota

ORIGINAL CHICKEN A LA KING

¼ c. green pepper, chopped
1 c. mushrooms, thinly sliced
2 T. flour
¾ t. salt
2 c. light cream
3 c. cooked chicken, cut up
1 t. onion juice
1 T. lemon juice
3 egg yolks
½ t. paprika
¼ c. soft butter
¼ c. pimento, diced

Cook green pepper and mushrooms in 2 T. butter until tender. Push vegetables aside; blend flour and salt into butter. Gradually stir in cream; cook until sauce thickens, stirring. Add chicken; heat thoroughly, stirring. Add onion and lemon juice. Blend egg yolks, paprika, and butter. Add mixture to bubbling chicken and stir to blend; heat. Add pimento. Garnish with parsley; serve in cheese toasted bread cups. Yield: 8 servings.

Mrs. Edith A. Camp, Lostant H.S.
Lostant, Illinois

NOODLE-CHICKEN DISH

1 stewing chicken or 2 cans tuna
2 cans condensed cream of mushroom soup
2 cans Chinese noodles
1½ c. celery, diced
½ c. onion, chopped
½ c. salted almonds, cashews or peanuts

Stew chicken; remove meat from bones and cut in small pieces. Combine all ingredients except half can of noodles. Pour mixture into greased casserole and sprinkle noodles on top. Bake at 350°F. for 1 hour or until set. Yield: 6 servings.

Mrs. Kenneth Fitzhugh, Oak Crest Jr. H.S.
Cardiff-by-the Sea, California

PLANTATION CHICKEN

1 c. celery, diced
1 med. onion, chopped
2 T. green pepper, minced (opt.)
5 T. butter
6 T. flour
3 c. milk
1 can cream of mushroom soup
4 c. cooked chicken, diced
2 T. pimento, minced
¼ t. salt
1 c. soft bread crumbs
1 c. American cheese, grated

Cook celery in 1-inch of boiling water until tender or saute with onion and green pepper in butter until soft. Blend in flour to make a paste. Add milk and cook over hot water, stirring constantly, until smooth. Add mushroom soup, chicken, and pimento; heat. Add salt. Pour mixture into a greased 2-quart casserole. Mix crumbs and cheese; sprinkle over casserole. Bake at 375°F. for 30 minutes or until golden brown and bubbling hot. NOTE: If desired, buttered corn flakes may be substituted for bread crumbs and cheese. Casserole may be prepared and refrigerated overnight before baking. Yield: 10-12 servings.

This recipe submitted by the following teachers:
Karen DeWald, Waterloo H.S.
Waterloo, Wisconsin
Mrs. JoAnne Tuttle, Spencer H.S.
Spencer, Iowa
Mrs. Judy Elzenga, Tyler Public School
Tyler, Minnesota

RING AROUND THE CHICKEN

1½ c. sifted flour
3 t. baking powder
¾ t. salt
½ to ¾ t. poultry seasoning
½ c. plus 2 T. milk

Sift dry ingredients together; cut shortening in until fine. Add milk, mixing thoroughly. Spoon into an 8-inch ring mold. Bake 15 minutes at 450°F. Unmold on hot platter. Serve with hot creamed chicken in center. Yield: 6 servings.

Mrs. Mabel L. Shipe, East Forest Joint School
Marienville, Pennsylvania

SCALLOPED CHICKEN

CHICKEN:
1 5-lb. chicken
1 carrot
1 onion, sliced
2 t. salt
1 bay leaf
Pinch of basil

Cook chicken with remaining ingredients until tender. Bone meat and remove skin; cut into slices. Chop skin and cook giblets.

DRESSING:
1½ loaves of 2 day-old Italian bread
½ c. margarine
1 bunch of parsley, chopped
6 green onions, chopped
2 lge. stalks of celery with tops, chopped
1 t. poultry seasoning
Pepper to taste
1 t. salt
6 T. chicken broth

Crumble bread. Saute parsley, onions and celery in margarine for 5 minutes; mix into bread crumbs lightly with a fork. Grind cooked giblets and add to dressing; add seasonings and lightly mix in broth.

SAUCE:
1 c. chicken fat
1 c. sifted flour
2 c. milk
4 c. chicken broth
2 t. salt
4 eggs, beaten
Buttered bread crumbs

Melt fat; add flour and blend until smooth. Heat milk and broth; do not boil. Add to butter mixture, stirring constantly. Add salt and cook until thickened, stirring constantly. Add eggs; cook 3-4 minutes. Add ground skin. Place dressing in a large greased casserole; cover with half of sauce. Add sliced chicken; pour on remaining sauce. Top with buttered bread crumbs. Bake at 375°F. for 20 minutes.

Grace Setness, Stagg H.S.
Stockton, California

SCALLOPED CHICKEN

4 c. cooked chicken
1 c. celery, finely chopped
1½ c. soft bread crumbs
2 T. parsley, minced
2 t. salt
4 eggs, slightly beaten
2 c. chicken stock

Cut chicken in large pieces. Alternate layers of chicken, celery, crumbs and parsley in greased casserole. Add salt and eggs to chicken stock; mix thoroughly and pour over chicken. Bake in pan of hot water at 350°F. for 1 hour. Yield: 6-8 servings.

Alberta Hawkins, Lakeview H.S.
Battle Creek, Michigan

SCALLOPED CHICKEN

4 c. chicken broth
Poultry seasoning
Dried celery leaves
¼ t. sage
1 bay leaf
Pinch of ginger
1 c. milk
½ c. butter
¾ c. flour
2 c. bread cubes
5 c. cooked chicken, diced

Add seasonings to broth; bring to a boil and strain. Add half of broth to milk; heat. Blend butter and flour; add to milk mixture. Cook for 15 minutes or until creamy; stir occasionally. Pour remaining broth over bread cubes. Place a layer of chicken in a greased casserole; add layers of gravy and bread cubes. Repeat layers; bake at 350°F. for 30-40 minutes. Yield: 8-10 servings.

Mrs. R. E. Hieronymus, Clinton H.S.
Clinton, Illinois

SCALLOPED CHICKEN CASSEROLE

1 4 to 5-lb. stewing chicken, cut up
Salt and pepper
½ c. butter
½ c. flour
2½ c. chicken broth
1½ c. milk
2 eggs separated
½ t. salt
2 c. fresh bread crumbs
1 6-oz. can sl. mushrooms, drained

Simmer chicken until tender; refrigerate meat and broth for several hours. Arrange chicken in greased baking dish; sprinkle with salt and pepper. Melt butter; stir in flour, 2 cups broth and milk. Cook until thickened. Remove from heat; stir in beaten egg yolks and remaining ingredients except egg whites. Fold in beaten egg whites. Pour over chicken. Bake 1 hour at 325°F. Yield: 8-10 servings.

Dorothy Carson, Willamette H.S.
Eugene, Oregon

SEASONED CHICKEN SUPREME

Salt
Monosodium glutamate
1 pkg. chicken breasts or thighs
1 can cream of mushroom soup
1 can mushrooms, stems and pieces
Paprika
Parsley (garnish)

Season chicken; put into casserole. Pour soup over pieces; add mushrooms and sprinkle generously with paprika. Bake covered for 1 hour; remove cover last 5 minutes. Yield: 6 servings.

Mrs. Owen J. Main, Casey Community Unit C-1
Casey, Illinois

SCALLOPED CHICKEN WITH MUSHROOMS

1 c. milk
1 can cream of mushroom soup
2 c. dried bread crumbs
½ c. butter, melted
2 c. cooked chicken, diced
½ t. salt
Dash of pepper
¾ c. cheese, grated
2 T. pimentos, diced

Add milk to mushroom soup; heat and stir until well mixed. Combine bread crumbs and melted butter. Arrange alternate layers of buttered bread crumbs, chicken, salt, pepper, cheese and mushroom soup. Add remaining bread crumbs and pimento. Bake at 350°F. for 25-30 minutes. Yield: 5-6 servings.

Mrs. Betty L. Smith, Southwestern H.S.
Piasa, Illinois

SCALLOPED CHICKEN IN CASSEROLE

3 c. chicken broth
3 eggs, slightly beaten
½ loaf bread, cubed
1 c. cracker crumbs
1 t. salt
¾ c. celery, diced
2 T. onion, chopped
3 c. cooked chicken, chopped
1 can sliced mushrooms
Buttered crumbs

Pour broth and eggs over bread and crackers; mix thoroughly. Add salt, celery and onion. Fold in chicken and mushrooms. Pour in greased baking pan. Top with buttered crumbs. Bake slowly at 300°F. until a knife comes out clean when inserted. Yield: 12 servings.

Mrs. Harold R. Byers, Wolcott H.S.
Wolcott, Indiana

PRESSED TURKEY MOLD

4 c. cooked turkey, coarsely ground
1 bay leaf
3 c. turkey broth
1 chicken bouillon cube
¼ t. liquid onion or ½ t. onion salt
½ t. salt
Dash of pepper
½ t. celery salt
1 T. unflavored gelatin
½ c. cold water

Cook turkey and bay leaf in broth for 5 minutes; remove bay leaf. Add bouillon cube and seasonings. Dissolve gelatin in water; stir into mixture. Cook 5 minutes. Pour mixture into a lightly oiled mold; chill until set.

Mrs. Violet Wagle, Paramount H.S.
Paramount, California

FAVORITE TURKEY SCALLOP

1 c. celery, diced
½ c. water
½ c. butter, melted
2½ c. toasted bread cubes
Milk
¼ c. flour
¼ t. poultry seasoning
⅛ t. pepper
½ t. salt
1 c. turkey, diced

Cook celery in water until tender. Pour ¼ cup butter over toasted cubes. Combine celery liquid with enough milk to make 2 cups. Gradually stir flour and milk mixture into remaining butter; stir constantly until thickened. Add seasonings. Place half of bread cubes in a 1½-quart casserole; add turkey and celery. Top with remaining bread cubes. Pour sauce over bread; bake at 350°F. 20-30 minutes or until thoroughly heated. Garnish with parsley. Yield: 4 servings.

Mrs. Constance Ackerson, Grand Ledge H.S.
Grand Ledge, Michigan

HOLIDAY TURKEY CASSEROLE

6 T. butter
1½ c. celery, diagonally sliced
1 med. onion, minced
6 T. flour
1 t. salt
Dash of pepper
3 c. milk
1 can cream of mushroom soup
2 c. cooked ham, cubed
2 c. roast turkey, sliced or cubed
2 T. pimento, minced
¼ t. dried basil
3 T. cooking Sherry
½ c. grated Cheddar cheese
Parsley sprigs

Saute celery and onion in butter until tender. Stir in flour, salt and pepper; add milk. Cook, stirring constantly, until thickened. Add soup, ham, turkey, pimento, basil and Sherry; add additional seasonings if desired. Pour into a 2-quart casserole; top with cheese and refrigerate. Bake, uncovered, at 350°F. for 1 hour. Garnish with parsley. Yield: 8 servings.

Sister Josita Prokosch, OSB
Father Pierz Memorial H.S.
Pierz, Minnesota

"GOODBYE TURKEY" CASSEROLE

5 T. sifted flour
1 t. salt
¼ t. onion salt
¼ c. butter, melted
2½ c. milk or light cream
1⅓ c. instant rice
1½ c. turkey or chicken broth
½ c. American cheese, grated
1½ c. cooked asparagus
2 c. turkey, sliced
2 T. slivered almonds, toasted

Stir flour, half of salt and onion salt into melted butter; mix until smooth. Add milk; stir while cooking until thickened. Pour rice directly from box into 2-quart shallow baking dish. Combine broth with remaining salt and pour over rice. Sprinkle half of cheese over rice. Top with asparagus; add turkey. Pour on sauce. Sprinkle with remaining cheese. Bake at 375°F. for 20 minutes. Top with almonds. Yield: 6 servings.

Mrs. Evelyn Schmidt, Monte Vista H.S.
Spring Valley, California

PERFECT TURKEY CASSEROLE

1 can cream of chicken soup
½ c. milk
1 can or cup boned turkey or chicken
2 c. cooked noodles
2 T. diced pimento
1 T. chopped parsley or ½ t. parsley flakes
2 T. buttered bread crumbs

In 1½-quart casserole, blend soup and milk. Add turkey, cooked noodles, pimento and parsley. Sprinkle crumbs on top. Bake at 375°F. about 30 minutes. NOTE: Cream of mushroom, celery, or Cheddar cheese soup may be substituted for the chicken soup to lend variety. One 7-oz. can tuna may be substituted for the turkey. Yield: 4 servings.

Mrs. Rubye R. Hill, York Community H.S.
Thomson, Illinois

SCALLOPED TURKEY

4 c. cooked turkey, diced
6 c. dry bread cubes
¼ c. butter, melted
4¾ c. chicken broth
¾ t. sage
¾ t. salt
¼ t. pepper
2 T. minced onion
¼ c. chicken fat
½ c. flour

Place diced chicken in a 13x9x2-inch pan. Combine bread cubes, butter, sage, ¾ cup chicken broth, seasonings and onion; place on top of chicken. Blend chicken fat and flour; slowly stir in remaining broth. Cook, stirring constantly, until thickened and smooth. Pour over dressing; bake at 350°F. oven for 40 minutes. Yield: 10-12 servings.

Lorraine B. Klebeck, Artesia H.S.
Artesia, California

TURKETTI

1¼ c. noodles or spaghetti
1½-2 c. cooked turkey or chicken
¼ c. pimento, diced
¼ c. green pepper, diced
½ sm. onion, diced
1 can cream of mushroom soup
½ c. broth or water
½ t. salt
⅛ t. pepper
1¾ c. sharp Cheddar cheese, grated

Cook noodles; drain. Add turkey, pimento, pepper and onion to noodles. Place in a greased casserole. Pour soup and broth mixture over casserole; season. Add part of cheese to mixture; sprinkle cheese over top. Cook 45 minutes at 350°F. NOTE: All ingredients may be combined and put in casserole. Yield: 8-10 servings.

This recipe submitted by the following teachers:
Mrs. Fleta Bruce, Hamburg Community School
Hamburg, Iowa
Mrs. Jane Barber, Bodcaw School
Rosston, Arkansas

HOLIDAY TURKETTI

1¼ c. spaghetti
2 c. turkey
¼ c. pimentos, minced
¼ c. green peppers, chopped
1 can cream of mushroom soup
1 c. turkey broth
⅛ t. salt
⅛ t. pepper
½ sm. onion, diced
1½ c. cheese, grated

Cook spaghetti in boiling salted water until tender; drain and rinse in hot water. Combine spaghetti with remaining ingredients saving ½ cup grated cheese. Add more seasoning if needed. Sprinkle cheese over top. Bake covered at 350°F. for 1 hour. Yield: -8 servings.

Mrs. Karl Joehrendt, Paoli Community H.S.
Paoli, Indiana

TURKEY CHOW MEIN

1 can chow mein noodles
1 c. cooked turkey or chicken, chopped
1 can cream of celery soup
1 c. milk
1 c. almonds, sliced or chopped
1 c. celery, chopped
1 sm. onion, minced

Line casserole with half can of chow mein noodles. Combine remaining ingredients; add chicken mixture. Cover with remaining noodles. Bake at 400°F. for 30 minutes. Yield: 4-5 servings.

Lorna Mulder, Holmen H.S.
Holmen, Wisconsin

TURKEY LOAF

1 c. broken spaghetti
1 c. bread crumbs
1 c. cooked turkey or chicken, diced
1½ c. milk, scalded
2 T. butter, melted
¾ c. American cheese, grated
¼ c. green ppeper, diced
3 T. pimento, chopped
1 t. salt
⅛ t. pepper
¼ t. paprika
2 eggs, slightly beaten

Cook spaghetti in boiling salted water; drain. Combine spaghetti with remaining ingredients in a large mixing bowl. Turn into a greased loaf pan or a 1½-quart casserole. Set in a pan of hot water. Cook at 300°F. for 1 hour. Serve plain or with mushroom sauce. Yield: 6 servings.

Dorothy Davey, Jr. H.S
Iron Mountain, Michigan

TURKEY SOUFFLE

½ c. butter
¾ c. flour
1¼ qt. milk, heated slightly
2¼ t. salt
1½ c. bread crumbs
1 oz. powdered chicken stock
12 eggs, separated
1 lb. cooked turkey, boned

Melt butter; add flour and stir until smooth Add salt; cook until thickened. Combine crumbs, chicken stock and well beaten yolks; mix well. Fold in turkey. Fold in beaten egg whites. Set in a pan of water. Bake at 350°F. for 1 hour and 30 minutes. Yield: 12 servings.

Mrs. Joy R. Murray, Potterville H.S.
Potterville, Michigan

TURKEY STROGANOFF

¼ c. green pepper, chopped
2 T. onion, chopped
2 T. butter or margarine
1 can condensed cream of mushroomsoup
½ c. sour cream
2 c. cooked noodles
1 c. cooked turkey, diced
½ t. paprika

Cook green pepper and onion in butter until tender. In a 1-quart casserole, blend. soup and sour cream; stir in remaining ingredients. Bake at 350°F. for 30 minutes. Yield: 4 servings.

Sister Mary Ambrose, Sacred Heart H.S.
Salina, Kansas

TURKEY TETRAZZINI

4 T. butter or fat
1 med. onion, chopped
½ c. celery, chopped
2 c. turkey, cut in strips
6 oz. uncooked fine spaghetti
1 t. salt
¼ t. pepper
1 can cream of chicken soup
2 c. turkey broth
1 4-oz. can sliced mushrooms, drained
½ c. Parmesan cheese, grated
Paprika

Place electric skillet on 225°F. or place over low heat. Melt butter; add onion and celery and cook until clear. Arrange turkey in layer; add spaghetti. Mix salt, pepper, chicken soup and broth; pour over spaghetti. Place mushrooms over top. Sprinkle with Parmesan cheese and paprika. Cover; cook for 35 minutes. Yield: 4-6 servings.

Mrs. Robert F. Warren, Rochelle Township H.S.
Rochelle, Illinois

MARY'S TURKEY TETRAZZINI

¼ c. butter or margarine
¼ lb. fresh mushrooms, sliced
¼ c. flour
2 c. turkey broth or gravy
1 T. onion, grated
1 c. light cream or evaporated milk
Salt and pepper
2 c. cooked turkey, diced
1 8-oz. pkg. spaghetti
½ c. cheese, grated

Melt butter; add mushrooms and cook 5 minutes. Stir in flour; add broth, onion and cream. Heat to boiling, stirring constantly. Season to taste. In a buttered 2-quart casserole put alternate layers of spaghetti, chicken and mushroom sauce, finishing with thin layer of spaghetti. Sprinkle with cheese. Bake at 400°F. for 20 minutes. Yield: 5-6 servings.

Mrs. Mary McKenna, McLoughlin Jr. H.S.
Medford, Oregon

ZELMA'S TURKEY CASSEROLE

1 c. onion, finely chopped
1 c. green pepper, finely chopped
1 c. celery, cut into strips
1 stick butter
2-3 c. cooked chicken or turkey, diced
1 4-oz. can mushrooms
3 cans cream of chicken soup
1 lge. can chow mein noodles
1 3-oz. pkg. slivered almonds

Lightly saute' onion, green pepper and celery in butter. Combine diced chicken, mushrooms and soup; add sauted ingredients and blend well. Line casserole with noodles; pour mixture over noodles. Top with additional noodles and sliced almonds. Bake 40 minutes at 350°F. Yield: 6-8 servings.

Mrs. June Letcher, Mount Shasta H.S.
Mount Shasta, California

Combination Meat Casseroles

AFRICAN CHOP SUEY

1 lb. veal
1lb. pork
1 onion, chopped
½ c. uncooked rice
1 c. cream chicken soup
1c. mushroom soup
1 c. celery, diced
1 c. mushrooms
1 c. water

Brown veal and pork with onions. Add the remaining ingredients and place in a greased casserole. Bake 2 hours and 30 minutes at 350°F. Yield: 8 servings.

Marge Blanchard, Clarenceville Jr. H.S.
Livonia, Michigan

ALL-IN-ONE SUPPER CASSEROLE

1 can of cream of chicken soup
½ c. milk
1 c. cooked chicken, diced
1 c. julienne strips of cooked ham
¼ t. marjoram, crushed
¼ t. rosemary, crushed
1 c. peas, drained
1 8-oz. pkg. frozen French-fried potato puffs

Combine soup, milk, chicken, ham, marjoram, rosemary and peas. Pour into 1½-quart casserole. Top with potato puffs. Bake at 425°F. for 40-45 minutes. NOTE: One-half a 10-ounce package of frozen peas, thawed enough to break apart, may be substituted for canned peas. Yield: 4-5 servings.

Addie Moum, Washington Jr. H.S.
Fergus Falls, Minnesota

AMERICAN CHOP SUEY

2 lb. mixed ground beef and pork
2 medium onions, chopped
2 c. celery, diced
1 8-oz. pkg. uncooked macaroni
2 c. tomato soup
2 soup cans hot water
2 t. salt
Pepper
¼ c. soy sauce
1 c. American cheese, grated
Buttered bread crumbs

Brown meat well, but slowly to develop the flavor. Add onions and celery; cook until onions are golden brown. Combine all ingredients except cheese and bread crumbs. Put in buttered casserole; cover and cook at 350°F. for about 1 hour. Remove cover and stir in cheese. Top with crumbs and continue baking until brown. NOTE: This dish may be cooked in a heavy kettle on a surface burner turned very low. More liquid may be needed while cooking if a considerable sum boils away.

Janet Low, Adams H.S.
Adams, Minnesota

APPLESAUCE MEAT BALLS

¾ lb. ground beef
¼ lb. ground pork
½ c. thick unsweetened applesauce
½ c. soft bread crumbs
1 egg, well beaten
1¼ t. salt
⅛ t. pepper
¼ c. onion, minced
Flour
2 T. fat
¼ c. catsup
¼ c. water

Combine beef, pork, applesauce, bread crumbs, egg, salt, pepper and onion. Form into 12 balls. Roll lightly in flour and brown in hot fat. Place in 1½-quart casserole; cover with catsup, water and fat meat balls were browned in. Cover; bake at 350°F. for 1 hour. Yield: 4-6 servings.

Josephine Sherman, Clarinda Community H.S.
Clarinda, Iowa

BEV'S MEAT BALLS

1 lb. ground beef
½ lb. pork sausage
2 c. cracker crumbs
1 egg, beaten
1 c. milk
½ medium onion, finely chopped
2 t. salt
½ t. pepper
⅛ t. sage

Mix all ingredients; gently form into small 1½-inch meat balls. Brown balls in small amount of lard. Put in covered casserole. Bake 1 hour at 350°F. Yield: 6 servings.

Mrs. Doris A. Seal Bradley, Kelso H.S.
Kelso, Washington

BILL AND JULIE'S HOT DISH

1½ lb. pork steak, cubed
1½ lb. veal steak, cubed
2 c. celery, chopped
1 T. onion, browned
1 c. green pepper, cubed
1 1-lb. can cashew nuts, or less
¾ c. uncooked rice
1 can mushroom soup
1 c. cream of chicken soup
1 c. mushroom stems and pieces, undrained
2 soup cans water

Brown meat and mix with all remaining ingredients. Bake in a large casserole at 325°F. for 2 hours. Yield: 16 servings.

Mrs. Nora Estrem, Battle Lake H.S.
Battle Lake, Minnesota

BUFFET CHICKEN CASSEROLE

1 5-lb. chicken
Salt
Celery tops (opt.)
1 onion, sliced
1 bay leaf
1 4-oz. can mushrooms
1 c. ripe olives, sliced
1 12-oz. pkg. flat noodles
⅓ c. minced onions
⅓ c. green pepper
1 can mushroom soup
1½ c. processed cheese, grated
1 c. frozen peas
⅛ t. pepper
½ t. celery salt
1 c. cooked ham, diced

Half cover chicken with boiling water; add 1 tablespoon salt, celery tops, sliced onion and bay leaf. Simmer covered for 1½ hours; remove chicken from broth and cool. Cut off meat in large pieces. Skim fat from broth; reserve fat. To broth add mushroom and olive juices; measure and add water to make 6 cups. Bring to boil; add noodles. Cook until barely tender. In 2 tablespoons chicken fat saute minced onion, green pepper and mushrooms for 5 minutes. Add half of olives to chicken. To undrained noodles, add soup, cheese, peas, pepper, ½ teaspoon salt and the celery salt. In 3-qt. casserole arrange noodles and chicken in layers, ending with noodles. Top with ham and remaining olives. Bake at 325°F. 1¼ hours or until bubbling. NOTE: This casserole freezes well. Yield: 10-12 servings.

Mrs. Harriet Okino, Waiakea Intermediate School
Hilo, Hawaii

CAROLINA MEAT PIE

1 lb. shoulder veal, cut in 1-in. cubes
1 small slice ham, cubed
1 t. salt
½ t. pepper
1 T. butter
2 onions, chopped
2 carrots, diced
2 T. flour
1 qt. boiling water
½ c. tomato catsup
Pastry for 9-in. pie pan

Sprinkle meats with salt and pepper. Brown meats in butter. Add onion and carrot. Sprinkle with flour; add boiling water combined with catsup. Simmer 30 minutes until meat is tender. Add potatoes. Cook until tender and the stew is rich and thick. Line deep baking pan with pastry. Add stew. Pierce center. Bake at 375°F. until brown, 30-35 minutes.

Mrs. June Cessna McIsaac, Hampton Township Jr.-Sr. H.S.
Allison Park, Pennsylvania

CAPE COD CHICKEN-TUNA PIE

1 10-oz. pkg. pie crust mix
¼ t. poultry seasoning
2 T. yellow corn meal
1 can condensed cream of chicken soup
2 T. water
1-2 chicken bouillon cubes
1 13-oz. jar boned chicken, cut in large pieces
1 7-oz. can tuna, coarsely flaked

Make pie crust by package directions for 2-crust pie; add seasoning and corn meal. Stir in liquid. Fit half of pastry into 9-inch pie pan. Heat soup; add water and bouillon cubes. Add chicken and tuna; pour into pastry-lined pan. Cover with top crust and bake at 400°F. for about 40 minutes, or until golden brown. Yield: 6 servings.

Mrs. Robert Berkner, Public H.S.
Lamberton, Minnesota

CHICKEN-HAM AND BACON CASSEROLE

8 chicken breasts or thighs
8 strips bacon
8 slices ham or dried beef
1 can cream of mushroom soup
1 soup can sour cream

Wrap each piece of chicken in a strip of bacon. Place each on a slice of ham or wrap in a slice of dried beef. Arrange in a casserole. Cover with mushroom soup mixed with sour cream. Bake 2 hours at 350°F. NOTE: Chicken may be boned if desired. This casserole may be prepared ahead of time and baked just before serving. Yield: 4-6 servings.

Mrs. Marguerite Crews, Lewisburg Jr. H.S.
Lewisburg, Pennsylvania

CHICKEN AND HAM CASSEROLE

1 c. buttered bread crumbs
1 c. diced baked ham
1 can of mushroom soup
1 c. cooked diced chicken

Spread half of crumbs on bottom of casserole. Spread ham on crumbs. Mix mushroom soup and chicken. Spread on top of ham. Cover with remaining bread crumbs. Bake at 350°F. for 1 hour. Yield: 4-6 servings.

Mrs. Vivian Harwood, Harbor Beach Community School
Harbor Beach, Michigan

CHOP SUEY

1 lb. veal, diced
1 lb. pork, diced
2 sm. or 1 lge. bunch celery, diced
3-4 medium onions, chopped
2-3 T. soy sauce
½-¾ pkg. noodles
1 sm. can mushrooms
1 can tomato soup
2-3 T. molasses

(Continued on Next Page)

Brown meat; add celery, onions, soy sauce. Simmer for a few minutes. Add noodles, tomato soup, mushrooms and molasses. Place in casserole and bake at 350°F. 1 hour or longer. Yield: 10-12 servings.

Mrs. Evelyn Suomi, Washington H.S.
New London, Wisconsin

CHOP SUEY CASSEROLE

1 lb. veal, cubed
1 c. celery, chopped
1 c. onion, chopped
½ c. green pepper, chopped
6 T. Shoyu sauce
½ lb. pork, cubed
3 T. shortening
1 c. rice
1 c. mushroom soup
1 c. chicken and rice soup
Chow mein noodles

Combine all ingredients except noodles; place in a buttered casserole. Bake 1 hour and 45 minutes at 350°F. Add a little chicken soup or water if mixture seems dry. About 5 minutes before taking from oven, sprinkle chow mein noodles over top. Yield: 4-5 servings.

Mrs. Irma Ewing, Mackinaw City H.S.
Mackinaw City, Michigan

CHOW MEIN HOT DISH

1 lb. mixed pork and veal, cubed
1 onion, finely chopped
Butter, melted
1 t. vinegar
1 t. dry mustard
1 can mushrooms
1 lge. can chow mein noodles
1 c. half and half cream
1 can cream of chicken soup
1 c. cashew nuts
Salt and pepper to taste

Brown meat and onion in butter. Pour water over to cover; add vinegar and mustard and simmer 1 hour. Mix in remaining ingredients. Bake ½ hour, or until heated, at 350° F. Yield: 4-5 servings.

Corinne Anderson, Morgan Park H.S.
Duluth, Minnesota

CITY CHICKEN SUPREME

1 lb. pork, cubed
1 lb. veal, cubed
Salt to taste
Bread crumbs
Fat
1 can whole tomatoes
1 stalk celery
2 small onions
2 carrots
½ c. water

Place alternate meat cubes on small skewer. Salt to taste. Bread the meat on the skewer. Fry in fat until golden brown. Place in casserole; pour tomatoes over. Add celery, onions, carrots and water. Bake at 350°F. for 2 hours. If sauce is too thick, add more water. Yield: 4-6 servings.

Mrs. Linda Coombs, Centauri H.S.
LaJara, Colorado

COMBINATION VEAL AND PORK SOUFFLE

1 lb. veal steak
1 lb. pork steak
1 can chicken-rice soup
1 c. water
8 slices white bread, toasted, buttered and cubed
6 eggs, separated
Salt and pepper

Cube the meat; brown. Add soup and water and simmer for 2 hours. Add bread cubes. Add well beaten egg yolks. Add the stiffly beaten egg whites. Season to taste. Pour into a buttered casserole or flat dish and place in pan of water. Bake 35 minutes at 350°F. Serve with mushroom sauce. Yield: 8 servings.

Nora Peterson, Junior College & Roosevelt H.S.
Virginia, Minnesota

EMERGENCY CASSEROLE

2 T. green pepper, chopped
2 T. celery chopped
Butter
1 c. chicken a la king
1 can tuna, flaked
1 c. mushroom soup
¼ c. milk
1 lge. pkg. chow mein noodles

Saute green pepper and celery in small amount butter. Combine chicken, tuna, soup and milk. Place alternate layers of noodles, soup mixture, green pepper and celery in buttered casserole, beginning and ending with noodles. Bake at 350°F. for 30 minutes. Yield: 4-6 servings.

Florence B. Hicks, Bellmar Jr. H.S.
Belle Vernon, Pennsylvania

FAMILY SUCCESS CASSEROLE

1 lb. ground beef
1 lb. ground pork
1 medium onion, chopped
1 lge. green pepper, chopped
Bacon fat
1 1-lb. pkg. egg noodles, cooked
Salt and pepper to taste
1 sm. pkg. cream cheese or ¾ c. grated Parmesan cheese
3 T. Worcestershire sauce
2 10½-oz. cans tomato soup
2 cans water

Fry meats, onion and green pepper in bacon fat until lightly brown and tender. Add cooked noodles and other ingredients. Bake about 1 hour and 15 minutes at 325°F. Yield: 12 servings.

Mrs. A. W. Cummings, Kingsford H.S.
Kingsford, Michigan

FRICKADELLARS

1 lb. ground beef
½ lb. ground veal
3 med. potatoes, cooked and mashed
1 med. onion, finely chopped
2½ c. sifted flour
1 egg, beaten
4 T. milk
2½ t. salt
1 can cream of mushroom soup
¼ c. mushrooms, sliced

Combine all ingredients, except 1 cup flour, soup and mushrooms. Shape mixture into 32 meat balls. Roll in 1 cup flour. Fry in hot fat until browned. Place in greased casserole in layers with soup between each layer. Top with mushrooms. Bake at 325°F. for 1 hour. Yield: 6-8 servings.

Mrs. Jeanne Rumburg, Marlington H.S.
Alliance, Ohio

HAM AND CHICKEN WITH NOODLES

½ lb. egg noodles
1 T. salt
3 qts. boiling water
2 cans cream of chicken soup
1 c. ham, diced
1 c. chicken, diced
1 t. sweet basil
¼ t. poultry seasoning
¼ t. celery salt
Pepper

Cook noodles in boiling salted water until tender, about 7 minutes. Drain and rinse. Combine all ingredients. Place in greased baking dish. Heat in 350°F. oven for 20 to 25 minutes. Yield: 6 servings.

Alice Fetterman, Punxsutawney Area Jr. H.S.
Punxsutawney, Pennsylvania

HAM BALLS

1 lb. ham, ground
1 lb. veal or beef
1 lb. pork
2 c. crumbs
1 c. milk
2 eggs
1 c. brown sugar
½ c. water
½ c. vinegar
1 T. prepared mustard

Have butcher grind and mix the three kinds of meat together. Add crumbs, milk and eggs and form into balls. Place in a large covered casserole. Combine remaining ingredients and pour over the balls. Bake in a 350°F. oven for 2 hours. Yield: 8 servings.

Mrs. Marcia Miller, Petoskey H.S.
Petoskey, Michigan

HEARTY SUPPER CASSEROLE

¾ lb. veal cubed
¾ lb. pork, cubed
½ medium onion, diced
1 sm. green pepper, chopped
½ t. salt
1 8-oz pkg. medium noodles
1 can mushroom soup
1 c. whole-kernel corn
¼ lb. process cheese, diced
½ c. bread crumbs

Cover veal and pork with water; add onion, green pepper and salt. Simmer until meats are tender. Boil noodles in salted water until tender. Drain and place in a buttered casserole. Combine meat mixture and mushroom soup; add to casserole. Cover with layers of corn and cheese; top with crumbs. Bake at 350°F. for 25 minutes. Yield: 6 servings.

Mrs. Margery Hamm, Ashtabula H.S.
Ashtabula, Ohio

HOLIDAY TURKETTI

2-2½ c. spaghetti or elbow macaroni
3-4 c. turkey
1 c. ham, diced
2 cans undiluted cream of mushroom soup
1 c. turkey broth
1 sm. onion, grated
3 c. cheese, grated
½ c. pimento, minced
½ c. green pepper, diced
¼ t. celery salt
¼ t. pepper

Cook spaghetti until barely tender; rinse with hot water and drain. Combine all ingredients except 1 cup cheese. Pour mixture into a 3-quart casserole. Top with reserved cheese. Refrigerate overnight. Bake 1 hour at 350°F. Yield: 10 servings.

Dorothy Williams, Hot Springs County H.S.
Thermopolis, Wyoming

HOLLYWOOD CASSEROLE

2 lbs. pork, cubed
2 lbs. veal, cubed
2 stalks celery, diced
1 med. onion, diced
½ c. water
2 8-oz. pkg. noodles
1 can cream of chicken soup
2 cans cream-style corn
1 c. American cheese, grated
Salt and pepper

Simmer pork, veal, celery and onion in water until meat is tender. Strain, saving broth. Cook noodles. Place all ingredients in a large baking dish or roaster. Bake at 300°F. for 45 minutes. If more liquid is needed, use broth. Yield: 25 servings.

Sandra A. McNellis, Shakopee Public School
Shakopee, Minnesota

HUNTERS' STEW

½ lb. salt pork, cubed
½ lb. salami, sliced and cut into ½-in. strips
1 3 to 4-lb. broiler-fryer, cut up
4 whole carrots, pared
2 leeks or green onion, sliced 1-in. thick
4 sprigs parsley
2 whole cloves
1 bay leaf
¼ t. crushed thyme
1 T. salt
½ t. pepper
3 beef bouillon cubes
3 c. hot water
1 c. dry white wine
2 10-oz. pkg. frozen California Brussels sprouts
¼ c. flour
¾ c. water

Brown pork and salami in Dutch oven or large saucepan; remove from drippings and set aside. Brown chicken in hot drippings. Pour off drippings. Return pork and salami to saucepan. Stir in carrots, leeks, parsley, seasonings, bouillon cubes, hot water and wine. Simmer, covered, for 45 minutes or until tender. Add Brussels sprouts. Cover and cook 10-15 minutes longer, or until tender. Blend flour and ¾ cup water; stir into stew. Stir over medium heat until slightly thickened. Yield: 6-8 servings.

Photograph for this recipe on page 87

JOHN MARZETTI

1 lb. ground beef
½ lb. ground pork
1 lge. onion, chopped
1 stalk celery, chopped
1 green sweet pepper, chopped
1 pkg. extra fine noodles, cooked
2 cans tomato soup
1 t. salt
½ lb. cheese, grated

Partially brown pork and beef in a very large skillet. Add onion, celery and pepper; cook until clear. Add noodles, tomato soup and salt; mix well. Pour into large baking dish and cover with cheese. Bake at 350°F. for 45 minutes. Yield: 6 servings.

Mrs. Margaret Ewbank, North Central School
Ramsey, Indiana

JOHNNY MARZETTI

1 lge. onion, chopped
2 T. fat, melted
1 lb. ground beef
½ lb. ground pork
1 8-oz. pkg. wide noodles
1 can cream-style corn
1 can condensed tomato soup
1 can tomato sauce
Salt and pepper
Cheese, grated

Cook onion in fat until transparent. Add meat; cook, stirring until browned. Cook noodles in boiling salted water until tender. Drain and rinse; mix with corn, soup and tomato sauce. Combine with meat mixture and season to taste. Place in greased casserole; top with cheese. Bake at 350° F for 1 hour. Yield: 8-10 servings.

Dorothy Riggs, Senior H.S.
Anderson, Indiana

LASAGNA ITALIANA

1 clove garlic, minced
1 medium onion, sliced
3 T. olive oil
½ lb. Italian sweet sausage
1 lb. ground beef
1 8-oz. can tomato sauce
1 No. 2 can tomatoes
1½ t. salt
¼ t. pepper
½ t. oregano
1 8-oz. pkg. broad noodles, cooked
½ lb. sliced Mozzarella cheese
½ lb. Ricotta cheese
⅓-½ c. grated Parmesan cheese

Saute garlic, onion and crumbled beef in oil; add sausage and brown. Add tomato sauce, tomatoes and seasonings; simmer 20-30 minutes or until slightly thickened. Place a layer of half the noodles in a rectangular baking dish; cover with half of Mozzarella cheese. Sprinkle with half of Ricotta cheese; cover with half of meat sauce. Top with half of grated cheese. Repeat layer. Bake at 350°F. for 35 minutes. Cut in squares to serve. Yield: 10 servings.

Mrs. Susan Dartley, Saddle Brook H.S.
Saddle Brook, New Jersey

LUNCHEON DELIGHT

1½ lb. lean veal, cubed
1½ lb. lean pork, cubed
1 pkg. fine noodles, broken
1 lge. green pepper, chopped
2 cans chicken with rice or noodle soup
⅜ lb. American cheese, grated
1 sm. jar pimento, chopped
1 No. 2 can whole-kernel corn
Cracker crumbs

Boil meat until tender in just enough water to cover. Add noodles, green pepper and soup. Boil until noodles are tender. Add cheese and pimento. Place in buttered baking dish. Cover with corn and sprinkle top with cracker crumbs. Bake at 350°F. for 30 minutes to 1 hour. Yield: 18 servings.

Mrs. Lois Watts, Bismarck Sr. H.S.
Bismarck, North Dakota

MACARONI MULLIGAN

½ lb. sausage
1 T. bacon drippings
1 onion, finely chopped
1 lb. ground beef
1 8-oz. pkg. macaroni, cooked
1 No. 2½ can tomatoes
1 T. parsley, chopped
2 t. salt
⅛ t. pepper

Brown the pork in bacon drippings; add onion and brown. Add ground beef. Stir until mixture is a golden brown. Add cooked macaroni, tomatoes, parsley and seasonings. Cover and bring to steaming point; reduce heat to simmer and continue cooking for 45 minutes, or until mulligan is done. Yield: 6 servings.

Mrs. Ramona Norstedt, Hemet Union Sr. H.S.
Hemet, California

MEAT-NOODLE CASSEROLE

½ lb. veal, cubed
½ lb. pork, cubed
Butter
Salt and pepper to taste
½ c. water
1 pkg. wide noodles, cooked
1 can mushrooms
1 can cream of mushroom soup
1 soup can water

Brown veal and pork in butter. Add salt and pepper to taste. Add ½ cup water; simmer for 1 hour. Add noodles, mushrooms, soup and water. Put in casserole and cover. Bake at 350°F. for 35-40 minutes. Yield: 4-6 servings.

Mrs. Patricia Johansen, Rockford H.S.
Rockford, Minnesota

ONE-DISH MEAL

1½ lb. pork, cubed
1½ lb. beef, cubed
2 T. fat
1 can peas
1 can kidney beans
6 stalks celery, chopped
2 c. carrots, diced
2 c. potatoes, diced
2 onions, chopped
2 qts. tomatoes
Salt and pepper to taste
¼-½ c. flour

Brown meat in the fat. Combine with remaining ingredients except flour and place in greased baking dish. Bake in 350°F. oven for 1 hour and 30 minutes. Mix flour with a little water and thicken casserole before serving. Yield: 15 servings.

Mrs. Mary Esther Rowe, Swartz Creek H.S.
Swartz Creek, Michigan

MOCK CHOW MEIN

1 c. onion, chopped
1 c. celery, diced
1 lb. veal and pork, cubed
1 c. rice, uncooked
1 can mushroom soup
1 t. salt
2 soup cans water
2-3 T. soy sauce
Chow mein noodles (opt.)

Saute onions and celery; add meat and saute until brown. Put in baking dish; add remaining ingredients. Bake at 350°F. for 2 hours, stirring occasionally. If desired, sprinkle chow mein noodles on top near end of baking time. Yield: 6 servings.

Ardeth Doherty, LeSueur H.S.
LeSueur, Minnesota

MUSHROOM MEAT

3 lb. veal
1½ lb. pork
1 c. peas
1 c. mushrooms
1 qt. milk
¾ t. salt
⅛ t. pepper
½-¾ c. buttered bread crumbs

Cook veal and pork until tender in 2 cups of salted water. Cut meat in cubes and place in buttered casserole; add peas and mushrooms. Thicken the quart of milk and pour over the top of meat. Add salt and pepper. Cover with buttered bread crumbs. Bake at 350°F. for 30 minutes. Yield: 6-8 servings.

Marian Ebinger, North Muskegan H.S.
North Muskegan, Michigan

OYSTER AND HAM-NOODLE CASSEROLE

½ c. cooked ham, chopped
¼ c. onion, chopped
2 T. margarine
1 can frozen oyster stew
Dash of Tabasco sauce
2 T. flour
½ c. milk
1½ c. cooked noodles
Parmesan cheese

Brown ham and cook onion in margarine. Add oyster stew and Tabasco sauce. Heat until thawed. Make paste of flour and milk. Pour into soup mixture; simmer 3-4 minutes, stirring constantly until thick and smooth. Do not boil. Combine sauce and noodles in 1-quart casserole. Refrigerate. When ready to use, heat thoroughly in 370°F. oven for 25 minutes. Sprinkle cheese on top. Place under broiler until brown. Yield: 4 servings.

Mrs. Marguerite Craig, Fulton School
Swanton, Ohio

PINEAPPLE HAM

PINEAPPLE GLAZE:
1 8-oz. can pineapple slices
⅔ c. brown sugar, packed
2 t. vinegar
1 t. catsup
½ t. dry mustard

Drain syrup from pineapple slices. Combine syrup with brown sugar, vinegar, catsup and dry mustard. Mix well.

1 lb. raw ham, ground
½ lb. pork steak, ground
½ lb. bulk pork sausage
2 eggs, beaten
½ c. milk
1 8½-oz. can crushed pineapple
2 T. onion, grated
1½ t. dill weed
1½ t. dry mustard
1 c. fine dry bread crumbs

Have butcher grind meat. Mix meats with eggs, milk, undrained pineapple, onion, seasonings and crumbs. Blend thoroughly. Shape into 8-inch round loaf on lightly greased shallow baking pan or round casserole. Bake in 350°F. oven for 1 hour. Brush with pineapple glaze. Continue baking another 15 minutes, brushing on glaze every 5 minutes. Arrange pineapple slices on loaf 5 minutes before taking from oven, securing with toothpicks, if needed. Garnish with Maraschino cherries. Yield: 10-12 servings.

Mrs. Hazel M. Huckaby, Fowler H.S.
Fowler, Colorado

PORK AND VEAL CASSEROLE

1 lb. boneless pork, cubed
¼ lb. boneless veal, cubed
¼ c. butter
1 8-oz. pkg. medium noodles
½ c. green peppers, chopped
½ c. pimento, chopped
1 No. 2 can green peas and juice
1 can cream of chicken soup
½ lb. Cheddar cheese, grated
1 t. salt
½ c. slivered almonds

Brown meats in butter; add other ingredients except almonds and mix well. Pour into 3-quart casserole. Bake at 350°F. for 1 hour. Last 10 minutes of baking remove from oven and sprinkle with slivered almonds. Return to oven and finish baking. Yield: 6-8 servings.

Levern Gayman, Sr. H.S.
SanLuis Obispo, California

SAUERKRAUT AND BEEF SPECIAL

1 med. onion, chopped
¼ c. green pepper, chopped
2 T. olive or salad oil
1 lb. ground chuck
2 cans tomato sauce
1 can stem and pieces mushrooms
1 T. salt
1 T. chili powder
1 can sauerkraut
6 frankfurters

Cook onion and green pepper in oil until limp. Add ground chuck in broken pieces and cook until brown and crumbly. Add tomato sauce, mushrooms, salt and chili powder; simmer 15 minutes. Add sauerkraut and frankfurters in pieces; blend with sauce until heated throughout. Yield: 6 servings.

Mrs. Katherine L. Burdick, Arvin H.S.
Arvin, California

SAUSAGE MARZETTI

¾ lb. ground beef
¼ lb. sausage
1 lge. onion, chopped
½ pkg. noodles, cooked
1 pimento, cut in small pieces
1 med. green pepper, diced
1 can tomato soup
1 can mushroom soup
Salt and pepper to taste

Combine all ingredients and put in lightly buttered casserole. Bake at 375°F. for 45 minutes. Yield: 6 servings.

Mrs. Ethel Haun, Sr. H.S.
Junction City, Kansas

SAUSAGE TAMALE PIE

½ lb. link sausage, sliced
1½ lb. ground beef
1 lge. onion
1 T. chili powder
2 t. salt
¼ t. pepper
1 2-oz. can whole-kernel corn, drained or 1 pkg. frozen corn
2 8-oz. cans tomato sauce
1 c. milk
½ c. corn meal
1 sm. can pitted ripe olives
1 c. cheese, grated

Brown sausage; add beef and onion. Stir in seasonings, corn, tomato sauce and milk; simmer for 20 minutes. Add corn meal and olives. Pour in 2-quart casserole; top with cheese. Bake at 325°F. for 40 minutes.

Mrs. Elaine Thompson, Tolleson Union H.S.
Tolleson, Arizona.

SHIP WRECK

1 to 1½ lb. ground beef
½ lb. ground ham (opt.)
½ c. onions, sliced
4 raw medium potatoes, sliced
½ can kidney beans
¼ c. uncooked rice
½ c. celery, cut up
1 can tomato soup

Brown and season meats; place meat and other ingredients except soup in layers in a greased casserole until all are used. Top with soup and enough water to cover ingredients. Bake covered at 350°F. for 1 hour. Yield: 8 servings.

Mrs. Lois Simmonds, DeSoto H.S.
DeSoto, Wisconsin

SPAGHETTI ORIENTAL

½ lb. ground beef
½ lb. ground pork
Bacon drippings
1 sm. onion, minced
1 c. celery, diced
1½ c. Chinese vegetables, drained
½ c. liquid from Chinese vegetables
4 oz. spaghetti, cooked and drained
1 10½-oz. can tomato soup
¾ c. sharp cheese, shredded
1½ t. salt

Cook beef and pork in hot drippings until browned. Add onion, celery, and Chinese vegetables. Cook for 10 minutes. Mix with hot spaghetti. Add the tomato soup, liquid from vegetables, cheese and salt; simmer for 30 minutes, or place in buttered baking dish and bake for 45 minutes at 350°F. Yield: 6 servings.

Leola A. Davis, Enterprise H.S.
Enterprise, Oregon

SPECIAL CASSEROLE

2 lb. beef, cubed
1 lb. pork, cubed
Butter
5 c. hot water
1½ c. uncooked rice
1 can mushroom soup
2 c. celery, chopped
1 can mushroom stems
1 lge. onion, diced
½ c. soya sauce
Salt and pepper to taste

Brown the beef and pork cubes in butter. Add the hot water and simmer. Combine the rice, soup, celery, mushroom stems, onion and soya sauce. Bring to a boil. Combine the meat with the soup mixture. Season with salt and pepper. Place in an oiled baking dish. Bake at 350°F. until well done, about 1 hour. Yield: 8 servings.

Marval Klecker, Viroqua H.S.
Viroqua, Wisconsin

CURRIED SHRIMP CASSEROLE

1 4-oz. can sliced mushrooms
2 5-oz. cans shrimp
¼ c. butter
¼ c. onion, chopped
¼ c. celery, chopped
¼ c. flour
1 t. curry powder
½ t. salt
⅛ t. pepper
½ t. monosodium glutamate
2 c. chopped leftover ham or 1 can Spam, chopped
3 c. cooked rice or noodles

Drain liquid from the mushrooms and shrimp. Add enough milk to liquid to make 2 cups. Melt butter in saucepan over low heat. Add onions and celery, cooking until onion is transparent. Blend in flour and seasonings. Heat until mixture bubbles, stirring constantly. Remove from heat; gradually add liquid. Return to heat and bring mixture rapidly to boiling. Cook until sauce thickens. Blend mushrooms, shrimp and ham into sauce. Serve over rice or noodles, or combine and bake at 325°F. for 20-30 minutes. NOTE: This mixture may be frozen for later use. Yield: 6 servings.

Mrs. Delores Linaman Ginsbach, Sisseton H.S.
Sisseton, South Dakota

STUFFED CABBAGE CASSEROLE

12 lge. cabbage leaves
¾ lb. ground pork
¾ lb. ground beef
¾ c. cooked rice
1 t. salt
¼ t. pepper
¼ t. powdered garlic
1 can tomato soup
1 sm. can tomato sauce
4 strips uncooked bacon

Cook cabbage leaves in boiling water a few minutes to soften; drain and remove core end. Combine pork, beef, rice, salt, pepper, garlic and ¼-½ cup cold water. Mix thoroughly and divide into 12 sections. Place each section on cabbage leaf; roll, beginning at wide end. Place each roll into casserole dish. Mix soup, ¼ cup water and tomato sauce. Pour over cabbage rolls. Place strips of bacon on top. Bake at 350°F. for 45 minutes to 1 hour. Yield: 6 servings.

Mrs. Sadie M. Jacques, Newfound Memorial H.S.
Bristol, New Hampshire

TAMALE PIE

⅓ c. salad oil
1 t. butter
1 onion, minced
1 clove garlic, cut up
1¼ lb. ground beef
¼ lb. ground pork
2 t. chili powder
1 t. salt

(Continued on Next Page)

1 can cream-style corn
2 cans tomato soup
½ c. ripe olives
1 egg
1 c. milk
1 c. yellow corn meal

Heat oil and butter in a skillet. Add onion, garlic, meats and seasonings; cook until brown. Add corn, soup and olives; mix well. Add egg, milk and corn meal. Pour into casserole. Bake in 350°F. oven for 45 minutes to 1 hour. Yield: 8 servings.

Mrs. Ruth Radcliffe, Riverside Jr. H.S.
Billings, Montana

VEAL AND BEEF BAKED DISH

½ lb. ground beef
½ lb. ground veal
1 c. onions, diced
½ c. celery, diced
1 t. salt
Dash of pepper
1 can cream of mushroom soup
1 can cream of chicken soup
2 T. soy sauce
1 c. instant rice
1¾ c. water

Brown the beef, veal and onions. Add the celery and seasonings and finish browning. Add remaining ingredients and mix. Put in a 1½ or 2-quart casserole and bake at 375°F. for 1 hour. Yield: 6 servings.

Mrs. Esther Towers, Kiel H.S.
Kiel, Wisconsin

VEAL-PORK CASSEROLE

1 lb. veal, diced
½ lb. pork, diced
Fat
Onion, chopped
1 c. cream of chicken soup
1 can mushroom soup
½ c. uncooked rice
1 c. celery, diced
Buttered crumbs

Brown meats in a little fat; add onion and brown. Add remaining ingredients except crumbs; pour into casserole. Top with crumbs. Bake at 350°F. for 1 hour and 30 minutes.

Eleanore Moehrke, Hancock H.S.
Hancock, Michigan

WILD RICE JAMBALAYA

½ c. wild rice
½ c. regular rice
2 c. celery, chopped
1 8-oz. can mushrooms, drained
¼ c. onion, chopped
½ lb. pork, cubed
½ lb. veal, cubed
¼ c. fat
2-3 T. soy sauce
1 can mushroom soup
½-¾ c. water

Cook separately wild rice and regular rice. Saute celery, mushrooms, onion, pork and veal in hot fat. Combine with drained cooked rice. Add soy sauce, mushroom soup and water. Bake covered in 2-quart greased casserole at 350°F. for 2 hours. Yield: 6-8 servings.

Mrs. Marlyus Emerson, Bertha-Hewitt H.S.
Bertha, Minnesota

VEGETABLE-GIBLET CASSEROLE

1 pkg. bread cubes
1 c. milk
½ lb. ground beef
½ lb. sausage
1 med. onion, chopped
Giblets, chopped or ground
3 carrots, chopped or ground
1 apple, chopped or ground
1 potato, chopped or ground
1 c. celery, diced
2 eggs
1 t. marjoram or sage
1 t. salt
½ t. pepper

Mix bread cubes and milk in a large bowl. Brown meats, onion and giblets; add to bread mixture. Add remaining ingredients. Pour into a greased baking dish. Bake at 350°F. for 1 hour and 30 minutes. NOTE: The mixture may also be used for stuffing wild game. Yield: 10-12 servings.

Mrs. Marjorie Mattie, Boscobel H.S.
Boscobel, Wisconsin

VERY SPECIAL CASSEROLE

¼ c. margarine
¼ c. flour
¼ t. salt
½ t. dry mustard
⅛ t. pepper
1½ c. light cream
2 egg yolks, slightly beaten
1½ c. cooked ham cubes or strips
1 c. cooked chicken cubes or strips
¾ t. grated lemon peel
Frozen asparagus or broccoli

Melt margarine over low heat. Blend in mixture of flour, salt, mustard and pepper. Heat until mixture bubbles. Remove from heat and add the cream gradually, stirring constantly. Return to heat and bring rapidly to boiling, stirring constantly. Cook 1 to 2 minutes longer. Vigorously stir about 3 tablespoons of the mixture into the egg yolks. Immediately and thoroughly blend into mixture in the saucepan, stirring constantly. Cook 2 to 3 minutes over low heat. Mix in the ham, chicken and lemon peel. Frozen vegetables as desired may be added at this point and allowed to just cook through. NOTE: If desired, ¾ cup evaporated milk plus ¾ cup reconstituted powdered milk may be substituted for cream. Yield: 6-7 servings.

Katherine DeKay, Alameda Jr. H.S.
Pocatello, Idaho

Variety Meat Casseroles

ASPARAGUS-CORNED BEEF CASSEROLE

2 c. creamettes
1 can mushroom soup
3 T. butter
3 T. flour
3 c. milk
½ lb. Velveeta cheese, chopped
1 can corned beef, finely chopped
2 No. 2 cans asparagus, drained
1 can pimento
Mushrooms (opt.)
Potato chips, crushed

Cook creamettes in unsalted boiling water; drain. Add mushroom soup; heat until blended. Make white sauce with butter, flour and milk. Add cheese; let melt. Arrange layers of creamettes, corned beef, asparagus, pimento and mushrooms in a greased casserole. Pour sauce over casserole; top with potato chips. Bake at 350°F. for 40-50 minutes. Yield: 15 servings.

Mrs. Vera Smith, Flandreau Indian School
Flandreau, South Dakota

BAKED EGGS ON CORNED BEEF HASH

1 can corned beef hash
4 eggs
Salt and pepper

Heat oven to 400°F. Spread warmed, moist corned beef hash in well greased shallow baking dish. With bottom of custard cup make 4 deep hollows in hash. Slip eggs in hollows. Bake 15-20 minutes until eggs are set. Yield: 4 servings.

Mrs. Lillian Whaley, New Monroe Community
School
Monroe, Iowa

CORNED BEEF CASSEROLE

2 c. cooked macaroni or noodles
1 can corned beef, minced
1 can cream of chicken soup
½ c. milk
2 T. onion, grated
¼ lb. pimento cheese, cubed
¼ c. buttered crumbs or potato chips

Combine all ingredients except crumbs; pour into a buttered casserole. Top with crumbs. Bake at 325°F. for 45-60 minutes or until crumbs are brown. Yield: 4-6 servings.

Mrs. Marilyn Orban, Atherton H.S.
Flint, Michigan

CORNED BEEF SUPREME

2 c. uncooked macaroni
1 c. corned beef, cubed
¼ lb. sharp American cheese, cubed
1 can mushroom soup
¼ c. onion, chopped

Cook macaroni only partly done. Mix all ingredients. Place in a casserole and bake 1 hour at 350 F. Yield: 8 servings.

Lorna Carswell, River Valley H.S.
Spring Green, Wisconsin

BEEF-NOODLE HOT DISH

1 8-oz. pkg. wide noodles
1 15-oz. can corned beef hash
¼ lb. processed cheese, cubed
½ cup onion, chopped
1 can cream of chicken soup
½ c. milk
¾ c. potato chips, crushed

Cook noodles in salt water. Alternate noodles and corned beef hash in layers in a casserole. Add cheese cubes and onion. Pour soup and milk over the top of mixture. Sprinkle the potato chips over the top. Bake at 350°F. for 45 minutes, or until cheese is melted. Yield: 6-8 servings.

Mrs. Florence Wiest, Wishek Public School
Wishek, North Dakota

CORNED BEEF-NOODLE CASSEROLE

¼ c. onion, chopped
¼ c. green pepper, chopped
Butter
1 8-oz. pkg. noodles, cooked
1 12-oz. can corned beef, cut in pieces
¼ lb. sharp cheese, diced
1 can mushroom soup
Stuffed olives (opt.)
Buttered crumbs

Saute onion and green pepper in butter. Combine all ingredients except crumbs. Top with crumbs. Bake at 375°F. for 30 minutes: Yield 6-8 servings.

Margaret Zachariah, Director of Home Economics
Lansing Public Schools
Lansing, Michigan

DELUXE CORNED BEEF CASSEROLE

1½ c. broken noodles
1 can cream of mushroom or chicken soup
½ c. evaporated milk
12-ounce can corned beef, cut up
1 c. process American cheese, grated
¼ to ½ c. onion, finely cut
½ c. potato chips, crumbled

Cook noodles in unsalted water; drain. Combine soup, evaporated milk, corned beef, cheese, onion and noodles in a 3-quart bowl. Pour into a greased 1½-quart casserole. Top with potato chips. Bake at 425°F. for 15 minutes or until bubbly hot. NOTE: If desired, 1 tablespoon dehydrated onion may be used. Yield: 4 servings.

This recipe submitted by the following teachers:
Doreen Nielsen, Murray H.S.
Murray, Utah
Mrs. Virginia Christensen, North Sevier H.S.
Salina, Utah
Gloria K. David, Gay Jr. H.S.
Harlingen, Texas

EASY CORNED BEEF CASSEROLE

1 8-oz. pkg. noodles
1 can corned beef
1 can cream of mushroom soup
½ c. American cheese, grated
1 c. cooked peas (opt.)
¼ c. buttered bread crumbs

Cook the noodles in salted water as directed on package; drain. Add the remaining ingredients except crumbs; mix well. Place in greased baking dish; top with crumbs. Bake in 350°F. oven for 30 minutes or until brown. Yield: 12 servings.

Mary B. McGlone, St. Rose Academy
Vincennes, Indiana

FAVORITE CORNED BEEF DINNER

1 pkg. macaroni, spaghetti or noodles
1 12-oz. can corned beef, chopped
¼ lb. American cheese, cubed
1 10½ or 11-oz. can condensed cream of chicken
    or mushroom soup
1 c. milk
⅛ t. pepper (opt.)
¼ to ½ c. onion, chopped
½ to 1 c. buttered crumbs, chips or corn flakes
Olives (garnish)

Cook macaroni in boiling salted water; drain and rinse. Combine all remaining ingredients except macaroni, crumbs and olives. Alternate layers of macaroni and beef mixture in greased 2-quart casserole. Top with crumbs and olives, if desired. Bake at 350-375°F. for 30-60 minutes. Garnish with parsley and olive slices. NOTE: If desired, macaroni may be mixed with beef mixture rather than layered. Yield: 6 servings.

This recipe submitted by the following teachers:
Lola Crown, Celina Sr. H.S.
Celina, Ohio
Maud Chase, Tinora H.S.
Defiance, Ohio
Mrs. Paula E. Compton, Custer County H.S.
Miles City, Montana
Mrs. Bruce Miller, Glencoe H.S.
Glencoe, Minnesota
Mrs. Carol Schutts, Marshfield Sr. H.S.
Marshfield, Wisconsin
Mrs. Muriel F. Richards, Battle Creek H.S.
Battle Creek, Nebraska
Lorene L. Arent, Wausa H.S.
Wausa, Nebraska
LaVonne Dupraz, Tracy H.S.
Tracy, Minnesota
Marylou Rideout, Wasilla Area H.S.
Wasilla, Alaska
Mrs. Linda Knutson, Central Cass H.S.
Casselton, North Dakota
Mrs. Marie Strand, Jr. H.S.
Stillwater, Minnesota
Mrs. Cecile Poling, North Shore Jr. H.S.
Houston, Texas
Princess L. Egbert, Grants Pass Sr. H.S.
Grants Pass, Oregon

HASH CASSEROLE

1-1½ c. American cheese, grated
2 cans corned beef hash
2 cans condensed cream of mushroom soup

Reserve enough grated cheese for top. Combine other ingredients; mix lightly. Pour into lightly greased casserole. Sprinkle grated cheese over top. Bake in preheated 350°F. oven until thoroughly heated and cheese is bubbly, 30-40 minutes. Yield: 6-8 servings.

Helen Green, St. Charles H.S.
St. Charles, Illinois

HASH AND LIMA BEAN CASSEROLE

1 c. tomato catsup
2 cans corned beef hash
2 pkg. or cans lima beans, cooked and drained
8 oz. American cheese, grated
6 T. milk
¼ t. prepared mustard

Mix catsup and beef hash. Pat mixture in bottom of 13 x 9 inch greased pan. Over top of hash spread the lima beans. Top lima beans with cheese mixed with milk and mustard. Bake at 350°F. for 35 to 40 minutes. Yield: 6 servings.

Kay Morgan, Vanjalia H.S.
Vanjalia, Illinois

HOT CORNED BEEF CASSEROLE

1 c. or more creamettes, cooked
1 or 2 cans asparagus, drained
1 can corned beef
2 c. white sauce
1 can mushroom soup
¼ lb. or more cheese

In a greased pan arrange creamettes, asparagus and corned beef in layers. Combine white sauce, mushroom soup and cheese; pour over layers. Bake 40-50 minutes at 350°F. Yield: 10 servings.

Mrs. Ruth Kentfield, J. M. Wright Technical
School
Stamford, Connecticut

LUNCHEON CORNED BEEF

1 8-oz. pkg. noodles
¼ lb. Velveeta cheese
1 can cream of chicken soup
1 lge. can evaporated milk
1 sm. can pimento
1 sm. onion, chopped
1 can corned beef
2 c. buttered corn flakes

Cook noodles and drain. Melt cheese in soup and milk. Combine all ingredients except corn flakes. Pour in casserole; top with corn flakes. Bake at 350°F. for 45 minutes. Yield: 12 servings.

Mrs. Ardelle Grove, Canton H.S.
Canton, South Dakota

MACARONI CASSEROLE WITH CORNED BEEF

1 8-oz. box macaroni
1 can cream of chicken soup
Milk
1 can corned beef, broken up
½ lb. cheese, diced
Pepper to taste

Cook macaroni according to directions on box. Rinse in cold water and drain. Place in casserole. Add cream of chicken soup; rinse soup can with milk and add. Add corned beef and cheese. Heat for 30 minutes at 350°F. Yield: 4-6 servings.

Barbara Hughes, Wilmot H.S.
Wilmot, South Dakota

MUSHROOM-CORNED BEEF DISH

1 pkg. shell macaroni
1 can corned beef
1 can mushroom soup
1 can cream of chicken or celery soup
Dash of Worcestershire sauce
3 T. onion, minced
¼ c. butter
1 c. sharp cheese, grated
1 8-oz. can mushrooms
Buttered bread crumbs

Boil macaroni for 6-8 minutes; blanch quickly. Place in casserole with corned beef which has been broken into small pieces. Heat soups, Worcestershire sauce, onion and butter; add grated cheese and mushrooms with liquid. Pour over macaroni and corned beef. Cover with bread crumbs. Bake for 30 minutes at 350°F. NOTE: Lobster or tuna may be substituted for corned beef. Add milk if casserole becomes too dry. Yield: 8-10 servings.

Mrs. Ardyce Gilbert, Scotland H.S.
Scotland, South Dakota

POTATO-CORNED BEEF CASSEROLE

2 c. potatoes, cooked and sliced
1 12-oz. can corned beef
Onion, sliced
3 hard-cooked eggs
2 T. butter
2 T. flour
2 c. milk
½ t. salt
Pepper
1 c. cheese, grated
⅓ c. buttered crumbs

In greased casserole place layers of potatoes, slices of corned beef and onions. Cut eggs in half crosswise and push into mixture, cut side up. Make white sauce of butter, flour, milk and seasoning. Add cheese to sauce; heat until melted and pour over all. Add crumbs to top. Bake at 350°F. for 30 minutes. Yield: 5-6 servings.

Mrs. D. L. Keller, Grant Jr. H.S.
East Detroit, Michigan

PEAS AND CORNED BEEF

1 12-oz. pkg. frozen peas
1 12-oz. can corned beef
2 c. medium white sauce
2 T. pimentos, chopped
2 c. hot mashed potatoes

Cook frozen peas for 5 minutes. Break corned beef into bite-size pieces. Place half of beef into greased casserole. Spread peas over beef. Place rest of beef over layer of peas. Pour white sauce and pimentos over beef and peas. Top with mashed potatoes. Brown at 375°F. for 15-20 minutes. Yield: 6 servings.

Mrs. J. B. Morris, Gooding H.S.
Gooding, Idaho

PIMENTO-CORNED BEEF HOT DISH

2 8-oz. pkgs. noodles
1 can cream of mushroom soup
1 can cream of celery soup
2 lge. cans evaporated milk
2 12-oz. cans corned beef, cubed
½ lb. processed American cheese, cubed
1 T. onion, minced
1 sm. jar pimentos, minced
Potato chips, crushed

Combine all ingredients except potato chips. Pour into casserole. Top with crushed potato chips. Bake at 350°F. for 30 minutes or until golden brown. Yield: 20 servings.

Mrs. Betty Rogers, Wakefield H.S.
Wakefield, Nebraska

QUICK CORNED BEEF DINNER

1 can condensed cream of chicken soup
½ c. evaporated milk
1 12-oz. can corned beef, cut up
1 c. American process cheese, grated
⅓ c. onion, finely chopped
1½ c. unsalted, cooked noodles
½ c. potato chips, crumbled

Combine soup, milk, corned beef, cheese, onion and noodles in a 1½-quart casserole. Top with potato chips. Bake at 425°F. for 15 minutes or until bubbly hot. Yield: 4 servings.

Mrs. Margery Bartlett, Milwaukee Jr. H.S.
Saginaw, Michigan

YANKEE RED FLANNEL HASH

1½ c. canned or cooked corned beef, finely chopped
3 c. cooked potatoes, finely chopped
1½ c. cooked or canned beets, finely chopped
⅓ c. onions, finely chopped
⅓ c. milk
1 t. salt
Few drops of Tabasco sauce
3-4 T. fat

Toss together all ingredients lightly except fat; season to taste. Melt fat in skillet; spread hash evenly over bottom of skillet. Cook over medium heat until under side is brown and crusty. Top with onion rings. Bake at 275°F. for 20 minutes. Serve warm from oven. Yield: 4 servings.

June Kreutzkampf, Maquoketa Sr. H.S.
Maquoketa, Iowa

CAULIFLOWER AND BEEF CASSEROLE

1 c. bread crumbs
2 T. butter, melted
¼ c. Italian cheese, grated
1 4-oz. pkg. macaroni
1 can mushroom soup
¾ c. milk
1½ c. cooked cauliflower
2½ oz. dried beef
1-3 T. green peppers, chopped
Dash of pepper

Mix bread crumbs with melted butter; add cheese. Cook macaroni until tender; drain. Mix mushroom soup with milk; add cooked macaroni. Add cooked cauliflower, dried beef, green pepper and black pepper. Put mixture into a buttered casserole. Place crumb mixture on top. Bake at 350°F. for 25-30 minutes. Yield: 4-6 servings.

Vera Vilmann, Ashland H.S.
Ashland, Wisconsin

CHIPPED BEEF AU GRATIN

½ pkg. egg noodles
2 T. butter
3 T. flour
1½ c. milk
¼ lb. Cheddar cheese, shredded
½ c. sliced mushrooms
4-5 oz. chipped beef
2 T. pimento, minced
¼ t. pepper
⅓ c. buttered bread crumbs

Cook noodles in salted water; drain. Make sauce of butter, flour, milk and cheese. Saute mushrooms in butter; add to sauce. Saute chipped beef in same butter until edges curl. Combine sauce, noodles and beef; add pimentos and pepper. Place in casserole; top with crumbs. Bake at 375°F. for 30 minutes. Yield: 4-6 servings.

Joyce J. Terrass, Coordinator, Homemaking and
Family Life Education
Wichita, Kansas

COMPANY BEEF-NOODLE CASSEROLE

2 lbs. noodles
2 cans mushroom soup
½ c. catsup
½ lb. dried beef, sliced fresh
1 T. onion juice
1½ cans evaporated milk
½ lb. mushrooms
Butter

Boil noodles in salt water and drain. Combine mushroom soup, catsup, cut dried beef, onion juice, milk and noodles. Blend well and place in a casserole dish; bake in 350°F. oven for 1 hour. Fry mushroom caps in butter until brown on top; place on top of baked casserole. Yield: 15-17 servings.

Geneura Lanning, Wapakoneta H.S.
Wapakoneta, Ohio

CORN AND BEEF SUPREME

¼ c. onion, chopped
¼ c. green pepper, chopped
1 T. fat
¼-½ lb. dried beef, cut up
1 c. sliced mushrooms (opt.)
2 c. med. white sauce
2 egg yolks, beaten
1 t. prepared mustard
Salt and pepper to taste
1 No. 2 can whole kernel corn, drained
½ c. sharp cheese, grated (opt.)
¼ t. paprika (opt.)

Saute onion and green pepper in fat. Add beef and mushrooms; fry until beef curls at edges. Combine white sauce, egg yolks and mustard; add to beef mixture. Add salt, pepper and corn. Pour into a greased 1½-quart baking dish. Sprinkle with cheese and paprika, if desired. Bake at 350° F. for 30 minutes. NOTE: If desired, ½ teaspoon dry mustard may be substituted for prepared mustard. For variety cream-style corn may be used; reduce white sauce to 1-1½ cups. Yield: 8 servings.

This recipe submitted by the following teachers:
Sister M. Del Rey, PBVM, St. Mary H.S.
Dell Rapids, South Dakota
Caroline N. Daniels, Freedom Area H.S.
Freedom, Pennsylvania

DELUXE DRIED BEEF CASSEROLE

1 can mushroom soup
1 c. milk
1 c. grated Cheddar cheese
3 T. minced onion
1 c. uncooked elbow macaroni
1 4- or 5-oz. pkg. dried beef, cut up
2 hard-cooked eggs, sliced (opt.)
1 T. chopped pimento (opt.)

Combine soup and milk, stirring until creamy. Add other ingredients, folding in eggs last. Cover and refrigerate for 3-4 hours or overnight. Bake uncovered for 1 hour at 350°F. Yield: 4 servings.

This recipe submitted by the following teachers:
Mrs. Helen B. Brewer, Walla Walla H.S.
Walla Walla, Washington
Loretta Sawin, Dickson County Community H.S.
Chapman, Kansas
Madge Landis Capel, Woden H.S.
Woden, Texas
Mrs. Virginia Johnson, Ind. #837
Madelia, Minnesota
Mrs. Jack Copeland
Tellico Plains, Tennessee
Mrs. Esta Newman, Bluffs H.S.
Bluffs, Illinois
Amy H. Redfearn, Cheraw H.S.
Cheraw, South Carolina

DO-AHEAD DRIED BEEF CASSEROLE

3 T. onion, finely chopped
3 T. green pepper, finely chopped
2 T. butter
1 can cream of mushroom soup
1 c. milk
1 c. cheese, shredded
1 c. uncooked elbow macaroni
¼ lb. dried beef, cut in bite-size pieces
2 hard-cooked eggs, sliced

Saute onion and green pepper in butter until straw-colored. Stir soup until creamy. Add milk, cheese, onion, green pepper, uncooked macaroni and dried beef. Fold in eggs. Pour into buttered 1½-quart baking dish. Refrigerate 3 to 4 hours or overnight. Bake uncovered at 350°F. for 1 hour. NOTE: Pour boiling water over dried beef and drain well before using to remove salt. Yield: 4-6 servings.

Bette D. Jenness, Linesville Conneaut Summit
Joint Schools
Linesville, Pennsylvania

DRIED BEEF CASSEROLE

¼ lb. sliced dried beef
1 can cream of chicken soup
½ c. milk
½ c. celery, chopped
1 pkg. frozen green peas, cooked and drained
¼ T. garlic salt
¼ t. ground black pepper
1 5-oz. can chow mein noodles
Butter

Cut dried beef into bite size pieces. Cover with boiling water; drain. Dilute soup with milk; add to beef. Mix in celery, peas, garlic salt and pepper. Arrange in alternate layers with chow mein noodles in 1½-quart buttered casserole, beginning and ending with noodles. Dot the top with butter. Bake at 375°F. for 30 minutes. Garnish with chopped celery and sliced ripe olives, if desired. Yield: 4 servings.

Mrs. Carolyn Arthur, Mayville H.S.
Mayville, Wisconsin

DRIED BEEF SUPREME

¼ lb. dried beef, cut in bite size pieces
2 T. margarine or butter
¾ c. milk
1 c. Cheddar cheese, grated
3 hard-cooked eggs, sliced

Fry beef in margarine until slightly browned. Add the mushroom soup, milk and cheese, stirring constantly. When cheese is melted, simmer mixture for 15 minutes. Add eggs and serve in a toast cup, on toast, over chow mein noodles, or over rice. Yield: 4-6 servings.

Mrs. Joanne Beck, St. Anne H.S.
St. Anne, Illinois

EGG-CHIPPED BEEF CASSEROLE

2 cans cream of mushroom soup
1 pt. milk
1 pkg. creamettes, cooked
¼ lb. chipped beef
¼ lb. mild Cheddar cheese, cubed
1 sm. onion, minced
4 hard-cooked eggs, chopped
½ c. buttered cracker crumbs

Mix soup and milk; beat until well blended. Add the rest of the ingredients except crumbs; pour into a buttered baking dish. Bake at 350°F. for 1 hour. Sprinkle the crumbs on top and bake for 15-20 minutes longer. Yield: 10 servings.

Mrs. Betty Eggland, Stanhope Jr. H.S.
Stanhope, Iowa

LAYERED DRIED BEEF CASSEROLE

1 4-oz. pkg. dried beef
½ c. celery, chopped
1 8½-oz. can peas
1 10½-oz. can creamed chicken soup
1 10½-oz. can mushroom soup
⅛ t. pepper
1 5-oz. can chow mein noodles
A few sprigs parsley (opt.)

Cut the dried beef in chips; pour boiling water over and drain off at once. Mix all ingredients except the noodles; arrange mixture in a casserole in layers with the noodles, ending with noodles on top. Bake 30 minutes at 375°F. Yield: 10 servings.

Mrs. Avis Thompson, Tigerton H.S.
Tigerton, Wisconsin

SCHOOL-DAY CASSEROLE

1 6-oz. pkg. macaroni
¼ to ½ lb. dried beef
¼ c. green pepper, chopped
4 T. butter
4 T. flour
2½ c. milk
1 c. sharp American cheese, grated

Cook the macaroni in boiling, salted water 7 minutes; drain. Cook meat in butter until edges curl. Add green pepper and saute. Blend in flour; add milk. Cook until thick, stirring constantly. Add ¾ cup cheese. Combine sauce and macaroni; pour into greased 1½-quart casserole. Top with remaining cheese. Bake at 350°F. for 30 to 40 minutes. Yield: 6 servings.

NOTE: For less sauce use 3 tablespoons butter and flour with 1½ cup milk. Yield: 6 servings.

This recipe submitted by the following teachers:
Mrs. Doris Kirk, St. Croix Falls H.S.
St. Croix Falls, Wisconsin
Emma E. Bunyard, Jenks Public School
Jenks, Oklahoma
Mrs. Gladys Evans, Central H.S.
Camp Point, Illinois

NOODLES AND BEEF BAKE

¼ lb. dried beef, cut into bite size pieces
2 T. butter
3 c. med. white sauce
1 c. American cheese, grated
1 8-oz. pkg. noodles, cooked and drained
½ c. buttered bread crumbs

Lightly brown dried beef in butter. Prepare white sauce and blend in cheese. Stir in dried beef. Add noodles and pour into a 2-quart baking dish. Top with buttered bread crumbs and bake for 30 minutes at 350°F. Yield: 6-8 servings.

Lois Gruneberg, Loyalsock Township Jr-Sr. H.S.
Williamsport, Pennsylvania

PEAS AND BEEF CASSEROLE

¼ lb. dried beef
½ c. celery, chopped
8½ oz. canned or frozen peas
1 c. condensed cream of chicken soup
1 c. condensed cream of mushroom soup
¼ t. pepper
1 c. pimento
1 t. onion, grated
1 5-oz. can Chinese noodles
Parsley (garnish)
Ripe olives (garnish)

Cut dried beef into pieces. Combine with all other ingredients except noodles. Arrange alternate layers of noodles and beef mixture in buttered 1½-quart casserole, ending with noodles. Bake at 375°F. for 30 minutes. Garnish with parsley and ripe olives. Yield: 6-8 servings.

Mrs. Bernice Peterson,
Anthon-Oto Community School
Anthon, Iowa

QUICK DRIED BEEF CASSEROLE

¼ c. onion, chopped
¼ c. celery, chopped
¼ lb. dried beef, shredded
¼ c. fat
4 T. flour
2 c. milk
2 c. cooked macaroni
½ t. salt
¼ t. pepper
1 T. parsley, minced
⅓ c. American cheese, grated

Cook onion, celery, and dried beef in hot fat until onion is golden brown. Stir in flour; add milk gradually and stir until slightly thickened. Add macaroni, seasonings and parsley. Pour into greased casserole dish. Sprinkle with cheese. Bake at 350-400°F. for 15-20 minutes. Yield: 4-5 servings.

This recipe submitted by the following teachers:
Mrs. Phyllis Garnick, Ord Public Schools
Ord, Nebraska
Mrs. Rose Kivett, Clarks Public
Clarks, Nebraska

VEGETABLE-BEEF CASSEROLE

6 c. water
1 T. salt
¾ c. uncooked rice
½ c. onions, chopped
½ c. green peppers, chopped
2 T. fat
5 oz. dried beef, cut up
1 sm. can whole-kernel corn
4 oz. mushrooms, sliced
1 can cream of vegetable soup
Seasoning to taste
½ c. milk
½ c. American cheese, grated
3 T. Italian cheese, grated

Heat 6 cups of water until it comes to a boil. Add salt and rice and cook until tender. Saute onions and green peppers in fat until tender. Add beef and continue to saute until edges turn up. Remove from heat and add corn, mushrooms, soup and milk. Blend all ingredients except cheeses until evenly spread throughout. Pour into greased 1½-quart baking dish. Blend cheeses and sprinkle over top. Bake at 350°F. for 30 minutes. Yield: 6-8 servings.

Mrs. Ruth F. Harris, Whitefield H.S.
Whitefield, New Hampshire

BARBECUED FRANKFURTERS

½ medium onion, chopped
1 T. butter
½ t. black pepper
1 t. prepared mustard
1 t. paprika
½ c. catsup
¼ c. vinegar
½ c. water
4 t. Worcestershire sauce
12 frankfurters

Saute onion in butter until clear. Add dry seasonings, catsup, vinegar, water and Worcestershire sauce. Bring to a boil. Cut 3-inch slits in each frankfurter. Place in a flat baking pan, slit-side up. Pour sauce over frankfurters and bake in 350°F. oven for 25 minutes. Baste frankfurters with sauce. Yield: 4-6 servings.

Kathylene Mosier, Kane Area Sr. H.S.
Kane, Pennsylvania

FRANKFURTER CROWN WITH CORN
STUFFING

½ c. green pepper, chopped
¼ c. onion, chopped
6 T. butter or margarine, melted
2 1-lb. cans cream-style corn
2 eggs, beaten
4 c. soft bread crumbs
1 t. salt
½ c. dry bread crumbs
1½ lbs. frankfurters, halved crosswise

(Continued on Next Page)

Cook green pepper and onion in 4 tablespoons butter until onion is golden but not brown. Add corn, eggs, soft bread crumbs and salt; mix lightly. Combine dry bread crumbs with 2 tablespoons butter. Place corn mixture in round baking dish, mounding in center; sprinkle top with buttered crumbs. Bake uncovered at 350°F. for 25 minutes; stand frankfurters, cut end down, in a crown around edge of stuffing. Continue baking for 15 minutes longer. Yield: 6-8 servings.

Linda Phillips, Knox H.S.
Knox, Indiana

FRANKFURTER-CABBAGE CASSEROLE

4 frankfurters
1 T. onion, minced
3 T. fat or salad oil
3 c. raw cabbage, shredded
1½ T. flour
¾ t. prepared mustard
⅛ t. pepper
¾ t. salt
1 c. milk
1 T. parsley, minced
¾ c. cooked macaroni
¼ c. soft bread crumbs

Halve frankfurters lengthwise, then crosswise. Saute onion in 2½ tablespoon fat. Add cabbage; cover and simmer 2 minutes. Add flour and seasonings. Slowly stir in milk; cook, stirring, until thickened. Stir in frankfurters, parsley and macaroni. Pour into 1-quart casserole. Top with crumbs combined with ½ tablespoon fat. Bake in 425°F. oven for 15 minutes. Yield: 2-3 servings.

Mrs. Edith D. Snapp, Orange Glen H.S.
Escondido, California

FRANKLY CORNY CASSEROLE

½ c. butter
1 T. onion, chopped
3 T. flour
1 T. mustard
½ t. salt
2 c. milk
1 lb. skinless frankfurters, cut into 1-in. pieces
2 c. canned peas, drained
1 12-oz. pkg. corn bread mix
½ c. American cheese, shredded

Melt butter in large skillet; add onion and brown lightly. Blend in flour, mustard and salt. Add milk and cook until thickened, stirring constantly. Stir in frankfurters and peas; heat until boiling. Pour into a greased 13 x 9 x 2-inch baking dish. Prepare corn bread batter according to directions on the p a c k a g e. Drop batter by the tablespoonfuls around the edges of the hot mixture. Sprinkle cheese in the center. Bake at 375°F. for thirty minutes or until corn bread topping is golden brown. Yield: 8 servings.

Sister M. Roseann, C.D.P. Bishop Guilfoyle H.S.
Altoona, Pennsylvania

HOT DOG CASSEROLE

8 hot dogs
1½ c. boiling water
½ t. salt
⅛ t. pepper
1 t. Worcestershire sauce
1 T. onion, finely chopped
1½ c. potatoes, diced
2 c. medium white sauce
½ c. sharp cheese, grated or buttered crumbs

Add hot dogs to boiling water and simmer for 5 minutes; cool slightly. Cut into 1-inch rounds. Combine all ingredients except cheese. Put into baking dish; top with cheese or crumbs. If cheese is used, add to casserole last 5 minute of baking. Bake at 465°F. for 20-25 minutes. Yield: 6 servings.

Mrs. Marlene Harris, Mather H.S.
Munising, Michigan

HOT FRANKFURTER-POTATO SALAD

6 frankfurters, sliced
2 T. cooking oil
1 med. onion, chopped
4 c. cooked potatoes, sliced
1 lge. dill pickle, chopped
1 t. capers (opt.)
¼ c. vinegar
1 T. prepared mustard
1 t. salt
⅛ t. pepper
3 hard-cooked eggs, whites sliced

Lightly brown frankfurter slices in hot oil. Remove frankfurters; cook onion in the oil about 5 minutes, stirring occasionally. Add remaining ingredients except egg yolks. Stir salad lightly while heating it through. Grate the egg yolks and use as a golden garnish. Yield: 6 servings.

Mrs. Dorothy Schofield, Marion Local
Chesterhill, Ohio

PENNIES FROM HEAVEN CASSEROLE

4 lge. potatoes, sliced
1 t. onion, minced
1 t. sweet pepper flakes
1 t. salt
1 lb. wieners, sliced
1 can condensed cream of celery soup
1 can milk

Cook potatoes, onion and sweet pepper flakes in boiling salted water for 5 minutes. Drain, saving liquid. Place layers of potatoes, wieners, and soup mixed with milk in a buttered casserole. Add more milk or reserved liquid until it may be seen through the top layer. Bake at 350°F. for 1 hour, or until potatoes are soft. NOTE: If desired, frozen peas, beans, carrots or mixed vegetables may be added. Yield: 6-8 servings.

Naomi Ross, Freedom Area Schools
Freedom, Pennsylvania

MIXED BEAN BARBECUE

1 10-oz. pkg. green lima beans
1 1-lb. can red kidney beans, drained
1 No. 2½-can pork and beans
1 envelope onion soup mix
¾ c. chili sauce
¼ c. molasses
1 t. dry mustard
Dash of Tabasco
1 lb. frankfurters, cut in ½-in. pieces

Cook lima beans without salt and drain. Combine all the ingredients in a large casserole. Bake 1 hour at 350°F.

Mrs. Dorothy Anderson, Montrose H.S.
Montrose, South Dakota

'TATER DOGS

8-10 frankfurters
1 pkg. instant mashed potato flakes
1½ c. boiling water
3 T. butter
3 T. onion, chopped
1 t. parsley flakes
½ c. sour cream
Salt to taste
1 egg, beaten
1½ c. potato chips or crumbs

Heat frankfurters in boiling water; drain. Prepare potato flakes by stirring into boiling water; whip thoroughly. Melt butter; add onion and parsley. Cook very slowly; do not get too brown. Remove from heat and add sour cream, salt, mustard, and egg. Add to the potatoes. Completely cover individual frankfurters with potato mixture; roll in crushed potato chips or other crumbs. Bake in buttered dish for 25 to 30 minutes at 350°F. NOTE: This recipe won third prize in a national recipe contest for teachers. Yield: 8 servings.

Mary Jane Anderson, Rancho Alamitos H.S.
Garden Grove, California

PENNY SUPPER

6 wieners, thinly sliced
4 med. potatoes, cooked and diced
2 T. onion, minced
¼ c. soft butter
1 c. cooked peas
1 t. prepared mustard
1 c. cream of mushroom soup
Salt and pepper

Combine wiener slices, reserving a few for top, with potatoes, onion and butter in casserole. Mix in rest of ingredients and dot with wiener slices. Bake at 350°F. for 25-30 minutes.

Mrs. Verna Zeeb, Tripp H.S.
Tripp, South Dakota

HEART CASSEROLE

1 veal heart or ½ beef heart
5 carrots, sliced
1 lge. onion, sliced
3 stems celery, sliced
5 med. potatoes, sliced
1½ t. salt
¼ t. pepper
2 cans mushroom soup
1 soup can water

Soak heart for 1 hour in cold water. Simmer heart until tender in water. Slice heart and arrange a row of overlapping slices down the middle of roasting pan. Arrange vegetables on each side of the heart slices. Sprinkle salt and pepper over vegetables and meat. Mix mushroom soup with water and pour over vegetables and meat. Cover roaster and bake until vegetables are tender at 350°F. Yield: 7 servings.

Naomi F. Stock, Lakota H.S.
West Chester, Ohio

ITALIENE HEART CASSEROLE

¾ c. diced cooked heart
3 T. fat, melted
½ No. 2 can spaghetti with tomato sauce
1 T. pimento, chopped
Cheese, grated
¾ c. cooked string beans
½ T. flour
½ c. boiling water
⅜ T. salt
⅛ t. pepper
Buttered crumbs

Brown heart in fat. Combine spaghetti, pimento, ⅛ cup cheese and string beans; add heart and place in baking dish. Blend flour with remaining fat; add water, salt and pepper. Cook until thick, stirring constantly. Add to heart mixture. Cover with buttered crumbs mixed with cheese and bake at 350°F. for 30 minutes. Yield: 4 servings.

Sandra Gill, Bruce H.S.
Bruce, Wisconsin

BRAISED KIDNEY IN CASSEROLE

2 beef kidneys
¼ c. onions, chopped
½-1 c. celery, chopped
2 T. margarine or other fat
½ t. salt
Dash of pepper
2-4 T. cooking wine
Toast points

Clean kidney, being careful to remove all white membrane and fat. If kidney has a strong odor, cover cleaned kidney with boiling water. Let stand 5 minutes; drain. Saute onions and celery in margarine until lightly browned. Add kidney, salt, pepper and 2 tablespoons wine or 1 tablespoon vinegar. Place in casserole; cover. Place in preheated oven at 350°F. for 20 minutes. Remove cover and leave in oven until kidney is done, about 10 to 20 minutes. Add remaining cooking wine and serve with toast points. NOTE: This can be cooked in a skillet. Do not boil; simmer. Yield: 4 servings.

Ora Goodrich, Coudersport Area H.S.
Coudersport, Pennsylvania

LIVER CASSEROLES

CHICKEN LIVERS GOURMET

1 4-oz. can sliced mushrooms
¼ c. flour
1½ t. salt
¼ t. pepper
1 lb. fresh chicken livers
2 T. instant minced onion
3 T. butter
¼ t. Worcestershire sauce
1⅔ c. evaporated milk
½ c. sliced celery
2 c. "instant" rice
2 T. lemon juice
2 T. chopped dried parsley

Drain mushrooms; reserve liquid. Mix flour with salt and pepper. Coat chicken livers in flour mixture. Gently cook mushrooms, minced onion and chicken livers in butter over medium heat about 10 minutes or until livers are browned. Add mushroom liquid and Worcestershire. Cover and cook over very low heat about 5-8 minutes or until livers are tender. Remove from heat and slowly stir in evaporated milk and celery. Return to low heat and cook, covered, about 5 minutes or until thickened. Prepare rice according to package directions. Just before serving, stir lemon juice and dried parsley into liver mixture. Serve over hot cooked rice. NOTE: 1 pound frozen chicken livers, thawed, may be substituted for the fresh.

Photograph for this recipe on page 97

CHICKEN LIVERS WITH RICE

¼ c. butter
3 T. onion, minced
1 5-oz. pkg. instant rice
½ lb. chicken livers, cut into 1-in. pieces
Seasoned flour
1 can cream of chicken soup
½ c. milk
1 T. chopped parsley
Pinch of dried basil

Melt 1 tablespoon butter in saucepan; add onion and cook until tender. Add to rice. Roll livers in flour; saute in remaining butter. Combine livers, rice, soup, and remaining ingredients in a casserole. Bake at 375°F. for 30 minutes. Yield: 5-6 servings.

Mrs. Mabel S. Werner, Millburn H.S.
Millburn, New Jersey

CHICKETTI

1 lb. chicken livers, chopped
2 T. cooking oil
1 med. onion, chopped
2½ c. water
1 8-oz. pkg. uncooked spaghetti
2 T. celery leaves, chopped
½ t. salt
1 can cream of chicken soup

Brown chicken livers in cooking oil. Stir in all other ingredients except soup. Cover and simmer 30 minutes, stirring occasionally. Add soup during last 10 minutes of cooking time. Yield: 4-6 servings.

Frances Alsup, Kopperl H.S.
Kopperl, Texas

BRAISED LIVER CASSEROLE

1 lb. beef liver
¼ c. flour
1½ t. salt
¼ t. pepper
2 T. shortening, melted
1 onion, sliced
1 c. meat stock or bouillon
1 can tomato soup or 1 c. canned tomatoes
2 carrots, sliced
2 potatoes, sliced
1 sm. bay leaf

Cut liver into 2-inch square pieces. Roll in flour with salt and pepper. Brown in shortening. Add onion and brown. Remove liver and onions from fat and blend in remaining flour left from dredging the liver; stir in meat stock and soup or tomatoes. Combine gravy with liver and vegetables. Add bay leaf and pour into casserole. Cover and bake for 1 hour at 350°F. Yield: 6 servings.

Dorothy Angelos, Central H.S.
Deer River, Minnesota

EASY LIVER CASSEROLE

5 strips bacon
1 lb. liver
4 T. flour
Salt to taste
1 can tomato soup
3-4 T. green pepper, minced
1-2 T. onion, minced
¼ t. chili powder

Cut up bacon; fry in skillet until crisp. Remove. Dredge liver in flour with salt. Brown in bacon fat. Pour on tomato soup. Add green pepper, onion and chili powder. Sprinkle bacon on top. Cover and simmer 20 to 25 minutes. Yield: 4-6 servings.

Meroe E. Stanley, Northville H.S.
Northville, Michigan

LIVER AND APPLE CASSEROLE

2 T. flour
Salt and pepper
1 t. dry mustard
1 lb. calf liver, thinly sliced
1 oz. fat
2 cooking apples, peeled and sliced
2 onions, peeled and sliced
6 strips bacon, halved
½ pt. water

Mix flour, salt, pepper and mustard; coat liver slices with mixture. Brown lightly in heated fat. Fill a greased casserole dish with alternate layers of liver, apples, and onions; top with pieces of bacon. Add water. Cover and cook in the center of a 350°F. oven for 1 hour and 30 minutes, removing cover for the last 20 minutes.

Mrs. Karen Richards, Ottawa Sr. H.S.
Ottawa, Kansas

LIVER DELUXE

2 lb. liver, sliced ¼-in. thick
¼ c. flour
½ t. salt
¼ t. pepper
¼ c. salad oil
½ c. onion, chopped
¼ c. green pepper, chopped
1 garlic clove, minced
3 carrots, sliced
3 stalks celery, sliced
1 pt. tomato sauce
1 c. water
1½ c. uncooked elbow macaroni

Roll liver in mixture of flour, salt and pepper. Brown in heated oil in heavy skillet. Remove from pan and saute onion, green pepper and garlic. Add carrots, celery, tomato sauce and water. Simmer 10 minutes. Put macaroni in lightly oiled casserole. Cover with liver. Pour sauce over all. Cover and bake at 325°F. for 1 hour or until liver is tender. Yield: 4 servings.

Mrs. Robert Gonser, Rome City Jr. H.S.
Rome City, Indiana

LIVER LYONNAISE

1 lb. sliced liver
3 T. flour
2 t. salt
¼ t. pepper
3½ c. potatoes, cubed
1 c. onions, sliced
1 can condensed cream of celery soup
½ c. milk

Cut liver into 1½-inch cubes. Blend flour, half of salt and half of pepper. Roll liver in flour mixture and brown in skillet. Remove liver and then brown potatoes and onions. Combine liver, potatoes and onions in 1½-quart baking dish. Combine soup, milk, and remaining salt and pepper; pour over casserole. Cover and bake 40 minutes at 375°F. Yield: 6 servings.

Mrs. Darlene Wright, Brock Public School
Brock, Nebraska

LIVER AND RICE SKILLET

1½ c. cereal flakes, crushed
1 t. paprika
2 t. salt
1 lb. liver, sliced
3 T. shortening
½ c. onion, finely chopped
1 c. rice
1 can cream of tomato soup
1 soup can water

Combine cereal flakes, paprika and half of salt. Coat liver with mixture. Brown in hot shortening in heavy skillet. Remove from skillet. Lightly brown onion and rice in skillet. Stir in soup, water and remaining salt. Bring to a boil; place liver slices on top of rice. Reduce heat and simmer 20 minutes or until rice is tender. Yield: 4 servings.

Helen Wales, Public School
Breckenridge, Minnesota

POTATO-LIVER CASSEROLE

5 slices bacon
1½ lbs. beef liver
¼ c. flour
1 lge. onion, sliced
2 c. celery, diced
1 green pepper, diced
1 c. tomatoes
1 t. salt
⅛ t. black pepper
2 lb. sm. new potatoes, scraped
¾ c. hot water

Pan broil bacon in heavy skillet. Remove from pan and brown liver that has been dredged in flour. Move liver to one side of pan. Saute onion, celery and green pepper until soft. Add remaining flour and stir until smooth. Add tomatoes, salt and pepper. Cook until thickened and smooth. Add the potatoes. Cover tightly and bake 45 minutes at 350°F. or until potatoes are soft. Remove lid; arrange bacon. Reheat for 5 minutes. Yield: 5 servings.

Mrs. Marion R. Compton, Haston H.S.
Dearborn Heights, Michigan

VEGETABLE-LIVER CASSEROLE

½ c. flour
½ t. paprika
¼ t. pepper
1 t. salt
1½ lb. beef liver, cut into 2-in. pieces
¼ c. shortening
1 lge. onion, diced
3 lge. sticks celery, diced
6 carrots, cut into 1-in. pieces
3 med. potatoes, cut into 1-in. cubes
1 No. 303 can tomatoes or 2 c. tomato juice
1 bay leaf
1 beef bouillon cube

Blend flour and seasonings in a bag. Drop liver into bag and shake until coated. Saute quickly in hot shortening. Remove liver to a 2½-quart casserole. Add vegetables to liver. Pour tomatoes into frying pan; add bay leaf and simmer a few minutes. Add bouillon cube and stir until dissolved. Pour over casserole. Bake covered for 1 hour and 30 minutes at 350°F. Remove lid and bake 30 minutes longer. If more liquid is needed, add a small amount of hot water or beef broth. Yield: 6 servings.

Adele E. Bast, Wilson Joint H.S.
West Lawn, Pennsylvania

LUNCHEON MEAT CASSEROLES

CAMPER'S CASSEROLE

1 can luncheon meat, sliced
4 lge. potatoes, sliced
1 lb. carrots, sliced
1 onion, sliced
Salt and pepper to taste

Lightly brown meat slices. Add layers of potatoes, carrots and onion. Season. Cover tightly; simmer for 25 minutes. Yield: 4 servings.

Cynthia Ebert, Ripon Sr. H.S.
Ripon, Wisconsin

MEAT 'N' POTATO SUPPER

1 12-oz. can luncheon meat, cut in strips
1 med. onion, thinly sliced
2 T. shortening
1 can cream of mushroom soup
½ c. milk
2 c. cubed potatoes, cooked
2 T. parsley, chopped
Salt
Dash of pepper

Lightly brown luncheon meat and onion in shortening. Blend in soup and milk. Add potatoes, parsley, salt and pepper. Cook over low heat about 10 minutes; stir. Yield: 4 servings.

Mrs. Claudia M. Thomsen, North Fremont H.S.
Ashton, Idaho

QUICK CASSEROLE DISH

1 can luncheon meat
6-8 whole cloves
1 No. 3 can sweet potatoes
½ c. brown sugar
1¼ c. pineapple with juice
1 T. butter or margarine

Place meat in a lightly greased casserole; stick cloves in top of meat. Place sweet potatoes around meat. Sprinkle brown sugar over casserole; top with pineapple. Dot with butter; cover. Bake at 350°F. for 20-30 minutes.

Lucille L. Stewart, Lake Ville Memorial H.S.
Otisville, Michigan

FULL O' BOLOGNA

1½ c. or ½ lb. bologna, sliced or cubed
2 c. raw potatoes, sliced or cubed
1 med. onion, diced
1 c. carrots, diced (opt.)
6 T. flour
½ t. salt
¼ t. pepper
3 T. margarine or butter
2 c. milk

Arrange ingredients except margarine and milk in alternate layers in greased 7 or 8-inch baking dish. Dot with butter. Pour milk over all. Bake 1 hour and 15 minutes at 350°F. Yield: 4-6 servings.

Mrs. Georgina Irelan, Grand Blanc H.S.
Grand Blanc, Michigan

MACARONI-BOLOGNA ROLL

1 8-oz. pkg. macaroni
4 c. boiling water
1 c. thin white sauce
1½ c. cooked peas
Salt and pepper
Paprika
1 lb. bologna, uncut
½ c. sharp cheese, grated

Add macaroni to boiling water; cover and cook slowly for 14-18 minutes. Do not drain. Add white sauce and peas; season to taste with salt, pepper and paprika. Cut bologna down the center, being careful not to cut all the way through. Place in an oiled baking dish. Pile macaroni mixture in the center of the bologna roll; cover with cheese. Bake at 350°F. for 30 minutes. Serve hot, sliced crosswise. Yield: 4-6 servings.

Barbara J. Smith, Antwerp H.S.
Antwerp, Ohio

BOLOGNA-NOODLE CASSEROLE

3 c. cooked noodles
1 c. bologna, chopped
½ t. salt
⅛ t. pepper
1 c. milk
½ c. cracker or bread crumbs
1 T. fat

Arrange alternate layers of noodles and bologna in a greased baking dish. Add salt, pepper and milk; cover with crumbs. Dot with fat and bake at 400°F. for 30 minutes. NOTE: Use macaroni or spaghetti instead of noodles if desired. Yield: 6 servings.

Mrs. Johnnie Mae Proctor, Dilley H.S.
Dilley, Texas

GARDEN CASSEROLE

1½-2 c. white sauce
1 can corn
1 can peas
1 can Spam, diced
1 T. onion, finely cut
2 hard-cooked eggs, sliced
Buttered bread crumbs

Combine all ingredients except crumbs. Place in casserole. Cover mixture with crumbs. Heat for 30-40 minutes at 350°F. NOTE: If desired, cheese may be added to white sauce. Yield: 6-8 servings.

Irene Decker, Humboldt H.S.
Humboldt, Kansas

HARRIET'S CASSEROLE

5 med. potatoes, sliced
Flour
Salt and pepper
1 can Spam or left over ham
2 onions
2 or 3 carrots, thinly sliced
2 or 3 celery sticks, with leaves, thinly sliced
Juice from canned meat
Cheese
1 can evaporated milk
Bread crumbs
Paprika (opt.)

Place one layer potatoes in bottom of greased casserole. Sprinkle with flour, salt and pepper. Add layers of meat and layers of vegetables until all are used. Pieces or slices of cheese can be put throughout. Each layer is sprinkled with flour and seasonings. Pour milk with meat juice over the top, making sure it is mixed through. Place pieces of cheese on top and bake covered about 1 hour at 350°F. Add buttered, browned bread crumbs to the top when casserole is almost done. Sprinkle with paprika if desired.

Patricia Copeland, Pinckney Community Schools
Pinckney, Michigan

HANDY HAM CASSEROLE

1½ T. butter
2 T. flour
½ t. salt
⅔ c. bean liquid
½ c. Spam
Onion
4 hard-cooked eggs, chopped
1 can lima beans, drained
Cornflakes

Make white sauce by blending butter, flour and salt with bean liquid. Grind meat with a little onion. Mix meat, eggs and beans. Alternate layers of meat mixture and sauce in casserole. Top with cornflakes. Bake at 350°F. about 30 minutes or until mixture bubbles. Yield: 6 servings.

Mrs. Oral M. Esch, Holland Sr. H.S.
Holland, Michigan

HAM TOP CASSEROLE

1 can Spam
1 8-oz. pkg. creamettes or macaroni
1 can cream of celery soup
½ c. milk
¼ t. black pepper
1 T. pepper or mango, chopped
1 T. onion, minced
¼ lb. Cheddar cheese, cubed

Cut 3 slices of Spam; cube the remaining Spam. Cook macaroni or creamettes. Combine soup, milk, black pepper, chopped pepper and onion. Place over low heat. Add cheese; stir all until cheese melts. Add cubed Spam and pour over macaroni in a 2-quart casserole. Garnish with slices of Spam. Bake 15 minutes at 325°F. Yield: 9 servings.

Sara Sue Chowning, Sullivan H.S.
Sullivan, Indiana

MACARONI-HAM LOAF

3 c. cooked macaroni
1 sm. onion
½ green pepper
⅛ lb. cheese
1 can meat, Spam, Prem etc.
¾ c. hot milk
¼ c. butter
¾ c. bread crumbs
2 eggs, separated
1 can cream of mushroom soup

Grind the cooked macaroni, onion, pepper, cheese and meat with the coarse blade of the food grinder. Mix the milk, butter, bread crumbs and beaten egg yolks together. Combine the two mixtures. Fold in the beaten egg whites. Pour into greased casserole and bake in 350°F. oven for 30 minutes. Top with mushroom soup and return to oven for a few minutes until the soup is hot. Yield: 8 servings.

Mrs. Reva Wilson, Drummond H.S.
Drummond, Montana

NOODLE-HAM HOT DISH

1 c. Spam
½ green pepper
½ c. celery
½ onion
2 pimentos
1 pkg. fine egg noodles, cooked
1 can mushroom soup
Buttered bread crumbs or potato chips

Grind Spam, green pepper, celery, onion and pimento. Add noodles and soup. Place in casserole. Top with buttered bread crumbs. Bake 1 hour at 300-350°F. NOTE: If desired, 1 can mixed vegetables may be substituted for green pepper, celery and pimento. Yield: 6 servings.

Mrs. Dorothy Schulz, McLaughlin H.S.
McLaughlin, South Dakota

LUNCHEON LOAF

1 can Spam, ground
1 sm. can evaporated milk
1 c. oatmeal
1 can chicken noodle soup
2 eggs, beaten
1 med. onion, chopped

Mix ingredients. Pack into greased loaf pan. Bake for 30 minutes at 300°F. Yield: 8 servings.

Patricia Morgan, Laurel H.S.
Laurel, Montana

RICE AND HAM

1 can Spam, cubed
1 green pepper, chopped
1 T. onion, chopped
1 c. raw carrots, grated
¾ c. uncooked rice
½ lb. very sharp Cheddar cheese, grated
1 can cream of celery soup
3 c. milk

Combine all ingredients. Bake at 350°F. for 2 hours in a covered dish, stirring occasionally. No salt is needed in this casserole. NOTE: If desired, cream of mushroom soup may be served over it as a sauce. Yield: 6-8 servings.

Janice Hagemeister, Mott H.S.
Mott, North Dakota

SNAPPY SUPPER SOUFFLE

1 can Spam, grated
2 c. sharp cheese, grated
3 eggs, beaten
1 c. milk
1 c. cracker crumbs
½ t. salt

Combine all ingredients in a 13x8x3 baking pan. Bake in 350°F. oven for 30 minutes, or until the center tests done. Serve with chili sauce or catsup. Yield: 8 servings.

Mrs. Keith Van Koevering,
Saugatuck Public School
Saugatuck, Michigan

SCALLOPED POTATOES AND HAM

3 T. cooking fat
3 T. flour
1 t. salt
½ t. pepper
1 sm. onion, minced
1 T. parsley, minced
2 c. milk
4 lge. potatoes, boiled
1 can Spam, sliced
1 c. buttered bread crumbs

Melt the fat; stir in flour. Add the salt and pepper. Add onion, parsley and milk. Cook, stirring until smooth and thickened. Slice the potatoes thin and place in layers in a casserole; top with Spam slices. Pour on sauce; sprinkle with bread crumbs. Bake at 375°F. for 30 minutes. Yield: 6 servings.

Ruth W. Wingo, Kaufman H.S.
Kaufman, Texas

SPAM SUEY

1 12-oz. can luncheon meat, diced
¼ c. butter or shortening
1 c. onions, finely cut
1 c. celery, cut in diagonal strips
1 t. salt
⅛ t. pepper
1 c. hot water
1 1-lb. can bean sprouts, drained
2 T. cornstarch
⅓ c. cold water
2 t. soy sauce

Sear meat in hot shortening quickly without browning or burning; add onions and fry for 5 minutes. Add celery, salt, pepper and hot water. Cover and cook for 5 minutes. Add bean sprouts. Mix and heat to boiling point. Add cornstarch mixed with cold water and soy sauce. Cook until thickened. Serve piping hot with fried noodles nested on rice. Yield: 4 servings.

Virginia Caffo, Port Allegany Union H.S.
Port Allegany, Pennsylvania

WONDER-FULL NELSON STYLE

1 can cream of mushroom soup
½ c. milk
1 can mixed vegetables, drained
1 med. onion, finely chopped
1 can Spam, cut in ½-in. cubes
2 c. wide noodles, cooked and drained
½ t. pepper

Mix soup, milk, vegetables and onion. Add Spam, noodles, and pepper; mix. Pour into greased casserole. Bake covered for 40 to 50 minutes at 350°F. Yield: 4 servings.

Mrs. Anthony G. Stone, Newell-Providence
Community School
Newell, Iowa

SALAMI MACARONI TOSS-UP

3 T. butter or margarine
3 T. flour
1 t. salt
⅛ t. pepper
½ t. dry mustard
1 t. Worcestershire sauce
1½ c. milk
1 T. onion, minced
½ c. American cheese, grated
1 c. salami, slivered
¼ c. sweet pickle, slivered
4 oz. elbow macaroni, cooked

Melt butter in top of double boiler. Stir in flour, salt, pepper, mustard and Worcestershire sauce. Gradually add milk, stirring constantly until thickened. Fold in onion, cheese, salami and pickle; mix lightly. Fold in macaroni. Pour into a greased casserole. Bake at 350°F. for 25 minutes. Yield: 4 servings.

Jean Passino, Keewatin-Nashwauk Jr. H.S.
Keewatin, Minnesota

SWEETBREAD CASSEROLES

SWEETBREAD-OYSTER CASSEROLE

2 c. med. white sauce
2 c. cooked sweetbreads, diced
1 pt. oysters
¼ lb. fresh mushrooms, sauted
2 T. parsley, chopped
2 T. onion, grated
Salt and pepper to taste

Combine white sauce with all ingredients; pour into casserole.
TOPPING:
1 c. yellow corn meal
¼ c. flour
1 t. baking powder
½ t. salt
1 t. sugar
¼ c. shortening, melted
1¼ c. milk

Mix dry ingredients; add melted shortening and milk. Stir until blended. Spread over creamed mixture and bake 30 minutes at 350°F. NOTE: White sauce should be made with oyster liquor plus enough milk to make 2 cups liquid. Yield: 4 servings.

Margaret Lopp, Chandler H.S.
Chandler, Arizona

SWEETBREADS AND CHICKEN CASSEROLE

¼ lb. mushrooms, sliced
1 T. onion, chopped
3 T. butter
¼ c. flour
1 c. chicken stock
½ c. milk
½ c. light cream
1 c. cooked chicken, diced
½ c. sweetbreads, cooked and chopped
½ c. blanched almonds
1 t. salt
Pepper to taste
Paprika
½ c. Sherry
Bread crumbs

Saute mushrooms and onions in butter until lightly browned. Stir in flour; add chicken stock and milk gradually. Stir until thick. Add cream, chicken, sweetbreads, almonds and seasonings; bring to a boil. Add sherry; pour into a buttered casserole. Cover with crumbs. Bake in 400°F. oven about 20 minutes. Yield: 4-6 servings.

Bonnie Van Kessel, Duluth Central
Duluth, Minnesota

VIENNA SAUSAGE CASSEROLES

EASY CASSEROLE

1 5-oz. box instant rice
1 4-oz. can Vienna sausage
1 can condensed tomato soup
American cheese slices

Prepare rice as directed on box. Slice Vienna sausage crosswise and brown in skillet. Add the cooked rice to the sausage. Stir in tomato soup. Mix ingredients together and top with slices of American cheese. Bake at 350°F. to melt cheese and brown slightly. Yield: 4 servings.

Betty Hoover, Wamego Rural H.S.
Wamego, Kansas

HAWIIAN BEANS

2 lge. cans pork and beans
3 T. molasses
2 cans Vienna sausages, cut into ½-in. pieces
1 can yams or sweet potatoes, cut into 1-in. pieces
1 onion, cut into rings
½ c. brown sugar
½ t. salt
½ t. dry mustard

Mix beans and molasses; add sausages and potatoes. Put in casserole. Top with onion rings. Combine remaining ingredients; sprinkle over top. Bake at 350°F. for 1 hour to 1 hour and 30 minutes. Yield: 12-16 servings.

Cara L. Newman, Madison Jr. H.S.
Rexburg, Idaho

LIMA-SAUSAGE CASSEROLE

2 pkgs. frozen lima beans
2 cans Vienna sausage
1 can tomato soup

Put beans in a 2-quart buttered casserole. Arrange sausages on top; Pour soup over top. Cover and bake at 350°F. for 20 minutes. Yield: 6 servings.

Blanche M. Burnett, Eminence Consolidated School
Eminence, Indiana

MEXICAN CORN PUDDING

2 c. cream-style corn
3 eggs, slightly beaten
½ c. fine cracker crumbs
1 t. onion, grated
2 T. green pepper, chopped
2 T. pimento, chopped
½ t. salt
¼ t. pepper
¼ t. dry mustard
2 cans Vienna sausages

Combine corn, eggs, cracker crumbs, onions, green pepper, pimento and seasonings. Slice 1 can sausages and add to mixture. Pour into a well greased 1-quart casserole. Bake in oven at 350°F. about 1 hour. For garnish, arrange remaining sausages over top of casserole for the last 15 minutes of baking time. Yield: 6 servings.

Mrs. Alice E. Stone, Sherrard Unit H.S.
Sherrard, Illinois

SCALLOPED POTATOES WITH VIENNA SAUSAGES

3 c. raw potatoes, sliced
8 Vienna sausages, diced
1 8-oz. can sliced mushrooms
¼ c. flour
1 t. salt
⅛ t. pepper
3 T. onion, minced
1 c. milk
1 tomato, sliced
¼ c. American cheese, grated
Parsley

Arrange about half the potato slices, sausages, and mushrooms in a greased casserole. Sprinkle with half the flour, salt, pepper and onion. Pour milk over all. Cover and bake for 45 minutes at 350°F. Remove from oven. Top with tomato slices and cheese. Bake uncovered for 30 minutes longer. If desired, garnish with parsley. Yield: 3-4 servings.

This recipe submitted by the following teachers:
Dorothy Marie Salter, Midlothian H.S.
Midlothian, Texas
Mrs. Ollie Lee Arter, Kiowa H.S.
Kiowa, Oklahoma

SAUSAGE AND CORN CASSEROLE

7 Vienna sausages
1 No. 2 can whole kernel corn
½ green pepper, chopped
Salt and pepper
2 c. med. white sauce
1½ c. cracker crumbs

Cut sausages; mix with corn and green pepper. Season to taste. Layer crumbs, corn mixture and sauce. Top with buttered crumbs; bake at 350°F. for 20 minutes. Yield: 5 servings.

Louise Fiqueiredo, Leonville H.S.
Leonville, Louisiana

VIENNA SAUSAGE CREOLE

1 med. onion, sliced
½ green pepper, cut in strips
½ c. celery, sliced
2 T. shortening
1 No. 303 can tomatoes
1 8-oz. can tomato sauce
1-2 t. chili powder
1 t. sugar
½ t. salt
1 8-oz. can Vienna sausage, drained and cut in thirds

In large frying pan cook onion, green pepper, and celery in shortening for 5 minutes. Add tomatoes, tomato sauce and seasonings; mix well. Simmer for 10 minutes. Add sausage; stir carefully. Heat thoroughly. May be served over rice. Yield: 4 servings.

Mrs. Gail Patton, Hollywood Jr. H.S.
Memphis, Tennessee

Seafood Casseroles

CLAM PIE

1 9-in. pie crust, unbaked
1½ c. mashed potatoes
1 c. chopped onions, cooked
1 c. minced clams, drained
12 hard-cooked eggs, chopped
Clam juice

In uncooked pie crust layer potatoes, onions, clams, chopped eggs and clam juice. Repeat layers twice, ending with eggs and juice. Cover with vented top crust. Bake at 450°F. for 10 minutes. Reduce heat to 350°F. Bake 1 hour. Yield: 8 servings.

Betty R. Heal, Cherry Hill H.S.
Cherry Hill, New Jersey

DEVILED CLAMS

3 T. olive oil
¼ c. onion, diced
1 garlic clove, minced
½ t. oregano
1 t. parsley
½ c. bread crumbs
1 can minced clams or 8 fresh clams, ground
⅛ t. salt
Parmesan cheese

Saute the onion, garlic, oregano and parsley in olive oil until onion is soft. Remove from heat and add bread crumbs, clams with juice and salt. Spoon either into clean clam shells or individual baking cups. Sprinkle Parmesan cheese on top. Place shells in pan of water and bake at 350°F. for 30 minutes. Yield: 2 servings.

Mrs. Joan Law, F. D. Roosevelt Jr. H.S.
Bristol, Pennsylvania

CRAB-ARTICHOKE CASSEROLE

1 No. 2 can artichoke hearts
½-¾ lb. fresh crab meat or 2 6½-oz. cans
1 sm. can sliced mushrooms
2 T. butter
Worcestershire sauce
¼ c. Sherry
1½ c. well-seasoned med. cream sauce
¼ c. Parmesan cheese, grated

Drain the artichoke hearts and arrange in a buttered shallow baking dish. Sprinkle crab meat over the artichoke hearts. Drain mushrooms and saute in butter for about 5 minutes; arrange over crab meat. Add Worcestershire sauce and Sherry to cream sauce; season to taste and pour over casserole. Top with cheese and bake at 375°F. for 20 minutes. Yield: 4 servings.

Dorothy Deare O'Rear, Bellevue Sr. H.S.
Bellevue, Washington

CRAB DELIGHT

1 lge. green pepper, diced
1½ T. butter
6 t. flour
1 t. dry mustard
2 c. tomato juice
½ lb. Velveeta cheese, cubed
2 8-oz. cans crab meat
2 eggs, slightly beaten
½ c. all-purpose cream
1⅓ c. rice, cooked
Salt and pepper to taste
1 c. crushed potato chips

Cook green pepper for 5 minutes in butter. Blend flour and dry mustard; add to green pepper and blend. Blend in tomato juice. Add cheese; stir until cheese is melted. Add crab meat, eggs and cream. Blend mixture with rice. Salt and pepper to taste. Place in a shallow buttered pan. Sprinkle with crushed potato chips. Bake at 350°F. for 30 minutes. Cut in squares and serve. Yield: 10-12 servings.

Dorothy S. Giller, Narbonne H.S.
Harbor City, California

CRAB MEAT-CHEESE CASSEROLE

10 T. butter, melted
2 T. flour
2 c. cream, scalded
¼ c. natural Swiss cheese, grated
¼ c. Parmesan cheese, grated
Salt
Cayenne pepper
3 c. crab meat, flaked

Make white sauce of 2 tablespoons butter, flour and cream. Add cheese; stir until melted. Add remaining butter, beating hard. Season with salt and cayenne. Arrange crab meat in shallow buttered casserole. Pour sauce over crab meat. Place under a moderately hot broiler for 8 to 10 minutes until a golden brown. Yield: 6-8 servings.

Sister Miriam Joseph S.C.L.
Bishop Hogan H.S.
Kansas City, Missouri

CRAB MEAT EN CASSEROLE

2 T. butter, melted
1 can cream of mushroom soup
2 egg yolks, slightly beaten
1 can crab meat or fresh crab
2 T. lemon juice
Salt and pepper to taste
Paprika to taste
Buttered bread crumbs

Combine butter and soup; heat thoroughly. Gradually add mixture to egg yolks. Add crab meat, lemon juice and seasonings. Pour into greased casserole and sprinkle with buttered bread crumbs. Bake at 375°F. until thoroughly heated and crumbs are brown. Yield: 4 servings.

Carolyn Law, State Supervisor,
Home Economics Education
Montpelier, Vermont

CRAB MEAT CASSEROLE

½ c. butter, melted
⅔ c. flour
2⅔ c. milk
2 6½-oz. cans crab meat, flaked
4 c. celery, chopped
2 pimentos, chopped
½ c. green pepper, chopped
⅓ c. slivered blanched almonds
4 hard-cooked eggs, chopped
2 t. salt
1 c. sharp Cheddar cheese, shredded
1 c. buttered bread crumbs

Blend butter and flour in a saucepan. Remove from heat and slowly add milk. Return to heat and cook, stirring constantly, until the white sauce thickens. Add crab meat, celery, pimento, green pepper, almonds, eggs and salt. Pour into a 2-quart casserole. Top with cheese and bread crumbs; bake at 350°F for 45 minutes. Yield: 8 servings.

Sister M. Benedict, O.S.B., Sacred Heart Academy
Minot, North Dakota

CRAB MEAT DELIGHT

4 T. butter, melted
6 T. flour
½ t. salt
1½ c. milk
2 eggs, well beaten
½ c. cheese, grated
1½ c. crab meat
1 c. buttered bread crumbs

Make a white sauce of the butter, flour, salt and milk. Add the eggs and cheese, cooking until well blended. Put crab meat into a greased 1½-quart casserole and pour sauce over it. Top with buttered crumbs and stir quickly until well mixed. Bake casserole about 20-25 minutes at 350°F. to heat through and brown top. Yield: 4 servings.

Mrs. Esther P. Leeds, Piscataquis Community H.S.
Guilford, Maine

CRAB-MUSHROOM CASSEROLE

2 c. cooked rice
1½ c. fresh crab, flaked
¾ c. mayonnaise
1 2-oz. can sliced mushrooms
1 sm. green pepper, chopped
1 sm. onion, diced
1 c. tomato juice
Salt and pepper to taste
¾ c. sharp cheese, grated

Mix all ingredients except the cheese; pour mixture into greased 2-quart casserole. Sprinkle cheese on top. Bake for 1 hour in a 350°F. oven. NOTE: For variation cracker crumbs or potato chips may be sprinkled over cheese. Yield: 6 servings.

Mrs Robert A. Riffenburg, Fortuna Union H.S.
Fortuna, California

CRAB MEAT CHASSEUR

4 lge. mushrooms or 1 4-oz. can mushrooms
3 T. butter
2 T. shallots or chives, finely chopped
2 T. tomato paste
1 c. heavy cream
1 lb. crab meat
Salt and pepper to taste
2 egg yolks
¼ c. heavy cream
1 t. parsley
1 t. tarragon
1 t. chives
Dash of Cognac

Saute mushrooms in butter for 5 minutes in skillet or chafing dish. Add shallots; stir until liquid evaporates. Add tomato paste; cook for 5 minutes. Pour in cream; simmer until blended. Add crab, salt and pepper; stir gently. Heat, but do not break up crab. Mix egg yolks and cream; add to crab mixture. Add seasonings and Cognac. Keep hot; serve over rice. Yield: 6 servings.

Marilyn Lindsey Maynard, Barnum Jr. H.S.
Birmingham, Michigan

CRAB SOUFFLE

8 slices bread
2 c. crab meat
½ green pepper, chopped
⅓ c. onion, chopped
1 c. celery chopped
1 c. mayonnaise
4 eggs, beaten
2 c. milk
1 can mushroom soup
½-1 cup cheese, grated

Cut each slice of bread into fourths; lay on bottom of baking dish. Spread mixture of crab, pepper, onion, celery, and mayonnaise over the bread. Pour mixture of beaten eggs and milk over the top and refrigerate overnight. Pour heated mushroom soup over top. Sprinkle with cheese. Bake for 1 hour at 325°F. Yield: 8 servings.

Mrs. Marrel Hughes, Nooksack Valley H.S.
Nooksack, Washington

CRAB SUPREME

1 c. canned crab meat
1 c. soft bread crumbs
1 c. cream
1½ c. mayonnaise
1 T. parsley, minced
6 hard-cooked eggs, diced
1 t. onion, minced
½ t. salt
Pepper to taste
½ c. buttered fine dry bread crumbs

Mix all ingredients except buttered dry crumbs and place in a buttered casserole. Top with buttered crumbs. Bake in a 350°F. oven for 20 minutes. Yield: 6-8 servings.

Mrs. Mary Lou Hayes, Altamont, H.S.
Altamont, Utah

DEVILED CRAB

4 T. butter
2 T. flour
1 c. milk
½ t. salt
1 8-oz. can crab meat
½ t. paprika
¼ t. pepper
½ t. prepared mustard
1 T. chopped parsley
1 T. lemon juice
3 hard-cooked eggs
3 slices toasted bread, cubed

Melt 2 tablespoons butter in a saucepan; add flour and salt. Add milk gradually and cook over low heat, stirring constantly until sauce boils and thickens. Fold in remaining ingredients except bread cubes and remaining butter; mix until well blended, but do not mash. Mix bread cubes with remaining melted butter. Place layer of cubes on bottom of buttered casserole. Cover with crab mixture; repeat layers, ending with bread cubes. Bake for 20 minutes at 375°F. or until crumbs are a golden brown and mixture is heated through. Yield: 6 servings.

Ardis Boyd, Beaver Creek Public School
Beaver Creek, Minnesota

LUNCHEON CRAB BAKE

1 6½- or 7½-oz. can crab meat
1 c. soft bread crumbs
1 c. mayonnaise or salad dressing
¾ c. milk
6 hard-cooked eggs, finely chopped
⅓ c. onion, chopped
¼ c. stuffed green olives, sliced
¾ tsp. salt
Dash of pepper
½ c. buttered soft bread crumbs

Break crab meat in chunks, removing any bony bits. Mix with remaining ingredients except buttered crumbs. Pile in greased individual dishes or a 1-quart casserole. Top with buttered crumbs. Bake at 350°F. for 20 to 25 minutes or until hot through. Trim with stuffed olive slices. Yield: 6 servings.

Ann Clinton, Limestone H.S.
Bartonville, Illinois

DEVILED CRAB IMPERIAL

½ cube butter
1 T. flour
1½ c. milk
¼ t. salt
½ T. onion juice
½ T. lemon juice
1 t. Worcestershire sauce
1 t. fresh parsley, finely chopped
Dash of cayenne pepper
¼ t. celery salt
1 T. Sherry wine
2 eggs, well beaten
1 lb. fresh or frozen crab meat
⅓ c. buttered bread crumbs

Melt butter in heavy saucepan; blend in flour. Add milk; stir constantly until smooth and thickened. Add seasonings and Sherry; mix well. Add eggs; heat, but do not boil. Fold in crab. Spoon into 6 crab shells or baking dish. Cover lightly with crumbs. Place shells on cookie sheet. Bake at 350-400°F. for 15 minutes. Finish under broiler if a more golden color is desired. Yield: 6 servings.

Mrs. Inez W. Johnson, Sunnyside H.S.
Tucson, Arizona

KING CRAB CASSEROLE

8 slices white bread
2 c. Kodiak king crab or shrimp
½-¾ c. mayonnaise
1 onion, finely chopped
1 green pepper, finely chopped
Pimento (opt.)
1 c. celery, finely chopped
4 eggs, beaten
3 c. milk
1 t. salt (opt.)
1 can mushroom soup
1 c. American cheese, grated
Paprika to taste (opt.)

Dice half of bread into a greased 16-inch baking pan. Combine crab, mayonnaise, onion, green pepper, pimento and celery; place over bread. Trim crust from remaining bread and place in slices over crab mixture. Mix eggs, milk and salt; pour over casserole. Refrigerate overnight. Pour undiluted soup over top; sprinkle with cheese and paprika. Let stand at room temperature for 1 hour. Bake at 325°F. for 1 hour. NOTE: If desired, onion and green pepper may be sauted in 2 tablespoons butter before adding to casserole. Casserole may be place in oven immediately after refrigerating; bake at 350°F. for 20 minutes. Top with soup and cheese: bake for 1 hour longer. One can cream of celery soup may be added with mushroom soup. Yield: 6-8 servings.

This recipe submitted by the following teachers:
Mrs. Agnes C. Huffman, Thomas Downey H.S.
Modesto, California
Letha A. Chastain, Pamplico Public Schools
Pamplico, South Carolina
Abbie E. Dale, Edmonds Sr. H.S.
Edmonds, Washington
Mrs. Evelyn Pence, Bend Jr. H.S.
Bend, Oregon
Mrs. Esther Nelson, Leuzinger H.S.
Lawndale, California
Mrs. Helen M. Godwin, Northwest Guilford H.S.
Greensboro, North Carolina
Cathy O'Farrell, St. Helens Sr. H.S.
St. Helens, Oregon

UPSIDE-DOWN CRAB MEAT CORN BREAD

1 c. crab meat, flaked
1/3 c. mushrooms
2 c. cooked mixed vegetables
1/4 c. ripe olives, sliced
Dash of pepper
1/8 t. salt
Dash of paprika
1 can condensed cheese soup
1/4 c. flour
3/4 c. corn meal
1 t. baking powder
1 T. sugar
1/2 t. salt
1/4 t. soda
3/4 c. sour milk
1 1/2 T. butter, melted

Mix together crab meat, mushrooms, vegetables and olives. Add pepper, salt and paprika. Combine mixture with the cheese soup in a buttered casserole. Combine flour, corn meal, baking powder, sugar, salt and soda. Add sour milk; stir in the melted butter and mix until smooth. Pour over top of meat-vegetable mixture. Bake at 325°F. for 30 minutes or until corn bread is done. Invert on a plate for serving. Yield: 6-8 servings.

Mrs. Marlys Folkers, Ellsworth Public School
Ellsworth, Minnesota

CAPE COD BAKED STUFFED HADDOCK

2 haddock fillets or 1 whole haddock, split and
   cleaned
1 onion, minced
3 T. butter
1 t. parsley, minced
3 c. stale bread crumbs
1 egg
1 t. salt
1/8 t. pepper
1 T. water
6 slices bacon
4-6 tomatoes
Whole-kernel corn

Wipe fish and dust with salt and pepper. Brown onion in butter; add parsley, crumbs, egg and seasonings. Moisten with water. Spread mixture between fillets or stuff whole fish. Skewer opening closed. Place fish on a well greased, paper lined baking pan; lay strips of bacon on fish, or brush with softened butter. Stuff tomatoes with corn. Arrange around fish in pan. Bake at 375°F. for 1 hour to 1 hour and 15 minutes. Transfer to a hot platter. Garnish with parsley and lemon slices. Serve with cucumber sauce. Yield: 4-6 servings.

Lillian P. Dunbar, Abington H.S.
Abington, Massachusetts

BAKED HADDOCK WITH MUSHROOM SAUCE

2 lb. fillet of haddock
Salt to taste
1 sm. onion, thinly sliced
1 can undiluted cream of mushroom soup
1 c. med. sharp cheese, grated
1 c. sm. bread cubes, slightly buttered

Remove skin from fish. Wash the fish and place in a buttered baking dish. Sprinkle with salt and slices of onion. Bake in a 400°F. oven about 20 minutes. Heat the undiluted mushroom soup and pour over the baked fish. Sprinkle with cheese. Cover with bread cubes. Cook until sauce begins to bubble. Yield: 6 servings.

Louise Temple, Exeter H.S.
Exeter, New Hampshire

ELEGANTE FILLETS

1 lb. frozen fish fillets, thawed
Fresh ground pepper
2 T. butter
1 can frozen condensed cream of shrimp
   soup, thawed
1/4 c. Parmesan cheese, grated
Paprika

Arrange fish in a buttered 9-inch pie plate. Dash with pepper; dot with butter. Spread soup over fillets; sprinkle with cheese and paprika. Bake at 400°F. for 25 minutes. Serve with lemon wedges. NOTE: For fish, use sole, haddock, halibut or cod. Yield: 4 servings.

Mrs. Helen C. Sockman, Mechanicsburg Jr. H.S.
Mechanicsburg, Pennsylvania

HOT HALIBUT SALAD SOUFFLE

6 slices white bread
2 c. cooked halibut, flaked
1/2 c. green pepper, chopped
1/2 c. onions, chopped
1/2 c. celery, finely chopped
1/2 c. mayonnaise
Dash of pepper
3/4 t. salt
2 eggs, beaten
1 1/2 c. milk
1 can condensed cream of mushroom soup
1/2 c. sharp process cheese, shredded

Cube 2 slices of bread; place in bottom of slightly greased 9x9x2-inch baking dish. Combine halibut, vegetables, mayonnaise and seasonings; spoon over bread cubes. Trim crust from remaining bread; arrange slices on top of mixture. Combine eggs and milk; pour over all. Cover and chill 1 hour to 24 hours. Spoon soup over top. Bake at 325°F. for 1 hour or until set. Sprinkle cheese over top last few minutes of baking. Yield: 6 servings.

Mrs. Meryl R. Fishback, Franklin Jr. H.S.
Yakima, Washington

FISH GOURMET

3 lb. halibut, ¾-inch thick
⅓ c. lime or lemon juice
¼ c. butter, melted
½ t. salt
¼ t. fresh ground pepper
1 t. sweet basil
Generous pinch of marjoram
1 can frozen cream of shrimp soup, thawed
1 c. sour cream
½ c. tiny fresh water shrimp
3-4 green onions and tops, thinly sliced

Wash, dry and cut fish into 6 pieces; trim. Place in shallow baking dish. Pour the lime juice over the top and soak for 30 minutes, turning once. Discard juice. Pour the butter over the fish and spread with seasonings. Broil 10 minutes, basting with butter mixture. Remove from heat; baste again. Cool. This can be done in advance and covered with foil. Mix soup and sour cream; spoon over fish. Bake 30 minutes at 325°F. Serve from baking dish. Garnish with shrimp and tiny pieces of onion. Yield: 6 servings.

Bertha Boyd, University H.S.
Los Angeles, California

LOBSTER-ARTICHOKE CASSEROLE

4 5-oz. lobster tails, cooked
1 8-oz. can artichoke hearts, drained
Butter or margarine
1 green pepper, cut into strips
1 sm. onion, peeled and quartered
¼ c. unsifted all-purpose flour
1¾ t. salt
½ t. paprika
⅛ t. pepper
2½ c. milk
1 egg, beaten
½ T. Worcestershire sauce
1 t. lemon juice
2 c. hot seasoned mashed potatoes

Remove lobster meat from shells; cut into bite-size chunks. Cut artichoke hearts in half; gently toss with lobster and set aside. In hot butter in a saucepan, saute green pepper and onion until tender, about 5 minutes. Remove from heat. Lift out vegetables; combine with lobster mixture. Into same saucepan, add ⅓ cup butter. When melted, add the flour, salt, paprika and pepper and stir until smooth. Gradually stir in milk. Bring to boiling, stirring; boil 1 minute. Stir some of hot mixture into egg; pour back into saucepan. Cook, stirring, over low heat about 5 minutes, or until thickened. Add lobster mixture along with rest of the ingredients, except mashed potatoes; mix well. Gently reheat. Spoon into 4 15-ounce casseroles. Put mashed potatoes into pastry bag, using rosette tip; pipe around edge of each casserole. Run casserole under broiler 2 to 3 minutes or just until potatoes are nicely browned. Yield: 4 servings.

Mildred M. Newbold, Sparks Jr. H.S.
Sparks, Nevada

LOBSTER CASSEROLE

¼ lb. butter or margarine, melted
⅓ pkg. oyster crackers, crushed
1 can frozen shrimp soup, thawed
½ lb. lobster meat
1 t. Parmesan cheese
Parsley (garnish)

Combine butter and crushed crackers. Stir in the thawed shrimp soup. Fold in the lobster and cheese. Bake at 350°F. for forty minutes. Serve garnished with fresh parsley. Yield: 5 servings.

Dorothy B. Tobey, Hampton Jr. H.S.
Hampton, New Hampshire

LOBSTER CASSEROLE SUPREME

½ c. butter
1 c. flour
1½ t. salt
8 c. milk
4 c. Cheddar cheese, shredded
5 c. lobster, chopped
⅔ c. ripe olives, chopped
1 8-oz. can sliced mushrooms
8 hard-cooked eggs, sliced
3 c. packaged biscuit mix

Melt butter in large saucepan; remove from heat. Stir in flour and salt until smooth. Gradually add 7 cups of the milk, blending well. Cook and stir over low heat until thickened. Stir in 2 cups of cheese; cook until melted. Add lobster, olives, mushrooms and hard-cooked eggs. Place mixture in a 2-quart casserole dish. Add remaining 1 cup of milk to biscuit mix. Roll dough ¼-inch thick. Cover with remaining 2 cups cheese. Roll dough as for a jelly roll. Cut into ½-inch slices. Cover lobster mixture with biscuits. Bake at 425° F. for 15 minutes, or until biscuits are browned. Yield: 16 servings.

Phyllis J. Hill, Paradise Valley H.S.
Phoenix, Arizona

LOBSTER-MUSHROOM CASSEROLE

1 lb. mushrooms, sliced
5½ T. butter
3 T. flour
1 t. salt
⅛ t. paprika
1½ c. milk
2 c. lobster meat
2 egg yolks
½ c. cream
½ c. Sherry
⅓ c. bread crumbs
1½ T. butter

Saute mushrooms for 2 minutes in 4 tablespoons butter. Add flour, salt and paprika; cook stirring constantly over low heat for 1 minute. Slowly stir in milk; cook and stir for 3 minutes. Add lobster. Beat egg yolks with cream and add to meat mixture. Add Sherry; stir and cook until well heated. Pour into buttered casserole. Cover with bread crumbs. Dot with remaining butter. Bake at 450°F. for 10 minutes. Yield: 4-6 servings

Mrs. Ruth Schaffer, Annville-Cleona H.S.
Annville, Pennsylvania

STUFFED LOBSTER SUPREME

8 rock lobster tails
9 T. butter
4 T. flour
1 t. salt
1 t. paprika
Few grains of cayenne pepper
2 c. light cream
2 T. lemon juice
¼ c. cracker crumbs
¼ c. Parmesan cheese

Cook lobster in boiling salted water; drain. With scissors cut meat away and dice; save shells. Saute lobster meat in 8 tablespoons butter 2 or 3 minutes; blend in flour, salt, paprika, cayenne. Slowly stir in cream; cook until mixture thickens and boils 1 minute. Stir in lemon juice. Spoon filling into lobster shells; sprinkle lightly with mixture of cracker crumbs, cheese and 1 tablespoon melted butter. Bake in shallow pan at 450°F. for 12 minutes. Yield: 8 servings.

Mrs. LaVerne Macy, Fort Morgan H.S.
Fort Morgan, Colorado

LOBSTER PIE

1 c. milk
1 T. flour
6 T. butter, melted
2 c. condensed mushroom soup
1½ lb. boiled lobster, cut in 2-inch pieces
½ pt. tomalley
1 c. fine bread crumbs
¼ c. buttered crumbs

Combine milk and flour and cook until creamy. Add 2 tablespoons butter. Combine the sauce, mushroom soup and lobster. Pour into large shallow casserole. Combine tomalley, remaining butter, and fine crumbs. Form into patties ¼-inch thick. Cover lobster mixture with patties. Top with buttered crumbs. Bake at 375°F. for 30 minutes until a golden brown. Yield: 6 servings.

Olga E. Sachs, Melrose H.S.
Melrose, Massachusetts

LOBSTER PIE

3 1-lb. lobsters, boiled
½ c. butter, melted
2 T. flour
½ t. dry mustard
½ t. salt
Dash of pepper
1 c. milk
½ c. cream
4 egg yolks
4 slices bread, buttered

Remove meat from lobster, reserving the tomalley. Cook lobster slowly in ¼ cup butter until heated. Heat the remaining ¼ cup butter in saucepan; add flour, salt, pepper and mustard. Cook until thickened, about one minute, stirring constantly. Remove from heat and slowly blend in the butter drained from the lobster meat. Add milk and cream slowly; continue cooking and stirring. Beat egg yolks. Gradually stir at least half of hot mixture into egg yolks, then blend into remaining mixture in saucepan. Cook 3 minutes over hot water until sauce is smooth and thick. Add the lobster and pour the mixture into a shallow 1½-quart casserole. Crumble buttered bread crumbs in coarse pieces. Add tomalley. Mix well and sprinkle over the pie. Bake 20 to 30 minutes in a 350°F. oven until brown. Yield: 4-6 servings.

Mrs. Sereen N. Taylor, Waterville H.S.
Waterville, Maine

ESCALLOPED OYSTERS

1 qt. oysters
Salt and pepper
1-1½ c. fresh cracker crumbs
5 T. butter
½ c. milk

Butter the sides of a 1½-quart casserole. Place a layer of oysters on bottom. Season with salt and pepper. Sprinkle generously with fresh cracker crumbs; dot with butter. Repeat until oysters have been used, ending with crumbs and butter. This can be prepared ahead of time and refrigerated for several hours. Pour milk over the top. Bake 45 minutes at 350°F. Yield: 8-10 servings.

Margaret S. Nelson, Delmar H.S.
Delmar, Delaware

BERTIE'S OYSTERONI

1½ c. celery, finely chopped
4 T. onion, finely chopped
4 T. butter, melted
4 T. flour
1 t. salt or to taste
2 c. milk
1 T. Worcestershire sauce
2 doz. lge. or 3 doz. sm. oysters
1½ c. macaroni, cooked
½ c. bread crumbs
¼ c. cheese, grated

Mix celery and onion. Blend butter, flour and salt. Add milk. Cook for 10 minutes slowly. Add Worcestershire sauce. Add vegetables and oysters. Arrange in buttered casserole, alternating layers with macaroni, and salting to taste. Top with bread crumbs and cheese. Bake at 350°F. until heated through and slightly brown on top, about 30 minutes. Yield: 8-10 servings.

Alberta Ball Bickerdike, East Pike School
Milton, Illinois

LAYERED SCALLOPED OYSTERS

½ c. stale bread crumbs
1 c. cracker crumbs
½ c. butter, melted
1 pt. oysters
Salt and pepper
¼ c. oyster liquor
2 T. cream

Mix bread and cracker crumbs in melted butter; put a thin layer in bottom of a shallow buttered baking dish. Cover with oysters and sprinkle with salt and pepper; add half each of oyster liquor and cream. Repeat layers and cover top with remaining c r u m b s. Bake 30 minutes at 425-450°F. NOTE: Do not make more than 2 layers of oysters, as inner layers will not be well cooked. Sprinkle each layer with mace, nutmeg, celery or parsley, if desired. Yield 4 servings.

This recipe submitted by the following teachers:
Mrs. Margaret P. Samson
Western Wayne Jointure H.S.
Lake Ariel, Pennsylvania
Mrs. Ruth William, Mt. Sterling H.S.
Mt. Sterling, Kentucky

OYSTERS AU GRATIN

5 slices buttered toast
1 pt. fresh oysters
1 c. American cheese, grated
2 eggs, beaten
½ c. milk
½ t. paprika
1 t. prepared mustard
Salt and pepper to taste

Place toast squares, oysters and cheese in layers in casserole. Add eggs to which milk and seasonings have been added. Bake at 375°F. for 30 minutes. Cover for a few minutes at first. Remove cover to allow to brown. Yield: 4-5 servings.

Mrs. Minnie G. Burke, Los Gatos H.S.
Los Gatos, California

OYSTER PUDDING CASSEROLE

6 slices buttered bread
1 pt. oysters
3 t. salt
Dash of cayenne pepper
½ lb. Cheddar cheese, chopped
3 eggs
½ t. mustard
¼ t. paprika
1½ c. milk

Put three slices buttered bread into ungreased casserole. Cover with oysters. Sprinkle with 2 teaspoons salt and cayenne and cover with cheese. Repeat layers. Beat eggs slightly; add mustard, paprika, 1 teaspoon salt and milk. Pour over ingredients in casserole. Bake in 350°F. oven for 30 or 40 minutes. Yield: 4-6 servings.

Carolyn M. Smet, Newmarket H.S.
Newmarket, New Hampshire

SCALLOPED CORN AND OYSTERS

¼ c. celery, finely chopped
1 can frozen condensed oyster stew, thawed
1 1-lb. can cream-style corn
2 c. med. cracker crumbs
1 c. milk
1 egg, slightly beaten
¼ t. salt
Dash of black pepper
2 T. butter, melted

Combine celery, oyster stew, corn, 1½ cup crumbs, milk, egg and seasonings. Pour into greased 1½-quart casserole. Mix butter with remaining cracker crumbs; sprinkle over top. Bake at 350°F. for 1 hour or until knife inserted halfway to center comes out clean. Yield: 8 servings.

Marlyce Zebley, Bellmar Jr. H.S.
Belle Vernon, Pennsylvania

SCALLOPED OYSTER CORN

4 c. cream-style corn
½ c. cream
1 t. salt
¼ t. pepper
16 med. canned oysters
3 c. cracker crumbs
½ c. butter, melted
1 c. liquid from oysters

Combine corn, cream, salt, pepper and oysters. Toss crumbs with melted butter. Layer crumbs and oyster mixture in a buttered casserole, beginning and ending with crumbs. Pour oyster liquid over all to moisten. Bake at 375°F. for 40 minutes. Yield: 8 servings.

Mrs. Avis E. Colgrove, Fort Lupton H.S.
Fort Lupton, Colorado

SCALLOPED CORN AND OYSTERS

5 c. coarse cracker crumbs
2 pt. oysters, drained
2 No. 2 cans whole-kernel corn, drained
1 c. butter or margarine, melted
⅔ c. milk or light cream
Salt and pepper

Place one-third of crumbs in a large buttered baking dish. Arrange layers of half the oysters and corn over the crumbs. Top with another third of crumbs; repeat layers. Combine butter and milk; pour over casserole. Season to taste. Bake at 350°F. for 40-45 minutes. Yield: 12 servings.

Mrs. Ruth Dow, Modesto H.S.
Modesto, California

SCALLOPED OYSTERS

½ c. butter or margarine, melted
1½ c. coarse cracker crumbs
1 pt. oysters and liquor
Paprika

Lightly mix cracker crumbs and butter. Place one half of buttered crumbs in baking dish. Pour oysters and oyster liquor over crumbs. Put remaining crumbs on top of oysters. Do not salt. Use dish or casserole large enough for only 1 layer, as this becomes soggy if more is used. Bake at 450°F. for 20 minutes. Sprinkle paprika on top. Yield: 4 servings.

Mrs. Ruth McLaughlin, New London Local H.S.
New London, Ohio

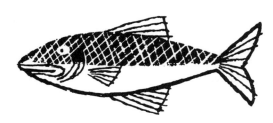

BAKED SALMON CASSEROLE

1 1-lb. can salmon, drained
1 egg
3 c. tomatoes
¼ t. pepper
2 T. sugar
½ t. salt
½ c. onion, diced
3 T. shortening
3½ c. bread crumbs
1 t. lemon juice
½ c. cheese, grated

Separate salmon into chunks; mix with all ingredients except cheese. Pour into greased baking dish; sprinkle with cheese. Bake at 375°F. until brown. Yield: 6 servings.

Margaret S. Yoder, Upper Perkiomen H.S.
East Greenville, Pennsylvania

BUBBLING FISH BAKE

¼ c. onion, chopped
2 T. butter or margarine
1 can condensed cream of mushroom soup
½ c. milk
1 c. sharp Cheddar cheese, shredded
2 c. cooked macaroni or noodles
1 8-oz. can salmon or tuna, drained and flaked
2 T. buttered bread crumbs

Cook onion in butter until tender Stir in soup, milk, ¾ cup cheese, macaroni and fish. Pour into a 1½-quart casserole. Top with bread crumbs and remaining cheese. Bake in a 350°F. oven for 30 minutes or until lightly browned and bubbling. Yield: 4 servings.

Mrs. Dalthea Black, Hopewell-Loudon H.S.
Bascom, Ohio

CASSEROLE OF SALMON

2 c. canned salmon, drained and flaked
2 T. minute Tapioca
¼ t. salt
Dash of pepper
Dash of paprika
1 c. milk
2 T. butter

Combine all ingredients. Pour into greased casserole. Bake at 400°F. for 25 minutes, stirring mixture twice during first 10 minutes of baking. NOTE: Small baking powder biscuits may be baked on top of mixture. Place biscuits on mixture after it has baked 10 minutes; return to oven and bake 12 to 15 minutes longer, or until biscuits are browned. Yield: 6 servings.

Mrs. Nannie C. Edwards, Oxford Area H.S
Oxford, Pennsylvania

FRIDAY RICE SPECIAL

1⅓ c. instant rice
½-⅔ c. milk
½ lb. process American cheese, thinly sliced
¾ t. salt
Dash of pepper
1 7¾-oz. can salmon
¼ c. stuffed olives, chopped
Stuffed olives, sliced (garnish)

Cook rice as label directs. In a double boiler combine milk, cheese, salt and pepper; heat, stirring constantly, until well blended and smooth. In a 1½-quart casserole arrange layers of cooked rice flaked fish, olives, and cheese sauce, ending with sauce. Bake uncovered at 350°F. for 30 minutes. NOTE: Tuna may be substituted for salmon. Yield: 6 servings.

This recipe submitted by the following teachers:
Mrs. Clara Mae Chatham, Smithville H.S.
Smithville, Oklahoma
Sister M. Alvera, St. Josephs Academy
Chickasha, Oklahoma
Catharine Ida Moyer, Salisbury H.S.
Allentown, Pennsylvania

DEVILED SALMON

1 can red salmon, flaked
1 c. undiluted tomato soup
¼ sm. onion
¼ sm. green pepper
3 T. butter
½ t. salt
1 t. prepared mustard
1 slice lemon with peel

Put salmon in a buttered casserole. Put all remaining ingredients into a blender. Blend until green pepper is chopped. Pour over salmon and bake at 350°F. for 30 minutes. Yield: 4 servings.

Nettie-Adelyn Landau, E. C. Best School
Fallon, Nevada

FRIDAY SALMON CASSEROLE

¾ c. rice
1 qt. boiling water
3 t. salt
2 T. parsley, chopped
4 T. fat, melted
4 T. flour
2 c. milk
½ t. celery salt
¼ t. nutmeg
2 T. lemon juice
1 c. American cheese, grated
1½ c. salmon, flaked

Cook rice in the boiling water with 2 teaspoons salt. Toss cooked rice with parsley; pour into a greased casserole. Blend fat and flour. Gradually stir in milk. Cook 20 minutes until thick. Remove sauce from heat; add remaining 1 teaspoon salt, seasonings, lemon juice and cheese. Stir until the cheese is melted. Add salmon. Pour mixture over rice. Bake at 375°F. for 30 minutes. Yield: 6 servings.

This recipe submitted by the following teachers:
Mrs. Lorraine Criswell, Prichard H.S.
Grayson, Kentucky
Winifred Bryant, Madison Heights H.S.
Anderson, Indiana

MACARONI SCALLOP

1 c. macaroni
1 6-oz. can salmon, flaked
1 T. onion, chopped
1 T. green pepper, chopped
Salt to taste
1 c. thin white sauce
Buttered crumbs

Cook macaroni in boiling salted water; drain and rinse. Alternate layers of macaroni and salmon in buttered casserole. Sprinkle each layer with onion, green pepper and salt. Pour white sauce over macaroni and top with buttered crumbs. Bake at 350°F. for 30 minutes. Yield: 6 servings.

Eileen Miller, McCook Sr. H.S.
McCook, Nebraska

JIFFY SALMON CASSEROLE

1 can pink salmon
½ can peas
2 eggs
½ can mushroom soup
1 can fried noodles

Combine all the ingredients in a buttered casserole, saving ½ cup of noodles for topping. Bake 20 minutes in a 350°F. oven. Yield: 4 servings.

Mrs. Olith Hamilton, Maple Valley H.S.
Nashville, Michigan

MUSHROOM-SALMON LOAF

2 c. salmon, drained and flaked
1½ c. dry bread crumbs
1 t. dried minced onion (opt.)
½ c. green pepper, minced (opt.)
2 eggs, slightly beaten
1 can cream of mushroom soup

Combine ingredients and mix lightly. Pack firmly into a greased small loaf pan. Bake in 350°F. oven for 1 hour. Pour off juice and turn out on a warm platter.

MUSHROOM SAUCE:

1 can cream of mushroom soup
¼ c. milk

Combine soup and milk; heat, stirring constantly. Pour over salmon loaf or serve in a side dish. Yield: 6 servings.

This recipe submitted by the following teachers:
Mrs. Arlene Bazzoon, Tarkington H.S.
Cleveland, Texas
Mrs. Alma Burtis, Williams H.S.
Williams, California

SALMON CREOLE

½ pkg. instant potatoes
1 med. onion, chopped
¾ c. green pepper, chopped
2 T. cooking oil
1 c. basic white sauce
1 1-lb. 1-oz. can creamed corn
1 1-lb. can salmon

Cook instant potatoes according to package directions; keep warm. Cook the onion and green pepper in oil for 10 minutes or until tender, but not brown. Stir in white sauce, corn and liquid from salmon. Mix and heat to simmering. Add flaked salmon and heat. Pour mixture into a 6-cup casserole; surround with a border of the mashed potatoes. If desired, place under broiler for 2 or 3 minutes. Garnish with a green pepper "flower." NOTE: For a pretty glaze on the potatoes, brush lightly with a mixture of 1 tablespoon milk and 1 tablespoon cooking oil before broiling. Yield: 4-6 servings.

Janice Walther, Lakota H.S.
Kansas, Ohio

SALMON-CHEESE PIE

2-2¼ c. sifted flour
3 t. baking powder
½ t. salt
⅓ c. shortening
2 eggs, beaten
½-⅔ c. milk
1 1-lb. can red salmon
1 T. onion, grated
2 T. salmon juice
¼ lb. Cheddar cheese, thinly sliced

Sift together flour, baking powder and salt. Cut in shortening until mixture resembles coarse meal. Combine eggs with milk and add to dry ingredients; mix only until all flour is moistened. Roll out two-thirds of dough on well floured pastry cloth to an 11-inch circle. Fit into 9-inch pie pan or layer cake pan. Flake salmon into bowl; add onion and salmon juice. Pour into dough lined pan; cover with cheese. Roll out remaining one-third of dough to a 7-inch circle; place on top of cheese. Bake at 375°F. for 20 to 30 minutes. Serve hot with vegetable sauce.

VEGETABLE SAUCE:

¼ c. butter
¼ c. flour
1 t. prepared mustard
2 c. milk
½ t. salt
2 c. any cooked vegetable or ¼ c. parsley, chopped

Melt butter in saucepan; blend in flour and mustard. Mix well. Gradually stir in milk. Cook over low heat until thick, stirring constantly. Add salt and green vegetable. Serve with salmon pie. Yield: 6 servings.

This recipe submitted by the following teachers:
Mrs. Elvira Schmidt, Siren H.S.
Siren, Wisconsin
Judith Graf, Greenfield H.S.
Milwaukee, Wisconsin

SALMON LASAGNA

¼ c. onion, chopped
⅓ c. green pepper, chopped
2 T. butter or margarine
1 6-oz. can tomato paste
¾ c. water
⅓ t. salt
⅛ t. pepper
½ t. basil
2 7¾-oz. cans salmon, drained and flaked
¼ lb. lasagna noodles, cooked
4 oz. Mozzarella cheese, finely sliced
¼ c. Parmesan cheese, grated

Saute onion and green pepper in butter until tender. Add tomato paste, water, seasonings and salmon. Layer noodles, salmon mixture and cheeses in a 9x9x2-inch baking dish, ending with cheese on top. Bake in a 375°F. oven for 25 minutes. Serve hot. Yield: 6 servings.

Mrs. Betty Lou James, Western H.S.
Russiaville, Indiana

SALMON LOAF

1 1-lb. can pink salmon
2 eggs, beaten
½ c. milk
1 c. soda cracker crumbs
Dash of onion salt
Dash of celery salt

Place salmon in mixing bowl; break into small pieces with a fork. Beat eggs; add milk and pour over salmon. Add cracker crumbs, onion and celery salt. Mix together and pour into 1½-quart oiled casserole. Bake 45 minutes at 350°F. Yield: 6-8 servings.

Mrs. Cecilia A. McLean, Becker H.S.
Becker, Minnesota

SALMON LOAF

1 1-lb. can salmon
1 can cream of celery soup
1 c. fine dry bread or cracker crumbs
2 eggs, slightly beaten
½ c. onion, chopped
1 T. lemon juice

Crush bones and flake salmon; mix thoroughly with other ingredients. Pack into greased loaf pan. Bake at 375°F. for 1 hour or until browned. Cool for 10 minutes; loosen sides and turn out on platter. This may be served with celery soup-parsley sauce. Yield: 4-6 servings.

Mrs. Iva W. Ammon, Beth Center Jr. H.S
Brownsville, Pennsylvania

SALMON LOAF

3 c. salmon
1-2 eggs
1 slice of onion, chopped
1 c. bread crumbs
1 t. salt
2 slices bacon, finely chopped
1 T. parsley, chopped
1 c. milk
¼ t. pepper

Mix all ingredients thoroughly; press into a greased bread pan. Bake at 350°F. for 30-40 minutes.

SAUCE:

2 T. butter or margarine
2 T. flour
¼ t. salt
Dash of pepper
1 c. milk
Chopped parsley or hard-cooked egg

Melt butter in saucepan over low heat. Blend in flour and seasonings. Add milk all at once. Cook quickly, stirring constantly until mixture thickens. Add parsley or egg. Serve over salmon loaf. Yield: 6-8 servings.

Mrs. Agnes Husenko, Mark Morris H.S.
Longview, Washington

SALMON AND NOODLE CASSEROLE

1 pkg. noodles
1 can cream of mushroom soup
1 can milk
½ c. cheese, cubed
1 med. can salmon
1 sm. bag potato chips, crushed

Cook noodles in boiling salted water until tender; drain and rinse. Heat together the soup, milk and cheese. Stir salmon in carefully. Put a layer of noodles in a greased casserole. Pour half the sauce on the noodles; add the remaining noodles and sauce. Top with crushed potato chips. Bake at 350°F. for 30 minutes. NOTE: Any chopped meat may be substituted for salmon. Yield: 6 servings.

Edna Mae Van Tuyl, Linn Rural H.S.
Linn, Kansas

SALMON AND RICE BALLS

1 lb. canned salmon
1 c. cooked rice
½ c. bread crumbs
1 T. onion, minced
2 t. green pepper, chopped
1 t. salt
2 eggs, slightly beaten
1 can cream of mushroom soup
½ c. water

Mix all ingredients except soup and water. Roll mixture into small balls. Place in shallow baking dish. Cover with soup and water. Bake 30 minutes at 350°F. Yield: 6 servings.

Myrtle B. Sellie, Ellis Jr. H.S.
Austin, Minnesota

SALMON SHELL CASSEROLE

1 8-oz. pkg. macaroni
¼ c. onion, minced
¼ c. parsley, minced
¼ c. butter or margarine, melted
⅓ c. enriched flour
½ t. salt
Dash of pepper
3 c. milk
1 c. sharp cheese, shredded
2 T. pimento, chopped
1 c. salmon, drained and flaked
Buttered bread crumbs

Cook macaroni in boiling, salted water until tender, 7 minutes. Drain. Saute onion and parsley in butter for 5 minutes, stirring occasionally. Stir in flour, salt and pepper. Add milk gradually, stirring constantly. Blend in cheese, then pimento and salmon. Add macaroni to salmon mixture and pour into lightly greased 2-quart casserole. Top with buttered crumbs. Bake at 350°F. for 25 minutes. Yield: 4-6 servings.

Mrs. Ruth Tamblyn, Muskegon Heights H.S.
Muskegon Heights, Michigan

SALMON SOUFFLE

2 T. butter
2 T. flour
1 can salmon, drained
1 c. milk
½ t. salt
4 eggs, separated

Melt butter; blend in flour. Flake salmon and add to butter mixture. Add milk and salt; cook for 3 minutes, stirring constantly. Add the hot mixture to beaten egg yolks. Fold in stiffly beaten egg whites. Pour mixture into buttered casserole. Bake in a 350°F. oven for 30-35 minutes. Serve immediately. Yield: 6 servings.

Aldeth T. Robinson, Gallia Academy H.S.
Gallipolis, Ohio

SALMON TETRAZZINI

½ c. shortening
½ c. flour
2 c. hot chicken broth or bouillon
½ t. salt
⅛ t. pepper
⅛ t. nutmeg
1 1-lb. can salmon
½ c. cream
½-¾ lb. spaghetti
1 sm. can mushrooms
2 T. butter
½ c. Parmesan cheese, grated
½ c. bread crumbs

In a saucepan melt shortening and stir in flour. Gradually stir in hot chicken broth and cook, stirring constantly until sauce is smooth and thickened. Stir in salt, pepper and nutmeg. Stir in liquid from salmon and cook for eight minutes, stirring constantly. Stir in cream and keep hot, stirring occasionally. Cook spaghetti in rapidly boiling salted water until tender; drain. Saute mushrooms in butter until lightly browned, stirring several times, 5-7 minutes. Mix half the sauce with spaghetti and mushrooms and pour into a baking dish or deep platter. Make a hole in center of spaghetti. Mix remaining sauce with the flaked salmon and pour into hole in spaghetti. Sprinkle with Parmesan cheese mixed with bread crumbs; brown lightly at 350°F. for 20 minutes. Yield: 10 servings.

Mrs. Ann Guth, Palisade H.S.
Palisade, Colorado

SCALLOPED SALMON

1 lge. can salmon
1 T. lemon juice
2 med. eggs, well beaten
½ t. salt
½ t. monosodium glutamate
¼ t. seasoned salt
¼ t. paprika
2 T. margarine, melted
1 c. cracker crumbs, finely chopped
¼ c. celery leaves, finely chopped
2 T. parsley, finely chopped
1 t. onion, finely chopped
1½ c. evaporated milk, undiluted

(Continued on Next Page)

Pour salmon into mixing bowl. Mince and mash bones and skin. Add all remaining ingredients to the salmon. Stir until well blended. Pour into a well greased casserole. Sprinkle with paprika. Set the casserole in a pan of hot water. Place in a 350°F. oven and bake about 1 hour or until mixture becomes set. Serve hot with creamed peas for a sauce. Yield: 4 servings.

Mrs. Lois Whitener, Peary Jr. H.S.
Gardena, California

SCALLOPED SCALLOPS

3 T. butter
3 T. flour
1 c. scalded milk
1 lb. scallops
½ c. thin cream
2 T. pimento
1 T. parsley, diced
Salt and pepper
½ c. buttered crumbs

Melt butter; blend in flour. Add milk and stir until thickened. Place scallops in ½ cup boiling water and simmer 10 minutes. Add scallops, water and cream to white sauce. Add pimento and parsley; season to taste. Pour into buttered casserole. Sprinkle with buttered crumbs. Bake 25 minutes at 350°F. Yield: 6 servings.

Mrs. Dorothy W. Gove, Wareham H.S.
Wareham, Massachusetts

CHINESE FRIED RICE WITH SHRIMP

¼ c. salad oil
1 c. white rice
1 envelope chicken noodle soup mix
2½ c. boiling water
½ lb. fresh or canned shrimp, cleaned and cut up
2 eggs, slightly beaten
¼ t. salt
Few grains of pepper
1½ T. soy sauce
2 sm. scallions, sliced

In a large skillet, heat 2 tablespoons salad oil and saute rice until golden brown. Combine soup mix and water and stir into rice. Cover and simmer 30 minutes or until liquid is absorbed. In another skillet, heat remaining oil and saute shrimp quickly, about 1 minute. Add eggs, stirring constantly, and cook 1-2 minutes. Add salt, pepper and soy sauce. Stir shrimp-egg mixture into soup-rice mixture; heat 2-3 minutes. Serve topped with scallions. Yield: 4-6 servings.

Ruth Metaweh, Villard H.S.
Villard, Minnesota

CORN AND SHRIMP SOUFFLE

6 lge. ears of corn
3 eggs, separated
½ t. salt
2 t. sugar
1 T. butter, melted
1½ lb. fresh shrimp, cooked

Scrape corn kernels from cob and stir into well-beaten egg yolks; add seasonings, butter and shrimp. Fold in stiffly beaten egg whites. Pour into greased souffle dish; cover and place in pan of hot water. Bake at 300°F. for 1 hour, or until firm. Remove cover the last 15 minutes of baking time to brown top. Yield: 6 servings.

Mrs. Winifred C. Hobart, Akron-Fairgrove H.S.
Fairgrove, Michigan

CREOLE SHRIMP

1 sm. onion, chopped
1 sm. green pepper, chopped
1 stalk celery, cut in strips
2 T. butter, melted
1 can tomato soup
½ c. water
1 sm. can mushrooms
2 c. cooked shrimp
Salt to taste
Rice, cooked

Saute onion, green pepper and celery in butter until tender. Add soup, water and mushrooms. Simmer until flavors are blended. Add shrimp; cook for 10 minutes. Add salt. Serve over hot steamed rice. Yield: 4 servings.

Mrs. Dorothy C. Daggert, Warsaw H.S.
Warsaw, Illinois

CREOLE SHRIMP IN RICE RING

2 lb. fresh shrimp
1 lge. onion, chopped
1 clove garlic, minced
4 stalks celery, chopped
2 T. salad oil
3½ c. tomatoes
Salt and pepper
2 bay leaves
1 sprig thyme
Dash of Tabasco sauce
2 c. rice
¼ c. butter, melted

Cook shrimp; clean, removing black line. Brown onion, garlic and celery in hot salad oil; add tomatoes, seasonings and Tabasco sauce. Cook 40 minutes. Add shrimp; cook 10 minutes. Cook rice. Add melted butter, salt and pepper; pack firmly in greased 10-inch ring mold. Let stand 30 minutes in pan of hot water or in moderate oven at 350°F. Unmold on hot platter; fill center with creole shrimp. Yield: 6-8 servings.

Betty Davis, Arapahoe H.S.
Arapahoe, Nebraska

DELUXE SHRIMP HOT DISH

2 cans cream of mushroom soup
1 8-oz. can mushrooms
½ c. Parmesan cheese
½ t. dry mustard
½ lb. carton sour cream
1-1½ lb. frozen shrimp
1 pkg. cut frozen broccoli
Paprika

Mix mushroom soup, mushrooms, Parmesan cheese, dry mustard and sour cream. Boil frozen shrimp for 10 minutes; add to the soup mixture. Layer the mixture in buttered casserole with the frozen broccoli. Garnish with paprika. Bake at 325°F. about 45 minutes. Serve with rice. Yield: 6 servings.

Grace Lamusga, Hosterman Jr. H.S.
Robbinsdale, Minnesota

DEVILED SHRIMP CASSEROLE

6 hard-cooked eggs, deviled
6 T. butter
4 T. flour
2 c. milk
1 t. salt
1½-2 c. shrimp
½ c. buttered cracker crumbs

Place deviled eggs, cut-side up, in the bottom of a lightly buttered casserole. Melt butter in saucepan; blend in flour and salt. Add milk all at once. Cook quickly, stirring constantly, until mixture thickens. Gently stir in the shrimp. Pour sauce mixture over the eggs. Sprinkle with buttered crumbs. Bake at 350°F. until bubbly. Yield: 6 servings.

Mrs. B. H. McPhee, Northview H.S.
Covina, California

MACARONI-SHRIMP CASSEROLE

1 2-oz. can mushroom stems and pieces
Milk
¼ c. onion, chopped
1 T. butter or margarine
1 can frozen condensed shrimp soup, thawed
1 c. cooked shrimp, sliced
½ c. sharp process cheese, shredded
1 T. parsley, chopped
Dash of pepper
2 c. cooked elbow macaroni
1 T. fine dry crumbs

Drain mushrooms, saving liquid. Add milk to liquid to make ¾ cup. Cook mushrooms and onion in butter until onion is tender. Add soup, liquid, shrimp, half the cheese, parsley, pepper and macaroni. Pour mixture into 1½-quart casserole. Top with crumbs and the rest of the cheese. Bake at 375°F. for 30 minutes. Sprinkle with more parsley, if desired. Yield: 4 servings.

Mrs. Joan Quilling, Central H.S.
Superior, Wisconsin

FRIDAY SHRIMP

1 lb. frozen shrimp
2 T. butter
1 can frozen shrimp soup
1½ c. instant rice
1½ c. water
1 t. salt
2 T. butter
1 pkg. frozen peas

Prepare frozen shrimp according to directions on package. Melt butter in electric fry pan; add shrimp and shrimp soup. Boil water, salt and 1 tablespoon butter in saucepan; add rice and allow to stand for 12 minutes. Prepare frozen peas according to directions on box; add 1 tablespoon butter. Surround shrimp in fry pan with alternate layers of rice and peas. Yield 4-6 servings.

Mrs. Mary Eriksen, Brandywine Heights H.S.
Topton, Pennsylvania

SHRIMP CASSEROLE

¾ lb. cooked shrimp
½ c. celery, chopped
¼ c. green pepper, chopped
3 T. onion, chopped
5 T. butter or other fat, melted
6 T. flour
1 t. salt
1 can mushroom soup
1½ c. milk
¼ c. dry bread crumbs

Cut large shrimp in half. Cook vegetables in 4 tablespoons butter until tender; blend in flour and salt. Combine soup and milk; add to vegetable mixture and cook until thick, stirring constantly. Add shrimp and pour into a well greased casserole. Combine remaining butter and crumbs; sprinkle over top of casserole. Bake at 400°F. for 10 minutes or until brown. Yield: 6 servings.

Ruth Adams, Claymont H.S.
Claymont, Delaware

SHRIMP CASSEROLE

¾ c. onion, chopped
¾ c. green pepper, chopped
1 c. raw rice
2 lb. raw shrimp or 1 lb. cooked shrimp
1 can condensed tomato soup
1 c. cream
½ c. Sherry
Pinch of salt
3 T. cooking oil
1 T. lemon juice
½ c. sliced almonds
Paprika

Saute onion and green pepper. Mix with rice and shrimp. Add tomato soup, cream, Sherry and salt; mix well. Put in casserole and sprinkle with cooking oil, lemon juice, almonds and paprika. Bake at 350°F. for 1 hour. Yield: 4-6 servings.

Mrs. Eva Huston, Edmunds Jr. H.S.
Burlington, Vermont

SHRIMP CASSEROLE

1 7-oz. pkg. noodles
1 sm. can pimentos
½ lb. cheese, grated
1 can shrimp

Partially cook noodles. Drain, saving ½ cup liquid. Add remaining ingredients to noodles including the ½ cup liquid. Bake at 350°F. for 30 minutes. Yield: 6-8 servings.

Mrs. Ann Nesshoefer, Mallard Community H.S.
Mallard, Iowa

SHRIMP CASSEROLE BAKE

8 slices day old bread
2 c. shrimp, cooked or canned
1 3-oz. can mushrooms, drained
½ lb. sharp American cheese, grated
3 eggs
2 c. milk
½ t. salt
½ t. dry mustard
Pepper and paprika to taste

Butter each slice of bread; cut in cubes. Place half the cubes in a 8x11x12-inch baking dish. Add shrimp, mushrooms and half the cheese. Add remaining bread and cheese. Beat together eggs, milk and seasonings; pour over casserole. Bake at 325-350°F. for 40-45 minutes. NOTE: Ground ham may be used in place of shrimp. Yield: 6 servings.

Mrs. Vera Graham, Enderlin H.S.
Enderlin, North Dakota

SHRIMP CASSEROLE SPECIAL

2 lb. raw shrimp
⅓ c. onion, finely chopped
2 garlic cloves, put through a press
2 T. butter
1 c. raw long grain white rice
3½ c. cooked tomatoes
2 c. consomme
1 piece of bay leaf
3 T. parsley, chopped
½ t. cloves
½ t. marjoram
1 t. chili powder
Few grains of cayenne
1 T. salt
⅛ t. pepper

Cook shrimp for 6-8 minutes. Drain; shell and cool. Saute onion and garlic puree in butter. Place mixture in a 3-quart casserole. Add shrimp, rice, tomatoes, consomme and seasonings. Stir to blend. Cover tightly; bake 1 hour and 15 minutes at 350°F. Yield: 6 servings.

Laurel A. Rizzi, San Juan H.S.
Citrus Heights, California

SHRIMP CASSEROLE WITH WILD RICE

1 can cream of mushroom soup
2 T. green pepper, chopped
2 T. onion, chopped
2 T. butter, melted
1 T. lemon juice
2 c. cooked wild rice
½ t. Worcestershire sauce
1 t. dry mustard
¼ t. pepper
½ c. cheese, cubed
½ lb. uncooked shrimp, cleaned

Combine all ingredients. Pour into 1½-quart casserole and bake at 375°F. for 30-35 minutes. Yield: 4 servings.

Mrs. Josephine Rummler, Belding Area Schools
Belding, Michigan

SHRIMP AND CHEESE CASSEROLE

6 slices bread
½ lb. Old English cheese, sliced
1 lb. prepared shrimp, cooked
¼ c. margarine, melted
3 whole eggs, beaten
½ t. dry mustard
Salt to taste
1 pt. milk

Break bread in pieces about size of quarter. Break cheese into bite size pieces. Arrange shrimp, bread and cheese in several layers in greased casserole. Pour melted butter over layers. Combine eggs, mustard and salt. Add the milk. Mix and pour over ingredients in casserole. Refrigerate, covered, for at least 3 hours or overnight. Bake 1 hour in 350°F. oven, covered. NOTE: If you increase amount of shrimp, you improve the dish. When doubling the recipe, use 3 pounds of prepared shrimp. Yield: 4-6 servings.

Mrs. Rex Todd Withers, Chief, Home Economics
and Family Life Education Service
Lansing, Michigan

SHRIMP AND CHEESE CASSEROLE

⅓ c. butter
⅓ c. flour
3 c. milk
2 c. sharp American cheese, grated
2 lb. boiled shrimp, peeled and drained
½ t. salt
½ t. pepper
½ c. bread crumbs
Garlic to taste

Melt butter; blend in flour. Add milk. Cook, stirring constantly until sauce thickens. Add 1½ cup cheese, shrimp, salt and pepper. Turn into buttered baking dish; sprinkle top with bread crumbs mixed with remaining cheese. Bake at 400°F. for 20 minutes. Yield: 8-10 servings.

Evelyn Cotney, Northeast District Supervisor
Home Economics Education
Montevallo, Alabama

SHRIMP CREOLE

1½ green peppers, diced
3-4 cloves garlic, minced
3 lge. onions, chopped
6 T. salad oil
1 T. salt
⅛ t. pepper
½ t. dried rosemary
½ t. paprika
6 dashes of Tabasco sauce
2 lge. cans tomatoes
3 lb. cleaned shrimp
4 c. seasoned, cooked rice
1 c. parsley, chopped

Saute pepper, garlic and onions in oil. Add seasonings and tomatoes; simmer for 15 minutes, stirring occasionally. Add shrimp and cook until shrimp turn pink. Serve from skillet or platter surrounded by rice and parsley. Yield 6-8 servings.

Mrs. Ann W. Allen, Martinsville H.S.
Martinsville, Indiana

SHRIMP CREOLE

½ c. onion, chopped
½ c. green pepper, chopped
½ c. celery, chopped
1 sm. clove garlic, minced
½ c. margarine
1 lge. can stewed tomatoes
1 c. tomato juice
½ c. tomato paste
3 t. salt
1 bay leaf
2 t. sugar
2 t. Worcestershire sauce
2 cans shrimp

Saute onion, green pepper, celery and garlic in margarine over medium heat for 5 minutes. Add tomatoes, juice, paste and seasonings. Cook uncovered for 30-40 minutes longer, stirring occasionally. Add shrimp during last five minutes of cooking. Serve with hot buttered rice. Yield: 6-8 servings.

Mrs. Rhoda Lubetkin, Columbia H.S.
Maplewood, New Jersey

SHRIMP CREOLE

1 lb. shrimp, cooked and deveined
½ c. onion, chopped
¼ garlic clove, minced
½ c. celery, chopped
⅓-½ c. green pepper, chopped
2 T. butter or margarine
1 can tomato puree
2 c. canned tomatoes
2 c. water
½ t. Worcestershire sauce
½ t. Tabasco sauce
½ t. salt
1½ c. uncooked rice, cooked

Saute onion, garlic, celery and green pepper in butter over moderate heat for 5 minutes. Add puree, tomatoes and water; simmer for 10 minutes. Add sauces and salt; simmer for 1 hour. Add shrimp for the last 10 minutes of cooking time. Serve over rice in casserole. Yield: 4 servings.

This recipe submitted by the following teachers:
Jean Zink, Chrisman H.S.
Chrisman, Illinois
Mrs. Virginia H. Culbertson, Mid-Carolina H.S.
Prosperity, South Carolina

SHRIMP CREOLE DELUXE

½ c. onion, chopped
⅔ c. celery, chopped
⅔ c. green pepper, chopped
2 T. butter or margarine, melted
1 T. flour
¾ t. salt
⅛ t. cinnamon
⅛ t. nutmeg
Dash of pepper
1 1-pt. 2-oz. can tomato juice
1 8-oz. can tomato sauce
½ t. Worcestershire sauce
1½ T. vinegar or lemon juice
1½ t. brown sugar
2 lb. shrimp, cooked
2 c. rice, cooked

Saute onions, celery and green pepper in butter until tender. Combine flour, salt, cinnamon, nutmeg and pepper; stir into onion mixture. Gradually add tomato juice and tomato sauce. Add Worcestershire sauce, vinegar and brown sugar. Simmer for 15-20 minutes. Add shrimp and heat. Serve over cooked rice. Yield: 8 servings.

SHRIMP CREOLE FOR A CROWD:

2 c. onion, chopped
2 c. celery, chopped
2½ c. green pepper, chopped
¼ c. butter or margarine, melted
¼ c. flour
2 T. salt
1 t. cinnamon
1 t. nutmeg
½ t. pepper
2 1-qt. 14-oz. cans tomato juice
3 8-oz. cans tomato sauce
2 t. Worcestershire sauce
3 T. vinegar or lemon juice
¼ c. brown sugar
10-12 lb. shrimp, cooked
20 c. rice, cooked

To prepare, follow same method as above, simmering for 30 minutes before adding shrimp. NOTE: This may be frozen. Yield: 50 servings.

Mrs. Sarah B. Plumb, Middlesex H.S.
Middlesex, New Jersey

SHRIMP DE JONGHE

1 lge. clove garlic
¾ c. butter
1 t. salt
1 pinch of tarragon
1 pinch of majoram
1 c. fine bread crumbs
1 c. dry Sherry
1 lb. cooked shrimp
Chopped parsley

Mash garlic until almost paste; add butter, salt and spices. Cream together until well blended. Add crumbs and Sherry; blend. In buttered baking dish alternate shrimp and bread crumb mixture, sprinkling with parsley. Bake in 40°F. oven for 20-25 minutes. Yield: 6 servings.

Mrs. Dorothy Maxwell, Westville H.S.
Westville, Illinois

SHRIMP FONDUE

4 slices bread
1 c. cooked shrimp
¼ c. mayonnaise
2 T. onion, chopped
½ green pepper, chopped
1 c. celery, finely sliced
2 eggs
1½ c. milk
½ t. salt
¼ t. pepper
½ c. mushroom soup
½ c. grated Cheddar cheese
Paprika

Cut half of the bread into cubes; arrange them in a deep 9-inch square greased baking dish. Mix the shrimp, mayonnaise, onion, green pepper and celery and spread over the cubed bread. Trim crusts from the remaining 2 slices of bread and place over shrimp mixture. Beat eggs slightly; stir in milk, salt and pepper. Pour over bread. Let stand 1 hour. Bake at 325°F. for 15 minutes. Remove from oven and spoon the undiluted soup over the top. Sprinkle with cheese and paprika. Return to oven and continue baking 1 hour longer. Yield: 6 servings.

Mary Jane Jacobs, Perris Valley Jr. H.S.
Perris, California

SHRIMP AND RICE

1 9-oz. pkg. frozen shrimp
2 c. cooked rice
2 c. light cream
3 T. catsup
2 T. butter, melted
1 T. Worcestershire sauce
¼ t. Tabasco sauce

Cook shrimp according to package directions. Mix all ingredients in casserole and bake 45 minutes at 350°F. Yield: 4-6 servings.

Judith Unze, Elk River H.S.
Elk River, Minnesota

SHRIMP AND RICE

1 t. onion, chopped
2 T. butter
1 lb. cooked and cleaned shrimp
1 c. hot boiled rice
⅔ c. light cream
½ t. salt
¼ t. celery salt
3 T. tomato catsup

Cook onion in butter for 5 minutes, stirring constantly. Add shrimp, rice and cream. When thoroughly heated, add salt, celery salt and tomato catsup. Simmer until cream is absorbed, or put in casserole and bake for 20 minutes at 350°F. Yield: 4 servings.

Elsa Graham, Moorestown Jr. H.S.
Moorestown, New Jersey

SHRIMP MARENGO

3½ lb. shrimp
7 slices bacon
1 clove garlic, crushed
1 c. onions, chopped
1 lb. mushrooms, wiped and sliced
1 35-oz. can Italian tomatoes
1 6-oz. can tomato paste
1 10½-oz. can consomme
1¼ t. sweet basil
1 t. monosodium glutamate
1¼ t. oregano
1 T. sugar
6 T. prepared mustard
3 drops liquid hot pepper
¼ c. flour

Cook the shrimp 7 minutes in lots of water; cut bacon and fry until crisp. Remove bacon and reserve. Saute shrimp in bacon drippings with garlic. Add onions and mushrooms; saute a few minutes longer. Pour in tomatoes, tomato paste and consomme. Add seasonings. Cook 10 minutes, stirring often; taste for seasoning and correct if needed. Mix flour with enough cold water to make a smooth paste. Stirring briskly, add mixture to the shrimp mixture and cook one minute. This dish should be prepared in advance, as it improves with a stay in the refrigerator. Yield: 8 servings.

Lillian Mattson, Moses Lake H.S.
Moses Lake, Washington

SHRIMP-TOMATO CASSEROLE

2 c. cooked shrimp, shredded
2 c. cooked rice
1 c. mayonnaise
2 T. onion, chopped
1 t. salt
¼ t. pepper
Dash of Tabasco
Dash of paprika
1 8-oz. can seasoned tomato sauce
6-8 med. tomatoes

Combine all ingredients except tomatoes. Fill hollowed out tomato shells with mixture. Bake at 350°F. for 30 minutes. Yield: 6-8 servings.

Mrs. Vera Moe, Pierceton H.S.
Pierceton, Indiana

SHRIMP AND NOODLE CASSEROLE

⅓ c. margarine
⅓ c. flour
2 c. milk
Salt and pepper
2 c. Cheddar cheese, grated
1 8-oz. pkg. noodles, cooked
2 c. small deveined shrimp
2 c. whole-kernel corn, cooked
1 6-oz. can sliced mushrooms
2 T. buttered crumbs

Make a cream sauce with margarine, flour and milk, adding salt and pepper to taste. Stir in cheese, stirring until cheese melts. Add the noodles, shrimp, corn and mushrooms to sauce. Blend and pour into greased casserole. Top with buttered crumbs. Bake 30 minutes in a 400°F. oven Yield: 6 servings.

Jo Ann Staff, Choteau H.S.
Choteau, Montana

SWEET AND PUNGENT FRIED SHRIMP

SAUCE:
1 9-oz. can crushed pineapple
½ c. green pepper, finely chopped
⅓ c. pimento, finely chopped
1 clove garlic, minced
½ c. vinegar
½ c. sugar
½ t. salt
1 T. soya sauce
3 dashes Tabasco sauce
¾ c. cold water
3 T. cornstarch

Combine all ingredients except ¼ cup cold water and cornstarch; bring mixture to a boil. Blend cornstarch and water; stir into sauce. Boil for 3 minutes.

SHRIMP:
1 lb. shrimp
½ c. flour
½ t. salt
2 T. water
1 egg, beaten
Fat or oil

Cook shrimp; shell and clean. Add flour, salt and water to egg; stir until smooth. Dip shrimp in batter; fry in deep fat until golden. Drain. Arrange shrimp with hot sauce in serving dish. Serve with rice or noodles. Yield: 4 servings.

Mrs. Eugenia Holderith, Franklin Schools
Franklin, New Jersey

SWEET AND PUNGENT SHRIMP

1 lb. fresh, canned or frozen shrimp
1 9-oz. can sliced or chunk-style pineapple
½ c. brown sugar
½ c. vinegar
2 T. soy sauce
1¼ c. water
3 T. cornstarch
1 green pepper, cut in strips
1 tomato, cut in wedges

Cook and clean shrimp. Drain pineapple, reserving syrup. Combine pineapple syrup, brown sugar, vinegar, soy sauce and 1 cup water. Bring to a boil, stirring until sugar is dissolved. Combine ¼ cup cold water and cornstarch; add to hot syrup mixture, stirring constantly until thick. Add green pepper, tomato and shrimp; heat thoroughly. Serve on rice or noodles. Yield: 6 servings.

Mrs. Jerrard Gould, Seymour Jr. H.S.
Seymour, Connecticut

FILET OF SOLE PANE

1 4½-oz. jar sliced mushrooms, drained
3 T. melted butter or margarine
½ c. chopped pecans
1½ lb. sole fillets
1 egg, well beaten
¼ c. milk
½ t. salt
¾ c. fine bread crumbs
Parsley and lemon slices

Saute mushrooms in butter until lightly browned. Stir in pecans; sprinkle lightly with salt and pepper. Spread mixture on fillets. Roll tightly and skewer with toothpicks. Combine egg, milk and salt. Dip fish in egg mixture then roll in bread crumbs. Place in well greased 8-inch square casserole. Bake in preheated 400°F. oven about 20 minutes or until fish flakes easily. Garnish with parsley and lemon slices. Yield: 6 servings.

Photograph for this recipe on page 113

THOMPSON STREET FISH AND RICE

2 c. water
1 t. salt
1 c. uncooked rice
1 lge. Bermuda onion
2 T. butter
¾ t. oregano
6 lge. peeled tomato slices
½ t. salt
Black pepper
1 lb. sole fillets
1 t. paprika
1 T. lemon juice
1 8-oz. can tomato juice
8 slices American cheese

Combine water, salt and rice in 2-quart saucepan. Bring to a vigorous boil. Turn heat as low as possible. Cover; simmer for 14 minutes. Remove from heat, but leave lid on for 10 minutes. Cook onion in butter until soft. Arrange in greased casserole; pour rice over onion. Sprinkle with oregano. Top with tomato slices. Season with salt and pepper. Cut fish fillets into serving pieces; spread over tomato layer. Sprinkle with paprika and lemon juice. Pour tomato juice over; cover with cheese. Bake 30 minutes at 350°F. or until cheese bubbles and top is brown. Yield: 6 servings.

Shannon Bauman, Riverside H.S.
Painesville, Ohio

GREEK FISH

4-5 slices fillet of sole
Seasoned salt
Pepper
Juice of ½ lemon
3 T. butter
1 17-oz. can peas
2 t. cornstarch
1 c. stewed tomatoes
8-10 small cooked whole onions

Roll up fish into individual rolls. Arrange in baking dish. Sprinkle with seasoned salt, pepper and lemon juice. Dot with 1 tablespoon butter. Bake at 425°F. for 5 minutes. Melt 2 tablespoons butter in saucepan; add ¼ cup liquid from the peas, ½ teaspoon seasoned salt, the cornstarch and stewed tomatoes. Simmer 5 minutes. Add peas and onions. Spoon over and around fish. Bake 10 minutes more, or until fish is tender. Yield: 4-5 servings.

Polly Powell, Nordhoff H.S.
Ojai, California

POACHED LAKE SUPERIOR TROUT

1 3 to 4-lb. dressed lake trout
½ c. milk
½ c. water
4 slices lemon
½ t. allspice
½ t. salt
1 sprig parsley
2 c. white sauce
1½ T. lemon juice
2 hard-cooked eggs, chopped

Place fish in skillet; add milk, water, lemon slices, allspice, salt and parsley. Cover and cook over low heat for 20 minutes until tender. Remove to hot platter. Combine white sauce, lemon juice and eggs; pour over fish. Yield: 6 servings.

Dorothy Maltby, Muskegon H.S.
Muskegon, Michigan

BASIC TUNA CASSEROLE

1 8-oz. pkg. elbow macaroni
2 4-oz. cans chunk-style tuna fish
1 8-oz. can cream of mushroom soup
Potato chips

Prepare macaroni according to package directions. Drain; rinse and place in 2-quart casserole. Add tuna and soup; mix well. Top with broken potato chips. Bake 30 minutes at 350°F. Yield: 4-6 servings.

Horma M. Lemon, Rudyard Township School
Rudyard, Michigan

MAIN DISH TUNA CASSEROLE

½ c. mayonnaise
2 T. flour
1½ c. milk
1 T. onion, finely chopped
½ t. salt
⅛ t. black pepper
1 6-oz. can tuna
1 T. lemon juice
3 c. cooked macaroni or noodles
1 can peas, drained
½ c. Cheddar cheese, shredded
Crushed potato chips

Blend mayonnaise and flour in saucepan; stir in milk gradually. Add onion, salt and pepper. Bring to a boil, stirring constantly. Sprinkle tuna with lemon juice in greased 1½-qt. casserole. Add macaroni, peas and cheese. Pour sauce over all. Cover with crushed potato chips. Bake in 350°F. oven for 30 minutes. Yield: 6 servings.

Mrs. Floyd Plake, Shawswick H.S.
Bedford, Indiana

TUNA-ASPARAGUS CASSEROLE

2 c. macaroni or noodles
1 can tuna, flaked
1 sm. can asparagus
¼ lb. sharp Cheddar cheese, shredded
1 can cream of mushroom soup

Cook noodles according to package directions; drain and rinse thoroughly. Place noodles in a greased 2-quart casserole. Add tuna, asparagus, half the cheese, and the mushroom soup; mix lightly. Put remaining cheese on top and bake at 350°F. until heated through and cheese is lightly browned on top, 20-30 minutes. Yield: 6 servings.

Sharon Lampman, Ruthton H.S.
Ruthton, Minnesota

TUNA CASSEROLE

1 c. macaroni, cooked
½ c. cheese, diced
1 can tuna
½ c. milk
1 c. potato chips, crushed
Salt (opt.)

Pour macaroni in casserole. Mix in cheese, tuna, milk and salt; cover with crushed potato chips. Bake in covered casserole at 375°F. for 30 minutes. Remove cover for last 10 minutes to brown top. Yield: 4 servings.

Barbara Gilhaus, ABL H.S.
Broadlands, Illinois

TUNA CONFETTI CASSEROLE

1 pkg. macaroni and cheese mix
2 c. hot cooked peas
1 7-oz. can tuna, flaked
1 can cream of celery soup
½ c. milk
2 T. pimento, chopped
½ t. salt

Prepare macaroni and cheese mix as package directs. Combine with remaining ingredients and place in greased casserole. Bake at 350°F. for 25 to 30 minutes. Yield: 4 servings.

Mrs. Patsy Sachse Edmunds, Crete-Monee H.S.
Crete, Illinois

TUNA-MACARONI CASSEROLE

1 c. macaroni, cooked
1 8-oz. can stewed tomatoes
1 8-oz. can green beans, drained
1 6-oz. can chunk-style tuna
Seasonings (opt.)
Bread crumbs (opt.)

Mix macaroni, undrained tomatoes, beans and tuna. Place mixture in a 1-quart casserole; top with seasonings or bread crumbs if desired. Bake at 350°F. for 30 minutes in a covered casserole. Yield: 4 servings.

Ellen F. Dow, Roaring Fork H.S.
Carbondale, Colorado

TUNA FISH CASSEROLE

2 T. onions, chopped
1 can mushroom soup
2 c. potato chips, crushed
1 can tuna fish
½ t. salt
½ t. pepper
2 c. cooked macaroni
½ c. cheese, shredded

Heat onions and mushroom soup. Put a layer of potato chips on bottom of greased baking dish. Combine all ingredients except cheese and chips. Put in the dish. Cover with a layer of cheese and a layer of potato chips. Bake at 350°F. for 30 minutes. Yield: 6 servings.

Nancy Newey, Grace H.S.
Grace, Idaho

TUNA-MACARONI CASSEROLE

1 can mushroom soup
1 c. milk
1 T. onion, chopped
1 T. pimento, chopped
2 T. green pepper
2 c. cooked elbow macaroni
1 can tuna fish
¼ lb. cheese

Combine soup, milk, onion, pimento and green pepper; cook over low heat. Add cheese and stir until melted. Mix macaroni and tuna fish; add cheese. Bake at 350°F. for 20-30 minutes. Yield: 6 servings.

Velma R. Dill, Williamsport School
Williamsport, Indiana

TUNA FISH CASSEROLE

1 c. dry macaroni
1 t. butter or margarine
⅓ c. milk
1 can cream of chicken soup
1 6-oz. can tuna fish
½ c. mixed vegetables or peas and carrots
1 t. onion, chopped (opt.)
Salt and pepper to taste
Potato chips, crushed (opt.)

Prepare macaroni by following instructions on box. Melt butter in bottom of casserole; add milk, soup, tuna and vegetables; mix. Onion may be added if desired. Add cooked macaroni and stir. Add salt and pepper to taste. Sprinkle crushed potato chips over top. Bake in 350°F. oven for about 30 minutes. Yield: 4 servings.

Mrs. Patricia T. Stealey, Mapletown Jr.-Sr. H.S.
Greensboro, Pennsylvania

TUNA-MACARONI CASSEROLE

2 T. onion, chopped
2 T. butter, margarine or oil
1 can condensed cream of celery soup
1 c. milk
1 7-oz. can tuna, drained and rinsed
1 t. salt
Dash of pepper
¼ t. whole celery seed
1 c. sharp Cheddar cheese, coarsely chopped
2 c. elbow macaroni, cooked

Saute onion lightly in hot butter. Gradually stir in soup and milk. Fold in tuna, seasonings and half the cheese. Mix in drained macaroni. Place in casserole and top with remaining cheese. Bake at 350°F. for 10-15 minutes until cheese melts and casserole is bubbly.

Mrs. Marie Della Penna, Jefferson Union H.S.
Richmond, Ohio

TUNA MEDITERRANEAN

1 c. commercial sour cream
½ t. ground oregano (opt.)
2 7-oz. cans tuna
2 c. cooked elbow macaroni
½ c. ripe olives, sliced
¾ c. mushrooms, sliced
¼ c. green pepper, chopped
¼ c. cashew nuts, chopped (opt.)
2 T. pimento, chopped (opt.)
1 c. American cheese, grated

Mix all ingredients except cheese. Spoon into a 1½-quart casserole. Sprinkle cheese on top. Bake at 350°F. for 25-30 minutes. NOTE: If desired, cheese topping may be omitted. Yield 4-5 servings.

This recipe submitted by the following teachers:
Mrs. Richard P. Menninger, Miamisburg H.S.
Miamisburg, Ohio
Marilyn Kaelke, Dysart H.S.
Peoria, Arizona
Betty Bielenberg, Jefferson Community H.S.
Jefferson, Iowa
Blanche N. Strother, Stratford H.S.
Stratford, Texas

VEGETABLE-TUNA CASSEROLE

1 lb. shell macaroni
1 can chunk-style tuna
1 can condensed cream of mushroom soup
¼ c. onions, diced
1 6-oz. pkg. frozen mixed vegetables
Salt and pepper
1 c. potato chips, crushed

Cook shell macaroni according to directions on package; drain. Add tuna, soup, onion, vegetables and seasonings; mix until combined. Pour mixture into a greased 2-quart baking dish. Top with potato chips. Bake in 350°F. oven for 15 minutes. Yield: 8 servings.

Marjorie Arseneau, Bismarck H.S.
Bismarck, Illinois

BUSY DAY TUNA CASSEROLE

1½ c. broken noodles
1 can cream of mushroom soup
½ c. evaporated milk
1 7-oz. can tuna, drained
1 c. process American cheese, grated
⅓ c. onion, chopped
1½ c. potato chips, broken

Cook noodles in unsalted water. Drain and mix with mushroom soup, evaporated milk, tuna, cheese and onion. Pour into greased 1½-quart casserole. Top with potato chips. Bake at 425°F. for 15 minutes.

Ann Erickson, Southeast Junior High
Iowa City, Iowa

CHILE-TUNA CASSEROLE

2 t. chili powder
3 T. cream
2 c. cooked noodles
1½ c. med. white sauce
1 c. American cheese, grated
¼ c. parsley, chopped
1 t. salt
¼ t. pepper
1 can tuna

Blend chili powder with cream; add to white sauce. Combine remaining ingredients in white sauce. Pour into a greased casserole and bake covered at 350°F. for 30 minutes. NOTE: If desired, 1 can mushroom soup plus enough milk to make 1½ cups soup may be substituted for white sauce. Yield: 6 servings.

Mrs. Carol Russell, Edgewood H.S.
Ellettsville, Indiana

CHURCH SUPPER TUNA BAKE

¼ c. green pepper, diced
1 c. celery, sliced
1 med. onion, chopped
1½ T. butter
1 can cream of mushroom soup
⅔ c. milk
1 c. process cheese, shredded
1 9¼-oz. can tuna, drained
1 8-oz. pkg. med. noodles, cooked and drained
8 T. mayonnaise
¼ c. pimento, chopped
⅓ c. slivered almonds, toasted

Cook green pepper, celery and onion in butter for 5 minutes. Blend soup and milk; add cheese. Heat and stir until cheese melts. Combine tuna, noodles, mayonnaise and pimento. Pour cheese sauce over mixture. Turn into greased casserole dish. Sprinkle almonds over the top. Bake at 400°F. for 30-35 minutes, or until hot and bubbly. NOTE: Chicken may be used instead of tuna. Yield: 8 servings.

Mrs. Ray Robertson, Madison H.S.
Madison, Nebraska

LAYERED TUNA CASSEROLE

1 6-oz. pkg. egg noodles
1 6½-oz. can tuna
1 can condensed cream of mushroom soup
1 soup can water
½ c. corn flake crumbs

Cook noodles according to package directions. Drain tuna and rinse with water. Dilute soup with 1 can of water. Spread half of noodles in bottom of casserole; cover with layer of flaked tuna. Spread remaining noodles as a third layer. Cover with remaining tuna. Pour diluted soup over all. Top with corn flake crumbs. Bake at 350°F. for 30 minutes. Yield: 4-6 servings.

Edna L. House, North Knox H.S.
Edwardsport, Indiana

DEEP SEA HOT DISH

1 8-oz. pkg. noodles
1 sm. can mushrooms
1 can tuna
1 No. 1 can asparagus tips
1 sm. green pepper, diced
1 c. Cheddar or American cheese, grated
½ t. salt
Few grains of pepper
1 c. white sauce
1 10-oz. can mushroom soup
½ c. liquid from asparagus

Cook the noodles in salted boiling water until nearly tender; drain. Add remaining ingredients, reserving some cheese for topping. Put into buttered baking dish and bake in 350°F. oven for 30-35 minutes. Yield: 10-12 servings.

Mrs. Isabelle Staley, Huron H.S.
Huron, South Dakota

EPICURE'S DELIGHT

2 c. noodles
2 T. butter, melted
1½ T. flour
¾ t. salt
1 c. milk
¾ c. canned asparagus tips, drained
¾ c. tuna, flaked
2 T. green pepper, minced
Small pinch of paprika
1 3-oz. can button mushrooms, drained
1 t. Angostura bitters
⅔ c. grated Cheddar or Parmesan cheese
Parsley

Cook noodles in salted boiling water for 12-14 minutes; drain. Rinse with cold water and drain. Blend butter and flour in a saucepan. Add ½ teaspoon salt; gradually stir in milk. Cook until mixture begins to bubble. Add all remaining ingredients except cheese and parsley; mix gently. Pour into buttered casserole; sprinkle with cheese. Bake at 350°F. for 40 minutes. Garnish with parsley. Yield: 4-6 servings.

Juanita M. Driscoll, Newton South H.S.
Newton, Massachusetts

POT LUCK TUNA CASSEROLE

6 oz. med. noodles
1 can tuna
¼ c. pimento, chopped
1 t. salt
1 can mushroom soup
½ c. milk
¾ c. potato chips, crushed

Prepare noodles according to package directions. Place half of potato chips on bottom of casserole dish. Combine rest of ingredients; pour into casserole and sprinkle remaining potato chips on top. Bake at 350°F. for 30 minutes. NOTE: Any leftover vegetables may be added if desired. Yield: 6 servings.

Rita Higgins, Southeastern H.S.
South Charleston, Ohio

LAYERED HOT DISH

1 box Creamettes, cooked
1 can asparagus, drained
Asparagus liquid
¼ lb. Cheddar cheese, grated
1 can tuna
1 med. green pepper, finely cut
1 can mushroom soup
½ c. cream
Buttered crumbs

Place half of Creamettes in bottom of buttered casserole. Add layers of asparagus, cheese, tuna and green peppers. Add rest of Creamettes. Combine mushroom soup with asparagus liquid; add the cream. Pour over layered mixture and top with buttered crumbs. Bake one hour at 350°F. Yield: 8-10 servings.

Nima Fogelberg, Red Wing H.S.
Red Wing, Minnesota

QUICK TUNA BAKE

1 can cream of mushroom soup
¾ soup can milk
½ t. salt
Dash of pepper
1 8-oz. pkg. noodles, cooked
1 7-oz. can tuna, flaked
Buttered crumbs or crushed potato chips

Mix soup, milk and seasonings; add noodles and tuna. Pour into buttered casserole. Top with crumbs; bake at 350°F. for 20-30 minutes. NOTE: If desired, 2 sliced hard-cooked eggs may be added before baking. Yield: 6 servings.

Pearle Peterson, Perth Amboy H.S.
Perth Amboy, New Jersey

TOMATO TOPPED TUNA CASSEROLE

1 pkg. crinkly egg noodles
2 qt. boiling water
1 T. salt
2 cans tuna
1 can condensed mushroom soup
1 c. milk
1 c. Cheddar cheese, grated
1 tomato, sliced
Bread crumbs

Cook noodles in boiling water with salt for 4-6 minutes. Drain and rinse with cold water. Mix noodles with tuna, mushroom soup, milk and cheese. Pour into buttered casserole. Garnish with tomato slices and crumbs. Bake 15 minutes at 375°F. Yield: 6-8 servings.

Mrs. Bonnie Miller, Woodston Rural H.S.
Woodston, Kansas

TUNA-ASPARAGUS-NOODLE

2 c. milk
2 T. flour
2 T. butter
1 family-size can chunk tuna
1 can asparagus, drained
1 8-oz. pkg. noodles, cooked
4 hard-cooked eggs, cut-up
1 can mushroom soup
½ green pepper, chopped
1 cup cheese, grated
½ t. salt
1 cup buttered bread crumbs

Make a white sauce with the milk, flour and butter. Combine all ingredients except bread crumbs in buttered casserole. Top with bread crumbs. Bake 1 hour at 325°F. Yield: 8 servings.

Mary Jane Elliott, Constantine H.S.
Constantine, Michigan

TUNA-NOODLE CASSEROLE

½ lb. noodles
1 sm. can tuna
¾ t. onion powder
2 c. milk
Potato chip crumbs

Cook noodles in boiling salted water until tender; drain. Put in 1½-quart casserole. Stir in tuna and onion powder. Add milk and sprinkle potato chips on top. Bake at 350°F. for 30-40 minutes. NOTE: A can of mushroom soup may be substituted for the milk, and a can of vegetable beef soup may be substituted for the tuna. Yield: 4-5 servings.

Bonnie Macklin, Peebles H.S.
Peebles, Ohio

TUNA-NOODLE CASSEROLE

½ c. butter
2 T. onions, chopped
½ c. green pepper, minced
½ t. celery salt
⅛ t. paprika
⅜ t. pepper
¾ t. Worcestershire sauce
1 can condensed cream of mushroom soup
2 c. milk
3 c. tuna fish, rinsed and flaked
3 c. cooked noodles
6 T. pimento, chopped
1 T. lemon juice
1 can mushrooms (opt.)

Melt butter in large saucepan; add onions and green pepper and cook until soft. Add seasonings and mix; add remaining ingredients and mix. Bake uncovered at 375°F. oven for ½ hour. Yield: 8 servings.

Esther Wasson, Bridgeton H.S.
Bridgeton, New Jersey

TUNA-CHIP CASSEROLE

2 c. tuna
2 c. green peas
2 cans cream of mushroom soup
1 lge. onion, diced
1 13-oz. can evaporated milk
Salt to taste
1 8-oz. pkg. noodles, cooked
2 c. potato chips, crushed

Combine all ingredients except potato chips in a large casserole. Cover top with potato chips and bake at 400°F. for 30 minutes. Yield: 15 servings.

Bernice Stahl, Stagg H.S.
Stockton, California

TUNA-CORN CASSEROLE

1 5-oz. pkg. fine egg noodles, cooked
1 6½-oz. can white chunk-style tuna
1 can corn
½ c. pimento, chopped
1 can undiluted cream of mushroom soup
1 c. potato chips, crushed

Mix drained noodles, tuna, corn, pimento and soup. Place in 2-quart baking dish. Cover with potato chips. Bake in 375°F. oven for 30 minutes. Yield: 4-6 servings.

Mary Jean Steinheuser, Lemmon H.S.
Lemmon, South Dakota

TUNA-NOODLE CASSEROLE

1 can mushroom soup
½ c. milk
1 pkg. noodles, cooked and drained
1 c. tuna
1 c. peas
1 c. potato chips, crushed

In a 1-quart casserole blend mushroom soup, milk, noodles, tuna and peas. Bake at 450°F. for 15 minutes. Top with potato chips. Bake 5 minutes more. Yield: 6-8 servings.

Mrs. Carolyn Saxe, Edwards Sr. H.S.
Albion, Illinois

TUNA-NOODLE CASSEROLE

1 8-oz pkg. wide noodles
1 7-oz. can tuna, flaked
1 can cream of vegetable soup
1 t. salt
Dash of pepper
½ c. milk
1 c. potato chips, crushed

Cook noodles in two quarts of boiling salted water for 10 minutes or until tender; drain. Rinse with hot water; drain. Mix lightly with tuna, soup, salt, pepper and milk. Pour into greased 12x8x2 baking dish. Cover with potato chips. Bake in 350°F. oven for 25-30 minutes. Yield: 4-6 servings.

Mrs. Ruby Pinter, Colby H.S.
Colby, Wisconsin

TUNA-NOODLE CASSEROLE DELIGHT

4 c. water
2 c. noodles, uncooked
1 t. salt
½ c. milk
1 can cream of mushroom soup
1 7-oz. can tuna
1 pkg. frozen peas, slightly thawed or
    2 c. canned peas, drained
¼ c. bread crumbs

Heat water to boiling; add noodles and salt. Boil for 9 minutes; drain. Add milk to soup and mix well. Arrange half of noodles, half of tuna, half of peas, and half of soup mixture in layers in a greased casserole. Repeat layers. Sprinkle bread crumbs on top. Bake at 350°F. for 30 minutes. Yield: 6 servings.

Catherine R. Mordan, Millville H.S.
Millville, Pennsylvania

TUNA-NOODLE-EGG CASSEROLE

1 8-oz. pkg. noodles, cooked and drained
1 can chunk tuna, flaked
2 hard-cooked eggs, sliced
1 can mushroom soup
¼ soup can water
1 pkg. frozen onion rings

Place half of cooked noodles in buttered casserole. Arrange half of tuna and the eggs over noodles. Add another layer of noodles and the remaining tuna. Stir soup with water to thin. Pour over casserole; place in 350°F. oven. Bake for 20 minutes. Remove from oven; place frozen onion rings on top. Return to oven for 10 minutes or until onion rings are crisp. NOTE: This casserole may be prepared ahead and refrigerated until baking time. Yield: 6 servings.

Mary J. Smith, Triopia H.S.
Chapin, Illinois

TUNA ROMANOFF

1 c. cottage cheese
1 c. sour cream
2 T. onion, minced
2 T. pimento, chopped
2 t. Worcestershire sauce
⅛ t. Tabasco
2 c. hot cooked noodles
2 6½- or 7-oz. cans tuna
½ c. ripe olives, slivered

Mix cottage cheese, sour cream, onion, pimento and seasonings. Stir in noodles, tuna and olives. Pour into a greased 2-quart casserole. Bake 40 minutes at 350°F. Yield: 6 servings.

Mrs. Patricia Castle, Ridge Farm H.S.
Ridge Farm, Illinois

TUNA TETRAZZINI

1 4-oz. can sliced mushrooms
1 c. undiluted evaporated milk
¼ c. butter or margarine
2 T. flour
½ t. salt
⅛ t. pepper
1 7-oz. can tuna, flaked
4 oz. fine noodles, cooked
1 c. soft bread cubes

Drain mushrooms, reserving liquid; add water to liquid to make 1 cup. Mix with milk. Melt 2 tablespoons butter; blend in flour, salt and pepper. Add milk mixture and cook, stirring, until thickened. Add tuna, mushrooms and noodles. Put in 1½-quart casserole. Melt remaining 2 tablespoons butter; add bread and toss. Arrange around edge of casserole. Bake at 375°F. for 20 minutes. Yield: 4 servings.

Joyce Core, Bellefontaine H.S.
Bellefontaine, Ohio

SEAFOOD DELIGHT

2 c. fine noodles
1½ qt. boiling water
1½ t. salt
1 7-oz. can light tuna fish, rinsed,
    drained and flaked
1 1-lb. 3-oz. can green asparagus, drained
1 4-oz. can mushrooms, drained

Cook noodles in salted water until tender, about 15 minutes; drain and rinse with cold water. In a greased 2-quart casserole place layers of half the noodles, the tuna fish, asparagus, mushrooms, and remaining noodles.

CHEESE SAUCE:
3 T. butter
½ c. green pepper, chopped
3 T. flour
¾ t. salt
Dash of pepper
1½ c. milk
¼ lb. processed American cheese, grated

Melt butter in saucepan and cook green pepper until soft. Add flour and seasonings and blend well; add milk gradually. Stir and cook until thickened. Add cheese and stir until cheese is melted. Pour cheese sauce over casserole. Bake at 350°F. for 25 minutes. Yield: 6 servings.

Mrs. Magdalene Dhuey, Casco H.S.
Casco, Wisconsin

HOSTESS HOT DISH

1½ c. carrots, shredded
1 c. cheese, grated
1 T. onion, grated
1 c. rice, cooked
2 eggs, beaten
1 c. tuna
1 c. white sauce
1 can mushroom soup

Boil carrots for 5 minutes; drain. Add cheese, onion, rice and egg. Bake in greased ring mold or casserole in pan of hot water at 350°F. for 30 minutes. Mix tuna, white sauce and mushroom soup; serve over carrot-rice casserole. Yield: 8 servings.

Mrs. Alma Martin, St. Maries H.S.
St. Maries, Idaho

RICE-CRUSTED TUNA PIE

2⅔ c. cooked rice
1½ T. butter or margarine, melted
3 eggs
2 tomatoes
French dressing
1 6½- or 7-oz. can solid-pack tuna
1¾ c. Swiss cheese, finely grated
¾ c. scalded milk
¼ t. salt
⅛ t. pepper
⅛ t. nutmeg
Snipped scallions

Make rice crust by combining rice, butter and 1 slightly beaten egg; turn mixture into 9-inch pie plate. Press firmly against side and bottom of plate, keeping mixture heaped high on rim. Cut each tomato into 6 wedges and marinate in French dressing. Flake the tuna; sprinkle ¾ cup grated cheese over rice crust. Top it with half of tuna; add rest of cheese. Combine the milk, 2 eggs, salt, pepper and nutmeg; pour over cheese in rice-lined plate. Sprinkle remaining tuna on top. Bake pie at 400°F. for 25 minutes. Place tomato wedges around inner edge of rice rim and return to oven for 10 minutes, or until a silver knife inserted in center comes out clean. Sprinkle scallions around tomatoes. Serve pie in wedges. Yield: 8 servings.

Marcia E. Nordquist, Mossyrock H.S.
Mossyrock, Washington

SIMPLE TUNA HOT DISH

½ c. uncooked rice
1 can tuna
1 can cream of mushroom soup
1 c. milk
1 t. dehydrated onions (opt.)
Celery or celery salt (opt.)
Slivered almonds (opt.)

Combine all ingredients and place in a greased casserole. Bake for 1 hour at 350°F. Yield: 5 servings.

Mrs. Vera Duzan, Hinckley H.S.
Hinckley, Minnesota

RICE-TUNA PIE

2 tomatoes
French dressing
2⅔ c. cooked rice
1½ T. butter, melted
3 eggs
1¾ c. Swiss cheese, grated
1 6½ or 7-oz. can tuna, flaked
¾ c. scalded milk
¼ t. salt
⅛ t. pepper
⅛ t. nutmeg

Cut each tomato into 6 wedges; cover with French dressing. Combine cooked rice, butter, and 1 egg, slightly beaten. Pour into 9-inch pie plate. Press mixture firmly against side and bottom of pie plate; heap high on rim of plate. Sprinkle ¾ cup cheese over rice crust; top with a scant half of the tuna. Add rest of cheese. Pile high in center. Combine milk, 2 eggs, salt, pepper and nutmeg until well blended. Pour over cheese in rice-lined pie plate. Sprinkle remaining tuna on top. Bake pie at 400°F. for 25 minutes or until done. Place tomato wedges all around inner edge and bake 10 minutes longer. Yield: 8 servings.

Mrs. Jackie Bullock, Highland H.S.
Pocatello, Idaho

TUNA-CHEESE SOUPREME

1¼ c. condensed cheese soup
½ c. milk
2 c. cooked rice
1-2 cans tuna, drained and flaked
¼ c. parsley, chopped
½ c. corn flake crumbs or crushed Rice Krispies
1-2 T. margarine or butter, melted

Combine cheese soup and milk. Arrange layers of rice, tuna, parsley, and soup mixture in a greased casserole; repeat layers. Combine crumbs with butter. Sprinkle over tuna mixture. Bake at 425° for 15 minutes or until thoroughly heated. Yield: 6 servings.

This recipe submitted by the following teachers:
Mrs. Ann C. Cartzendafner, Bel Air Jr. H.S.
Bel Air, Maryland
Mrs. Sylvia Ostanek, Trenary H.S.
Trenary, Michigan

TUNA-RICE CASSEROLE

¾ c. milk
1 can undiluted mushroom soup
2½ c. cooked rice
1 7-oz. can tuna
¼ c. pimento, chopped
¼ c. parsley, chopped
½ c. blanched slivered almonds

Stir milk into soup; add other ingredients except ¼ cup almonds. Put mixture into 1½-quart baking dish. Sprinkle with reserved almonds. Bake at 350°F. for 30 minutes. Yield: 6 servings.

Loraine Burtch, Edison Jr. H.S.
Champaign, Illinois

TUNA WITH CHEESE SWIRLS

1 can light tuna
1 No. 303 can peas, drained
1 can chicken-rice soup
¼ t. salt
1 c. biscuit mix
⅓ c. milk
½ c. sharp process cheese, shredded

Combine tuna, peas, soup and salt in greased 1½-quart casserole. Bake at 375°F. for 10 minutes. Combine biscuit mix with milk. Stir just until dough follows fork around bowl. Turn out on lightly floured surface. Knead gently 10 times. Roll in 6x10-inch rectangle, ¼-inch thick. Sprinkle with shredded cheese; roll as for jelly roll, starting at the narrow end. Seal edge. Cut in ½-inch slices. Place atop hot casserole. Bake at 425°F. for 15 to 20 minutes or until biscuits are done. Yield: 6 servings.

Mrs. Elsie Nichols, San Jose H.S.
San Jose, Illinois

TUNA-RICE HOT DISH SUPREME

1 sm. box instant rice
1 can mushroom soup
2 cans tuna fish
1 8-oz. jar Cheez Whiz
4 stalks celery, finely cut
½ green pepper, finely cut
1 med. onion, finely cut
3 T. butter
Salt and pepper to taste
½ c. milk or cream

Cook the rice as directed on the package. Combine the soup, tuna and Cheez Whiz in a large pan and heat until the cheese melts and forms a smooth mixture; remove from heat, but keep warm. Brown the celery, pepper and onion in the butter. Mix all the prepared foods; pour into a greased baking dish. Season with salt and pepper. Pour milk over the top and add a few dabs of butter. Bake at 350°F. for 1 hour. Yield: 6-8 servings.

Mrs. Astrid Ahrens, Delavan Public School
Delavan, Minnesota

TUNA-RICE PRONTO

1⅓ c. instant rice
¼ c. oil
1 c. onion, chopped
1 c. celery, chopped
½ clove garlic, chopped
1½ c. water
2 c. tomatoes
1 T. flour
1 T. salt
1 t. curry powder
2 cans tuna fish

Brown rice in oil; add onion, celery and garlic. Cook until onion is clear. Add water, tomatoes, flour and seasoning. Cook 10 minutes. Add tuna and cook 5 minutes more. NOTE: Any cooked meat can be used. Yield: 6 servings.

Mrs. Louise Miller, Mesa Jr. H.S.
Roswell, New Mexico

ALMOND-TUNA CASSEROLE

2 pkg. frozen asparagus, cooked
2 cans tuna, drained and flaked
3 T. butter
3 T. flour
½ t. salt
Dash of pepper
1½ c. milk
2 T. Sherry
1 c Cheddar cheese, grated
2 T. slivered almonds

Place asparagus in a baking dish; top with tuna. Melt butter; blend in flour. Add salt and pepper. Stir in milk; cook over low heat until thickened, stirring constantly. Add Sherry and cheese; stir until cheese is melted. Pour over tuna; sprinkle top with almonds. Bake in 350°F. oven for 30 minutes or until hot. Yield: 6-8 servings.

Mrs. Nancy Dillon, Coronado H.S.
Scottsdale, Arizona

ARTICHOKE-TUNA CASSEROLE

2 9-oz. pkg. frozen artichoke hearts
1 t. salt
1 can condensed cream of celery soup, undiluted
⅓ c. dry white wine
2 7-oz. cans tuna, drained and flaked
⅓ c. packaged dry bread crumbs
1½ T. butter, melted
¾ c. cashews, coarsely chopped

Cook artichoke hearts as package directs; drain. In a small saucepan combine soup with wine; bring just to boiling, stirring occasionally. Remove from heat. In a 1½-quart casserole layer half of the artichokes, tuna, cashews and soup mixture. Repeat layers. Toss bread crumbs with butter; sprinkle over casserole. Bake uncovered for 25 minutes at 350°F. until crumbs are golden. NOTE: May be prepared the night before and refrigerated. Bring to room temperature and bake as directed. Yield: 6 servings.

Helen D. Humm, Loy Norrix H.S.
Kalamazoo, Michigan

BERNIE'S TUNA CASSEROLE

1 can condensed cream of mushroom soup
½ c. milk
1 7-oz. can tuna
1 hard-cooked egg, sliced
1 c. cooked peas
1½ c. crushed potato chips

In a saucepan, heat soup and milk. Alternate layers of tuna, eggs, peas and chips with milk and soup mixture in a 1-quart casserole. Top with chips. Bake at 350°F. for 30 minutes. Yield: 4-5 servings.

Doris E. Dean, Newark H.S.
Newark, Delaware

CASSEROLE DISH

½ lb. potato chips, crushed
1 can creamed corn
1 lge. can tuna
½ c. milk

Combine all ingredients except 1 cup potato chips. Pour in baking dish; sprinkle with remaining potato chips. Bake for 30 minutes at 375°F. Yield: 6 servings.

Ferial Abraham, Argyle H.S.
Argyle, Minnesota

CHARLIE THE TUNA PIE

Pastry for 2 crust pie
2 med. potatoes, diced
1 med. onion, diced
1½ c. carrots, diced
1 c. green peas
½ c. water
1½ t. salt
1 T. butter, melted
1 T. flour
⅛ t. pepper
1 c. milk
2 7-oz. cans white tuna
Paprika

Line a 1-quart baking dish with pastry. Boil vegetables together in water with ½ teaspoon salt until tender; drain. Make white sauce with butter, flour, 1 teaspoon salt, pepper and milk; add tuna. Alternate layers of vegetables and tuna mixture in the casserole; sprinkle with paprika. Cover with pie crust. Bake at 425°F. for 30-40 minutes. Yield: 6-8 servings.

Mrs. Maybelle Nichols, Ridgeville H.S.
North Ridgeville, Ohio

CHIPPER TUNA CASSEROLE

1 can condensed cream of celery soup
⅓-½ c. milk
1 6½ or 7-oz. can tuna
1-1¼ c. crushed potato chips
1 c. cooked or canned garden peas

Empty soup into 1-quart casserole. Add milk and stir until well mixed. Add drained tuna, all except ¼ cup potato chips, and green peas. Spread evenly over soup mixture. Sprinkle reserved potato chips over the top. Bake 25 minutes in a 350-375°F. oven. NOTE: If desired, the reserved chips may be added the last 5 minutes of baking. Yield: 6 servings.

This recipe submitted by the following teachers:
Mrs. Stella Forrest, Wake Forest H.S.
Wake Forest, North Carolina
Blanche Martin, Mowat Jr. H.S.
Lynn Haven, Florida
Mrs. Phyllis Buchanan, Valier Jr. H.S.
Valier, Illinois

GARDEN SUPPER CASSEROLE

2 c. soft bread, cubed
½ c. sharp cheese, grated
2 T. butter, melted
1 c. peas or other cooked vegetable
1½ c. med. white sauce
2 T. onion, chopped
1 c. tuna, flaked
1 lge. tomato, sliced

Mix bread cubes, cheese and butter; spread half of mixture in greased 1-quart casserole. Add peas. Combine white sauce, sauted onion, and tuna; pour over peas. Arrange tomatoes over top and cover with remaining crumb mixture. Bake 25 minutes at 350°F. NOTE: Chopped cooked meat or 3 hard-cooked eggs may be substituted for the tuna. Yield: 4-6 servings.

Murrel M. Eckert, San Manuel H.S.
San Manuel, Arizona

JACK STRAW TUNA CASSEROLE

1 4-oz. can shoestring potatoes
⅔ c. evaporated or whole milk
1 can cream of mushroom soup
1-2 cans tuna, drained
1 3-oz. can sliced mushrooms, drained (opt.)
¼ c. pimento, chopped (opt.)

Reserve 1 cup of potatoes for the top. Combine milk and soup; stir until smooth. Add tuna fish and remaining potatoes. Pour into a 6-cup casserole. Arrange reserved potatoes on top. Bake uncovered for 20-25 minutes in a 375°F. oven. NOTE: If desired, casserole may be baked at 325°F. for 40 minutes. Yield: 6 servings.

This recipe submitted by the following teachers:
Mrs. Kathryn Schermerhorn, Butterfield-Odin H.S.
Butterfield, Minnesota
Mrs. Phyllis L. Barton, Fort Hunt H.S.
Alexandria, Virginia
Mary Elizabeth Ball, Kentwood H.S.
Grand Rapids, Michigan

MOCK CREAMED CHICKEN

1 can tuna
1 can cream of mushroom soup
1 box frozen peas, partially cooked
½ c. ripe olives, sliced
1 sm. pkg. potato chips, crumbled
1 c. diluted evaporated milk

Place a layer of tuna, undiluted soup, drained peas, olives, and crumbled potato chips in casserole. Repeat layers, omitting top layer of potato chips until after milk has been added. Bake in 350°F. oven for 45 minutes to 1 hour. Yield: 4 servings.

Mrs. Helen Stanford, Union H.S.
Union, Oregon

ORIENTAL TUNA CASSEROLE

1 can tuna
1 can Chinese vegetables with water chestnuts
1 can cream of chicken or mushroom soup
½ c. celery, chopped
1 sm. pkg. cashew nuts
1 can Chinese noodles

Mix all ingredients except a few noodles; pour mixture into casserole. Top with reserved noodles. Bake at 350°F. for 30 minutes. Yield: 6 servings.

Mrs. Betty Nason, Hamilton H.S.
Hamilton, Montana

QUICK TUNA CASSEROLE

1 bag potato chips
1 No. 2 can peas
1 family-size can tuna
1 can mushroom soup
1 soup can whole milk

In a buttered casserole put layer of crushed potato chips. Follow with layers of peas and tuna. Top with layer of potato chips. Pour mixture of soup diluted with milk over top. Bake at 350°F. until brown and bubbling, about 30 minutes. Yield: 6-8 servings.

Doris R. Hohn, Saydel Sr. H.S.
Des Moines, Iowa

TUNA AU GRATIN

PASTRY:
1½ c. sifted flour
½ t. salt
½ c. shortening
4-5 T. cold water

Combine ingredients to make pastry; roll out to ⅛-inch thickness. Line pastry pan; flute edge. Prick with fork. Bake at 450°F. for 12 minutes or until light brown. Bake extra pieces to use for crumbs for topping.

FILLING:
1 can mushroom soup
¼ c. milk
2 T. flour
2 T. onion flakes
1 pkg. frozen peas, thawed
2 cans tuna
1 4-oz. can pimento, chopped
1 c. cheese, grated

Combine in saucepan soup, milk, flour and onion flakes. Cook until thickened. Remove from heat. Add peas, tuna and pimento. Place in baked shell. Top with pastry crumbs and cheese. Bake at 425°F. for 12 to 15 minutes until cheese melts. Yield: 6 servings.

This recipe submitted by the following teachers:
Mrs. Hazel R. Dees, Delmar H.S.
Paris, Texas
Mrs. Edna Locker, Weyauwega H.S
Weyauwega, Wisconsin

TUNA-AVOCADO CASSEROLE

2 med. avocados
1 box frozen peas, thawed
4 slices bacon, fried
1 can cream of chicken soup
½ c. milk
½ onion, chopped
2 7-oz. cans tuna, flaked
¼ t. pepper
1 c. corn chips, crushed

Peel and cut avocados into ½-inch cubes; place in a greased casserole. Place thawed peas on top of avocados. Crumble the fried bacon and sprinkle on top. In a saucepan heat the soup, milk and onion; cook on low heat for 5 minutes. Add the tuna and pepper. Pour mixture over avocados and sprinkle with corn chips. Bake in a 375°F. oven for 20 minutes. Yield: 6 servings.

Mrs. Kikuye S. Kohashi, Hilo H.S.
Hilo, Hawaii

TUNA BAKE

1¼ c. water
1 can vegetarian vegetable soup
3 T. flour
1 6½-oz. can tuna, drained and flaked
Prepared biscuit mix
½ c. sharp cheese, grated
2 T. pimento

Mix ¼ cup water with soup; heat. Mix 1 cup water with flour; stir into soup. Cook, stirring until thickened. Add tuna. Turn into baking dish. Mix biscuit mix according to directions on package. Roll into 3x10 rectangle. Sprinkle with cheese and pimento. Roll like jelly roll. Cut into 12 slices and place on tuna mixture. Bake 15 minutes at 400°F. Yield: 4-6 servings.

Mrs. J. S. Grant, Carson City H.S
Carson City, Michigan

TUNA-CHIP CASSEROLE

1 can cream of mushroom soup
   or 1 cup med. white sauce
1 can chunk-style tuna
4 c. potato chips
1 No. 2 can peas, drained

Prepare white sauce or put mushroom soup in bowl. Add tuna and mix until tuna is of fine texture. Add 2 cups crushed chips and the peas, folding in gently. Line casserole dish with 2 cups whole chips, reserving 8 to 10 large chips. Place tuna mixture in casserole; top with large chips. Bake in 350°F. oven for 30 minutes. Yield: 6-8 servings.

Judith C. Hughes, Jefferson Township H.S.
Dayton, Ohio

TUNA-CHIP CASSEROLE

1 med. bag potato chips
1 can chunk tuna
1 can peas
1 can mushroom soup
1½ c. milk

Grease casserole. Put in a layer of crushed potato chips, a layer of peas and a layer of tuna. Pour one-fourth of heated soup-milk mixture over all. Repeat layers until ingredients are all used. Bake at 350°F. for 30 minutes. Yield: 6-8 servings.

Mrs. James L. Koster, Independent Dist.
Lake Benton, Minnesota

TUNA-GREEN PEA CASSEROLE

1 can mushroom soup
⅓-½ c. milk
1 can tuna, drained and flaked
1 can pimento, drained (opt.)
1 can English peas, drained
1-2 c. potato chips, crushed

Mix soup and milk; alternate layers of tuna, soup mixture, pimento, peas, and chips in casserole. Top with chips. Bake at 350-400°F. for 20-25 minutes or until bubbly hot. NOTE: If desired, all ingredients may be mixed together, reserving ¼ cup chips for topping. If frozen peas are substituted, bake at 350°F. for 40 minutes. Yield: 4-6 servings.

This recipe submitted by the following teachers:
Emma Joe Thomas, Burkeville H.S.
Burkeville, Texas
Mrs. Jessie L. Fielding, Plant City H.S.
Plant City, Florida
Mrs. Elaine Smith, New London H.S.
New London, Iowa
Mrs. Gary W. Oxley, Creighton H.S.
Creighton, Nebraska
Hazel Sluder, Wirth Jr. H.S.
Cahokia, Illinois
Eleanor Foreman, Tawas Area H.S.
Tawas City, Michigan
Mrs. Lois E. Boy, Syracuse H.S.
Syracuse, Kansas
Mrs. Diana Costello, W. F. George H.S.
Iowa Park, Texas
Jacqueline Olson, Lakota Public School
Lakota, North Dakota

CHOPSTICK TUNA

1 can condensed cream of mushroom soup
¼-½ c. water
1 3-oz. can chow mein noodles
1 6½ or 7-oz. can tuna, flaked
½-1 c. celery, sliced
¼-¾ c. toasted cashews
1 can mushrooms (opt.)
¼ c. onion, chopped
2 T. pimento, finely diced (opt.)
2-4 T. green pepper, chopped (opt.)
Salt and pepper to taste
Mandarin orange sections (garnish)
¼ c. green grapes, sliced (garnish)

Combine soup and water. Add 1 cup chow mein noodles, the tuna, celery, cashews, mushrooms, onion, pimento, green pepper and seasonings. Toss lightly to mix. Place in baking dish. Sprinkle remaining noodles over top. Bake at 325°F. for 40-60 minutes. Garnish with drained Mandarin orange sections and grapes. NOTE: For quicker baking, bake at 350-375°F. for 15-20 minutes or until thoroughly heated. Noodles for top may be crushed, if desired. Yield: 4-5 servings.

This recipe submitted by the following teachers:
Barbara Ray, Olathe H.S.
Olathe, Colorado
Mary Elizabeth Kloos, Helix H.S.
LaMesa, California
Mrs. Pauline Lentz, Walhalla H.S.
Walhalla, North Dakota
Mrs. Mildred Fanta, Soldiers Grove H.S.
Soldiers Grove, Wisconsin
Mrs. Charles F. Wilcox, Eagle Jr. H.S.
Eagle, Idaho
Mrs. Margaret Fagot, Fairbury-Cropsey H.S.
Fairbury, Illinois
Win McMullin, Dawson County H.S.
Glendive, Montana
Mrs. Betty J. Anderson, Wilder Jr. H.S.
Savannah, Georgia
Marjorie C. Gould, Kirkland Jr. H.S.
Kirkland, Washington
Sara Lu Greeley, Preston H.S.
Preston, Minnesota
Annjanette Emery, Wilson H.S.
Wilson, Arkansas
Mrs. Niva J. Reddick, Largo Sr. H.S.
Largo, Florida
Ruth Schudel, Bowen H.S.
Bowen, Illinois
Sally Hildebrand, Enumclaw H.S.
Enumclaw, Washington
Mrs. Mayme W. Day, Refugio H.S.
Refugio, Texas
Mrs. Nettie Waller, Central H.S.
Deer River, Minnesota
Mrs. C. D. Rosson, Blanche H.S.
Taft, Tennessee
Mrs. Carmel Provencal, Pompano Sr. H.S.
Pompano, Florida
Ines Bressan, Washington Jr. H.S.
Springfield, Illinois
Mrs. Alverna M. Thomas, Lewiston Sr. H.S.
Lewiston, Idaho
Lacquita Olson, Colman H.S.
Colman, South Dakota
Pearl Oliver, Cadillac Jr. H.S.
Cadillac, Michigan
Mrs. Betty Tasker, Rice Lake H.S.
Rice Lake, Wisconsin
Mrs. Webster Intermill, Chassell H.S.
Chassell, Michigan
Mrs. Verona Lechler, Beach H.S
Beach, North Dakota

CASHEW HOT DISH

1 3-oz. can chow mein noodles
1 can mushroom soup
1 can tuna
¼ lb. cashew nuts
1 c. celery, diced
¼ c onion, minced
Dash of pepper
Dash of salt
1 can Mandarin oranges

Combine half of noodles, the soup, tuna, nuts, celery, onion, pepper and salt. Mix well and place in 2-quart casserole. Top with reserved noodles. Bake at 350°F. for 30 to 40 minutes. Garnish with Mandarin oranges. NOTE: If cashew nuts are salted, omit the dash of salt. Yield: 4-6 servings.

Mrs. Wilma Sonne, Plankinton Independent
Plankinton, South Dakota

CHEESE BISCUIT-TUNA CASSEROLE

2 c. med. white sauce
Salt and pepper to taste
1 c. tuna
¼ c. stuffed olives, sliced

Season white sauce with salt and pepper. Pour into 2-quart casserole. Add tuna separated in large pieces. Add olives.

BISCUITS:
2 c. sifted flour
3 t. baking powder
1 t. salt
¼ c. shortening
¾ c. milk
¾ c. American cheese, cubed

Combine all ingredients except cheese to make biscuit dough. Roll to ¼ to ⅓-inch thickness. Sprinkle with cheese cubes. Roll as for a jelly roll; cut in pieces. Drop into white sauce mixture. Bake at 450°F. for 25 minutes. Serve hot. Yield: 6 servings.

Mrs. Ruth Arrell, Halstad H.S.
Halstad, Minnesota

EXCELLENT CHINESE CASSEROLE

1 c. onions, diced
1 c. celery, diced
1 c. water chestnuts, diced
1 can flaked tuna
1 can evaporated milk
1 can Chinese fried noodles
1 can mushroom soup
1 c. cashew nuts

Mix all ingredients except nuts; place in baking dish. Top with cashew nuts. Bake 1 hour at 350°F. Yield: 8 servings.

Mrs. Geraldine Marrs, Homer H.S.
Homer, Illinois

FESTIVE TUNA CASSEROLE

⅓ c. green pepper, chopped (opt.)
3 T. onions, chopped
3 T. fat
1 t. salt
6 T. flour
1 can chicken-rice soup
1½ c. milk
1 7-oz. can tuna, flaked
1 T. lemon juice (opt.)
Cheese, crackers or potato chips

Cook green pepper and onion in hot fat until golden; blend in salt and flour. Add soup and milk; cook until sauce is thick, stirring constantly. Add tuna and lemon juice. Pour mixture into greased baking dish and top with cheese. Bake at 425°F. for 30 minutes. Yield: 6-8 servings.

This recipe submitted by the following teachers:
Mrs. Barbara Tyner, Runnelstown H.S.
Hattiesburg, Mississippi
Mrs. Martha Swingle, Northwestern H.S.
West Salem, Ohio

FISH AND CHIPS

2 c. potato chips, crushed
6 hard-cooked eggs, diced
1 can cream of mushroom soup
½ c. milk
1 sm. onion
1 can tuna
Salt and pepper to taste

Combine all ingredients except 1 cup of potato chips. Pour into a greased 1-quart casserole. Sprinkle remaining potato chips over top. Bake 25 minutes at 400°F. Yield: 6 servings.

Diane D. Rutherford, Evansville H.S.
Evansville, Minnesota

MEAL IN ONE CASSEROLE

¼ c. butter
2 T. onion, chopped
¼ c. sifted flour
1 t. salt
⅛ t. pepper
2 c. milk
1 c. cooked celery
1 7-oz. can tuna fish
2 T. pimento, chopped
2 hard-cooked eggs, sliced
Biscuits

Brown onion in butter; blend in flour and seasoning. Add milk gradually. Cook until thickened, stirring constantly. Add celery and other ingredients. Pour into a 1½-quart casserole and top with biscuits. Bake at 450°F. about 15 minutes, or until biscuits are browned and sauce is bubbling. Yield: 6 servings.

Evelyn Mangold, Warrensburg-Latham H.S.
Warrensburg, Illinois

OLIVE-TUNA CASSEROLE

¼ c. butter
¼ c. flour
2 c. milk
½ t. salt
1 c. cheese, grated
¾ c. stuffed olives
½ green pepper, minced
1 can tuna
2 c. soft bread cubes
¾ c. corn flakes

Make a white sauce of butter, flour, milk and salt; add cheese, olives, green pepper and tuna. Butter a casserole. Arrange layers of tuna mixture and bread cubes in the casserole. Top with corn flakes. Bake 30 minutes at 350°F. Yield: 4 servings.

Mrs. Gayle Grickson, Hankinson Public School
Hankinson, North Dakota

ORIENTAL CASSEROLE

1 3-oz. can Chinese noodles
1 can cream of mushroom soup
⅓ c. light cream or milk
1 T. A-1 sauce
1 5¼-oz. can tuna fish
¼ lb. whole cashews (opt.)
1 c. celery, diced
¼ c. onion, chopped
½ t. salt
Pepper

Mix half of noodles with all the other ingredients; pour into buttered casserole. Top with remaining noodles; bake 35 minutes at 350°F. May be served with soy sauce. Yield: 6 servings.

Helen Reesor, Colon H.S.
Colon, Michigan

SAUCY TUNA CASSEROLE

4 eggs, separated
2 c. cooked rice
1 c. milk
2 T. butter
½ c. parsley, chopped
1 c. cheese, grated

Beat egg yolks. Combine all ingredients, folding in beaten egg whites last. Pour into baking pan. Bake at 350°F. for 40 minutes; cut in squares. NOTE: Chicken or ham may be added if desired.

SAUCE:

3 c. thick white sauce
1 sm. bottle stuffed olives with juice
1 med. can mushrooms
1 med. can tuna
Salt to taste

Combine all ingredients; heat thoroughly. Serve over rice squares. Yield: 8 servings.

Mrs. Edith Donaldson, Gadsden H.S.
Anthony, New Mexico

PARTY CASSEROLE

2 cans tuna
2 cans undiluted mushroom soup
⅔ cup water
1 can mushrooms
1 can water chestnuts, thinly sliced
1 sm. pkg. sliced almonds
½ c. onion, sliced
2 c. celery, finely sliced
2 T. green pepper, chopped
1 lg. can chow mein noodles

Pour boiling water over tuna; drain. Mix all ingredients except noodles. Place in casserole; cover with noodles and bake at 350°F. for 1 hour. Yield: 4-5 servings.

Rose L. Kimpton, Liberty H.S.
Spangle, Washington

LAYERED TUNA-POTATO CHIP CASSEROLE

2 c. tuna
2 c. potato chips, slightly crushed
2 c. med. white sauce
¾ c. sliced mushrooms, sauted

Arrange ingredients in alternate layers in a buttered casserole. Top with a few more potato chips. Bake at 350°F. for 35 minutes. Yield: 4-6 servings.

Allyne Sue Doll, Ajo H.S.
Ajo, Arizona

SCALLOPED TUNA

2 cans light meat tuna
2 c. potato chips, crushed
3 c. med. white sauce
½ c. sauted mushrooms

Arrange ingredients in alternate layers in a buttered casserole, topping with a potato chip layer. Bake 35-45 minutes at 350°F. Yield: 6 servings.

Mrs. Vera Glades, West H.S.
Anchorage, Alaska

SEAFOOD SUPREME

1½ sm. can crisp noodles
¼ c. onion, minced
1 c. celery, chopped
1 7-oz. can tuna or crab
1 can cream of mushroom soup
¼ c. milk
1 c. unsalted cashew nuts (opt.)

Place half of noodles in bottom of greased casserole. Mix remaining ingredients; pour over noodles. Top with remaining noodles. Bake at 325°F. for 40 minutes. Yield: 4-6 servings.

Mrs. Helen Sageman, LeRoy Community School
LeRoy, Michigan

SPEEDY TUNA CASSEROLE

1 med. pkg. potato chips
1 can tuna
1 can cream of mushroom soup
½ soup can water

Crumble potato chips over bottom of small casserole dish. Add a thin layer of tuna. Top with soup heated with water. Repeat layers until all ingredients are used. Sprinkle top with potato chip crumbs. Bake in 350°F. oven for 30 minutes. Yield: 4-5 servings.

Goldie Farmer, Mt. Carmel H.S.
Mt. Carmel, Illinois

TUNA BAKE WITH CHEESE SWIRLS

3 T. onion, chopped
⅓ c. green pepper, chopped
3 T. fat
1 t. salt
6 T. flour
1 10½-oz. can condensed cream of chicken soup
  or chicken-rice soup
1½ c. milk
1 7-oz. can tuna
1 T. lemon juice

Brown onion and pepper in hot fat. Add salt and flour; blend. Add soup and milk; cook until sauce is thick and smooth. Add flaked tuna and lemon juice. Pour into greased casserole.

CHEESE SWIRLS:
2 c. flour
½ t. salt
3 t. baking powder
4 T. shortening
⅔-¾ c. milk
½-1 c. American cheese, grated
¼ c. pimento, finely chopped (opt.)

Sift together dry ingredients; cut in shortening. Add milk all at once and mix just until dough follows fork around bowl. Turn on lightly floured surface and knead gently for 30 seconds. Roll dough ¼-inch thick. Sprinkle with cheese and pimento. Roll like jelly roll. Slice and place on tuna mixture. Bake at 450°F. for 15 minutes. Reduce heat to 425°F. and bake for 15 minutes, or until brown. NOTE: If desired, spread dough with butter. Sprinkle with 2 tablespoons chopped parsley and 2 tablespoons chopped pimento. Casserole may be baked at 425°F. for the entire 30 minutes. Yield: 6 servings.

This recipe submitted by the following teachers:
Mrs. Betty Larsen, Orland School
Madison, South Dakota
Evie Wirchainski, Horace Mann Jr. H.S.
Miami, Florida
Nana E. James, Southeastern H.S.
Hammond, Louisiana
Cathy M. Koszegi, Stockbridge H.S.
Stockbridge, Michigan
Mrs. Corrine Olsen, Waterville H.S.
Waterville, Kansas

SCALLOPED TUNA CASSEROLE

2 7-oz. cans tuna
¾ c. sauted mushrooms
2 c. potato chips
3 c. med. white sauce

Arrange ingredients in alternate layers in buttered 1½-quart baking dish. Top with potato chips. Bake 35 minutes at 350°F. Yield: 5-6 servings.

Mrs. Phyllis Ann Stewart,
Fritchton-South Knox School Corporation
Vincennes, Indiana

TUNA-APPLE CASSEROLE

1 can tuna, flaked
2 apples, peeled and diced
½ c. celery, chopped
⅓ c. stuffed olives, chopped
1 med. bag potato chips, crushed
1 can mushroom soup

Combine tuna, apples, celery and olives. Arrange alternating layers of fish mixture and potato chips in a casserole. Pour mushroom soup over entire mixture. Place in an oven at 350°F. until mixture is hot, 30 to 40 minutes. Yield: 4-5 servings.

Bessie L. Alford, Adult Home Economics Class
Quincy, Illinois

TUNA CASSEROLE

1 can tuna
¼ c. onion, chopped
¼ c. cashew nuts
1 can mushroom soup
¼-1 c. milk
1 c. celery, chopped
1 can chow mein noodles

Combine all ingredients. Bake at 350°F. for 40 to 60 minutes. Yield: 6 servings.

This recipe submitted by the following teachers:
Geraldlyn Watts, Nederland H.S.
Nederland, Texas
Mrs. Earl Hagg, Belle Plaine H.S.
Belle Plaine, Minnesota

TUNA CASSEROLE

1 can tuna, flaked
1 can mushroom soup
½ bag potato chips
¼ t. pepper (opt.)
¼ t. salt (opt.)

Combine all ingredients, mixing thoroughly. Place in a casserole and bake for 25-35 minutes at 350-375°F. NOTE: If desired, ingredients may be layered rather than mixed. Yield: 4-6 servings.

This recipe submitted by the following teachers:
Irma Scott, Fayetteville H.S.
Fayetteville, North Carolina
Pauline Waggener, Du Quoin Township H.S.
Du Quoin, Illinois
Mrs. Eleanor Finley, Rastraver H.S.
Belle Vernon, Pennsylvania

TUNA AU GRATIN

1 9-oz. can tuna
½ c. cottage cheese
5 slices bread, cut in ½-in. cubes
4 T. butter
1 T. flour
1 t. paprika
1½ c. milk
½ c. Cheddar cheese, shredded

Combine tuna, cottage cheese and half of bread cubes; spread mixture in bottom of shallow 1¼-quart baking dish or individual casseroles. In saucepan melt 2 tablespoons butter; blend in flour and paprika to form a smooth paste. Gradually add milk; heat, stirring constantly, until mixture thickens. Add cheese; continue heating, stirring constantly, until cheese melts. Pour sauce over tuna mixture; top with reserved bread cubes. Melt remaining butter and pour over bread. Bake 25-30 minutes at 350°F. Yield: 4 servings.

Mrs. Ruth Andreason, Genoa-Kingston H.S.
Genoa, Illinois

TUNA AND CHIPS IN CASSEROLE

2 T. butter
2 T. flour
½ t. salt
½ t. pepper
2 c. milk
2 t. Worcestershire sauce
1 c. potato chips, crumbled
2 7-oz. cans tuna, drained and flaked

Melt butter; blend in flour, salt and pepper. Add milk and cook, stirring constantly until thick and smooth. Add Worcestershire. Cover bottom of greased 1½-quart casserole with ¼ cup potato chips. Top with one-fourth of tuna. Repeat layers; top with potato chips. Pour sauce over and bake at 350°F. for 30 minutes. Yield: 4 servings.

Brenda Craig, Elverado H.S.
Elkville, Illinois

TUNA CHOW CASSEROLE

1 3-oz. can chow mein noodles
1 can cream of mushroom soup
¼ c. water
1 7-oz. can tuna, rinsed
¼ lb. cashew nuts, rinsed
1 c. celery, diced
1 c. cream of chicken soup
¼ c. onion, minced
½ t. thyme
½ t. marjoram
1 T. butter
Mushrooms (opt.)
Green pepper, diced (opt.)

Combine all ingredients; except a few chow mein noodles; put into greased casserole. Sprinkle with reserved noodles. Bake for 30 minutes at 350°F. Yield: 6 servings.

Sister M. Aloysius, PBVM, O'Gorman H.S.
Sioux Falls, South Dakota

TUNA CHOW MEIN

1 c. celery, chopped
¼ c. onion, chopped
2 T. green pepper, chopped
1 T. butter
1 can tuna
1 can cream of mushroom soup
¼ c. milk
¼ c. water
1 3-oz. can chow mein noodles
¾ c. salted cashew nuts
¼ t. monosodium glutamate
¼ t. pepper

Saute celery, onion and green pepper in butter. Combine all ingredients except ⅓ cup noodles. Pour into buttered 1½-quart baking dish; sprinkle with remaining noodles. Bake 30 minutes at 350°F. Yield: 4-6 servings.

Myrtle Bergstrom, Maple Grove School
Muskegon, Michigan

TUNA CHEESE TARTS

TART SHELLS:
1½ c. sifted flour
¾ t. salt
¾ c. cheese, shredded
8 T. shortening
4-5 T. water

Sift flour and salt into bowl. Add cheese; cut in shortening. Add water by tablespoons, tossing mixture with fork. Shape into shells for individual pie pans.

TUNA FILLING:
6 T. onion, finely chopped
6 T. green pepper, finely chopped
3 T. butter, melted
1 can cream of celery soup
¾ c. process cheese, shredded
2 6½-oz. can tuna
6 T. pimento, finely chopped

Saute onion and green pepper in butter until tender. Add soup and cheese; heat and stir until blended. Stir in tuna and pimento. Pour into tart shells. Add upper crust; bake at 400°F. for 40-45 minutes. Yield: 6 servings.

Frances Shipley, Coon Rapids Community School
Coon Rapids, Iowa

TUNA-CHIP DINNER

½ lb. potato chips
1 9-oz. can chunk tuna
1 12-oz. pkg. mixed frozen vegetables
1 c. milk
1 can cream of mushroom soup

Crush a layer of chips in bottom of casserole. Place tuna in layer; add a layer of cooked vegetables. Top with chips. Mix milk with soup and pour over top. Place in 350-400°F. oven for 30 minutes or until heated through. Yield: 6 servings.

Margaret Dyke, Air Academy H.S.
United States Air Force Academy, Colorado

TUNA-CHOW MEIN CASSEROLE

1 sm. can tuna
1 can chow mein noodles
1 can condensed mushroom soup
1 c. celery, diced
½ c. water

Combine all ingredients except half of noodles. Pour mixture in a greased 1½-quart casserole. Sprinkle the remaining noodles over top. Bake at 400°F. for 30 minutes. Yield: 6-8 servings.

Mrs. Dorothy Congrove, Concordia H.S.
Concordia, Kansas

TUNA-CHOW MEIN CASSEROLE

1 can white meat tuna, flaked
2 cans chow mein noodles
1 can cream of mushroom soup
1 c. milk
½ c. cashews
½ c. black olives, chopped

Combine tuna with chow mein noodles in a 2-quart casserole. Blend mushroom soup and milk; pour over casserole mixture. Add cashews and black olives. Bake at 350°F. for 35-45 minutes. Yield: 6 servings.

Mrs. Susan Mahoney, Gerrish Higgins H.S.
Roscomnas, Michigan

TUNA DELIGHT

1½ c. onion, sliced
1½ c. celery or bean sprouts, diced
1 can chow mein noodles
1 can cream of celery soup
1 can cream of mushroom soup
1 can tuna
Crumbs

Combine all ingredients except crumbs. Pour into casserole. Cover with crumbs. Bake at 350°F. for 30 minutes. Yield: 6 servings.

Mrs. Margaret Tarsa, Weidman Community School
Weidman, Michigan

TUNA-GREEN PEPPER CASSEROLE

¼ c. butter
¼ c. flour
2 c. milk
1½ c. American cheese, grated
½ c. stuffed olives
½ c. green pepper, minced
1 can tuna, flaked
2 c. soft bread, cubed
¾ c. corn flakes

Make a white sauce with the butter, flour and milk. Add 1 cup cheese, olives, green pepper, tuna and bread cubes. Put in a buttered baking dish. Top with remaining cheese and corn flakes. Bake at 350°F. for 20 minutes. NOTE: If desired, salmon, chicken, or ham may be substituted for tuna. Yield: 6 servings.

Doris Kirk, Fridley Jr. H.S.
Minneapolis, Minnesota

TUNA HOT DISH

2 T. butter
2 c. milk
2 T. flour
3 eggs, separated
1 can tuna
2 sm. pkg. chow mein noodles
½ c. blanched almonds

Make white sauce with butter, milk, flour and egg yolks. Add tuna, chow mein noodles and almonds. Fold in beaten egg whites. Pour into a loaf pan; bake at 350°F. for 45 minutes. If desired, serve with a hot mushroom sauce. Yield: 8 servings.

Mrs. Evelyn Attendorf, Warren H.S.
Warren, Minnesota

TUNA-LEMON PIE

1 firm unpeeled lemon, sliced
1 6½- or 7-oz. can tuna
2 T. onion, minced
1 t. green pepper, minced
¼ c. fresh bread crumbs
½ t. dry mustard
2 T. lemon juice
⅓ c. catsup
1 egg, well beaten
¼ lb. process Cheddar cheese, sliced
6 T. milk
1 c. packaged biscuit mix
Thin white sauce (opt.)

Heat oven to 400°F. Arrange slices of unpeeled lemon in bottom of greased 9-inch pie plate. Mix tuna, onion, green pepper, bread crumbs, mustard, lemon juice, catsup and egg. Spread over lemon slices. Top with cheese slices. Stir milk into biscuit mix. Spread dough over cheese layer. Bake uncovered 15-20 minutes or until light brown. Loosen edges; quickly invert onto serving plate. Cut into six wedges. Serve hot as is or topped with thin white sauce. Yield: 6 servings.

Mrs. Doris Smith, Dayton H.S.
Dayton, Washington

TUNA PIE

1 sm. onion, chopped
2 T. butter
2 T. flour
1 c. milk
1 can tuna
1 can chicken gumbo soup
1 T. lemon juice
Unbaked biscuits

Brown onion in butter; add flour and mix well. Add enough milk to make a thick gravy. Add tuna and soup. Add seasonings. Top with biscuits. Bake in a 450°F. oven until lightly browned. Yield: 4-6 servings.

Kathleen Kane, Ames-Bern School
Amesville, Ohio

TUNA SURPRISE CASSEROLE

2 T. butter
¼ c. onion, chopped
3 c. celery, chopped
1 can tuna
1 can cream of mushroom soup
1 can cream of celery soup
3 T. milk
1 T. soy sauce
1 can chow mein noodles
½ c. cashew nuts, chopped

Melt butter; add onion and celery and cook until tender. Add tuna fish, soups, milk, soy sauce, half of noodles and nuts. Put into a greased 1½-quart casserole. Cover with remaining noodles and nuts. Bake at 350°F. for 25 minutes. Yield: 6 servings.

Janice H. Geraets, Aurora-Hoyt Lakes H.S.
Aurora, Minnesota

BAKED SEAFOOD

1 c. celery, chopped
1 green pepper, chopped
¼ c. onion, chopped
7 T. butter, melted
3 T. flour
1½ c. milk
1 T. Worcestershire sauce
1 ½-lb. can crab
1 ½-lb. can shrimp
1 c. mayonnaise
1 c. uncooked rice, cooked

Cook celery and green pepper and onion in 4 tablespoons butter until tender. Combine 3 tablespoon butter, flour and milk in double boiler for a white sauce. Add vegetables, Worcestershire sauce, crab, shrimp and mayonnaise. Line baking dish with cooked rice. Spread seafood mixture in dish. Place buttered crumbs on top. Bake at 325°F. for 20 minutes. NOTE: Fresh seafood may be substituted for canned. Yield: 7-8 servings.

Velma Gillet, Lillis Vejlupek, Jean Branstator
Judson Jr. H.S.
Salem, Oregon

BAKED SEAFOOD CASSEROLE

1 lb. combined crab and lobster
1 lb. cooked deveined shrimp
1 c. mayonnaise
½ c. green pepper, chopped
¼ c. onion, minced
1½ c. celery, finely chopped
½ t. Worcestershire sauce
2 c. potato chips, crushed
Paprika

Mix ingredients except potato chips and paprika. Fill baking pan with mixture and completely cover with crushed potato chips. Sprinkle with paprika and bake at 400°F. for 20 to 25 minutes. Yield: 12 servings.

Lois H. Colman, Las Plumas H.S.
Orville, California

BAKED SHRIMP-CRAB SALAD

1 green pepper, chopped
1 onion, chopped
1 c. celery, finely cut
1 can crab meat, shredded
1 can shrimp
⅔ to 1 c. mayonnaise
½ t. salt
Pepper to taste
1 t. Worcestershire sauce
1 c. buttered bread crumbs or cracker crumbs

Combine green pepper, onion and celery. Remove tendons from crab meat and flake. Remove black line from shrimp and cut into pieces. Mix crab and shrimp with vegetables. Add mayonnaise and seasonings. Place in buttered baking dish. Cover top with bread crumbs mixed with butter. Bake at 350°F. until top is nicely browned, about 30 minutes. Yield: 8 servings.

This recipe submitted by the following teachers:
Mrs. Maud Rhea Sharer, Wheeler H.S.
Fossil, Oregon
Mary Peare Bragg, Rancocas Valley Regional H.S.
Mount Holly, New Jersey
Ellen Morgan Schenck, Wilson H.S.
West Lawn, Pennsylvania
Mrs. Ramona K. deSilva, Washington Jr. H.S.
Yakima, Washington
Mrs. Sudie M. Bell, Isola H.S.
Isola, Mississippi
Annie Lillian Brewton, Escambia H.S
Pensacola, Florida
Mrs. Maxine Williams, Prentiss H.S.
Prentiss, Mississippi
Elizabeth Pond, Portland Jr. H.S.
Bloomington, Minnesota
Mrs. Helen L. Phelps, Roseland H.S.
Roseland, Nebraska
Mrs. Ralph H. Dunn, Jerome H.S.
Jerome, Idaho
Helen McMahon, Lowell H.S.
Lowell, Michigan
Mrs. Charles Simpson, McEwen H.S.
Athena, Oregon
Mrs. Mildred Drinkard, West Lauderdale H.S.
Collinsville, Mississippi

INDIA CURRY SAUCE

¼ c. onion, chopped
½ c. apple, chopped
¼ c. celery, chopped
¼ c. butter
1½-2 t. curry powder
⅛ t. ginger
2½ c. chicken stock
3 T. flour
2 egg yolks, beaten slightly
½ c. cream
Salt and pepper to taste
1¼ lb. frozen shrimp
1 can crab meat

(Continued on Next Page)

Cook onion, apple and celery in butter for 5 minutes; blend in curry powder and ginger. Add 2 cups chicken stock; simmer for 15 minutes. Blend flour with remaining stock; stir into onion mixture. Cook until thick and smooth. Add egg yolk. Cook over low heat for 2 minutes. Add remaining ingredients. Serve in pastry shells. Yield: 6 servings.

Mrs. Alice Sheppard, South Jr. H.S.
Grand Forks, North Dakota

SALMON-TUNA MEIN CASSEROLE

½ c. onion, finely chopped
½ c. celery, finely chopped
2 T. butter or margarine
1 can condensed cream of mushroom soup
1 7-oz. can tuna, coarsely flaked
½ 7½-oz. can salmon, coarsely flaked
Dash of pepper
½ t. monosodium glutamate
1 can chow mein noodles

Saute onion and celery in butter until tender. Add condensed soup and stir. Drain oil from tuna and salmon; flake coarsely and add to mixture. Add pepper and monosodium glutamate. Simmer for 2 minutes and remove from heat. Cover bottom of buttered casserole with chow mein noodles. Pour salmon-tuna mixture over noodles and top with remaining noodles. Bake in 350°F. oven for 15 minutes. Yield: 4-5 servings.

Mrs. Helen Ota, Pahoa H.S.
Pahoa, Hawaii

SEAFOOD DELIGHT

2 T. butter
2 T. flour
⅛ t. salt
Pepper to taste
½ t. Worcestershire sauce
½ c. milk
1 can frozen cream of shrimp soup
1 c. fresh or canned shrimp
1 6-oz. can crab or lobster
1 c. cooked scallops
2 T. pimento, chopped
1 sm. can sliced mushrooms (opt.)
Buttered bread crumbs

Melt butter in top of double boiler; stir in flour and seasonings. Add milk; stir until smooth and thickened. Add frozen shrimp soup; heat until dissolved. Add drained seafood, pimento and mushrooms. Pour into greased casserole; top with bread crumbs. Bake at 375°F. until topping is browned, 25-30 minutes. NOTE: If desired, French-fried onion rings or crushed potato chips may be substituted for bread crumbs. Yield: 4-5 servings.

Mrs. Charlotte Thompson, Claremont Jr. H.S.
Claremont, New Hampshire

RICE AND SEAFOOD CASSEROLE

2 c. boiled rice
1 sm. can crab meat
1 can shrimp
1 t. salt
½ t. paprika
¼ t. dry mustard
2-3 T. Sherry (opt.)
2 c. med. white sauce
½ c. buttered bread crumbs
½ c. cheese, grated

Place boiled rice in a greased casserole or in individual ramekins; top with crab and shrimp. Add seasonings and Sherry to white sauce; pour over rice and seafood. Top with buttered crumbs, cheese and a dash of paprika. Bake at 375°F. for 25 minutes or until browned. Yield: 4-6 servings.

Mary Lou Fraser, Grace Davis H.S.
Modesto, California

SEAFOOD CASSEROLE

1 med. green pepper, chopped
1 med. onion, chopped
1 c. celery, chopped
1 6½-oz. can tuna
1 5¾-oz. can shrimp
½ t. salt
⅛ t. pepper
½ t. Worcestershire sauce
1 c. mayonnaise
1 sm. can button mushrooms
1 c. buttered bread crumbs

Combine all ingredients except crumbs. Pour mixture in buttered casserole. Sprinkle bread crumbs on top. Bake 30 minutes at 350°F. Yield: 4 servings.

Mrs. Beverly Johnson, Slinger H.S.
Slinger, Wisconsin

SEAFOOD NEWBERG

1 sm. can shrimp
1 can crab meat
2 cans tuna
1 T. onion
1 T. lemon juice
1 T. Worcestershire sauce
Dash of Tabasco
½ t. dry mustard
2 c. med. white sauce
¾ c. corn flakes, crushed
¼ c. butter, melted

Drain and flake all seafood and place in a greased casserole. Add seasonings to white sauce; pour over fish. Combine corn flakes and butter. Cover fish with mixture. Bake 20 minutes at 425°F. Yield: 4 servings.

Mrs. Lew Renard, Blair H.S.
Blair, Nebraska

COMBINATION SEAFOOD CASSEROLE

2½ c. celery, diced
1 can crab meat
1 can shrimp
1 can tuna
1 sm. green pepper, chopped
4 hard-cooked eggs, diced
1½ c. mayonnaise
1½ t. salt
1 sm. onion, diced
Buttered crumbs

Precook celery just until tender. Mix all ingredients together except crumbs. Spread ingredients in greased 9-inch square pan and top with buttered crumbs. Bake at 350°F. for 30 minutes. Cut in squares and serve hot with quarters of lemon or tartar sauce. Yield: 8 servings.

Margaret Morgan, Austin H.S.
Austin, Minnesota

SEAFOOD GOURMET

1 6½-oz. can crab meat
1 6½-oz. can rock lobster
1 c. cooked shrimp, halved
3 c. cooked rice
1 c. diced celery, partially cooked
2 T. chopped parsley
Dash of pepper
Pinch of thyme
1 t. salt
1 c. milk
½ c. light cream
½ c. catsup
½ c. Cheddar cheese, grated
½ c. buttered bread crumbs

Remove bones from crab; place crab meat in a buttered 2-quart casserole. Cut lobster into pieces; add to crab. Add shrimp, rice, celery, parsley and seasonings. Combine milk, cream and catsup; add to seafood. Mix lightly. Sprinkle with cheese and crumbs. Bake at 375°F. for 25-30 minutes. Yield: 6 servings.

Dorothy J. McCabe, Blakely Borough Jr.-Sr. H.S.
Peckville, Pennsylvania

SEAFOOD-NOODLE CASSEROLE

1 c. lobster or crab meat
1 c. white tuna
3 c. cooked egg noodles
½ c. margarine
8 T. flour
1 tsp. salt
¼ t. pepper
1 qt. milk
1 t. dry mustard
1 t. onion, grated
½ t. paprika
Grated cheese

Melt butter; stir in flour, salt and pepper. Stir in milk gradually; cook until thickened and smooth. Add mustard, onion and paprika, to 2 cups of sauce. Pour into a large casserole. Add egg noodles. Mix lobster or crab with tuna and remaining white sauce; put on top of noodles. Cover with grated cheese. Bake at 325°F. for 1 hour. Yield: 6 servings.

Mrs. Miriam R. Eames, Sharon H.S
Sharon, Massachusetts

SEAFOOD PIE

1 c. crab flakes, fresh or canned
1 c. shrimp, fresh or canned
3 eggs, beaten
⅓ c. butter, melted
¾ t. mustard
¼ t. paprika
½ t. Worcestershire sauce
1 t. salt
1½ c. undiluted evaporated milk
1 T. pimento, chopped
½ c. cracker crumbs

Mix crab and shrimp. Stir in eggs and butter. Add seasonings and milk. Place the mixture in a well buttered casserole. Sprinkle with pimento and cracker crumbs. Bake at 325°F. for 50 to 60 minutes. Yield: 6 servings.

Mrs. Jean Puckett, Klamath Union H.S.
Klamath Falls, Oregon

SHRIMP-TUNA CURRY

1 med. onion, chopped
½ green pepper, seeded and chopped
3 T. butter
2 cans cream of celery soup
¼ c. milk
1 c. cooked small shrimp
1 7-oz. can tuna, flaked
1 t. curry powder
2 hard-cooked eggs, sliced
Parsley, chopped (garnish)

Saute onion and green pepper in butter until limp and wilted. Add the soup and milk and mix well. Stir in shrimp, tuna and curry powder; simmer for 30 minutes, stirring occasionally. Gently stir in sliced eggs and serve immediately in a rice or noodle ring. Garnish with parsley. Yield: 6-8 servings.

Maude P. Whitcomb, Appleton Academy
New Ipswich, New Hampshire

SEAFOOD SUPREME

2 cans undiluted cream of shrimp soup
1 can lobster meat
1 can crab meat
1 can tuna fish or shrimp
Croutons or buttered crumbs

Heat oven to 350°F. Mix all ingredients except croutons; pour into buttered 2-quart baking dish. Top with croutons or buttered crumbs. Bake 30-40 minutes. Yield: 6-8 servings.

Barbara Ann Dunbury, Woburn H.S.
Woburn, Massachusetts

TUNA-SHRIMP CASSEROLE

¾ pound rice
½ lb. cheese, cubed
2 cans tuna
1 can shrimp
1 green pepper, cut
1 sm. can pimento, cut
5 hard-cooked eggs
4 c. med. white sauce

Boil and blanch rice. Spread the remaining ingredients in a flat pan in layers alternately with the medium white sauce. Have a layer of rice, cheese and white sauce on top. Bake 30-45 minutes at 375°F. Yield: 12 servings.

Margaret Konesky, Starbuck H.S.
Starbuck, Minnesota

VERSATILE SEAFOOD

1 can tuna
1 can crab meat
1 can shrimp
2 T. French dressing
½ c. cucumber, diced
2 T. radishes, sliced
1 T. capers
2 T. lemon juice
1 c. mayonnaise
Salt and pepper to taste

Combine tuna, crab meat, shrimp and French dressing; chill. Add the remaining ingredients and toss lightly. Serve in lettuce cups, in patty shells, or as a hearty main dish with macaroni. Yield: 4-6 servings.

Mrs. Marlys Schneider, Washington H.S.
Sioux Falls, South Dakota

BAKED FISH WITH TAPIOCA DRESSING

4 T. instant tapioca
1¾ t. salt
1 c. milk, scalded
1 c. hot water
2 lb. fish
⅛ t. pepper
2 thin slices bacon, salt pork or 4 t. butter
2 onions, thinly sliced
1 green pepper, chopped
1 cup canned tomatoes

Add tapioca and ¾ teaspoon salt to milk and water; cook in double boiler for 15 minutes or until tapioca is clear, stirring frequently. Clean and wash fish. Sprinkle with salt and pepper. Gash fish and insert slices of pork, or dot with butter. Place on thin layer of vegetables in greased baking pan. Place remaining vegetables around fish and pour tapioca mixture over all. Bake at 350°F. for 1 hour, or until fish is done, basting frequently. Yield: 6 servings.

Mrs. Larry Stomm, Auburn H.S.
Auburn, Indiana

FISH AND RICE CASSEROLE

1 T. lemon juice
1 t. Worcestershire sauce
1½ t. salt
Dash of paprika
1½ lb. fish fillets
2 T. onion, minced
Dash of pepper
¼ c. parsley, chopped
¼ c. butter, melted
1⅓ c. instant rice
¼-½ t. oregano
1⅓ c. boiling water

Combine lemon juice, Worcestershire sauce, 1 teaspoon salt and paprika. Dip fish in mixture. Combine remaining ingredients. Cover and let stand 5 minutes. Mix with the fish mixture. Spoon into a greased casserole; cover and bake at 350°F. for 30 minutes. Yield: 6 servings.

Ann Derrick, Amarillo H.S.
Amarillo, Texas

Meat-Vegetable Casseroles

ADAPTABLE SIX-LAYER DINNER

Potatoes, ground
Rice
Carrots, ground
Onion, ground
Hamburger
Cooked tomatoes

Place potatoes in greased casserole; sprinkle with a thin layer of rice. Add layers of carrots, onion and meat. Top with tomatoes. Bake at 350°F. for 2 hours to 2 hours and 30 minutes. Yield: 1-100 servings.

Mrs. Barbara Fitts, Garfield H.S.
Garfield, Washington

AMERICAN SUKIYAKI

2 onions, diced
1 stalk celery, diced
1 bunch carrots, diced
1 can bamboo shoots, diced
¼ c. butter
1½ lb. beef sirloin, cut in slivers
1 c. beef broth, heated
4 t. soy sauce

Saute vegetables in butter for 7 minutes. Add beef; saute 7 minutes longer. Add hot beef broth and soy sauce. Serve over fluffy white rice. Yield: 4 servings.

Mrs. Dianne Fynboh, Onamia H.S.
Onamia, Minnesota

BAKED CHILI

2 lb. hamburger
1 med. onion, chopped
1 c. uncooked macaroni
1 t. salt
1 qt. whole tomatoes
1 can chili beans
¼ t. rosemary leaves

Brown hamburger and onion; remove excess fat. Combine all ingredients in a casserole. Bake at 350-375°F. for 1 hour. Yield: 8 servings.

Helèn Ruth McElwee
Southeast Fountain School Corporation
Veedersburg, Indiana

BARLEY HOT DISH

1½ lb. hamburger
1 onion
1 c. celery
1 sm. green pepper (opt.)
1½ c. barley, uncooked
1 No. 2 can peas with liquid
1 No. 2 can tomatoes
1 can cream of mushroom soup

Brown hamburger, onion, celery and green pepper. Place in casserole. Add parsley, undrained peas, tomatoes and mushroom soup. Bake at 350°F. for 1 hour or until done. Yield: 8 servings.

Mrs. Delores Sandbeck, Dilworth H.S.
Dilworth, Minnesota

BEAN-BURGER CASSEROLE

1 lb. ground beef
1 sm. onion, chopped
1 lge. can pork and beans
2 cans tomato soup
2 T. brown sugar
1 T. mustard

Saute meat and onion until tender. Put into greased casserole. Add remaining ingredients; mix well. Bake at 400°F. for 45 minutes. Yield: 6-8 servings.

Janet Oyler, Garden City Sr. H.S.
Garden City, Kansas

BEATNICK CASSEROLE

1 lb. ground beef
1 onion, sliced or chopped
1 T. fat
1 can tomato soup
½ c. water
1 can green beans
1 c. cooked noodles
1 c. Cheddar cheese, shredded
Oregano or thyme (opt.)
Garlic (opt.)

Brown the hamburger and onions in the fat. Combine with the remaining ingredients, using half the cheese in the casserole and other half to top the casserole. Pour into a greased casserole and bake 20 to 25 minutes in a 375°F. oven. NOTE: If desired, any other vegetable may be substituted for beans. Yield: 4-6 servings.

Agnes Dervishian, Caruthers Union H.S.
Caruthers, California

BEEF-CRUST CASSEROLE

1½ lb. ground beef
½ c. onion, chopped
2 t. salt
¼ c. catsup
2 cans cream of mushroom soup
1 10-oz. pkg. frozen peas and carrots
½ c. converted rice, uncooked
½ c. water
½ t. salt
1 c. chow mein noodles

Combine meat, onion, salt, catsup; use to line 2½-quart casserole. Combine soup, vegetables, rice, water and salt; pour into meat shell. Cover; bake at 350°F. for 1 hour and 15 minutes. Top with noodles; bake, uncovered, 15 minutes. NOTE: Unbaked casserole may be refrigerated and baked when needed. Yield: 6 servings.

Janice Ann Schuster, Grand Rapids H.S.
Grand Rapids, Ohio

BEEF-CORN DISH

1-1½ lb. ground beef, browned
1 med. onion, sliced
1 No. 303 can cream-style corn
1 No. 2½ can tomatoes
1½ c. rolled cracker crumbs
Salt and pepper
2 t. Worcestershire sauce

Into a baking dish put a layer of the cooked meat and onion. Add a layer of corn. Top with tomatoes. Sprinkle with a covering of cracker crumbs. Season to taste with salt, pepper and the Worcestershire sauce. Bake 1 hour at 350°F. Yield: 6 servings.

Mrs. Wm. J. Buyske, Troy H.S.
Troy, Montana

BEEF AND EGGPLANT CASSEROLE

2 t. butter, melted
¾ c. soft bread crumbs
1 lb. ground chuck
¼ c. onion, shredded
1 clove garlic, mashed
3 T. fat, melted
2 med. eggplants, pared and cubed
2 t. salt
Dash of pepper
Dash of thyme
1 can tomato paste
1 c. evaporated milk
1 c. tomato soup, undiluted

Toss butter and crumbs. Brown beef, onion and garlic in fat. Add eggplant, salt, pepper and thyme. Cover; simmer 10 minutes or until eggplant is tender. Stir in tomato paste, milk, and soup. Pour into 2-quart casserole. Top with buttered crumbs. Bake at 375°F. for 30 minutes or until crumbs are browned.

Brenda J. Payne, Lewis-Palmer H.S.
Monument, Colorado

BEEF LOAF-SCALLOPED POTATO CASSEROLE

4 c. raw potatoes, sliced
1 T. onion, chopped
2 t. salt
⅝ t. pepper
1 t. parsley, chopped
1 lb. ground beef
¾ c. evaporated or whole milk
½ c. fine soda cracker crumbs
¼ c. catsup
¼ c. onion, chopped

Arrange potatoes in a greased 2-quart casserole. Sprinkle with onion, 1 teaspoon salt, ½ teaspoon pepper and parsley. Mix remaining ingredients. Place over the potatoes. Bake at 350°F. for 1 hour to 1 hour and 30 minutes. Serve hot. Yield: 4-6 servings.

Bethany Radtke, Marine City Ward, Cottrell H.S.
Marine City, Michigan

BEEF-MUSHROOM CASSEROLE

1 med. onion, minced
½ green pepper, minced
2 T. butter
1½ lb. ground beef
1 c. cooked rice
1 c. tomato juice
1 4-oz. can mushrooms
1 c. peas, cooked and drained
Salt and pepper to taste

Brown onions and pepper in butter. Stir ground beef into mixture; cook until redness has left meat. Mix with remaining ingredients. Place in greased baking dish; bake at 350°F. for 45 minutes. Yield: 4-6 servings.

Mrs. Marjorie Wilcox, Swartz Creek H.S.
Swartz Creek, Michigan

BEEF NEAPOLITAN

⅓ c. onion, chopped
3 cloves garlic, crushed
1 c. carrots, diced
1½ c. celery diced
¼ c. salad oil
1½ lb. ground chuck
1 6-oz. can mushroom caps
½ c. cooking Sherry
1 6-oz. can tomato paste
1 1-lb. 3-oz. can tomatoes
1 T. salt
½ t. pepper
½ t. oregano
1 8-oz. pkg. shell macaroni
½ c. buttered bread crumbs
1 c. grated sharp Cheddar cheese
Parmesan cheese

Saute onion, garlic, carrots and celery in hot oil until golden brown. Add beef, stirring until lightly browned. Add mushrooms, Sherry, tomato paste, tomatoes, salt, pepper and oregano; simmer, uncovered, for 1 hour and 30 minutes. Cook macaroni; drain well. Stir into meat sauce. Pour into 3-quart casserole. Top with Cheddar cheese and crumbs. Bake at 350°F. for 30 minutes. Serve sprinkled with Parmesan cheese. Yield: 12 servings.

Mrs. Joan Grube, Hartford Jr. H.S.
Croton, Ohio

BEEF AND POTATO LOAF

1 lb. ground lean beef
¾ c. evaporated milk
½ c. cracker crumbs or oatmeal
¼ c. catsup
5 T. onion, chopped
2 t. salt
¼ t. pepper
4 c. raw potatoes, thinly sliced
1-3 t. parsley flakes

(Continued on Next Page)

Combine beef, milk, crumbs, catsup, 4 tablespoons onion, 1 teaspoon salt and ⅛ teaspoon pepper; mix thoroughly. Arrange potatoes and 1 tablespoon onion in a greased 2-quart casserole. Sprinkle with remaining salt, pepper and parsley flakes. Spread meat mixture evenly over potatoes. Decorate top with more catsup if desired. Bake at 350°F. for 1 hour, until potatoes are tender. Yield: 4 servings.

This recipe submitted by the following teachers:
Susanne Davis, Ruby H.S.
Ruby, South Carolina
Mrs. Evelyn Bosak, Osways Valley Jr. H.S.
Shinglehouse, Pennsylvania
Brenda Joyce Cox, Allendale H.S
Allendale, Illinois

STUFFED PEPPERS

8 green peppers
1 sm. onion, chopped
1 lb. ground beef
2 T. fat
4 med. tomatoes, chopped
1½ c. cut, fresh corn
Salt and pepper
Buttered crumbs

Remove top and seeds from green peppers. Parboil 5 minutes; drain. Brown onion and meat in fat; add tomatoes, corn and seasonings. Stuff peppers and top with buttered crumbs. Stand upright in greased baking dish. Add small amount of water. Cover and bake at 350°F. for 1 hour. Yield: 8 servings.

Donna Campbell, Pine Valley H.S.
Halfway, Oregon

BEEF-TOMATO DISH

1 sm. onion, chopped
1 sm. green pepper, chopped
1 T. fat
½ lb. ground beef
¾ t. salt
1 egg, beaten
1 c. cream-style corn
1 med. tomato, thinly sliced
Buttered bread crumbs

Saute onion and pepper in the fat until onion becomes transparent. Add the ground beef and salt; cook until the meat separates into small particles. Remove from heat. Stir in egg. In casserole place ½ cup of corn. Spread half the meat mixture over corn. Cover with half of the tomato slices. Repeat with remaining corn, meat and tomato. Top with buttered bread crumbs. Bake in a 350°F. oven for 30 minutes. Yield: 4-6 servings

Sarah Beth Galloway, Bonneville H.S.
Idaho Falls, Idaho

BEEF-VEGETABLE CASSEROLE

1½ lb. beef, cut in 1-inch cubes
2 T. fat
2 T. flour
1 t. salt
2 t. paprika
1½ t. chili powder
¼ t. pepper
1 No. 2 can tomatoes
6 med. onions, cut in half
1 c. celery, sliced
½ c. carrots, sliced
1 c. uncooked noodles

Brown beef in hot fat. Mix flour and seasonings; add to meat. Stir in tomatoes and cook over low heat for 1 hour. Add remaining ingredients. Pour into 2-quart casserole. Cover. Bake at 350°F. for 1 hour or until vegetables and meat are tender. Yield: 8 servings.

Helen Madsen, Gaylord Community School
Gaylord, Michigan

BERNICES ZITONI

2 onions, chopped
2 sm. green peppers, chopped
1 clove garlic, minced
½ c. oil
2 cans tomato soup
1 can tomato paste
1 can corn
1 can mushrooms
2 c. browned hamburger or other meat or chicken
1 c. Swiss cheese, grated
1 lb. spaghetti, cooked
1 c. cheese, grated

Cook onions, green peppers and garlic in oil until tender. Add tomato soup and tomato paste; cook 5 minutes. Add the corn, mushrooms, meat and Swiss cheese. Mix with cooked spaghetti. Place in greased baking dish; sprinkle with grated cheese and a few mushrooms. Bake for 30 minutes at 325°F. Yield: 8-10 servings.

Mrs. Ruth Hockersmith, Medford Sr. H.S.
Medford, Oregon

BEST HOT DISH

1 lb. ground beef
2 sm. onions, finely chopped
1 c. whole-kernel corn
½ c. mushroom pieces
1 can condensed tomato soup
½ c. sliced stuffed olives
½ t. salt
½ t. chili powder
1 lb. macaroni, cooked
¼ lb. rich cheese, grated

Brown ground beef; add onions. Add remaining ingredients and stir thoroughly. Bake at 325°F. for 45 minutes. Yield: 4-6 servings.

Mrs. Mary Zurawski, Alexander H.S.
Nekoosa, Wisconsin

THE BISHOP'S BEANS

½ c. milk
1 c. soft bread crumbs
1½ t. salt
⅛ t. pepper
½ t. chili powder
1½ lb. ground beef
5 T. fat
1¼ c. onions, sliced
2 8-oz. cans tomato sauce
2 med. green peppers, sliced
3 No. 2 cans red kidney beans

Combine milk, bread crumbs, 1 teaspoon salt, pepper, chili powder and ground beef. Form mixture into small balls, using 1 tablespoons for each. Wet hands to prevent sticking. Brown meat balls in fat; remove meat. Cook onions and ½ teaspoon salt in same fat until soft. Add tomato sauce and green peppers; simmer 8-10 minutes. Put beans in shallow casserole; add tomato sauce and a border of meat balls. Bake at 350°F. for 40-50 minutes. Yield: 8 servings.

Mrs. Helen Wilson, State Supervisor
Home Economics Education
Boise, Idaho

BUSY DAY CASSEROLE

1½ lb. ground beef
2 c. tomatoes
1 med. onion, chopped
Salt and pepper
4 potatoes, thinly sliced
1 box frozen corn
1 box frozen peas
Cheese, grated

Grease bottom and sides of deep baking dish. Place raw ground beef, tomatoes and onion in bottom of dish. Add a layer of floured potatoes. Top with frozen corn and frozen peas. Cover; bake 2 hours at 350°F. Top with cheese before serving. Yield: 12 servings.

Shirley Umberger, Elwood Public School
Elwood, Nebraska

CABBAGE ROLLS WITH TOMATO SAUCE

8 lge. cabbage leaves
1 lb. ground beef
1 t. salt
¼ t. pepper
2 T. onion, chopped
1 c. cooked rice
1 egg
1 can tomato soup
1 c. water

Pour boiling water over cabbage leaves and bring to boil; drain. Season meat; add onion, rice and egg. Place a portion of the filling in each cabbage leaf and fasten with toothpicks. Place rolls in casserole and cover with tomato soup mixed with water. Bake covered at 350°F. for 45 minutes, and uncovered for 15 minutes. Yield: 8 servings.

Mrs. Esther E. Smith, Cowanesque Valley
Joint School
Westfield, Pennsylvania

BRUSSELS SPROUTS AND BEEF RAGOUT

1½ lb. cubed beef chuck
2 T. flour
2 T. butter or margarine
2 c. beef stock or bouillon
½ c. California Burgundy
2 bay leaves
1 clove garlic, crushed
1 t. salt
½ t. thyme
Freshly ground black pepper to taste
12 whole new potatoes, pared or 6 med. potatoes, pared and quartered
8 whole small onions or 4 leeks, cut in pieces
4 carrots, quartered
2 10-oz. pkg. frozen California Brussels sprouts
½ lb. mushrooms
¼ c. chopped mint or parsley

Coat beef with flour, brown in butter in Dutch oven. Add stock, wine, seasonings, potatoes, onions and carrots. Heat to boiling point. Cover and cook over low heat for 20 minutes. Add remaining ingredients; cover and simmer 25 minutes or until tender. Garnish with additional fresh mint as desired. Yield: 6 servings.

Photograph for this recipe on page 151

CABBAGE CASSEROLE

1 med. onion, chopped
2 T. margarine or butter
1 lb. ground beef
1 t. salt
Dash of pepper
1 med. cabbage
2 c. American cheese, grated
1½ c. sour cream
1 c. buttered bread crumbs
¼ c. wine (opt.)

Brown onion in the margarine. Add ground beef and brown; season. Cut up cabbage into pieces about 1-inch square; add to the ground beef mixture. Cover and cook slowly until the cabbage turns translucent, about 10 minutes. Add cheese and sour cream; mix thoroughly. Put in greased casserole; top with buttered crumbs. Bake at 375°F. for about 45 minutes. NOTE: May be reheated for second day servings. Yield: 6 servings.

Eva Risnel, Mira Costa H.S.
Manhattan Beach, California

CALICO BEAN HOT DISH

½-1 lb. hamburger
¼-½ lb. bacon, cut in small pieces
½-1 c. onion, chopped
½ c. catsup
⅓-½ c. packed brown sugar
1-3 t. mustard
2-6 t. vinegar
Salt to taste
1 No. 2 can pork and beans
1 No. 2 can kidney beans
1 No. 2 can lima beans

(Continued on Next Page)

Saute hamburger, bacon and onion until lightly brown. Drain only a small amount of liquid from beans. Thoroughly mix all ingredients. Bake, uncovered, for 1 hour and 30 minutes to 2 hours in a 300°F. oven. For faster cooking, place dish in 350°F. oven for 40 minutes. Yield: 8-10 servings.

This recipe submitted by the following teachers:

Mrs. Iris Hart, Okabena H.S,
Okabena, Minnesota

Mrs. Frances Reed, Anthony Jr. H.S.
Minneapolis, Minnesota

Sally Rae Fischer, Princeton H.S.
Princeton, Minnesota

CASSEROLE DISH

1½ lb. ground beef
1 T. fat
2 8-oz. can tomato sauce
1 t. salt
⅛ t. pepper
½ pkg. elbow macaroni
2 T. butter, melted
1 c. cottage cheese
1 3-oz. pkg. cream cheese
¼ c. milk
1 T. vinegar
½ c. whole green onions, chopped
3 T. green pepper, chopped
1¾ c. whole-kernel corn, drained

Brown ground beef in fat; remove from heat. Stir in tomato sauce and seasonings. Cook macaroni; drain. Mix melted butter with macaroni. Combine cottage cheese, cream cheese, milk, vinegar, onions and green peppers. Spread one-third of meat mixture on bottom of well greased 2½-quart casserole. Put half of macaroni in layer on top of meat; layer half of corn. In fourth layer put all of cheese mixture. Cover with another layer of meat mixture, rest of macaroni and corn. Top with remaining meat. Bake at 350°F. for 30-40 minutes. Yield: 8 servings.

Mrs. Gayle Pfeil, Monona Grove H.S.
Madison, Wisconsin

CASSEROLE LAYER DINNER

2-3 raw potatoes, sliced
½ c. raw rice
2 sm. onions, sliced
2 green peppers, sliced
1 lb. ground beef
1 No. 1 can tomatoes
½ c. water
2 t. sugar
Salt and pepper to taste

Arrange the potatoes, rice, onions and green peppers in layers in a large casserole. Brown the beef and put on top of the layers. Pour tomatoes and water over meat. Sprinkle sugar and seasonings over top. Bake in a 350°F. oven for 2-3 hours or until vegetables are soft. Yield: 6 servings.

Martha Sterrett, Franklin Area Jr. H.S.
Murrysville, Pennsylvania

CASSEROLE OF GROUND BEEF

1 lb. lean ground beef
¼ lb. wide noodles, uncooked
1 T. Worcestershire sauce
3 t. chili powder
1 t. salt
3 T. onion, chopped
1 No. 2½ can tomatoes
1 pkg. frozen mixed vegetables
⅓ lb. sharp cheese, grated

Combine all ingredients except cheese. Pour into casserole; cover. Bake at 350°F. for 45 minutes. Sprinkle with cheese. Continue baking, uncovered for 30 minutes. Yield: 6 servings.

Mrs. Effie S. Gaynon, Leonard Schools
Saxtons River, Vermont

CEDRIC ADAMS' CASSEROLE

2 lb. ground beef, separated into particles
Salt and pepper
1 onion, minced
½ head lge. cabbage, finely shredded
1 can condensed tomato soup

Place a layer of ground beef in the bottom of a large casserole. Salt and pepper to suit taste. Sprinkle a layer of onion and a layer of cabbage over the beef. Continue to alternate layers until casserole is filled. Cover mixture with undiluted soup. Bake in 350°F. oven 1 hour and 30 minutes to 2 hours, or until cabbage is tender. Yield: 6 servings.

Mrs. Audrey Krengel, Hawley Public H.S.
Hawley, Minnesota

CHEESE LASAGNA

½ c. onion, chopped
3 T. olive oil
½ t. garlic salt
½ t. parsley, chopped
½ t. oregano
1 t. basil
1¾ t. salt
½ t. sugar
¼ t. pepper
1 No. 2½ can tomatoes
1 6-oz. can tomato paste
½ lb. lasagna noodles
2 lb. cottage cheese
¾ lb. American cheese
Parmesan cheese

Brown onion in oil; add seasonings, tomatoes and tomato paste. Simmer for 20 minutes. Cook noodles according to package directions in boiling salted water. Place a layer of noodles, cottage cheese, American cheese and sauce. Repeat layers; top with Parmesan cheese. Bake at 350°F. for 1 hour. Yield: 16 servings.

Mrs. Forrest A. Stewart, Sandoval
Community Unit #501 H.S.
Sandoval, Illinois

CHILI CON CARNE

1 T. bacon fat
½ of med. onion, minced
1 clove garlic
1 c. ground beef
1 t. salt
Dash of pepper
¼ t. chili powder
½ c. cooked or canned kidney beans
1 c. canned tomatoes
¼ c. cheese, grated (opt.)

Melt bacon fat. Add onion and garlic; saute for three minutes. Add the meat after removing the garlic. Brown meat for 3 minutes, stirring constantly. Add seasonings, beans and tomatoes. Pour into a greased casserole and top with cheese. Bake in 375°F. oven for 15 to 20 minutes. NOTE: This may also be done in a covered fry pan or cooked over low heat on top of stove. Yield: 3-4 servings.

Sister M. Herbert, St. Joseph Academy H.S.
Cleveland, Ohio

CHIP 'N' CHILI CASSEROLE

1 lb. hamburger
½ c. onion, chopped
½ c. celery, chopped (opt.)
1 1-lb. can chili with beans
1 c. American cheese, grated
1 c. corn chips

Brown hamburger, onion and celery in frying pan. Add chili and simmer about 5 minutes. Put half of the hamburger mixture in the bottom of casserole dish; add half of corn chips and half of cheese. Add the remaining hamburger mixture, corn chips and cheese. Bake at 350°F. for about 20 minutes. Yield: 6-8 servings.

Nona L. Dutson, Marsh Valley H.S.
Arimo, Idaho

CHOW MEIN CASSEROLE

1 lb. ground beef
2 T. butter
½ c. onion, chopped
1 c. celery, chopped
1 4-oz. can mushroom stems and pieces
1 can mushroom soup
1 can bean sprouts, undrained
½ c. water
¼ c. soy sauce

Brown beef in butter. Add onion; brown. Pour into 2-quart casserole. Stir in remaining ingredients. Bake at 350°F. for 1 hour. Yield: 6 servings.

Mrs. Allan P. Cobb, Mosinee H.S.
Mosinee, Wisconsin

CONNECTICUT SUPPER

2 lge. onions, chopped
2 T. fat
2 lb. beef chuck, cut in 1-inch cubes
1 c. water
2 lge. potatoes, sliced ⅛-in. thick
1 10½-oz. can cream of mushroom soup
1 c. commercial sour cream
1¼ c. milk
1 t. salt
¼ t. pepper
1 c. Cheddar cheese, grated
½ c. cereal flakes, crushed

Brown onions in fat. Add meat and water; cover. Simmer 50 minutes. Pour into oblong baking dish. Place potato slices over meat. Blend soup, cream, milk, salt and pepper. Pour evenly over the top. Sprinkle with cheese and cereal flakes. Bake at 350°F. for 1 hour and 30 minutes or until done. Yield: 6-8 servings.

Susan Snell, Montour H.S.
McKees Rocks, Pennsylvania

CORN AND HAMBURGER CASSEROLE

1 c. macaroni
1 lb. hamburger
1 onion, diced
1 green pepper, diced
1 can tomato soup
1 can whole-kernel corn
¼ lb. cheese, grated

Cook macaroni in boiling water. Brown hamburger, onion and pepper. Add soup, corn and cheese. Put in casserole; bake at 325°F. for 1 hour. Yield: 6-8 servings.

Jean Davis, Fast Jr. H.S.
Great Falls, Montana

COWBOY CASSEROLE

1 lb. ground beef
3 T. fat
1 clove garlic
2½ t. salt
1¼ c. minced onion
½ c. minced green pepper
1 t. chili powder
1 No. 2 can tomatoes
½ c. uncooked rice
1 No. 2 can kidney beans, undrained

Cook ground beef in fat until lightly browned. On cutting board thinly slice garlic; sprinkle with salt and mash thoroughly to a pulp. Add to beef with onion, green pepper and chili powder. Cook 5 minutes; remove from heat and add tomatoes. Combine rice and kidney beans in 2-quart casserole. Add hot tomato mixture. Bake, covered, for 1 hour in a 350°F. oven. Yield: 6-8 servings.

Mrs. Dorothy M. Hardin, Lebanon
Community H.S.
Lebanon, Illinois

ECONOMY ONE DISH MEAL

¾ c. onion, sliced
2 c. raw potatoes, sliced
1 lb. ground beef
½ c. uncooked rice
1 c. celery, chopped
1 No. 303 can red kidney beans
2 c. canned tomatoes
Salt and pepper

Arrange ingredients in layers in a buttered 3-quart casserole, seasoning each layer slightly with the salt and pepper. Cover and bake in 350°F. oven for 2 hours. Yield: 6 servings.

Mrs. Marjorie Corsaw, Cuba H.S.
Cuba, Illinois

EDNA'S CHINESE CASSEROLE

1 lb. hamburger
1 c. onion, chopped
2 T. fat, melted
½ c. uncooked rice
1 can cream of chicken soup
1 soup can water
2 T. soy sauce
1 10-oz. pkg. frozen peas
1 c. celery, cut diagonally in 1-in pieces
½-¾ c. sliced almonds
2 T. butter, melted

Saute meat and onion in fat until light brown. Toss together meat mixture, rice, soup, water and soy sauce. Pour into greased shallow casserole. Bake in preheated 350°F. oven for 45 minutes. Toss in peas and celery; bake for 15 minutes longer. Brown almonds in butter; sprinkle over casserole. Yield: 6 servings.

Irma I. Whitehead, Grace M. Davis H.S.
Modesto, California

EGGPLANT AND ROUND BEEF CASSEROLE

1 lge. onion, chopped
¼-½ c. butter
1 lb. ground beef
½ c. tomato sauce
½ c. water
1 t. salt
⅛ t. pepper
1 med. eggplant

Saute onion in 2 tablespoons fat until yellow. Add ground beef and cook until brown. Combine tomato sauce, water, salt and pepper; pour over meat mixture. Bring to boil and cook 5 minutes. Slice eggplant and brown lightly in remaining butter. Place layer of egg plant in 1½-quart casserole; add a layer of meat drained from sauce, another layer of eggplant, and another of meat. Pour sauce over all. Bake uncovered at 350°F. for 20-30 minutes. Yield: 5-6 servings.

Vivian Werk, Lebanon H.S.
Lebanon, Ohio

ERNIE'S SPECIAL

2 eggs, beaten
¼ c. milk
1 c. soft bread crumbs
1 lb. ground beef
2 t. salt
1 No. 2 can cream-style corn
2 t. mustard
¼ c. onion, finely chopped

Combine eggs, milk, and crumbs. Add remaining ingredients; pour into baking dish. Bake at 350°F. for 50 minutes. Yield: 4-6 servings.

Mrs. Margaret Hempel, Lennox H.S.
Lennox, South Dakota

FAVORITE SEVEN LAYER CASSEROLE

1 c. uncooked rice
1 can whole-kernel corn, drained
Salt and pepper to taste
2 8-oz. cans tomato sauce
¾ sauce cans water
¼-½ c. onion, chopped
¼-½ c. green pepper, chopped
¾ lb. ground beef
4 strips bacon, halved

Place rice and corn in layers in a 2-quart baking dish. Season to taste. Pour 1 can tomato sauce and ½ can water over the layers. Add layers of the onion and green pepper. Cover with a layer of seasoned ground beef. Pour remaining can of tomato sauce and ¼ can water over casserole. Top with bacon strips. Cover; bake at 350°F. for 1 hour; uncover and bake 30 minutes longer. Yield: 6 servings.

This recipe submitted by the following teachers:
Helen Perman, Athens H.S.
Athens, Alabama
Mrs. F. E. Johnson, North Chattanooga
Jr. H.S.
Chattanooga, Tennessee
Eleanor Avery, Larned H.S.
Larned, Kansas
Ruth Darnell, Neoga Community
Unit District #3
Neoga, Illinois
Mrs. Shirley Luna, Southcross Jr. H.S.
San Antonio, Texas

FIVE-IN-ONE DISH

½ lb. hamburger
3 med. potatoes, sliced
4 stalks celery, diced
1 med. onion, diced
2 c. tomatoes

Place hamburger on the bottom of a greased 2-quart casserole. Cover with layers of potatoes, celery, and onions. Pour tomatoes over the top. Bake in 350°F. oven for 1 hour. Yield: 6-8 servings.

Mrs. Doris Balbach, Warren Community H.S.
Warren, Illinois

FRENCH RAGOUT WITH OLIVES

1 c. spaghetti, broken up
2 lb. ground chuck
1 No. 3 can tomatoes
2 onions, chopped
2 green peppers, chopped
7 stalks celery, chopped
1 t. salt
1 t. pepper
1 No. 303 can small peas with liquid
1 4-oz. can sliced mushrooms, drained
1 c. ground pecans
3 t. butter or margarine
¼ c. grated Parmesan cheese
1 4-oz. can ripe pitted olives

In Dutch oven cook spaghetti in boiling salted water until tender. Drain; add chuck, tomatoes, onions, green peppers, celery, salt, pepper, peas, mushrooms and pecans. Mix well. Turn mixture into 3-quart casserole. Dot with butter. Sprinkle with Parmesan cheese. Bake at 350°F. for 1 hour or until slightly browned and hot in center. Garnish edge with drained olives. Yield: 6 servings.

Catherine Dicks Myers, State Supervisor
Home Economics Education
University Park, New Mexico

FRESH POTATO-BEEF HASH

1 lb. ground beef
3 T. fat
2 c. raw potatoes, coarsely grated
½ c. onions, minced
¼ c. green peppers, chopped
½ t. salt
Pepper to taste
¼ c. chili sauce

Brown beef in hot fat; add potatoes and remaining ingredients except chili sauce. Cover; cook on high until steaming. Reduce heat and simmer for 20-25 minutes. Remove cover and spread chili sauce over top. Broil under broiler to brown and crisp the top of the hash. NOTE: If a moist heat hash is preferred, add ½ cup beef stock, or bouillon cube plus water, to hash before cooking. Yield: 6 servings.

Rosetta Skinner, Inman Rural H.S.
Inman, Kansas

GLORIFIED STEW

1 lb. ground beef
1 sm. onion
1 can vegetable soup
1 can cream of mushroom soup
2 med. potatoes, sliced
2 carrots, sliced

Brown hamburger and onion; mix with soups. Place potatoes and carrots in bottom of baking dish. Pour the hamburger mixture on top. Bake one hour at 350°F. Yield: 6-8 servings.

Mrs. Wm. Keiner, Madison Central H.S.
Madison, South Dakota

FROZEN VEGETABLE-BEEF

1 lb. ground chuck
2 T. salad oil
1 c. onions, chopped
1 No. 303 can tomatoes
1½ t. salt
¾ t. chili powder
¼ t. monosodium glutamate
1 pkg. frozen mixed vegetables
¼ lb. medium noodles, uncooked
1½ c. cheese, grated

Brown beef in hot oil for 10 minutes. Add onions, tomatoes, salt and chili powder. Sprinkle the vegetables with monosodium glutamate. Combine vegetables, uncooked noodles and meat in a 2-quart casserole. Bake 45 minutes at 350°F. Top with cheese and bake 20 minutes more. Yield: 8-10 servings.

Mrs. Merle K. Heckler, Windber Area H.S.
Windber, Pennsylvania

GOULASH

5 slices bacon, cubed
1 lge. onion, chopped
1½ lb. hamburger
1 can peas
1 can whole corn
1 can baby lima beans
2 cans spaghetti in tomato sauce
2 c. canned tomatoes
2 t. paprika
2 t. salt
1 t. pepper

Fry bacon until golden brown; add onion and hamburger and brown. Add peas, corn, beans, spaghetti, tomato and seasonings. Simmer about 30 minutes. May be placed in casserole and bake at 350°F. for 45 minutes. Yield: 10 servings.

Mrs. Velda Roesler, Chandler H.S.
Fulda, Minnesota

GREEN BEANS AND HAMBURGER

1 med. onion, minced
3 T. butter
1½ lb. ground beef
1½ t. salt
½ t. pepper
¼ t. celery seed
¼ t. Worcestershire sauce
1 bay leaf
1 1-lb. can tomatoes
2 c. green beans, cut in 1-inch pieces
6 T. milk
½ c. water

Cook onion in butter for 5 minutes. Add beef and cook, stirring frequently for 5 minutes longer. Add remaining ingredients and simmer for 30 minutes. Yield: 6 servings.

Mrs. Beulah Buhr, Grant Park H.S.
Grant Park, Illinois

GROUND BEEF CASSEROLE

1 lb. lean ground beef
1 med. onion, chopped
1 No. 2 can cream-style corn
3 c. mashed potatoes
3 T. butter, melted
Brown meat and onion, stirring until crumbly. Pour into greased 2-quart casserole; top with corn and potatoes. Sprinkle with butter. Bake at 350°F. for 20 minutes or until golden brown. Yield: 4-6 servings.

Mrs. Frances E. Smith, Alpena H.S.
Alpena, South Dakota

GROUND BEEF CASSEROLE

2 lb. ground beef
1 c. celery, diced
1 sm. onion, diced
1 can cream-style corn
½ lb. cooked noodles, drained
1 can cream of mushroom soup
½ lb. med. cheese, cubed
1 c. buttered bread crumbs
Brown beef, celery and onion. Add corn, noodles, soup and cheese. Place in buttered casserole and top with bread crumbs. Bake at 350°F. for 30 minutes. NOTE: Half of the casserole may be frozen for later use. Yield: 10 servings.

Mrs. Arvella Curtis, Fulton H.S.
Middleton, Michigan

GROUND BEEF AND CORN CASSEROLE

2 lb. ground beef
1 pkg. macaroni rings
2 cans cream-style corn
2 cans chicken rice soup
2 t. salt
½ t. pepper
Brown meat. Cook macaroni; drain and mix with meat. Add corn, soup and seasoning. Bake 45 minutes at 350°F. Yield: 15 servings.

Mrs. Marianne Abramowski, Madison H.S.
Madison, Minnesota

GROUND STEAK LAYER DINNER

Potatoes, sliced
⅓ c. uncooked rice
1½ lb. ground steak
Onion, sliced
Sliced carrots or green pepper
1 qt. tomatoes
1 T. salt
1 T. sugar
Pepper
Place a thick layer of sliced potatoes in a deep well buttered baking pan. Wash rice and sprinkle over potatoes. Cover with ground steak; add a thick layer of onion and a layer of carrots or green pepper. Add salt and sugar to tomatoes and pour over layers. Sprinkle lightly with pepper and bake at 350°F. for 2 hours. Yield: 6 servings.

Mrs. Evelyn Van Vleet, Garden City Sr. H.S.
Garden City, Kansas

HAMBURGER-BEAN CASSEROLE

1 lge. or 2 sm. cans pork and beans
1 can lima beans
1 can kidney beans
1 can butter beans
1 can cut string beans
½ lb. hamburger
1 lge. onion, chopped
6 T. brown sugar
½ c. catsup
1 T. vinegar
1 t. salt
Chili powder (opt.)
Drain and save liquid from beans. Brown hamburger with onion. Add bean liquid, brown sugar, catsup, vinegar, salt and chili powder. Bring to a boil. Pour over mixture of beans in large casserole. Bake at 350°F. for 2 hours. Yield: 20 servings.

Mrs. Irene Louise Hogan, North Kitsap Jr. H.S.
Poulsbo, Washington

HAMBURGER-BEAN SPROUT CASSEROLE

1½ lb. ground beef
1 onion, browned
1 can cream of chicken soup
1 can cream of mushroom soup
2 T. soy sauce
1 can bean sprouts, finely cut
¾ c. rice
Combine all ingredients. Bake at 350°F. for 1 hour and 30 minutes, stirring twice while baking. Yield: 12 servings.

Mrs. Marge Harouff, Pierce H.S.
Pierce, Nebraska

HAMBURGER-CABBAGE CASSEROLE

1½ lb. hamburger
1 sm. onion, chopped
1 t. salt
⅛ t. pepper
1 2-lb. head cabbage
1 can cream of tomato soup
Brown hamburger and onion; add seasoning. Put a layer of cabbage in a greased 1½-quart casserole. Add a layer of hamburger. Repeat layers until dish is filled. Pour soup over mixture. Bake at 350°F. for 35 to 45 minutes, or until cabbage is done. Yield: 8-10 servings.

Genevieve Overvaag, Mountain Lake H.S.
Mountain Lake, Minnesota

HAMBURGER-CHIP CASSEROLE

1 can shoestring carrots
1 lb. hamburger, fried with onion
1 can peas
1 can cream of chicken soup
½ soup can water
1 pkg. potato chips
In a casserole arrange in layers the carrots, meat, peas, soup with water, and chips. Repeat with another set of layers. Put chips on top. Bake at 350°F. for ½ hour. Yield: 4-6 servings.

Mrs. Shirley Keenlance, Manawa H.S.
Manawa, Wisconsin

HAMBURGER-CORN CASSEROLE

4 lb. ground beef
3 med. onions, chopped
3 12-oz. cans whole-kernel corn, drained
3 cans condensed cream of chicken soup
3 cans condensed cream of mushroom soup
3 c. dairy sour cream
¾ c. pimento, chopped
2 t. salt
1½ t. monosodium glutamate
¾ t. pepper
9 c. med. noodles, cooked and drained

Brown meat. Add onion; cook until tender but not brown. Add remaining ingredients except noodles; mix well. Add noodles. our into two oblong cake pans.

CRUMB TOPPING:
3 c. soft bread crumbs
½ c. butter, melted
¾ t. paprika
¾ c. parsley, chopped

Combine crumbs, butter and paprika. Sprinkle across casserole in diagonal rows. Bake at 350°F. for 45 minutes until hot. Top with parsley. Yield: 24 servings.

Barbara Jo Pulley, Highland H.S.
Highland, Illinois

HAMBURGER-CORN CASSEROLE

1½ lb. ground beef
1 c. onion, chopped
1 12-oz. can whole-kernel corn, drained
1 can cream of chicken or mushroom soup
1 can chicken-noodle soup (opt.)
1 c. sour cream
¼ c. pimento, chopped
¾ t. salt
½ t. monosodium glutamate
¼ t. pepper
3 c. cooked noodles
1 c. soft bread crumbs
3 T. butter, melted

Brown meat; add onions and cook until tender. Drain off fat. Add corn, soup, sour cream, pimento and seasoning; mix well. Stir in noodles. Pour into 2-quart casserole. Mix crumbs with butter and sprinkle over top. Bake in 350°F. oven for 30 minutes.

This recipe submitted by the following teachers:
Marie E. Myrick, Rogers H.S.
Florence, Alabama
Mrs. Darleen Kvas, Mt. Iron H.S.
Mount Iron, Minnesota

HAMBURGER HARVEST CASSEROLE

1 lb. ground chuck
1 c. onion, minced
1 No. 2 can tomatoes
1 T. Worcestershire sauce or 1 t. curry or chili powder
2 t. salt
2 c. potatoes, thinly sliced
⅓ c. flour
1 pkg. frozen cut corn, partially thawed
1 pkg. frozen lima beans, partially thawed
1 green pepper, slivered
1½ c. American processed Cheddar cheese, grated

Combine meat, onion, tomatoes, spice, and salt. Pat in 1-inch layer in 3-quart casserole. Add layers of remaining ingredients except cheese. Cover; bake at 375°F. for 45 minutes. Sprinkle with cheese; continue baking, uncovered, for 30 minutes or until vegetables are tender. NOTE: If desired, canned corn and beans may be used; add cheese before baking. Bake at 350°F. for 1 hour. Yield: 8 servings.

This recipe submitted by the following teachers:
Mrs. Marcia Chapman, Central H.S.
Independence, Oregon
Betty Mac Spadden, Salinas H.S.
Salinas, California

HAMBURGER-NOODLE CASSEROLE

1 lb. ground beef
¾ c. onion, chopped
¾ c. green pepper, chopped
¼ c. shortening
1 1-lb. can cream-style corn
1 8-oz. can tomato paste
1 sm. can tomato soup
1 T. A-1 sauce
1½ t. salt
¼ t. pepper
1 8-oz. pkg. egg noodles, cooked
1 c. Cheddar cheese, grated, (opt.)

Brown ground beef, onion, and green pepper in shortening. Add corn, tomato paste, tomato soup, A-1 sauce, salt and pepper. Bring to a boil. In a two-quart casserole alternate layers of cooked noodles and meat mixture until casserole is nearly filled. If desired, cheese may be sprinkled on top. Bake at 350°F. for 45 minutes. Yield: 4-6 servings.

Sister M. Coletta, C.S.C. Holy Cross H.S.
Riverside, New Jersey

HAMBURGHETTI CASSEROLE

1 8-oz. pkg. spaghetti
1 10-oz. can tomato soup
1 c. cooked lima beans
1 c. cooked green peas
1 lb. ground beef
Seasonings to taste
1 T. butter
½ c. American cheese, grated

Cook spaghetti until tender; drain. In casserole mix spaghetti, soup, lima beans and peas. Brown hamburger; add seasoning to taste. Add to spaghetti mixture. Top with butter and cheese. Bake in 350°F. oven for 30 minutes. NOTE: May substitute cream of mushroom or cream of celery for tomato soup. Yield: 4-6 servings.

Mrs. George Meyer, Iowa-Grant H.S.
Livingston, Wisconsin

HAMBURGER-STUFFED TOMATOES WITH CORN

6 lge. tomatoes
1 lb. hamburger
1 med. onion, minced
2½ t. salt
¼ t. pepper
½ t. Worcestershire sauce
3 c. corn
3 T. margarine, melted
½ c. soft bread crumbs

Cut tops from tomatoes; scoop out and reserve pulp. Sprinkle inside of tomatoes with salt; turn upside down to drain. Cook hamburger and onion until meat loses its red color, using a small amount of fat if necessary. Add tomato pulp, 1½ teaspoon salt, ⅛ teaspoon pepper and Worcestershire sauce. Cook rapidly, uncovered, for 5 minutes or until liquid evaporates; stir occasionally. Fill tomatoes with mixture. Combine corn with 2 tablespoons margarine, 1 teaspoon salt, and ⅛ teaspoon pepper. Put in deep 9-inch pie-pan. Arrange tomatoes on top of corn. Add remaining margarine to crumbs; mix well. Sprinkle on tomatoes. Bake at 375°F. for 25 minutes. Yield: 6 servings.

Mrs. Beulah Pullen, Lewis Cass H.S.
Logansport, Indiana

HE-MAN CASSEROLE

2½ lb. round steak
3 c. macaroni
3 lge. onions, chopped
3 cloves garlic, chopped
1 green pepper, chopped
1 can tomato sauce
2 t. oregano
1 t. cumin seed
1 t. chili powder
1 sm. can peas
1 c. ripe olives, chopped
1 c. green olives, chopped
1 c. mushrooms, chopped
1 c. grated cheese
1½ c. tomato juice

Cut steak in 1-inch pieces and brown in a small amount of fat. Cook macaroni according to package directions. Mix all ingredients. Bake in 350°F. oven for 45 minutes. NOTE: If mixture seems dry add more tomato juice. Yield: 10-12 servings.

Ruth R. Kolar, Absarokee H.S.
Absarokee, Montana

ITALIAN DELIGHT

½ lb. long spaghetti
1 lb. hamburger
¼ c. margarine, melted
2 sm. onions, chopped
1 green pepper, chopped
1 can pitted olives
2 cans tomato sauce
1 can water
1 sm. can mushrooms
½ lb. cheese
1 can whole-kernel corn
1 t. paprika
1 T. Worcestershire sauce
¼ t. garlic salt
½ t. pepper
1 T. chili powder
½ t. poultry seasoning
½ t. cumin
½ t. oregano
½ t. salt

Cook spaghetti in boiling salted water. Brown meat in margarine, add onion and pepper before meat is completely browned. Add remaining ingredients. Bake for 1 hour in a 325°F. oven. Yield: 14 servings.

Mrs. Erma Jean Crider, Sanger Union H.S.
Sanger, California

JACKPOT DISH

1 lb. ground round steak
1 med. onion, chopped
1 can tomato soup
1½ c. water
Salt and pepper to taste
½ 8-oz. pkg. noodles, cooked
1 No. 2 can creamed corn
1 sm. can ripe olives, sliced (opt.)
1 c. cheese, grated (opt.)

Mix all ingredients except cheese as for meat loaf; place in buttered baking dish. Sprinkle with cheese. Bake at 350°F. for 45 minutes. NOTE: If desired, meat and onion may be browned in 2 tablespoon fat before combining. Yield: 8 servings.

This recipe submitted by the following teachers:
Mrs. Bess Snyder Mohl, Petersburg H.S.
Petersburg, West Virginia
Mrs. Vera Grimm, Holgate H.S.
Holgate, Ohio
Mrs. Elizabeth C. Totman, Waterville Jr. H.S.
Waterville, Maine

KRAUT CASSEROLE

1 lb. ground beef
1 med. onion, chopped
½ c. raw rice, cooked
1 qt. tomatoes, cut up
1 2½ can sauerkraut
Salt and pepper to taste
Monosodium glutamate (opt.)

Brown ground beef in skillet. Add onions and cook until golden. Mix all ingredients in a large casserole. Bake one and one half hours at 350°F. Yield: 8-10 servings.

Lone Bolstad Olson, Woodland Jr. H.S.
Duluth, Minnesota

LIMA BEAN-CORN BARBECUE

1½ lb. ground beef
3 T. fat
1 med. onion, chopped
1 med. green pepper, chopped
1 can tomato soup
Juice from lima beans
1 T. chili powder
1 T. prepared mustard
1 T. Worcestershire sauce
1½ T. salt
1 1-lb. can baby lima beans, drained
1 10-oz. can whole-kernel corn, drained
1 can water chestnuts, sliced

Brown meat in fat. Add onion and green pepper; cook just until tender. Mix soup, juice from beans, chili powder, mustard, Worcestershire sauce and salt. Stir in meat mixture. Cover and simmer for 20 minutes. Add remaining ingredients; cook for 15 minutes.

Dorothy Kimbley, Jeffersonville H.S.
Jeffersonville, Indiana

MACARONI-HAMBURGER CASSEROLE

1 lb. hamburger
2 c. macaroni
1 sm. onion
Salt & pepper
1 can tomatoes, stewing

Cook macaroni. Brown hamburger, add onions, salt and pepper. Add tomatoes and simmer. Rinse macaroni and add to hamburger and tomato mixture. Simmer 10-15 minutes. Yield: 4 servings.

Mrs. Grady Rostberg, Brownton Public School
Brownton, Minnesota

MEAT BALL CASSEROLE

1 egg
1¼ c. milk
1 c. soft bread crumbs
1 t. dry mustard
½ t. celery salt
¼ t. pepper
¼ t. nutmeg
3 T. onion, grated
1 lb. ground beef
¼ c. flour
2 T. cooking fat
1 can condensed cream of mushroom soup
1 pkg. frozen mixed vegetables
½ t. salt

Combine egg, ½ cup milk, crumbs, mustard, celery salt, pepper, nutmeg, onion and beef. Form into small balls using 1 tablespoon mixture for each. Roll lightly in flour. Brown in hot fat for 12 minutes. Freeze in plastic container. Combine ¾ cup milk and soup in casserole; add meat balls, vegetables and salt. Bake, uncovered, at 375°F. for 30 minutes. Cover; continue baking for 15 minutes. Yield: 8 servings.

Rose Marie Romero, Rio Grande H.S.
Albuquerque, New Mexico

MACARONI RING CASSEROLE

1 lb. hamburger
1 med. onion, chopped
½ c. celery, chopped
1 No. 2 can whole-kernel corn
1 can mushroom soup
¼ c. soy sauce
1 8-oz. pkg. macaroni rings, cooked

Brown hamburger, celery and onions. Add remaining ingredients. Pour into greased casserole. Bake at 300°F. for 30-45 minutes. Yield: 6 servings.

Mrs. Jane Outcalt, Clayton H.S.
Clayton, Wisconsin

MEAT-CARROT CASSEROLE

2 c. carrots
1 c. hamburger
2 T. butter
Few grains nutmeg and cloves (opt.)
Salt to taste
⅛ t. pepper
1 t. sugar
3 T. flour
2 onions, chopped
2 c. tomatoes

Cook carrots until tender. Brown the meat in butter. Place all the ingredients in a casserole and bake covered about one hour at 350°F. NOTE: More carrots and meat may be added if desired. Yield: 4-6 servings.

Vades Koonst, Sherman County H.S.
Moro, Oregon

MEAT BALL-VEGETABLE CASSEROLE

2 lb. ground beef
2 eggs, slightly beaten
1 c. soft bread crumbs
1 c. applesauce
1 t. salt
¼ t. pepper
Fat
1 can condensed tomato soup
½ c. water
1 onion, chopped
1 green pepper, chopped
½ c. carrots, chopped
½ c. celery, chopped

Combine beef, eggs, bread crumbs, applesauce, salt and pepper; mix lightly. Shape into 3-inch balls and brown in small amount of fat. Arrange in a 3-quart casserole. Blend together soup and water. Stir in remaining vegetables. Pour mixture over meat balls; blend slightly. Bake at 350°F. for about 1 hour, or until the vegetables are tender. Yield: 6-8 servings.

Mrs. Lois J. Latteman, Washington H.S.
Washington, New Jersey

MEAT BALL STEW EN CASSEROLE

2 lb. potatoes, quartered
1½ lb. sm. white onions
1 bunch sm. carrots, halved lengthwise
1 pkg. frozen peas, thawed
2 lb. ground beef
1 egg
1 c. dry bread crumbs
¾ t. marjoram
2½ t. salt
¾ t. Worcestershire sauce
⅔ c. milk
⅓ c. hot salad oil
1½ lb. sm. fresh mushrooms
1 can cream of mushroom soup
¾ t. nutmeg
¾ t. A-1 sauce
¾ t. onion salt or monosodium glutamate

Place potatoes, onion and carrots in saucepan with 1-inch boiling salted water; cover. Cook 20 minutes or until barely tender. Add peas; cover. Remove from heat. Lightly mix beef, egg, crumbs, marjoram, salt, Worcestershire sauce and milk. Drop by teaspoonfuls into hot oil; brown quickly. Remove from skillet. Saute mushrooms in remaining oil until tender; remove. Heat remaining ingredients in skillet. Arrange potato mixture, meat and mushrooms in 3-quart casserole. Bake at 400°F. for 35 minutes or until browned and bubbly. Yield: 8 servings.

Barbara Bird, Stilwell Jr. H.S.
Alma, Michigan

MEAT-VEGETABLE PIE

1 lb. ground lean beef
1 T. salad oil or melted fat
1 c. onions, chopped
½ med. green pepper, cut into strips
1 c. celery
1½ c. carrots, thinly sliced
1½ t. salt
Dash pepper
1 beef bouillon cube
¾ c. boiling water
4 med. potatoes, cooked
1 egg, beaten

Lightly brown beef in hot oil, stirring frequently. Add onions; cook 5 minutes, stirring occasionally. Stir in green pepper, celery, carrots, 1 teaspoon salt and pepper. Dissolve bouillon cube in water; add to meat mixture. Cover; simmer for 1 hour or until vegetables are tender. Mash potatoes; blend in egg, ½ teaspoon salt and dash of pepper. Line greased 9-inch pie pan with even layer of potato mixture about 1-inch thick, building edge up to ½-inch above edge of pie pan. Bake at 400°F. for 20 minutes or until lightly browned. Pour in meat mixture. Serve.

Ann Davis, Box Elder H.S.
Brigham City, Utah

MEAT LOAF CASSEROLE

⅔ c. dry bread crumbs
1 c. milk
1½ lb. ground beef
2 eggs, beaten
¼ c. onion, grated
1 t. salt
Pepper
4 potatoes, pared
1 can pork and beans or canned baked beans
½ c. brown sugar
½ c. catsup

Soak bread crumbs in milk; add meat, eggs, onion and seasonings. Mix well. Form in a loaf and place in a greased casserole. Add pared potatoes around outside of loaf. Pour pork and beans around potatoes. Mix brown sugar and catsup and pour over top of casserole. Bake at 350°F. for 1 hour and 30 minutes. Yield: 4 servings.

Mrs. Joyce Goggin, Villa Grove H.S.
Villa Grove, Illinois

MEAT-VEGETABLE CASSEROLE

1 lge. onion, chopped
1 pod garlic or garlic salt
½ stick butter
1 lb. round steak ground
1 t. salt
½ t. pepper
2 8-oz. cans tomato puree
1 can mushroom soup
1 8-oz. can cream corn
1 8-oz. can whole-kernel corn
1 8-oz. can button mushrooms
1 No. 2 can tomato juice
1 sm. pkg. noodles
½ lb. Cheddar cheese, grated
1 can pitted black olives

Saute onion and garlic in butter; add meat and brown. Add salt, pepper, tomato puree, mushroom soup, corn, mushrooms, tomato juice and noodles. Bake at 350°F. for 30 to 40 minutes. Just before serving, add cheese and olives; bake until cheese is melted. Yield: 6-7 servings.

Phyllis P. Nash, Conestoga Sr. H.S.
Berwyn, Pennsylvania

MEXICAN BEANS

1 lb. ground beef
1 onion, diced
1 sm. green pepper, diced
1 No. 303 can creamed-style corn
1 t. chili powder
1 lge. can pork and beans
Salt & pepper
Bacon strips

Saute ground beef, onion, and green pepper. Add corn, pork and beans and seasoning. Place in casserole. Put bacon strips on top and bake in 350°F. oven for 35 minutes. Yield: 6-8 servings.

Mrs. Carol Paynter, Mineral Point H.S
Mineral Point, Wisconsin

MEXICORN MIX

1 sm. box corn bread mix
1½ lb. hamburger
1 sm. onion, diced
1 green pepper, diced
1 can Mexicorn
1 can vegetable soup
1 t. chili powder
Salt and pepper to taste

Bake corn bread according to package directions. Brown hamburger, onion and green pepper. Add corn, soup and seasonings. Crumble baked corn bread into mixture; mix well. Put in casserole; bake at 350°F. for 30-40 minutes. Yield: 4-6 servings.

Betty G. Quick, Barrington H.S.
Barrington, Illinois

MINNESOTA HAMBURGER CASSEROLE

4 or 5 raw potatoes, sliced
1 lb. raw ground beef
1 can vegetable or vegetable beef soup
1 can cream of mushroom soup
Salt and pepper

Put potatoes in bottom of a greased 2-quart casserole. Brown meat and spread over potato layer. Add vegetable soup and top with mushroom soup. Season with salt and pepper. Bake, covered, at 325°F. about 2 hours or at 400°F. for 1 hour or until potatoes are tender. NOTE: If desired, raw beef may be added without browning. Ingredients may be mixed rather than layered Yield: 6-8 servings.

This recipe submitted by the following teachers:
Mrs. Patricia Larson, Milaca H.S.
Milaca. Minnesota
JoAnn Helblad, McIntosh H.S
McIntosh, Minnesota
Diane Stenberg, Eden Valley H.S.
Eden Valley, Minnesota

MIXED VEGETABLE HOT DISH

1½ lb. ground beef
1 lge. onion, chopped
1 c. celery, diced
1 T. fat
2 cans mushroom soup
1 can chicken-rice soup
1 can mixed vegetables and juice
2 c. chow mein noodles
2-4 T. soy sauce
1 sm. can mushrooms and juice (opt.)

Brown meat, onion and celery in fat. Drain off excess fat. Mix with remaining ingredients. Bake at 350°F. for 1 hour. NOTE: If desired, 2 packages frozen mixed vegetables, cooked, may be used. Yield: 10-14 servings.

This recipe submitted by the following teachers:
Mrs. Ruth Gamache Weber
Brandon Valley H.S.
Brandon, South Dakota
Genevieve Olson, Osseo Sr. H.S.
Osseo, Minnesota

MOCK CHOW MEIN

1-1½ lb. hamburger
1 onion, diced
1 c. celery, diced
1 sm. green pepper, diced (opt.)
1 can mushroom soup
1 can chicken-rice soup
2 cans water
½ c. raw rice
2-3 T. soy sauce
1 can mixed vegetable soup
Potato chips, crushed

Brown meat. Combine all ingredients except potato chips in a casserole. Cover and bake at 350°F. for one hour, stirring occasionally. Uncover and bake another ½ hour. When serving, sprinkle crushed potato chips over the top. Yield: 6-8 servings.

Sandra M. Cuchna, LaFarge H.S.
LaFarge, Wisconsin

MULLIGAN

½ lb. elbow macaroni
1 lb. hamburger
1 med. onion, finely cut
1 can tomato soup
¾ c. milk
1 No. 2 can dark red kidney beans
1 t. salt
½ t. pepper
½ c. cracker crumbs

Cook macaroni in boiling salted water until tender; drain. Brown hamburger and onion; break hamburger into small bits. Mix tomato soup and milk; add to hamburger mixture. Combine macaroni, hamburger mixture, kidney beans, salt and pepper. Place in greased 1½-quart casserole. Sprinkle cracker crumbs over top. Bake at 350°F. for 35 minutes. Yield: 6 servings.

Mrs. M. Judelle Jones, Turlock H.S.
Turlock, California

NELLIE SANK'S DUTCH POTATOES

Potatoes, sliced
Onions, sliced
Bacon, slices
Salt and pepper

The amount of potatoes and onions is determined by size of casserole used. Place potato and onion slices in cold water; let stand 10-15 minutes. Cover bottom of casserole with bacon slices. Fill casserole two-thirds full with potato slices. Sprinkle lightly with salt and pepper. Fill remainder of casserole with onion slices; sprinkle with salt. Top with bacon slices. Cover; bake at 350°F. for 1 hour.

Mrs. Nancy Zebrun, Forbes H.S.
Kantner, Pennsylvania

NOODLE CASSEROLE

1 lb. hamburger
½ c. onion
1 T. oil
½ c. water
1 8-oz. pkg. cream cheese
12 oz. canned corn
1 can mushroom soup
4 c. cooked noodles

Fry meat and onion in oil. Add remaining ingredients. Pour into buttered casserole. Bake at 350°F. for 30 minutes. Yield: 8 servings

Mrs. Janet T. Rose, Hempfield Union Sr. H.S.
Landisville, Pennsylvania

ONE-DISH DELICIOUS DINNER

1 lb. ground chuck
¼ c. onion, chopped
1 clove garlic, minced
1 No. 303 can stewed tomatoes
½ pkg. spaghetti sauce mix
½ t. chili powder
1 2½-oz. can mushrooms, sliced
½ pkg. frozen green beans
¼ 8-oz. pkg. vermicelli
1 T. oil
1 c. corn chips, crushed
Salt and pepper to taste
3 sl. Cheddar cheese

Brown meat, onion and garlic together. Add tomatoes, spaghetti sauce mix, chili powder, mushrooms, and beans; simmer. Cook vermicelli in boiling water with oil until tender. Drain; place in buttered casserole. Sprinkle with ½ cup corn chip crumbs. Pour in meat mixture; add salt and pepper. Top with cheese slices and remaining crumbs. Bake at 325°F. for 40 minutes. Yield: 4-6 servings.

Susan Holbrook, Blackford H.S.
San Jose, California

ONE-DISH DINNER

½ onion, finely chopped
2 green peppers, chopped
1 T. cooking oil
1 lb. ground chuck
1½ t. salt
2 c. tomatoes
2 c. corn
Buttered bread crumbs

Lightly brown onion and green peppers in oil; add meat and salt and brown well. Put one-third of meat mixture, tomatoes, and corn in layers in a casserole. Repeat layers twice. Top with crumbs. Bake at 350°F. for 45-60 minutes. Yield: 6 servings.

Mrs. Gloria Love, Cumberland Vally Sr. H.S.
Mechanicsburg, Pennsylvania

ONE-DISH MEAL

Potatoes, sliced
Onions, sliced
Carrots, sliced
Uncooked rice
Green pepper rings
Ground beef
Whole canned tomatoes or raw tomatoes, sliced
1 can cream of mushroom soup
Salt and pepper

Place ingredients in layers in greased casserole. Salt and pepper each layer. Add enough liquid to cover all layers. Bake at 350°F. for 1 hour and 30 minutes. Yield: 3-4 servings.

Mrs. Donald Berkland, Minnesota Lake
Public School
Minnesota Lake, Minnesota

ONE-DISH MEAL

2 c. raw potatoes
1 c. onion, chopped
2 c. raw ground beef
1 No. 2 can tomatoes
1 c. green pepper, chopped
Salt

In a greased casserole place layers of potatoes, onion, beef, tomatoes and green pepper. Season each layer to taste. Cover; bake at 250°F. for 2 hours and 30 minutes. Yield: 6 servings.

Mrs. Louise B. McIntosh, Tipton H.S.
Tipton, Indiana

ONE-HOUR CASSEROLE

6 potatoes, sliced
1 can vegetable soup, undiluted
1 can cream of mushroom soup, undiluted
½ lb. ground beef
1 sm. onion, chopped

Slice potatoes into greased 1½-quart casserole. Add both cans of soup. Bake for 50 minutes at 350°F. Brown ground beef and onion; place on top of potato mixture and bake an additional 10 minutes. Yield: 6 servings.

Mrs. Barbara Hiller, Winnebago
Community School
Winnebago, Minnesota

PAT'S HOT DISH

1 lb. hamburger
½ pkg. dry onion soup
1 can cream of chicken soup
½ can water
1 pkg. frozen mixed vegetables
1 pkg. frozen Tater Tots

Lightly brown hamburger. Add onion soup; brown. Stir in chicken soup, water and mixed vegetables. Pour into casserole. Place Tater Tots on top. Bake at 350°F. for 45 minutes. Yield: 6 servings.

Mrs. Fred Lamppa, Chisholm Sr. H.S.
Chisholm, Minnesota

POTATO AND HAMBURGER HOT DISH

1½ lb. hamburger
1 onion, chopped
Salt and pepper to taste
1 can vegetable soup
1 can vegetable beef soup
4-5 med. potatoes, sliced
1 can mushroom soup

Brown hamburger and onions. Season. Combine vegetable soups and ⅓ can water. Alternate layers of potatoes, soup mixture and hamburger in greased casserole. Repeat until all are used. Blend mushroom soup and ⅓ can water; pour over layers. Bake at 350°F. for 2 hours. Yield: 8-10 servings.

*Mrs. Dallas Sturlaugson, Benson County
Agricultural and Training School
Maddock, North Dakota*

QUIVERSEC STEW

¾ lb. hamburger
1 T. fat, melted
¼ c. onion, chopped
1 No. 303 can mixed vegetables
1 T. sugar
Water
½ c. catsup
1 t. Worcestershire sauce
½ t. salt
¼ t. pepper
2 T. flour

Brown hamburger in fat; add onion and cook until tender. Add mixed vegetables, sugar, ⅓ cup water, the catsup, Worcestershire sauce, salt and pepper. Simmer for 15 minutes. Mix flour and ½ cup water to a smooth paste. Add to simmering stew; stirring until thickened. Serve in toast cups, over chow mein noodles or cornbread squares. NOTE: The title is a combination of the words "quick, versatile, economic." Yield: 4 servings.

*Mrs. Gladys Wirth, Liberty Community
Unit #2 H.S.
Liberty, Illinois*

RED GOLD CASSEROLE

1 1-lb. pkg. raw carrots
1 lb. ground beef
1 onion, chopped
½ c. green pepper, chopped
Salt and pepper to taste
½ t. poultry seasoning
1 1-lb. can tomatoes or 2 c. tomato puree

Peel carrots and cut into cubes or slices; cook in small amount of water until barely tender. Brown meat, onion and green pepper; add seasonings. Combine meat mixture, carrots and tomatoes; pour into baking dish. Bake uncovered at 350°F. for 30 minutes. Yield: 4-6 servings.

*Mrs. Stanley Murdock, Paoli Community H.S.
Paoli, Indiana*

RICE CASSEROLE

1½ lb. hamburger
1 onion, chopped
2 cans tomato soup
1 can peas, undrained
1 can sm. mushrooms
1½ c. cooked minute rice
4 sl. bacon

Brown hamburger and onion; season to taste. Combine with remaining ingredients except bacon. Pour into greased casserole. Place bacon on top. Bake at 350°F. for 1 hour. Yield: 4-6 servings.

*Eileen Loken, DeSmet H.S.
DeSmet, South Dakota*

SCALLOPED TOMATOES WITH HAMBURGER

½ lb. hamburger
2 c. canned tomatoes
2 T. onion, finely chopped
1 T. green pepper, finely chopped
½ t. salt
1 t. sugar
¾ c. cracker crumbs
2 T. butter
¼ c. grated cheese

Brown hamburger in small amount of oil. Combine tomatoes, onion, green pepper and salt. In a greased casserole, put alternate layers of tomato mixture, hamburger and cracker crumbs. Dot with butter. Bake at 365°F. for 20-30 minutes. Top with grated cheese during last 10 minutes of baking. Yield: 4-5 servings.

*Ruth I. Schwarz, Galesburg Sr. H.S.
Galesburg, Illinois*

SEVEN LAYER CASSEROLE

1 c. uncooked rice
1 c. whole-kernel corn, drained
1 No. 303 can stewed tomatoes
½ c. water
½ c. onion, finely chopped
½ c. pepper, finely chopped
1 lb. ground beef
Salt and pepper to taste

Place uncooked rice in a 2-quart casserole. Add a layer of corn, half the tomatoes and water, onions, green pepper, and uncooked beef. Salt and pepper each layer. Pour remaining tomatoes and water over beef; season to taste. Cover and bake for 1 hour at 350°F. Remove cover and bake 30 minutes longer. Yield: 4-6 servings.

*Janice Olson, Jim Hill Jr. H.S.
Minot, North Dakota*

SHEPHERD'S PIE

¼ c. onion
1 lb. ground beef
½ t. salt
2 c. peas or green beans
2 c. carrots
4-5 potatoes, mashed

Saute onion and salted beef. Place in baking dish. Add layers of peas and carrots. Cover with potatoes. Bake at 350°F. until potatoes are well browned. NOTE: Any combination of vegetables may be used. This is an excellent way to use leftovers. Yield: 6 servings.

Mrs. Iris Hendershot, Southern Fulton H.S.
Warfordsburg, Pennsylvania

SHIPWRECK

3-6 med. potatoes
½-1 lb. hamburger
½ t. salt
¼ t. pepper
1 med. onion
1 15-oz. can kidney beans
1 can tomato soup

Slice the potatoes in a greased casserole and crumble the hamburger on top. Sprinkle on half the salt and pepper. Slice the onion and spread over the hamburger. Spread kidney beans over onion. Cover all with the undiluted tomato soup. Add remaining salt and pepper; bake for 1 hour and 30 minutes in a 375°F. oven. Yield: 6 servings.

This recipe submitted by the following teachers:
Mrs. Ben Henderson, Belle Fourche H.S.
Belle Fourche, South Dakota
Joanne C. DeVuyst, St. Louis H.S.
St. Louis, Michigan

SIX LAYER BEEF DINNER

6 med. potatoes
Salt and pepper
1 T. rice
1 lb. ground beef
Butter
1 onion, chopped
1 green pepper, finely chopped
1 can tomatoes
Sugar

Slice potatoes into buttered baking dish; season with salt. Add rice. Brown meat in butter; season with salt and pepper. Place over rice in casserole. Lightly saute onions; place over meat. Add a layer of green pepper. Pour on tomatoes seasoned with salt, pepper, and a little sugar. Dot with butter. Cover and bake 1 hour and 30 minutes at 350°F. Yield: 6 servings.

Betty Herbel, Lignite Public School
Lignite, North Dakota

SIX-LAYER CASSEROLE

2 c. raw potatoes, sliced
2 c. celery, chopped
1 lb. ground beef
1 c. raw onions, sliced
1 c. green pepper, minced
2 c. cooked tomatoes
2 t. salt
¼ t. pepper
Green pepper rings

Place potatoes, celery, beef, onions, minced green pepper and tomatoes in layers in a greased 2-quart casserole, seasoning each layer with salt and pepper. Garnish with green pepper rings. Bake at 350°F. for 2 hours. Yield: 6 servings.

Mrs. Gaylord N. Webster, Mattanawcook Academy
Lincoln, Maine

SPECIAL STUFFED MEAT LOAF

¼ lb. ground beef
1 potato, grated
1¼ t. salt
¼ t. pepper
¼ t. sage
2 T. tomato juice
1 c. canned whole-kernel corn
1 onion, thinly sliced
1 c. whole tomatoes, drained

Combine beef, potato, salt, pepper, sage and tomato juice. Spread half of mixture in greased loaf pan. Add layers of corn, onion and tomatoes. Season with salt and pepper. Cover with remaining meat mixture. Bake at 350°F. for 1 hour. Yield: 6 servings.

Mrs. Gladys Hetherton, Cascade H.S.
Cascade, Montana

STEAK IN SAUCE

1 1½-lb. round steak
2 T. oil
Salt and pepper
1 clove garlic, minced
1 med. onion, finely chopped
1 can tomato paste
1 can tomato sauce
1 No. 2 can tomatoes, mashed
5-6 potatoes, sliced
Dash of oregano (opt.)
1 sprig parsley, chopped

Brown steak in oil; season. Add remaining ingredients. Cook on medium heat for 45-50 minutes or bake at 350°F. for 45-60 minutes or until potatoes are done. Yield: 4-5 servings.

Mrs. William Potzner, Weatherly Area H.S.
Weatherly, Pennsylvania

STUFFED GREEN PEPPERS

4 green peppers
1 lb. hamburger
1 sm. onion, chopped
2 stalks celery, chopped
1 c. rice, cooked
1-2 t. salt
1 qt. stewed tomatoes
½ c. catsup

Precook cleaned green peppers in salted water for 5 minutes. Saute meat and onion until brown. Stir in remaining ingredients. Stuff into peppers. Place in greased baking dish, putting excess filling around edge. Bake at 375°F. for 45 minutes.

Verna J. Erickson, Hyre Jr. H.S.
Akron, Ohio

STUFFED GREEN PEPPER

1 lb. hamburger
1 lge. onion, chopped
2 T. fat
2 lge. potatoes, cubed
2½ c. of tomatoes
1 t. salt
Pepper to taste
6-8 green peppers

Slightly brown hamburger and onions in fat. Add remaining ingredients except peppers. Stuff into peppers. Bake at 350°F. for 1 hour and 30 minutes. NOTE: For Green Pepper Goulash add 1 cubed green pepper to meat mixture. Pour into casserole and bake as above. Yield: 6-8 servings.

Helen A. Alberda, Manhattan H.S.
Manhattan, Montana

STUFFED PEPPER CASSEROLE

4 med. green pepper
1½ lb. ground beef
2 T. onions
½ t. salt
¼ t. pepper
1½ c. rice
1 c. corn
1 8-oz. can tomato sauce

Cut tops off of peppers and clean out inside. Cook peppers and tops in water to cover for 20 minutes. Brown ground beef and onions. Add seasonings, rice, corn and tomato sauce. Heat until bubbly. Spoon filling into peppers. Put into casserole dish. If too much filling, put extra around the peppers in the dish. Bake for 25-30 minutes at 350°F. Yield: 4 servings.

Barbara Coddington, Dinuba H.S.
Dinuba, California

STUFFED PEPPERS

8 lge. green peppers
½ lb. ground beef
1 c. course dry bread crumbs
1 t. salt
¼ t. pepper
1 T. onion, chopped
1 10½-oz. can tomato soup

Remove stem and seeds from green peppers; boil for 5 minutes. Drain; place in small baking dish. Stuff with mixture of beef, bread, salt, pepper, onion and half of soup. Dilute remaining soup with ½ can of water; pour over peppers. Bake at 350°F. for 1 hour. Yield: 8 servings.

Mrs. Nancy Fleming, John Dewey Jr. H.S.
Denver, Colorado

SUNDAY NIGHT SUPPER

1 lb. hamburger
½ 10-oz. pkg. egg noodles, cooked
1 can whole-kernel corn
1 can cream of mushroom soup
1 can cream of chicken soup
Salt and pepper to taste
½ c. Wheaties

Brown hamburger in shortening. Stir in noodles, corn, soups, salt and pepper. Pour into lightly greased casserole; sprinkle with Wheaties. Bake at 350°F. for 30 minutes. Yield: 6-8 servings.

Mrs. Kay D. Anderson Vymola, Warren H.S.
Warren, Minnesota

SWEDISH STEW

1 lb. hamburger
Salt and pepper to taste
1 t. sweet basil
2 c. potatoes, sliced
2 c. carrots, finely sliced
1 c. onions, finely sliced
1 No. 2½ can tomatoes
½ c. fine bread crumbs

Put hamburger in the bottom of greased casserole, covering the entire bottom. Salt and pepper to taste. Sprinkle sweet basil over top. Place potatoes, carrots and onions in layers on top of meat. Pour tomatoes over top. Sprinkle bread crumbs over top. Bake 1 hour at 350°F., or until all vegetables are tender. Yield: 4 servings.

Mrs. Elaine West, Wattsburg Area H.S.
Wattsburg, Pennsylvania

TAG

¼ c. onion, chopped
2 garlic cloves, chopped
1 green pepper, chopped
4 T. cooking oil
1 lb. ground beef
2 cans tomato sauce
½ pkg. noodles
1 No. 2 can whole-kernel corn
1 lge. can mushrooms, sliced
1 sm. can ripe olives, chopped
1 c. sharp cheese, grated

Brown onions, garlic and green pepper in cooking oil. Add ground beef and brown. Stir in tomato sauce; cook for 15 minutes. Cook noodles as directed on package. Add noodles, corn, mushrooms and olives to the meat mixture. Place all ingredients in a baking dish; top with cheese. Bake for 40 minutes at 325°F. Yield: 8 servings.

Marianne Blanchard, Southeastern Jr. H.S.
Battle Creek, Michigan

TAGLARRINA

½ lb. hamburger
3 T. onions, chopped
1 c. Tomato Juice
3 T. green pepper, chopped or Ortega green chilis
½ c. whole-kernel corn
3 T. ripe olives, chopped
1 t. salt
1 c. egg noodles, cooked
½ lb. unpasteurized American cheese, grated

Fry hamburger until brown; add the onions and cook 5 minutes. Add the tomato juice, chopped pepper or chili, corn and olives. Simmer 30 minutes. Add noodles and arrange in a casserole. Cover with grated cheese. Bake at 250°F. for 1 hour, or until top is bubbly and crusty. Yield: 8 servings.

Mrs. Ruth J. Reisdorfer, Seligman H.S.
Seligman, Arizona

TALLARINA

1 lb. hamburger
1 lge. onion, chopped
1 clove garlic, minced
Cooking oil
Salt to taste
1 T. soya sauce
1 T. Tabasco sauce
1 med. can tomatoes
1 sm. can whole-kernel corn
4 to 6-oz. noodles, cooked
½ lb. cheese, grated

Brown meat, onion and garlic in oil until onion is golden and tender. Add salt, soya sauce and Tabasco sauce; cook 5 minutes. Stir in tomatoes; simmer for 15 minutes. Add corn and noodles. Pour into baking dish; cover with cheese. Bake at 350°F. for 30-45 minutes. Yield: 6 servings.

Lois J. Smeltzer, Eastern Lebanon County H.S.
Myerstown, Pennsylvania

TAMALE PIE

1 egg, beaten
½ c. milk
½ c. yellow corn meal
1 onion
1 lb. ground beef
1 sm. can tomato sauce
1 sm. can shoepeg corn
1 sm. can pitted olives
Salt and pepper
Chili powder (opt.)
Few drops of garlic oil (opt.)
Slices of tilamuk cheese

Beat egg; add milk and corn meal. Fry onion and meat until brown; add tomato sauce, corn, olives, salt and pepper, chili powder and garlic oil. Combine egg mixture with meat mixture; pour into greased baking dish. Top with corn meal mixture. Cover the top with slices of cheese. Bake at 300°F. for 45 minutes. Yield: 6 servings.

Mrs. Elizabeth Platt, Chaffey H.S.
Ontario, California

THREE-SOUP CASSEROLE

1 lb. ground beef
1 T. butter
1 onion, sliced
1 c. celery, diced
1 c. water
1 can mushroom soup
1 can vegetable soup
1 sm. can mushrooms
1 can chicken-rice soup
1 8-oz. pkg. chow mein noodles

Brown ground beef to crumbly stage. Add butter, onion, celery and water. Cook covered in skillet for 10 minutes. Add soups, mushrooms and noodles. Blend well. Pour into large buttered casserole. Bake at 350°F. for 30 minutes. Yield: 8 servings.

Mrs. Bonnie Shaw, Clarkfield Public School
Clarkfield, Minnesota

VEAL-CORN HOT DISH

1 lb. veal, cubed
¾ c. water
2 cans chicken broth
½ lb. noodles, cooked
1 can corn
½ green pepper, finely cut
½ sm. can pimento
¾ lb. Cheddar cheese, cubed
1 t. salt
½ t. pepper
1 t. monosodium glutamate
¼ c. toasted almonds

Brown meat and simmer in water and 1 can of broth until tender. Add all ingredients except almonds. Bake for 1 hour at 350°F. Sprinkle almonds on top before serving. Yield: 12 servings.

Mrs. Dewey Huber, Sr. H.S.
Chippewa Falls, Wisconsin

VEGETABLE-MEAT BALL CASSEROLE

1 lb. ground beef
1 egg
¼ c. bread crumbs
2 med. carrots, grated
2 med. potatoes, grated
1 sm. onion, chopped
1 can cream of mushroom soup
2 c. white sauce

Mix all ingredients, except soup and white sauce. Shape into balls; dust with flour and brown in fat. Place in a casserole dish. Add the soup to the white sauce and pour over the vegetable meat balls. Bake at 325°F. for 45 minutes. NOTE: This can be prepared the day before and baked on the desired day. Yield: 4-6 servings.

Gloria R. McHenry, East Jr. H.S.
Mesa, Arizona

VEGETABLE-MEAT CASSEROLE

1 lb. ground beef
1 onion, ground
1 c. carrots, ground
2 c. tomatoes
1 c. whole-kernel corn
½ c. uncooked rice
1 green pepper, chopped
2 c. boiling water
1 T. sugar
2 t. salt
Pepper

Brown meat; add rest of ingredients. Stir. Put into casserole; cover. Cook in 350°F. oven for 2 hours. Yield: 6 servings.

Mrs. Nel L. Estill, Maxwell Union H.S.
Maxwell, California

VENETIAN VEAL CASSEROLE

2 lb. veal, cubed
1 t. paprika
Salt and pepper
⅓ c. water
¼ c. onion, diced
¼ c. green pepper, diced
¼ c. celery, diced
1 lb. broad noodles
1 box frozen peas, cooked
1 c. sour cream
1 sm. can sl. mushrooms
1 can cream of mushroom soup, diluted with milk
Soy sauce

Brown veal cubes sprinkled with paprika in a small amount of fat; salt and pepper to taste. Add water; cover and simmer until tender. Boil onions, green pepper and celery in salted water. After 5 minutes drop in noodles and cook until tender; drain. Combine all ingredients. Place in a buttered casserole dish. Bake at 350°F. until bubbly. Yield: 8-10 servings.

Carol Steele, Vulcan Jr. H.S.
Vulcan, Michigan

VEGETABLE AND HAMBURGER EN CASSEROLE

2 green peppers, chopped
1 med. onion, chopped
4 T. shortening
1 lb. hamburger
1½ t. salt
¼ to ½ t. pepper
2 eggs (opt.)
2 c. whole-kernel corn
4 med. tomatoes, sliced
¼-½ c. dried bread crumbs
Butter

Lightly brown green pepper and onions in shortening. Thoroughly blend in meat and seasonings. Remove from heat and stir in eggs if desired. Put 1 cup of corn in baking dish; add a layer of tomatoes and a layer of half the meat mixture. Repeat layers. Cover with bread crumbs. Dot generously with butter. Bake at 350-375°F. for 35 minutes. Yield: 6 servings.

This recipe submitted by the following teachers:

Mrs. Hobert Keller, Rabun County H.S.
Clayton, Georgia

Mrs. Ann Fate, Harvard Public Schools
Harvard, Nebraska

Mrs. Mildred Mayfield, Medina H.S.
Medina, Texas

WANDA'S CASSEROLE

1 lb. ground beef
1 sm. onion, chopped
½ green pepper, chopped (opt.)
Fat
1 t. salt
Dash of pepper
6 med. potatoes, sliced
1 can cream of mushroom soup

Brown hamburger, onion and green pepper in a little fat. Season with salt and pepper. Butter a 2-quart casserole and put half the hamburger mixture in a layer on the bottom. Cover with half the potatoes; season potatoes to taste with salt and pepper. Cover potatoes with half the undiluted soup. Repeat layers, starting with hamburger and ending with soup. Cover casserole and bake in a 350°F. oven for 1 hour or until potatoes are done. Yield: 4 servings.

Wanda June Newlin, Atwood-Hammond H.S.
Atwood, Illinois

WESTERN CASSEROLE

1 lb. ground beef
1 sm. onion, chopped
1 No. 2 can tomatoes
1 No. 2 can red kidney beans
½ c. uncooked rice
½ t. salt
Dash of pepper
1 t. chili powder

Cook ground beef and onion over medium heat until meat loses its red color. Combine meat, onion, and remaining ingredients in casserole. Bake uncovered at 350°F. for 1 hour, stirring several times during baking period. Yield: 4 servings.

Mrs. Russell Welsh, Harlem H.S.
Loves Park, Illinois

WILD RICE CASSEROLE

1 c. wild rice
1 lb. chop suey meat or ground beef
1 sm. green pepper, cubed
2 c. celery, chopped
1 onion, chopped
1 carrot, shredded
1 can bean sprouts and liquid
1 can mushrooms
1 can cream of mushroom soup
1 T. soy sauce
1 T. Worcestershire sauce
Salt and pepper to taste

Soak rice in water for 2 hours; drain. Brown meat. Add remaining ingredients and rice. Pour into buttered casserole; dot with butter. Bake at 375°F. for 1 hour, adding water as needed. Yield: 15 servings.

Regina Johnson, Ely Memorial H.S.
Ely, Minnesota

YUM-YUM HAMBURGER CASSEROLE

1 lb. hamburger
1 green pepper, chopped
1 med. onion, chopped
2 T. fat
1 box macaroni rings, cooked
1 can chicken-rice soup
1 can creamed corn
½ t. pepper
Salt to taste

Brown meat, green pepper and onion in fat. Combine all ingredients except crumbs. Bake at 350°F. for 1 hour. Last few minutes sprinkle with crumbs; brown lightly. Yield: 12-15 servings.

Mrs. Melba Olverson, Clark H.S.
Clark, South Dakota

ZUCCHINI-BEEF STEW

⅓ c. onion, thinly sliced
1 clove garlic
3 T. fat
1 lb. beef, pork or veal, cubed
2 8-oz. cans tomato sauce or 2 c. canned tomatoes
¼ c. water
2 t. salt
¼ t. pepper
3-4 med. potatoes, cubed
1 1½-2-lb. zucchini, unpared
1 No. 303 can green beans or 1 pkg. frozen green beans

Saute onion and garlic in hot fat until tender. Add meat; brown. Stir in tomato sauce, water and seasoning. Boil 5 minutes. Add potatoes; cook 5 minutes. Halve zucchini lengthwise; cut crosswise into 3-inch strips. Cook with meat mixture for 10-15 minutes or until tender, adding water if necessary. Stir in beans; continue cooking for 10 minutes. Yield: 5-6 servings.

Virginia Martell, Dept. of Home and Family
Southern Illiois University
Carbondale, Illinois

PORK CASSEROLE

1 lb. pork, diced
2 sm. onions, chopped
1 c. celery, chopped
1 can cream of mushroom soup
1 can chicken soup
1 c. cooked peas
1 c. instant rice
2 T. soy sauce
Pinch of Oregano
Worcestershire sauce to taste
1 can mushrooms (opt.)

Brown pork; add onion and celery and saute. Stir in remaining ingredients. Place in a greased casserole and bake at 375°F. for 30 minutes. Yield: 6 servings.

Florence Sutton, T. L. Handy H.S.
Bay City, Michigan

BILL'S NEW YEAR'S PORK SPECIALTY

4 lb. pork loin
Salt and pepper to taste
⅛ t. garlic powder
3-4 T. butter, melted
1 lge. onion, finely chopped
2 No. 2½ cans sauerkraut, undrained
¼ c. barley, uncooked

Season pork with salt, pepper, and garlic powder. Roast at high temperature until well browned. Remove from oven. Saute onion in butter. Combine onion, sauerkraut and barley. Place pork in casserole. Top with sauerkraut mixture. Cover. Bake at 300°F. for 2 hours. Add water as needed to keep moist. Uncover last 15 minutes. Yield: 6 servings.

Mrs. Anna Marie Rittinger, South Lake H.S.
St. Clair Shores, Michigan

CANADIAN BACON CASSEROLE

2 T. butter, melted
¾ c. brown sugar
1 No. 2 can sweet potatoes
⅛ t. cinnamon
¼ t. salt
½ lb. Canadian bacon, sliced
1 No. 2 can pineapple slices
⅓ c. pineapple juice
2 T. butter, cut in small pieces

Pour butter in a shallow baking dish. Add ¼ cup brown sugar. Place sweet potatoes in rows. Sprinkle with cinnamon, salt and remaining brown sugar. Arrange bacon strips and pineapple slices alternately over sweet potatoes. Cover with pineapple juice; top with butter. Bake at 350°F. for 40 minutes, baste occasionally. Yield: 4 servings.

Irene E. Krause, Shawano Sr. H.S.
Shawano, Wisconsin

CORN CHOWDER

12 sl. bacon, finely cut
4 sm. onions, chopped
½ c. green pepper, chopped
2 c. carrots, diced
2 c. diced celery or cabbage
8 c. whole-kernel cooked corn
6 c. milk
1 t. pepper
4 t. salt

Fry bacon with onion. Add other vegetables and a small amount of water. Simmer until tender. Add the corn and milk and heat to boiling. Add seasonings. Serve with crackers. Yield: 20 serving

Sister M. Alcantara, O.S.F., St. Francis de Sales
Chicago, Illinois

CHOP-TOP CASSEROLE

1½ c. dried white beans
1 lge. onion
1 bay leaf
1 t. rosemary
1½ t. salt
4 thick lean pork chops
Garlic salt
Black pepper
1 1-lb. can stewed tomatoes

Cook beans as directed on package, adding whole onion, bay leaf, rosemary and salt. When beans are tender, remove the onion and bay leaf. Drain some of the water from beans. Brown chops; sprinkle with garlic salt and pepper as they brown. Remove chops from skillet; pour tomatoes into skillet and blend with meat juices. Add beans. Pour into 2-quart casserole. Arrange chops on top. Bake uncovered at 350°F. for 1 hour. Yield: 4 servings.

Marilyn Cerny, E. J. Lederle Jr. HS.
Southfield, Michigan

EASIEST PORK CHOP-POTATO CASSEROLE

4 lean chops, ¾-inch thick
2 t. salt
½ t. pepper
4 c. raw potatoes, thinly sliced
1 sm. onion, minced
½ c. milk
1 can condensed cream of mushroom soup

Heat oven to 325°F. Trim fat from chops; arrange chops in bottom of 12x8x2-inch baking dish. Sprinkle with half the salt and pepper. Mix potatoes and onions; place over pork chops. Sprinkle with remaining salt and pepper. Gradually add milk to mushroom soup, stirring until smooth. Pour over potatoes. Bake for 45 minutes. Yield: 4 servings.

Mrs. Beverly Sampson, Redfield H.S.
Redfield, South Dakota

PORK CHOP CASSEROLE

5 pork chops
1 t. salt
⅛ t. pepper
1 No. 2 can baked beans
1 c. chili sauce
1 T. brown sugar
1 t. Worcestershire sauce
1 med. green pepper

Brown pork chops on both sides; season with salt and pepper. Place chops in 3-quart greased casserole. Combine baked beans, chili sauce, brown sugar and Worcestershire sauce. Pour over pork chops. Garnish with green pepper rings. Bake at 375°F. for 1 hour. Yield: 5-6 servings.

Mrs. Bessie Hutchins, Grady Municipal School
Grady, New Mexico

PORK CHOPS EN CASSEROLE

5 thick loin or rib chops
1 T. fat
Salt and pepper
1 No. 2 can cream-style corn
⅓ c. green pepper, diced
½ c. hot water

Brown pork chops slowly on both sides in hot fat. Sprinkle with salt and pepper. Mix corn and green pepper. Alternate layers of corn mixture and chops in buttered casserole. Add water; cover. Bake at 350°F. for 45 minutes. Uncover and continue baking for 15 minutes. Yield: 5 servings.

Avis Prochaska, Glasco H.S.
Glasco, Kansas

PORK CHOP-MUSHROOM CASSEROLE

6 pork chops
1 No. 2 can peas
1 2½-oz. can sl. mushrooms
2 T. flour
½ T. salt

Brown salted chops in skillet, place in casserole. Drain peas & mushrooms, reserving liquid. Cover chops with drained peas and mushrooms. Remove all but 2 tablespoons fat from skillet. Blend in flour and salt. Combine reserved liquids; add enough water to make 1½ cups liquid. Gradually stir liquid into flour mixture. Cook until thickened, stirring constantly. Cover and bake at 350°F. for 1 hour. Yield: 4-6 servings.

Mrs. Lucille Nally, Bishop McNamara H.S.
Kankakee, Illinois

PORK CHOP-POTATO SCALLOP

4 pork chops
1 can cream of mushroom soup
½ c. sour cream
¼ c. water
2 T. parsley, chopped
4 c. potatoes, thinly sliced
⅛ t. salt
⅛ t. pepper

Brown pork chops. Blend soup, sour cream, water and parsley. In 2-quart casserole alternate layers of potatoes, sprinkled with salt and pepper, and sauce. Top with chops. Cover and bake at 375°F. for 1 hour and 15 minutes. Yield: 4 servings.

Darla Havelka, Sparland H.S.
Sparland, Illinois

PORK CHOP-POTATO SCALLOP

4 pork chops
1 can cream of mushroom or celery soup
½ c. cream
¼ c. water
¼ c. onion, chopped
¼ c. celery, chopped
4 c. potatoes, thinly sliced
Salt and pepper

In skillet, brown chops. Remove chops and pour soup, cream and water into skillet. Add onions and celery and cook about 5 minutes. In a 2-quart casserole alternate layers of potatoes and soup mixture. Sprinkled with salt and pepper. Top with chops. Cover and bake at 375°F. for 1¼ hours. Yield: 4 servings.

Mrs. Suzanne Elliott Gregory, Richard Jr. H.S.
Detroit, Michigan

PORK CHOP-CORN CASSEROLE

5 or 6 pork chops
Salt and pepper
Corn flakes
1 can cream-style corn

Season chops to taste. Roll corn flakes into chops on both sides. Spoon cream-style corn on top of each chop. Bake at 250°F. for 2 hours. Yield: 3-4 servings.

Mrs. Janet Sutton, LeRoy H.S.
LeRoy, Illinois

PORK CHOP-VEGETABLE CASSEROLE

6 pork chops
6 med. potatoes, quartered
6 carrots, halved lengthwise
1 can cream of mushroom soup

Brown pork chops; place in baking pan. Arrange potatoes and carrots around meat. Dilute soup with equal amount of water; heat. Pour over meat and vegetables. Cover. Bake at 350°F. for 40 minutes. Yield: 6 servings.

Mrs. Bernece Crimmings, Rockford Sr. H.S.
Rockford, Iowa

PORK AND SAUERKRAUT CASSEROLE

4 pork loin chops
2 t. salt
Dash of pepper
1 med. onion, grated
1 No. 2 can sauerkraut
1 c. tomato juice
4 t. brown sugar
4 med. potatoes

Arrange pork chops in 2-quart casserole dish; season with salt and pepper. Place onion over each chop. Mix drained sauerkraut with tomato juice; place mixture on each chop. Sprinkle with brown sugar. Bake 1 hour at 350°F. Place whole peeled potatoes in casserole; bake 30 minutes longer. Yield: 4 servings.

Lois Clarchick, Plum Sr. H.S.
Pittsburgh, Pennsylvania

ASPARAGUS MEAL IN A DISH

2 doz. asparagus stalks
1 can mushroom soup
Oregano
Garlic salt
Onion flakes
Seasoning salt
½ t. salt
Monosodium glutamate
½ c. ham, Spam or shrimp, diced
½ c. Cheddar cheese, diced
3 hard-cooked eggs, diced
Potato chips, crushed

(Continued on Next Page)

Snap washed asparagus off at tender point; cut in 1-inch lengths. Cook in no more than ¼ cup water for 5 to 7 minutes or until nearly tender. Remove asparagus; add soup to asparagus liquid and warm. Add seasonings, meat, cheese and egg. Arrange alternate layers of asparagus and sauce in a buttered casserole. Top with potato chips. Bake at 325°F. for 30 minutes. NOTE: If desired, cream of celery or chicken soup may be used. Yield: 6 servings.

Ruth C. Peabody, Sunnyside Jr. H.S.
Sunnyside, Washington

BROCCOLI-HAM CASSEROLE

1 lb. fresh or 1 10-oz. pkg. frozen broccoli
1½ T. butter
1½ T. flour
½ t. salt
1½ c. milk
1½ c. cooked ham, chopped
2 T. green pepper, chopped
1 T. parsley
2 hard-cooked eggs, chopped
¼ c. American cheese, grated
¼ t. lemon juice
2 T. butter, melted
1 c. bread crumbs

Cook broccoli. Make white sauce with butter, flour, salt and milk. Cook until medium thick. Cut cooked broccoli into one-inch pieces and place in buttered 1½-quart casserole. Combine ham, green pepper, parsley, eggs, cheese and lemon juice. Cover broccoli with ham mixture. Combine melted butter with bread crumbs and spread over top. Pour white sauce over casserole. Bake at 350°F. for 20 minutes. Yield: 5-6 servings.

Mrs. Patsy Steffensen, Lake Norden H.S.
Lake Norden, South Dakota

CORN AND HAM HOT DISH

1 onion, chopped
½ green pepper, diced
1 lb. hamburger or ground ham
½ pkg. cooked macaroni rings
1 No. 2 can cream-style corn
1 can chicken-rice soup
1 t. salt
Dash of pepper
Pimento (opt.)

Brown onion, green pepper and meat. Combine with other ingredients. Bake 1 hour at 350°F. NOTE: If ham is used, omit salt. If desired, chicken may be substituted for meat. Yield: 8-10 servings.

Mary Sargent, North H.S.
Minneapolis, Minnesota

HAM-ASPARAGUS CASSEROLE

2 c. cooked ham, diced
2 c. cooked asparagus
4 hard-cooked eggs, sliced
1 c. medium white sauce
1 c. potato chips, crushed

Alternate layers of ham, asparagus and eggs in a buttered casserole. Pour white sauce over all. Top with potato chips. Bake 30 minutes at 350°F. Yield: 4 servings.

Eleanor L. Lewis, Grove City Sr. H.S.
Grove City, Pennsylvania

HAM-CORN CASSEROLE

1 can whole-kernel corn
2 c. cooked noodles
½ c. green pepper, chopped
1 egg, beaten
1 lb. ham, finely ground
¾ c. cheese, diced
1½ c. cornflakes

Mix all ingredients except corn flakes and butter. Pour into buttered casserole. Top with cornflakes and butter. Bake at 350°F. for 30 minutes. Yield: 4-6 servings.

Naomi Haumont, Bridgeport H.S.
Bridgeport, Nebraska

HAM 'N' CORN PUDDING

2 T. flour
2 T. sugar
1 t. salt
2 c. milk
3 eggs, beaten
2 T. melted butter
2 c. corn
1½ c. ham, chopped

Combine dry ingredients; add milk, eggs and butter. Stir in corn and ham. Pour into buttered casserole. Bake at 325°F. for 40 minutes. Yield: 8 servings.

Louise Barton, Herrin H.S.
Herrin, Illinois

HAM AND GREEN BEAN CASSEROLE

1 sm. onion, diced
2 T. butter
1 can cream of potato soup
½ c. milk
1 c. cooked ham, diced
1 pkg. frozen cut green beans, cooked
Grated cheese

Cook onion in butter until tender. Stir in soup and milk. Add ham and beans. Place in a buttered 2-quart casserole. Sprinkle with cheese. Bake at 350°F. for 25 minutes. NOTE: A one-pound can of cut green beans, drained, may be substituted for frozen beans. Yield: 4-6 servings.

Mrs. Nancy Stewart, Melvindale H.S.
Melvindale, Michigan

HAM-NOODLE CASSEROLE

3 T. butter or margarine
2 T. flour
1 c. milk
1 c. cheese, shredded
1 t. salt
2 T. catsup
1 T. horseradish, or less
2 c. cooked ham, chopped
1 c. cooked peas, green beans, or lima beans
4 c. cooked noodles
¼ c. dry bread crumbs

Melt 2 tablespoons butter in a saucepan. Blend in flour, mixing well. Add milk slowly, stirring until thick and smooth. Add cheese and cook slowly, stirring until melted. Add salt, catsup, horseradish, ham, vegetable and noodles. Blend well. Pour into casserole. Mix crumbs with remaining butter. Sprinkle over casserole. Bake at 350°F. for 30 minutes. Yield: 6-8 servings.

Mrs. Robert T. Olson, Canby H.S.
Canby, Minnesota

HAM-POTATO CASSEROLE

1 sl. of ham, ½-inch thick
4 med. potatoes, sliced
1 sm. onion, chopped
Salt and pepper to taste
Milk

Cut ham slice into pieces. Arrange layers of ham, potatoes and onion in a buttered casserole. Season. Add enough milk to cover. Bake at 350°F. for 1 hour. Yield: 5-6 servings.

Mrs. Ruth Reich, Meyersdale Area H.S.
Meyersdale, Pennsylvania

HAM-POTATO AND CHEESE CASSEROLE

¾ lb. cooked ham, cut into small pieces
1 sm. onion, finely cut
4-5 potatoes, thinly sliced
3 T. flour
½ t. salt
¼ t. pepper
1 c. sharp cheese, grated
1 c. milk
2 T. butter

Layer half of ham, onion and potatoes. Sprinkle over half of flour, salt, pepper and cheese. Repeat layers. Heat milk and butter together. Pour over casserole. Cover; bake at 350°F. for 40 minutes. Uncover to brown; bake until potatoes are tender or about 25 minutes longer. Yield: 4 servings.

Mrs. Mary M. Reese, Lakeland Joint H.S.
Mayfield, Pennsylvania

HAM SUPREME

1 8-oz. pkg. macaroni
3 c. cured ham, diced
1 No. 2 can green peas
3 c. Cheddar cheese, grated
Salt and pepper
½ pt. heavy cream
1 stick butter
1 c. chopped mushrooms
1 No. 2½ can tomatoes
Fine bread crumbs

Cook and drain macaroni. Cover bottom of large greased shallow casserole with half of macaroni. Add layer of half of ham, canned peas and liquid and grated cheese. Season to taste with salt and pepper. Repeat layers. Pour cream over top. Dot with butter; add chopped mushrooms. Add juice and tomatoes over all. Cover with bread crumbs and dot with remaining butter. Bake for 2 hours and 30 minutes at 250°F. Yield: 8 servings.

Mrs. Velma Shaffer, State Supervisor
Home Economics Education
Little Rock, Arkansas

HAM-VEGETABLE CASSEROLE

2 c. frozen corn
2 c. frozen peas and carrots
2 c. frozen succotash
1 t. salt
¼ t. pepper
3 T. onion, chopped
1 can condensed cream of mushroom soup
Ham slices, cut ¼-inch thick

Place frozen vegetables in greased 3-quart casserole. Sprinkle with salt, pepper and onion. Spread soup over the top. Cover with foil and bake at 400°F. for 40 minutes. Stir vegetables, spreading them evenly over the bottom of the casserole. Cover with ham. Return to oven and bake, uncovered, for 10 minutes. Turn meat and continue baking for 10 minutes. Yield: 8 servings.

Mrs. Lorena Nattress
Madison Consolidated H.S.
Lore City, Ohio

HUNTER'S DREAM

½ lb. bacon, cubed
1 lb. raw ham
1 can tomatoes
1 can corn
1 can lima beans
1 can mushrooms
1 pkg. spaghetti

Fry bacon until crisp; add ham and brown. Add tomatoes, corn, beans and mushrooms. Cook spaghetti slightly underdone. Add to mixture. Pour into casserole; bake at 300°F. for 45 minutes. Yield: 8-10 servings.

Mrs. Doris Schlumpf, Durand Unified Schools
Durand, Wisconsin

LETTUCE PIE

½ lb. smoked or boiled ham
6 green onions or equivalent dried onions, finely diced
1 head of lettuce, finely cut
Salt and pepper to taste
4 eggs
Unbaked pastry shell

Cook and grind ham. Cook onions in a small amount of water for a few minutes. Add lettuce, ham, pepper and salt. Cook until tender; cool. Stir in one egg at a time until thoroughly mixed. Pour into unbaked pastry shell. Bake at 425°F. for 20 to 30 minutes. Yield: 8 servings.

Fern E. Ruck, Rangely H.S.
Rangely, Colorado

OLD SOUTH CASSEROLE

6 med. sweet potatoes
½ c. pecans, chopped
1 c. cooked ham, cubed
1½ c. pineapple juice
¼ c. granulated sugar
¼ c. brown sugar
1 T. cornstarch
2 T. butter or margarine, melted

Wash potatoes and boil until tender. Peel and cut in half lengthwise. Place in buttered baking dish with pecans and ham. Mix pineapple juice, sugars, cornstarch and butter; pour over potatoes. Bake 1 hour at 300°F. Baste several times during baking with syrup in dish. Yield: 6 servings.

Mrs. Louise Frame, Coraopolis Jr. H.S.
Coraopolis, Pennsylvania

SCALLOPED HAM AND POTATOES

¾ lb. cooked ham, thinly sliced
1 sm. onion, minced
4-6 pared raw potatoes, thinly sliced
3 T. flour
½ t. salt
¼ t. pepper
1 c. process sharp American cheese, grated
1 c. milk
2 T. butter or margarine
¼ c. catsup

Arrange ham in a greased casserole; top with onion. Top with half of potatoes; sprinkle with half of flour, salt, pepper and cheese. Repeat layers. Heat milk with butter; pour all over. Bake covered for 40 minutes at 350°F. Uncover and dot with catsup. Bake for 30 minutes, or until potatoes are tender. NOTE: If desired, 1 can thinly sliced luncheon meat may be used in place of ham. Yield: 4-6 servings.

Joanne F. Jordan, Bailey Jr. H.S.
West Haven, Connecticut

POTATO-HAM CASSEROLE

6 med. potatoes, sliced ¼-inch thick
6 med. onions, sliced ¼-inch thick
12 sl. ham
Salt and pepper
1 8-oz. can tomato sauce

Arrange layers of one-third of potatoes, onion and ham in greased casserole. Season. Repeat layers twice. Top with tomato sauce. Cover. Bake at 350°F. for 1 hour or until potatoes are tender. Yield: 6 servings.

Mrs. Nancy Carlson, Oregon Community H.S.
Oregon, Illinois

WIKIWIKI HAM BAKE

1 sl. cooked ham, ¾-inch thick
1 1-lb. 4-oz. can pineapple chunks
½ c. brown sugar, firmly packed
1 1-lb. can whole sweet potatoes
12 marshmallows

Cut ham into 6 pieces; brown. Drain syrup from pineapple; stir in brown sugar until dissolved. Pour over ham in frying pan; heat to boiling. Pile ham in middle of 2-quart baking dish; arrange sweet potatoes around edge. Tuck pineapple chunks between potatoes; add hot syrup. Bake at 400°F. for 15 minutes. Place marshmallows around edge; bake 5 minutes until marshmallows are brown. Yield: 6 servings.

Carol L. Neff, Columbia H.S.
Columbia, Pennsylvania

APPLE-PORK AND BEANS CASSEROLE

1 lb. mild pork sausage
2 1-lb. cans pork and beans
2 c. pared apples, sliced
⅓ c. brown sugar
1 T. prepared mustard
2 T. lemon juice
¼ c. tomato catsup

Shape pork sausage into balls and cook over direct heat until browned. Mix beans, apples, brown sugar, mustard and lemon juice thoroughly. Drain sausage and add to bean mixture. Place into greased 2½-quart casserole. Top with catsup. Bake at 350°F. for 1 hour. Yield: 6-8 servings.

Mrs. Arlene Voecks, Wells H.S.
Wells, Minnesota

CORN-SAUSAGE CASSEROLE

½ lb. pork sausage
1 c. celery, diced
2 T. onion, minced
1 t. salt
4 c. bread cubes
1 No. 2 can whole-kernel corn

Brown sausage, celery, onion and salt in skillet. Mix bread cubes and corn in buttered casserole, liquid and all. Add sausage mixture. Mix well. Bake in 350°F. oven for 30 minutes. NOTE: This may also be used as a stuffing for poultry. Yield: 6-8 servings.

Leona B. Ziesemer, Joliet Township H.S.
and Junior College
Joliet, Illinois

CORN AND SAUSAGE CASSEROLE

2 No. 303 cans cream-style corn
¾ lb. bulk pork sausage
2 eggs, slightly beaten
⅓ c. milk
¼ t. salt
¾ c. cracker crumbs, finely rolled

Mix corn, pork sausage, eggs, milk, salt and ½ cup cracker crumbs. Pour into buttered casserole. Top with remaining ¼ cup cracker crumbs. Bake at 375°F. for 30 minutes. Yield: 6-8 servings.

Mrs. Esther Cain, Brodhead H.S.
Brodhead, Wisconsin

DUTCH LIMA CASSEROLE

1½ c. lge. dry lima beans
2½ t. salt
12 link sausages
1 onion, thinly sliced
2 unpeeled apples, sliced
¼ c. brown sugar
1 T. vinegar
½ c. catsup

Soak rinsed beans in 3½ cups water; add 1½ teaspoons salt. Bring to a boil; cook until tender. Fry sausages until half done; remove 8 from pan. Pour off all but 2 tablespoons fat; add onion and apple. Cook for 5 minutes. Cut remaining sausages into pieces. Sprinkle with sugar, vinegar and remaining salt. Drain beans; reserve ¾ cup liquid. Stir catsup and bean liquid into sausage mixture. Combine all ingredients. Pour into casserole. Bake at 350°F. for 1 hour. Yield: 4-6 servings.

Mrs. Claris Crotton, Browns Valley H.S.
Browns Valley, Minnesota

LENTIL SURPRISE CASSEROLE

1 c. lentils
2½-3 c. water
2 c. canned tomatoes
2 stalks celery, chopped
1 sm. onion, chopped
1 lb. link sausages
2 T. steak sauce

Cook lentils in water for 1 hour or until done and all water is absorbed. Place half of lentils in lightly greased casserole; mix in tomatoes. Add layers of celery, onion, and sausages. Sprinkle with steak sauce. Cover with remaining lentils. Bake at 350°F. for 1 hour. Yield: 6 servings.

Mrs. Linda M. Lewis, Kendrick H.S.
Kendrick, Idaho

LIMA BEAN-CORN AND SAUSAGE CASSEROLE

1 lb. pork sausage
1 pkg. frozen lima beans
1 can cream-style corn
1 can whole-kernel corn
1 c. bread crumbs

Slice sausage and brown in skillet. Pour off fat as sausage browns, but save ½ cup of the fat. Prepare lima beans as package instructs. Mix the cream-style corn and the whole-kernel corn. Pour half of corn mixture into the bottom of an ungreased 2-quart casserole. Sprinkle half of lima beans over corn mixture. Break sausage slices in forths and sprinkle half of sausage over lima bean layer. Repeat layers. Top the casserole with bread crumbs. Pour ½ cup sausage fat over casserole. Bake 30 minutes at 350°F. Yield: 8-10 servings.

Marilyn Hampton, Kenyon H.S.
Kenyon, Minnesota

MEAL-IN-A-CASSEROLE

1 med. onion, thinly sliced
2 med. potatoes thinly sliced
2 c. canned corn
½ t. salt
⅛ t. pepper
Dash of paprika
1 lb. sausage
1 c. tomato sauce

Place onion, potatoes, corn, salt, pepper, and paprika in greased casserole. Form sausage into balls or patties; place on vegetables. Top with tomato sauce. Cover; bake at 350°F. for 45-60 minutes. Remove lid; bake 15-20 minutes or until potatoes are tender and casserole browned. Yield: 4-6 servings.

Marget Condell, Snohomish Sr. H.S.
Snohomish, Washington

SAUSAGE-POTATO CASSEROLE

1 sm. onion, chopped
2 T. butter or margarine
1 lb. pork sausage
4 peeled raw potatoes, thinly sliced
1 No. 303 can cream-style corn
Salt and pepper
1½ c. milk, heated

Brown the onion in butter. Add the sausage and brown well. Arrange the potatoes in a layer in a greased casserole; add a layer of the corn, then a layer of sausage. Sprinkle the layer with salt and pepper. Repeat layers. Pour the heated milk over all. Bake in a 350°F. oven for 1 hour or until the potatoes are tender. Yield: 6-8 servings.

Mrs. Winifred Iverson, Pierre Sr. H.S.
Pierre, South Dakota

SAUSAGE-VEGETABLE CASSEROLE

1½ lb. sausage
6 med. potatoes, sliced
2 med. onions, sliced
Salt and pepper to taste
1 No. 2 can cream-style corn

Shape sausage into patties; fry until brown. Arrange potato and onion slices in casserole; season with salt and pepper. Pour corn over potato and onion slices; top with sausage patties. Bake at 350°F. until potatoes and onions are tender, about 45 minutes. Yield: 6 servings.

Nellie Merrill, St. David H.S.
St. David, Arizona

SWEET POTATO-SAUSAGE CASSEROLE

½ lb. sausage
¾ c. apple slices, thinly cut
2 T. brown sugar
1 c. mashed sweet potatoes
¼ t. salt
1 t. butter or margarine
¼ c. milk
Parsley (garnish)

Place sausage in the casserole dish. Arrange the apple slices on the sausage; sprinkle with brown sugar. Combine sweet potatoes, salt, butter and milk. Beat until light and fluffy. Place the potato, mixture over the apple slices. Bake for one hour in a 350°F. oven. Serve very hot. Garnish with parsley, if desired. Yield: 4 servings.

Frances Rodriguez, Espanola H.S.
Espanola, New Mexico

SWEET POTATO BAKE

2 lb. sweet potatoes
1 lb. pork link sausages, fried
1 pt. sweet applesauce

Cook, peel and mash sweet potatoes; keep hot. Spread in bottom of buttered 1½-quart casserole. Top with layer of pork sausages; top with a thick layer of applesauce. Bake uncovered 15-20 minutes at 350°F. Yield: 4-6 servings.

Blanche Maxwell, Spring Valley Public Schools
Spring Valley, Wisconsin

ZUCCHINI AND SMOKED SAUSAGE

1 zucchini squash, sliced
¼ c. celery, diced
¼ c. onion, diced
¼ c. green pepper, chopped
1 can stewed tomatoes
1 c. smoked sausages, cut in rings
1 T. parsley flakes
1 t. oregano
1 t. salt
½ t. pepper
½ c. Velveeta cheese, ¼-inch slices

Overlap half of squash slices in greased casserole. Sprinkle with half of celery, onion, green pepper, tomatoes sausages and seasonings. Repeat layers. Place stripes of cheese on top. Bake at 350°F. for 35-40 minutes or until vegetables are tender. NOTE: Two fresh tomatoes, chopped may be substituted for canned tomatoes. Yield: 6 servings.

Betty N. Davis, Masontown Jr. H.S.
Masontown, Pennsylvania

BARBECUED LIMA BEANS AND SPARE RIBS

1 c. lima beans
3 c. tomato juice
2 t. salt
1 lb. spareribs
½ med. onion, chopped
⅛ t. pepper
½ t. dry mustard
½ t. Tabasco sauce
¼ c. dark molasses

Soak beans overnight in ¾ cup tomato juice. Add half of salt; cover and simmer until beans are tender. Do not boil. Pour half the beans into a greased casserole. Rub remainder of salt over spareribs and place over beans. Add onion. Mix pepper, mustard, Tabasco sauce and molassas with remaining tomato juice; pour over beans. Cover and bake for 1 hour and 30 minutes at 325°F. Uncover and bake until brown, 20-30 minutes. Yield: 4-6 servings.

Mrs. Sarah Perry, North Webster H.S.
North Webster, Indiana

DUTCH OVEN SUPPER

1 T. margarine
¼ c. onion, chopped
¼ celery, chopped
1 sm. clove garlic
1 T. lemon juice
1 T. Worcestershire sauce
1 T. brown sugar
½ c. water
½ c. catsup
1 T. vinegar
½ t. dry mustard
½ t. salt
⅛ t. pepper
½ t. brown sugar
1½ lb. spareribs
1 No. 2 can sauerkraut
8 med. potatoes, peeled

In a saucepan melt margarine; add onions and celery and cook until golden. Add remaining ingredients except meat, potatoes and sauerkraut; simmer for 20 minutes. Brown sapreribs in heavy Dutch oven; add sauerkraut and sauce. Cover and cook until ribs are tender, about 1 hour. Turn ribs occasionally. Add potatoes and cook 20-30 minutes. Yield: 4 servings.

Barbara Myers Shaw, Hemlock H.S.
Hemlock, Michigan

CHICKEN-ALMOND VERMICELLI

8 oz. vermicelli
12 oz. boned chicken
2 chicken bouillon cubes
1½ c. boiling water
2 T. cornstarch
2 T. soy sauce
1½ t. salt
1 T. butter
1½ c. mushrooms, sliced
1c. celery, sliced
1 lge. onion, cut into 8 pieces
½ c. water chestnuts, sliced
1 10-oz. pkg. frozen broccoli, drained
2 T. toasted slivered almonds

Cook vermicelli in boiling salted water for 5-7 minutes or until tender; drain. Cut chicken into ¼-inch strips. Dissolve bouillon cubes in water. Blend soy sauce and cornstarch to a smooth paste; add to bouillon with salt. Cook chicken in butter, stirring constantly, 3-4 minutes; remove chicken. Cook mushrooms in remaining liquid until soft. Add celery, onion and chestnuts; cook 2-3 minutes. Stir in bouillon mixture; stir in chicken and broccoli. Bring to a boil. Serve over hot vermicelli; sprinkle with almonds. Yield: 4-6 servings.

Mrs. William Crolly, Abraham Clark H.S.
Roselle, New Jersey

BUFFET SUPPER CASSEROLE

1 4 to 5-lb. chicken, cooked
½ c. onion, chopped
½ c. green pepper, chopped
1 4-oz. can mushrooms
Liquid from mushrooms
Butter, melted
6 c. chicken stock
1 c. pitted ripe olives, chopped
Liquid from olives
1½ pkg. noodles
3-4 t. pimento, chopped
1 pkg. frozen peas
Celery salt to taste
Salt and pepper to taste
1½ c. sharp Cheddar cheese, grated

Remove bones from chicken; coarsely chop meat. Saute onion, green pepper and mushrooms in butter. Combine stock and liquid from mushrooms and olives; bring to a boil. Add noodles; cook until tender. Stir in chicken, mushroom mixture, olives, pimento, peas and seasonings. Pour half of mixture into 3-quart baking dish; sprinkle with half of cheese. Repeat layers. Bake at 325°F. for 1 hour. Yield: 8-10 servings.

Clela Wilson, Bardolph H.S.
Bardolph, Illinois

CHEESEY CHICKEN CASSEROLE

1 4-lb. chicken, cooked
2 c. milk
2 8-oz. pkg. cream cheese
1 t. salt
¾ t. garlic salt
1½ c. Parmesan cheese, shredded
2 10-oz. pkg. frozen broccoli, cooked

Remove skin and bones from chicken; thinly slice meat. Chill. Blend milk, cream cheese, salt and garlic salt in double boiler until smooth and thoroughly heated. Stir in half of Parmesan cheese. Arrange broccoli in 2-quart greased casserole; cover with 1 cup of cheese mixture. Top with chicken slices; cover with remaining cheese mixture. Sprinkle with ¼ cup Parmesan cheese. Bake at 350°F. for 25-30 minutes. Remove; let stand 5 minutes. Serve with remaining cheese. Yield: 8 servings.

Mrs. Ruth Irwin, Shawnee H.S.
Wolf Lake, Illinois

CHICKEN-ARTICHOKE CASSEROLE

1 3-lb. fryer, cut up
1½ t. salt
½ t. pepper
6 T. butter
¼ lb. mushrooms, cut in large pieces
2 T. flour
⅔ c. chicken consomme or bouillon
3 T. Sherry
1 12 to 15-oz. can artichoke hearts

(Continued on Next Page)

Sprinkle chicken with salt, pepper and paprika; brown in 4 tablespoons butter. Place in large casserole. Saute mushrooms in remaining butter for 5 minutes; sprinkle with flour. Stir in consomme and Sherry. Cook for 5 minutes. Arrange artichoke hearts between chicken pieces. Pour on mushroom sauce. Cover; bake at 375°F. for 40 minutes. Yield: 6 servings.

Barbara M. Shea, Memorial H.S.
Manchester, New Hampshire

CHICKEN AND BISCUIT CASSEROLE

1 can cream of mushroom soup
2 T. flour
2 T. instant minced onion
½ c. milk
1½ c. American cheese, shredded
1 10-oz. pkg. frozen peas
2 c. cooked chicken, diced
1 4-oz. can pimento, chopped
Salt and pepper to taste
1 can refrigerator biscuits

Combine soup, flour, onion and milk; cook until thickened. Remove from heat. Blend in 1 cup cheese until melted. Stir in peas, chicken, pimento, salt and pepper. Heat thoroughly. Pour into 8 to 9-inch baking dish. Place biscuits around edge. Bake at 400°F. for 20 minutes. Sprinkle with remaining cheese. Bake 5-10 minutes longer or until golden brown. Yield: 6 servings.

Arlene Reinford, Upper Perkiomen H.S.
East Greenville, Pennsylvania

CHICKEN DIVAN

5 lb. chicken breasts
1 T. salt
1 c. water
1 lge. bunch broccoli
1 c. Parmesan cheese, grated
2 c. med. white sauce
¼ t. nutmeg
½ c. Hollandaise sauce or mayonnaise
½ c. heavy cream, whipped
1 t. Worcestershire sauce

Sprinkle chicken with salt; add water. Cover and simmer for 45 minutes or until tender. Remove from bone and cut into thin slices. Cook and drain broccoli; place in a shallow buttered baking dish. Place chicken on broccoli; sprinkle with half the cheese. Combine white sauce with remaining ingredients except cheese; mix carefully and pour over chicken. Sprinkle with remaining cheese. Bake at 300°F. for 30 minutes. Slip under broiler to brown. Yield: 8 servings.

Dianne Huber, South Mountain H.S.
Phoenix, Arizona

CHICK DIVAN

1 5-lb. chicken
2 t. salt
2 c. med. white sauce
¼ t. nutmeg
1 c. Hollandaise sauce
½ c. whipped cream
3 T. Sherry
1 t. Worcestershire sauce
1 lge. bunch broccoli
1 c. Parmesan cheese, grated

Pressure cook the seasoned chicken; remove meat from bone. Combine white sauce, nutmeg, Hollandaise sauce, whipped cream, Sherry and Worcestershire sauce. Cook the broccoli. Arrange chicken slices in casserole. Place broccoli over all. Pour sauce over and sprinkle with cheese. Broil until lightly browned. Yield: 8 servings.

Mrs. Jacob O. Cozad
Indianola Community School
Indianola, Iowa

CHICKEN BISCUIT MEDLEY

½ c. chicken fat or butter
¾ t. salt
2 c. chicken stock
1 c. milk
2 c. cooked chicken, diced
1 c. carrots, diced
1 c. celery, chopped
Biscuits, unbaked

Heat chicken fat or butter in saucepan; stir in flour and salt. Gradually add chicken stock and milk, stirring constantly until sauce is thickened. Place chicken, carrots and celery in 2-quart casserole. Pour hot sauce over and stir until well blended. Top with biscuits. Bake at 400°F. for 15 minutes. Yield: 8-10 servings.

Sue Comer, Pendleton H.S.
Pendleton, Indiana

CHICKEN-CORN CASSEROLE

1 sm. pkg. noodle dumplings
1 sm. jar boned chicken
1 pkg. whole-kernel corn
1 sm. can mushrooms
2 T. butter
2 T. flour
1 c. milk
½ lb. cheese, cut up

Cook noodles according to package directions; add chicken, corn and mushrooms. Pour into casserole. Melt butter in sauce pan; mix in flour and slowly add milk. Add cheese; cook slowly until sauce thickens and cheese melts. Pour cheese sauce over casserole and stir in. Sprinkle cracker crumbs or potato chips over top if desired. Bake at 350°F. for 1 hour. Yield: 4-6 servings.

Norma Strube, Hopkins Township H.S.
Granville, Illinois

CHICKEN CASSEROLE WITH HOMEMADE NOODLES

2 lge. eggs
1 c. flour
1 2½ to 3-lb. chicken, cut up
Salt and pepper to taste
1 10-oz. pkg. frozen peas
1 can mushroom soup
½ c. milk
Seasoned salt

Beat eggs until frothy; stir in flour with fork. Roll out very thin on lightly floured surface. Cut into narrow strips. Let stand several hours or overnight. Cover chicken with water; add seasoning. Cook until tender; remove from broth. Cut into bite-size pieces. Cook noodles in broth until tender. Broth will be mostly absorbed. Place noodles in 9-inch casserole; sprinkle with peas. Cover with mixture of soup and milk; sprinkle with seasoned salt. Bake at 350°F. for 35 minutes to 1 hour or until peas are done. NOTE: May be frozen. Yield: 6-8 servings.

Mrs. W. C. Morris, Chesaning H.S.
Chesaning, Michigan

CHICKEN HOT DISH

1 cooked chicken, cut up
2 cans mushroom soup
2 cans celery soup
2 cans mushrooms
½ c. celery, chopped
1 can peas
Salt and pepper to taste
3 pkg. cooked shell macaroni
Milk or cream

Combine all ingredients; add enough milk or cream to make it moist. Bake at 350°F. for 1 hour.

Mrs. Allan Nelson, Karlstad H.S.
Karlstad, Minnesota

SAVORY CHICKEN CASSEROLE

2 lb. chicken legs
2 T. shortening
1 can cream of chicken soup
½ can water or milk
1 t. poultry seasoning
1 t. salt
Dash of pepper
1 pkg. frozen lima beans
1 pkg. frozen corn
6 sm. onions

Brown chicken in shortening; place in 2-quart casserole. Combine soup and water. Add remaining ingredients. Cover; cook 15 minutes. Pour over chicken. Cover. Bake at 375°F. for 1 hour. Uncover; bake 15 minutes longer or until chicken is tender. Yield: 6-8 servings.

Bessie M. Sarchet, Meadowbrook H.S.
Byesville, Ohio

CHICKEN LOAF

4 eggs, beaten
1¼ c. milk
½ c. chicken broth
½ t. salt
¼ t. pepper
1 c. salt bread crumbs
1 T. onion, chopped
3 c. cooked, chicken, chopped
1 10-oz. pkg. frozen peas and carrots
1 can cream of mushroom soup

Combine eggs and ¾ cup milk. Add remaining ingredients except soup and ½ cup milk. Mix well. Pour into greased loaf pan or casserole. Place in shallow pan of hot water. Bake at 350°F. for 45-50 minutes. Serve with mushroom sauce made from soup and ½ cup milk. Yield: 8 servings.

Mrs. Marian Wilson, Hopkins Academy H.S.
Hadley, Massachusetts

CHICKEN POLYNESIAN

3 pkg. frozen chicken breasts or other parts
1 1½-lb. bag frozen sm. potatoes
2 10-oz. pkg. frozen peaches
Salt to taste
8-10 whole cloves

Thaw chicken, potatoes and peaches. Sprinkle with salt. Arrange chicken and potatoes in a large casserole; top with peaches and peach juice. Sprinkle with cloves. Cover with foil; bake at 350°F. for 1 hour or until tender. Yield: 6-8 servings.

Mrs. Carolyn Gregory, Western H.S.
Latham, Ohio

CHICKEN TERRAPIN

2½ c. chicken broth
½ c. flour
1 T. salt
⅛ t. pepper
⅛ t. paprika
1 sm. can mushrooms
2 hard-cooked eggs, cubed
2 c. peas
1 c. pimento pods
2 stalks celery, chopped
1 T. onion, minced
4 c. cooked chicken, chopped
4 c. chow mein noodles
1 T. lemon juice

Thicken broth with flour, salt, pepper, paprika; cook until like creamed chicken. Add mushrooms, eggs, peas and pimento. Cook a few minutes. Add celery and onion; fold in chicken pieces. Pour over noodles; bake at 350°F. for 20-30 minutes. Sprinkle with lemon juice. Yield: 12 servings.

Mrs. Phyllis Houk, Decatur H.S.
Decatur, Indiana

CHICKEN TETRAZZINI

2 sl. bacon, chopped
⅓ c. onion, minced
½ c. green pepper, minced
½ lb. American cheese, grated
¼ c. pimento, cut up
¼ c. slivered almonds
1¾ c. cooked peas
2 c. cooked chicken, cut up
1 8-oz. pkg. macaroni, cooked

Fry bacon until crisp. Lightly brown onion and green pepper in drippings. Add remaining ingredients. Heat thoroughly using chicken stock to moisten when needed. Yield: 8 servings.

Mrs. Janis Linderoth,
Stephenson Consolidated Schools
Stephenson, Michigan

DELUXE GREEN BEAN CASSEROLE

2 cans French-style green beans, drained
1 c. diced cooked chicken, ham or tuna
2 T. pimento, chopped
1 5-oz. can water chestnuts, drained and sliced
1 can cream of mushroom soup
½ c. milk
1 can French-fried onion rings
½ c. American cheese, grated

In a buttered 1½-quart casserole arrange layers of green beans, meat, pimento, water chestnuts, and soup-milk mixture. Repeat layers. Arrange onion rings over top. Sprinkle cheese over onion rings. Bake at 350°F. until thoroughly heated and cheese is browned, about 30 minutes. Yield: 6 servings.

Mrs. Virginia Smith, North H.S.
Evansville, Indiana

FRIED CHICKEN CASSEROLE

2 frying chickens, cut up
4 T. vegetable fat
3 pkg. frozen broccoli
½ t. salt
¼ t. pepper (opt.)
2 cans condensed cream of chicken soup
½ c. milk
¾ c. buttered bread crumbs
½ c. cheese, grated

Brown chicken in fat quickly. Arrange frozen broccoli in bottom of greased rectangular baking dish with the browned pieces of chicken on top. Sprinkle with salt and pepper. Blend cream of chicken soup with milk and pour over all. Blend bread crumbs with cheese and sprinkle over all. Bake at 325°F. for two hours, or longer if pieces of chicken are large. Yield: 5-6 servings.

Mary Reece, Warsaw Community H.S.
Warsaw, Indiana

DELUXE CHICKEN CASSEROLE

4 chicken breasts
2 pkg. frozen broccoli stalks
¼ c. melted butter
2 c. chicken stock
1 c. milk
½ c. flour
1 c. light cream
1 t. salt
⅓ c. white Sauterne
¼ lb. Cheddar cheese, grated
½ c. slivered almonds
Paprika

Cook chicken breasts in salted water until tender; cut in slices. Cook broccoli until not quite tender. Make a white sauce out of remaining ingredients except cheese, almonds and paprika. Arrange broccoli in a buttered casserole; pour in half of sauce. Arrange sliced chicken over sauce; sprinkle with half of almonds. Cover with remaining sauce, almonds, cheese and paprika. Bake at 350°F. for 30 minutes. Yield: 4 servings.

Mrs. Bonnie Davis, Felton H.S.
Felton, Minnesota

MAIN-DISH CHICKEN CASSEROLE

1 4-lb. stewing hen
Salt and pepper
3-4 celery stalks, cubed
1 sm. whole onion
2 c. buttered bread crumbs
½ 8-oz. pkg. noodles, cooked
1 t. parsley, minced
1 c. cooked or frozen peas
2-3 T. butter or chicken fat, melted
3 T. flour
Dash of paprika
1 c. milk or chicken broth
8 uncooked biscuits

Stew chicken for 3½-4 hours with salt, pepper, celery and onion. Chill; remove bones and cube meat. Line a greased casserole with buttered bread crumbs. Add a layer of noodles; sprinkle with 1 teaspoon salt, ⅛ teaspoon pepper and parsley. Add a layer of chicken and a layer of peas. Sprinkle with bread crumbs. Repeat layers. Blend butter, flour, ¼ teaspoon salt, ⅛ teaspoon pepper and a dash of paprika in a double boiler. Stir until smooth and bubbly. Remove from heat. Stir into the liquid. Cook until thickened, stirring constantly. Pour over layers in casserole. Sprinkle with bread crumbs. Bake at 350°F. until sauce is thick and crumbs are browned. Top with biscuits and bake 12 minutes longer. NOTE: If desired, crushed potato chips or corn chips may be substituted for crumbs. Casserole may be garnished with parsley or slices of red bell pepper. Yield: 6-8 servings.

Berniece M. Cobb, Westminster H.S.
Westminster, Colorado

CLASSIC TURKEY DIVAN

2 10-oz. pkg. frozen broccoli
¼ c. butter, melted
¼ c flour
2 c. turkey broth
½ c. heavy cream
3 T. cooking Sherry
½ t. salt
Dash of pepper
¼ c. Parmesan cheese, grated
18 slices turkey

Cook broccoli in boiling salted water; drain. Blend butter and flour. Add broth; cook, stirring until thickened. Stir in cream, Sherry, salt and pepper. Place broccoli in 13x9x2-inch baking dish. Cover with half of sauce. Top with turkey slices. Combine cheese and remaining sauce; pour over turkey. Sprinkle with additional cheese. Bake at 350°F. for 20 minutes or until thoroughly heated. Broil until golden. NOTE: Two fresh bunches of broccoli may be used instead of frozen. Yield: 6-8 servings.

Kay Carlson, Bellevue H.S.
Bellevue, Washington

TURKEY STROGANOFF

¼ c. green pepper, chopped
2 T. onion, chopped
2 T. butter
1 can cream of mushroom soup
½ c. sour cream
2 c. chop suey vegetables
1 c. cooked turkey, diced
1 can pimentos, chopped

Cook green pepper and onion in butter until tender. Blend with soup and sour cream in 1-quart casserole; stir in remaining ingredients. Bake at 350°F. for 30 minutes. Yield: 4 servings.

Winifred Cozzens, Capitan H.S.
Capitan, New Mexico

TUNA-NOODLE CASSEROLE

1 8-oz. pkg. noodles
2 boxes frozen mixed vegetables
4 T. butter, melted
4 T. flour
½ t. salt
⅛ t. pepper
2c. milk
1 6-oz. can tuna, drained
1 c. buttered bread crumbs

Boil noodles in salted water for 10 minutes. Boil vegetables for 2 minutes; drain. Blend butter, flour, salt and pepper; slowly stir in milk. Bring to a boil. Add tuna; boil 2 minutes. Combine cooked noodles and tuna sauce. Add vegetables; pour into greased casserole. Top with crumbs. Cover. Bake at 350°F. for 20 minutes. Remove cover; continue baking for 10 minutes. Yield: 8-10 servings.

Mrs. Marie B. King, Ligonier Valley H.S.
Ligonier, Pennsylvania

SEVEN SEAS CASSEROLE

1 can cream of mushroom soup
¼-⅓ c. onion, finely chopped
1⅓ c. water
1 t. lemon juice
¼ t. salt
Dash of pepper
1⅓ c. instant rice
1 box frozen green peas
1 can tuna
½ c. Cheddar cheese, grated
Paprika

Combine soup, onion, water, lemon juice, salt and pepper; bring to a boil over medium heat, stirring occasionally. Pour half of soup mixture into a greased 1½-quart casserole. Layer rice, peas and tuna; add remaining soup. Sprinkle with cheese and paprika. Cover and bake at 375°F. for 15-20 minutes. Cut through mixture with knife after 10 minutes of baking to help distribute soup mixture. Yield: 4 servings.

This recipe submitted by the following teachers:
Glennes Sauber, Hastings Public H.S.
Hastings, Minnesota
Mrs. Marjorie West, Northeast Vocational H.S.
Lauderdale, Mississippi

TUNA TREAT

1pkg. frozen peas
⅓ c. milk
1 can cream of mushroom soup
1 6½ to 7-oz. can tuna fish
4 eggs, separated
¼ c. Cheddar cheese, coarsely grated

Cook the frozen peas until tender, omitting salt. Heat oven to 400°F. In a 1½-quart casserole mix the milk and cream of mushroom soup until blended. Add drained peas. Empty the tuna into the casserole. Toss lightly until mixed. Put casserole into oven for 12 minutes. Beat egg yolks until lemon colored. Fold cheese into yolks. Beat whites until they stand in peaks. Push cheese and yolks onto whites and carefully fold them together. The more delicately these are folded, the higher the topping will be. Pour topping onto casserole. Bake 20 minutes longer. Yield: 6 servings.

Mrs. Robert C. Powell,
Atkinson Community H.S.
Atkinson, Illinois

Vegetable Casseroles

ARTICHOKE HEARTS ELEGANTE

1 pkg. frozen artichokes
1 T. dried minced onion, rehydrated
1 clove garlic, crushed
1 T. chopped parsley or ½ T. dried parsley
½ c. dry bread crumbs
1 t. salt
Freshly ground pepper
¼ c. olive oil
2 T. water
4 T. Parmesan or Romano cheese, grated

Cook artichokes in boiling, salted water 5 minutes; drain well. Place in buttered baking dish. Mix other ingredients and sprinkle over artichokes. Bake in 400°F. oven for 20 minutes or until soft. Yield: 4 servings.

Mrs. Robert Still, Clover Park
Vocational Technical School
Tacoma, Washington

ASPARAGUS-CHESTNUT CASSEROLE

2 cans asparagus spears
1 can cream of celery or mushroom soup
1 can water chestnuts, sliced
1 8-oz. can mushrooms, sliced
1 sm. jar pimento, chopped
4 hard-cooked eggs, chopped
1 can French-fried onion rings

Drain and arrange the asparagus spears in the bottom of a greased casserole. Dilute the soup with part of the asparagus juice until it is the consistency of a medium white sauce. Add water chestnuts, mushrooms, pimento and eggs. Stir until well mixed; pour over the asparagus. Top with the French-fried onion rings. Bake at 350°F. for 25 minutes. Yield: 6-8 servings.

Mrs. Jane Wisdom, Hillsboro H.S.
Hillsboro, Illinois

ASPARAGUS-EGG CASSEROLE

16 stalks asparagus
⅔ c. water
1 t. salt
2 T. butter
4 T. flour
1½ c. milk
4 hard-cooked eggs, quartered
Cracker crumbs

Cook asparagus until tender in the water with ½ teaspoon salt. Make white sauce with butter, flour, milk and ½ teaspoon salt. Drain asparagus water into white sauce. Put asparagus in casserole. Arrange eggs in layer over asparagus. Pour white sauce over all. Top with crumbs and bake at 350°F. for 20 minutes. Yield: 4 servings.

Mrs. Laurie Williams, Stromsburg H.S.
Stromsburg, Nebraska

ASPARAGUS-FLAKE CASSEROLE

2 10½-oz. cans green asparagus tips
2 10½-oz. cans mushroom soup
¼ t. salt
¼ t. pepper
¼ lb. sharp cheese, grated
1½ c. corn flake crumbs

Arrange asparagus tips on bottom of greased baking dish. Combine soup and seasonings; pour over asparagus. Sprinkle with cheese; top with crumbs. Bake at 300°F. for 30 minutes, or until golden brown. Yield: 6 servings.

Elsa Rinkenberger, Franklin Area Schools
Franklin, Pennsylvania

ASPARAGUS-MUSHROOM CASSEROLE

1 No. 2 can asparagus
1 can cream of mushroom soup
Butter as desired
1-1½ c. buttered crumbs

Heat asparagus and liquid, undiluted mushroom soup and butter in saucepan. Place in buttered casserole; top with buttered crumbs. Bake until nicely browned at 375°F. NOTE: Two cans French-style green beans may be substituted for the asparagus. Yield: 6-8 servings.

Mrs. Mary Stockslager, Farmersville School
Farmersville, Ohio

ASPARAGUS-NUT CASSEROLE

1 pt. canned asparagus, drained
1 sm. can mushrooms, drained
3 hard-cooked eggs, sliced
2 to 3 T. pecans
1 can cream of mushroom soup
3 oz. cheese crackers, crushed

Arrange ingredients in layers in a greased casserole, reserving some of the crushed cheese crackers for the top. Bake 30 minutes at 350°F. Yield: 6 servings.

Mabel V. Garst, Eaton H.S.
Eaton, Ohio

ASPARAGUS CASSEROLE

3 eggs
2 c. milk
1½ c. Ritz crackers, crushed
2 pimentos, diced
1 c. mild cheese, grated
¾ stick butter, melted
Dash of salt
Few grains of pepper
1 No. 303 can green tip asparagus

Beat eggs; add milk and blend. Add crushed crackers, pimentos, cheese, butter and seasoning. Mix well. Fold in asparagus. Pour into long oblong greased casserole. Bake at 350°F. for 35 to 40 minutes. Yield: 6-8 servings.

Lottie Barton Harris, Trafford H.S.
Trafford, Pennsylvania

ASPARAGUS CASSEROLE

2 c. milk
2 T. flour
2 T. butter
Salt and pepper to taste
1 can asparagus tips
6 hard-cooked eggs, sliced
Cracker crumbs

Make white sauce with milk, flour, butter and seasonings. Arrange a layer of asparagus in a baking dish. Add a layer of sliced eggs and a portion of white sauce. Repeat process until all of the ingredients are used, reserving some sauce to put on top. Sprinkle top with cracker crumbs and dot with butter. Bake 30 minutes in a 350°F. oven. Yield: 6 servings.

Mrs. Nina B. Moore, Sharpsville-Prairie H.S.
Sharpsville, Indiana

SCALLOPED ASPARAGUS

1 10½-oz. pkg. frozen asparagus
3 hard-cooked eggs, finely cut
1 4-oz. can mushrooms
1 t. salt
1½ c. med. white sauce
½ c. sharp cheese, grated
½ c. crumbs

Cook and drain asparagus as per directions on the box. Arrange in a 1½-quart casserole; add eggs, mushrooms and salt. Toss lightly to mix. Combine hot white sauce and cheese. Pour over the casserole. Top with the crumbs and bake for 30 minutes at 350°F. Yield: 4-6 servings.

Mrs. Elizabeth C. Nesbitt, Seeger Memorial
West Lebanon, Indiana

SCALLOPED ASPARAGUS-EGG
CASSEROLE

3 T. butter, melted
3 T. flour
1½ c. milk
¾ t. salt
Pepper to taste
½ c. Velveeta cheese, cubed
2 c. cooked seasoned asparagus pieces
3 hard-cooked eggs, chopped
1 c. buttered soft bread crumbs

Blend the butter and flour in a saucepan. Gradually add the milk, salt and pepper; cook until thickened, stirring constantly. Add the cheese and stir until it melts. Toss together the asparagus and eggs in a buttered baking dish. Pour the cheese sauce over the asparagus. Top with the bread crumbs and bake 25 minutes at 350°F. Yield: 6 servings.

Frances E. Smith, Rock Creek School
Bluffton, Indiana

SCALLOPED ASPARAGUS

2 c. canned asparagus
1 c. cheese, grated
4 hard-cooked eggs
1½ c. cream of celery soup
½ c. milk
Paprika
Salt and pepper
Buttered bread crumbs

Fill well oiled baking dish with alternate layers of asparagus, cheese, sliced egg, and soup to which milk has been added. Sprinkle with paprika, salt and pepper. Add bread crumbs. Bake at 400°F. for 30 minutes. Yield: 6 servings.

Maralyn Braford, Sparta Jr. H.S.
Sparta, Michigan

ASPARAGUS CASSEROLE

1 No. 2 can asparagus, cut
3 hard-cooked eggs, chopped
Salt and pepper to taste
1 can cream of mushroom soup
1 c. buttered coarse bread crumbs

Place drained asparagus in buttered baking dish. Arrange eggs in layer over asparagus. Sprinkle with salt and pepper. Pour soup over eggs; cover with crumbs. Bake at 350°F. until golden brown. Yield: 6 servings.

Clara E. Marshall, Flandreau Indian School
Flandreau, South Dakota

ASPARAGUS CASSEROLE

1 can cream of mushroom soup
2 cans asparagus spears, uncut
Cheese Ritz crackers

Dilute the soup with liquid from the asparagus. Into a greased casserole dish place a layer of broken Ritz crackers and a layer of asparagus. Repeat layers. Add the soup mixture and bake at 350°F. for about 30 minutes. A thin layer of chow mein noodles may be sprinkled on top if desired. Yield: 8 servings.

Mrs. Ann Klosterman, Wooster H.S.
Wooster, Ohio

ASPARAGUS CASSEROLE

½ c. milk
1 can cream of mushroom soup
4-5 c. cooked asparagus, cut up
⅔ c. cracker crumbs
½ c. sharp cheese, grated
1 T. butter

Blend milk and soup; heat to boiling. Place half of asparagus in bottom of greased 1½-quart casserole; top with half of soup mixture. Cover with half the crumbs and grated cheese. Repeat layers; dot with butter. Bake in 350°F. oven for 20 to 30 minutes or until bubbly. Yield: 6-8 servings.

Gladys M. Harris, Buchanan H.S.
Buchanan, Michigan

BAKED BEANS

2 lb. navy beans
1 box brown sugar
1½ t. salt
1 lb. bacon

Wash beans and soak overnight; drain. Place beans, sugar, salt and bacon in a roaster. Cover with hot water. Cover roaster and bake at 325°F. for 5 or 6 hours or until done. Yield: 20 servings.

Mrs. Jessye Mac Kay, Pollock School
Pollock, South Dakota

BAKED BEANS

1 16-oz. can pork and beans
2 T. brown sugar
¼ t. dry mustard
¼ c. catsup
2 sl. bacon, finely cut
3 T. onion, chopped
1 t. Worcestershire sauce

Mix all ingredients in baking dish. Bake covered in a 350°F. oven for 20 minutes; bake uncovered for 20 minutes longer. Yield: 6 servings.

Mrs. Vanora Fry, Little River H.S.
Little River, Kansas

BAKED BEAN CASSEROLE

1 lge. can baked beans in tomato sauce
1 sm. onion, minced
1 t. mustard
½ c. catsup
½ c. brown sugar
4 strips bacon

Combine the baked beans, onion, mustard, catsup and brown sugar in casserole. Place strips of bacon on top. Bake for 1 hour at 325°F. Yield: 6 servings.

Jean Brittingham, John M. Clayton School
Dagsboro, Delaware

EASY BAKED BEANS

2 16- to 18-oz. cans pork and beans
¾ c. brown sugar
1 t. dry mustard
6 slices bacon, cut in pieces
½ c. catsup

Empty 1 can pork and beans into bottom of greased casserole. Combine sugar and mustard; sprinkle half of mixture over beans. Top with remaining beans. Sprinkle rest of sugar-mustard mixture, chopped bacon and catsup over beans. Stir entire mixture together. Bake, uncovered, at 325°F. for 2½ hours. Yield: 8 servings.

Mrs. Wallace Schueler, Ceylon H.S.
Ceylon, Minnesota

BROWN SUGAR-BEAN CASSEROLE

3 lge. cans pork and beans
3 lge. onions
½ bottle catsup
1½ c. brown sugar
Ham or bacon strips

Mix all ingredients and pour into a greased casserole. Ham or bacon strips may be placed on top or mixed in. Bake at 275°F. for 2 hours and 30 minutes. Yield: 15 servings.

Mrs. Marvin L. Killgore, Gallup H.S.
Gallup, New Mexico

FIESTA BEANS

⅓ c. brown sugar, packed
½ c. strong coffee
1 T. vinegar
1 t. dry mustard
½ t. salt
2 lge. cans oven baked beans
1 onion, thinly sliced
¼ c. Brandy (opt.)
4 slices bacon, chopped or whole strips

Mix together in a saucepan the brown sugar, coffee, vinegar, mustard and salt; simmer for 5 minutes. Alternate layers of beans, hot sugar syrup, and onion rings in a 2-quart casserole. Cover and bake at 350°F. for 45 minutes. Stir in brandy; top with bacon squares. Continue baking uncovered until bacon is cooked, about 30 minutes. Yield: 8 servings.

This recipe submitted by the following teachers:
Mrs. Georgia M. Wilson, Prescott H.S.
Prescott, Arizona
Rudene Wilbanks, McEachern Jr. H.S.
Powder Springs, Georgia

SWEET-SOUR BAKED BEANS

8 bacon slices
4 lge. onions, peeled and cut in rings
½-1 c. brown sugar
1 t. dry mustard
½ t. garlic powder (opt.)
1 t. salt
½ c. cider vinegar
2 15-oz. cans dried lima beans, drained
1 1-lb. can green lima beans, drained
1 1-lb. can dark red kidney beans, drained
1 can new England-style baked beans, undrained

Fry bacon until crisp; drain and crumble. Place onion in skillet; add sugar, mustard, garlic powder, salt and vinegar. Cook 20 minutes, covered. Add onion mixture to combined beans. Add crumbled bacon. Pour into 3-quart casserole. Bake at 350°F. for 1 hour. Yield: 12 servings.

Nancy S. Snyder, Oregon Davis Jr.-Sr. H.S.
Grovertown, Indiana

OLD-FASHIONED BAKED BEANS

2 lb. dried navy beans
2 qt. cold water
1 med. onion, sliced
1 T. salt
4 t. cider vinegar
1 t. prepared mustard
2 T. brown sugar
½ c. molasses
¼ c. tomato catsup
1/16 t. black pepper
½ lb. salt pork, sliced

Pick over and wash beans thoroughly. Add cold water; cover and heat to boiling and simmer for 30 minutes. Drain, reserving the liquid. Place onion slices in bottom of a bean pot or a 10-cup casserole. Combine remaining ingredients except salt pork. Pour into the bean pot. Add the beans and enough hot drained liquid or water to cover, about 2½ cups. Arrange salt pork slices on top; cover and bake at 250°F. 7 to 8 hours. After 4 hours, remove 2 cups of beans and mash them. Stir them into the remaining beans. Cover and continue to bake. Add additional hot bean liquid or water as needed. Beans should be just covered with thick, luscious liquid. Remove cover 1 hour before end of cooking time to allow salt pork to brown. Yield: 10 to 12 servings.

Mrs. Beth Boyd, Rogue River H.S.
Rogue River, Oregon

PORK AND BEANS CASSEROLE

2 1-lb. cans pork and beans in tomato sauce
1 1-lb. can kidney beans, drained
1 envelope onion soup mix
½ c. catsup
½ c. water
1 T. prepared mustard
2 t. cider vinegar
4 slices bacon

In mixing bowl combine all ingredients except bacon. Pour into 2-quart casserole. Top with bacon slices. Bake at 400°F. for 30 minutes. Yield: 6-8 servings.

Mrs. Audrey Richards, Crivitz H.S.
Crivitz, Wisconsin

BAKED BEET CASSEROLE

4 T. butter, melted
4 T. cornstarch
1 c. water
4 T. brown sugar
¼ t. salt
3 T. horseradish
4 c. cooked beets
⅓ c. dry bread crumbs
3 T. butter

Blend butter and cornstarch; add water gradually and cook until mixture begins to thicken, stirring constantly. Add sugar, salt, horseradish and beets. Pour into greased baking dish. Cover with crumbs; dot with butter and bake at 375°F. for 20 minutes or until crumbs are browned. Yield: 6-8 servings.

Mrs. Ralph E. Johnson, Scottsville H.S.
Scottsville, Kentucky

BROCCOLI BAKED DISH

2 pkg. frozen broccoli
½ lb. American cheese, sliced
1 can celery soup
½ pkg. herb bread dressing

Cook broccoli for three minutes in salted water. Spread a layer of broccoli in a well buttered baking dish. Add layer of sliced cheese. Cover with undiluted soup. Moisten bread dressing with water. Crumble dressing over top of casserole. Bake at 350°F. for 30 minutes. Yield: 6 servings.

Doris L. Carlson, Ramsay School
Ramsay, Michigan

BROCCOLI CASSEROLE

¼ c. onion, minced
¼ c. butter or margarine
3 T. flour
½ c. water
8 oz. pasteurized cheese or Cheez Whiz
2 10-oz. pkg. frozen chopped broccoli, thawed and drained
3 eggs, well beaten

Saute onion in butter. Stir in flour; add water and cook until thick. Blend in cheese; add broccoli. Fold in eggs. Pour into greased 1½-quart casserole. Cover with buttered crumbs. Bake 1 hour at 325°F. Serve immediately. Yield: 8 servings.

Mrs. Jeanne Bunch, Van Buren H.S.
Van Buren, Ohio

BROCCOLI CASSEROLE

2 pkg. frozen broccoli spears, par-boiled
4 No. 300 cans sm. whole new white potatoes
2 No. 303 cans sm. onions
2 pkg. cheese sauce mix
2 cans Cheddar cheese soup
2 c. bread crumbs, browned in butter

Place alternate layers of broccoli, potatoes, and onions in a greased 4-quart casserole. Prepare cheese sauce as directed; add the soup and mix thoroughly. Pour sauce over vegetables. Top with browned bread crumbs. Bake at 350°F. for 1 hour Yield: 16 servings.

Mrs. Gary Wiltse, Powder River H.S.
Broadus, Montana

BROCCOLI-LIMA BEAN CASSEROLE

3 T. butter, melted
½ t. curry powder
2 to 3 c. bite-size Rice Chex
1 box frozen broccoli
1 box frozen sm. lima beans
1 can condensed cream mushroom soup
1 can condensed cream celery soup

Blend curry powder and butter in skillet. Add cereal and stir over low heat about 5 minutes to coat and crisp cereal. Cook vegetables, being careful not to overcook; drain well. Put broccoli in buttered casserole. Stir celery soup in can; pour over broccoli. Put half the Rice Chex over broccoli. Add lima beans; top with mushroom soup. Bake about 30 minutes at 350°F. During the last 5 minutes, add the rest of the Rice Chex on top. They may be left whole, or may be slightly crushed. Yield: 8 servings.

Lois Sandell, Nevada Community H.S.
Nevada, Iowa

BROCCOLI-NOODLE CASSEROLE

2 pkg. frozen chopped broccoli
2 med. onions, finely chopped
4 T. butter, melted
1 c. light cream
1 c. Swiss cheese
1 t. salt
⅛ t. nutmeg
¼ t. pepper
1 8-oz. pkg. thin noodles, cooked

Cook broccoli according to package directions; drain. Saute onions in butter until transparent; add cream. Heat, but do not boil. Add cheese and seasonings. Add noodles and broccoli; pour into a casserole. Bake at 350°F. for 30-40 minutes. Yield: 8-10 servings.

Mrs. Eloise Peterson, University H.S.
Spokane, Washington

BROCCOLI-CHEESE CASSEROLE

1 pkg. cut frozen broccoli
½ c. Cheddar cheese, shredded
1 can undiluted mushroom soup
Salt to taste
1 c. bread crumbs
2 T. butter, melted

Cook broccoli according to package directions. Spread broccoli in bottom of buttered casserole. Add cheese and mushroom soup. Season with additional salt to taste. Toss bread crumbs with butter and sprinkle over casserole. Bake in 350°F. oven for 20 minutes or until bread crumbs are browned. Yield: 6 servings.

Mrs. Ina P. Vance, Jefferson-Morgan H.S.
Jefferson, Pennsylvania

BROCCOLI-MUSHROOM CASSEROLE

2 pkg. frozen chopped broccoli
Salt to taste
1½ cans mushroom soup
1 can mushrooms
1 pkg. slivered almonds
1 stick margarine
Cracker crumbs

Cook broccoli until almost done. Drain and season to taste. Mix with mushroom soup, mushrooms and almonds in ungreased casserole. Melt margarine and brown enough cracker crumbs to take up grease. Cover top of casserole with crumbs. Bake at 350°F. for 30-45 minutes. Yield: 8 servings.

Mrs. Frances Cooper, Charlotte H.S.
Charlotte, Michigan

BROCCOLI RING

1 pkg. frozen chopped broccoli
2 eggs, beaten
¾ c. mayonnaise
½ pt. heavy cream
½ t. salt

Cook broccoli according to directions on package; drain and cool. Add eggs to broccoli. Add remaining ingredients. Put into greased mold; place mold in pan of water. Bake in 350°F. oven for 30 to 40 minutes or until knife inserted comes out clean. NOTE: The heavy cream is not whipped. Yield: 6-8 servings.

Mrs. Jean McOmber, Spring Lake H.S.
Spring Lake, Michigan

BROCCOLI-RICE CASSEROLE

2 c. cooked rice or 1 sm. carton instant rice
1 can cream of chicken soup
1 8-oz. jar Cheez Whiz
1 pkg. frozen broccoli
2 c. buttered crumbs

Combine all ingredients except crumbs; place mixture in a greased 8x12 pan. Top with crumbs. Bake for 30 minutes at 375°F. Yield: 8 servings.

Mrs. Betty Huey, Russell H.S.
Russell, Kansas

BRUSSELS SPROUTS WITH YAM FRILL

½ c. brown sugar
5 T. butter, melted
¾ c. orange juice
3 T. orange peel, grated
½ t. nutmeg
½ t. allspice
8 cooked yams, peeled and mashed
2 10-oz. pkg. frozen Brussels sprouts
¼ t. white pepper

Blend sugar, 2 tablespoons of butter, ¼ cup orange juice, 2 tablespoons orange peel, ¼ teaspoon nutmeg, and ⅛ teaspoon allspice into the mashed yams; whip until light and fluffy. Heat to serving temperature and keep hot. Cook Brussels sprouts according to directions on package; drain. Toss gently with remaining butter, orange juice, peel, nutmeg, allspice and white pepper. Cook over low heat. Yield: 6-8 servings.

Mrs. Olive Curtis, Mt. Baker Jr.-Sr. H.S.
Deming, Washington

GERMAN CABBAGE WITH CREAM

1 sm. head white cabbage
½ c. stock
1 onion, sliced
½ c. sour cream
½ T. flour
Pepper
Nutmeg, grated
Sugar
Pork sausages

Remove and discard outer leaves of cabbage. Coarsely chop cabbage. Pour boiling water over and drain thoroughly. Put in an earthenware casserole with stock and onion, previously cooked to a light yellow. Cover saucepan and cook over brisk heat until cabbage is tender. Put sour cream in a saucepan over a low heat. Stir in flour; season with a little pepper, nutmeg and sugar. Stir for a few minutes. Pour over cabbage. Serve with pork sausages. Yield: 4 servings.

Grace A. Kurz, Shannon H.S.
Shannon, Illinois

CABBAGE-ALMONDINE

1 med. head cabbage
1½ c. white sauce
1 c. Cheddar cheese, grated
1 c. sliced almonds
Bread crumbs

Wash cabbage; chop into bite-size pieces. Boil until tender; drain. Place layers of cabbage, white sauce, cheese and almonds in a casserole. Top with mixture of cheese and bread crumbs. Bake at 400°F. for 20 minutes until browned on top. Yield: 6-8 servings.

Lillian Majhannu, Adolfo Camarillo H.S.
Camarillo, California

BAKED CABBAGE AND TOMATOES

1 med. cabbage, coarsely chopped
1½ c. canned tomatoes, drained
Salt and pepper
2 c. buttered bread crumbs
½ lb. American cheese, grated

Cook cabbage until just tender; drain well. Place alternate layers of cabbage, tomatoes, crumbs, and cheese in a buttered casserole, lightly sprinkling each layer with salt and pepper. Top layer should be buttered crumbs. Bake at 350°F. for 30 minutes. Yield: 6-8 servings.

Mrs. Miles S. Carpenter, Tisbury School
Vineyard Haven, Massachusetts

CABBAGE AU GRATIN

4 T. butter
4 T. flour
2 c. milk
⅓ lb. Velveeta cheese, cubed
1 head cabbage, diced
¾ c. buttered cracker crumbs

Make a cream sauce using the butter, flour and milk. Add cheese and melt. Cook cabbage for 5 minutes in salted water. Put alternate layers of cabbage and sauce in casserole. Sprinkle crumbs on top. Bake in 325°F. oven about 30 minutes. Yield: 8 servings.

Mrs. Erleen Johnson, Clay H.S.
Oregon, Ohio

SCALLOPED CABBAGE

1 4-inch head of cabbage
7 T. butter
3 T. flour
¾ t. salt
Dash of pepper
1½ c. milk
2 c. bread crumbs

Cut cabbage into one inch pieces; cook in salted boiling water for 8-10 minutes or until just tender when pierced with a fork. Make a white sauce by melting 3 tablespoons butter; add flour, salt and pepper, stirring until blended. Slowly add milk; cook until thickened, stirring constantly. In a 2-quart baking dish, melt 4 tablespoons butter; add bread crumbs and coat with butter. Remove two-thirds of buttered crumbs. Spread remaining crumbs evenly in baking dish. Add half of cabbage, half of sauce and one-third of crumbs. Repeat layer. Bake 10-15 minutes at 350°F. Yield: 6-8 servings.

Ruth Bosley, Leavenworth H.S.
Leavenworth, Indiana

SCALLOPED CABBAGE

5 c. cooked cabbage
1 recipe med. white sauce
½ c. cheese, grated
1 c. buttered bread crumbs

Place cooked cabbage in buttered casserole dish. Pour the white sauce to which has been added the grated cheese over cabbage. Top with buttered crumbs. Bake at 400°F. for 15 minutes. Yield: 6-8 servings.

Ruth H. Hullinger, Oakhill H.S.
Converse, Indiana

CABBAGE-TOMATO-CHEESE DISH

3 c. cabbage, finely shredded
1½ c. stewed tomatoes
¾ t. salt
½ t. paprika
2 t. brown sugar
1 c. cheese, grated
1 c. bread crumbs
1 T. butter or 2 strips bacon, minced

Cook cabbage for 5 minutes; drain. Cook tomatoes and seasonings together. Alternate layers of cabbage and tomatoes in a buttered casserole. Sprinkle the layers with the cheese and bread crumbs. Dot the top with butter or bacon. Bake at 325°F. for about ½ hour, or until the crumbs are brown. Yield: 6 servings.

Mrs. Cyrus Deem, Jr., Decker H.S.
Decker, Indiana

CARROT CASSEROLE

6 lge. carrots
2 eggs, separated
1 sm. onion, diced
1 c. crumbs
2 T. butter
1 c. milk
Salt and pepper to taste

Cook carrots; drain and mash. Add all ingredients, folding in beaten egg whites last. Put into a buttered casserole. Bake at 350°F. for 1 hour.

Meredith Briggs, Box Edler H.S.
Brigham City, Utah

CARROT CASSEROLE

4 c. carrots, cut in lengthwise slices
2 c. med. white sauce
2 c. potato chips

In a greased baking dish place a layer of carrots, white sauce, and crushed potato chips, ending with layer of potato chips. Bake 45 minutes at 375°F. Yield: 6-8 servings.

Zelma M. Waldron, Plymouth Public School
Plymouth, Nebraska

BUFFET SCALLOPED CARROTS WITH CHEESE

1 sm. onion, diced or grated
¼ c. butter or margarine
¼ c. flour
1 t. salt
¼ t. dry mustard
⅛ t. pepper
¼ t. celery salt
2 c. milk
12 sliced carrots, cooked
½ lb. sharp process cheese, grated
3 c. buttered crumbs

Saute onions in butter until tender. Add flour, seasonings and milk; cook until thick. In a buttered 2-quart casserole arrange a layer of carrots and a layer of cheese; repeat layers until all is used, ending with cheese. Pour sauce over all. Top with crumbs. Bake uncovered for 25 minutes in a 350°F. oven. Yield: 8 servings.

Ruby Beto, Flandreau Indian School
Flandreau, South Dakota

CARROT CASSEROLE

3 c. carrots
3 T. butter
1 green pepper, finely chopped
1 sm. dry onion, finely chopped
¼ c. flour
1 lge. can evaporated milk
1 t. salt
Dash of pepper

Cook carrots in a small amount of salted water until just barely done; drain. Chop finely and measure 3 cups to use. Saute green pepper and onion in butter until clear. Add flour and blend well. Add milk and seasonings. Stir constantly on medium heat until it thickens and boils. Add carrots; mix well. Place in greased, covered casserole in 325°F. oven for 30-40 minutes. Yield: 8 servings.

Gene Taresh, East Nicolaus H.S.
East Nicolaus, California

CARROTS AND STRING BEANS AU GRATIN

2 c. cooked carrots
1 c. cooked string beans
½ t. salt
3 T. butter, melted
⅓ c. cheese, grated
1 egg, beaten
1 c. milk
1 c. buttered bread crumbs

Combine the carrots, string beans, salt, butter, cheese, egg and milk. Pour mixture into a buttered baking dish. Cover with buttered crumbs. Brown in oven at 350°F. for 25 minutes. Yield: 6 servings.

Martha Jane Zepp, Pequea Valley H.S.
Kinzers, Pennsylvania

CHEESE-CARROT CASSEROLE

¾ c. onion, diced
3 T. butter or margarine
3 T. flour
1½ c. milk
¾ c. American cheese, cubed
4 c. cooked sliced carrots
2 c. buttered bread crumbs

Cook diced onions until clear in margarine. Add flour; stir until mixture bubbles. Add milk; bring to a boil. Cook until thick. Add cheese and stir over low heat until cheese melts. Line a greased casserole dish with a layer of carrots. Alternate layers of carrots and sauce, ending with sauce layer. Top with buttered bread crumbs. Bake 30-45 minutes in 350°F. oven. Yield: 6-8 servings.

Valerie Leech, Cozad H.S.
Cozad, Nebraska

ZESTY CARROTS

1 bunch carrots
¼ c. carrot liquid
2 T. grated onion or 1 T. instant onion
¾ t. horseradish
½ c. mayonnaise
½ t. salt
¼ t. pepper
½ c. dry bread crumbs
¼ c. butter, melted

Cut carrots into crosswise slices. Cook until tender in small amount of water; drain, reserving ¼ cup liquid. Place carrots in buttered casserole. Mix carrot liquid, onions, horseradish, mayonnaise, salt and pepper. Pour over carrots. Top with crumbs mixed with melted butter. Bake at 375°F. for 15 to 20 minutes. Yield: 8 servings.

Ruth B. Royer, Warrior Run Area Schools
Turbotville, Pennsylvania

CAULIFLOWER A LA CURRY

2 T. butter
2 T. flour
1 c. milk
¼ lb. Velveeta cheese
¼ t. curry powder
1 head cauliflower
12-15 soda crackers, crumbled

Prepare cheese sauce with butter, flour, milk and cheese; add curry powder. Boil cauliflower until slightly tender; drain. Alternate layers of cracker crumbs, cauliflower, and cheese sauce in a buttered baking dish, ending with cracker crumbs. Place a few dots of butter on top. Bake at 350°F. until lightly brown and bubbly. Yield: 8 servings.

Mrs. Ada B. Dobson, Edison Jr. H.S.
Macomb, Illinois

CAULIFLOWER MOLD

2 eggs
1 can cream of celery soup
1 lge. head cauliflower, coarsely chopped
½ c. cheese, grated
½ c. soft bread crumbs
2 pimentos, chopped
2 T. onion, chopped
1 t. salt
⅛ t. pepper

Beat eggs slightly in large bowl; stir in remaining ingredients. Pour into buttered casserole. Set in pan of hot water. Bake at 375°F. for 50 minutes or until firm. Serve hot. Yield: 4-6 servings.

Voncile Owens, Sonora Union H.S.
Sonora, California

GOLDEN HEAD CASSEROLE

1 head cauliflower
Water
¾ t. salt
2 T. butter
2 T. flour
1 c. milk
1 c. cheese, grated

Boil whole cauliflower in water with ½ teaspoon salt for 15-20 minutes; drain. Place in a greased, deep casserole. Blend butter, flour and ¼ teaspoon salt in a double boiler; gradually stir in milk. Cook until thickened, stirring constantly. Add half of cheese; heat until melted. Pour over cauliflower. Sprinkle with remaining cheese and dot with butter. Bake at 325°F. for 30-40 minutes. Serve in casserole. Yield: 4-6 servings.

Mrs. Mary Thomas, Hortonville H.S.
Hortonville, Wisconsin

SEASIDE VEGETABLE BAKE

2 pkg. frozen cauliflower or
  1 med. head, cut into flowerettes
1 can frozen condensed cream of shrimp soup
½ c. milk
¼ c. sharp cheese, shredded
1 T. fine dry bread crumbs

Cook cauliflower in boiling salted water until tender. Drain and place in shallow baking dish. In saucepan heat soup and milk, stirring constantly until soup thaws. Pour over cauliflower. Sprinkle with cheese and crumbs. Bake at 375°F. for 20-25 minutes, or until bubbly and brown. Yield: 4 servings.

Barbara Widmyer, Conneaut Lake Area H.S.
Conneaut Lake, Pennsylvania

CELERY-CHEESE LUNCHEON BAKE

4 c. celery, cut in 1-inch slices
1½ c. sharp Cheddar cheese, shredded
1 can condensed cream of chicken soup
Butter
⅓ c. slivered blanched almonds, toasted

Cook celery slices in boiling salted water for 8 minutes; drain. In a greased casserole alternate layers of celery, cheese and soup, ending with soup. Dot with butter. Sprinkle almonds over top. Bake in 350°F. oven for 20 minutes, or until bubbly hot. Yield: 4 servings.

Florence Starkebaum, Kennewick H.S.
Kennewick, Washington

CELERY AND WATER CHESTNUTS

4 c. celery, cut in 1-inch slices
1 5-oz. can water chestnuts
1 can cream of chicken soup
¼ c. pimento, diced
¼ c. soft bread crumbs
¼ c. toasted slivered almonds
2 T. butter

Cook celery in small amount of water until crisp tender, about 8 minutes; drain. Mix celery with sliced water chestnuts, soup and pimento. Pour into buttered casserole. Toss crumbs, almonds and butter together; sprinkle over casserole. Bake at 350°F. for 35 minutes or until lightly browned and hot. Yield: 6 servings.

Freda H. Montgomery, Central Union H.S.
Fresno, California

SCALLOPED CELERY

2 c. celery
2 T. butter
2 T. flour
1 c. milk
¼ t. salt
Buttered crumbs

Cut celery into pieces and cook in salted water for 10-15 minutes; drain. Make a medium white sauce with butter, flour milk and salt. Arrange celery and sauce alternately in layers. Top with buttered crumbs. Bake for 25 minutes at 325°F. or until it bubbles. Yield: 4-6 servings.

Anne Olmstead, South Haven H.S.
South Haven, Kansas

BAKED CORN CASSEROLE

2 T. fat
1½ T. flour
1 c. milk
1 t. salt
⅛ t. pepper
2 c. corn
1 T. sugar
2 eggs, well beaten
½ c. buttered crumbs

Melt fat; add flour. Add milk gradually and bring to boiling point, stirring constantly. Add salt, pepper, corn and sugar; heat thoroughly. Remove from heat and add eggs. Pour into a greased baking dish and top with crumbs. Bake 25 minutes at 350°F. Yield: 6 servings.

Genevieve E. Snyder, Cocalico Union Sr. H.S.
Denver, Pennsylvania

BLENDER SCALLOPED CORN

2 slices bread
1 med. onion, sliced
1 green pepper, seeded and coarsely sliced
1 c. water
3 T. butter
1 t. salt
⅛ t. pepper
2 T. flour
1 c. milk
¼ t. cayenne
¼ t. dry mustard
1 10-oz. pkg. frozen corn, thawed
1 egg

Tear 1 slice of bread into pieces; place in a blender. Cover and blend for 5 seconds. Set aside to use for topping. Combine onion, pepper and water in blender. Cover and blend for 5 seconds. Pour into a sieve to drain. Saute mixture until soft in 2 tablespoons butter. Into blender put salt, pepper, flour, milk, butter, cayenne, mustard, corn, egg and remaining slice of torn bread. Cover and blend for 5 seconds. Pour into buttered casserole. Stir in onion mixture. Sprinkle with blended bread slice and dot with butter. Bake at 375°F. for 1 hour. Yield: 4 servings.

Mrs. Elizabeth W. Knape, Douglas Sr. H.S.
Douglas, Arizona

CRUSTY CORN CASSEROLE

1¼ c. fine cracker crumbs
10 T. butter or margarine, melted
¼ c. green pepper, finely chopped
1 T. onion, finely chopped
2 T. flour
1 c. milk
1 No. 2 can corn
½ t. salt
1 t. sugar
2 whole eggs or 4 yolks, slightly beaten

Blend cracker crumbs with 8 tablespoons butter; reserve ¼ cup of the mixture. Press remaining mixture evenly on bottom and sides of a deep 9-inch pie plate. Saute green pepper and onion in remaining butter until onion is transparent. Blend in flour and cook until bubbly. Add milk all at once. Cook until thickened, stirring constantly. Add remaining ingredients; mix well. Pour mixture into crust; top with reserved crumbs. Bake at 400°F. until knife inserted in center is clean, 25-30 minutes. Yield: 5 servings.

Agnes Obester, Lilly-Washington H.S.
Lilly, Pennsylvania

CORN POTLUCK

6 lean slices bacon
1 c. milk
2 17-oz. cans corn
3 hot dog buns, finely crumbled
¾ t. salt
½ t. chili powder
1 c. Cheddar cheese, coarsely grated
1 4-oz. can sliced mushrooms

Fry bacon until crisp; drain well and break into bits. Mix bacon with milk and corn. Add hot dog bun crumbs. Stir in salt, chili powder, cheese and mushrooms. Mix well; bake uncovered in an 8-cup casserole at 350°F. for 50 minutes. If desired, garnish with crisp bacon slices. Yield: 8 servings.

Mrs. Marilyn Telander, Chandlerville H.S.
Chandlerville, Illinois

FRESH CORN PUDDING

12 lge. ears corn
2 T. butter, melted
3 T. tapioca
1½ t. salt
⅛ t. pepper
1 T. sugar
1 qt. milk, scalded
5 eggs, separated
Green or red pepper rings (opt.)

Grate or cut corn from cob. Combine butter, tapioca, salt, pepper and sugar, blending well. Add milk gradually, stirring until smooth. Cook in double boiler, stirring until tapioca is cooked. Remove from heat; add corn and beaten egg yolks. Fold in stiffly beaten egg whites. Place in 1½-quart baking dish; decorate top with pepper rings. Place dish in a pan of hot water. Cover and bake at 350°F. for 30 minutes. Remove cover and bake 30 minutes longer, or until knife inserted in center comes out clean. Yield: 10-12 servings.

Marie G. Reid, Rochester Area Jr.-Sr. H.S.
Rochester, Pennsylvania

PENNSYLVANIA DUTCH CORN PUDDING

1 c. dried corn
2 c. hot milk
2 egg, beaten
1 t. salt
1 c. cold milk
1 T. butter

Grind the dried corn in a food mill. Pour hot milk over it and let set for 1 hour. Add eggs, salt and cold milk. Pour into greased baking dish. Dot with butter. Place baking dish in shallow pan filled with water 1-inch deep. Bake at 350°F. for 1 hour. NOTE: If desired, sprinkle paprika over top. Yield: 6 servings.

Lucy M. Bamberger, Eastern Lebanon County H.S.
Myerstown, Pennsylvania

DELECTABLE CORN

2 T. onion, chopped
2 T. green pepper, chopped
2 T. pimento, chopped
2 T. butter
2 c. steamed rice
1 c. cheese, grated
3 eggs
1 t. salt
2 cans cream-style corn
Paprika

Saute onion, green pepper and pimento in butter, until well cooked. Combine rice, two-thirds of the cheese, the eggs and the salt. Mix well and add the sauted vegetables. Stir in corn. Pour in greased 1½-quart casserole. Top with remaining cheese. Sprinkle with paprika. Bake at 425°F. for 15 minutes. Yield: 8-10 servings.

Mrs. Dorothy Campbell, Riverside H.S.
Milan, Washington

SCALLOPED CORN

6 T. butter, melted
2 T. flour
1 c. milk
Dash of pepper
1 can cream-style corn
1 T. sugar
1 t. salt
1 c. bread crumbs
Cheese, grated

Make a white sauce using 2 tablespoons butter, flour, milk and pepper. Add the corn, sugar and salt; mix well. Combine remaining butter and bread crumbs. Cover the bottom of a buttered baking dish with a layer of corn mixture. Sprinkle heavily with buttered crumbs. Repeat layers. Top with a layer of crumbs and a little grated cheese. Yield: 6-8 servings.

Edythe B. Swalstad, Cass Lake H.S.
Cass Lake, Minnesota

SCALLOPED CORN

1 sm. onion, finely chopped
2 T. butter
2 T. flour
1 t. salt
½ t. paprika
¼ t. nutmeg
1 1-lb. can cream-style corn
1 t. baking powder
1 egg, beaten
½ c. buttered cracker crumbs

Cook onion in butter until lightly browned. Add flour and seasonings; mix well. Stir in corn, baking powder and egg. Pour into buttered casserole. Cover with buttered cracker crumbs and bake at 350°F. for 30 minutes. Yield: 4 servings.

Mrs. Marjorie Campbell, Larimore H.S.
Larimore, North Dakota

CREOLE EGGPLANT

1 lge. eggplant
1 onion, chopped
½ green pepper, chopped
1½ c. fresh or canned tomatoes
1½ c. soft bread crumbs
Salt to taste
1 c. buttered cracker crumbs

Peel eggplant and cut into ½-inch cubes. Cook until tender in small amount of salted boiling water. Brown onion and pepper; add to eggplant. Add tomatoes, bread crumbs and salt. Pour into baking dish; cover with cracker crumbs. Bake in 350°F. oven for 20 minutes. Yield: 4-5 servings.

Helen Tussey, Sugar Valley Area School
Loganton, Pennsylvania

EGGPLANT AMERICAN

1 med. eggplant
Cooking oil
1 c. onions, chopped
1 c. green pepper, diced
1 c. ripe olives, halved
1 t. salt
2 c. cheese, grated
1 8-oz. can tomato sauce
1 c. bread crumbs
2 T. butter, melted

Pare eggplant; dice and cook in small amount of oil until lightly browned and transparent. Add onion, green pepper, olives and salt. Place half of eggplant mixture in buttered 2-quart casserole. Cover with half of the grated cheese. Add remaining eggplant mixture. Cover with cheese. Pour tomato sauce over top. Mix bread crumbs with butter and sprinkle on top. Bake at 375°F. for 50 minutes. Yield: 6-8 servings.

Catherine M. Nugent, Amador Valley H.S.
Pleasanton, California

EGGPLANT AU GRATIN

1 med. eggplant
2 T. butter, melted
2 T. flour
¼ t. salt
⅛ t. pepper
1 c. milk
½ c. nippy American cheese, grated
Cracker crumbs

Wash, pare and cube eggplant. Cook covered in boiling water 10 to 15 minutes. Blend butter, flour and seasonings over low heat. Remove from heat and slowly add milk. Stir over heat until thick. Add cheese. Place half of cooked eggplant into greased casserole; add half of cheese sauce. Repeat layers. Top with cracker crumbs. Bake at 350°F. for 20-30 minutes. Yield: 4-6 servings.

Elizabeth Collings, North Kansas City H.S.
North Kansas City, Missouri

EGGPLANT AU GRATIN

1 lge. eggplant
2 eggs, slightly beaten
24 Ritz crackers, finely rolled
½ c. salad oil
2 8-oz. cans tomato sauce
¼ t. garlic powder
1 clove garlic, chopped
1 T. parsley flakes
¼ t. basil
1 t. oregano
1 6-oz. pkg. Mozzarella cheese

Pare eggplant and cut crosswise into ¼-inch slices; dip in eggs, then in crumbs. Saute in oil until golden brown. Combine tomato sauce, remaining crackers and seasonings. Simmer gently for 10 minutes. Alternate slices of eggplant, sauce, and slices of cheese in a 1-quart buttered baking dish. Bake at 350°F. for 30 minutes. Yield: 4-6 servings

Velma Jane Adams, Burwell Public Schools
Burwell, Nebraska

EGGPLANT BORDELAISE

1 med. eggplant
1 sm. clove garlic
3 T. salad oil
⅓ c. flour
2 lge. tomatoes, peeled
1 sm. onion, chopped
1 c. Cheddar cheese, grated
¼ t. pepper
½ t. salt

Peel eggplant and cut into ¼-inch slices. Rub skillet with garlic; pour oil in skillet and heat to about 350°F. Flour eggplant and brown in skillet. Arrange tomato slices and eggplant slices alternately in 1½-quart casserole. Sprinkle each layer with onion and cheese. Sprinkle salt and pepper over the top. Cover casserole and bake at 375°F. for 20 minutes. Yield: 6 servings.

Mrs. Joan Bergdolt, Harlem H.S.
Loves Park, Illinois

EGGPLANT CASSEROLE

1 eggplant
1 egg, well beaten
½ c. flour
Fat
1 onion, diced
1 can pizza sauce
Salt and pepper
¼ c. Parmesan cheese, grated

Slice eggplant thin. If desired, soak eggplant in salt water for 30 minutes Drain and dip slices in egg, then in flour. Fry until slightly brown. Saute onion until golden brown; add pizza sauce. Season to taste. Heat until simmering. Put eggplant slices in casserole; sprinkle with Parmesan cheese. Add onion sauce mix. Bake at 325°F. for 45 minutes to 1 hour. Yield: 4-5 servings.

Inez Waechter, Anna Jonesboro Community H.S.
Anna, Illinois

EGGPLANT CASSEROLE.

2 med. eggplants
4 t. salt
1 lge. egg
2 T. milk
1 c. fine bread crumbs
4 T. butter, melted
¾ onion, chopped
1 lge. can tomatoes
1 T. sugar
½ t. pepper
2 c. Cheddar cheese, shredded

Cut eggplant in ½-inch slices; sprinkle with 3 teaspoons salt. Let stand 15-20 minutes. Beat egg and milk. Dip eggplant slices into milk mixture and then into bread crumbs. Lightly brown eggplant slices in 2 tablespoons butter; add more butter if needed. Place slices in 2-quart shallow dish. Brown onion in 2 tablespoons butter. Add tomatoes, sugar, 1 teaspoon salt and the pepper. Simmer until mixture thickens, 20 minutes. Stir in 1⅓ cups cheese. Pour mixture over eggplant. Sprinkle with ⅔ cup Cheddar cheese. Bake at 350°F. for 35 to 45 minutes. Yield: 8-10 servings.

Mrs. Rex Todd Withers, Chief Home Economics & Family Life Education Service Lansing, Michigan

EGGPLANT CASSEROLE

6 T. butter
2 c. cooked eggplant, cubed
1 T. onion, chopped
1 t. salt
¼ t. black pepper
1 c. milk
¼ t. sage
1 c. cracker crumbs
1 c. American cheese, cubed
2 eggs, beaten

Add butter to hot eggplant; mix until melted. Add remaining ingredients; mix well. Pour into greased casserole dish. Bake at 325°F. until center rises, about 30 minutes. Yield: 6-8 servings.

Mrs. Carladon Fowler, Mulberry Grove H.S. Mulberry Grove, Illinois

EGGPLANT EN CASSEROLE

1½-lb. eggplant, peeled and diced
6 T. butter
2 onions, sliced
3 tomatoes, peeled and diced or 1½ c. canned tomatoes
1 c. cheese, grated
1 t. salt
Pepper
1 c. dry bread crumbs

Saute eggplant slowly for 5 minutes in 3 tablespoons butter. Place in a buttered casserole with alternate layers of onions, tomatoes and ¾ cup cheese; season each layer with the salt and pepper. Top with crumbs which have been mixed with remaining cheese; dot with remaining butter. Bake at 375°F. until vegetables are tender and top is nicely browned, about 35 minutes. Yield: 5 servings.

This recipe submitted by the following teachers:
Naomi Alice Prichard, Eel River-Perry Consolidated H.S. Huntertown, Indiana
Mrs. A. J. Robertson, Quitman H.S. Quitman, Arkansas

EGGPLANT CASSEROLE

4 c. eggplant, diced
½ t. salt
⅓ c. milk
1 can mushroom soup
1 egg, slightly beaten
½ c. onion, chopped
¾ c. herb seasoned stuffing or bread crumbs

Cook eggplant in salted water until tender, 6 or 7 minutes. Gradually stir milk into soup. Blend in egg; add drained eggplant, onion and stuffing. Toss lightly to mix. Pour into greased baking dish.

TOPPING:

1 c. herb dressing, finely crushed
  or ½ c. crushed cracker crumbs
2 t. butter, melted
1 c. sharp American cheese, shredded

Toss dressing with butter; sprinkle over casserole. Top with cheese. Bake at 350°F. for 20 minutes. Yield: 6 servings.

This recipe submitted by the following teachers:
Mrs. Naomi Blatt, Fairfield Union H.S. Lancaster, Ohio
Mrs. Annette B. Mix, Carlisle County H.S. Bardwell, Kentucky

EGGPLANT-TOMATO CASSEROLE

1 lge. eggplant, peeled and sliced
¼-⅓ c. flour
¼. c. vegetable oil
1 green pepper, sliced
1-2 onions, chopped
4 tomatoes, sliced
Salt and pepper
1 t. sugar
⅓ c. dry bread crumbs
¼ c. American cheese, grated

Coat eggplant slices in flour; brown in hot oil. Arrange a layer of eggplant in a greased casserole. Top with a layer of green pepper slices and a thin layer of onions. Add a layer of tomato slices; season with salt, pepper and sugar. Repeat layers. Bake at 375°F. for 1 hour. Top with bread crumbs and cheese. Bake 15-20 minutes longer until vegetables are tender and cheese is melted. Yield: 6 servings.

Mrs. Evelyn E. McConnell, Allen Jr. H.S. Camp Hill, Pennsylvania

EGGPLANT-TOMATO SOUP CASSEROLE

1 lge. onion, chopped
1 med. green pepper, chopped
2 T. oil
1 med. eggplant
1 egg
3 T. milk
Cracker crumbs or meal
Salt
1½ c. Cheddar cheese, grated
1 can cream of tomato soup

Saute onion and green pepper in oil. Peel eggplant and slice ¼-inch thick. Beat egg with milk. Dip eggplant slices in egg mixture, then in crumbs. Deep fry until golden brown. Place on paper toweling and salt lightly. Place a layer of eggplant in a 9x9x2 baking dish. Add a layer of onion mixture; sprinkle with cheese. Repeat layers until all eggplant is used. Pour soup over casserole; sprinkle with remaining cheese. Bake at 350°F. for 30-40 minutes. Yield: 6-8 servings.

Mrs. Shirley Rusche, Norte Vista H.S.
Arlington, California

EGGPLANT-VEGETABLE CASSEROLE

1 eggplant
3 med. onions
1 green pepper, sliced
⅓ c. butter, fat or oil
6 tomatoes, sliced
2 t. salt
½ t. pepper
2 c. cheese, grated

Pare and slice eggplant; cut slices in quarters. Prepare onions in same manner. Brown eggplant, onion and green pepper in fat. Place in lightly greased casserole alternately with tomatoes. Season each layer. Bake 30 minutes at 350°F.; remove and add cheese. Bake 20 minutes or until vegetables are tender. Yield: 6 servings.

Elizabeth Hine, Susquehanna Consolidated School
Susquehanna, Pennsylvania

SCALLOPED EGGPLANT

1 lge. eggplant
2 T. butter
1 can mushroom soup
½ c. bread crumbs
1 t. sugar
3 T. sharp Cheddar cheese, grated

Peel eggplant; slice in ½-inch slices. Cook in boiling water until tender. In casserole place a layer of eggplant; cover with half of butter, soup, bread crumbs, sugar and cheese. Repeat layers. Bake at 350°F. for 30 minutes. Yield: 6 servings.

Margaret H. Roush, Union Local H.S
Belmont, Ohio

BEAN A LA ONIONS

1 No. 1 can cut green beans
½ can French-fried onions
1 c. med. white sauce

Drain beans. Add white sauce and place in a casserole. Place in moderate oven for 15 minutes. Place onions on top of casserole. Place in oven again for 10 minutes. Serve hot. Yield: 4 servings.

Mrs. Lynda Beatty, Jackson Center School
Jackson Center, Ohio

GREEN BEAN-ONION CASSEROLE

1 can condensed cream of mushroom soup
½ c. milk
2 c. frozen or canned green beans
1 can onion rings

Combine mushroom soup and milk; stir until completely combined. Pour soup mixture over green beans. Add half the onion rings and stir. Pour into a casserole and top with remaining onion rings. Bake in a 350°F. oven for 30 minutes. Yield: 4-6 servings.

Relda E. Smith, Crestview H.S.
Ashland, Ohio

GREEN BEAN-ONION CASSEROLE

1 lb. string green beans, cooked
1 8-oz. pkg. frozen onion rings
1 can mushroom soup

Combine green beans, onion rings and mushroom soup in casserole. Bake at 350°F. for 20-30 minutes. Yield: 6 servings.

JoAnn Greenman, Herscher H.S.
Herscher, Illinois

GREEN BEAN-ONION CASSEROLE

2 cans cut green beans
1 can boiled onions
¼ c. butter, melted
¼ c. flour
Salt and pepper
1 sm. can evaporated milk
1 can fried onions

Drain beans and onions, reserving liquid. Arrange in buttered casserole. Use 1½ cups mixed liquid from vegetables. Combine butter, flour, seasonings, milk and 1½ cups mixed vegetable liquid for white sauce. Pour sauce over vegetables. Top with fried onions. Cover and bake for 30 minutes at 350°F. Remove lid the last few minutes to crisp the onion rings. Yield: 6-8 servings.

Mrs. Mary E. Van Fleet, Indio H.S.
Indio, California

STRING BEAN-ONION CASSEROLE

2 cans French-style green beans
Salt and pepper to taste
1 can celery or mushroom soup
Cheese slices
1 can French-fried onions

Heat beans and season to taste; drain. Mix soup with beans. Put mixture in 2-quart dish casserole. Put cheese slices on top, then onion rings. Bake about 20 minutes in 350°F. oven. Yield: 6-10 servings.

Mrs. Deborah Hoppenstedt, Magnolia-Swaney H.S.
McNabb, Illinois

BEAN-ONION CASSEROLE

2 cans early garden green beans
1 can chop suey vegetables
1 can undiluted cream of celery soup
1 can undiluted cream of mushroom soup
1 can of small stewed onions
½ c. slivered almonds

Combine beans, chop suey vegetables and soups in a casserole. Place onions on top and sprinkle with slivered almonds. Bake 40-45 minutes at 350°F. Yield: 8 servings.

Mrs. Helen Wilson, Washington H.S.
Sioux Falls, South Dakota

BAKED GREEN BEANS

1 10-oz. pkg. frozen French-style green beans
1 10½-oz. can cream of mushroom soup
1 4-oz. can sliced mushrooms
1 5-oz. jar bacon-cheese spread
1 3½-oz. can French-fried onions
3 slices crisp bacon, crumbled

Cook beans by package directions and drain. Combine soup, mushrooms and cheese spread. Toss beans with mixture and place in a 6-cup casserole. Top with French-fried onions and crumbled bacon. Bake at 325°F. for 30 minutes. Yield: 6 servings.

Mrs. Carolyn L. Peterson, Morton School
Kinnear, Wyoming

BEANS ORIENTAL

1 No. 2 can French-style green beans
½ No. 2 can bean sprouts
1 can sliced water chestnuts
4 slices crisp bacon, crumbled
1 can mushroom soup, undiluted
Potato chips, crushed

Drain the beans, bean sprouts and water chestnuts. Combine vegetables with bacon and soup. Place in a casserole and top with potato chips. Bake for 35 minutes at 350°F. Yield: 8 servings.

Mrs. Twyla Lyon, Boron H.S.
Boron, California

DEVILED GREEN BEAN CASSEROLE

1 med. onion, chopped
½ green pepper, chopped
2 pimentos, chopped
3 T. butter, melted
1 can tomato soup
2 c. cooked green beans, drained
2 t. prepared mustard
1 c. Cheddar cheese, grated

Cook onion, pepper, and pimentos in butter until the onion is transparent. Remove from heat. Stir in tomato soup, green beans and prepared mustard. Pour into buttered casserole. Sprinkle cheese on top. Bake at 350°F. for 25-30 minutes. Yield: 4 servings.

Ann Rust, Edison Jr. H.S.
Champaign, Illinois

EASY BAKED GREEN BEANS

1-2 pkg. frozen French-style beans
1 can cream of mushroom soup
1 can or pkg. French-fried onions or 1 c. dry bread crumbs

Partially cook beans. Mix with soup in 1½-quart baking dish. Top with French-fried onions. Bake at 375°F. for 15 to 20 minutes until beans are tender. NOTE: If desired, beans may be completely cooked before placing in casserole. Bake at 350°F. for 20-30 minutes. Yield: 6-8 servings.

This recipe submitted by the following teachers:
Pauline Curry, Dos Palos H.S.
Dos Palos, California
Elaine L. Deets, Moshannon Valley Jr.-Sr. H.S.
Houtzdale, Pennsylvania
Sue Hicks, Harrison County H.S.
Cynthiana, Kentucky

GREEN BEAN CASSEROLE

1 can green beans, drained
1 can mushroom soup
1 can French-fried onion rings

Place green beans in a baking dish; add undiluted soup and top with French-fried onion rings Thoroughly heat at 325-350°F. for 30-35 minutes. NOTE: If desired, onion rings may be sprinkled on top of casserole before end of baking time. Cauliflower may be substituted for beans. Yield: 6-8 servings.

This recipe submitted by the following teachers:
Mrs. Arlee Rylander Barton, Burnet H.S.
Burnet, Texas
Mrs. Dorothy Hoban,
Millington Community School
Millington, Michigan
Jean D. Alexander, Creswell H.S.
Creswell, North Carolina
Marjorie Vaughn, Mercer H.S.
Savannah, Georgia
Mrs. Hallie Christensen, Truman H.S.
Truman, Minnesota
Mrs. Kathryn Leischner, DeLand-Weldon H.S.
DeLand, Illinois

GREEN BEAN CASSEROLE

1 can condensed mushroom soup
¼ c. milk (opt.)
1 t. soy sauce
1 can French-fried onions
3 c. cooked French-style green beans, drained
Dash of pepper

In 1-quart casserole stir soup, milk and soy sauce until smooth; mix in half of onions, all beans and pepper. Bake in a 350°F. oven for 20 minutes or until bubbling. Top with remaining onions. Bake 5 minutes more. Yield: 6 servings.

This recipe submitted by the following teachers:
Gussie Mae Beard, Pelican H.S.
Pelican, Louisiana
Margaret N. Phillips, Grant Community H.S.
Fox Lake, Illinois

GREEN BEAN CASSEROLE

1 pkg. French-style green beans
1 can cream of chicken soup
3 T. water
¼ c. cheese, grated
¼ c. cracker crumbs

Cook beans according to directions; stir in undiluted chicken soup plus 3 tablespoons water. Place in casserole and sprinkle with cheese, then cracker crumbs. Bake at 400°F. for 10 minutes.

Ruth E. Sproat, Fishers H.S.
Fishers, Indiana

GREEN BEAN-ALMOND CASSEROLE

2 cans French-style green beans
1 can cream of mushroom soup
¼ c. buter or margarine
Salt and pepper to taste
1 can French-fried onion rings
1 sm. pkg. slivered almonds

Drain the green beans; put into a greased casserole dish. Heat soup with the butter to melt it; add salt and pepper to taste. Pour over green beans. Bake in a 350°F. oven for 35 minutes. About the last 10 minutes, add the onion rings and slivered almonds. Yield: 8-10 servings.

Elda Kaufman, Central Jr. H.S.
Clifton, Illinois

GREEN BEAN BAKE

2 10-oz. pkg. frozen cut green beans
1 5-oz. can water chestnuts, sliced
¼ c. onion, minced
2 cans condensed cream of mushroom soup
Salt
1½ oz. Parmesan cheese
½ c. toasted almonds

Place alternate layers of all ingredients except almonds in a 3-quart baking dish. Top with toasted almonds. Bake covered at 350°F. for 1 hour or until beans are tender. Yield: 6 servings.

Eleanor E. McCrimmon, Mount Pleasant H.S.
Mount Pleasant, Michigan

GREEN BEAN CASSEROLE

1 can French-cut green beans
1 can onion rings
Pinch of salt and pepper
1 can cream of mushroom soup

Drain the beans, reserving half of the liquid. Place beans in a casserole. Place onion rings over beans; sprinkle with salt and pepper. Pour soup over top. Rinse soup can with bean liquid and add to casserole. Bake at 400°F. for 20-25 minutes. Yield: 8 servings.

Mable E. Allen, Joppa Community H.S.
Joppa, Illinois

GREEN BEAN CASSEROLE

2 cans green beans, drained
½ c. cheese, grated
1 can cream of mushroom soup
1 can onion rings or 1 pkg. frozen onion rings

Carefully mix beans and cheese into mushroom soup. Pour into buttered casserole. Top with onion rings. Bake at 350°F. for 30 minutes until hot and bubbly. NOTE: If desired, 2 packages cooked frozen green beans may be used. Yield: 8-10 servings.

Mrs. Beverly Skrovig, Baltic H.S.
Baltic, South Dakota

GREEN BEAN CASSEROLE

1 can sliced or French-cut beans
1 can mushroom soup
1 can French-fried onion rings
½ c. cheese, grated
Paprika (opt.)

Drain beans, reserving ¼ cup liquid; blend bean liquid with the soup. Make a layer of beans, using half the beans. Add half of onion rings. Repeat for a second layer of each. Pour the soup mixture over this. Top with cheese. Sprinkle with paprika. Bake at 350°F. for 30 minutes or until hot. NOTE: If desired, 2 cans whole green beans may be used. Yield: 6 servings.

This recipe submitted by the following teachers:
Mrs. Hazel P. Kimbrough, Spade H.S.
Spade, Texas
Jean Cline, Rowan County H.S.
Morehead, Kentucky
Martha Wilson, Basic H.S.
Henderson, Nevada

GREEN BEAN SPECIAL

3 c. cooked and seasoned green beans
1 can cream of mushroom soup
½ c. slivered almonds
1 can French-fried onion rings

Cook green beans in boiling salted water until crisply done; drain. Add undiluted mushroom soup and mix gently. Place half the beans in a greased casserole; cover with almonds. Add remaining beans and cover with French-fried onion rings. Reheat at 375°F. for 10 minutes. Yield: 6 servings.

Virginia B. Firth, John Bassalt Moore H.S.
Smyrna, Delaware

GREEN BEAN CASSEROLE

2 No. 303 cans French-style green beans
2 cans condensed cream of mushroom soup
2 t. instant onion flakes
½ t. salt
¼ t. pepper
¾ c. cheese crackers or potato chips, crushed
¼ lb. margarine or butter

Drain beans, reserving liquid. Combine beans, soup, onion flakes, salt and pepper. Add one-half to three-fourths cup of bean liquid. Mix lightly and place in casserole. Sprinkle crumbs on top and dot with butter. Bake at 350°F. for 30 minutes or until golden brown. Yield: 6-8 servings.

Mrs. Carol Stephenson, North Adams H.S.
North Adams, Michigan

GREEN BEAN-SOUR CREAM CASSEROLE

5 T. butter, melted
2 T. flour
1 t. salt
Dash of pepper
½ t. onion, grated
1 c. dairy sour cream
2 No. 303 cans green beans, drained
⅔ c. cheese, grated
½ c. corn flake crumbs

Combine 4 tablespoons butter and flour. Add seasonings, onion and sour cream. Fold in the beans. Place in a 2-quart casserole. Sprinkle cheese over top, then crumbs. Dot with remaining butter and bake at 350°F. for 30 minutes. NOTE: If desired, 2 packages frozen French-style beans may be used. Yield: 6-8 servings.

Karen A. Fry, Bellevue H.S.
Bellevue, Washington

GREEN BEAN SUPREME

1 to 2 12-oz. cans sliced green beans
4 T. butter or margarine, melted
¼ c. onions, chopped
1 can cream of mushroom soup
½ c. dry bread crumbs

Heat beans; drain. Saute onions in 2 tablespoons butter. Combine beans, onion mixture and soup. Pour into 1½-quart casserole. Top with bread crumbs which have been mixed with remaining melted butter. Bake in 350°F. oven for 20-25 minutes. NOTE: If beans are not preheated, extend oven time to 30 minutes. For an extra quick dish, heat drained beans and soup together before combining with other ingredients, and bake 15 minutes. Yield: 6-8 servings.

Mrs. Martha Engelberg, Mason Co. Eastern,
Custer, Michigan

GREEN BEAN SURPRISE

2 T. butter
2 T. flour
1 c. sour cream
½ c. onion, diced
Salt and pepper to taste
2 cans French green beans, drained
½ c. Swiss cheese, grated
½ c. buttered corn flake crumbs

Melt butter; add flour, sour cream, onion, salt and pepper to make white sauce; thicken. Add green beans and half of cheese. Place in casserole; top with remaining cheese and buttered corn flake crumbs. Bake at 400°F. for 20 minutes until bubbly. Yield: 6-8 servings.

Mrs. Dorothye Hansen, Marshall H.S.
Marshall, Michigan

HEAVENLY BEANS

2 No. 2½ cans whole green beans
1 8-oz. can water chestnuts, sliced
1 No. 2½ can bean sprouts
1 can cream of mushroom soup
Milk
1 c. Cheddar cheese, grated
French-fried onion rings

Combine beans, water chestnuts and bean sprouts in layers in 2-quart casserole, adding slightly diluted mushroom soup and cheese last on each layer. Place French-fried onion rings on top; cover casserole and place in oven for 30 minutes at 350°F. Remove cover for last 10 minutes. Yield: 8-12 servings.

Joyce Littlejohn, Highland H.S.
Pocatello, Idaho

SCALLOPED SNAP BEANS

2 T. butter or margarine
3 T. all purpose flour
1 c. milk
½ c. liquid drained from beans
1 T. prepared mustard
¼ c. cheese, finely cut
½ t. salt
⅛ t. pepper
2 c. canned or leftover snap beans, drained
¼ c. buttered crumbs

Melt butter; add flour and blend well. Add milk slowly and cook, stirring constantly, until thickened; add liquid from beans, mustard and cheese. Stir until cheese is melted; add salt and pepper. Put alternate layers of beans and sauce into a small greased, uncovered casserole. Top with buttered crumbs and bake in a preheated 350°F. oven for 1 hour. Yield: 5 servings.

Mrs. Joan Sloat, Franklin Jr. H.S.
Pocatello, Idaho

STRING BEANS CREOLE

1 qt. canned string beans, drained
6 slices lean bacon
⅓ c. onion, chopped
⅓ c. green pepper, chopped
3 T. butter
2 c. canned tomatoes
½ t. salt
⅛ t. pepper
1 c. American cheese, shredded
Bread crumbs

Drain beans, saving ¼ cup of the liquid. Cut bacon into small pieces and fry until almost crisp. Add beans and reserved bean liquid to bacon; cook 10 minutes. Cook onions and green pepper in butter until tender; add tomatoes and cook until sauce is thick. Season with the salt and pepper. Combine mixtures and pour in baking dish; Sprinkle with cheese and crumbs. Bake at 375°F. until cheese is melted and crumbs are browned. Yield: 6 servings.

Fern A. Soderholm, Willmar Jr. H.S.
Willmar, Minnesota

STRING BEAN DISH

2 cans green beans
Salt and pepper to taste
Bacon grease
1 can mushroom or celery soup
½ c. milk
1 doz. saltine crackers
Onion rings

Combine green beans, salt, pepper and bacon grease; cook as usual and drain. Add remaining ingredients except onion rings; cook until liquid partially cooks down. Pour into casserole; top with onion rings. Bake at 350°F. until onion rings are crisp. Yield: 6-8 servings.

Mrs. Delores Dorton, Manchester H.S.
Manchester, Ohio

UNUSUAL GREEN BEANS

3 9-oz. pkgs. quick French-style green beans
1½ c. water
1½ t. salt
1 5-oz. can water chestnuts, sliced
2 cans condensed cream of celery soup
⅛ t. pepper
½ c. milk
1-2 cans French-fried onion rings

Combine beans, water and salt in saucepan; cover. Bring quickly to a boil over high heat, separating beans with fork, if necessary, to hasten thawing. When water boils, reduce heat to cook gently until thawed but still slightly crisp, about 4 minutes. Drain. Layer beans and water chestnuts in a 2-quart greased casserole. Mix celery soup and pepper with the milk. Pour over the mixture in the casserole. Bake in 350°F. oven for 25 minutes. Top with French-fried onions and bake until golden brown, 10 minutes or more. Yield: 8-10 servings.

Mrs. Lola Schall, York Public Schools
York, Nebraska

SWISS GREEN BEAN CASSEROLE

4 T. butter
2 T. flour
½-1 t. salt
¼ t. pepper (opt.)
2-3 t. sugar
3-4 t. onion, grated
1 c. sour cream
2 cans whole green beans or 2 pkg. frozen green beans, cooked
1-2 c. processed Swiss cheese, grated
1 c. corn flakes, slightly crushed

Melt 2 tablespoons butter; blend in flour, salt, pepper, sugar and onion. Stir in sour cream and heat through; do not boil. Stir in green beans and cheese. Turn into a greased casserole. Top with corn flakes and dot with remaining butter. Bake at 350°F. 20 minutes. NOTE OPTIONAL METHOD: Make a paste of 2 tablespoons melted butter, flour, salt and sugar. Remove from heat and add onion, sour cream and cheese. Mix sauce until cheese melts. Pour sauce over beans and put in a casserole. Melt remaining butter; mix with corn flakes. Sprinkle mixture on casserole. Bake at 350°F. for 20 minutes. Yield: 6-8 servings.

This recipe submitted by the following teachers:
Mrs. Rosetta Haire, Wellington H.S.
Wellington, Illinois
Mrs. Barbara L. Hastings, Cherry Hill H.S.
Inkster, Michigan

VEGETABLE-CHEESE CASSEROLE

2 pkg. frozen green beans, lima beans or mixed vegetables
1 c. American cheese, grated
1 sm. can evaporated milk
1 can mushroom soup
1 can cream of chicken soup
1 can French-fried onion rings

Parboil vegetable for 4 minutes; place in greased casserole. Add cheese, milk and soups in layers. Bake 45 minutes at 350°F. Top with onion rings the last 20 minutes of baking. Yield: 8 servings.

Mrs. E. J. Foley, Belview H.S.
Belview, Minnesota

BARLEY AND PEAS CASSEROLE

2 c. pearl barley
1 pkg. frozen peas
3 T. butter or margarine
1 med. onion, diced
1 c. chicken broth or soup
Salt

Cook barley and peas as directed on packages. In a large skillet melt margarine and lightly brown onions. Add barley, peas and broth; season to taste. Heat about 5 minutes and serve. Yield: 6-8 servings.

Gwen Morgenstern, Hamden H.S.
Hamden, Ohio

CASSEROLE OF PEAS

1 No. 2 can peas
2 hard-cooked eggs, chopped
¼ t. salt
Pepper
1 T. flour
1 T. butter
1 c. buttered cracker crumbs
½ c. cheese, grated

Drain peas, reserving juice. Place peas in a buttered casserole. Add eggs and seasonings. Pour liquid from peas into a saucepan and heat. Thicken with flour; add butter and pour over the peas. Brown buttered crumbs slightly. Mix crumbs with cheese and pour over the peas. Bake for 30 minutes at 350°F. Yield: 6 servings.

Mrs. Beulah Meyers, Ayersville H.S.
Defiance, Ohio

CREOLE ENGLISH PEAS

1 sm. onion, chopped
1 med. green sweet pepper, diced
1 1-lb. can tomatoes
1 T. butter
Salt and red pepper to taste
1 c. cheese, grated
1 1-lb. can small English peas, drained

Cook onion, green pepper and tomatoes until thick. Add butter, red pepper and salt. Cook until very little juice is left. Blend half of cheese into mixture. Add peas; mix and pour into casserole. Spread top with the remaining cheese. Bake at 350°F. for 20 minutes. Yield: 4-6 servings.

Mrs. Rowena McCarty, Beaumont H.S.
Beaumont, Mississippi

SPLIT PEA CASSEROLE

1½ c. green split peas
3 T. onion, chopped
Salt and pepper
2½ T. butter
4 T. flour
1 c. milk
1 No. 2 can tomatoes
1½ c. cooked rice
Buttered bread crumbs

Soak the peas overnight in water; add onion and cook until tender, but not mushy. Add ¾ teaspoon salt toward the end of the cooking time. Drain and boil the liquid down to ½ cup. In a saucepan melt the butter; stir in the flour. Add the split pea liquid and milk, stirring constantly. Cook until thickened. Season with salt and pepper to taste. Drain the tomatoes and sprinkle with salt. Place the peas, hot sauce, tomatoes and cooked rice in alternate layers in a buttered baking dish. Cover with crumbs. Bake at 375°F. for 25 to 30 minutes. Serve with bacon if desired. Yield: 6-8 servings.

Mrs. Marjorie P. Kibelbek, Beth Center Jr. H.S.
Brownsville, Pennsylvania

VEGETABLE CASSEROLE

1 c. thick white sauce
1 c. sharp cheese, grated
1 can tomato soup
1 sm. can pimento, drained and chopped
1 lge. can small English peas, drained
1 onion, finely chopped
1 green pepper, finely chopped
½ c. almonds

Combine white sauce, cheese and soup. Mix all vegetables together. Alternate layers of sauce and vegetables in a baking dish. Top with almonds. Bake at 350°F. for 30 minutes. Yield: 15 servings.

Mrs. Alton D. Lewis, Lexington H.S.
Lexington, Tennessee

CHEESE-STUFFED PEPPERS

6 med. green peppers
6 bacon strips
⅓ c. onion, chopped
3 c. cooked rice
3 c. Cheddar cheese, shredded
2 T. pimento, chopped
½ t. salt
½ c. bread crumbs
Bacon curls (garnish)
1 can green beans or 1 pkg. frozen beans, cooked and seasoned

Cut off tops of green peppers; remove seed and membrane. Cook 5 minutes in boiling salted water; drain. Cut bacon in small pieces; saute with onion until crisp and brown. Drain on absorbent toweling. In a mixing bowl combine bacon and onion, rice, cheese, pimento and salt; toss to blend. Spoon into green pepper cups, packing lightly. Place peppers in baking dish. Bake about 30 to 40 minutes at 375°F. Garnish with bread crumbs over the top and bacon curls if desired. Place green beans around the peppers to serve. Yield: 6 servings.

Mrs. Lola S. Pevehouse, Tascosa H.S.
Amarillo, Texas

CREOLE PEPPER CASSEROLE

8 lge. sweet peppers
¾ c. water
1½ T. butter
1½ T. flour
1 c. sweet milk
Salt to taste
1 can mushroom soup
1½ c. cheese, grated
1 c. bread or cracker crumbs

Coarsely grind peppers. Cook in water until tender; drain well. Make a cream sauce of butter, flour, milk and salt; mix with mushroom soup and peppers. Put mixture in buttered casserole; add cheese and bread crumbs. Bake for 30 minutes at 300°F. Yield: 6-8 servings.

Grace Evelyn Miller, Todd County Central
Elkton, Kentucky

PEPPER CASSEROLE

7 lge. green peppers
¼ lb. margarine
2 c. bread crumbs
½ lb. sharp cheese
3 eggs, beaten
2 c. evaporated milk
1 t. salt
¼ t. black pepper

Cook green peppers until tender. Place a layer of green pepper strips in a buttered casserole; dot with margarine. Cover with a layer of bread crumbs and cheese. Repeat layers until all green pepper has been used. Combine eggs, milk, salt and pepper. Pour over green pepper. Cook at 325°F. until eggs and milk set, about 40 minutes. Yield: 10 servings.

Mrs. Doran Ingram, Scottsboro H.S.
Scottsboro, Alabama

HOMINY CASSEROLE

1 No. 2½ can hominy
1 egg, beaten
½ c. cheese, grated
3 T. red chili sauce or catsup
3 T. onion, chopped
Salt and pepper to taste
Buttered crumbs

Drain hominy. Add egg, cheese, chili sauce, onion, salt and pepper; mix well. Put in greased baking dish; cover with buttered crumbs. Bake at 400°F. until top is brown. Yield: 6 servings.

Lillian S. Ealy, Gadsden H.S.
Anthony, New Mexico

HOMINY PIMENTO CASSEROLE

1 lge. onion, minced
1 lge. green pepper, minced
4 T. margarine, melted
3 T. flour
1½ c. milk
1 c. mushrooms
1 sm. can pimento
½ t. Tabasco
½ t. seasoned salt
½ t. dry mustard
1 c. sharp Cheddar cheese, grated
1 c. ripe olives, pitted and chopped
2 No. 2 cans of hominy, rinsed
1 t. salt
1 c. slivered almonds

Saute onion and green pepper in margarine until tender. Add flour; gradually stir in milk. Cook until thickened, stirring constantly. Add other ingredients except almonds. Place in long baking dish. Top with almonds. Bake at 325°F. until bubbly and slightly brown. Yield: 8 servings.

Nina Swindler, Newbern H.S.
Newbern, Tennessee

SOUTH COAST HOMINY

1 onion, minced
1 green pepper, chopped
½ stick butter
3 T. flour
1 t. salt
½ t. dry mustard
Tabasco sauce to taste
Monosodium glutamate
Seasoned salt
1½ c. milk
1 c. sharp Cheddar cheese, shredded
1 c. sliced mushrooms, drained
1 can sliced pimentos
3 c. white hominy

Saute onions and peppers in butter; add flour and seasonings. Add milk gradually; cook until thickened, stirring constantly. Add remaining ingredients except hominy and almonds. Rinse hominy in cold water; drain well. Mix with sauce. Place in casserole; top with almonds. Bake at 325°F. for 30 minutes. Yield: 12 servings.

Jacquie Eddleman, Dongola H.S.
Dongola, Illinois

BAKED LIMA BEANS

2 c. dried lima beans
2 t. salt
½ t. dry mustard
½ c. syrup
⅛ t. pepper
1 c. sour cream
3 strips bacon

Soak beans overnight. Cook slowly until tender; add 1 teaspoon salt and ¼ teaspoon dry mustard when partly cooked. Drain and place in 3-quart casserole. Add syrup, 1 teaspoon salt, ¼ teaspoon dry mustard and pepper. Mix well. Add the cream; lay strips of bacon on top. Cover and bake 1 hour at 375°F. Yield: 6-8 servings.

Elfrieda Schmidt, Adam Kolb Intermediate
Bay City, Michigan

BAKED LIMA CASSEROLE

2 c. lima beans, washed
1 med. onion, chopped
¼ lb. bacon, finely chopped
¼ c. molasses
1½ T. brown sugar
2 t. salt
1 t. dry mustard
¼ c. catsup
1 c. tomato juice or puree
3-4 whole slices bacon

Place lima beans, onion, chopped bacon in layers in baking dish, beginning and ending with beans. Combine remaining ingredients except bacon slices and pour over beans; top with bacon slices. Bake covered for 4 to 6 hours at 250°F. Uncover the last 30 minutes. Add water or tomato juice during baking, if needed. Yield: 6-8 servings.

Mrs. Lucy W. Martin, Murtaugh H.S.
Murtaugh, Idaho

BAKED LIMAS IN SOUR CREAM

1 lb. dried lima beans
Water
2 t. salt
¾ c. butter
¾ c. brown sugar
2 t. dry mustard
1 T. molasses
1 c. sour cream

Soak limas overnight in water Drain; cover with fresh water. Add 1 teaspoon salt and cook until tender, about 30-40 minutes. Drain again; rinse under hot water and put in 2-quart casserole. Dab butter over hot beans. Mix brown sugar, dry mustard and remaining salt and sprinkle over beans. Stir in molasses; add sour cream and mix gently. Bake at 350°F. for 1 hour. NOTE: This casserole may be prepared ahead of time and refrigerated until baking time. Yield: 8-10 servings.

Margaret Ann Ramsdale, Hutchinson H.S.
Hutchinson, Kansas

LIMA BEAN CASSEROLE

1 lb. lima beans
Salt and pepper to taste
6-7 slices bacon, cut in 2-in. pieces
¼ c. green peppers, chopped
½ c. onion, chopped
3 T. sugar
3 T. flour
1 No. 2½ can tomatoes

Soak beans overnight. Cook in pressure cooker for 25 minutes or until skins burst; season to taste. Cook bacon slightly; remove from skillet. Saute green pepper and onion in bacon fat for 5 minutes. Add sugar, 1 teaspoon salt, flour and tomatoes. Cook until thick. Put drained beans in casserole. Cover with tomato mixture; top with bacon. Bake 30 minutes at 350°F. Yield: 6 servings.

Mrs. Glen Wuester, Beattie H.S.
Beattie, Kansas

LIMA BEAN CASSEROLE

1 can lima beans, drained
4 slices bacon
1½ T. onion, chopped
1 can pizza sauce
⅓ c. pkg. herb seasoned stuffing mix

Place beans in a greased 1-quart casserole. Partially cook bacon in a small skillet. Remove bacon; drain on paper towel. Cook onion in bacon drippings until tender. Combine onion, pizza sauce and half of stuffing mixture and lima beans; mix well. Place in casserole. Sprinkle remaining stuffing and bacon on top. Bake in preheated 350°F. oven uncovered for 30 minutes. Yield: 2-3 servings.

Mary Ellen Weyer, Fenton H.S.
Fenton, Michigan

LIMA BEAN MEDLEY

2 c. celery, diced
1 sm. onion, diced
1 green pepper or pimento, diced
2 T. cooking oil
2 c. boiling water
2 c. tomatoes
2 c. lima beans, partially cooked
Salt and pepper
½ pkg. noodles
Bacon or hamburger (opt.)

Cook celery, onion and pepper in oil until brown. Add water and simmer until nearly done; add tomatoes, beans, salt and pepper. Simmer longer, adding water if necessary. Add noodles when nearly done; cook until noodles are tender. NOTE: If desired, noodles may be cooked separately; serve bean mixture over noodles. Yield: 8 servings.

Edna Strout, Amity Union H.S.
Amity, Oregon

SPANISH LIMAS

1 med. onion, chopped
1 green pepper, chopped
2 T. butter
2 c. tomato juice
1 t. salt
Pepper
1 t. Woreestershire sauce
2 c. cooked lima beans
1½ c. cheese, grated

Fry the onion and green pepper in the butter. Add the tomato juice and cook slowly for ten minutes. Add seasonings and drained lima beans. Simmer slowly for twenty minutes. Put lima bean mixture and cheese in alternate layers in a casserole. Bake at 350°F. for 20 to 30 minutes. Yield: 8 servings.

Elizabeth McClure, Greencastle H.S.
Greencastle, Indiana

LIMA BEAN-MUSHROOM CASSEROLE

3 pkg. frozen baby lima beans
1 lge. can mushrooms, drained
3 T. butter, melted
5 sm. or 2 lge. onions, chopped
Salt and pepper
1 can cream of mushroom soup
½ pt. half and half cream

Cook beans for 5 minutes; drain. Saute mushrooms in butter; remove mushrooms. Saute onion in remaining butter. Place a layer of beans, a layer of onions, and a layer of mushrooms in a casserole. Sprinkle generously with salt and pepper. Blend soup and cream; pour over casserole. Bake at 350°F. for 1 hour to 1 hour and 30 minutes. Yield: 10-12 servings.

Mrs. Pauline Norberg, Parma H.S.
Parma, Idaho

LIMAS O'BRIEN

2 c. cooked dried limas
1 sm. onion, chopped
2 T. pimento, chopped
1 c. cheese, grated
1 c. med. white sauce
½ t. salt
⅛ t. pepper

Mix all ingredients; place in buttered baking dish. Bake in 360°F. oven about 20 minutes. Garnish with onion rings, pimento strips or parsley before serving. Yield: 6-8 servings.

Harriett Smith Reed, Milltown H.S.
Milltown, Indiana

OKRA AND CHEESE CASSEROLE

½ lb. okra
4 med. unpeeled tomatoes, sliced
1 lb. American cheese, cubed
1 onion, finely chopped
Salt and pepper to taste

Cut tips and ends from okra and slice crosswise. Arrange ingredients in alternate layers, beginning with tomatoes and ending with cheese. Add seasonings to each layer. Bake for 40 minutes in covered casserole. Yield: 4 servings.

Mrs. Frances W. Utley, Lyon County H.S.
Eddyville, Kentucky

SPANISH OKRA

¼ lb. tender okra, cut ¼-in. thick
2 lge. fresh tomatoes, diced
3 T. onion, chopped
4 T. butter
1 t. salt
2 T. chili powder
3 drops Tabasco sauce
1 c. water

Mix okra, tomatoes, onions and salt. Saute in butter for 5 minutes. Add chili powder, Tabasco sauce and water; mix well. Cover and simmer over low heat until vegetables are tender and the mixture has thickened. Yield: 6-8 servings.

Mrs. Georgia Short, Dell City H.S.
Dell City, Texas

SCALLOPED ONIONS

6 lge. sweet onions
4 T. butter
4 T. flour
2 c. milk
2 c. med. cheese, grated

Peel, slice and separate onions into rings. Place in casserole. Make white sauce of butter, flour and milk. When thick, add cheese and stir until dissolved. Pour over onions. Bake for 1 hour and 30 minutes at 350°F. Yield: 6 servings.

Katie Jackson, Cass City H.S.
Cass City, Michigan

SCALLOPED ONIONS AND ALMONDS

12 sm. onions
1 c. celery, diced
4 T. butter
3 T. flour
1 t. salt
Few grains of pepper
1 c. milk
½ c. light cream
½ c. blanched almonds, slivered
Paprika
Grated Parmesan cheese (opt.)

Wash and peel onions; cook in boiling salted water until tender. Drain. Cook celery in boiling salted water until tender. Make a white sauce of butter, flour, salt, pepper, cream and milk. In a buttered casserole arrange alternate layers of onions, celery, almonds and white sauce. Sprinkle the top with paprika and cheese. Bake in a preheated 350°F. oven until bubbly and delicately brown. Yield: 8 servings.

Carolyn W. Baxley, Paul Knox Jr. H.S.
North Augusta, South Carolina

CREAMED ONION CASSEROLE

2 lbs. small white onions
1 can mushroom soup
¼ c. milk
½ c. English walnuts or pecans, chopped
Salt and pepper
½ c. sharp cheese, grated

Cook onions slowly in salted water until almost tender but firm, not more than 10-15 minutes. Drain and put in greased casserole. Mix soup, milk and nuts; season to taste and pour over onions. Top with cheese and bake at 350°F. about 30 minutes, or until well browned. Yield: 6 servings.

Mabel Jones, Snow Hill H.S.
Snow Hill, Maryland

ONION SUPREME

7 c. sliced onions
¼ c. butter or margarine
½ c. top milk
½ c. buttermilk
1 egg, well beaten
1 t. salt
Biscuit crust

Cook onions in butter over direct heat until soft and browned. Combine top milk, buttermilk, egg and salt with onions. Line casserole dish with biscuit crust; pour mixture into crust. Bake for 20 minutes in 425°F. oven. Yield: 6 servings.

Mrs. Imogene D. Crawford, East Henderson School
Flat Rock, North Carolina

BETTY'S ARISTOCRATIC POTATOES

4 med. cooked potatoes, mashed
1½ c. cream style cottage cheese
½ c. sour cream
2 T. butter
2 eggs
1 t. salt
1 T. mixed salt and white pepper
1 c. chopped almonds, toasted
Potato petals (garnish)
Olive petals (garnish)
Pimento (garnish)

Combine all ingredients except almonds and garnishes. Sprinkle top with almonds; garnish with potato and olive petals with pimento centers. Bake at 350°F. for 30 minutes. Yield: 4 servings.

Mrs. Dorothy Stutzman, Freehold Regional H.S.
Freehold, New Jersey

CASSEROLE OF MASHED POTATOES WITH CARROTS

4 med. potatoes
½ c. sour cream
½ c. carrots, shredded
½ t. salt
1 T. butter

Boil potatoes in salted water until tender; drain. Mash until well blended. Add sour cream until of proper consistency. Add carrots and season. Place in buttered casserole. Top with butter. Bake in 375°F. oven until lightly browned, about 20-30 minutes. Yield: 4-6 servings.

Judy S. Vaughn, Oblong Township H.S.
Oblong, Illinois

CHANTILLY POTATO PIE

4-5 potatoes
Milk
Butter or margarine
Seasonings to taste
1 9-in. baked pie shell
1 c. sharp Cheddar cheese, shredded
½ heavy cream, whipped

Cook potatoes; mash and whip with milk, butter and seasonings. Spoon potatoes into pie shell. Fold cheese into whipped cream; spread mixture over potatoes. Bake at 450°F. for 10-15 minutes. Yield: 6 servings.

Verlyne Foster, Rolette H.S.
Rolette, North Dakota

CHEESE AND POTATO CASSEROLE

6 lge. potatoes
12 oz. Cheddar cheese, grated
2 T. onion, grated
Salt and pepper

Boil potatoes; cool, peel and grate. Toss onion with potatoes. Arrange alternate layers of potatoes and cheese, ending with cheese, in a buttered casserole. Sprinkle layers with salt and pepper. Bake at 350°F. for 40 minutes. Yield: 6 servings.

Mrs. Lorraine Kerr, Cranberry Area H.S.
Seneca, Pennsylvania

CREAM OF POTATO

2 c. raw potatoes, diced
1 onion, minced
2 celery stalks, diced
2 c. boiling water
4 T. butter or margarine, melted
3 T. flour
1 t. salt
2 c. milk, scalded
1 T. parsley, minced

Cook potatoes, onion, and celery in boiling water, covered, until tender. Blend butter, flour and salt; gradually add the milk. Cook until smooth and thick, stirring constantly. Sieve the potatoes, onions and celery; combine with the white sauce. Heat well; sprinkle with parsley and serve. Yield: 6 servings.

Sister Mary Anthony, Cathedral H.S.
Trenton, New Jersey

MAINE POTATO SCALLOP

4 lge. potatoes, thinly sliced
1 lge. onion, chopped
1 can cream of chicken soup
¼ c. milk
4 slices cheese
Parmesan cheese, grated
Paprika
Salt and pepper to taste

Combine potato and onion in casserole. Mix in soup and milk; cover with cheese. Sprinkle with Parmesan cheese and paprika. Use salt and pepper throughout mixture. Bake at 350°F. for 1½ hours. Yield: 6-8 servings.

Mrs. Karlene Mahaney, Boothbay Region H.S.
Boothbay Harbor, Maine

MASHED POTATO CASSEROLE

6 potatoes
½ c. milk
¼ c. butter
2 eggs, beaten
2 t. salt
1 t. onion seasoning
⅛ t. pepper
¼ c. onion, grated
1½ c. American cheese, grated

Cook potatoes until tender; mash. Add milk and whip. Add butter, eggs, seasonings, onions and 1 cup cheese; mix well. Pour into a buttered 1½-quart casserole. Bake 40 minutes in 375°F. oven. Add remaining cheese; bake 10 minutes longer. Yield: 6 servings.

Mrs. Frances Bondurant, Cairo H.S.
Cairo, Illinois

O'BRIEN AU GRATIN POTATOES

1 gal. boiled potatoes, chopped
2 T. parsley, chopped
4 T. onion, chopped
8 T. pimento, chopped
2 T. green pepper, chopped
Salt and pepper to taste
3 c. cheese, grated
½ c. milk
Butter

Place vegetables in baking dish; sprinkle with salt, pepper and cheese. Add milk; dot with butter. Bake 40 minutes at 375°F. Yield: 10-12 servings.

Mrs. Katheryn Chambers, Wayne City School
Wayne, Nebraska

POTATOES AU GRATIN

½ c. American cheese, grated
2 c. med. white sauce
4 med. boiled potatoes, sliced
½ green pepper, chopped
1 c. buttered crumbs

Add cheese to warm white sauce, stirring until blended. Place alternate layers of potatoes, white sauce and peppers in a greased casserole. Top with crumbs. Bake covered for 20 minutes at 350°F.; uncover and bake an additional 10 minutes. Yield: 6 servings.

Sue Miller, Waldron H.S.
Waldron, Indiana

POTATO-CHEESE SCALLOP

6 lge. potatoes
¼ c. grated onions
1 t. salt
¼ t. pepper
2 c. cottage cheese
1 c. sour cream
1½ c. Cheddar cheese, grated
Paprika

Peel and slice potatoes; place in baking dish. Sprinkle onion, salt and pepper over potatoes. Combine cottage cheese and sour cream; spoon over potatoes. Top with cheese; sprinkle with paprika and bake 20 minutes at 350°F. Yield: 8 servings.

Elizabeth Skaggs, Cerro Gordo H.S.
Cerro Gordo, Illinois

POTATO SCALLOP

1 qt. diced potatoes, cooked
¼ c. green pepper, chopped
¼ c. onion, chopped
¼ c. pimento, chopped
1 T. parsley, chopped
¼ lb. American cheese, cubed
Salt and pepper to taste
½ c. butter, melted
½ c. milk
½ c. milk
¼ c. corn flakes, crushed

Mix vegetables, parsley, cheese and seasonings; place in a casserole. Pour butter and milk over casserole. Sprinkle top with corn flake crumbs. Bake 1 hour at 350°F. Yield: 8 servings.

Mrs. Lillian Nayes, Simle Jr. H.S.
Bismarck, North Dakota

SCALLOPED POTATOES

1½ c. onions, thinly sliced
4½ c. potatoes, sliced
3 t. salt
3 T. butter or margarine
7 t. flour
⅛ t. pepper
⅛ t. paprika
1¾ c. milk

Add onions, potatoes and 2 teaspoons salt to boiling water in saucepan. Boil, covered, for 5 minutes. Melt butter in top of double boiler; stir in flour, 1 teaspoon salt, pepper and paprika. Add milk. Cook over boiling water, stirring constantly, until smooth and thickened. Arrange one-third of drained potatoes and onions in a greased 1½-quart casserole. Pour on one-third of the sauce. Continue alternating layers, finishing with sauce. Bake at 400°F. for 35 minutes. Yield: 4 servings.

Marguerite Steele, Green Springs H.S.
Green Springs, Ohio

SCALLOPED POTATO CASSEROLE

1 T. onion, grated
1 can cream of mushroom, celery or chicken soup
    soup
½ to 1 soup can milk
1 t. salt (opt.)
⅛ t. pepper
6 potatoes, peeled
1 c. ham, spam or other boiled meat, grated
½ c. cheese, grated

Combine onions, soup, milk and seasoning in saucepan; cook until onions are done. Lay potatoes in layers alternately with meat and cheese in a greased casserole, reserving some cheese for top. Pour soup mixture over casserole; top with cheese. Bake 20 minutes at 325°F. Yield: 6-8 servings.

Sevola Fulgham, Safford H.S.
Safford, Arizona

SCALLOPED POTATOES

6 potatoes, peeled and sliced
½ sm. onion, diced
1 can cream of mushroom soup
1 soup can milk
Salt and pepper

In a well greased 2-quart casserole place layer of potatoes, onion and soup mixed with milk. Salt and pepper each layer. Continue making layers until all ingredients are used. Bake in 350°F. oven for 1 hour 15 minutes. Yield: 8-10 servings.

Rosemary Freeborn, Santiam H.S.
Mill City, Oregon

SCALLOPED POTATOES

5 c. pared white potatoes, thinly sliced
1 t. salt
¼ t. pepper
¼ c. onion, thinly sliced or 1 t. onion soup mix
1 can cream of celery soup
½ c. Cheddar cheese, grated

Place potatoes in buttered baking dish. Add seasonings, onion and undiluted soup. Sprinkle with cheese. Bake at 350°F., covered, for 45 minutes. Uncover; bake 15 minutes, or until tender. Yield: 6 servings.

Mrs. Florence Welty, Ligonier Valley Jr. H.S.
Ligonier, Pennsylvania

APPLESAUCE SAUERKRAUT

4 c. rinsed sauerkraut, drained
2 c. sweetened applesauce
½ t. caraway seed
1 T. butter or bacon fat

Combine all ingredients; place in buttered 2-quart casserole. Bake 45 minutes at 375°F. Yield: 6 servings.

Alice M. Downs, Rowe Jr. H.S.
Milwaukee, Oregon

SOYBEAN LOAF

1 c. soybeans
1 sm. onion
1 c. walnut meats, ground
1 c. toasted bread crumbs
½ c. cream
2 eggs, slightly beaten
1 T. butter or vegetable oil
Salt to taste

Soak the beans overnight or longer. Pour off the water; put the beans in cold water. Cook until tender, usually takes about 2 hours. When nearly cooked, add onion. When well done, make a puree of beans. Add other ingredients and mix well. Press mixture into a baking dish; bake 45 minutes at 350-400°F. Serve with cranberry or other tart jelly. Yield: 8 servings.

Mrs. Diane Caviezel, Enumclaw Public School
Enumclaw, Washington

CHEESEY SPINACH

6 c. steamed spinach
Salt and pepper to taste
1 c. sharp cheese, grated
4 slices bread
3 T. butter or margarine, melted

Spread a layer of steamed spinach in the bottom of a well buttered baking dish. Season to taste. Add a layer of grated cheese. Repeat layers until the spinach and cheese are used. Top with seasoned buttered crumbs which have been made from the 4 slices of bread and 3 tablespoons butter. Bake in a 375°F. oven until the crumbs are browned and the cheese is melted. Yield: 4-6 servings.

Mrs. Janet P. Berkebile, Penn Manor H.S.
Millersville, Pennsylvania

SPINACH SOUFFLE

1 c. chopped spinach or Swiss chard, cooked
1 c. thick cream sauce
3 eggs, separated
¼ t. cream of tartar
3-4 T. butter
4 T. flour
¼ t. salt
1 c. milk

Melt butter; blend in flour and salt. Let bubble up together. Remove from heat. Add milk. Cook over low to medium heat until thickened, stirring constantly. Blend spinach into cream sauce; add well beaten egg yolks. Add cream of tartar to egg whites; beat until stiff. Fold into vegetable mixture. Pour into ungreased 1½-quart baking dish; make groove with spoon 1-inch from edge. Bake in pan of hot water 1-inch deep in preheated 350°F. oven for 50-60 minutes until puffed and golden brown. Yield: 4 servings.

Helen C. Larson, Central H.S.
Crosby, Minnesota

SPINACH SOUFFLE

5 T. butter, melted
3 T. flour
½ t. salt
½ t. pepper
1 c. milk
1 c. cooked, chopped spinach
3 eggs, separated
½ c. cheese, grated
½ c. fine bread crumbs

Blend 3 tablespoons butter, flour, salt and pepper. Add milk; stir and cook until boiling. Add drained spinach and well beaten egg yolks. Fold in cheese and beaten egg whites. Put into buttered baking dish and cover with bread crumbs mixed with remaining butter. Place dish in shallow pan of boiling water. Bake at 350°F. until firm in center, about 25-30 minutes. Yield: 6 servings.

Mrs. Audra Taylor, Jacksonville H.S
Jacksonville, Illinois

SPINACH CASSEROLE

2 pkg. frozen spinach, cooked
1 carton sour cream
½ pkg. onion soup mix
Buttered bread crumbs
Cheese, grated

Combine spinach, sour cream and soup mix; put in casserole. Cover with buttered bread crumbs and grated cheese. Bake for 30 minutes at 350°F. Yield: 8 servings.

Twila Palmer, I. C. Ranum School
Denver, Colorado

SPINACH SUPREME CASSEROLE

2 strips bacon, diced
2 stalks celery and leaves, diced
1 lge. onion
2 boxes frozen spinach
1 can mushroom soup, undiluted
½ c. sm. bread cubes
4 T. butter
Black pepper

Fry bacon with celery and onions. Add spinach and soup. Place in a 2-quart casserole. Combine bread crumbs, butter and plenty of pepper; top casserole with mixture. Bake at 375°F. for 30 minutes. NOTE: Do not add salt. Yield: 12 servings.

Lois C. Smith, Troy H.S.
Troy, Ohio

SQUASH-SWISS CHEESE CASSEROLE

1½-2lb. yellow squash
1 med. onion, chopped
1 bay leaf
3 sprigs parsley or 1 t. dried parsley
¼ t. thyme
2 T. butter, melted
2 T. flour
1 c. milk
Dash of salt
½ t. seasoning salt
Dash of Worcestershire sauce
2 egg yolks, beaten
6 T. Swiss cheese, grated
Dash of cayenne pepper
Buttered bread crumbs

Slice squash into ⅓-inch pieces; pour over it enough boiling salted water to cover. Add onion, bay leaf, parsley and thyme. Cook until barely tender; drain. Remove parsley sprigs and bay leaf. Blend butter and flour; gradually stir in milk. Cook until smooth and thickened, stirring constantly. Add salt, seasoning salt and Worcestershire sauce. Stir in beaten egg yolks, 3 tablespoons cheese and cayenne. Add squash; pour into buttered baking dish. Mix remaining cheese with an equal amount, or more, of buttered bread crumbs. Sprinkle over casserole. Bake at 300°F. for 35 minutes, or until top is bubbly and brown. Yield: 6 servings.

Carolyn Hixson, Tyner Jr. H.S.
Tyner, Tennessee

PATTY PAN SQUASH CASSEROLE

2 med. patty pan squash
1 med. onion, sliced
Salt and pepper
¼ c. cracker crumbs
Butter
1 c. milk
Parmesan cheese

Cover bottom of a greased baking dish with slices of raw unpeeled squash. Add layer of onion. Sprinkle with salt, pepper and crumbs. Dot with butter. Repeat layers until all ingredients have been used. Add milk. Sprinkle generously with Parmesan cheese. Bake, covered, at 350°F. for 25 minutes. Yield: 4 servings.

Mrs. Gaynelle C. James, Gardner H.S.
Gardner, Illinois

SQUASH CASSEROLE

1½ lb. yellow summer squash, cooked and mashed
1 carrot, grated
1 sm. onion, chopped
¾ c. sour cream
1 can cream of chicken soup
½ c. bread crumbs
½ stick butter, melted

Combine squash, carrot, onion, sour cream and soup; pour into casserole. Sprinkle with bread crumbs and pour over melted butter. Bake in 350°F. oven for 30-40 minutes. Yield: 8-10 servings.

Sara C. Rambo, Pottsgrove H.S.
Pottstown, Pennsylvania

SQUASH OR EGGPLANT CASSEROLE

1½ c. cooked squash or eggplant
1 c. Cheddar cheese, grated
1 egg, beaten
¾ c. milk
1 T. butter
¼ t. salt
5 saltine crackers, crushed
1 green pepper, chopped
Black pepper to taste
Parmesan cheese
Catsup

Mix all ingredients except Parmesan cheese and catsup. Pour into a greased casserole. Sprinkle top with Parmesan cheese and dot with catsup. Bake at 425°F. until brown, 20 to 25 minutes. Yield: 4-6 servings.

Madeline H. Cleere, Lawrence County H.S.
Moulton, Alabama

SQUASH-PECAN CASSEROLE

1 can mushroom soup
2 eggs, beaten
2 c. cheese, grated
4 c. cooked squash, sliced or cubed
½ to ¾ c. pecans, chopped
Buttered bread crumbs

Mix the undiluted soup with the eggs and cheese. Place half of squash in a buttered baking dish and pour over half the mushroom mixture. Sprinkle with half the pecans. Repeat layers. Top with bread crumbs. Place in a 350°F. oven and bake until crumbs are a golden brown. Yield: 8-10 servings.

Mrs. Marie Lovil, McLeod H.S.
McLeod, Texas

CHEESE-ZUCCHINI CASSEROLE

12 zucchini, washed and cut into ½-inch cross-
    wise slices
12 med. tomatoes, peeled and sliced
1 lge. bermuda onion, sliced
1½ c. cracker crumbs
1 c. cheese, grated
Salt and pepper to taste
1 T. brown sugar (opt.)
Basil (opt.)

Alternate layers of squash, tomatoes and onion in a buttered casserole. Sprinkle each layer with cracker crumbs, cheese, salt and pepper; dot with butter. Sprinkle brown sugar and basil on tomatoes if desired. Top layer should be cheese. Bake at 350°F. for 1 hour 15 minutes. Yield: 8 servings.

Dorothy A. Rathsack, Lake Mills H.S.
Lake Mills, Wisconsin

ZUCCHINI CASSEROLE

3 c. unpeeled zucchini squash, sliced
1½ c. water
1½ t. salt
1 med. onion, chopped
½ green pepper, chopped
½ green pepper, chopped
2 T. corn oil
1 lb. ground beef
2 c. toasted bread cubes
1 c. American cheese, diced
2 T. uncooked rice
1 can condensed tomato soup
¾ c. water
⅛ t. pepper
⅛ t. paprika

Boil squash in 1½ cups water with 1 teaspoon salt. Saute onion and green pepper in corn oil; drain on paper towel. Brown ground beef in skillet. Mix squash, remaining ½ teaspoon salt, and all ingredients in a casserole. Bake in 325°F. oven for 1 hour. Yield: 6 servings.

Mrs. Lee W. Schorzman, Ritzville H.S.
Ritzville, Washington

LAYERED ZUCCHINI CASSEROLE

3 zucchini or yellow squash, cut in ¼-inch
    slices
2 med. onions, sliced
⅓ to ½ c. butter
Salt and pepper to taste

Place one-third of squash slices in casserole; cover with a thin layer of onion slices. Dot with butter; sprinkle with salt and pepper. Repeat procedure twice. Bake at 350°F. for 1 hour. Temperature and time may be varied to 300°F. for 1 hour and 30 minutes or to 375°F. for 45 minutes to accompany other foods in oven. NOTE: For color contrast, use a combination of the two types of squash. Yield: 4-6 servings.

Mrs. Douglas Gunn, East Haven Jr. H.S.
East Haven, Connecticut

ZUCCHINI CRISP

6 med. zucchini squash
1 t. salt
1 T. vinegar
2 T. butter or margarine, melted
2 T. flour
¼ t. paprika
½ t. dry dill
1 c. cream

Slice washed squash as for shoestring potatoes. Sprinkle with salt and add vinegar. Let set for 15 minutes. Pour off liquid. Cook squash in butter, stirring often, for about 10 minutes. Add flour and stir until smooth. Add paprika, dill and cream. Stir constantly until liquid is smooth and seasonings are well blended. Remove from heat and serve. Yield: 6 servings.

Mrs. Hazel Stivers, Madera School District
Madera, California

ZUCCHINI-NOODLE BAKE

1 1-lb. pkg. regular noodles
7 T. butter
4 T. flour
2 t. salt
1 t. dry mustard
1 tall can evaporated milk
1½ c. water
1 t. Worcestershire sauce
1 c. Cheddar cheese, grated
1 lge. onion, chopped
6 med. zucchini, trimmed and cut in ½-inch
    slices

Cook noodles in boiling salted water following label directions; drain. Melt 4 tablespoons butter; stir in flour, 1 teaspoon salt and mustard. Cook, stirring constantly, just until mixture bubbles. Stir in evaporated milk, water and Worcestershire sauce; continue cooking and stirring until sauce thickens and boils 1 minute. Stir in cheese until melted. Pour over noodles; toss lightly to mix. Spoon into a shallow 8-cup baking dish. Saute onion in 3 tablespoons butter just until soft. Stir
(Continued on Next Page)

in zucchini; sprinkle with remaining salt. Steam until tender. Push noodles to edges of dish to make a shallow well in middle. Fill with zucchini. Cover with foil. Bake at 350°F. for 30 minutes, or until noodles are golden. Yield: 8 servings.

Mrs. Barbara Woodhull, White Cloud H.S.
White Cloud, Michigan

APPLE-SWEET POTATO CASSEROLE

1 2-lb. can sweet potatoes, sliced lengthwise
2 c. peeled apples, sliced ¼-inch thick
¾ c. maple blended syrup
¼ c. butter, melted
1 t. salt

Place potatoes in greased 12x8x2-inch baking dish. Arrange apple slices on top of potatoes. Combine syrup, butter and salt; pour over potatoes and apples. Cover and bake at 350°F. for 45 minutes. Remove cover and bake another 30 minutes, or until apples are tender, basting frequently. NOTE: 4 cups sliced cooked potatoes may be used instead of canned potatoes. Casserole may be made ahead of time and reheated. Add syrup, if needed. Yield: 8 servings.

This recipe submitted by the following teachers:
Maggie Beth Watts, Era H.S.
Era, Texas
Mrs. JoAnne Davis, Oakdale H.S.
Oakdale, California
Mrs. Mildred Crow, Alvarado H.S.
Alvarado, Texas

SWEET POTATO-APPLE CASSEROLE

2 lge. sweet potatoes
2 apples
2 T. brown sugar
1 t. butter
½ c. orange juice
1 t. liquid non-caloric sweetener
Cinnamon or nutmeg

Wash and scrub the potatoes. Cook in water to cover for 20 minutes. Drain, peel and slice ¼-inch thick. Peel the apples and slice thin. In a baking dish arrange alternate layers of potatoes and apples, sprinkled with brown sugar and dotted with butter. Mix the orange juice and sweetener and pour over all. Sprinkle with cinnamon or nutmeg. Bake at 375°F. for 45 minutes or until tender and brown. Yield: 6 servings.

Mrs. Irene Wells, Grant County Rural H.S.
Ulysses, Kansas

APPLES AND SWEET POTATOES

1½ lb. apples, quartered
4 med. sweet potatoes, sliced
1 c. water
¾ c. sugar
½ c. butter
2 T. cornstarch

Place apples and sweet potatoes in a buttered casserole. Combine remaining ingredients; cook until very thick. Pour over the apples and sweet potatoes. Bake at 325°F. until tender and lightly browned. NOTE: If desired, this may be covered with marshmallows before baking. Yield: 6 servings.

Gertrude Quinby Brubaker Portage Area Schools
Portage, Pennsylvania

GOLDEN GLOW SWEET POTATOES

6 med. sweet potatoes, halved or quartered
2 c. miniature marshmallows
3-4 T. butter
⅓ to ½ c. cream
¼ c. (firmly packed) brown sugar
1 t. nutmeg
¾ t. salt
½ t. cinnamon

Cover sweet potatoes with boiling salted water. Cook until tender; drain and mash. Combine potatoes, 1½ cups marshmallows and remaining ingredients. Whip until fluffy. Pile lightly into greased casserole. Bake at 350°F. for 15 minutes. Remove from oven; top with remaining marshmallows. Bake 15-20 minutes, or until marshmallows are lightly browned. Yield: 6 servings.

Mrs. Wilma Christian Mitchell, Smithville H.S.
Smithville, Ohio

PINEAPPLE-SWEET POTATO BAKE

1 No. 2 can whole sweet potato or 2½ c. cooked
 fresh sweet potatoes
3 T. butter or margarine
½ t. salt
¼ c. orange juice
1 c. crushed pineapple
Butter
10 marshmallows, halved

Mash potatoes; add butter, salt and orange juice. Beat until light and fluffy. Add crushed pineapple. Pour into buttered casserole. Dot with butter. Bake at 350°F. for about 45 minutes. During last 10 minutes, top with marshmallows. Bake until marshmallows are golden. Yield: 6 servings.

Mrs. Mary Schierholt, Ludington H.S.
Ludington, Michigan

SWEET POTATO-ORANGE CASSEROLE

6 med. sweet potatoes
2 oranges
1 c. dark brown sugar
1 T. cornstarch
¼ c. butter

Partially cook sweet potatoes; cool and peel. Cut in halves or quarters. Arrange potatoes and thin slices of one orange in buttered casserole. Make a thick smooth syrup by boiling together the juice of one orange, brown sugar, cornstarch and butter. Pour syrup over potatoes; bake at 325°F. for 1 hour. Yield: 6 servings.

Mrs. Nancy R. Handshaw, South Redlands
School District
Detroit, Michigan

TROPICAL STYLE SWEET POTATOES

4 c. cooked or canned sweet potatoes, mashed
1 14-oz. can crushed pineapple, drained
4 T. butter, melted
1 t. salt
¼ c. brown sugar
⅛ t. cinnamon
½ c. coconut

Combine mashed sweet potatoes with ¾ cup of the pineapple, 2 tablespoons of the butter, salt, brown sugar and cinnamon; beat well. Place in a 1½-quart casserole and heat. Combine remaining butter and pineapple; add coconut. Mix well and sprinkle over casserole. Bake at 375°F. about 40 minutes. Yield: 6 servings.

Mrs. Barbara Barker, Arlington H.S.
Arlington Heights, Illinois

YAMS IN PEPPER CUPS

2 med. green peppers, cut in half
2 c. mushrooms, chopped
1 med. onion, chopped
¼ c. butter or margarine, melted
1 1-lb. can yams, drained and mashed
1 egg, beaten
1 t. salt
¼ t. pepper

Cook green peppers, covered, in boiling salted water for 5 minutes; drain. Saute mushrooms and onion in butter over low heat for 5 minutes. Combine mushroom mixture, yams, egg, salt and pepper; mix well. Stuff green pepper halves with yam mixture. Place in greased baking dish. Bake, uncovered, at 350°F. for 30 minutes. NOTE: If desired, 4 medium yams may be used instead of canned yams. Cook, peel and mash yams before adding to mixture. Yield: 4 servings.

Jean M. Suttle, Lathrop H.S.
Fairbanks, Alaska

CANDIED SWEET POTATOES

1 No. 3 can dry pack sweet potatoes
1 c. white sugar
½ to ¾ c. sweet cream

Place potatoes in greased casserole. Burn sugar in skillet; turn off heat. Add cream; stir until dissolved into thin syrup. Pour over potatoes. Bake at 300°F. at least 1 hour and 30 minutes. Uncover last 15 minutes for browning. Yield: 6-8 servings.

Ruby B. Rendall, Almond H.S.
Almond, Wisconsin

BAKED TOMATO CASSEROLE

7 T. butter
2 c. onions, thinly sliced
1 T. sugar
1 t. salt
2½ c. cooked tomatoes
1 c. soft bread crumbs
⅛ t. pepper
Cheddar cheese, grated

Melt 4 tablespoons butter in a saucepan. Add onions; sprinkle with sugar and salt. Cover; cook gently over low heat for 25 minutes. Do not brown. Arrange onions in a shallow casserole. Add tomatoes, half of bread crumbs, and the pepper. Top with cheese. Brown remaining bread crumbs in 3 tablespoons butter; sprinkle over casserole. Bake at 350°F. for 20 minutes. NOTE: When doubling the recipe, heat casserole before adding cheese and top crumbs. Add cheese and crumbs and bake until browned. Yield: 4 servings.

Louise Hagen, LaSalle H.S.
St. Ignace, Michigan

TOMATO CASSEROLE

3 slices stale or frozen bread
1 No. 2½ can tomatoes
½ t. salt
Dash of pepper
1 T. sugar
1 T. cornstarch
1 sm. onion, finely chopped
Cheddar cheese strips

Break bread into pieces and place in buttered 6x10x2 baking dish. Combine tomatoes, seasonings, sugar and cornstarch. Cook over medium heat until slightly thickened; pour over bread. Sprinkle with onion. Decorate with cheese strips. Bake at 350°F. for 30 minutes. Yield: 6 servings.

Mrs. Ellen Schiefer, Mohawk H.S.
Sycamore, Ohio

BAKED TOMATOES

5 strips bacon
1 sm. onion, diced
½ sm. green pepper, diced
½ t. salt
1 pt. tomatoes
4 c. dried bread, broken into pieces

Cut bacon into pieces and cook slightly. Add onion and green pepper; cook until bacon is crisp. Add bread crumbs and stir. Add tomatoes and mix. Put in well oiled casserole; bake 30 minutes or more at 350°F. Yield: 10 servings.

Mrs. Edna Coleman, Holton H.S.
Holton, Kansas

TOMATO CASTELLANO

2 c. tomato puree
2 c. brown sugar
½ c. water
Pinch of salt
1 c. butter or margarine, melted
4 c. cubed bread

Combine tomato puree, brown sugar, water and salt; cook for 5 minutes. Pour butter over bread cubes and mix well. Pour tomato mixture over bread cubes and mix. Place mixture in greased baking pan and set in a pan of hot water. Bake 45 to 60 minutes at 350°F. Yield: 6 servings.

Mrs. Fern Gordon, Cheboygan H.S.
Cheboygan, Michigan

TOMATO PUDDING

3 c. soft bread cubes
⅓ c. butter or margarine, melted
1 c. brown sugar
1½ c. water
2 6-oz. cans tomato paste
½ t. salt
Dash of pepper

Toast bread cubes in butter until lightly browned. Combine brown sugar, water, tomato paste, salt and pepper; simmer 5 minutes. Combine bread cubes and tomato mixture and pour into greased 1-quart casserole. Bake uncovered in a preheated 350°F. oven for 1 hour and 30 minutes. NOTE: If desired, 2 cups tomato puree may be substituted for the tomato paste. Reduce water to ½ cup. Cook as directed. Yield: 6 servings.

Juliann W. Cook, University School
Ann Arbor, Michigan

DOG PATCH TURNIPS

1 lb. turnips
4 T. butter, melted
4 T. flour
1 T. onion, minced
⅓ c. water in which turnips were cooked (pot liquor)

⅓ c. cream
Salt and pepper to taste
3 eggs, separated

Wash, pare and slice turnips. Cook until soft, about 30 minutes. Drain and mash, reserving water. Blend butter and flour. Gradually add onions, water and cream. Add mashed turnips and seasonings. Add to well beaten egg yolks. Fold in stiffly beaten egg whites. Pour into buttered baking dish. Cover; bake at 350°F. until thoroughly heated. Yield: 6 servings.

Frances Moore, Kingfisher H.S.
Kingfisher, Oklahoma

WINTER TURNIPS

6-8 bacon slices
1 med. turnip, cubed
1 med. onion, sliced
1 t. salt
½ t. sugar
¼ t. Tabasco
Bacon drippings

Saute bacon to desired crispness. Reserve bacon for garnish. Combine turnip, onion, salt, sugar and Tabasco in large kettle. Add water to cover. Add bacon drippings. Cook about 30 minutes or until turnip is tender. Drain. Add bacon pieces; toss. Yield: 4-6 servings.

Photograph for this recipe on page 185

PINWHEEL VEGETABLE CASSEROLE

8 sm. carrots, cooked
8 sm. onions, cooked
1½ c. cooked green beans
1 c. cooked peas
4 T. flour
½ c. butter or margarine
2 c. milk
½ lb. cheese, grated
Salt and pepper to taste
Biscuit dough

Place the well drained vegetables in a casserole. Make a cream sauce with 4 tablespoons butter, flour and milk. Add the cheese and stir until it is melted. Season to taste and pour over the vegetables. Roll out biscuit dough; spread with remaining melted butter. Roll like jelly roll; slice 1-inch thick. Cover casserole with pinwheel biscuits and bake at 425°F. for 20 minutes or until the biscuits are a light brown.

Rose Marie Whiteley, Deuel County H.S.
Chappell, Nebraska

CORN AND SQUASH

2 c. corn
2 c. squash
1 t. salt
4 T. butter
1 c. cereal flakes, crushed

Cook corn and squash in small amount of water until soft. Add salt and 2 tablespoons butter to mixture. Melt 2 tablespoons butter and mix with cereal flakes; do not crush too fine. Place layer of flakes on bottom of casserole. Add corn mixture. Sprinkle remaining flakes on top. Bake 375°F. until brown. NOTE: If desired, canned corn may be used; add to cooked squash. Yield: 4-6 servings.

Elizabeth J. Schue, Hanover Jr. H.S.
Hanover, Pennsylvania

FOUR-BEAN CASSEROLE

8 slices bacon
4 lge. onions, chopped
¾ c. brown sugar
1 t. dry mustard
½ t. garlic powder
1 t. salt
½ c. vinegar
2 15-oz. cans butter beans
1 No. 1 can lima beans
1 No. 1 can kidney beans
1 11-oz. can pork and beans

Fry bacon crisp and crumble. In large kettle combine onions, brown sugar, mustard, garlic powder, salt and vinegar. Cook for 20 minutes. Drain all beans except pork and beans. Add beans to onion mixture. Mix well; top with bacon. Bake 1 hour at 350°F. Yield: 12-15 servings.

Mrs. Barbara Beyer, Clinton H.S.
Clinton, Minnesota

HARVEST CASSEROLE

1 head cauliflower
6 carrots, cut into pieces
1 can green beans
2 T. butter
2 T. flour
½ t. salt
1 c. evaporated milk
1 c. vegetable stock
1 8-oz. Cheez Whiz
Cracker crumbs or crushed potato chips

Break cauliflower into pieces; soak in salt water for 10 minutes. Drain; cook until partly tender. Cook carrots until partly tender. Cook green beans. Make white sauce in a double boiler with butter, flour, salt, evaporated milk and vegetable stock; add Cheez Whiz. Put vegetables and sauce in casserole; top with crumbs. Bake at 350°F. for 30 minutes. Yield: 6-8 servings.

Mrs. Doris Slack, White Pigeon H.S.
White Pigeon, Michigan

GARDEN FRESH CASSEROLE

6 med. potatoes, sliced
2 onions, diced
4 carrots, sliced
1 lb. green beans
Salt and pepper
⅓ c. butter
½ c. buttered crumbs

In a well greased casserole place a layer of potato, onion, carrots and beans broken in 1-inch pieces. Repeat layers. Season with salt and pepper. Dot with butter. Garnish with a ring of buttered crumbs. Cover tightly and bake at 350°F. for 1 hour to 1 hour and 30 minutes, or until tender. Yield: 4-6 servings.

Mrs. Ann Manzer, Mountain View H.S.
Kingsley, Pennsylvania

LIMA BEAN-ZUCCHINI CASSEROLE

1 pkg. frozen lima beans
1 pkg. frozen zucchini or 1 lb. fresh zucchini
1 can condensed cream of mushroom soup
½ soup can water
Salt and pepper to taste
¼ c. slivered almonds

Alternate layers of lima beans and zucchini in buttered casserole. Mix soup with water; pour over vegetable mixture. Season to taste. Top with slivered almonds. Bake at 350°F. for 20 minutes or until bubbly. Yield: 4-6 servings.

Mrs. Marlene Figone, Armijo Union H.S.
Fairfield, California

MIXED VEGETABLES WITH ALMONDS

1 pkg. frozen or fresh cauliflower
1 pkg. frozen or fresh green beans
1 pkg. frozen or fresh peas
½ c. milk
1 can cream of chicken soup
1 6-oz. pkg. Cheddar cheese, shredded
1 sm. jar pimento, chopped
1 can small round onions
½ c. slivered almonds

Cook cauliflower, beans and peas until half done. Add milk to soup and heat with cheese. Combine all ingredients except almonds. Place in greased dish and cover with slivered almonds. Bake 30 minutes at 350°F. NOTE: This recipe may be prepared in advance. Yield: 10 servings.

Mrs. Meril T. Kenyon, Holyoke H.S.
Holyoke, Colorado

MIXED VEGETABLE CASSEROLE

1 pkg. mixed frozen vegetables
1½ c. scalded milk
1 c. soft bread crumbs
¼ c. butter, melted
1 sm. can pimento, chopped
1 T. parsley, chopped
1½ T. onion, chopped
1½ c. mild cheese, grated
3 eggs, beaten
Salt and pepper
Paprika to taste

Mix all ingredients together and bake slowly at 300°F. for 1 hour. Yield: 8 servings.

Mrs. Martha Waltner, Freeman Academy
Freeman, South Dakota

SCALLOPED VEGETABLE WITH CHEESE

2-3 c. desired vegetable
2 T. butter or margarine
2 T. flour
½ t. salt
1 c. milk, scalded
½ c. cheese, grated or cubed
½-¾ c. buttered crumbs

Cook vegetable in boiling salted water just until tender. Melt butter; blend in flour and salt. Gradually stir in milk; add cheese. Cook until cheese melts and sauce reaches boiling point, stirring constantly. Alternate layers of vegetable and cheese sauce in a greased baking dish. Top with buttered crumbs. Bake at 400°F. until crumbs are browned. NOTE: For vegetable, use frozen or fresh broccoli, cauliflower, Brussels sprouts, or ½ head cabbage. Yield: 6 servings.

Mrs. Helen Phillips, Metamora H.S.
Metamora, Ohio

SWEET-SOUR BAKED BEANS

8 slices bacon
4 lge. onions
½ to 1 c. brown sugar
1 t. dry mustard
1 t. salt
½ t. garlic salt (opt.)
1 t. salt
½ c. vinegar
2 15-oz. cans dried lima beans
1 1-lb. can green lima beans
1 1-lb. can red kidney beans
1 1-lb. can pork and beans

Pan fry bacon until crisp; drain and crumble. Peel and cut onion in rings. Place onions, sugar, mustard, salt, garlic salt and vinegar in pan. Cook 20 minutes, covered. Add onion mixture to beans. Add crumbled bacon. Pour into 3-quart casserole. Bake 1 hour at 350°F. Yield: 12 servings.

Mrs. Ardes Hasleton, Underwood Public School
Underwood, Minnesota

VEGETABLE CASSEROLE AU GRATIN

2 T. butter
2 T. flour
¼ t. salt
⅛ t. pepper
¼ t. dry mustard
1 c. milk, scalded
½ c. processed American cheese, cut up
2 c. mixed vegetables
Bread crumbs

Melt butter; blend in flour, salt and pepper. Add mustard. Gradually stir in milk. Cook over low heat until thickened, stirring constantly. Add cheese and continue cooking until the cheese melts and forms a smooth sauce. Place vegetables and sauce in a buttered casserole; sprinkle with bread crumbs. Dot with butter and bake at 350°F. for 25-30 minutes. Yield: 6 servings.

Dorothy L. O'Malley, North Arlington H.S.
North Arlington, New Jersey

VEGETABLE CASSEROLE DELIGHT

2 pkg. frozen mixed vegetables
½ c. boiling water
½ c. butter, melted
1½ c. warm milk
¼ c. sifted flour
½ c. green onion tops, chopped
⅓ c. Cheddar cheese
1 T. Parmesan cheese
1 t. salt
¼ t. white pepper
¼ c. pimento, cut into strips
2 c. pulled bread cubes

Cook mixed vegetables in boiling water for seven minutes. Melt ¼ cup butter; add flour. Stir until blended. Gradually stir in warm milk and blend. Add cheese and stir until melted. Add cooked vegetables and seasonings. Pour into casserole. Top with bread crumbs; pour remaining melted butter over casserole and bake 30 minutes in preheated 350°F. oven. Yield: 6-8 servings.

Mrs. Irma D. Bonebreah, Central H.S.
Martinsburg, Pennsylvania

VEGETABLE-TAPIOCA CASSEROLE

2 c. long carrot strips
2 c. celery, diced
½ c. onions, diced
½ c. green pepper, sliced
1 c. cut green beans
2 c. tomatoes
½ c. bean juice
2 t. salt
1 T. sugar
3 T. minute tapioca
1½ T. butter

Mix all ingredients. Bake 2-3 hours at 350°F., or until done. NOTE: May be kept in freezer, if any is left over. Yield: 10 servings.

Lucile Cooper, Algoma H.S.
Algoma, Wisconsin

Skillet Meals

AMERICAN CHOW MEIN

2 lb. round beef steak, cubed
2 lb. pork steak, cubed
3 T. butter
2 c. celery, chopped
2 c. onions, chopped
2 T. salt
3 T. soy sauce
Liquid from bean sprouts
2 T. dark molasses
3 cans bean sprouts, drained
½ c. canned mushrooms
1 can horse chestnuts
3 T. cornstarch

Cook meats in butter until almost tender. Cook celery and onions separately with water to cover. Add to meats with the seasonings. Cook for 5 minutes. Add bean sprout liquid; simmer for 20 minutes. Add molasses, bean sprouts, mushrooms and chestnuts. Thicken with a paste made from cornstarch. Simmer for 15 minutes. Serve over cooked, fluffed rice. Add extra soy sauce, if desired. Yield: 12 servings.

Mrs. Elizabeth Richard, Lakewood H.S.
Woodland, Michigan

AUSTRIAN BEEF GOULASH

2 lb. beef chuck, cut in 1-in. cubes
¼ c. butter
3 med. onions, sliced in rings
1 t. paprika
Dash of pepper
Dash of garlic salt
½ t. salt
1 med. bay leaf, crumbled
1 T. wine vinegar
2 beef bouillon cubes
1 c. boiling water
3 T. flour
1 c. evaporated milk
2 med. dill pickles, diced

Brown meat lightly in butter. Add onion rings and cook until transparent. Stir in seasonings and vinegar. Dissolve bouillon cubes in boiling water and pour over meat. Stir to blend well. Cover and simmer over low heat about 2 hours, or until meat is tender. Remove from heat. Sprinkle flour over meat, stirring to blend in smoothly. Return to medium heat and cook, stirring occasionally, until slightly thickened. Add evaporated milk and pickles; stir until heated through. Serve over hot cooked noodles. Yield: 6 servings.

Photograph for this recipe on page 217

BEEF WITH SOUR CREAM

⅓ c. flour
1 t. salt
1 t. freshly ground pepper
2 lb. round or Swiss steak, cut in 1-in. cubes
¼ c. salad oil
1 c. water or tomato juice
3 T. onion, grated
½ t. thyme
½ bay leaf
3-4 med. potatoes, cubed (opt.)
1 pkg. frozen peas and pearl onions
1 c. sour cream
1 T. horseradish

Mix flour, salt and pepper. Dredge meat in flour mixture; brown quickly in hot oil on all sides. Add water, onion, thyme, bay leaf and potatoes; cover tightly. Simmer 45 minutes or until potatoes are tender. Add peas and onions; simmer 10 minutes or until tender. Stir in sour cream and horseradish; heat thoroughly. Do not boil. Remove bay leaf. NOTE: Frozen peas without pearl onions may also be used. Yield: 4-6 servings.

Mrs. Joyce Henrich, James Ford Rhodes H.S.
Cleveland, Ohio

BEEF STROGANOFF

½ c. onion, chopped
⅓ c. butter
1 lb. round steak, cubed
1 t. salt
⅛ t. pepper
1 4-oz. can mushrooms
1 can cream of chicken soup, undiluted
1 c. sour cream

Saute onion in butter. Add beef; brown well. Add salt, pepper, mushrooms and soup; simmer for 15-20 minutes. Stir in sour cream; heat thoroughly. Serve over noodles, brown rice or mashed potatoes. Yield: 4-6 servings.

Ann Kathman, Miller Jr. H.S.
Aberdeen, Washington

BEEF STROGANOFF

1 lb. round steak, ¼ to ½-inch thick
3 T. fat
⅔ c. water
1 3-oz. can broiled sliced mushrooms
1 pkg. onion soup mix
1 c. sour cream
2 T. flour
½ lb. noodles, cooked

Remove fat from steak. Cut steak diagonally across grain into ¼ to ½-inch thick strips. Brown quickly in fat. Add water, mushrooms and onion soup mix. Heat just to boiling. Blend together sour cream and flour and add to mixture. Cook, stirring until mixture thickens; sauce will be thin. Serve over hot noodles. Yield: 5-6 servings.

This recipe submitted by the following teachers:

Ruth Anderson, Chartiers Houston H.S.
Houston, Pennsylvania

Patricia Potzler, Sr. H.S.
Albert Lea, Minnesota

BEEF STROGANOFF

3 c. onion, chopped
⅓ c. fat
2 lb. round steak, thinly sliced
1 can or 1 lb. mushrooms
1 can tomato soup
1 can tomato paste
1 c. sour cream
1 t. salt
Dash of pepper
1 t. Worcestershire sauce

Saute onion in fat; add meat and mushrooms. Cook until brown. Combine remaining ingredients; pour over meat mixture. Cover; simmer one hour. Serve on rice. Yield: 6 servings.

Mrs. Pat Skrocki, Parchment H.S.
Parchment, Michigan

COMPANY STROGANOFF

2 lb. round steak
¼ c. flour
½ c. onions, chopped
6 T. butter
1½ t. salt
⅛ t. pepper
½ c. water
1 can condensed cream of mushroom soup
1 4-oz. can mushrooms, undrained
1 c. sour cream

Cut steak in thin strips; dredge in flour. Brown with onions in butter. Add seasonings and water. Cover and simmer gently until almost tender, about 1 hour, stirring occasionally. Add soup and mushrooms; stir to mix. Cook gently until beef is tender, about 30 minutes. At serving time heat mixture piping hot and stir in sour cream. Serve over poppy seed noodles. Yield: 10 servings.

Mrs. Mary E. Schwartz, Artesia H.S.
Artesia, California

STROGANOFF TENDERLOIN

1 lb. trimmed beef tenderloin, sliced ¼-in. thick
¼ c. butter
6 oz. mushrooms, sliced
½ c. onion, chopped
1 can condensed beef broth
1 c. sour cream
2½ T. flour
Salt and pepper to taste

Cut beef into strips ¼-inch wide; brown quickly in butter. Push meat to one side; add mushrooms and onion. Cook until tender, but not brown. Add beef broth; heat just to boiling. Blend sour cream with flour; stir into broth. Cook, stirring constantly until thickened. Add salt and pepper. Serve over rice or buttered noodles. Yield: 4-5 servings.

Mrs. Judith Harrison, Pacific H.S.
Langlois, Oregon

BEEF STROGANOFF IN RICE RING

1 lb. sirloin, cut in ¼-in. strips
5 T. flour
1 t. salt
7 T. butter
1 c. mushrooms, sliced
1 clove garlic, minced
½ c. onion, chopped
1 T. tomato paste
1¼ c. beef broth
2 T. cooking Sherry (opt.)
1 c. sour cream

Dredge meat in 2 tablespoons flour seasoned with the salt; brown in 4 tablespoons butter. Add mushrooms, garlic and onion; cook 3-4 minutes. Remove from pan. Make gravy of 3 tablespoons butter, 3 tablespoons flour, tomato paste and beef broth. Add meat mixture and Sherry; blend. Add sour cream. Heat, but do not boil.

RICE RING:

1 c. long grain rice, cooked
3 t. butter, melted
2 c. frozen peas, cooked
3 T. pimento, diced
6 T. Parmesan cheese

Combine all ingredients and pack into ring mold. Unmold on serving platter. Serve with stroganoff. Yield: 5-6 servings.

Eileen Brenden, Independent District
Mahnomen, Minnesota

BOEUF A LA MODE

4 lbs. round steak, cubed
1 clove garlic
2 onions, chopped
2 sm. carrots, diced
1 c. celery stalks, diced
¼ c. suet or butter
2 c. red wine
2 c. tomato puree
1 t. salt
10 peppercorns
2 bay leaves

Sear meat in deep heavy pot. Cook garlic, onions, carrots and celery in fat for 5 minutes on low heat; add to the meat. Add wine, tomato puree, salt, peppercorns and bay leaves. Cook slowly until tender, about 3 hours. Add small amounts of water as necessary to keep meat from burning. Yield: 4-6 servings.

Catherine Wiedenhoeft, Platteville H.S.
Platteville, Wisconsin

MRS. McCARTHY'S IRISH STEW

2 lb. beef chuck, cut in 1-in. cubes
2 T. fat
4 c. boiling water
1 clove garlic
1 med. onion, sliced
3 beef bouillon cubes
½ t. pepper
6 carrots, quartered
3 potatoes, cut in 1-in. cubes
1 lb. sm. white onions
1 can mushroom soup
1 can mushrooms
1 pkg. frozen peas

Thoroughly brown meat in hot fat; add water, garlic, sliced onion and seasonings. Simmer covered about 2 hours. Add carrots, potatoes and small onions. Continue cooking 30 ot 40 minutes, or until vegetables are tender. Add mushroom soup, mushrooms and frozen peas. Cook 5 minutes more. Serve with salt sticks. Yield: 8 servings.

Mrs. Patricia Langston, Alamosa H.S.
Alamosa, Colorado

VEAL AND EGG SHORTCAKE

3 T. butter
4 T. flour
1 c. cream of mushroom soup
2 c. milk
½ t. salt
⅛ t. pepper
3 c. veal, cooked and diced
4 hard-cooked eggs, chopped
Baking powder biscuits

Melt butter; add flour and stir until smooth. Add soup and milk; cook until creamy. Add seasoning, veal and eggs; heat thoroughly. Serve between halves and on top of hot biscuits. Yield: 6-8 servings.

Mrs. Leah W. Little, Roosevelt H.S.
Johnstown, Colorado

VEAL-NOODLE CASSEROLE

1½-2 lb. veal round steak, ½-inch thick
Butter and shortening
1 pkg. dry onion soup
½-1 c. hot water
6-8 oz. medium or wide noodles
1 pt. sour cream

Cut veal in 1-inch squares. Roll in seasoned flour; brown in a mixture of butter and other shortening. Sprinkle with onion soup; pour hot water over meat. Cover and cook slowly for 45 minutes to 1 hour. Boil noodles in salted water; drain. Pour sour cream over meat mixture; mix well. Heat through and pour over noodles to serve. Yield: 4-6 servings.

Mrs. Mary E. Jackson, Bad Axe H.S.
Bad Axe, Michigan

BEEF-BACON CASSEROLE

1 lb. ground beef
3-4 slices bacon, chopped
1 med. onion, chopped
1 can tomatoes
1 c. shell macaroni
1 can mushrooms
⅓ can kidney beans (opt.)
Salt and pepper to taste
Chili powder

Brown ground meat, bacon and onion. Add tomatoes and cook slowly for about 30 minutes. Cook macaroni in salted water until done; add to meat mixture. If mixture is to too dry, add small amount of tomato sauce. Add mushrooms and kidney beans. Add seasonings to taste. Yield: 4-6 servings.

Mary Chappell, Bloomington H.S.
Bloomington, Wisconsin

BURGER-MACARONI

1 c. macaroni, uncooked
1½ lb. hamburger
1 sm. onion, finely cut
1 can tomato soup
Dash of celery salt
Dash of garlic salt
Salt and pepper to taste

Cook macaroni. Crumble hamburger and fry with onion. Add the soup and simmer. Add celery and garlic salts. Stir in cooked macaroni. Add salt and pepper. Heat thoroughly. Yield: 6-8 servings.

Betty Henderson, Jordan H.S.
Sandy, Utah

CAMPERS' BEEF-A-RONI

¾ c. onion, chopped
¼ c. butter
1 lb. ground beef
1 No. 2½ can tomatoes
2 t. salt
1 T. Worcestershire sauce
Dash of Tabasco
1 c. uncooked macaroni

Saute onion in butter until clear. Add ground beef and brown lightly. Add remaining ingredients except macaroni; bring to a boil. Add macaroni; cover and simmer gently for 15-20 minutes or until macaroni is tender. Remove cover; cook until mixture is thickened. Yield: 4-6 servings.

Mrs. Barbara Adams, Beavercreek H.S.
Xenia, Ohio

GOULASH

1 lb. hamburger
1 onion, diced
1 T. fat
2 c. cooked macaroni
2 c. canned tomatoes
1 t. Worcestershire sauce
1 t. salt
Dash of Tabasco sauce

Brown hamburger and onions in fat in large skillet. Add the remaining ingredients and simmer for at least 20 minutes. The longer this simmers, the more flavorful it is. When simmering for a longer period, add liquid to keep the goulash moist. Yield: 4-6 servings.

Mary Badger, M.S.D. Monroe H.S.
Winamac, Indiana

GROUND BEEF GOULASH

1 lb. ground beef
1 med. onion, diced
2-3 stalks of celery, diced
2 c. uncooked macaroni
½ can tomato soup or 1 c. whole canned
   tomatoes
Salt and pepper to taste
Garlic salt to taste

Saute ground beef, onions and celery until brown and tender; pour off excess grease. Cook macaroni as directed on the box; drain and add to meat mixture. Add tomato soup and seasoning. Simmer 15-20 minutes before serving. Yield: 10 servings.

Mrs. Sharon Domeier, Renville Public H.S.
Renville, Minnesota

JIFFY MACARONI SUPPER

½ lb. ground beef
1 onion, chopped
2 T. butter
1 c. elbow macaroni
2 c. tomato juice
½ t. salt
⅛ t. pepper
1 c. cheese, cubed

Brown beef and onion in melted butter. Add macaroni, stirring until coated with fat. Stir in tomato juice, salt and pepper. Reduce heat; cook for 15 minutes, stirring occasionally. Sprinkle with cheese; continue cooking for 5 minutes or until cheese is partially melted. Yield: 4 servings.

Ruth Behrends, Balyki H.S.
Bath, Illinois

MACARONI-HAMBURGER SKILLET

1 lb. hamburger
3 sm. onions, sliced
3 T. fat
2 c. cooked tomatoes
1 c. macaroni
1 t. salt
¼ t. pepper

Brown hamburger and onions in fat. Add tomatoes, macaroni and seasonings. Bring to a boil and reduce heat; cover and simmer for 20 minutes. Yield: 6 servings.

Sandra Parrish, Miami Trace H.S.
Washington Court House, Ohio

MEXICAN RING CASSEROLE

½ lb. ground beef
1 sm. onion, chopped
1 T. green pepper, chopped
½ t. salt
Pepper to taste
1 t. chili powder
1 c. carrots, thinly sliced
2 8-oz. cans tomato sauce
½ c. water
½ c. ring macaroni
1 No. 300 can kidney beans

Brown beef. Add remaining ingredients except beans; cover. Simmer for 15-20 minutes. Add beans; heat thoroughly. Yield: 6-8 servings.

Mrs. Carol Dibble, S.R.U. Schools
East Smithfield, Pennsylvania

SKILLET MACARONI AND BEEF

1 lb. ground beef
½ lb. macaroni
½ c. onion, minced
½ c. green pepper, chopped
2 8-oz. cans tomato sauce
1 c. water
1 t. salt
¼ t. pepper
1½ T. Worcestershire sauce

Cook beef in large skillet until no longer red. Remove from skillet; cook macaroni, onion and green pepper in drippings until macaroni is yellow. Return meat to skillet along with tomato sauce, water, salt, pepper and Worcestershire sauce. Cover and simmer 25 minutes. Yield: 6 servings.

Mrs. Joyce Miller, Hiland H.S.
Berlin, Ohio

DELUXE HAMBURGER

1 lb. ground beef
1 t. salt
¼ t. pepper
1 med. onion, chopped
1 c. celery, chopped
1 bell pepper, chopped
⅛ t. ground allspice
½ t. cumin seed
2 c. fine dry noodles
1 No. 2 can tomatoes
½ c. water

Brown hamburger in electric skillet. Add seasonings, onions, celery and green pepper; cook covered for 10 minutes. Add remaining ingredients; simmer covered for 30 minutes. Yield: 6 servings.

Mrs. Ruth L. Auge, Jr. H.S.
Belen, New Mexico

HAMBURGER HEAVEN

1 lb. ground beef
Salt to taste
1 c. celery, chopped
½ c. onions, chopped
¼ c. green peppers, chopped
2 c. thin noodles, uncooked
1 No. 2 can tomato juice
½ lb. American cheese, sliced
1 sm. can pitted olives, sliced

Brown meat; season with salt. Add celery, onion, green pepper, noodles, tomato juice and ¼ cup water. Cover; bring to a boil. Reduce heat; simmer for 30 minutes, adding more water if necessary. Add cheese and olives the last few minutes of cooking. Yield: 6 servings.

Mrs. Elizabeth Tomer, Hanford H.S.
Hanford, California

HAMBURGER SKILLET DINNER

1 lb. ground chuck
1 T. salad oil or melted shortening
1 sm. onion, chopped
1 med. green pepper, cut into strips
1 No. 2 can stewed tomatoes
1 lge. can pitted olives, sliced
Olive liquid
½ lb. nippy cheese, grated
½ t. salt
½ t. monosodium glutamate
¼ t. coarsely ground black pepper
4 oz. dry noodles

Brown meat in oil; add onion and green pepper and brown. Add tomatoes, olives, olive liquid, cheese and seasonings; stir in dry noodles. Cover and simmer for 25 minutes. Serve hot. Yield: 6 servings.

Mary Ann Page, Clearfield H.S.
Clearfield, Utah

NOODLE-BEEF CASSEROLE

½ c. onion, chopped
1 lb. ground beef
½ t. salt
Pepper to taste
¼ t. oregano
1 No. 2 can tomatoes
4 oz. noodles

Brown onions and ground beef in large skillet. Add salt, pepper and oregano. Add tomatoes and bring to a boil. Add dry noodles; lower heat to simmer. Simmer 20 minutes, covered. Serve with grated Parmesan or Romano cheese. Yield: 5 servings.

Mrs. Elizabeth Stark, Upland H.S.
Upland, California

NOODLE STROGANOFF

¼ c. onion, chopped
1 clove garlic
¼ c. butter
1 lb. ground chuck
1 6-oz. can mushrooms and juice
3 T. lemon juice
1 can condensed consomme
1 t. salt
¼ t. pepper
2 c. noodles
1 c. sour cream

Saute onions and garlic in butter; add ground chuck and cook. Stir in remaining ingredients except noodles and sour cream; simmer uncovered for 5 minutes. Stir in noodles; cover and cook 10-12 minutes or until noodles are tender. Mix in sour cream; heat quickly, but do not boil. Yield: 6 servings.

Louise Shirts, Clearfield H.S.
Clearfield, Utah

PATIO SKILLET SUPPER

1 green pepper, chopped
1 sm. onion, chopped
1 lb. hamburger or more
2 T. oil
1 clove garlic
1 No. 2 can tomatoes
1 c. pitted ripe olives
½ c. liquid from olives
½ lb. Cheddar cheese, finely cubed
½ t. salt
½ t. monosodium glutamate or season salt
¼ t. coarse black pepper
1 8-oz. pkg. thin uncooked noodles

Quickly brown green pepper, onion and meat in oil in a large skillet; add the remaining ingredients. Cover the skillet and when steam appears, remove cover and stir mixture. Replace cover; reduce heat and simmer for 20 minutes or until noodles are cooked. Yield: 4-6 servings.

Mrs. W. R. Dale, Jr., Artesia H.S.
Artesia, California

QUICK SKILLET MEAL

1 med. onion, chopped
1 lb. hamburger
2 T. salad oil
1 pkg. egg noodles, cooked
3-4 slices American cheese
1 can cooked tomatoes

Brown onion and hamburger in oil. Add layer of noodles. Top with cheese slices. Cover with tomatoes. Reduce heat; simmer until thoroughly heated and cheese is melted. Yield: 4-6 servings.

Mrs. Mary Laub, Hurst-Bush H.S.
Hurst, Illinois

YANKEE NOODLE

1 lb. ground beef or lean sausage
1 onion, chopped or sliced
1 No. 2½ can tomatoes
Salt and pepper to taste
8 oz. noodles

Brown meat and onion; drain off excess fat. Add tomatoes and seasonings; bring to a boil. Add uncooked noodles; cover. Cook 20 minutes before lifting the cover. Yield: 4-6 servings.

Mrs. Charlotte Russell, Litchfield H.S.
Litchfield, Michigan

AMERICAN CHOP SUEY

1 lb. ground beef
1 t. salt
1 c. celery, diced
¾ c. instant rice
1 mango, diced (opt.)
1 c. tomato sauce
1 2-oz. can mushrooms
1 t. garlic salt

Brown beef; add remaining ingredients. Simmer for 25-30 minutes. Yield: 4-6 servings.

Mary Jo Oldham,
North Gallatin Community Unit H.S.
Ridgway, Illinois

HE-MAN SPANISH RICE

1 lb. ground beef
½ c. onion, chopped
¼ c. green pepper, chopped
1 t. salt
⅛ t. chili powder
½ sm. clove garlic, minced
1 can tomato soup
1 c. water
1 t. Worcestershire sauce
⅓ c. rice

Cook beef, onion, green pepper, salt, chili powder, and garlic in skillet until beef is browned and crumbly. Add remaining ingredients. Cover; cook 30 minutes or until rice is tender, stirring often. Yield: 3-4 servings.

Mrs. Grace S. Wells, Huntington Local H.S.
Chillicothe, Ohio

HAMBURGER SKILLET DISH

¾ c. rice
2 T. shortening
¼ c. onion, chopped
¼ c. celery, chopped
1 lb. hamburger
1 No. 2 can tomatoes
2 t. salt
⅛ t. pepper
1 t. sugar
1 c. meat stock or bouillon
1 t. Worcestershire sauce

Brown rice slowly in hot fat, stirring frequently. Add onion, celery and hamburger; brown. Add remaining ingredients. Cover; simmer 45 minutes or until rice is tender. Yield: 4 servings.

Zona Kay Bunger, Fairmont Public Schools
Fairmont, Nebraska

MEXICAN LUNCHEON DISH

½ lb. ground beef
½ green pepper, chopped
1 sm. onion, chopped
2 T. butter
2 c. tomatoes
1 c. canned kidney beans
½ c. carrots, diced
1 sm. can mushrooms
½ c. uncooked rice
2 T. sugar
Dash of chili powder
Salt and pepper to taste

Brown meat, green pepper and onion in butter; add remaining ingredients. Cover and cook on high heat until steaming. Turn heat to low or warm and cook for 20-25 minutes. NOTE: If desired, recipe may be doubled. Yield: 4 servings.

This recipe submitted by the following teachers:
Carol L. Stager, West Allegheny Jr. H.S.
Oakdale, Pennsylvania
Ruby Lucking, Quincy Jr. H.S.
Quincy, Illinois

STROGANOFF-STYLE CASSEROLE

1 c. quick cooking rice
½ lb. lean ground beef
½ t. salt
1 c. onions, thinly sliced
1 T. butter or margarine
1 can cream of chicken soup
1 2-oz. can mushrooms
½ c. sour cream
¼ c. dill pickles, chopped
Paprika

Cook rice as directed on box. Brown meat with salt and onions in butter; add soup and mushrooms with liquid. Cook slowly until hot. Serve over rice. Top with sour cream mixed with pickles and sprinkled with paprika. Yield: 4 servings.

Gwladys Jeanneret, Kettle Falls, H.S.
Kettle Falls, Washington

POOR MAN'S STROGANOFF

1 sm. onion, chopped
2 T. green pepper, minced
2 T. butter
2 lb. ground beef
½ T. salt
1 carton sour cream
1 can tomato soup
1 sm. can mushrooms
Dash of Worcestershire sauce
2 drops Tabasco sauce
2½-3 c. rice, cooked

Cook onion and green pepper in butter until tender. Add beef and salt; brown. Drain off excess liquid. Add remaining ingredients except rice; simmer 30 minutes, stirring occasionally. Serve over rice. Yield: 8 servings.

Lorraine Traybiatowski, Browerville Public School
Browerville, Minnesota

RICE-A-BURG

½ lb. hamburger
½ c. green pepper, chopped
¼ c. onion, chopped
¼ t. salt
⅛ t. pepper
1 c. instant rice, cooked

Brown meat, seasonings, onion and green pepper; stir frequently. Combine with rice to serve. Yield: 4 servings.

Mrs. Brenda D. Flint, Vilas H.S.
Alstead, New Hampshire

SPRINGTIME SKILLET DINNER

2 T. fat, melted
1 clove garlic, minced
1 c. onion, finely diced
½ lb. ground beef
½ c. uncooked rice
5-6 c. water
1 c. carrots, finely diced
1 c. potatoes, finely diced
1-2 t. soy sauce
1 T. salt
⅛ t. pepper
Parsley (garnish)

Brown garlic in fat in 10-inch skillet. Remove garlic. To oil add onion and beef. Cook until browned, stirring. Add uncooked rice and water. Simmer uncovered over low heat for 40 minutes. Add carrots and potatoes. Continue simmering until tender, 20 minutes. Season with soy sauce, salt and pepper. Serve hot, garnished with parsley. Yield: 6 servings.

This recipe submitted by the following teachers:
Nancy Moffett Badertscher, Bath H.S.
Lima, Ohio
Mrs. Jack Rainwater, Lynn H.S.
Lynn, Arkansas

VOSTA CUA

1 lb. hamburger
Salt and pepper
1 T. fat
1 can red kidney beans
½-1 bottle catsup
2 c. rice

Season meat and shape into patties. Fry patties in fat until done. Add kidney beans and catsup. Cook until beans are done. Serve on cooked hot rice. NOTE: This is a good picnic dish to make over an open fireplace. Yield: 6 servings.

Florence T. Shaffer, Berwick Area Sr. H.S.
Berwick, Pennsylvania

JUTE

1½ lb. ground beef
1 med. onion, chopped
1 can spaghetti
1 can peas
½ c. celery, chopped
Salt and pepper

Brown meat and onion; pour off excess fat. Add remaining ingredients; cook until celery is tender. Add juice of peas if needed for moisture. Yield: 4 servings.

Shirley Erickson, Mira Loma H.S.
Sacramento, California

ITALIAN SPAGHETTI

1 lb. beef hamburger
3 sm. cans tomato sauce
1 can tomatoes
1 t. garlic salt
½ t. oregano
⅛ t. pepper
¼ t. salt
⅓ c. sugar
¾ c. brown sugar
¼ c. molasses
1 bay leaf

Brown hamburger; add remaining ingredients. Simmer about 1 hour. Serve over spaghetti. Yield: 6-8 servings.

Mrs. Glennys Pacsmag, Napavine H.S.
Napavine, Washington

QUICK SPAGHETTI

1 lb. ground beef
1 med. onion, chopped
½ t. salt
1½ c. tomato juice
¾ c. catsup
1 c. spaghetti, broken into 1-inch pieces

Crumble beef into cold skillet with onion and salt; cook until browned. Stir in remaining ingredients; cover. Bring to a boil; reduce heat. Simmer 1 hour without removing cover. Yield: 4-6 servings.

Mrs. Dorothy B. Gifford, Sepulveda Jr. H.S.
Sepulveda, California

SAVORY SAUCE SPAGHETTI

½ lb. ground beef
¼ lb. ground pork
1 t. instant onion
1 sm. green pepper, sliced
½ c. ripe olives, sliced
1 2-oz. can mushrooms, drained
1 8-oz. can tomato sauce
1 No. 2 can seasoned tomatoes
2 c. water
2 t. salt
¼ t. pepper
1 t. Worcestershire sauce
6 drops Tabasco sauce
4 oz. spaghetti

Brown meats. Add onion and green pepper; cook 5 minutes. Add olives, mushrooms and tomato sauce; mix lightly. Stir in tomatoes, water, salt, pepper and sauces. Add spaghetti; bring to boil. Cover; reduce heat. Simmer 40 minutes. Uncover; simmer 15 minutes longer. NOTE: May be kept warm in oven indefinitely. Yield: 6 servings.

Mrs. Alberta F. Hickey, Camas H.S.
Camas, Washington

SPAGHETTI-BEAN CASSEROLE

1 lb. ground beef
1 small onion
Salt and pepper to taste
1 can kidney beans
1 can spaghetti

Brown beef and onion. Season with salt and pepper. Add kidney beans and spaghetti. Cook until thoroughly heated. Yield: 4 servings.

Mrs. Judy Howard, Mid-County Jr. H.S.
Lacon, Illinois

SPAGHETTI AND MEAT BALLS

1 lb. ground beef
¼ c. fine bread crumbs
1 c. onion, chopped
2 t. salt
½ t. pepper
⅔ c. evaporated milk
2 T. butter
¼ c. green pepper, chopped
4½ c. tomato juice
1 sm. bay leaf, crumbled
½ t. oregano
1 7-oz. pkg. spaghetti
⅛ c. Parmesan cheese, grated

Mix beef, crumbs, half of onion, salt, pepper and milk. Shape into 12 balls. Melt butter in pan; saute meat balls. Push meat balls to sides of pan to form a ring. Place green pepper and rest of onion in center; cook. Pour juice over all. Add spaghetti. Sprinkle oregano and bay leaf over top. Simmer covered for 40 minutes. Sprinkle with cheese. Yield: 6 servings.

Mrs. Vivian B. Barnes, Argyle H.S.
Argyle, Wisconsin

SPICY ITALIAN SPAGHETTI

1 lb. long spaghetti
1 T. shortening
2 T. onions, finely chopped
1 lb. ground beef
1½ T. chili powder
Red pepper to taste
Salt and pepper
1 c. cheese, grated

Cook spaghetti as directed on package. Melt shortening; add onions and cook until brown. Add ground beef; lower heat and cook slowly until well done. Add chili powder, red pepper, salt and pepper; cook until well seasoned. Pour spaghetti onto hot platter; add meat sauce and sprinkle with cheese. Serve hot. Yield: 8 servings.

Mrs. Floretta Brock, Laguna-Acoma Jr.-Sr. H.S.
New Laguna, New Mexico

TOP-RANGE SPAGHETTI

1 lb. hamburger
1 c. onions, chopped
1 T. butter
2½ c. tomato juice
¼ t. mace
¼ t. allspice
½ t. dry mustard
1 t. salt
1½ c. thin spaghetti
¼ t. pepper

Brown hamburger and onion in butter. Add tomato juice and seasonings. When boiling, sprinkle cut spaghetti over top. Do not stir. Cover; simmer for 30 minutes. Yield: 3-4 servings.

Margaret M. Warth, Washington H.S.
Massillon, Ohio

BUSY DAY SKILLET SUPPER

1 lb. ground beef
4 med. potatoes, thinly sliced
1 med. onion, thinly sliced
1 t. salt
¼ t. pepper
½ t. oregano
1 can mushroom soup
1½ soup can buttermilk

Brown beef, stirring constantly. Cover with potato and onion slices. Sprinkle with salt, pepper and oregano. Combine soup and buttermilk; pour over all. Cover; simmer until potatoes and onions are tender. Yield: 4-6 servings.

Kathryn Davis, Community H.S.
Pinckney, Illinois

BEAN 'N' BEEF SKILLET CASSEROLE

1 med. onion, chopped
½ lb. ground round
1 No. 300 can pork and beans
Salt and pepper to taste

Combine onion and meat in cold skillet; cook, slowly until done. Drain off excess grease. Add pork and beans, salt and pepper. Heat thoroughly. NOTE: Reheats well. Yield: 4 servings.

Helena Tidrow Raine, Morro Bay H.S.
Morro Bay, California

CHINAMAN PIE

1 lb. hamburger
1 sm. onion, chopped
2 T. vegetable shortening
1½ t. salt
⅜ t. pepper
1 can cream style corn
3 med. potatoes, cooked
3 T. warm milk
2 T. butter

Saute onion and hamburger in shortening until browned; add 1 teaspoon salt and ¼ teaspoon pepper. Put into greased casserole. Pour in corn. Mash potatoes with milk, butter and remaining seasonings. Pour over casserole. Bake for 20 minutes at 350°F. Yield: 4 servings.

Rita M. Roy, Murdock Jr.-Sr. H.S.
Winchendon, Massachusetts

DINNER IN A SKILLET

½ lb. ground beef
1 egg, beaten
1 c. milk
¼ c. fine bread crumbs
1½ T. onion, minced
1 t. salt
¼ t. dry mustard
2 T. flour
2 T. salad oil
1 can tomato or cream of mushroom soup
1½ c. cooked mixed vegetables or 1 pkg. frozen
    mixed vegetables

Combine beef, egg, ¼ cup milk, bread crumbs, onion, ½ teaspoon salt and dry mustard. Shape into twelve 1-inch meat balls. Sprinkle with flour. Heat oil in skillet; brown meat balls on all sides. Arrange around sides of skillet. Into center of skillet gradually pour the soup combined with the remaining ¾ cup milk. Top with the vegetables and remaining salt. Cover. Simmer 10 or 12 minutes. If frozen vegetables are used, cook 25 minutes. Yield: 4-6 servings.

Mrs. Rosamond Fuller, Danube H.S.
Danube, Minnesota

FRYING PAN SUPPER

1 lb. ground beef
2 T. shortening
3 stalks celery, chopped
2 large onions, sliced
2-3 potatoes, cut into strips
2 c. cabbage, shredded
2 t. salt
½ c. water

Brown beef in shortening, stirring frequently. Add layers of vegetables. Sprinkle with salt; add water. Cover tightly; simmer for 15 minutes or until vegetables are tender. Yield: 4 servings.

Barbara Leistikow, Williamsburg H.S.
Williamsburg, Iowa

HAMBURGER AND BEAN CASSEROLE

½ lb. hamburger
1 sm. onion
1 med. can pork and beans
¼ c. catsup
¼ c. brown sugar

Brown hamburger and onion. Remove any pork from pork and beans. Add beans, catsup and brown sugar to meat mixture. Heat thoroughly. Yield: 4 servings.

Marilyn Harder, Wheaton H.S.
Wheaton, Minnesota

HAMBURGER GOULASH

1 lb. hamburger
½ c. onion, chopped
½ c. green peppers, chopped
1 No. 2½ can tomatoes
1 No. 303 can chili beans
1 No. 303 can whole-kernel corn
1 T. salt
½ t. pepper

Brown hamburger with onion and green pepper. Add remaining ingredients; cover. Simmer for 1 hour. Yield: 4-6 servings.

Fern Parrish, Laramie H.S.
Laramie, Wyoming

HAMBURGER HASH

1 med. onion, chopped
1½ lb. hamburger
1 T. shortening
Salt and pepper to taste
2½ c. raw potatoes, diced
2 T. catsup
1 sm. can red kidney beans (opt.)

Brown onion and hamburger in shortening, stirring often. Add seasonings, potatoes and catsup. Cook covered until potatoes are done. If beans are used, they should be added when potatoes have first started to become tender. Yield: 6-8 servings.

Mrs. Jean Hamm, Southern H.S.
Racine, Ohio

HAMBURGER CASSEROLE

1 lb. ground beef
Salt and pepper to taste
¼ c. flour
¼ c. margarine
2 c. milk
6 boiled potatoes, diced
1 10-oz. pkg. frozen peas, cooked
1 c. buttered crumbs (opt.)

Brown ground beef. Add salt and pepper to taste. Remove from pan. In same pan blend and heat flour, margarine, and ½ teaspoon salt. Add milk; cook on medium heat until mixture boils. Remove from heat; add potatoes, peas and browned meat. Serve, or turn into 2-quart casserole. Top with buttered crumbs and bake at 350°F. for 20-30 minutes, or until top is lightly browned. NOTE: Cream of mushroom soup or cream of celery soup may be substituted for white sauce, if desired. Yield: 6 servings.

Carolyn Doelker, Manchester H.S.
Manchester, Michigan

HAMBURGER STROGANOFF

½ c. onion, minced
¼ c. butter
1 lb. ground beef
1 clove garlic, minced
2 T. flour
2 t. salt
¼ t. monosodium glutamate
¼ t. pepper
¼ t. paprika
1 lb. mushrooms
1 can cream of chicken soup
1 cup sour cream
Snipped parsley

Saute onion in butter until golden. Stir in remaining ingredients except soup, sour cream and parsley; saute for 5 minutes. Add soup; simmer, uncovered, for 10 minutes. Stir in sour cream; sprinkle with parsley. NOTE: For Hamburger Czarina substitute mushroom soup for mushrooms. Yield: 4-6 servings.

Mrs. Dorothy Shirley, Live Oak Union H.S.
Live Oak, California

HURRY-UP SKILLET DINNER

1½ c. soft bread crumbs
½ c. water
1 egg, slightly beaten
½ c. non-fat dry milk
2½ t. salt
⅛ t. pepper
1 lb. ground beef
3 T. flour
2 T. shortening
1 c. onion, sliced
1 1-lb. can green beans
Liquid from green beans
2 c. potatoes, finely cut
¼ c. water

Mix crumbs and water in 2½-quart mixing bowl; let stand until soaked. Add egg, dry milk, 1½ teaspoon salt, ⅛ teaspoon pepper and beef. With wet hands shape into 16-20 meat balls; roll in flour. Brown meat balls in hot shortening. Add onion; cook slowly for 5 minutes. Add liquid drained from green beans, potatoes, water, 1 teaspoon salt, and dash of pepper. Cover; cook slowly for 15 minutes or until potatoes are tender, adding more water if needed. Add green beans; heat thoroughly. Yield: 4-6 servings.

Ortus Velma Burns, Lemont Township H.S.
Lemont, Illinois

MEAL-IN-A-FRYING PAN

1 lb. ground beef
2 T. shortening
2 T. onion, chopped
1 1-lb. can whole tomatoes
1 1-lb. can pork and beans
1 t. salt
¼ t. pepper
1 t. prepared mustard

Brown beef in hot shortening. Stir in onion, tomatoes, beans and seasonings. Cover and simmer approximately 30 minutes, stirring occasionally to prevent scorching. Yield: 5 servings.

Clotile Pease, Robbinsdale H.S.
Minneapolis, Minnesota

MEAL-IN-ONE

1 lb. hamburger
1 med. onion, chopped
Salt and pepper to taste
1 can cream of chicken soup
1 can vegetable soup
1 c. water
2½ c. potatoes, diced

Crumble and brown hamburger with onion. Season. Stir in soups and water. Sprinkle with potatoes; simmer 1 hour or until potatoes are tender. NOTE: May also be baked at 350°F. for 1 hour. Yield: 6 servings.

Karen Jodock, Cooperstown Public School
Cooperstown, North Dakota

MEXICAN SKILLET SUPPER

1 lb. hamburger or sausage
2 c. pasta
2 c tomatoes
1 c. water
¼ c. green pepper, diced
1 sm. onion, diced
Chili powder to taste
Salt and pepper to taste
1 c. sour cream

Brown meat; add remaining ingredients except cream. Cover; cook 20 minutes. Fold in sour cream. Yield: 6 servings.

Carole N. Hustead, Central School
Idaho Falls, Idaho

MEAT BALL STEW

1½ lb. ground lean beef
1 envelope spaghetti sauce mix
½ c. corn flake crumbs
3 eggs
4 T. oil
6 carrots, cut into 1-inch pieces
2 green peppers, cut into 1-inch squares
1 c. water
1 can beef gravy
1 family size can tomato sauce
2 cans whole potatoes
2 No. 2 cans sm. white onions

Combine beef, sauce mix, crumbs and eggs; shape into 36 meat balls. Lightly brown in oil. Add carrots, green pepper and water; simmer until vegetables are tender. Stir in gravy, tomato sauce, potatoes and onions; heat thoroughly. Yield: 8 servings.

Mrs. Dorthea Brown Kurtz,
Hellertown-Lower Saucon H.S.
Hellertown, Pennsylvania

MEAT BALL-VEGETABLE DISH

½ c. bread crumbs
½ c. milk
1 lb. ground beef
1½ t. salt
Few grains of pepper
2 T. onion, diced
2 T. shortening
3 c. potatoes, sliced
1 pkg. frozen peas
4 carrots, cut in thirds
1 c. water

Combine crumbs, milk, beef, 1 teaspoon salt, pepper and onion; shape into 12 meat balls. Roll in flour; brown in shortening on all sides. Add vegetables and water; season with salt and pepper. Cover; simmer for 30 minutes or until vegetables are tender. Yield: 4 servings.

Mrs. Patsy Stowers, North H.S.
Evansville, Indiana

SKILLET DINNER

1 lb. ground beef
¼ c. onion, chopped
1 T. margarine
2 T. flour
1½ t. salt
Dash of pepper
¼ c. light cream
2 carrots
2 c. green beans
4-6 potatoes
1 can condensed consomme
2 T. tapioca

Combine beef, onions, margarine, flour, salt, pepper and cream. Form into balls; brown. Add vegetables. Mix consomme and tapioca; add to vegetables and meat balls. Cover and simmer for 1½ - 2 hours. Yield: 4-6 servings.

Judith A. Maggert, Grant Community H.S.
Fox Lake, Illinois

SKILLET STEW

1 lb. ground beef
1½ lb. potatoes, cut into strips
2 c. celery, cut in 1-inch pieces
½ c. onion, thickly sliced
1 c. green pepper, diced
2 t. salt
¼ t. pepper
2 c. canned tomatoes

Form beef into 6 patties; brown in a small amount of fat. Drain off fat. Add raw vegetables and seasonings; top with tomatoes. Cover; simmer for 30 minutes or until potatoes are done. Quarter patties before serving. Yield: 6 servings.

Mrs. Lois Farrington
Mesick Consolidated Schools
Mesick, Michigan

AUTUMN SKILLET DINNER

1 lb. pork sausage
¾ c. celery, chopped
½ c. onion, chopped
½ c. green pepper, chopped
1 can tomato soup
1 c. water
1 2-oz. can mushrooms, drained
1 7-oz. can whole-kernel corn, drained
⅓ c. sharp cheese, grated
2 c. med. noodles

Form sausage into tiny balls; brown. Remove from skillet; drain off most of fat. Stir in celery, onion, green pepper and soup; blend in water. Add remaining ingredients and sausage balls. Cover; simmer 20 minutes stirring once or twice. NOTE: Ingredients may be combined in casserole. Cover; bake at 350°F. for 1 hour and 15 minutes, stirring several times. Yield: 6 servings.

Mrs. Sharon Eich, Whiteford H.S.
Ottawa Lake, Michigan

BACON-MACARONI AND CHEESE

¾ lb. bacon, diced
1 c. onions, chopped
1 qt. milk
2 t. celery salt
½ t. pepper
¼ t. Tabasco sauce
2 c. elbow macaroni
1 c. cheese, grated
½ c. pimento, chopped

In large skillet cook bacon and onion over low heat for 15 minutes. Drain off drippings. Add milk, celery salt, pepper and Tabasco. Heat to boiling point. Gradually add macaroni so that milk continues to boil. Simmer uncovered for 20 minutes, stirring often. Add cheese and pimento; stir until cheese melts. Serve hot. Yield: 4-6 servings.

Mary Lumsden, New Holland-Middletown H.S.
New Holland, Illinois

AMERICAN CHOP SUEY

½ lb. pork or chicken, diced
2 med. onions, finely chopped
1 med. green pepper, finely chopped
3 med. mushrooms, finely chopped (opt.)
1 c. celery, diced
1½ t. salt
1 c. meat stock
2 c. cooked rice

Brown meat and onion. Add green pepper, mushrooms, celery, salt and meat stock. Cook until all is tender. Serve hot on rice. Yield: 6 servings.

Mrs. Alice A. Lovely, Walter S. Parker Jr. H.S.
Reading, Massachusetts

JAMBALAYA

1 lb. smoked sausage, cut into pieces
2 c. onions, sliced
½ c. whole green onions, sliced
½ c. parsley, chopped
½ c. green pepper, chopped
2 c. celery, chopped
1 sm. clove garlic
2 c. water
2 t. salt
⅛ t. red pepper
1 c. uncooked rice

Brown sausage; remove from pan. Add vegetables to drippings; cook until well done and browned. Add sausage, water and seasonings; bring to a boil. Add rice; cover and cook over low heat for 30 minutes without stirring. Stir gently and cook 15 minutes longer. Add more water if necessary. Yield: 5-6 servings.

JoAnna Littrel, Columbus Community School
Columbus Junction, Iowa

MEAL IN A SKILLET

1 lb. bulk or sm. link pork sausage
4 med. potatoes, diced
2 med. onions, thinly sliced
1 c. boiling water
1 No. 2 can cream corn
1 c. tomato sauce, soup, or canned tomatoes
⅛ t. pepper
½ t. salt
Dash of paprika

Brown the sausage in a heavy skillet which has a cover. Remove excess fat; add potatoes, onions and boiling water. Cook until vegetables are tender, about 10 minutes. Add remaining ingredients; heat well over medium heat. Yield: 6-8 servings.

Jessie Hollenbeck, Manistique H.S.
Manistique, Michigan

GOO FOOYU

1 lb. sausage
1 lge. onion, chopped
1 stalk of celery or 1 can celery soup
2 pkg. dry chicken soup mix
1 c. rice
4 c. water

Brown sausage and onions. Add celery, or celery soup, chicken soup, rice and water. Cover; cook over medium heat until rice is done. Yield: 6 servings.

Sandra Harden, Salem Public H.S.
Salem, South Dakota

SAUSAGE SKILLET

1 lb. little link sausage
2 T. water
1 onion, chopped
½ green pepper, chopped
6 pieces celery, diced
1 can tomato soup
½ c. catsup
1 can kidney beans, drained

Place sausage in cold frying pan. Add water; cover and simmer until water evaporates. Remove cover; increase heat and brown sausage evenly. Add onions, green pepper, celery, tomato soup and catsup. Cover and simmer slowly for 30 minutes. Add kidney beans and heat. Yield: 6 servings.

Mrs. Edith M. Newsom, McArthur H.S.
McArthur, Ohio

SPANISH RICE WITH BACON

1 lb. sliced bacon
½ c. onion, diced
¼ c. green pepper, diced
2 cans tomato soup
2 c. cooked rice
2 t. salt
1 bay leaf
¼ t. pepper
1 c. water

Cut bacon into bits and fry until crisp and brown; drain on absorbent paper. Saute onion and green pepper in ¼ cup bacon fat until tender. Add tomato soup, rice, water and seasonings. Cook over low heat for 10-15 minutes, stirring frequently. Remove bay leaf before serving. Garnish with bacon bits. NOTE: Mixture may be baked in a casserole for 20 minutes at 325°F. Yield: 4-6 servings.

Eleanor Otto, Brookville H.S.
Brookville, Indiana

PORK SKILLET MEALS

SWEET-SOUR PORK ON RICE

1½ lb. lean shoulder pork
2 T. fat
¼ c. water
¾ c. green peppers, cut in strips
¼ c. onions, sliced
1 No. 2 can pineapple chunks
¼ c. brown sugar
2 T. cornstarch
½ t. salt
⅓ c. vinegar
1 c. pineapple juice
1 T. soy sauce
½ c. slivered almonds

Cut pork in strips 2-inches long and ½-inch wide. Brown slightly in hot fat. Add water. Cover and cook in electric skillet at 300°F. for 1 hour. Add pepper slices, onion slices, and drained pineapple and saute. Combine the brown sugar, cornstarch, salt, vinegar, pineapple juice and soy sauce; mix and cook in a saucepan until slightly thick. Stirring constantly. Pour over hot cooked pork. Cover and simmer 10 minutes. Serve over cooked rice. Garnish with slivered almonds. Yield: 6 servings.

Mrs. Margarette C. Weeks, Highland Jr. H.S.
Highland, California

DUTCH CHOPS

4 loin pork chops
1 can mushroom soup
1 No. 2 can sauerkraut
Salt and pepper to taste

Brown pork chops. Pour in soup; add sauerkraut and seasoning. Simmer for 30 minutes. Yield: 4 servings.

Mrs. Peter W. Johnson, Hays H.S.
Hays, Kansas

ONE-DISH MEAL

4 thick pork chops
4 med. potatoes, sliced
2 med. onions, sliced
2-4 parsnips, cut in ½-in. lengthwise slices
1 can mushroom soup

Brown chops; pour off excess fat. Top chops with onion rings, potatoes and parsnips. Cover with soup; season. Simmer or bake at 350°F. for 1 hour and 30 minutes. NOTE: One and one-half pound chopped chuck may be used instead of pork chops. Yield: 4 servings.

Susan B. Raudlett, Molly Stark Jr. H.S.
Bennington, Vermont

PORK-ASPARAGUS MEAL

4 pork chops, 1-in. thick
¼ c. salad oil
2 med. tomatoes
1½ lb. fresh asparagus or 1 10-oz. pkg. frozen asparagus spears
1 6- to 8-oz. can chopped mushrooms
1 t. salt
¼ t. ground black pepper

Cook pork chops in oil at 375°F. in an electric skillet for about 30 minutes. They should be well done. Cut thin slices off tops and bottoms of tomatoes; cut each into 2 crosswise slices. Wash and trim fresh asparagus or thaw frozen asparagus just enough to separate. Arrange asparagus and tomato slices over chops; add mushrooms and liquid. Sprinkle with salt and pepper. Cover; lower heat to simmer and cook 12-15 minutes. Yield: 4 servings.

Mrs. Susan Dohrmann, School District #245
Glenville, Minnesota

PORK CHOP CASSEROLE

6 pork chops, ¾-in. thick
3 c. boiling water
6 chicken bouillon cubes
1 c. uncooked rice
½ c. celery, diced
Dash of Tabasco sauce
¼ t. pepper
6 onion slices
6 tomato slices
6 green pepper rings

Brown chops in a preheated 360°F. electric skillet. Remove from pan. Turn control to simmer. Pour water into skillet; add bouillon and stir until dissolved. Add uncooked rice, celery, Tabasco and pepper; stir well. Place chops on rice; top each chop with a thick slice of onion, tomato, and green pepper. Cover; cook for 45 minutes or until tender. Add more water if necessary. Yield: 6 servings.

Laura L. Franklin, Las Animas H.S.
Las Animas, Colorado

PORK AND RICE CASSEROLE

4 pork chops
Salt and pepper
Mustard
½ c. chicken soup
½ c. uncooked rice
1 c. cold water

Salt and pepper chops; spread mustard on both sides. Brown in skillet; add remaining ingredients. Cover; cook for 1 hour over medium to low heat. Yield: 4 servings.

Ruth L. Smith, Hillman Community School
Hillman, Michigan

230

PORK CHOPS IN WINE

1 carrot, peeled and thinly sliced
4 pork chops
¾ c. white wine
1 clove garlic
Sprig of thyme
1 onion, chopped
Salt and pepper
2 egg yolks
3 T. thick cream

Put carrots, chops, wine, garlic, thyme, onion, salt and pepper into skillet. Cover tightly and cook 40 minutes over low heat. Remove chops and keep warm. Beat egg yolks into cream. Strain liquid in which meat was cooked and pour into cream mixture. Heat carefully, do not allow to boil. When piping hot, pour over warm chops and serve immediately. Yield: 4 servings.

Nita P. Lowery, South Mountain H.S.
Phoenix, Arizona

PORK CHOP SKILLET MEAL

4 T. fat
4 pork chops, 1-in. thick
4 slices Bermuda onion, ¼-in. thick
4 rings green pepper
4 T. uncooked rice
3 c. tomatoes, canned or stewed
1 c. celery, diced

Heat fat in skillet on high heat. Turn heat to medium low and brown chops well, approximately 15 minutes. Place a slice of onion and one pepper ring on each pork chop. Place one tablespoon rice in each ring. Pour tomatoes around the meat. Add celery; cover. Simmer for one hour. Yield: 4 servings.

Dorothy Heidlebaugh, Mendon Union H.S.
Mendon, Ohio

SPANISH PORK CHOPS

4 shoulder pork chops, cut ¾-in. thick
1 T. shortening
½ c. rice
1 c. onions, sliced
¼ c. green pepper, chopped
2 t. salt
¼ t. black pepper
½ t. paprika
1 t. sugar
1 20-oz. can tomatoes, juice, or puree

If using electric fry pan, set dial to 325°F. Brown pork chops in shortening. Add remaining ingredients. Cover skillet and cook for 1 hour and 15 minutes; stir occasionally. Add small amount of water as needed for rice. Yield: 4 servings.

Mrs. Marion R. Hessler, Gov. Mifflin H.S.
Shillington, Pennsylvania

POTATOES AND PORK CHOPS

8 pork chops
6-8 potatoes
1-1½ c. water
Salt and pepper to taste

Brown both sides of chops in heavy skillet. Remove chops. French cut potatoes. Put potatoes in skillet; cover with water. Lay browned chops on top of potatoes. Add salt and pepper. Cover and simmer for about 1 hour, or until potatoes are tender and most water gone. Yield: 4 servings.

Rozella Orosz, Monroeville H.S.
Monroeville, Ohio

SPANISH PORK CHOPS

6 pork chops
2 T. shortening
½ c. uncooked rice
1 qt. tomatoes
½ green pepper, diced
2 teaspoons salt
Pepper

Brown pork chops in melted shortening. Add remaining ingredients; cover. Bring to boil and simmer 1 hour. Yield: 6 servings.

Mary Ann DeVore, Fort Recovery H.S.
Fort Recovery, Ohio

TOMATOES AND PORK CHOPS

6 pork chops
2 T. shortening
½ c. rice
3 T. onion, chopped
3 T. green pepper, chopped
3¾ c. strained tomatoes or juice
2 t. salt
¼ t. pepper

Salt, pepper and flour pork chops; brown in hot fat on both sides. Add remaining ingredients; cover. When steaming reduce heat. Simmer for 45 minutes without removing lid. Yield: 6 servings.

Mrs. Jean Jacobs, Community Unit H.S.
Valmeyer, Illinois

CHICKEN DIVAN

2 boxes frozen broccoli spears, uncooked
5 chicken breasts, cooked
2 cans condensed cream of chicken soup, undiluted
1 c. sharp Cheddar cheese, grated
Paprika

Place the broccoli spears on the bottom of an electric skillet, arranging in one layer. Cover broccoli with sliced cooked chicken. Cover meat with undiluted soup and spread over top evenly. Sprinkle grated cheese and paprika over all; cook in covered electric skillet for 30 minutes at 375°F. NOTE: Turkey may be used instead of chicken. Yield: 6 servings.

Barbara McColgin, Union Area Jr.-Sr. H.S.
New Castle, Pennsylvania

CHICKEN PILAF

1 lge. onion, chopped
2 T. butter
1 cooked chicken, cut up
2 c. long-grain rice
1 No. 2½ can tomatoes
1 8-oz. can tomato sauce
1 t. salt, or to taste
Pepper to taste
¾ t. cinnamon

Saute onion in butter. Add chicken; brown slightly. Add rice, tomatoes and tomato sauce. Cover; cook until rice is done. Add chicken broth or water if needed. Stir in salt, pepper and cinnamon. Yield: 6-8 servings.

Britta Callamaras, Del Oro H.S.
Loomis, California

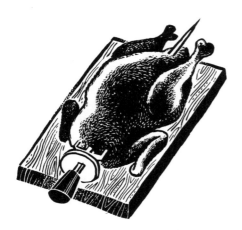

CHICKEN TETRAZZINI

2 7-oz. can chicken
2 cans cream of mushroom soup
1 2-oz. jar stuffed olives, sliced
1 4-oz. can sliced mushrooms
¼ c. milk
¼ c. Parmesan cheese, grated
2 T. onion, grated
1 T. parsley, chopped
1 t. salt
⅛ t. pepper
⅛ t. thyme
⅛ t. marjoram

Mix all ingredients. Pour into cold electric skillet; set temperature at 190°F. Cover, with vent closed; cook 30 minutes. Yield: 6-8 servings.

Mrs. Myrna McNair, Palestine H.S.
Palestine, Illinois

MODERNIZED CHICKEN ALMOND

2 T. margarine
¾ c. celery, cut in 1-in. pieces
¼ c. onion, sliced
2 c. cooked chicken, diced
½ c. canned mushrooms
1 T. cornstarch
3 T. soy sauce
1 c. canned clear consomme
1 c. almonds, toasted
Cooked rice

Melt butter; add celery and onion. Stir and cook 2 minutes. Add chicken and mushrooms; heat 8 minutes. Combine cornstarch, soy sauce and consomme; stir slowly into chicken mixture. Stir and cook slowly for 5 minutes. Stir in almonds. Serve hot on fluffy rice. Yield: 6 servings.

Sylvia Hayashi, Crescenta Valley H.S.
La Crescenta, California

SKILLET CHICKEN TETRAZZINI

1 T. butter or margarine
1 med. onion, chopped
1 stalk celery, chopped
2 c. cooked chicken, cut in strips
6 oz. uncooked fine spaghetti
1 t. salt
¼ t. pepper
1 can cream of chicken soup
2½ c. chicken broth or bouillon
1 3- to 4-oz. can sliced mushrooms
½ c. grated Parmesan cheese
Paprika

Melt butter in skillet. Add onion and celery; cook until clear. Arrange chicken in layer over this, then add spaghetti. Mix salt, pepper, soup and broth or bouillon. Pour over spaghetti being careful to moisten all of spaghetti. Place mushrooms over top. Sprinkle with Parmesan cheese and paprika. Cover and cook over high heat until steam escapes. Reduce heat immediately to simmer and cook 30 minutes. Yield: 4-6 servings.

Mrs. Edith Kreidler, St. Joseph H.S.
St. Joseph, Michigan

TURKEY TETRAZZINI

3 T. butter
1 med. onion, chopped
½ c. celery, chopped
2 c. cooked turkey, chopped
6 oz. spaghetti, uncooked
1 t. salt
¼ t. pepper
1 can cream of chicken soup
2 c. turkey broth
1 4-oz. can sliced mushrooms, drained
½ c. Parmesan cheese, grated
Paprika

(Continued on Next Page)

Saute onion and celery in butter until clear. Arrange layers of turkey and spaghetti. Combine salt, pepper, chicken soup and broth; pour over spaghetti being sure it is moistened. Top with mushrooms; sprinkle with cheese and paprika. Cover; cook slowly for 35 minutes. Yield 4-6 servings.

Beverly Anderson, Gridley Community H.S.
Gridley, Illinois

ALA PILAF

2 T. butter
1 T. onion, chopped
1 T. green pepper, chopped
2 c. water
2 beef bouillon cubes
1 c. Ala

Melt butter; add onion and pepper. Add water and the bouillon cubes. Stir until dissolved. Add the Ala. Cover and steam 20-30 minutes. Serve as an accompaniment to fowl. Browned hamburger or sausage may be added to make this a complete one-dish meal. NOTE: Ala is a processed whole wheat. Yield: 6 servings.

Mrs. Winifred Robinson, Homedale H.S.
Homedale, Idaho

HAZEL'S RICE DISH

1 stick margarine or butter
1 c. celery, chopped
½ c. onions, chopped
1 sm. box rice
1 can chicken-rice soup
2 cans water
1 sm. can sliced mushrooms

Melt butter in skillet; add celery and onions and brown thoroughly. Add remaining ingredients; cover and simmer until rice is cooked. Yield: 4-6 servings.

Mrs. John C. Griswold,
Carrollton Community Unit H.S.
Carrollton, Illinois

KIDNEY BEAN MEDLEY

¼ c. fat
½ c. green pepper, diced
2 med. onions, sliced
1 c. celery, diced
2½ c. canned kidney beans
1 t. salt
½ t. paprika
2 T. sugar
1 6-oz. pkg. elbow macaroni or spaghetti, broken
3½ c. canned tomatoes

Cook green pepper, onion and celery in fat until onion is clear. Sprinkle with beans, seasonings, sugar and macaroni. Do not stir. Top with tomatoes. Cover tightly; heat until steaming. Reduce heat; cook for 45 minutes. Stir to mix lightly. Yield: 6 servings.

Mrs. Ella Harrison, Windsor H.S.
Stockport, Ohio

ELECTRIC SKILLET MACARONI AND CHEESE

¼ c. butter
2 c. water
1½ t. salt
½ lb. macaroni
¾ c. milk
½ lb. cheese
Parsley

Preheat skillet to 250°F. Melt butter; add water, salt and macaroni. Bring to a boil, stirring occasionally. Turn temperature control to 200°F. Simmer with vent open, stirring occasionally, approximately 15 minutes. Stir in milk and cheese. Sprinkle with parsley. Yield: 4-5 servings.

Maxine King, Unity H.S.
Mendon, Illinois

RED BEANS AND RICE

½ c. onions, chopped
2 T. fat
1⅓ c. instant rice
1 t. salt
⅛ t. pepper
Liquid from beans plus tomato juice to make 2 c.
2 c. red kidney beans, drained
½ c. sharp cheese, grated

Saute onions in the fat over medium heat until tender, but not brown; stir occasionally. Add rice, salt, pepper and liquid. Bring quickly to a boil over high heat, uncovered, fluffing rice gently once or twice with a fork. Do not stir. Cover and simmer gently for 3 minutes. Remove from heat. Let stand 10 minutes. Add beans to rice mixture. Reheat, mixing lightly. Arrange in serving dish. Serve with cheese on the top. Yield: 4-6 servings.

Wilma Keeler, Cadillac H.S.
Cadillac, Michigan

SHRIMP NEWBURG

1 can frozen condensed cream of shrimp soup
¼ c. milk
1 10-oz. pkg. frozen peas
1 8- to 12-oz. pkg. frozen cooked and deveined
  shrimp
2 T. sharp cheese spread or ¼ c. cheese, cubed
1-2 T. mustard
1 t. lemon rind, grated (opt.)
1 can chow mein noodles

Combine soup and milk in skillet. Place block
of peas in center; arrange shrimp around block.
Add cheese spread and mustard. Cover; cook slowly for 15 minutes. Stir to blend. Add lemon
rind. Cover; cook 5 minutes. Serve on noodles.
Yield: 4 servings.

Elizabeth L. Stephenson, Brighton H.S.
Brighton, Colorado

TUNA-BROCCOLI CASSEROLE

1 pkg. frozen broccoli
1 sm. can tuna
1 can cream of chicken soup
2 T. mayonnaise
1 T. lemon juice
⅛ t. curry
Salt and pepper

Cook broccoli according to directions. Combine
remaining ingredients; heat thoroughly. Pour over
broccoli. Yield: 4 servings.

Helen McSparrin, Quakertown H.S.
Quakertown, Pennsylvania

TUNA TREASURE

1 pkg. frozen mixed vegetables
1 can cream of celery soup
½ soup can water
1 7-oz. can tuna fish
1 pkg. buttermilk refrigerator biscuits
2 T. butter, melted
Parsley

Place frozen vegetables that have been broken
up in large skillet. Add soup, water and tuna;
stir to mix. Place biscuits on top. Pour butter
over biscuits and sprinkle with parsley. Cover
skillet. Cook on high heat until steaming. Reduce
heat to low; simmer for 20 minutes. Yield: 6
servings.

Susan Leitzinger, West Branch Area H.S.
Morrisdale, Pennsylvania

WASH DAY SPAGHETTI

1 8-oz. pkg. shell macaroni
5 slices bacon, diced
1 med. onion, diced
1 can tomato sauce
1 can water

Prepare macaroni according to directions on package. Fry bacon and brown onions. Add tomato
sauce and water to cooked bacon and onions.
When macaroni is ready, drain and add to tomato
sauce mixture. Cook until sauce is about the
consistency of tomato sauce. Yield: 6-7 servings.

Mrs. Madeleine Beckman, Astoria H.S.
Astoria, Illinois

Cereal, Pasta, Egg & Cheese Dishes

BARLEY PILAF

½ lb. mushrooms, thinly sliced
4 T. butter or margarine
2 med. onions, coarsely chopped
1¾ c. barley
1 qt. rich chicken broth

Saute mushrooms in 2 tablespoons butter for 4-5 minutes; remove from skillet. Heat remaining butter and cook onions until they look wilted; remove from skillet. Pour in barley and cook very slowly until it turns a delicate brown. Add mushrooms and onions to barley and place in a large casserole. Pour on 1¾ cups chicken broth; cover tightly and bake 30 minutes at 350°F. Remove lid and add 1¾ cups chicken broth; bake 30 more minutes. If barley looks dry, add remaining broth. Avoid over cooking. Delicious served with wild game. Yield: 6-8 servings.

Mrs. Frances Dailey, Greater Greensburg
Salem Sr. H.S.
Greensburg, Pennsylvania

BREAKFAST CHEESE GRITS

¾ c. quick grits
3 c. boiling water
½ lb. sharp Cheddar cheese, grated
¾ stick butter
1 t. salt
2 eggs, beaten
Paprika

Cook grits in boiling water until thick; remove from heat. Stir in cheese and butter. Add salt and eggs, stirring until well mixed. Pour into an oiled casserole. Bake at 350°F. for 1 hour. Sprinkle generously with paprika the last 10 minutes of baking. Yield: 6-8 servings.

Armalea Hopperstad, Independence
Community College
Independence, Kansas

CHEESY GRITS CASSEROLE

1 qt. milk
1 c. quick grits
1 stick butter
¾ t. salt
¼ lb. Swiss cheese
¼ lb. Cheddar cheese
1 sm. can Parmesan cheese

Combine milk, grits, butter and salt; cook until firm. Pour into greased baking dish; chill. Cut into squares and slice horizontally. Combine cheeses; put a layer of mixture between sliced grits and on top. Bake at 300°F. for 25 minutes. Yield: 8-10 servings.

Zelma Pipes, Oak Ridge H.S.
Oak Ridge, Louisiana

BROILED MACARONI AND CHEESE

12 oz. macaroni
1 sm. onion, finely chopped
2 stalks of celery, finely chopped
4 T. butter or margarine
⅓ c. flour
3 c. milk
1 t. salt
Dash of pepper
¾ t. mustard
½ lb. American cheese, grated

Cook macaroni in boiling salted water until tender. Drain thoroughly and pour into a buttered casserole. Simmer onion and celery in melted butter for 5 minutes. Blend in flour; add milk, salt and pepper. Cook until sauce boils and thickens, stirring constantly. Remove from heat and add mustard and cheese, stirring until blended. Pour hot cheese sauce over hot macaroni. Place under broiler to brown. Yield: 6 servings.

Mrs. Mary M. Radford, Centralia Local School
Chillicothe, Ohio

EASY MACARONI AND CHEESE

2 c. uncooked macaroni
2 T. butter
2 T. flour
1 c. milk
1 c. Velveeta cheese
1 t. onion flakes

Cook macaroni in salted water; drain. Make white sauce using butter, flour and milk. Add cheese and onion, stir until cheese melts. Mix with macaroni. Bake at 350°F. for 1 hour. Yield: 6-8 servings.

Mrs. Joann Fell, Bettsville Local School
Bettsville, Ohio

FAVORITE MACARONI AND CHEESE

1 c. broken macaroni
1½ T. butter
½ t. salt
⅛ t. pepper
Dash of cayenne
1½ c. milk
⅓ lb. Cheddar cheese, grated or chopped
1 c. buttered soft bread crumbs

Cook macaroni according to package directions; drain and rinse. Melt butter; add flour and blend thoroughly. Add salt, pepper and cayenne. Add milk all at once; cook over moderate heat, stirring constantly until thickened. Add 1 cup of cheese to hot white sauce; stir until blended. Combine with macaroni. Sprinkle a layer of crumbs in a greased 1-quart baking dish. Add macaroni mixture. Top with remaining cheese and crumbs mixed together. Bake at 400°F. for 30 minutes or until sauce is bubbly and top is well browned. Yield: 4 servings.

Mrs. Sally McConnell, North Findley Street School
Punxsutawney, Pennsylvania

KAREN'S CASSEROLE

1 box elbow macaroni, cooked
¼ lb. Longhorn cheese
1 can Spam
1 med. green pepper
1 med. onion
4 lge. carrots
Salt and pepper to taste
1½ c. soda crackers, crushed
4 eggs, separated
1½ c. milk
⅓ c. butter, melted
1 can of cream of chicken soup

Coarsely grind macaroni, cheese, meat and vegetables. Add seasonings, cracker crumbs, beaten egg yolks, milk and butter. Beat egg whites and fold into mixture. Place in a casserole or loaf pan; bake 1 hour at 300°F. Slightly dilute soup and spread over casserole to serve. Yield: 8 servings.

Karen Mae Lindstrom, Anaheim H.S.
Anaheim, California

LENTEN DISH

2 c. macaroni
2 T. green pepper, chopped
1 t. onion
2 T. butter
1 sm. can mushrooms
1 can mushroom soup
¼ c. cheese, grated

Cook macaroni for 15 minutes. Add green pepper and onion to butter and brown. Combine all ingredients except cheese; sprinkle cheese on top. Bake 425°F. for 25 minutes. Yield: 6 servings.

Mrs. Emma Raboin, Carney H.S.
Carney, Michigan

MACARONI-BEEF CASSEROLE

1 6-oz. pkg. macaroni
¼ lb. dried beef, broken up
¼ c. green pepper, chopped
¼ c. butter
¼ cup flour
2½ c. milk
1 c. cheese, grated

Cook the macaroni in boiling salted water until tender; drain. Fry beef and green pepper in butter. Add flour and mix. Gradually add milk; cook until thick, stirring constantly. Add ¾ cup cheese. Combine sauce and macaroni; pour into greased 1½-quart casserole. Top with remaining cheese. Bake in 350°F. oven for 30 minutes. Yield: 6 servings.

Edith Wilcoxen, Valley H.S.
Fairview, Illinois

LENTEN MACARONI AND CHEESE

1 pkg. macaroni, cooked
1 can mushroom soup
½ lb. Cheddar cheese, cubed
½-¾ c. milk
⅛ t. pepper
½ t. salt
½ sm. onion, chopped

Thoroughly blend all ingredients; pour into a casserole. Bake 30-45 minutes at 350°F. Yield: 6-8 servings.

Mrs. Jeannine N. Brady, Crosby H.S.
Crosby, North Dakota

MACARONI AND CHEESE

4 T. butter, melted
4 T. flour
2 c. milk
1 t. salt
2 c. macaroni, cooked
⅓ lb. grated Cheddar cheese

Blend flour into butter to make a paste; add ½ cup milk. Stir constantly, adding remaining milk. Add salt. Place a layer of macaroni in a baking dish; sprinkle with grated cheese. Repeat layers; cover with sauce. Top with buttered crumbs if desired. Bake at 375°F. for 30 minutes. Yield: 4-6 servings.

Mrs. Marguerite Stetson, Parrish Jr. H.S.
Salem, Oregon

OLD-FASHIONED MACARONI AND CHEESE

1 c. macaroni
1½ c. scalded milk
1 c. soft bread crumbs
5 T. melted butter
½ green pepper, minced
1 sm. jar pimento, finely chopped
⅛ t. pepper
1 T. parsley, finely chopped
¼ t. onion salt (opt.)
½ t. salt
3 eggs, separated

Break macaroni in half; cook according to directions. Pour scalded milk over bread crumbs; add butter, green pepper, pimento, parsley and seasonings. Add egg yolks and blend well; add to cooked macaroni. Beat egg whites until frothy; fold into macaroni mixture and pour into a well buttered casserole. Bake at 350°F. for 50 minutes. Yield: 6 servings.

Sister Mary Ignatius, O.S.F. Madonna H.S.
Chicago, Illinois

MACARONI-CHEESE DISH

1 8-oz. pkg. elbow macaroni
2 cans cream of chicken soup
⅓ c. onions, chopped
2 T. pimento, chopped
4 hard-cooked eggs, diced
½ lb. Cheddar cheese, diced
½ lb. fresh mushrooms (opt.)
2 T. butter (opt.)

Cook macaroni according to package directions, reducing salt to 1 teaspoon; rinse and drain. Combine soup, onions, pimento, eggs and cheese with macaroni. Saute mushrooms in butter and add. Bake in a 2-quart casserole 25-30 minutes at 350°F. Yield: 6-8 servings.

This recipe submitted by the following teachers:
Mrs. Lila Wilkins, Smylie Wilson H.S.
Lubbock, Texas
Mrs. L. O. Lockwood, Whitewater H.S.
Cedar Grove, Indiana

PEANUT ACCENT FOR MACARONI AND CHEESE

1 12-oz. pkg. macaroni, cooked
5 T. butter or margarine, melted
3 T. flour
1½ t. salt
Cayenne pepper (opt.)
2¼ c. milk
1 c. Cheddar cheese, grated
1⅓ c. salted peanuts, chopped
⅓ c. fine buttered crumbs

Blend flour and seasonings into melted butter; add milk and cook slowly until thickened, stirring constantly. Arrange alternate layers of cooked macaroni, grated cheese and chopped peanuts in a greased 2-quart baking dish, saving some peanuts and cheese for the top. Cover with white sauce and sprinkle with buttered crumbs, peanuts and cheese; bake at 375°F. for 20 minutes. Yield: 6 servings.

Beverly Butts, Medford H.S.
Medford, Oregon

BAKED MACARONI WITH TOMATOES AND CHEESE

1 8-oz. pkg. macaroni
1 med. onion, chopped
2 T. butter
1 med. green pepper, cut in pieces
1 19-oz. can tomatoes
1 6-oz. can tomato paste
1 t. salt
¼ t. pepper
¾ lb. sharp Cheddar or American cheese

Place macaroni in a shallow, 2-quart casserole. Fry onion in butter until brown; add ½ cup water and all remaining ingredients except cheese. Bring to a boil; pour over macaroni. Cut 9 thin slices of cheese; shred remaining cheese. Add grated cheese to macaroni and stir lightly. Bake at 325°F. for 1 hour; stir once during baking. Top with sliced cheese, bake 5 minutes or until cheese melts. Yield: 4-6 servings.

Helen Sanecki, Cadillac Jr. H.S.
Detroit, Michigan

SPECIAL MACARONI AND CHEESE

1¼ c. scalded milk
¾ c. soft bread crumbs
3 T. butter
1½ c. macaroni, cooked
½ t. onion, chopped
1 t. salt
½ c. or more grated cheese
2 eggs, well beaten

Pour milk over crumbs and butter; add remaining ingredients in order listed. Mix thoroughly and place in greased casserole. Set in a pan of hot water; bake at 350-375°F. for 45 minutes or until lightly browned. Yield: 6 servings.

Helen Foote, Summit H.S.
Frisco, Colorado

QUICK MACARONI AND CHEESE

3 c. macaroni
2 T. salt
Butter or margarine
¾ lb. Longhorn cheese, cubed
1 sm. can tomato sauce
6-8 soda crackers, crumbled

Cook macaroni until tender in boiling salted water. Drain, leaving small amount of water. Add cheese and tomato sauce. Pour into greased 2-quart casserole. Top with cracker crumbs; dot with butter. Bake 25-30 minutes at 350°F. Yield: 6-8 servings.

Amy D. Thompson, Dolores H.S.
Dolores, Colorado

FRESH TOMATO MACARONI

4 lge. ripe tomatoes
2 T. brown sugar
2 t. salt
3 T. butter or margarine
1 c. processed cheese, coarsely grated
1 can cream of celery soup
1 8-oz. pkg. elbow macaroni, cooked

Skin tomatoes and cut into quarters; add sugar and salt. Cook over low heat 10-15 minutes or until juicy. Stir in butter, cheese and celery soup. Place a layer of macaroni in a greased baking dish; add a layer of sauce. Add remaining macaroni and tomato sauce. Bake at 375°F. for 30 minutes. Yield: 5-6 servings.

Sally Worth, Rancocas Valley Regional H.S.
Mount Holly, New Jersey

TOMATO-CHEESE MACARONI

2 c. uncooked macaroni
1 can condensed tomato soup
½ c. milk
2 c. Cheddar cheese, shredded
¼ c. parsley, chopped
2 T. buttered bread crumbs

Cook macaroni according to directions on package. Heat soup, milk and 1½ cups of cheese over low heat until cheese melts; add parsley. Blend with cooked macaroni; pour into a greased 2-quart casserole. Top with remaining cheese and buttered bread crumbs. Bake about 20 minutes at 400°F. Yield: 6 servings.

This recipe submitted by the following teachers:
Mrs. Betty Jo Hill, Carterville Community H.S.
Carterville, Illinois

Mrs. Gayle Jones, Gallatin H.S.
Gallatin, Tennessee

TOMATO-CHEESE-MACARONI BAKE

¼ c. onion, chopped
2 T. butter
1 can tomato soup
½ c. water
1 c. Cheddar cheese
2 c. cooked elbow macaroni
2 T. buttered bread crumbs

Lightly brown onion in butter. Stir in tomato soup, water and ¾ cup cheese; heat until cheese melts. Blend mixture with macaroni; pour into a greased 1½-quart casserole. Sprinkle ¼ cup shredded cheese and bread crumbs on top. Bake at 350°F. for 30 minutes. Yield: 4 servings.

Sister M. Pierre, Catherine McAuley H.S.
Brooklyn, New York

HORN OF PLENTY

1 T. onion, minced
3 T. butter
1 c. hot milk
1 t. salt
1 T. parsley
⅛ t. pepper
2 T. pimentos, minced
1 c. sharp cheese, diced
1 egg, slightly beaten
1½ c. cooked macaroni
1 c. soft bread crumbs

Cook onion in butter until clear; add milk, seasonings, pimento, cheese and egg. Heat until cheese is melted. Place macaroni in a casserole; top with crumbs. Cover with sauce. Bake at 325°F. for 35 minutes. Yield: 6-8 servings.

Emma K. Maughan, Weber County H.S.
Ogden, Utah

SCHOOL DAY FAVORITE

¼ lb. dried beef
3 T. butter, melted
3 T. flour
1½ c. milk
1 c. sharp cheese, grated
1 8-oz. pkg. macaroni, cooked

Blend beef, butter and flour; add milk and cook until thickened, stirring constantly. Add ¾ cup cheese. Combine sauce and macaroni; pour into a casserole. Top with remaining cheese. Bake at 350°F. for 30-40 minutes. Yield: 8 servings.

Mrs. Thelma Hause, Stevens H.S.
Claremont, New Hampshire

MACARONI AND HAM LOAF

½ c. butter
1½ c. scalded milk
2 c. cooked macaroni
1½ c. bread crumbs
1 c. grated cheese
1-2 c. cooked ham, chopped
4 eggs, slightly beaten
1 med. onion, minced
1 green pepper, minced
3 pimentos, minced
3 sprigs of parsley, minced (opt.)

Melt butter in hot milk. Carefully fold all ingredients together. Put into greased casserole; set in pan of water and bake at 350°F. for 1 hour. Serve with mushroom sauce. Yield: 12 servings.

This recipe submitted by the following teachers:
Mrs. Merle Twesme, Arcadia H.S.
Arcadia, Wisconsin

Ruth McDaniels, Neah-Kah-Nie H.S.
Rockaway, Oregon

MACARONI AND HAM CASSEROLE

2 lb. smoked ham, ground
½ lb. macaroni, cooked
1 T. mustard
1 med. onion, diced
2 eggs, beaten
Milk to cover

Combine ham, macaroni, mustard and onions. Place in a buttered casserole. Pour eggs and milk over casserole. Bake at 325°F. for 1 hour. Yield: 6-8 servings.

Eliza Ninmann, Gresham H.S.
Gresham, Wisconsin

MACARONI LOAF

1 c. macaroni, cooked
1 c. cheese, grated
1 c. soft bread crumbs
1 T. onion, chopped
1 T. chopped parsley
1 sm. pimento, chopped
½ c. melted butter
1 sm. green pepper, chopped (opt.)
1 c. scalded milk
3 eggs, separated

Combine all ingredients except egg whites. Beat egg whites until stiff; fold into mixture. Pour into a casserole; bake in a pan of water for 1 hour and 30 minutes at 350°F. Serve with mushroom sauce. NOTE: Egg yolks and whites may be beaten together and added. Yield: 6 servings.

This recipe submitted by the following teachers:
Sister Moira, OSB Saint Boniface H.S.
Cold Spring, Minnesota
Mrs. Billie Nowlin, Rising Star H.S.
Rising Star, Texas

MACARONI SOUFFLE

1½ c. scalded milk
1 c. soft bread crumbs
1½ c. Cheddar cheese, grated
1 c. cooked macaroni
3 eggs, separated
1 T. parsley, chopped
⅛ t. pepper
1 t. salt
1 T. onion, grated
¼ c. pimento, diced
3 T. melted butter or margarine

Pour hot milk over soft bread crumbs; add cheese. Cover and let stand until cheese melts. Add macaroni. Combine beaten egg yolks, parsley, salt, onion, pimento and melted shortening; add to cheese mixture. Beat egg whites until stiff; fold into mixture. Pour into a greased casserole and bake at 350°F. for 35 minutes or until set. Serve with mushroom sauce. Yield: 6-8 servings.

This recipe submitted by the following teachers:
Pauline K. Fish, Mount Lebanon H.S.
Pittsburgh, Pennsylvania
Catherine Stall, Greenville H.S.
Greenville, Michigan

MACARONI MOUSSE

1½ c. milk, scalded
¼ c. butter, melted
1 pimento, chopped
3 eggs, well beaten
1 c. macaroni, cooked
1 green pepper, diced
1 T. parsley, chopped
½ c. Cheddar cheese, grated
1 c. soft bread crumbs
1 T. onion, chopped

Combine all ingredients in order listed; pour into a greased 10x8-inch casserole. Bake at 350°F. for 40 minutes.

SAUCE:

1½ c. milk
4 T. flour
1 T. butter
¼ t. salt
Dash of paprika
1 can whole mushrooms
½ c. mushroom liquid
1 can shrimp

Combine milk, flour and butter; heat until thickened, stirring constantly. Add remaining ingredients; heat and mix well. Serve with macaroni mousse. Yield: 12 servings.

Elnor Alkio, McCune Jr. H.S.
Pendleton, Oregon

MACARONI PUFF

1 15¼-oz. macaroni in cheese-cream sauce
½ c. bread crumbs
2 T. pimento, chopped
2 T. green pepper, finely chopped
2 eggs, separated
¼ t. salt

Combine macaroni, crumbs, pimento, green pepper, beaten egg yolks and salt. Beat egg whites stiff and fold in mixture. Put in greased casserole. Bake for 45 minutes at 350°F. Yield: 4 servings.

Mrs. Phyllis Groninger, Tuscarora Valley H.S.
Port Royal, Pennsylvania

MOCK RAVIOLI

½ lb. ground round steak
1 clove garlic, minced
1 med. onion, chopped
1 can tomato paste
1 can tomato sauce
2 t. salt
1 t. oregano
1 t. basil
1 t. rosemary
¾ c. spinach juice
½ c. grated cheese
½ c. bread crumbs
¼ c. oil

(Continued on Next Page)

2 eggs
1 pkg. frozen spinach
½ lb. butterfly macaroni, cooked

Brown meat, half of garlic and onion; add tomato paste and sauce, 1 teaspoon salt, seasonings and spinach juice. Simmer 15 minutes. Combine remaining garlic and salt with cheese, bread crumbs, oil, eggs and spinach. Place layers of meat sauce, macaroni, spinach mixture, macaroni and sauce in a casserole. Top with Parmesan cheese if desired. Bake 1 hour at 300°F. Yield: 6 servings.

Joyce Sullivan, Saratoga H.S.
Saratoga, California

APPLE PIE CASSEROLE

2 c. cooked noodles
4 apples, pared
4 T. butter
1 t. cinnamon
¾ c. sugar

Cook noodles. Cut pared apples in eighths. Melt 2 tablespoons of butter in baking dish. Add half of noodles and apples. Sprinkle with half of cinnamon and sugar mixture; cover with remaining noodles. Dot with butter; sprinkle sugar-cinnamon mixture. Bake at 350°F. for 30-40 minutes. Yield: 6 servings.

Mrs. Judith B. Lindley, Bellflower Twp. H.S.
Bellflower, Illinois

BACON-NOODLE-CHEESE BAKE

½-¾ lb. hamburger
1½ c. fine noodles, cooked
1 No. 303 can tomatoes
½-1 t. salt
⅛ t. pepper
Bread crumbs
Grated American cheese
Bacon slices, halved

Brown meat. Combine meat, noodles, tomatoes and seasonings in a greased 2-quart casserole. Cover with a ¼-inch layer of bread crumbs and a layer of cheese. Top with bacon. Bake at 350°F. until bacon is browned. Yield: 6 servings.

Ruth Lang, Cromwell H.S.
Cromwell, Connecticut

BAKED NOODLES SUPREME

1 med. pkg. of noodles
1 can cream of mushroom soup
1 can cream of chicken soup
Bread crumbs

Cook noodles in boiling salt water. Place in baking dish. Heat soups and pour over noodles. Top with bread crumbs. Bake at 350°F. until soup bubbles. Let bake 10-15 minutes after soup begins to bubble. Yield: 6 servings.

G. Kathleen Booth, Grove City H.S.
Grove City, Ohio

BEEF AND NOODLE CASSEROLE

2 T. onion, finely chopped
2 T. fat
1 lb. hamburger
1½ t. salt
⅛ t. pepper
1 8-oz. pkg. wide noodles, cooked
1 can condensed cream of tomato soup
½ c. cheese, shredded

Fry onion in hot fat; add hamburger and brown thoroughly. Combine meat, seasonings, noodles and soup in a 3-quart casserole. Top with cheese. Bake at 350°F. for 30 minutes. Yield: 6-8 servings.

Mrs. Rosalyn Petersen, Federal Way H.S.
Federal Way, Washington

BERNICE'S FAVORITE CASSEROLE

½ green pepper, minced
½ c. celery, minced
½ c. onion, minced
1 T. butter
1 can chow mein noodles
¼ lb. salted cashew nuts
1 7-oz. can tuna
1 can cream of chicken soup
½ soup can water

Saute green pepper, celery and onion in butter. Put into a 1½-quart casserole. Add noodles, nuts and tuna. Dilute soup with water; pour over casserole. Bake at 375°F. for 15 minutes. Yield: 4 servings.

Kathleen P. Burton, Star Valley H.S.
Afton, Wyoming

CHEESEBURGER-NOODLE LOAF

4 oz. broad noodles
½ lb. ground beef
1 egg
¼ c. catsup
2 T. onion, chopped
¾ t. salt
Dash of pepper
¼ c. raw carrot, shredded
2 T. green pepper, chopped
2 T. butter, melted
2 slices American cheese
Buttered crumbs

Boil noodles until tender; drain and rinse. Mix ground beef, egg, catsup, onion, salt and pepper. Mix carrot, green pepper and butter with noodles. Place noodle mixture in a greased loaf pan. Spread meat mixture in a layer over noodles. Top with cheese; sprinkle with bread crumbs. Bake at 350°F. for 30 minutes. Yield: 4 servings.

Ruth Baumback, Harrisburg Union H.S.
Harrisburg, Oregon

CANADIAN HOT CASSEROLE

2 lb. ground beef
2 cloves garlic
4 8-oz. can tomato sauce
1 8-oz. pkg. cream cheese
1 pt. sour cream
6 green onions
1 lb. noodles, partially cooked
¼ lb. Cheddar cheese, grated
½ green pepper, diced

Shape ground meat into small balls and brown. Add garlic, tomato sauce, cream cheese, sour cream and onions; simmer for several minutes. Place noodles in casserole; pour beef mixture over noodles. Top with cheese and green pepper. Bake at 350°F. for 30 minutes. Yield: 4-6 servings.

Mrs. Barbara Arola, Murray H.S.
St. Paul, Minnesota

COMPANY CASSEROLE BAKE

1 lb. ground beef or veal
3 T. butter
2 8-oz. cans tomato sauce
½ lb. cottage cheese
1 8-oz. pkg. cream cheese, softened
¼ c. sour cream
⅓ c. scallions, snipped
1 T. green pepper, minced
½ lb. noodles, cooked

Saute meat in 1 tablespoon butter; stir in tomato sauce and remove from heat. Combine cottage cheese, cream cheese, sour cream, scallions and green pepper. Place half of noodles in a 2-quart casserole; cover with cheese mixture. Add remaining noodles; add remaining melted butter. Top with meat mixture. Bake 30 minutes at 350°F. Yield: 6 servings.

This recipe submitted by the following teachers:
Mrs. Dorothy Mitchell, Waterford H.S.
Waterford, Connecticut
Mrs. Kathryn O. Smith, Morristown H.S.
Morristown, Tennessee

CASSEROLE FOR COMPANY

1 8-oz. pkg. medium noodles
1½ lb. ground beef
2 T. butter
1 t. salt
Pepper to taste
¼ t. garlic salt
¼ t. celery salt
¼ t. rosemary, finely crushed
1 8-oz. can tomato sauce
1 c. creamed cottage cheese
1 c. sour cream
6 green onions, chopped
¼ c. green pepper, chopped
¾ c. American cheese, grated

Cook noodles until tender in boiling salted water; drain and rinse in cold water. Melt butter in skillet; add meat and stir until brown. Add salt, pepper, garlic salt, celery salt, rosemary and tomato sauce; simmer gently 5 minutes. Remove from heat. Combine cottage cheese, sour cream, onion, green pepper and noodles. Alternate layers of noodles and meat mixture in a 2-quart casserole. Top with grated cheese. Bake at 350°F. for 30 minutes. Yield: 6-8 servings.

Freda Teitzel, W. F. West H.S.
Chehalis, Washington

EASY CASSEROLE

1 lb. ground beef
½ lb. noodles
1 can mushroom soup
1 can cream of chicken soup
1 soup can water
1 c. celery, diced
¼-⅓ c. onion, finely chopped
½ t. salt
¼ t. pepper

Do not precook ingredients. Layer meat and noodles, celery and onion. Pour soups and water over layers. Sprinkle with salt and pepper. Bake 1 hour and 30 minutes at 350°F. Yield: 4-6 servings.

Donna Jean Pomerenke, Walnut Grove Public H.S.
Walnut Grove, Minnesota

GOURMET CASSEROLE

1 8-oz. pkg. thin noodles
1 c. mushroom soup
¾ c. stuffed olives, sliced
1¼ c. milk
½ c. onions, chopped
2 lb. ground beef
2 T. butter
½ lb. Cheddar cheese, chopped
2 T. chopped parsley
1 c. chow mein noodles

Cook noodles; drain. Add soup, olives and milk. Saute onions and meat in butter. Layer noodle mixture, meat, cheese and parsley in a casserole. Cover and bake at 350°F. for 50 minutes. Uncover; put chow mein noodles on top and bake 15 minutes more. Yield: 6-8 servings.

Mrs. June Barnett, Onekama Consolidated H.S.
Onekama, Michigan

HACIENDA HAMBURGER CASSEROLE

¾ lb. ground meat
¾ c. onions, chopped
2 T. oil
¼ c. ripe olives, sliced
1 c. celery, diced
1½ t. salt
¼ t. pepper
2 c. tomatoes
2 c. wide noodles
1 c. cheese, diced

(Continued on Next Page)

Brown meat and onion in oil. Remove from heat; add remaining ingredients. Mix well and place in casserole dish. Bake 45 minutes at 350°F. Yield: 4-6 servings.

Norah Baker, Klamath Union H.S.
Klamath Falls, Oregon

HAM-NOODLE CASSEROLE

2 T. butter
2 T. flour
1 c. milk
1 c. grated Cheddar cheese
1½ c. med. noodles, cooked
1 t. salt
2 T. catsup
1 T. horseradish
2 c. cooked ham, diced
1 c. cooked peas, drained
¼ c. soft bread crumbs, buttered

Melt butter over low heat; blend in flour. Gradually add milk; stir until smooth and thickened. Remove from heat; add cheese and stir until melted. Add remaining ingredients except crumbs. Mix well; pour into a 1½-quart casserole. Top with buttered crumbs. Bake at 350°F. until browned. Yield: 4 servings.

Faye B. Mitchell, Allen Consolidated School
Allen, Nebraska

HOT LUNCHEON DISH

1 pkg. egg noodles
1 sm. onion, chopped
Butter
1 lb. ground veal or beef
2 cans vegetable soup

Cook egg noodles in salted water for 10 minutes; drain. Fry onions in butter until crisp; add ground meat and brown. Mix together and bake at 400-425°F. for 30 minutes. Water may be added to prevent casserole from becoming dry. Yield: 6-8 servings.

Gudrun Harstad, Detroit Lakes H.S.
Detroit Lakes, Minnesota

JOE MAZETTI

2 T. fat
1 lb. hamburger
1 onion, sliced
1½ cans tomato soup or ½ can tomato paste
    and 1 c. water
1 sm. can mushrooms
6 stalks of celery, diced
½ green pepper, finely cut
1 T. lemon juice
Salt and pepper
½ lb. sharp cheese, chopped
1 8-oz. pkg. broad noodles

Melt fat; add meat and onions and cook until browned. Add remaining ingredients except noodles. Simmer 15 minutes to make a rich sauce. Cook noodles according to directions on package. Drain and mix with sauce. Cover; cook slowly 1 hour on top of stove or at 350°F. Yield: 6 servings.

Yvonne Elzinga, Payson H.S.
Payson, Utah

JOHN BAGHETTI

1 lb. pork, diced
1 lb. veal, diced
2 T. butter
1 c. celery, diced
3 med. onions, diced
2 T. green pepper, diced
1 pkg. med noodles, cooked
1 4-oz. can mushrooms
2 c. tomatoes
1 t. salt
⅛ t. pepper
1 T. Kitchen Bouquet

Brown meat in butter; add celery, onions and green pepper. Simmer until tender. Add remaining ingredients; bake in a greased casserole at 350°F. for 1 hour. Yield: 6-8 servings.

Mrs. Henrietta Mook, Mercer H.S.
Mercer, Pennsylvania

MEAT-CHEESE CASSEROLE

2½ c. noodles, cooked
5 T. butter
1 c. cottage cheese
6 oz. cream cheese
⅓ c. sour cream
½ c. onion, minced
2 T. green pepper, chopped
1 T. chives, chopped
1 t. salt
½ t. monosodium glutamate
¾ lb. ground beef
2 c. tomato sauce
½ t. Worcestershire sauce
3 drops Tabasco sauce

Blend 3 tablespoons butter into noodles; set aside. Thoroughly combine cheeses and sour cream; add chopped vegetables, ½ teaspoon salt and monosodium glutamate. Brown meat in remaining butter; stir occasionally to break up meat. Add tomato sauce, Worcestershire sauce, Tabasco sauce and ½ teaspoon salt. Pour a small amount of meat sauce in a casserole; add layers of half of noodles, cheese mixture and remaining noodles. Top with meat sauce. Bake at 350°F. for 50-60 minutes. Yield: 6 servings.

Mrs. Marilyn J. Fleener, Lakeview H.S.
Decatur, Illinois

NOODLE-BURGER CASSEROLE

1 lb. ground beef
¼ c. onion, chopped
1 t. salt
1 can condensed beef bouillon
1 1-lb. can tomatoes
1 4-oz. can mushrooms and liquid
1 8-oz. pkg. noodles
½ c. milk
1 c. Cheddar cheese, shredded
1½ t. parsley flakes
1½ t. Worcestershire sauce
⅛ t. pepper
1 T. flour

Brown ground beef; drain off fat. Stir in onions and salt. Add bouillon, tomatoes, mushrooms and liquid; bring to a boil. Add noodles; simmer 10 minutes or until tender. Add remaining ingredients except ½ cup of cheese. Place in a 2-quart casserole. Sprinkle with remaining cheese. Bake at 350°F. for 20-30 minutes, until cheese melts and is golden browned. Yield: 6 servings.

Mildred Bartosh, Dodge H.S.
Dodge, Nebraska

NOODLE CASSEROLE FOR A CROWD

2 qt. broken noodles
12 c. milk
24 eggs, separated
2½ lb. cheese, grated
8 c. bread crumbs
2 c. butter
2 T. pimento, finely chopped
Salt to taste
White pepper to taste
½ c. parsley, chopped
½ c. onions, finely chopped
1 T. paprika

Cook noodles in salted water; drain. Heat milk in double boiler; stir in beaten egg yolks. Remove from heat; add cheese. Add crumbs, butter, pimento, salt, pepper, parsley and onions. Beat egg whites; add to noodle mixture carefully. Put into buttered pan; sprinkle with paprika. Bake at 350°F. for 1 hour. Yield: 50 servings.

Sister Nicola Maria, Holy Names Academy H.S.
Spokane, Washington

NOODLE-CHEESE CASSEROLE

4 eggs
¾ c. sour cream
1 t. salt
½ t. onion salt
1 T. sugar
4 T. butter, melted
2 c. cottage cheese
5 c. cooked fine noodles
¼ c. fine bread crumbs

Beat eggs with sour cream, salt, onion salt and sugar. Blend in 2 tablespoons melted butter. Stir in cottage cheese and noodles. Place mixture in buttered 2-quart casserole. Mix bread crumbs with 2 tablespoons butter; sprinkle over top. Bake at 375°F. for 40 minutes. Yield: 6-8 servings.

Mrs. Caryl Wright, College Area Schools
State College, Pennsylvania

NOODLE HOT DISH

1 lb. hamburger
¼ c. onions, chopped
1 No. 2 can tomatoes
1 8-oz. can tomato sauce
½ lb. broad noodles
½ t. garlic salt
½ t. salt
¼ t. pepper
1½ t. oregano
2 T. olive oil
½ lb. sharp cheese, grated

Brown hamburger and onions. Add tomatoes, tomato sauce and seasonings. Simmer about 30 minutes. Cook noodles in salted water about 10 minutes; drain. Add hamburger mixture to noodles in a baking dish. Cover with grated cheese. Bake about 25 minutes at 325°F. Yield: 6 servings.

Mrs. Nancy Hoffman, McComb Local School
McComb, Ohio

NOODLE LOAF

1 8-oz. pkg. noodles
½ c. carrots, shredded
¼ c. green peppers, chopped
¼ c. butter
1 lb. ground beef
¼ c. onion, chopped
½ T. salt
¼ t. pepper
2 eggs
½ c. catsup
Cheese slices
Buttered bread crumbs

Cook noodles in salted water as directed on package; drain. Add carrots, green peppers and butter. Place in casserole. Combine remaining ingredients except cheese and crumbs; spread over noodle mixture. Cover with cheese slices and buttered bread crumbs. Bake 45 minutes at 350°F. Yield: 8 servings.

Mrs. Leona Bates, Lakewood Jr. H.S.
Woodland, Michigan

NOODLE-RIPE OLIVE CASSEROLE

1 8-oz. pkg. thin noodles
1 med. onion, diced
1½-2 lb. hamburger
½ green pepper, diced
1 garlic clove, chopped
2 T. oil
1 c. ripe olives, sliced
Salt to taste
2½ c. tomatoes
½ c. grated cheese
1 t. chili powder

Cook noodles in boiling water until tender. Brown onion, hamburger, green pepper and garlic in oil. Add olives, salt, tomatoes, cheese and chili powder. Alternate layers of noodles and meat mixture in a casserole. Bake at 375°F. for 35 minutes. Yield: 8 servings.

Donna Young, Buckley H.S.
Buckley, Michigan

NOODLES ROMANOFF

6 oz. broad noodles
2 c. sour cream
1 c. cottage cheese
¼ c. onion, finely chopped
1 t. Worcestershire sauce
½ t. salt
⅛ t. pepper
Paprika (opt.)
⅓ c. chives, chopped
Parmesan cheese

Cook noodles until tender; drain. Add 1 cup sour cream, cottage cheese, onion and seasonings. Turn into a 1½-quart casserole. Sprinkle with paprika. Bake at 350°F. for 45 minutes. Combine remaining sour cream with chives; put 1 tablespoon on each serving. Sprinkle with Parmesan cheese. Yield: 6 servings.

Mrs. Norma Gill, Chenoa H.S.
Chenoa, Illinois

NOODLES ROMANOFF

1 T. butter
1½ T. flour
1 c. milk
1 c. cottage cheese
1 c. sour cream
2 T. Parmesan cheese, grated
2 c. Cheddar cheese, grated
½ t. liquid garlic
1 T. onion, minced
1 8-oz. pkg. med. noodles, cooked
¼ c. buttered bread crumbs

Melt butter in saucepan; add flour and cook until bubbly. Add milk, stirring constantly until thickened. Add remaining ingredients except bread crumbs. Pour into baking dish. Sprinkle with bread crumbs. Bake at 375°F. for 20-25 minutes. Yield: 6 servings.

Cornelia M. Merwin, Lower Dauphin Joint School
Hummelstown, Pennsylvania

NUTTY NOODLE CASSEROLE

1½ lb. ground beef
½ c. onions, chopped
2 c. thin egg noodles
1 can mushroom soup
1 c. milk
2 oz. cheese
1 t. soy sauce
1 t. salt
16 stuffed olives, halved
4 oz. salted peanuts, chopped

Cook noodles in salted water. Saute beef and onions in small amount of shortening; add noodles. Dilute soup with milk and add to noodle and beef mixture. Add cheese, soy sauce and salt. Place mixture in a 2-quart casserole; top with olives. Sprinkle with peanuts. Bake at 350°F. for 30 minutes. Yield: 6-8 servings.

Donna Faye Reuther, Valier H.S.
Valier, Montana

NUTTY NOODLES

1 8-oz. pkg. fine noodles
2 lb. ground beef
1 med. onion, finely chopped
1 med. green pepper, chopped
1 can mushroom soup
1½ c. milk
½ lb. American Cheddar cheese, grated
1 can chow mein noodles
½ lb. salted mixed nuts

Cook noodles. Brown ground beef, onion and green pepper. Pour off grease; add to noodles. Cream in mushroom soup and milk. In medium oblong casserole, arrange alternate layers of beef, noodles and cheese. Bake covered at 350°F. for 30 minutes. Add chow mein noodles and nuts; bake uncovered for another 30 minutes. Yield: 8 servings.

Ann Callison, Ankeny H.S.
Ankeny, Iowa

PARTY HAM CASSEROLE

¼ lb. med. noodles
2 c. boiling water
1 t. salt
1 can cream of mushroom soup
1 T. onion, grated
2 t. mustard
1 c. sour cream
2 c. cooked diced ham
½ c. chow mein noodles or toasted slivered almonds

Cook noodles in salted water until tender; drain and rinse with cold water. Heat soup in a saucepan; add onion, mustard and cream. Mix and heat thoroughly. In a greased 1½-quart casserole, place layers of noodles, ham and sauce; repeat layers. Sprinkle with chow mein noodles or nuts. Bake at 325°F. for 30 minutes. Yield: 8-10 servings.

Mrs. Elizabeth Sweet, Mt. Morris H.S.
Mt. Morris, Illinois

SALMON-NOODLE CASSEROLE

1 8-oz. pkg. noodles
2 T. butter
2 T. flour
2 t. mustard
Salt and pepper to taste
1/8 t. nutmeg
2 c. milk
1 can salmon
2 T. lemon juice
1/4 c. parsley
2 T. peanut butter
1/2 c. bread crumbs

Cook noodles according to package directions. Melt butter; add flour, mustard, salt, pepper and nutmeg. Gradually stir in milk; cook 1 minute. Combine noodles and sauce; add salmon, lemon juice and parsley. Place in a greased casserole. Cut peanut butter into bread crumbs; sprinkle on top. Bake at 350°F. for 20-25 minutes. Yield: 6 servings.

Mrs. Elva Whitehouse, Galva H.S.
Galva, Illinois

SAUSAGE-NOODLE CASSEROLE

1 2-lb. pkg. pork sausage
1 med. onion, chopped
2 cans tomato soup
Dash of oregano
Garlic salt to taste
1 6-oz. pkg. noodles
Crumbs or Parmesan cheese

Brown sausage; drain off fat. Add remaining ingredients except noodles and crumbs; simmer 1 hour. Cook noodles in salted boiling water until tender; drain. Add to meat or arrange in casserole. Sprinkle with crumbs or grated cheese; brown quickly at 400°F. Yield: 6-8 servings.

Mrs. Marcella Hromy
Our Lady of Providence H.S.
Clarksville, Indiana

JAN'S SPANISH NOODLES

4 oz. fine noodles
1 onion, finely chopped
1 green pepper, chopped
Fat
1 lb. hamburger
1 No. 2½ can tomatoes
1 t. sugar
1/4 c. stuffed olives, chopped
1/4 lb. sharp cheese, grated
Salt and pepper to taste

Cook noodles in salted water; drain. Saute onions and peppers in fat; add hamburger and brown. Combine all ingredients; pour into oiled casserole. Bake 30 minutes at 350°F. Yield: 4 servings.

Martha Wreath Streeter, Wamego H.S.
Wamego, Kansas

SPANISH NOODLE CASSEROLE

1 lb. hamburger
1 onion, chopped
1/2 green pepper, chopped
1 can peas
1 can tomato soup
Salt and pepper to taste
1 pkg. noodles, cooked
Bacon strips
Bread crumbs

Saute hamburger, onion and pepper until browned. Add peas, soup, seasonings and noodles; blend well. Place in a casserole; cover with bacon and bread crumbs. Bake at 400°F. until bacon is browned and crisp. Yield: 6 servings.

Mrs. Anita Lewis, Cumberland Valley H.S.
Mechanicsburg, Pennsylvania

SOUR CREAM-NOODLE BAKE

1 8-oz. pkg. medium noodles
1 lb. lean ground beef
1 T. butter
1/8 t. pepper
1 t. salt
1/4 t. garlic salt
1 c. tomato sauce or puree
1 c. creamed cottage cheese
1 c. sour cream
1/2-1 c. green onions, chopped
3/4-1 c. sharp Cheddar cheese, shredded

Cook noodles in boiling salted water; rinse in cold water and drain. Brown meat in butter; add salt, pepper, garlic salt and tomato sauce. Simmer for 5 minutes. Combine cottage cheese, sour cream, onions and noodles. Alternate layers of noodle mixture and meat mixture in a 2-quart casserole, beginning with noodles and ending with meat. Top with shredded cheese. Bake at 350°F. for 20-25 minutes or until cheese is melted and browned. Yield: 8 servings.

This recipe submitted by the following teachers:
Mary Myers, Barry Community Unit
Barry, Illinois

Mrs. Alma Hicks, Elverado H.S.
Elkville, Illinois

TAMALE TALIARINI

1 bud of garlic, finely cut
2 T. butter
1 8-oz. pkg. noodles
2 sm. cans tomato sauce
1 sm. can whole-kernel corn
1 4½-oz. can ripe olives, chopped
1 can tamales, cut in 1-inch pieces
1/2 lb. cheese, grated

Saute garlic in butter. Cook noodles in boiling salted water; drain. Add 1 can tomato sauce, corn, olives and garlic. Put in greased casserole in layers alternately with tamales. Put grated cheese and can of tomato sauce on top. Bake at 350°F. for 30 minutes. Yield: 6 servings.

Mrs. Evelyn Gose Owens, Valley H.S.
Albuquerque, New Mexico

AMERICAN LASAGNA

1 lb. ground beef
2 cloves of garlic, chopped
1. T. hot fat
1 6-oz. can tomato paste
1 No. 2 can tomatoes
1 t. salt
¾ t. pepper
½ t. oregano
1 8-oz. pkg. wide noodles
1 8-oz. pkg. Swiss cheese, cut up
1 12-oz. carton cottage cheese

Brown ground beef and garlic in hot fat. Add tomato paste, tomatoes, salt, pepper and oregano. Cover and simmer 20 minutes. Cook noodles according to package directions. Alternate layers of cooked noodles, Swiss cheese, cottage cheese and meat sauce. Bake at 350°F. for 20-30 minutes. Serve with Parmesan cheese. Yield: 6-8 servings.

Mrs. Joan Bull, Dallas Jr. H.S.
Dallas, Oregon

AMERICAN CHEESE LASAGNA

1 box lasagna noodles, cooked
1 lb. ground beef
2 cloves garlic, crushed
2 T. oil
1 sm. onion, chopped
1 No. 2½ can tomatoes
½ t. crushed oregano
1 t. salt
⅛ t. pepper
1 T. butter
8 slices American cheese
3 hard-cooked eggs, sliced
Shredded cheese

Saute garlic in oil; remove garlic and add ground beef and brown. Add onion and saute for 5 minutes. Add tomatoes, salt, pepper, butter and oregano; simmer 30-60 minutes. Place alternate layers of meat sauce, noodles, sliced cheese and eggs in a casserole. Repeat layers; top with shredded cheese. Bake at 350°F. for 45 minutes. Yield: 6-8 servings.

Sui Inn Young, Waialua H.S.
Waialua, Hawaii

AMERICAN-STYLE LASAGNA

1 lb. ground beef
¼ t. garlic powder
½ c. Parmesan cheese, grated
2 6-oz. can tomato sauce
1½ t. salt
⅛ t. pepper
½ t. oregano
1 T. onion, chopped
1 8-oz. pkg. wde noodles
1 8-oz. pkg. Mozzarella cheese
1 12-oz. carton cottage cheese

Brown beef, garlic and Parmesan cheese; add tomato sauce, seasonings and onion. Cover and simmer 20 minutes. Cook noodles according to directions on package. In large casserole, alternate layers of meat sauce, noodles, cheese and cottage cheese. Bake at 350°F. for 25 minutes. Yield: 6 servings.

Mrs. Lorn Pracht, Prentice H.S.
Prentice, Wisconsin

BAKED LASAGNA WITH HOME-MADE NOODLES

NOODLES:

1 c. flour
2 egg whites
¼ t. salt

Combine flour, egg whites and salt; mix well. Add small portions of water until dough forms a soft ball. Divide dough into 2 sections; roll each half into a rectangle ¼ inch thick on a floured board. Cut into strips 2 inches wide and 4-6 inches long. Cook noodles in 2 quarts of salted water for 3-5 minutes.

1 lb. ground beef or Italian sausage
1 clove garlic, minced
3 T. parsley flakes
1 T. basil
3½ t. salt
1 1-lb. can tomatoes
2 6-oz. cans tomato paste
3 c. cream-style cottage cheese
2 eggs, beaten
½ t. pepper
½ c. grated Parmesan cheese
1 lb. Mozzarella cheese, thinly sliced

Brown meat; drain excess fat. Add garlic, 1 tablespoon parsley flakes, basil, 1½ teaspoons salt, tomatoes and tomato paste. Simmer uncovered for 30 minutes stirring occasionally. Combine cottage cheese, eggs, remaining seasonings and Parmesan cheese. Place half of noodles in a 13x9x2-inch baking dish; spread half of cottage cheese mixture over noodles. Add half of Mozzarella cheese and half of meat sauce. Repeat layers. Bake at 375°F. for 30 minutes. Let stand 10-15 minutes before cutting squares to serve. NOTE: If desired, one 10-ounce package of lasagna noodles may be used. Yield: 12 servings.

This recipe submitted by the following teachers:

Mrs. Paul Messersmith, Cornwall-Lebanon
Suburban Joint Schools
Cornwall, Pennsylvania

Mrs. Carole Childers, Johnston City H.S.
Johnston City, Illinois

Elizabeth G. Voland, Franklin Community H.S.
Franklin, Indiana

ANDERSON'S LASAGNA

1 lb. ground beef
1 med. onion, chopped
1 6-oz. can mushrooms
1 6-oz. can tomato paste
1¾ c. tomato juice
1½ t. salt
¼ t. pepper
1 t. garlic powder
½ t. oregano
½ t. parsley flakes
1 6-oz. pkg. broad noodles
1 c. American cheese, shredded
1 c. Swiss cheese, shredded
1 c. Mozzarella cheese, shredded

Brown ground beef and onions. Add mushrooms, tomato paste, tomato juice, salt, pepper, garlic powder, oregano and parsley flakes. Simmer over low heat for 30 minutes, stirring occasionally. Cook noodles by directions on package. Place noodles, cheese and sauce in a 2-quart casserole. Cook at 350°F. for 45 minutes. Yield: 6 servings.

Virginia Anderson, Bendle H.S.
Flint, Michigan

DELICIOUS LASAGNA

2½ c. tomatoes
1 6-oz. can tomato paste
2 cans tomato sauce
2 cloves garlic
3 T. dried parsley
1 T. basil
1 T. oregano
5 t. salt
Pepper
1 med. onion, diced
2 lb. hamburger
1 carton cottage cheese
2 eggs, beaten
½ c. Parmesan cheese
1 box lasagna noodles, cooked
1 lb. Mozzarella cheese, sliced

Combine tomatoes, tomato paste, tomato sauce, garlic, 1 tablespoon parsley, basil, oregano, 3 teaspoons salt, dash of pepper and onion; simmer for 2 hours. Brown hamburger and add to sauce. Combine the remaining 2 tablespoons parsley and 2 teaspoons salt with cottage cheese, eggs, ½ teaspoon pepper and Parmesan cheese. Place a layer of noodles in a greased 12x16-inch pan. Add a layer of sauce, a layer of cottage cheese mixture, and strips of Mozzarella cheese. Bake at 350°F. for 45-60 minutes. Yield: 8-10 servings.

Mrs. Kathryn Anderson, Iola-Scandinavia H.S.
Iola, Wisconsin

EASY LASAGNA

12-oz. wide noodles
1 lb. hamburger
1 onion, minced
1 T. green pepper, minced
½ t. garlic salt
32-oz. tomato sauce

1 lb. cottage cheese
1 lb. sliced American cheese
Parmesan cheese, grated

Cook noodles in 4-quarts of salted boiling water. Saute meat; add onion, pepper and garlic salt. Simmer 10 minutes. Add 1-quart tomato sauce. Drain noodles; rinse with cold water. Alternate layer of noodles, cheeses and remaining tomato sauce until dish is filled. Bake at 300°F. for 30 minutes. Yield: 10-12 servings.

Mrs. Clifton E. Whitney, Northfield H.S.
Northfield, Vermont

FLAVORFUL LASAGNA

1 lb. hamburger
½ onion, chopped
Olive oil
1 10½-oz. can tomato paste
2 garlic cloves, chopped
1 t. salt
½ t. pepper
2 T. oregano
¼ t. dried celery
1 tomato paste can water
1 carton smooth curd cottage cheese
1 pkg. lasagna noodles, cooked
½ lb. Mozzarella cheese
12 oz. Scamorze cheese

Brown onion and hamburger in olive oil; add tomato paste, garlic and seasonings. Add water and simmer 15 minutes. Add cottage cheese; stir until blended. Place alternate layers of noodles, cheese, and sauce in an oblong pan. Bake 30 minutes at 350°F. NOTE: For better flavor, let sauce stand overnight before using. Yield: 8 servings.

Mrs. Sandra K. Binder
New Athens Community H.S.
New Athens, Illinois

JANET'S LASAGNA

1-2 lge. onions
Olive oil
1-2 lb. hamburger
Garlic or garlic powder
1 No. 2½ can tomatoes
1 can tomato paste (opt.)
1-1½ T. Italian seasoning
½ lb. lasagna noodles
8 oz. Mozzarella cheese
Parmesan cheese, shredded or grated

Saute onions in oil; add hamburger and garlic and brown. Add tomatoes, tomato paste and seasoning; simmer 1 hour or until thickened. Cook noodles; drain. Layer noodles, meat and cheese in a greased casserole. Bake at 350°F. for 20 minutes. NOTE: 2 cans tomato puree and ½ puree can of water may be substituted for canned tomatoes. Yield: 6 servings.

Janet Vogel, Eureka H.S.
Eureka, Illinois

LASAGNA

1 lb. ground beef
¼ c. onion, minced
1 clove garlic, minced
1 6-oz. can tomato paste
1 No. 2½ can tomatoes
¼ t. pepper
2 t. salt
½ t. oregano
¼ t. basil
½ lb. lasagna noodles
½ lb. Mozzarella cheese
¾ lb. Romano cheese
½ c. grated Parmesan cheese

Cook ground beef, onion and garlic over medium heat until brown. Add tomato paste, tomatoes, salt, pepper, basil and oregano. Cook over low heat about 15 minutes. Cook lasagna noodles, adding a little cooking oil to keep from sticking; drain. Grease a 2½-quart casserole. Arrange layers of tomato and meat mixture, Parmesan cheese, noodles, Mozzarella and Romano cheese. Repeat with as many layers as desired, ending with meat mixture and Parmesan cheese. Bake at 350°F. for 30-35 minutes. Yield: 6-8 servings.

Mrs. G. Wayne Ross, Upper St. Clair H.S.
Bridgeville, Pennsylvania

LASAGNA WITH CLAM SAUCE

6 strips or 4-oz. lasagna noodles
1¾ t. salt
1 T. olive oil
2 qt. boiling water
1 10½-oz. can clams, minced
2 T. butter or margarine
¼ c. onion, finely chopped
½ clove garlic, finely chopped
2 T. flour
⅛ t. pepper
Dash of cayenne pepper
2 c. stewed tomatoes
⅓ c. grated Parmesan cheese
1 T. parsley, finely chopped
6 slices Mozzarella cheese

Cook noodles, 1½ t. salt and olive oil in boiling water until tender, stirring occasionally. Drain and rinse. Drain clams. Melt butter in saucepan; add onion and garlic. Saute gently about 3 minutes. Blend in flour, remaining salt, pepper and and cayenne pepper. Add tomatoes gradually and and cook until thickened, stirring constantly. Stir in Parmesan cheese, clams and parsley. Remove from heat. Make layers of lasagna and clam sauce in a greased baking dish. Top with Mozzarella cheese. Bake at 375°F. for 25-30 minutes or until mixture is bubbly and cheese melted. Yield: 4 servings.

Mary Woodmencey, West Brook Jr. H.S.
Paramus, New Jersey

LASAGNA

1¼ lb. ground beef
1¾ c. onion, chopped
½ clove garlic, crushed
½ c. green pepper, chopped
1 c. celery, diced
1 T. oil
1 No. 2½ can tomatoes
1 can tomato paste
2 t. salt
¼ c. water
½ t. sweet basil
1 t. oregano
1 t. vinegar
Dash of black pepper
2 bay leaves
1 sm. can mushrooms
¼ lb. lasagna noodles, cooked
½ c. cottage cheese
6 oz. Mozzarella cheese
¾ c. Parmesan cheese

Combine beef, onions, garlic, green pepper and celery; brown in oil. Add tomatoes, tomato paste, seasonings and mushrooms; simmer for 2-3 hours. Stir occasionally. Place alternate layers of sauce, noodles and cheese in a buttered casserole. Bake at 350°F. for 30 minutes. Yield: 6 servings.

Margaret Scholtz, Waldport H.S.
Waldport, Oregon

SHORT-CUT LASAGNA

1 lb. ground beef
3½ c. canned tomatoes
1 c. seasoned tomato sauce
1-2 envelopes spaghetti sauce mix
2 cloves garlic, minced
Salt to taste
1 8-oz. pkg. lasagna or wide noodles
1 8-oz. pkg. sliced Mozzarella cheese
1 c. cream-style cottage cheese
½ c. Parmesan cheese, grated

Brown meat slowly; spoon off excess fat. Add tomatoes, tomato sauce, spaghetti mix and garlic. Simmer 40 minutes, stirring occasionally. Salt to taste. Cook noodles in boiling salted water until tender; drain and rinse in cold water. Layer half of noodles, one-third of sauce, half of Mozzarella and half of cottage cheese. Repeat layers, ending with sauce. Top with Parmesan cheese. Bake at 350°F. for 25-30 minutes. Let stand 15 minutes; cut into squares. Yield: 6-8 servings.

This recipe submitted by the following teachers:
Mary Nan Fitch, Electra H.S.
Electra, Texas
Mrs. Eleanor Roberts
Thompsonville Community H.S.
Thompsonville, Illinois
Dorothy Faulk, Burkburnett H.S.
Burkburnett, Texas
Cora Mae Kintz, Mount Terrace H.S.
Mountlake Terrace, Washington

MACARONI LASAGNA

½ lb. macaroni
3 t. salt
1 lge. onion, diced
1½-2 lb. hamburger
3½ c. tomato juice
1 6-oz. can tomato paste
3 cloves, grated
1 lge. garlic bud, grated
1½ t. oregano flakes
1 t. sugar
½ lb. Old English cheese, cut in strips

Boil macaroni and 1 teaspoon salt in water. Cook about 20 minutes over low heat; do not drain. Fry ground beef until brown. Cook onion until brown. Pour off fat; add 1 teaspoon salt. Add tomato juice and paste. Grate cloves and garlic; add 1 teaspoon salt, oregano flakes and sugar. Blend sauce mix with macaroni, ground beef and cheese; top with a few strips of cheese. Bake at 350°F. for 30 minutes. If mixture seems dry, add boiling water. Yield: 8 servings

Mrs. Norine Bydalek, Franklin H.S.
Franklin, Nebraska

SOUR CREAM LASAGNA

1 8-oz. pkg. lasagna noodles
1 lb. ground beef
¼ t. garlic juice
½ t. salt
2 cans Spanish-style tomato sauce
1 3-oz. pkg. cream cheese
½ pt. sour cream
3 T. cottage cheese
6 green onions with tops, sliced
½ c. Cheddar cheese, grated

Cook noodles 20 minutes; rinse in cold water. Brown meat; add garlic juice, salt, tomato sauce and a little water. Simmer over low heat for 15 minutes. Combine all remaining ingredients except cheese. Alternate layers of noodles, meat sauce and cream cheese mixture in a 9x12-inch casserole; top with grated cheese. Bake at 350°F. for 45 minutes. Yield: 6-8 servings.

Mrs. Margaret J. Wahl, Schneider Vocational H.S.
Stockton, California

LASAGNA

1½ lb. ground beef
2 T. shortening
1 c. onion, chopped
2 cloves garlic, minced
1 12-oz. can tomatoes
2 6-oz. cans tomato paste
2½ t. salt
½ t. pepper
1 t. basil
1 t. oregano
1 bay leaf
1 pkg. broad noodles, cooked
½ lb. sliced Mozzarella cheese
¼ c. Parmesan cheese

Brown beef in shortening and pour off drippings. Add onion and garlic; cook until tender. Add tomatoes, tomato paste and seasonings; cover tightly and simmer. Remove bay leaf. Arrange half of noodles in a greased, oblong baking dish; add half of meat sauce and cover with strips of Mozzarella cheese. Repeat layers with remaining noodles, meat sauce and cheese. Sprinkle with Parmesan cheese. Bake at 350°F. for 30 minutes. Yield: 8 servings.

Mrs. Patricia Blair, Brownsburg H.S.
Brownsburg, Indiana

AFRICAN CHOW MEIN

5 t. salt
5 lb. ground beef
4 c. rice
10 med. onions, chopped
8 c. celery, chopped
3 4-oz. cans mushroom bits
8 cans mushroom soup
8 cans chicken and rice soup
8 c. water
Chow mein noodles

Brown meat; add onion and celery and heat. Combine remaining ingredients; add meat mixture. Bake 1½-2 hours at 325°F. Serve with chow mein noodles on top. Yield: 60 servings.

Judith Adams, Stillwater H.S.
Stillwater, Minnesota

CASHEW NUT CASSEROLE

3½ c. boiling water
1 c. rice
1 lb. ground beef
2 c. celery
1 sm. onion
1 T. brown sugar
5 T. soy sauce
1 sm. can mushrooms
½ c. cashew nuts

Pour boiling water over rice; let stand for a few minutes. Combine all ingredients except nuts. Bake at 350°F. for 1 hour and 30 minutes. Add cashew nuts 10 minutes before done.

Mrs. Karen Williams, Perham H.S.
Perham, Minnesota

CHEESE-RICE CASSEROLE

3 c. cooked rice
1 c. parsley, chopped
3 T. green pepper, chopped
2 T. onion, minced
2 eggs, well beaten
1 c. milk
1 t. Worcestershire sauce
1½ t. salt
1 c. sharp cheese, grated
¼ c. butter

Combine rice, parsley, green pepper and onion. Combine eggs, milk, Worcestershire sauce and salt in another bowl. Add to first mixture. Pour into a buttered baking dish. Sprinkle top with cheese and butter. Bake 30 minutes at 325°F. Yield: 6 servings.

Rose Hagopian, Arcata H.S.
Arcata, California

CHICKEN-RICE CASSEROLE

1 c. uncooked rice
¼ c. margarine
2 T. onion flakes
½ t. salt
1 can chicken and rice soup
½ soup can water
2 T. parsley flakes
Slivered almonds

Brown rice in margarine; pour into a buttered casserole. Add remaining ingredients. Bake 1 hour covered at 300-350°F. Uncover 5 minutes before serving; add parsley and almonds. Fluff up and serve. Yield: 5-6 servings.

Verna Buerge, Turlock H.S.
Turlock, California

JOHNNY MAZETTI

2 c. chopped celery
1 c. chopped onion
2 green peppers, chopped
1 lb. ground beef
1 can tomato soup, undiluted
1 can tomato paste
1 8-oz. can tomato sauce
1 c. water
2 t. salt
¼ t. pepper
½ c. sliced stuffed olives
½ lb. mushrooms, sliced and sauted
½ lb. wide noodles, cooked
2 c. grated sharp cheese

Saute celery, onion, and green pepper in drippings for 5 minutes. Remove from pan. Brown meat in same pan. Add celery, onion, and green pepper. Add tomato soup, sauce, paste, water, and seasonings. Cook slowly for 30 minutes. Add olives, mushrooms, and noodles; mix. Turn into 2½ quart casserole; cover with cheese and bake at 350°F. for 20 minutes. Yield: 8-10 servings.

Sonya Whittenburg, Reynolds H.S.
Troutdale, Oregon

CHOP SUEY BAKE

1 lb. ground beef
2 c. celery, cubed
1 lge. onion, chopped
1 c. rice
1 t. salt (opt.)
1 T. Kitchen Bouquet
1 T. molasses
¼ c. soy sauce
1 can cream of mushroom soup
3 c. hot water

Brown meat and onion. Combine all ingredients. Bake in buttered casserole for 1 hour and 30 minutes at 350°F. Yield: 4 servings.

Mrs. Sharon Harke, Elmwood Area Schools
Elmwood, Wisconsin

CURRIED RICE WITH TUNA

½ c. celery, chopped
1 can mushroom soup
3 c. cooked rice
2 cans tuna
1 t. curry powder
½ c. olives, sliced
1 T. onion, minced
½ t. salt
½ c. buttered bread crumbs

Cook celery in a small amount of water until tender. Combine remaining ingredients except bread crumbs; add celery and water. Spoon into a greased 2-quart casserole. Top with bread crumbs. Bake at 375°F. for 25-30 minutes. Yield: 4-6 servings.

Mrs. Ellen Dettmann, Sanford Jr. H.S.
Minneapolis, Minnesota

GREEN RICE WITH MUSHROOMS

1 onion, diced
1 sm. green pepper, chopped
⅓ c. butter or margarine
1 3-oz. pkg. pimento cream cheese
2 c. cooked rice
2 c. evaporated milk
2 eggs, beaten
1 c. parsley, ground
1 lb. or 1 lge. can mushrooms
½ c. corn flakes, crushed
1 t. paprika

Saute onion and green pepper until tender. Mix butter and cheese into hot rice. Add milk, eggs, parsley, mushrooms, onion and green pepper. Grease pan; fill with rice mixture. Sprinkle top with corn flakes and paprika. Bake in a pan of hot water at 350°F. for 40 minutes. Yield: 6-8 servings.

Mrs. Katherine Swain, La Mirada H.S.
La Mirada, California

GREEN RICE CASSEROLE

1 egg
1¼ c. milk
½ c. fresh parsley, finely chopped, or flakes
1 sm. garlic, finely chopped
1 sm. onion, minced
½ t. salt
Dash of pepper
2 T. olive oil
2 c. cooked rice
½ c. grated cheese

Beat egg; add milk, parsley, garlic, onion, salt and pepper. Put layer of olive oil and rice in baking dish. Pour liquid mixture over rice. Top with grated cheese. Bake at 325°F. for 30-40 minutes. Yield: 4-6 servings.

Rose Marie Tondl, Pound Jr. H.S.
Lincoln, Nebraska

GREEN RICE AND SAUCE

2 c. cooked rice
1 c. fresh parsley, chopped
1 c. American cheese, grated
¼ to ⅓ c. onion, grated
½ c. butter, melted
2 c. milk
2 eggs, well beaten
1 can cream of mushroom or shrimp soup

Mix all ingredients except soup and put into a well greased casserole. Bake at 350°F. for 35-45 minutes or until firm as in custard. Serve with soup diluted with ½ can liquid poured over individual servings. Yield: 6 servings.

Ardith Johnson, Butte Public School
Butte, Nebraska

MOCK CHOP SUEY

1½-2 lb. hamburger
1 c. onion chopped
¾ c. rice
1 c. celery, cut up
2 T. soy sauce
2 T. Worcestershire sauce
1 can cream of mushroom soup
1 can cream of chicken soup
2½ c. water
1 can chow mein noodles

Brown hamburger, onions and rice. Add remaining ingredients except noodles; cook 5 minutes. Put in casserole; cover with chow mein noodles. Bake 30 minutes at 350°F. or until rice is done. Yield: 8-10 servings.

Judith Klawiter, Ashland H.S.
Ashland, Wisconsin

HAMBURGER CHOP SUEY

2 lb. hamburger
1 c. onions, chopped
¼ c. soy sauce
1-2 sm. cans mushrooms
1 can mushroom soup
1 can celery soup
1 can chop suey vegetables
1 can bean sprouts
2 c. cooked rice

Brown onions and hamburger; add soy sauce and mix well. Add remaining ingredients; blend thoroughly. Pour into 2 medium casseroles; bake at 350°F. for 30-40 minutes. Yield: 12-14 servings.

Mrs. Lillian McKinney, Ashley Community School
Ashley, Michigan

HAMBURGER CHOW MEIN

1 sm. onion, chopped
1 lb. hamburger
1 c. celery, chopped
1 c. cooked rice
1 can mushroom soup
1 can cream of chicken soup
2 T. soy sauce
1 can chow mein noodles

Saute onions and hamburger in butter; drain. Cook celery in water until tender. Combine all ingredients except noodles. Put half of noodles in bottom of 2-quart casserole; add hamburger mixture. Top with remaining noodles. Bake at 350°F. for 1 hour. Yield: 4-6 servings.

Mrs. Norma Kay J. Isern, Moore H.S.
Moore, Montana

MUSHROOMS WITH RICE

1 lb. mushrooms, cut up
6 T. butter
½ t. salt
¼ t. pepper
¼ t. mace
1½ c. cooked rice
1½ c. seasoned white sauce
4 T. grated cheese

Saute mushrooms in butter; add seasonings. Add boiled rice to white sauce; combine with mushrooms. Pour into buttered baking dish; sprinkle grated cheese over top. Cook at 350°F. until browned. Yield: 6 servings.

Mrs. Barbara Sherwood, Saranac H.S.
Saranac, Michigan

INDIAN RICE

¼ c. onion, thinly sliced
3 T. slivered almonds
2 T. butter
¼ c. seedless raisins
2 c. hot, cooked rice

Cook onions and almonds in butter until golden. Add raisins and heat until puffy. Add mixture to rice; mix lightly. Sprinkle with curry powder. Yield: 5 servings.

Mrs. Jeanne Damhof, Manton H.S.
Manton, Michigan

POLYNESIAN RICE MINGLE

1 c. brown rice
1½ T. onion, minced
1½ T. soy sauce
2 chicken bouillon cubes
2 c. boiling water

Combine rice, onion and soy sauce in a 1-quart casserole. Dissolve bouillon cubes in boiling water; stir into rice mixture. Cover and bake at 350°F. for 30 minutes. Remove cover and bake 15 minutes longer. Garnish with pimento, chopped cashews and parsley. Yield: 6 servings.

Mrs. Donna Henriksen, Lena-Winslow H.S.
Lena, Illinois

RICE-HAMBURGER CASSEROLE

¾ lb. hamburger
3 med. onions, chopped
1 t. salt
1 c. celery, diced
1 can cream of mushroom soup
1 can chicken and rice soup
½ c. rice
2 c. water
2 T. green and red pepper, chopped (opt.)

Saute hamburger and onions until slightly browned; add salt. Put into greased 1½-quart casserole. Add celery and soups. Sprinkle dry rice over ingredients; toss together. Add water gradually and mix. Bake for 1 hour and 30 minutes at 325°F. Yield: 6 servings.

Kathryn Burkholder, Chosen Valley H.S.
Chatfield, Minnesota

RICE HOT DISH

1 c. rice
1 c. celery, chopped
1 lb. ground beef
1 lge. onion, chopped
1 can cream of mushroom soup
1 can cream of chicken soup
2 T. soy sauce

Cook rice for 15 minutes. Simmer celery in water until tender. Brown beef and onions. Combine all ingredients. Bake at 275°F. for 1 hour. Yield: 6 servings.

Mrs. Evelyn Piper, Minnewaukan H.S.
Minnewaukan, North Dakota

RICE AND MUSHROOM CASSEROLE

1 sm. box instant rice
½ c. onion, chopped
½ c. butter
1 can chicken and rice soup
1 can water
1 c. mushrooms and liquid
1 t. garlic salt
1 t. onion salt

Brown rice and onion in butter. Add soup, water, mushrooms and seasoning. Place in a covered casserole; bake for 45 minutes at 350°F. Yield: 10 servings.

Mary Beth Stine, Flora Township H.S.
Flora, Illinois

RICE PILAF

2½ T. butter or margarine
1 c. rice
⅓ t. monosodium glutamate
2 c. hot chicken broth
½ c. parsley, chopped
½ c. carrots, finely cubed
½ c. green onions, chopped
½ c. celery, chopped
¼ c. slivered almonds

Brown rice in butter with seasoning; pour into a casserole. Stir in broth; cover and bake 45 minutes at 350°F. Add remaining ingredients and toss lightly; bake 10 minutes. Yield: 4 servings.

Lois Pullen, Area Supervisor, Home Economics
Education, State Department of Education
Baton Rouge, Louisiana

RICE PILAF

1 c. butter
1 onion, chopped
1 can beef consomme
1 can water
1 c. rice

Melt butter; saute onions until yellow. Add consomme, rice and water. Bake in covered casserole at 350°F. for 1 hour. Yield: 6 servings.

Mrs. Louis Ivanish, Malta H.S.
Malta, Montana

QUICK PILAF

1 pkg. dry chicken-noodle soup
1 c. long grain rice
½ c. butter
2½-3 c. hot water

Brown noodles and rice in butter. Dissolve broth ball from package of soup in hot water. Mix browned rice and noodles with broth. Pour in casserole. Bake for 1 hour at 350°F. Yield: 4-6 servings.

Mrs. James M. Miller, Lakewood H.S.
Hebron, Ohio

TURKISH PILAF

1 sm. onion, chopped or 2 sm. cloves garlic
2 T. fat
1 c. rice
1 t. salt
2 c. boiling water
2 c. tomatoes
1 lb. beef, cubed

Brown onion in fat; add rice, seasonings, water, tomatoes and meat. Bake covered at 350°F. until rice is tender. NOTE: Variation: Meat may be omitted. Rice may be cooked in tomatoes and water. Casserole may be topped with grated cheese. Yield: 6 servings.

Cecile L. Herscher, Dowagiac Union H.S.
Dowagiac, Michigan

RICE PILAF

½ c. butter or margarine
1 lge. onion, thinly sliced
1 c. fresh mushrooms, sliced
½ c. green pepper, finely chopped
1 c. rice
Dash of dried thyme
2 c. chicken broth or bouillon
1 c. cooked shrimp or chopped ham

Saute onions in ¼ cup butter until golden. Add mushrooms and green pepper; cook until tender. Remove vegetables; heat remaining butter. Add rice and brown slightly, stirring constantly. Stir in vegetables and thyme. Heat chicken broth to boiling; stir into rice mixture. Add shrimp or ham; pour into a 1-quart casserole. Cover and bake 30-40 minutes at 350°F. Yield: 6 servings.

Susan Borchers, Fallbrook Union H.S.
Fallbrook, California

RICE CASSEROLE

1 c. uncooked rice
½ c. butter
1 med. onion, chopped
1 can cream of chicken soup
1½ soup cans water
1 sm. can mushrooms

Put all ingredients in a greased 2-quart casserole; mix lightly. Bake at 375°F. for 1 hour. Yield: 6 servings.

Beulah Riegel, Brookville School
Brookville, Ohio

RICE SIMPLICITY

1 c. rice, washed
1 can beef bouillon
1 can mushroom stems and pieces
1 stick butter or margarine

Combine rice, b o u i l l o n and mushrooms in a greased casserole. Top with butter. Cover and bake 1 hour at 325°F. Yield: 4 servings.

Agnes Kowitz Boulger, Bradley Bourbonnais
Community H.S.
Bradley, Illinois

RICE SUPREME

1 c. long grain rice
3 chicken bouillon cubes
¼ c. cooking oil
1½ c. cooked ham, cubed
¼ c. cooking oil
1½ c. cooked ham, cubed
¼ c. onion, chopped
1 clove garlic, minced
⅔ c. pineapple juice
2 T. ginger
2 t. soy sauce
2 t. curry powder
½ t. salt
1 med. green pepper, cut in strips
1 No. 2 can sliced pineapple strips
1½ lb. fresh shrimp

Cook rice and bouillon in 2 cups boiling water. Saute ham, onion and garlic in oil. Blend pineapple juice with seasonings; add with green pepper to ham mixture. Cut 4 pineapple slices into chunks; add to skillet. Cut shrimp in pieces, reserving 5-6 whole shrimp for garnish; add with rice to mixture. Toss well; heat thoroughly. Garnish with remaining pineapple and shrimp. Yield: 6 servings.

Eileen H. MacDonald, Jenifer Jr. H.S.
Lewiston, Idaho

RUSSIAN CHOW MEIN

3 c. boiling water
1 c. rice
1 lb. hamburger
3 c. celery, diced
1 c. onion, chopped
1 can mushroom soup
1 can cream of celery soup

Pour water over rice; let stand. Fry hamburger, celery and onion. Combine all ingredients; pour into a casserole. Bake at 350°F. covered for 45 minutes; uncover and bake 45 minutes longer. Yield: 6-8 servings.

Sharron Mallin, Martin Hughes H.S.
Buhl, Minnesota

RUSSIAN RICE

5 strips bacon
4 c. cooked rice
1 can tomatoes
Dill pickles, chopped
5 slices cheese, cut up
Salt
Pinch of sugar
1 med. bottle olives, cut up

Fry bacon until crisp; break into pieces. Add rice and toss. Add tomatoes, pickles, cheese, salt and sugar. Mix carefully with fork. Put in casserole. Bake at 350°F. for 25-35 minutes. Garnish with olives and bacon. Yield: 6 servings.

Myrna O'Neil, Ashland H.S.
Ashland, Kansas

SAVORY RICE

1 c. uncooked rice
1 stick butter or margarine
2 cans chicken consomme
2 onions, sliced

Brown rice in butter in skillet. Pour into casserole and add consomme and sliced onions. Bake at 350°F. for 1 hour.

Ruth Stovall, State Supervisor, Home Economics
Education, State Department of Education
Montgomery, Alabama

SPANISH RICE

⅓ c. onion, chopped
⅓ c. green pepper, chopped
3 T. butter, melted
1 c. instant rice
1 c. water
1 c. canned tomatoes
2 t. sugar
1 t. salt
⅛ t. pepper
1 bay leaf
3 T. Cheddar or Parmesan cheese, grated

Saute onion and green pepper in butter until onion is yellow. Add remaining ingredients except cheese; bring to a boil. Cover and simmer for 10-15 minutes or until rice is tender. Remove bay leaf. Serve hot, sprinkled with cheese. Yield: 4 servings.

Mrs. Helen C. Long, Southern Huntingdon H.S.
Orbisonia, Pennsylvania

SPANISH RICE AU GRATIN

1 c. rice, cooked
3 T. butter
1 c. onion, chopped
1 c. celery, chopped
⅔ c. green pepper, chopped
2 t. sugar
2 c. canned tomatoes
½ t. Worcestershire sauce
1 t. salt
1 t. monosodium glutamate
1½ t. chili powder
1½ c. grated Cheddar cheese

Saute onion, celery, and green pepper in butter until tender; add all remaining ingredients except cheese. Cook over low heat until liquid has been absorbed. Pour into a buttered casserole, top evenly with the cheese. Place under broiler 3-4 inches from heat until cheese is melted. Yield: 6-8 servings.

Sister Mary Giovanni, O.S.F.
Immaculate Conception Academy
Dubuque, Iowa

SPANISH RICE CASSEROLE

2 lb. ground round steak
2 T. butter
1 c. rice
2 med. onions, finely cut
1 No. 2½ can tomatoes
1 can tomato soup
1 sm. jar pimentos, cut up
Salt and pepper to taste
Sugar

Brown meat in butter until well cooked. Cook rice until done; pour water off and cold water on to flake rice. Cook onion and tomatoes for 20 minutes. Layer tomato soup, pimentos, meat, tomatoes and onion; mix well. Add cooked rice and season with salt, pepper and sugar. Bake 25-30 minutes at 350°F. Yield: 6-8 servings.

Mrs. Myrtle Hawk, Lincoln H.S.
Warren, Michigan

SPANISH RICE WITH HAMBURGER

2 sm. onions, chopped
1 green pepper, chopped
3 T. fat
1 lb. hamburger
1½ t. salt
¼ t. pepper
1 t. chili powder
4 c. cooked rice
2 c. tomatoes

Saute onions and peppers in fat until browned. Add hamburger, salt, pepper and chili powder. When meat is slightly browned, place alternate layers of cooked rice and meat mixture in a casserole. Pour tomatoes over dish and bake at 375°F. for 50 minutes. Yield: 6-8 servings.

Naomi Beiler, Selinsgrove Area H.S.
Selinsgrove, Pennsylvania

SU-CHAN ORIENTAL RICE CASSEROLE

1 6-oz. pkg. long grain wild rice mix
1 c. onion, chopped
1 c. celery, chopped
3 T. butter
2 T. soy sauce
1 3-oz. can broiled sliced mushrooms
1 5-oz. can water chestnuts
⅓ c. slivered almonds, toasted

Prepare rice mix according to directions on package. Cook onion and celery in butter until tender. Mix all ingredients. Bake in a 1½-quart casserole at 350°F. for 20 minutes. Yield: 8 servings.

Mrs. Frances Baratz, Clark Lane Jr. H.S.
Waterford, Connecticut

SUNNY JIM

1 c. cooked rice
1 c. Cheddar cheese, diced
1 c. dried bread crumbs
2 t. salt
1 sm. onion, minced
1 c. celery, diced
¼ c. margarine
1 c. milk

Combine cooked rice, cheese, bread crumbs and salt; place in greased 8-inch casserole. Brown onion and celery in butter; stir into rice mixture. Pour milk over all; bake at 350°F. for 1 hour. Yield: 6 servings.

Mrs. Joyce Marcy, Sandy Union H.S.
Sandy, Oregon

CASSEROLE OF WILD RICE

3 c. water
1 c. wild rice
1 lge. onion
1½ lb. ground beef
4 T. oil
1 can consomme
¼ t. celery salt
¼ t. onion salt
2 sm. cans sliced mushrooms
½ t. bay leaves
1 T. parsley
½ t. salt
2 cans chicken soup
½ c. almonds
¼ t. paprika
¼ t. pepper

Pour water over rice and let stand 30 minutes; drain. Brown onion and ground beef in oil. Add remaining ingredients. Refrigerate overnight. Bake at 350°F. covered for 2 hours; uncover and bake 1 hour. Yield: 12 servings.

Linda Oldenburg, Osseo Community Schools
Osseo, Wisconsin

EASY-TO-DO WILD RICE

½ lb. wild rice
1 med. onion, chopped
1 c. ripe olives, sliced
1 c. sharp cheese, cubed
1 No. 2½ can tomatoes
½ c. cooking oil
1½ c. hot water
1 t. salt

Wash wild rice and soak in water for 2 hours. Combine all ingredients. Place in covered casserole; bake for 3 hours at 325°F. NOTE: One 8-ounce box of wild rice-a-roni may be substituted for wild rice, in which case no soaking would be necessary. Yield: 6 servings.

Mrs. Cleo Cooper, Warden H.S.
Warden, Washington

WILD RICE CASSEROLE

1 c. wild rice
1 lge. onion, diced
1 bunch of celery, finely cut
1 lb. ground beef
1 lge. can tomatoes
1 can mushroom soup
Salt and pepper to taste

Pour boiling water over wild rice; let stand 5 minutes. Rinse rice; add water and boil 20 minutes. Drain. Boil onion and celery. Brown meat; add to rice, tomatoes and soup. Salt and pepper to taste. Bake for 1 hour at 350°F. Yield: 6-8 servings.

Gale Wolff, Byron H.S.
Byron, Minnesota

WILD RICE CASSEROLE DELUXE

1 lb. hamburger
1 onion, chopped
1 can chicken and rice soup
1 can cream of mushroom soup
½ c. white rice
½ c. wild rice
1 c. celery, chopped
2 soup cans water
1 t. soy sauce
Salt and pepper to taste

Brown meat and onion. Combine all ingredients. Bake for 1 hour and 30 minutes to 2 hours at 350°F. Yield: 8 servings.

Dorothy Loken, Campbell Ind. School Dist. 847
Campbell, Minnesota

WILD RICE STUFFING

1 c. wild rice, washed
3 qt. cold water
1 t. salt
1 lb. bulk pork sausage
1 c. onion, chopped
1 c. celery, chopped
1 can chopped mushrooms with liquid

Put wild rice in 3 quarts cold water with salt; bring to a boil. Rinse well in cold water. Saute sausage; pour off excess grease. Saute onions and celery in same pan. Combine all ingredients. Mixture may be used to stuff a fowl, or pour into casserole; cover and bake for 1 hour. NOTE: If used for stuffing, be sure to leave plenty of room for expansion. Yield: 6-8 servings.

Mary J. Sullivan, Central Jr. H.S.
White Bear Lake, Minnesota

WILD RICE DISH

1 c. wild rice
8 stalks celery
2 med. green peppers
Butter
1 sm. jar Cheese Whiz
1 can cream of celery soup
1½ cans milk
Chopped almonds (opt.)

Soak rice overnight. Saute celery and green pepper in butter. Combine all ingredients. Bake at 350°F. for 45 minutes. Yield: 6 servings.

Mrs. Eloise Hearin, Thomas Edisen Jr. H.S.
Springfield, Illinois

AMERICAN CHOP SUEY

1 sm. onion
3 T. shortening
½ lb. hamburger
1 c. spaghetti, cooked
1 can vegetable soup
1 can tomato soup
Salt and pepper to taste
Cracker crumbs

Saute onion in shortening until golden brown. Add hamburger and mix. Add spaghetti. Add vegetable and tomato·soup; season with salt and pepper. Put into greased casserole; top with cracker crumbs. Bake at 350°F. for 1 hour.

Marjorie Corliss, Belmont H.S.
Belmont, New Hampshire

AMERICAN RAVIOLI

1½ lb. ground round steak
1½ c. onion
2 T. butter
1 c. water
2 T. sugar
2 T. Worcestershire sauce
½ lb. cream cheese, finely cut
1 c. mushrooms
Salt and pepper to taste
1 pkg. spaghetti
2 pkg. Chinese noodles
½ lb. almonds, chopped

Brown meat and onions in butter. Add water, sugar, Worcestershire sauce, cheese, mushrooms, salt and pepper; cook 30 minutes. Cook spaghetti; mix with other ingredients. Bake 30 minutes at 350°F. Serve on noodles with almonds over top. Yield: 8-10 servings.

Mrs. Evelyn W. Hansen, Buffalo H.S.
Buffalo, Minnesota

BUSY DAY CASSEROLE

1 8-oz. pkg. uncooked spaghetti
1 lb. ground beef
1 T. fat
1 med. onion, minced
2 c. celery, diced
1 T. soy sauce
2 c. canned cooked tomatoes
1 c. grated cheese
1 t. salt
¼ t. pepper

Cook spaghetti until tender. Cook meat in fat until browned; add onion, celery and soy sauce. Gently mix in spaghetti, tomatoes, salt and pepper. Pour into a buttered 2-quart casserole; top with cheese. Bake at 350°F. for 45 minutes. Yield: 8 servings.

Helen M. McKinley, Oxnard H.S.
Oxnard, California

CELERY-CHEESE CASSEROLE

1 sm. box spaghetti
3 t. butter
3 t. flour
½ c. milk
½ c. cheese, chopped
½ c. cooked celery, chopped
2 T. onion, chopped
¼ t. salt
2 slices bread, crumbled

Cook spaghetti according to package directions; rinse and drain. Make a white sauce of butter, flour and milk; add cheese and stir until smooth. Combine all ingredients; pour into buttered casserole. Top with bread crumbs. Bake at 375°F. for 30 minutes. Yield: 6-8 servings.

Helen H. Wise, Manhum Township H.S.
Neffsville, Pennsylvania

COMPANY CASSEROLE

1 12-oz. box spaghetti
2 lb. hamburger
3 green peppers, chopped
2 lge. onions, chopped
1½ c. butter or margarine
½ c. mushrooms
⅔ c. pitted ripe olives
1 No. 303 can tomatoes
8 T. flour
2 c. milk
1 pt. half and half or light cream
1 lb. cheese, grated
6 slices bread, cubed

(Continued on Next Page)

Add spaghetti to 4 quarts of boiling, salted water. Cook until tender. Brown hamburger. Saute green peppers and onion in ½ cup butter. Add green peppers, onion, mushrooms, olives and tomatoes to hamburger. Make white sauce from ½ cups butter, the flour, milk, and half and half. Add cheese. Stir over low heat until cheese melts. Combine bread cubes with remaining ½ cup melted butter. Arrange spaghetti, hamburger mixture, cheese sauce and bread cubes in layers in a greased casserole. Bake for 45 minutes to 1 hour at 350°F. Yield: 12 servings.

Phyllis Gilmore, Homewood-Flossmoor H.S.
Flossmoor, Illinois

EAST INDIAN SPAGHETTI

1 lb. mixed ground beef and sausage
1 onion, chopped
1½ qt. stewed tomatoes
½ med. green pepper, chopped
1 sm. can pimento
1 4-oz. can mushrooms
1 t. salt
½ t. pepper
1 t. sugar
2 t. curry powder
½-¾ lb. thin spaghetti
½ lb. American cheese, sliced

Brown meat; pour off excess grease. Brown onions; add remaining ingredients except spaghetti and cheese. Simmer 30 minutes. Cook spaghetti as directed. Combine spaghetti and sauce; put into greased baking dish. Top with cheese. Bake 1 hour at 325°F. Yield: 10-12 servings.

Marilyn J. Mouchka, White Bear Lake H.S.
White Bear Lake, Minnesota

HAM CASSEROLE

2 lge. onions, chopped
3 green peppers, chopped
⅓ c. oil
2 lb. raw ham, diced
1 lge. can tomatoes
1 lb. spaghetti
1 lge. can mushrooms
Salt and pepper to taste
Paprika
1 lb. American cheese, sliced

Brown onions and peppers in oil. Add ham and brown. Add tomatoes; when hot add uncooked spaghetti and mushrooms. Season to taste. Simmer covered for 20 minutes. Add half of cheese; put in buttered casserole. Top with remaining cheese. Bake at 350°F. for 30 minutes. Yield: 8-10 servings.

Mrs. Lynn Ackerman, Ventura H.S.
Ventura, California

GERMAN HAM SPAGHETTI

1 8-oz. pkg. spaghetti
1 c. milk
2½ oz. Gruyere cheese, diced
2 eggs, beaten
2 c. cooked ham, chopped
1 T. parsley, chopped

Cook spaghetti in boiling salted water until tender, about 7 minutes. Drain and place in lightly greased 2-quart casserole. Scald milk; add cheese and heat until melted. Pour a little of the milk over the eggs, stirring constantly. Add milk and egg mixture to remaining milk and stir. Add ham; pour over spaghetti in casserole. Mix lightly, but thoroughly. Top with parsley. Bake at 350°F. for 20 minutes until brown and bubbly.

Mrs. Marion Morgan, La Grande H.S.
La Grande, Oregon

ITALIAN SPAGHETTI

1 T. salad oil
1 lb. ground beef
1 med. onion, finely chopped
1 No. 2½ can tomatoes, sieved
½ c. brown sugar
1 c. catsup
1 t. salt
¼ t. peppr
½ c. water
1 10-oz. pkg. thin spaghetti

Brown beef and onion in oil; add sieved tomatoes, brown sugar, catsup, salt, pepper and water. Simmer slowly for 20 minutes. Cook spaghetti according to directions; drain. Mix spaghetti and meat sauce; pour into a baking dish and bake 25 minutes at 350°F. Yield: 8 servings.

Mrs. Ruth Hale, Cheyenne-Eagle Butte H.S.
Eagle Butte, South Dakota

ITALIAN SPAGHETTI SAUCE

1 lb. ground round steak
Vegetable oil
1 med. onion, chopped
1 2½-oz. jar mushroom stems and pieces
16-20 sm. Spanish olives, sliced crosswise
1½ t. salt
½ t. pepper
1 t. garlic salt
½ t. Beau Monde seasoning
1 15-oz. can tomato sauce
1 15-oz. can undrained whole tomatoes

Brown meat in vegeable oil; add onion, mushrooms and olives. Add seasonings, tomato sauce and whole tomatoes. Simmer 45 minutes to 1 hour. Serve over long spaghetti. NOTE: If desired, substitute ¼ teaspoon onion salt and ¼ teaspoon celery salt for Beau Monde seasoning. Yield: 4 servings.

Mrs. Marlys Weinman, Planview H.S.
Plainview, Minnesota

SPAGHETTI SAUCE

1 lb. hamburger
1 onion, grated
2 t. salt
Dash of pepper
1 c. Romano cheese, grated
1 6-oz. can tomato paste
2 8-oz. cans tomato sauce
½ t. garlic powder
2 T. sugar
½ t. oregano

Brown hamburger and onion; add remaining ingredients and mix well. Simmer 1-2 hours. Serve sauce over spaghetti. Top with grated Parmesan cheese. Yield: 6-8 servings.

Mrs. Marilyn Breiding, Prospect H.S.
Mount Prospect, Illinois

MOR CASSEROLE

1 lb. hamburger
2 c. tomatoes, undrained
½ t. salt
⅛ t. pepper
1 T. chili powder
1 can whole kernel corn
½ sm. onion, chopped
½ pkg. spaghetti, cooked
¾ c. cheese, grated

Brown hamburger; pour off grease. Add tomatoes and seasonings; simmer for 30 minutes. Mix corn and chopped onion. Place spaghetti in a baking dish; cover with meat sauce. Add a layer corn and onion; top with cheese. Bake at 350°F. for 20-25 minutes. Yield: 6-8 servings.

Mrs. Pheba Downes, Mr. Vernon H.S.
Mount Vernon, Ohio

ROMAN HOLIDAY

¼ c. fat
1 onion, chopped
1 lb. hamburger
1 t. salt
⅛ t. pepper
2 c. cooked spaghetti
1½ c. tomatoes
¾ c. cheese, grated

Saute onion in fat; add meat and seasonings. Cook 5 minutes. Make a layer of spaghetti in baking dish; add meat mixture and drippings. Add another layer of spaghetti; pour in tomatoes. Cover; bake at 350°F. for 35 minutes. Remove cover and bake 10 minutes longer. Yield: 4-6 servings.

Mrs. Mary K. Adams, New Troy H.S.
New Troy, Michigan

SAVORY SPAGHETTI CASSEROLE

1 lb. ground beef
½ c. onions, chopped
¼ c. green pepper, chopped
2 T. butter
1 can condensed cream of mushroom soup
1 can condensed tomato soup
1 soup can water
1 clove of garlic, minced
1 c. sharp cheese, shredded
½ lb. spaghetti, cooked and drained

Cook beef, onions and green pepper in butter until meat is lightly browned and vegetables are tender; stir to separate meat. Add soups, water and garlic; heat. Blend with half cup of cheese and cooked spaghetti in a 3-quart casserole; top with remaining cheese. Bake at 350°F. for 30 minutes. Yield: 6-8 servings.

Mrs. Elsie Rosselit, Vassar H.S.
Vassar, Michigan

SPAGHETTI BAKE

2 T. shortening
½ lb. ground beef
1 sm. onion
1 c. catsup
1½ c. tomato juice
¼ t. pepper
1 c. uncooked spaghetti

Melt shortening; add meat and onion and brown. Add remaining ingredients; blend and pour into baking dish. Bake at 375°F. for 1 hour. Yield: 4 servings.

Mrs. Delores Hutton, New Lothrop H.S.
New Lothrop, Michigan

SPAGHETTI SKILLET DINNER

1½ lb. ground beef
¼ c. green pepper, chopped
⅓ c. onion, chopped
3 T. fat
½ c. celery, diced
½ c. carrots, diced
2 c. canned whole-kernel corn and liquid
⅔ c. sliced mushrooms and liquid
½ 8-oz. pkg. broken spaghetti
2 c. canned tomatoes
1½ t. salt
⅛ t. pepper

Brown beef, green pepper and onions in hot fat. Add celery, carrots, corn, mushrooms and spaghetti. Pour tomatoes over all; sprinle with seasoning. Cover and simmer for 30 minutes. Yield: 8-10 servings.

Mrs. Vera L. Scheff, Franklin Area H.S.
Murrysville, Pennsylvania

SPAGHETTI SUPREME

2 c. spaghetti
1 T. butter
1 onion, finely cut
1 green pepper, finely cut
¼ c. stuffed olives, sliced
¼ c. mushrooms
1 can tomato soup
2 c. American cheese, grated

Cook spaghetti. Melt butter; add onion, pepper, olives, mushrooms and soup and heat. Add cheese, stir until melted. Pour over spaghetti. Bake in buttered casserole at 350°F. for 30 minutes. Yield: 8 servings.

Frances R. LeClair, Superior East H.S.
Superior, Wisconsin

SPAGHETTI-SPANISH MICHEL

2 c. spaghetti
1 qt. tomatoes, fresh or canned
½ c. boiled ham
1 onion, diced
1 green pepper, diced
¼ t. pepper
½ t. salt

Break spaghetti into 1-inch pieces. Cook in 1-quart boiling water until tender. Add tomatoes; cook 15 minutes. Remove fat from ham; fry onions and green peppers slowly in fat until tender. Add chopped ham, onion, green pepper and seasonings to spaghetti and tomatoes. Put in casserole; bake 15 minutes at 350-400°F. Yield: 4 servings.

Mrs. Videllia M. Peters, Goodridge H.S.
Goodridge, Minnesota

TOMATO ITALIAN SPAGHETTI

1 lb. ground beef
1 sm. onion, chopped
½ c. green pepper, chopped
1 t. salt
½ t. pepper
½ t. chili powder
½ t. garlic salt
½ t. paprika
1 can tomato sauce
1 can tomato soup
1 can tomato paste
1 can mushrooms
Cooked spaghetti

Brown ground beef; add onion and pepper. Add seasonings; add mushrooms and tomato ingredients. Simmer for 1 hour. Serve over cooked spaghetti. Top with Parmesan cheese. Yield: 6-8 servings.

Mrs. Sandra Bendt, Clear Lake H.S.
Clear Lake, South Dakota

SPEEDY SPAGHETTI

1 lb. ground beef
1 1½-oz. pkg. spaghetti sauce mix
½ c. water
1 15-oz. can tomato sauce
1 No. 2½ can tomatoes
⅓ c. onion, minced
⅓ c. green pepper, diced
1 t. salt
¼ t. pepper
1 7-oz. pkg. thin spaghetti, broken

Place ground beef in skillet and flatten until it covers bottom of pan in thin layer. Combine spaghetti sauce mix with remaining ingredients except spaghetti. Add layers of spaghetti and tomato mixture on top of meat. Cover and cook for 20 minutes at 350°F. Yield: 6-8 servings.

Judy M. Newman, Jefferson Intermediate School
Port Huron, Michigan

VERMICELLI LOAF

1 c. vermicelli spaghetti
1 c. soft bread crumbs
1 c. cheese, grated
1 c. hot milk
3 T. butter, melted
3 eggs, separated
2 pimentos, finely cut
1 t. salt
1 T. onion, grated
1 T. chopped parsley

Cook vermicelli until tender. Combine all ingredients except egg whites. Fold in beaten egg whites. Bake 45 minutes at 350°F. Yield: 5-6 servings.

Mrs. Shirley Glenn, Centennial Jr. H.S.
Circle Pines, Minnesota

WESTERN SPAGHETTI

1½ lb. bottom round beef, cubed
5 c. tomato juice
2 c. water
½ c. onions, thinly sliced
½ c. stuffed olives, sliced
½ c. pitted ripe olives
1 8-oz. pkg. spaghetti
1 t. salt
½ t. pepper
2 c. American cheese, cubed

Brown beef in Dutch oven. Add tomato juice and water; simmer covered for 15 minutes or until meat is almost tender. Add remaining ingredients except cheese; cook over very low heat for about 30 minutes or until spaghetti and meat are tender. Add cheese and toss to blend. Yield: 6-8 servings.

Mrs. Ada Colguhoun, Pershing County H.S.
Lovelock, Nevada

BAGS OF GOLD

4 c. flour
2⅔ T. baking powder
1½ t. salt
5 T. shortening
1⅓ c. milk
1 lb. American cheese
5 c. tomato soup or chicken broth

Make up biscuit dough. Roll dough into round balls; put a smaller ball of cheese in center of each dough ball. Knead dough carefully around cheese. Drop balls into hot tomato soup; cover and cook slowly until dough is cooked through. Yield: 8 servings.

Mrs. Phyllis D. Larsen, Alameda Jr. H.S.
Las Cruces, New Mexico

BREAD AND CHEESE CASSEROLE

4 thin sl. buttered bread, remove crusts
1 lb. American cheese, cut in small pieces
3 eggs
4 c. milk
1 t. mustard
Salt and pepper to taste

In a well buttered baking dish, put slices of bread cut into quarters. Put alternate layers of bread and cheese. Beat up eggs in milk; add mustard, salt and pepper. Pour over cheese and bread. Let stand 1 hour. If necessary a little more milk may be added. Bake for 45 minutes at 325°F. Yield: 6 servings.

Sister Marianne, Bishop Miege H.S.
Shawnee Mission, Kansas

BROCCOLI-CHEESE STRATA

12 slices bread
¾ lb. sharp cheese, sliced
1 10-oz. pkg. frozen chopped broccoli, cooked
2 c. ham, finely diced
6 eggs, slightly beaten
3½ c. milk
2 T. minced instant onion
½ t. salt
¼ t. dry mustard

Cut 12 doughnuts and holes from bread; set aside. Fit bread scraps in bottom of 13x9x2-inch baking dish. Place cheese in a layer over bread; add a layer of broccoli and a layer of ham. Arrange bread doughnuts and holes on top of ham. Combine remaining ingredients; pour over bread. Cover and refrigerate at least 6 hours or overnight. Bake uncovered at 325°F. for 55 minutes. Let stand 10 minutes before cutting into squares. Yield: 12 servings.

Emma Andreae, Bellows Falls H.S.
Bellows Falls, Vermont

CHEESE CHOWDER

¼ c. onion, chopped
¼ c. carrot, diced
¼ c. celery, diced
¼ c. margarine
3 T. flour
½ t. salt
½ t. paprika
4 c. milk
1 can condensed beef consomme
2 c. Cheddar cheese, cubed

Cook onions, carrots and celery in butter until tender. Stir in flour, salt and paprika; cook 1-2 minutes. Add milk and consomme; cook, stirring constantly until thickened. Add cheese and stir until melted. Yield: 6 servings.

Mrs. Berta Pylkosz, Stowe H.S.
Stowe, Vermont

CHEESE DELIGHT

4 lge. slices of bread, cut in 1-inch cubes
½ lb. med. sharp cheese, grated
3 T. butter
½ t. salt
Paprika
2 eggs
2 c. milk

Place a layer of bread cubes in a buttered casserole. Top with a layer of cheese. Add butter, salt and paprika. Fill pan with layers, ending with cheese. Mix eggs and milk; pour slowly over casserole. Let stand 3 hours; bake at 350°F. for 45 minutes. Yield: 8 servings.

Mrs. Charlotte L. Heinlen, Coraopolis Jr. H.S.
Coraopolis, Pennsylvania

CHEESE DREAM HOT DISH

3 c. cooked rice
3 c. cooked macaroni
3 c. American cheese, cubed
3 c. soft bread, broken in small pieces
3 c. ham or 1 can Spam, cubed
4 eggs, well beaten
2 c. milk
Salt and pepper to taste

Combine all ingredients except eggs and milk. Add milk and eggs. Bake for 1 hour at 300°F. Yield: 12 servings.

Mrs. Charlotte Clarke, Central H.S.
Aberdeen, South Dakota

CHEESE FONDUE

½ stick butter
2½ T. mustard
12 slices or ½ loaf French bread
Cheddar cheese, sliced
3 eggs
3 c. milk
1 t. Worcestershire sauce
½ t. salt
Parmesan cheese
Paprika

Spread butter and mustard on bread; place in casserole. Top with sliced cheese. Combine eggs, milk, Worcestershire sauce and salt; pour over bread. Sprinkle top with Parmesan cheese and paprika. Refrigerate overnight. Bake at 350°F. for 1 hour. Yield: 6-8 servings.

Mrs. J.M. Klungle, Beecher H.S.
Flint, Michigan

CHEESE FONDUE

5 slices bread, remove crusts
Butter
1 t. salt
1 t. dry mustard
4 eggs, beaten
2 c. milk
½ lb. Cheddar cheese, grated

Butter bread and cut into ½-inch cubes. Mix salt and mustard; sprinkle over bread. Combine remaining ingredients; pour over bread cubes. Refrigerate overnight. Bake in a casserole in a pan of water for 1 hour at 350°F. Yield: 6 servings.

Marie Green, Newton Community H.S.
Newton, Illinois

CHEESE FONDUE

2 c. bread cubes
1½ c. milk
½ c. cheese, grated
3 eggs, separated
½ t. dry mustard
½ t. salt

Soften bread cubes in ½ cup milk. Combine cheese, remaining milk, beaten egg yolks, mustard and softened bread cubes. Whip egg whites and salt until stiff; fold in cheese and milk mixture. Pour into a buttered 2½-quart casserole. Bake at 350°F. for 40 minutes. Yield: 6 servings.

Mrs. Helen Wright, Stevenson H.S.
Stevenson, Washington

CHEESE LOAF

2 eggs, beaten
½ c. sugar
1 c. milk
1 T. butter
1 t. salt
1 T. mustard
½ c. vinegar
1 lb. cheese, cut in small chunks
1 sm. can pimento
1 c. cracker crumbs

Combine all ingredients except cheese, pimento and crumbs. Cook over low heat, stirring constantly until mixture thickens. Combine remaining ingredients; add to egg mixture, stirring until blended. Pour mixture into buttered casserole. Bake at 350°F. for 30 minutes. Yield: 6-8 servings.

Wanda Neudigate, Manchester H.S.
Manchester, Ohio

CHEESE PUDDING

6-8 slices of bread
¼ c. butter
2½ c. American cheese, grated
3-4 eggs, slightly beaten
2½ c. milk
1 t. salt
¼ t. dry mustard

Spread butter over bread; place half of bread in a buttered casserole. Add a layer of cheese; repeat layers. Combine remaining ingredients; pour over cheese. Set casserole in a pan of hot water; bake at 375°F. for 45 minutes or until firm. NOTE: Bread may be cubed if desired. Yield: 8 servings.

This recipe submitted by the following teachers:

Mrs. Wilborn N. Day, Lincoln Rural H.S.
Lincoln, Kansas

Elizabeth Neumeyer, D.C. Everest Jr.-Sr. H.S.
Schofield, Wisconsin

CHEESE RAREBIT

2 T flour
1 T. butter
Dash of cayenne pepper
¼ t. salt
¼ t. dry mustard
½ c. water
½ c. cheese, grated

Melt butter in top of double boiler; blend in flour, cayenne pepper, salt and mustard. Gradually add water, stirring constantly until thickened. Place over boiling water. Blend in cheese; stir occasionally until melted. Yield: 4 servings.

Marie Zeigler, Swanton Local H.S.
Swanton, Ohio

CHEESE STRATA

12 slices bread
½ lb. cheese, grated
4 eggs, beaten
2½ c. milk
¾ t. salt
⅛ t. pepper
¼ t. dry mustard

Arrange bread and cheese in alternate layers in greased baking dish with bread on bottom and top. Combine eggs, milk, and seasonings. Pour over bread and cheese; refrigerate 1 hour. Bake at 350°F. for 1 hour. Yield: 6 servings.

Mrs. Mary Alice Collins, Hancock Central H.S.
Maxwell, Indiana

CHEESE-TUNA CASSEROLE

6 slices bread
1 can tuna
½ lb. sharp cheese
½ t. dry mustard
3 eggs, slightly beaten
2 c. milk
Dash of salt

Break bread and cheese into bite size pieces; arrange in layers with tuna in a casserole. Mix eggs, milk and mustard; pour over mixture in casserole. Refrigerate overnight. Bake at 350°F. for 1 hour in covered casserole. Yield: 4 servings.

Mrs. Bonnie Johnson, Moscow H.S..
Moscow, Idaho

DAIRY SPECIAL CASSEROLE

¾ c. cooked ham, chopped
1¼ c. Cheddar cheese, grated
3 hard-cooked eggs, cut up
2 c. macaroni
1 can mushroom soup
2 c. milk

Combine all ingredients, tossing lightly. Put into greased casserole; refrigerate overnight. Remove from refrigerator 1 hour before baking. Bake 1 hour at 350°F. Yield: 6-8 servings.

Mrs. Harry Cooper, Richland Center H.S.
Richland Center, Wisconsin

CORN-CHEESE BAKE

1 No. 2 can cream-style corn
¾ c. milk
1 c. cracker crumbs
2 T. onion, grated
3 T. pimento
1 c. American cheese, grated
½ t. salt
Dash of pepper
2 T. butter

Combine corn and milk. Stir in remaining ingredients except butter. Pour into buttered 1½-quart casserole; dot with butter. Bake at 350°F. for 30 minutes until lightly browned. Yield: 6 servings.

Mrs. Jessie D. Lombard, Windsor H.S.
Windsor, Vermont

GOLDEN CHEESE BAKE

½ c. rice, cooked
2 c. carrots, shredded
1½ c. cheese, grated
⅓ c. milk
1 egg, beaten
1 T. minced onion
1 t. salt
Dash of pepper

Combine rice, carrots, 1¼ cup cheese and remaining ingredients. Pour into a greased baking dish; sprinkle with remaining cheese. Bake at 350°F. for 1 hour. Yield: 6 servings.

Mrs. Ivan Wood, Amanda Jr. H.S.
Middletown, Ohio

GRANDMA'S SUPPER DISH

8-10 slices hard bread
3 T. butter
8-10 slices sharp cheese
2 eggs, beaten
1⅓ c. milk
1 t. salt
1 t. pepper
1½ t. baking powder

Spread bread with butter; cover with cheese slices. Place in greased baking dish. Combine eggs, milk, salt, pepper and baking powder. Pour over bread and cheese. Bake at 375°F. about 40 minutes or until of custard consistency. Yield: 6 servings.

Armitage Coburn, Calhoun Jr. H.S.
West Homestead, Pennsylvania

SAVORY CREAMED MUSHROOMS

1 T. onion, chopped
¼ c. green pepper, chopped
¼ c. butter
¼ c. flour
2 c. milk
2 4-oz. cans mushrooms, drained
2 c. American cheese
3 hard-cooked eggs, sliced
3 T. pimentos
¼ c. stuffed olives, sliced

Saute onion and green pepper in butter. Stir in flour and milk; cook until thickened. Add mushrooms and cheese; heat until cheese melts. Add remaining ingredients. Serve over noodles or rice. Yield: 6 servings.

Mrs. Doris Henderson, Tower Hill H.S.
Tower Hill, Illinois

RING OF PLENTY

1½ c. cooked macaroni
1½ c. cheese, diced
1 c. soft bread crumbs
1 T. minced parsley
3 T. pimento, minced
2 T. butter, melted
1 T. onions, minced
1 egg, well beaten
1 c. scalded milk
1 t. salt
Dash of pepper

Mix all ingredients in order listed. Place in a well greased casserole or ring mold. Bake in a pan of water 35-40 minutes at 350°F. Yield: 6 servings.

Lucy White, Wethersfield H.S.
Kewanee, Illinois

WILSON'S HOT STUFF

¼ lb. boiled ham
¼ lb. American cheese
2 eggs
2 c. milk
1 c. cracker or bread crumbs
Dash of Worchestershire sauce
¼ t. onion powder
Salt and pepper to taste

Grind ham and cheese together. Combine all ingredients; pour into casserole. Bake at 375°F. for 45-60 minutes or until a knife inserted in middle comes out clean. Yield: 4 servings.

Maryann Imhoff, Harrison Park Jr. H.S.
Grand Rapids, Michigan

SANDWICH OMELET

3 eggs
1½ c. milk
Seasoning as desired
3 cheese sandwiches
Paprika

Beat eggs well; add milk and seasoning. Pour over 3 cheese sandwiches which have been placed in a well buttered baking pan. Sprinkle with paprika. Refrigerate overnight or for several hours. Bake at 300°F. until golden brown. Yield: 3 servings.

Hazel Edberg, Denair H.S.
Denair, California

CHEESE SOUFFLE

¼ c. butter
¼ c. flour
1 c. milk
1 c. grated cheese
1 t. salt
⅛ t. paprika
½ t. mustard
4 eggs, separated

Make white sauce of butter, flour and milk; add cheese and seasonings, stirring until cheese is melted. Remove from heat. Gradually stir in well beaten egg yolks and fold in stiffly beaten egg whites. Pour into an oiled casserole and put in pan of hot water. Bake at 350°F. for 50-60 minutes or until delicately browned and firm to touch. Test for doneness with knife. Serve at once. Yield: 4-6 servings.

Mrs. Frances Eldridge, Central H.S.
Clifton, Illinois

CHEESE SOUFFLE

3 T. butter
4 T. flour
⅛ t. pepper
1 t. salt
1 c. milk
½ c. cheese, grated
4 eggs, separated

Melt butter; add flour and seasonings. Add milk; cook over medium heat until a thick sauce is formed, stirring constantly. Add cheese and set aside to cool. Beat egg yolks until light; add white sauce, stirring. Beat egg whites until stiff and fold into mixture. Pour into a greased baking dish. Set in a pan of water. Bake at 350°F. for 1 hour. Yield: 4 servings.

Laura E. Kirsch, White River H.S.
White River, South Dakota

CHEESE SOUFFLE

10 sl. day-old bread
8 oz. sharp cheese
3 eggs
2 c. milk
1 t. salt
1 t. dry mustard
¼ t. pepper

Cut crusts off bread; butter bread well and cut into cubes. Place cubed bread and cheese in alternate layers in greased casserole. Mix remaining ingredients in blender or mixer and pour over bread and cheese. Set in pan of water. Bake 1 hour at 325°F. NOTE: May be made in advance and refrigerated. Have at room temperature to bake. Yield: 6 servings.

Mrs. Mildred G. Grundy
South Middleton Township H.S.
Boiling Springs, Pennsylvania

CHEESE SOUFFLE

1 c. milk, scalded
1 c. soft stale bread crumbs
1 c. cheese, cut up
1 T. butter
½ t. salt
2-3 eggs, separated

Combine milk, bread crumbs, cheese, butter and salt; cook over low heat until mixture is smooth, stirring with fork. Beat egg yolks until lemon colored; add to cheese mixture. Beat egg whites until stiff and fold into mixture. Pour into buttered 1-quart baking dish. Bake at 350°F. for 20 minutes or until firm. Yield: 6 servings.

Mrs. Mabel S. Pausch, Fairfield Local H.S.
Leesburg, Ohio

CARROT-CHEESE SOUFFLE

3 T. butter
3 T. flour
1 c. milk
½ t. salt
Dash of pepper
¼ lb. cheese, grated
1 c. cooked carrots, mashed
3 eggs, separated

Melt butter; add flour, milk and seasonings. Heat until thickened, stirring constantly. Add cheese and stir until melted. Add carrots. Beat egg yolks until thickened; add to cheese mixture. Fold in stiffly beaten egg whites. Pour into an ungreased baking dish; place in a pan of water. Bake 45 minutes at 325°F. Yield: 3-4 servings.

Mrs. Gladys M. Myers, St. Francis H.S.
St. Francis, Minnesota

CHEESE SOUFFLE WITH SAUCE

5 slices buttered bread, cubed
1 10-oz. pkg. sharp cracker barrel cheese, grated
3 eggs
1 T. mustard
2 c. milk
½ t. salt
¼ t. pepper

Place a layer of bread cubes in a 1½-quart buttered casserole; sprinkle with grated cheese. Repeat layers. Beat eggs; add mustard, milk, salt and pepper. Pour over cheese and bread layers. Let stand overnight, bake at 350-375°F. for 45 minutes or until firm. Serve with hot shrimp soup diluted with ½ cup milk if desired. Yield: 6 servings.

Mrs. Beth W. Wiley, Weiser H.S.
Weiser, Idaho

CHEESE SOUFFLE SUPREME

4 T. butter
4 T flour
1 t. salt
Dash of pepper
Dash of dry mustard
Few drops onion juice
1½ c. milk
1½ c. cheese, grated
4 eggs, separated

Melt butter; add flour and stir until smooth. Add salt, pepper, mustard and onion juice; stir in milk. When mixture comes to a boil, add cheese and stir until melted. Add beaten egg yolks. Fold mixture into stiffly beaten egg whites. Pour into a buttered baking dish and set in pan of hot water. Bake at 300°F. for about 1 hour or until firm. Yield: 5 servings.

Ruth C. Maud, South Lebanon H.S.
Lebanon, Pennsylvania

CHEESE SOUFFLE WITH TAPIOCA

⅓ c. tapioca
1 t. salt
2 c. scalded milk
⅓ c. Cheddar cheese, grated
6 eggs, separated

Add tapioca to salt and scalded milk; cook over boiling water for 3 minutes, stirring often. Add cheese and stir until melted. Beat egg yolks well; add some of the hot tapioca mixture, stirring constantly. Pour into mixture; cool until slightly thickened. Beat egg whites until stiff; fold into tapioca mixture. Turn into greased shallow baking pans. Set in pans of hot water. Bake at 350°F. for 45-50 minutes or until firm. Yield: 4 servings.

Mrs. Bertha Hale, North H.S.
Phoenix, Arizona

TOMATO-CHEESE SOUFFLE

2 T. butter or fat
4 T. flour
1 c. hot tomato juice
Salt and pepper to taste
¼ lb. grated cheese
3 eggs, separated

Blend butter and flour; add hot tomato juice, salt, pepper and grated cheese. Stir quickly to melt cheese; cool. Beat egg yolks and add; fold in stiffly beaten egg whites. Place in a greased baking dish; set in a pan of hot water and bake at 350°F. for 40-50 minutes. Yield: 5-6 servings.

Mrs. Margaret Swigart, Bainville H.S.
Bainville, Montana

BAKED EGGS

3 T. butter or margarine
2 med. onions, thinly sliced
Salt and pepper to taste
4 eggs
2 T. dried bread crumbs
4 sl. sharp American cheese

Saute onion slices in butter for 5 minutes; arrange slices in an 8-inch pie plate. Sprinkle lightly with salt and pepper. Carefully break eggs one at a time into a cup; slide onto top of onions. Sprinkle with salt, pepper, and crumbs; top with cheese slices. Bake, uncovered, 10 minutes at 350°F. Yield: 4 servings.

Mrs. Luana Hutchings, Moopa Valley H.S.
Overton, Nevada

CHICKEN SOUFFLE

1 can condensed cream of chicken soup
4 eggs, separated

Blend soup and beaten egg yolks. Beat egg whites until stiff; gently fold egg whites into soup mixture. Pour into individual greased casseroles. Set each in a pan of water. Bake at 300°F. for 30 minutes. Yield: 4-5 servings.

Carol Oberle, H.S.
Silver Lake, Kansas

CHINESE OMELET

3 c. cooked rice
¼ lb. Cheddar cheese, grated
1 T. butter, melted
3 egg, separated
1½ c. milk
1 t. (scant) salt
¼ t. paprika

Combine hot rice, cheese, butter, beaten egg yolks, milk, ¾ teaspoon salt and paprika in a casserole dish. Beat egg whites and ⅛ teaspoon salt until stiff. Fold into rice mixture. Set in pan of hot water. Bake at 350°F. for 50 minutes or until set. Yield: 4-6 servings.

Leila Steckelberg, Mount Vernon Union H.S.
Mount Vernon, Washington

DEVILED EGG CASSEROLE

12 hard-cooked eggs
½ t. salt
¼ t. pepper
½ t. dry mustard
3 T. salad dressing, vinegar or cream
1 T. (rounded) flour
1 T. butter or margarine
1½ c. milk
1 can mushroom soup

Cut eggs in half lengthwise. Remove yolks; Mash with fork and mix thoroughly with salt, pepper, dry mustard and salad dressing. Fill whites with yolk mixture, heaping it up lightly. Place eggs in well buttered, shallow baking dish in single layer. Melt butter; add flour and blend. Add milk gradually, stirring constantly until thickened. Add mushroom soup; mix well and heat until blended. Pour over eggs and bake 25 minutes at 350°F. Yield: 12-15 servings.

Mrs. Vera M. Troyer, Bennett County H.S.
Martin, South Dakota

EGG AND BACON CASSEROLE

½ c. chopped onion
1 T. butter
White sauce
½ c. cheese, grated
6 hard-cooked eggs, sliced
Potato chips, crushed.
6-7 slices bacon, fried crisp

Saute onion in butter until soft. Melt cheese in white sauce; add to onion mixture. Place ingredients in a buttered casserole in layers of egg, potato chips, bacon and white sauce. Repeat layers. Bake 10 minutes at 350°F. Yield: 6 servings.

Mrs. Ruth Fowler, Peabody H.S.
Peabody, Kansas

EGG AND BACON SOUFFLE CASSEROLE

¼ c. bacon, diced
3 sl. of bread
3 eggs, slightly beaten
1 c. milk
½ t. salt
¼ t. dry mustard
¼ t. paprika

Fry bacon until lightly browned; dice. Brush bread with bacon drippings; cut in pieces. Put in casserole. Alternate layers of bread and bacon. Combine eggs, milk and seasonings; pour over bread. Set in pan of hot water. Bake at 350°F. for about 45 minutes.

Ann Henryson, Alden Community School
Alden, Iowa

EGG CASSEROLE

¼ lb. potato chips, crumbled
3 T. melted butter
2 T. green pepper, finely chopped
2 T. flour
1 can mushroom soup
10 hard-cooked eggs
1 c. milk
1 t. salt
Pinch of garlic salt

Saute green pepper in butter for 3 minutes; add garlic salt. Add flour, mixing well; add milk and salt. Cook until thickened. Gradually stir in mushroom soup. Sprinkle a third of chips in a large greased casserole. Cut eggs in half lengthwise and place cut-side down on potato chips; cover with a third of chips. Cover with cooked mixture; sprinkle with remaining potato chips. Bake for 20 minutes at 375°F. Yield: 6-8 servings.

Mrs. Ruby G. Sabel, Oliver H.S.
Pittsburgh, Pennsylvania

EGG SOUFFLE

8 slices bread
4 T. butter
8 slices American cheese
1 c. ham, chopped
4 eggs
1 t. salt
2 c. milk

Cut crusts from bread; butter four slices. Put in bottom of pan, butter side down. Place a slice of cheese on each slice of bread. Sprinkle chopped ham over all. Lay another slice of bread on top, buttered side up. Place a slice of cheese on top and sprinkle with chopped ham. Mix eggs, salt and milk. Pour over mixture and allow to set overnight. Bake 1 hour at 350-375°F. Yield: 6-8 servings.

Jessie Chambers, East H.S.
Cheyenne, Wyoming

EGG SOUFFLE

14 sl. buttered bread, cubed
3 c. milk
6 eggs, beaten
1½ c. American cheese, grated
1 t. dry mustard
1 t. salt
Dash of pepper

Combine bread, milk, eggs, cheese and seasonings; stir just until blended. Put into a buttered casserole; bake 45 minutes at 350°F. Yield: 8 servings.

Mrs. Bertha Netzel, Wittenberg H.S.
Wittenberg, Wisconsin

EGGS DIVAN

6 hard-cooked eggs
1 can deviled ham
¼ t. Worcestershire sauce
½ t. grated onion
½ t. salt
½ t. dry mustard
1 T. milk
1 pkg. broccoli, cooked

Slice eggs lengthwise; remove yolks and mash. Add all ingredients except broccoli to yolks; mix well. Fill egg whites. Place broccoli in a buttered dish; place eggs on top.

CHEESE SAUCE:

2 T. flour
1½ T. butter, melted
⅛ t. dry mustard
½ t. salt
1 c. milk
½ c. sharp cheese, grated

Blend flour, butter and seasonings; add milk and cheese. Heat until thickened, stirring constantly. Pour over eggs; bake at 350°F. for 25 minutes. Yield: 4-5 servings.

Mrs. Frances McLaughlin, Connersville H.S.
Connersville, Indiana

HAM AND EGG PIE

2 c. med. white sauce
Unbaked pastry
3 c. ham, diced
8 hard-cooked eggs, sliced

Prepare white sauce using chicken bouillon. Line a casserole with half of pastry. Add alternate layers of ham, egg slices and white sauce. Cover with remaining pastry. Bake at 350°F. for 35-40 minutes or until crust is done. Yield: 8 servings.

Mrs. Louise Howard, Preble-Shawnee Local H.S.
Camden, Ohio

PICNIC CASSEROLE

1 can mushroom soup
1 pkg. noodles, cooked
Milk
3 hard-cooked eggs, chopped
¼ lb. American cheese, grated
1 can peas
1 pkg. potato chips, crushed
French-fried onion rings
1 T. butter

Combine soup and noodles; add enough mix to thin slightly. Place half of mixture in a buttered casserole. Add eggs, cheese, peas and potato chips in layers. Top with onion rings; dot with butter. Bake at 350°F. for 1 hour. Yield: 8 servings.

Mrs. Janice Larson, Iron River H.S.
Iron River, Michigan

ROLLED OMELET

2 eggs
4 T. cream, top milk or evaporated milk
Pinch of salt
Dash of pepper
1 T. butter

Combine all ingredients except butter with 25-30 strokes, using a fork. Melt butter over medium heat; pour in omelet. Roll with pancake turner or spatula to center. Cook until lightly browned; serve immediately. NOTE: Optional filling of crumbled ham, bacon, cheese, jelly or cranberry sauce may be used. Add before rolling omelet. Yield: 1 serving.

Ruth E. Carlson, Donovan H.S.
Donovan, Illinois

SCALLOPED BACON AND EGGS

¼ c. onion, chopped
2 T. butter
2 T. flour
1½ c. milk
1 c. American cheese, shredded
6 hard-cooked eggs, sliced
1½ c. potato chips, crushed
10 sl. crisp bacon, crumbled

Saute onions in butter until tender. Blend in flour; add milk gradually. Cook, stirring constantly until thickened, add cheese and stir until melted. Place layer of egg slices in 10x6-inch baking dish. Cover with half of cheese sauce, half of potato chips and half of bacon; repeat layers. Bake at 350°F. for 15-20 minutes. Yield: 4 servings.

Mrs. Betty Keeney, Gilbert Community School
Gilbert, Iowa

STUFFED EGGS AU GRATIN

6 hard-cooked eggs
½ t. dry mustard
1 T. vinegar
2 T. melted margarine
½ t. salt
1 sl. ham, finely chopped

Cut eggs in half lengthwise; remove and mash yolk. Add remaining ingredients; mix well. Fill whites with yolk mixture, place in a buttered shallow casserole.

SAUCE:
3 T. melted margarine
3 T. flour
1 t. salt
½ t. basil
2 c. milk
½ c. grated cheese

Melt margarine; blend in flour and add salt and basil. Gradually add milk; cook over low heat until thickened, stirring constantly. Pour over eggs; sprinkle with cheese. Bake at 350°F. for 25 minutes or until browned. Yield: 6 servings.

Alma Frerichs, Grants Pass H.S.
Grants Pass, Oregon

SOUFFLE CHOUX DE BRUXELLE

1 10 oz. pkg. frozen California Brussels Sprouts
3 T. butter or margarine
¼ c. flour
½ t. salt
1 c. milk
4 eggs, separated
1 c. grated Cheddar cheese

Cook Brussels sprouts according to package directions; drain if necessary. Chop fine. Blend flour and salt into melted butter in large saucepan. Gradually add milk and cook over low heat, stirring constantly, until thickened. Beat egg yolks. Blend in some hot milk mixture, then add to saucepan. Add cheese, cook 1 minute stirring constantly. Stir in sprouts; remove from heat. Beat egg whites until stiff but not dry; fold into hot mixture. Turn into ungreased 2-quart casserole. Bake at 300°F. for 1½ hours. Yield: 4-6 servings.

Photograph for this recipe on page 235

Convenience Casseroles

BEEF-VEGETABLE CURRY

1 clove garlic, minced
½ c. onions, chopped
½ stick butter, melted
2 lb. boneless beef, cut in ½-inch cubes
1½ T. curry powder
1 t. salt
1½ c. water
1 c. peeled, cored apples, sliced
½ c. golden raisins
½ c. Parmesan cheese, grated
2 T. flour
1 10-oz. pkg. frozen peas and carrots, thawed
1 10-oz. pkg. corn bread mix
1 c. Cheddar cheese, cubed

Saute garlic and onion in butter until tender; remove from skillet. Brown meat in same skillet. Stir curry powder and salt into drippings; add water, apples, raisins, cheese, browned onion and garlic. Cover and simmer 30 minutes or until meat is tender. Blend in flour; sprinkle peas and carrots over meat mixture. Prepare corn bread according to package directions. Fold cubed cheese into batter. Spread over meat mixture and bake in preheated 425°F. oven for 15-20 minutes. NOTE: This casserole may be baked and frozen. Thaw thoroughly before reheating. Yield: 8 servings.

Mrs. Jane Hutchins, Bangor H.S.
Bangor, Michigan

HAMBURGER-CREAM CHEESE CASSEROLE

1 lb. hamburger
1 onion, chopped
1 T. butter
1 t. salt
½ t. pepper
2 8-oz. cans tomato sauce
1 8-oz. pkg. noodles
1 c. creamed cottage cheese
1 8-oz. pkg. cream cheese
¼ c. sour cream
⅓ c. green onion, sliced
¼ c. green pepper, chopped

Brown hamburger and onion in butter; stir in salt, pepper and tomato sauce. Remove from heat. Cook noodles according to directions on package; drain. Combine cottage cheese, cream cheese, sour cream, green onion and green pepper. Spread half the noodles in 3-quart casserole. Cover with cheese mixture; top with remaining noodles. Pour hamburger mixture over top. Bake in 350°F. oven about 30 minutes. NOTE: This casserole may be frozen. Yield: 8-10 servings.

Mrs. Hazel Tassis, Imperial H.S.
Imperial, California

CASSEROLE FOR THE CROWD

1½ lb. ground beef
1 c. onion, chopped
1 12-oz. can whole-kernel corn
1 can condensed cream of chicken soup
1 can condensed cream of mushroom soup
1 c. sour cream
¼ c. pimento, chopped (opt.)
¾ t. salt
½ t. monosodium glutamate
¼ t. pepper
3 c. med. noodles, cooked and drained
1 c. buttered soft bread crumbs

Brown meat. Add onion; cook until tender but not brown. Add corn, soups, sour cream, pimento and seasonings; mix well. Gently fold in noodles. Pour into a 2-quart buttered casserole. Sprinkle crumbs over top. Bake at 350°F. until bubbly hot and crumbs browned. NOTE: May be frozen before baking. Yield: 10-12 servings.

Mrs. Maurietta W. Cusey, Wapella H.S.
Wapella, Illinois

FREEZER MEAT LOAF

1¼ lbs. ground beef
¼ lb. ground pork
¼ c. onion, minced
1 c. rolled oats, uncooked
2½ t. salt
¼ t. pepper
¼ tomato catsup
1 egg, well beaten
1 c. milk
1 12-oz. pkg. frozen mixed vegetables

Mix all ingredients except vegetables. Put meat mixture into a greased 1½-quart casserole. Bake at 375°F. for 1 hour. Seal casserole cover in place with freezer tape; freeze. Pour vegetables over loaf. Reheat in 350°F. oven before serving until piping hot all the way to the center, about 45 minutes. NOTE: Do not add vegetables if the meat loaf is to be frozen. Add vegetables before heating. Yield: 6 servings.

Mrs. Lucille Craddock, Benton Consolidated H.S.
Benton, Illinois

JOHNNIE MAZETTE

2 c. pepper, chopped
1 c. celery, chopped
2 c. onion, chopped
2 lb. ground beef
1 c. margarine or butter
1 c. stuffed olives, chopped (opt.)
1 4-oz. can sliced mushrooms with liquid
2 t. salt
2 cans tomato soup
1 can tomato sauce
2 c. American cheese, grated

(Continued on Next Page)

Saute pepper, celery, onion and ground beef in melted butter; add salt. Reduce heat to medium; cook 5 minutes. Stir in olives, mushrooms and liquid; cook 5 minutes. Cook noodles; drain. Pour noodles into a roasting pan; add sauce and stir gently until well mixed. Sprinkle grated cheese on top. Bake at 350°F. for 35 minutes. NOTE: Freezes very well. Yield: 12 servings.

Pearl E. Reuter, Fayetteville H.S.
Bedford, Indiana

HEARTY WESTERN CASSEROLE

½ c. onion, chopped
½ cube butter or margarine
1 8-oz. pkg. noodles, cooked
1 can corned beef
1 can cream of mushroom soup
1 c. milk
½ c. cheese, shredded
Potato chips, crushed

Saute onions in butter until light brown. Place corned beef in a large bowl and break into small pieces; add soup, cheese, milk, onions, and cooked noodles. Mix gently but thoroughly. Place in baking pan or casserole; cover top with potato chips. Bake at 350°F. for 35 minutes or until heated well and browned. NOTE: Casserole can be doubled and half frozen for future use. Yield: 7-10 servings.

Janet C. Clark, Rigby H.S.
Rigby, Idaho

A MAN'S CASSEROLE

3 med. onions, chopped
2 T. butter
4 c. medium noodles
2 lb. ground chuck
1 T. salad oil
2 t. salt
½ t. pepper
1 c. undiluted cream of celery soup
½ c. milk
1½ c. American cheese, grated
3 eggs, beaten

Saute onion in butter. Cook noodles until barely tender; rinse and drain. Brown meat in oil; add seasonings and cook 10 minutes. Add onions. In a 3-quart casserole arrange one-third of the noodles, half meat mixture, and half the soup diluted with milk. Repeat layers; arrange remaining noodles on top. Refrigerate or freeze. When ready to bake, sprinkle cheese on top; pour eggs over cheese. Do not mix. Bake uncovered at 350°F. for 1 hour or until bubbly and brown. Top will be very crispy. Yield: 8-10 servings.

Mrs. Judith H. Grigsby, Morristown H.S.
Morristown, Indiana

HUNTER'S DINNER

2 lb. veal or beef, diced
2 lb. pork, diced
2 onions, finely cut
1 bunch celery, finely cut
1 No. 303 can lima beans
Salt and pepper to taste
½ lb. shell macaroni
1 can mushrooms or soup
1 can tomato paste or 1-2 cans tomato soup

Simmer meat with onion and celery. Boil macaroni a little, but not done. Combine all ingredients in a roaster and bake 1½ to 2 hours at 350°F. If not enough moisture, add tomato juice or water. NOTE: Freezes well and is good reheated.

Mrs. Ann Vanvig, Belfield H.S.
Belfield, North Dakota

MEXICAN SPAGHETTI

1 lb. ground meat
1 med. bell pepper, diced
1 med. onion, diced
3 T. ground chili
1 8-oz. can tomato sauce
1 t. salt
1 t. pepper
1 t. garlic salt
1 12-oz. pkg. spaghetti

Brown ground beef; add peppers and onions. Cook until tender. Stir in ground chili, tomato sauce and remaining seasonings; simmer for 15 minutes. Cook spaghetti according to directions on package; drain and rinse with cold water. Combine with meat sauce. Serve immediately or pour into a casserole to store in freezer or refrigerator. If frozen, place directly into cold oven and bake at 200°F. for 20-25 minutes; increase temperature to 400°F. and heat 25-30 minutes or until piping hot. Yield: 4-6 servings.

Ruth A. Dunn, Marshall Jr. H.S.
Clovis, New Mexico

MOCK CHICKEN CASSEROLE

2-3 lb. coarsely ground pork
2 sm. onions, chopped
½ green pepper, chopped
9 c. water
3 pkg. dry chicken-noodle soup mix
2 c. instant rice
1 med. bunch celery, chopped
Salt and pepper to taste
1 c. toasted almonds

Brown pork, onion and green pepper. Bring water to a boil; add soup, rice and celery. Cook until celery is crisp but tender. Add meat mixture and seasoning. Pour into a large casserole; sprinkle almonds over top. Bake at 350°F. until hot. Add more water if necessary. NOTE: Casserole freezes well. Yield: 20-24 servings.

Mrs. Lillian Moran, Filer H.S.
Filer, Idaho

PINEAPPLE-HAM CASSEROLE

2 c. cooked ham, cut into bite-size pieces
2 T. butter or margarine
1 lge. green pepper, cut in strips
1 13½-oz. can frozen pineapple chunks, partially
   thawed
1 T. cornstarch
Pineapple syrup
2 T. brown sugar
2 T. vinegar

Fry ham in melted butter until lightly browned.
Add green pepper strips and pineapple chunks;
cook for 2-3 minutes. Make a smooth paste of
cornstarch and pineapple syrup; if necessary, ad1
enough water to make ¾ cup liquid. Stir into
the ham mixture along with brown sugar and vinegar. Cook, stirring constantly, until clear and thick.
Pour into containers and freeze for at least 24
hours. To thaw, remove from the freezer and
thaw in refrigerator; heat and eat. Yield: 4-6
servings.

Sandra Bartecchi, Robichaud H.S.
Dearborn Heights, Michigan

RICE-ALMOND CASSEROLE

1 lb. ground beef
1 c. onion, chopped
1 c. celery, chopped
1 c. green pepper, chopped
2 4-oz. cans mushrooms
2 c. boiling water
2 c. brown rice
4 cans cream of chicken soup
2 cans cream of mushroom soup
1 can chicken-rice soup
1 c. slivered almonds
¼ c. soy sauce

Brown beef, onion, celery and green pepper. Add
the mushrooms, water and rice; cover and simmer 15 minutes or until liquid is absorbed. Add
soups, almonds and soy sauce; mix well. Place
in large casserole or several small ones. Bake
45 minutes at 350°F. NOTE: Casserole may
be frozen for future use. Yield: 15-20 servings.

Mrs. Enid Hedrick, Bolsa Grande H.S.
Garden Grove, California

SOUR CREAM SUPREME

1½ lb. ground beef
1 clove of garlic, chopped
1 t. salt
1 t. sugar
Dash of pepper
2 8-oz. cans tomato sauce
1 sm. pkg. cream cheese
1 c. sour cream
5 green onions with tops finely cut
1 8-oz. pkg. macaroni
½ lb. Cheddar cheese, grated

Brown ground beef and garlic in large skillet;
add salt, sugar, pepper and tomato sauce. Simmer 20 minutes. Cook macaroni. Blend cream
cheese and sour cream until smooth; add green
onions. Grease large casserole dish; add a layer
of macaroni, a layer of cream mixture and a
layer of meat sauce. Repeat twice, ending with
meat sauce. Top with grated cheese. Refrigerate
overnight. Bake 45 minutes at 350°F. NOTE: This
dish freezes very well. Yield: 8 servings.

Mrs. Ruth Park, Bend H.S.
Bend, Oregon

TWIN SAUSAGE CASSEROLES

1 6-oz. can sliced mushrooms
6 chicken bouillon cubes
1 lb. pork sausage
1 lb. ground beef
2 c. celery, chopped
1 c. green pepper, chopped
½ c. Parmesan cheese, grated
1 t. salt
⅛ t. pepper
½ t. dried marjoram leaves
2 c. uncooked rice

Drain mushrooms and add enough water to liquid to make 5 cups. Add bouillon cubes and heat
to dissolve. Brown meats and drain off fat and
liquid. Combine meat with remaining ingredients
except bouillon. Line 2 casseroles with aluminum
foil. Divide mixture evenly in the casseroles.
Pour half of hot bouillon mixture over each casserole. Stir lightly to blend. Cover and bake in
350°F. oven for 15 minutes. Remove from
oven; leave covered and cool to room temperature. Freeze. When frozen, lift from casserole;
wrap. May store for 1 month. To serve, heat
unthawed in covered casserole at 350°F. for 1
hour and 30 minutes. Yield: 4-6 servings.

Mrs. Lee Iris Britton, Buhler Rural H.S.
Buhler, Kansas

CHICKEN DELUXE CASSEROLE

1 hen, cooked and cut up
1 qt. broth
1 loaf bread, cubed
1 c. finely chopped onions
1 c. finely chopped celery
1 4-oz. can pimentos
1 6-oz. can mushrooms
6 eggs, well beaten
Cracker crumbs

Combine all ingredients except crumbs; place in
a greased 2-quart casserole. Top with cracker
crumbs. Bake at 350°F. for 1 hour. NOTE: May
be frozen. Yield: 12 servings.

Mrs Florence Lemons, North Green H.S.
White Hall, Illinois

TURKEY-RICE SPECIAL

¾ lb. pork sausage
1 c. celery, chopped
1 c. onion, chopped
1 c. uncooked rice
3 cans chicken noodle soup
1-1½ c. water
½ c. blanched almonds, sliced
1 c. sliced turkey or chicken

Saute the sausage, celery, and onion on medium heat until meat is browned; add the remaining ingredients. Cover the skillet and turn to high until steaming. Reduce heat and simmer for 45 minutes. NOTE: This may be baked in a covered casserole at 325°F. for 1½ hours. Remove cover the last 20 minutes of baking time and top with crushed potato chips. May be frozen and reheated. Yield: 10-12 servings.

Charlyene Deck, Exeter Union H.S.
Exeter, California

MEXICAN CORN BREAD

2 c. corn meal
1 t. soda
1 t. salt
4 eggs
1½ c. milk
⅔ c. bacon grease
2 cans creamed corn
1 c. green chili, chopped
2 c. Cheddar cheese, grated

Sift corn meal, soda and salt together. Add eggs, milk and ⅓ cup bacon grease. Mix well. Add creamed corn; mix. Pour half of mixture into a heavy skillet or heavy casserole in which the remaining bacon grease is melted. Spread with chili and 1 cup of cheese. Add the remaining batter. Sprinkle with remaining cheese. Bake 45 minutes at 400°F. NOTE: This freezes with excellent results. Recipe is for altitude of 4000 feet; adjust accordingly. Yield: 8 servings.

Mercedes Hoskins, Lynn Jr. H.S.
Las Cruces, New Mexico

BAKED SWEET POTATO CASSEROLE

6 med. sweet potatoes
¼ c. brown sugar
¼ c. condensed milk
1 c. crushed pineapple, drained
½ c. nuts, chopped
9 marshmallows

Bake sweet potatoes; peel and mash while hot. Add brown sugar, condensed milk, pineapple and nuts; mix well. Pour into a buttered casserole. Top with marshmallows and brown at 400°F. NOTE: This is an excellent freezer casserole. Omit the marshmallows until the casserole is partially thawed; then top with marshmallows and finish baking. Yield: 8-10 servings.

Mrs. Gladys M. Clark, Cedar Vale H.S.
Cedar Vale, Kansas

CHICKEN-VEGETABLE CASSEROLE

1 2-lb. pkg. frozen peas
1½ c. chicken fat or ¾ lb. butter
2 c. sifted flour
3 T. salt
½ t. pepper
2½ qt. milk
1¼ qt. chicken stock or bouillon
½ c. onions, finely chopped
3 T. lemon juice
1¼ lb. spaghetti, cooked and drained
2 chickens, cooked and diced
1 lb. Cheddar cheese, grated

Cook peas and drain. Make cream sauce using chicken fat, flour, salt, pepper, milk and chicken stock; add onions. Cook until thickened. Add peas, lemon juice, spaghetti and chicken; mix well. Pour into 5 8x8x2-inch baking pans. Sprinkle with cheese. Bake at 350°F. for 30 minutes or until bubbly and heated through. NOTE: May be frozen before baking and baked as they are used. Yield: 30 servings.

Mrs. Margaret C. Hoffman, Victory H.S.
Harrisville, Pennsylvania

OPEN-FACED HAMBURGERS

1 lb. ground beef
½ c. catsup
¼ t. dry mustard
2 T. onion, chopped
½ c. Parmesan cheese, grated
Salt and pepper
8 hamburger buns split
Pickles
Olives

Combine all ingredients. Spread mixture on each half of bun. Broil 5 minutes. Serve immediately with pickles and olives. Yield: 8 servings.

Mrs. Mary Lou Demoise, Conestoga Valley H.S.
Lancaster, Pennsylvania

PIZZA TOASTIES

1½ lb. ground beef
1 t. salt
½ t. garlic salt
1 t. onion salt
½ t. black pepper
1 t. oregano
12 hamburger buns
Butter
2 c. Mozzarella cheese, grated

Toast hamburger buns lightly; butter. Combine ground beef and seasonings. Spread open-face buns, with ground beef mixture; broil 2-3 minutes. Sprinkle buns with grated cheese; return to oven until cheese melts. Yield: 6 double sandwiches.

Boni Standaert, Cashton Public Schools
Cashton, Wisconsin

SOUPER BURGERS

1 lb. ground beef
2 or 3 T. onion, chopped
½ c. tomato soup
½ t. horseradish
½ t. mustard
½ t. Worcestershire sauce
Salt to taste
Butter
Garlic salt
Celery salt
Paprika
French bread or rolls

Combine all ingredients except butter, salts, paprika and bread. Spread on French bread or French rolls cut lengthwise. This amount will be plenty for the bottom of four to six large French Rolls. Broil about 10 minutes or until done. Butter cut side of top piece of bread; sprinkle with garlic salt, celery salt and paprika. Place in oven about 30 seconds before serving. Yield: 6 servings.

Mrs. Loretta Wulf, Dell Rapids Public H.S.
Dell Rapids, South Dakota

HAM AND CHEESEWICHES

4 eggs, beaten
½ t. salt
¼ t. pepper
1½ c. milk
8 slices bread
2 c. baked ham, chopped
2 c. Wisconsin cheese, grated

Combine eggs, seasonings and milk. Place bread side-by-side in a long baking pan. Cover with ham; sprinkle with cheese. Pour over milk mixture. Refrigerate 5 hours or overnight. Bake at 300°F. for 30 minutes. Cut in squares; serve hot. Yield: 8-10 servings.

Elizabeth Sacker, Cherry Hill H.S.
Cherry Hill, New Jersey

OPEN-FACE DENVER SANDWICH

2 T. butter or margarine
1 pkg. refrigerated flaky rolls
4 eggs
¼ c. milk
¾ c. cooked ham, diced
2 T. onion, finely diced
2 T. parsley, chopped
¼ t. salt

Melt the butter or margarine in a 9-inch pie plate. Separate the 12 rolls; dip each into butter to coat both sides. Arrange in single layer in pie plate. Bake in 450°F. oven for 5 minutes. While rolls bake, beat eggs in medium size bowl; stir in milk, ham, onion, parsley and salt. Remove rolls from oven; reduce heat to 350°F. Spoon egg mixture over rolls. Bake 20 minutes longer or until custard is set. Cut into 4 wedges. Serve hot. Yield: 4 servings.

Carol Peterson, Estherville H.S.
Estherville, Iowa

WESTERN HAMBURGER SANDWICH

3 T. butter or fat
1 lb. hamburger
1 onion, grated
4 eggs, beaten
¼ c. cold water
1 t. mustard
1 t. salt
⅛ t. pepper
12 sl. buttered bread

Melt butter; add hamburger and onion. Brown slowly, stirring frequently. Combine eggs, water, mustard, salt and pepper; beat well. Pour over meat mixture. Fry, stirring slowly until eggs are set. Serve mixture between slices of buttered bread or toast. Yield: 6-8 servings.

Dora C. Fleming, Centerville H.S.
Sand Coulee, Montana

WESTERN RANCHO CANAPES

6 French roll buns
1 lb. mild processed cheese, softened
¾ lb. ground beef
½ t. salt
1 4-oz. can sliced mushrooms
½ t. oregano
1 8-oz. can tomato sauce
1 c. green onions, sliced

Cut French rolls in half lengthwise. Spread cheese on cut side of rolls. Brown ground beef until crumbly; drain off fat. Combine salt, mushrooms, oregano and tomato sauce with ground beef. Spoon over bread. Top with green onions. Bake at 450°F. for 5 minutes. Yield: 12 servings.

Mrs. Manuel Cox, Scappoose Union H.S.
Scappoose, Oregon

HAM FOOTBALLS

⅔ c. deviled ham
2 t. onion, minced
4 T. green pepper, chopped
¼ lb. process cheese, grated
4 T. piccalilli
2 T. catsup
6 sliced frankfurter buns
6 sl. process cheese

Combine ham, onion, green pepper, grated cheese, picalilli and catsup. Spread 3 tablespoons ham mixture on each bun half. Cut cheese slices into ¼-inch strips; arrange two strips parallel along length of buns. Cut remaining strips in half and lay them across long cheese strips to resemble a laced football. Place bun halves on a cookie sheet; heat in 400°F. oven for 10-15 minutes or until cheese has melted sufficiently. Yield: 12 open-faced sandwiches.

Phyllis Ann Lankalis, Diamond Jr. H.S.
Lexington, Massachusetts

SAUSAGE SANDWICH

1 lb. pork sausage links
2 T. water
16 T. applesauce
8 slices buttered toast
4 slices Velveeta cheese

Place sausage and water in a cold frying-pan. Cover tightly; cook slowly 5 minutes. Uncover pan; brown links. Spread 2 tablespoons applesauce on each of 8 slices of buttered toast. Arrange 2 pork sausage links on each slice of bread; top with a cheese strip. Broil sandwiches until cheese melts. Yield: 8 servings.

Mrs. Shirley Campbell, Alexis Community H.S.
Alexis, Illinois

HOT CHICKEN DINNER SANDWICH

6 firm, ripe tomatoes
1 30-oz. can boned chicken
1 can cream of chicken soup
½ lb. processed cheese, sliced
12 hamburger buns, split and toasted
24 slices or 1 lb. bacon, cooked until crisp

Cut each tomato into 4 slices; arrange in a greased shallow pan. Top each slice with a serving of chicken. Stir soup until smooth; spread over tomato and chicken. Place cheese slice on top of each mound. Bake in 450°F. oven for about 10 minutes. Serve each mound on half a toasted bun. Garnish with crisp bacon. Yield: 24 servings.

Mrs. Berneta B. Hackney
McGuffey-McDonald School
McGuffey, Ohio

HOT CHICKEN SANDWICHES

1 can cream of mushroom soup
1 T. onion, minced
½ of 2-oz. jar pimento, chopped
3 T. flour
¾ c. plus 3 T. milk
1½-2 c. chicken, diced
8 slices sandwich bread, crusts removed
2 eggs, beaten, slightly
2 c. potato chips, crushed
½ c. slivered almonds

Combine soup, onion and pimento in a pan. Blend flour with ¾ cup milk; add to soup mixture. Cook, stirring until thick. Add chicken. Place 4 slices of bread in a 9x9-inch pan. Cover with soup and chicken mixture. Place remaining slices of bread on top. Chill several hours or overnight. Mix eggs with remaining milk. Cut sandwiches in half. Dip both sides in egg mixture, then in crushed potato chips. Arrange on a buttered cookie sheet; top with almonds. Bake in 350°F. oven for 25 minutes. Yield: 4 servings.

Mrs. Diane Isakson, Chaska Public School
Chaska, Minnesota

SAUCY SALAD SANDWICH

2 c. chicken, tuna or turkey, chopped
1 c. celery, chopped
2 T. pickle relish
½ c. mayonnaise
1 c. cheese, grated
4 hamburger buns

Combine meat, celery, pickle relish, and mayonnaise. Spread on buns; making 8 sandwiches. Top each with cheese. Place on cookie sheet. Broil until cheese melts. Yield: 4 servings.

Mrs. Phyllis Wright, Faulkton H.S.
Faulkton, South Dakota

SAUCY TURKEY SANDWICHES

¼ c. flour
¼ c. butter or margarine, melted
1 pt. milk
6 oz. process cheese, grated
16 toast slices, crusts removed
1 c. whole cranberry sauce
16 slices cooked turkey

Blend flour into melted butter. Add milk; cook until thick, stirring constantly. Add cheese; stir until melted. Place 8 toast slices in shallow individual casseroles. Cover each toast slice with 2 tablespoons cranberry sauce, 2 slices turkey and another toast slice. Pour ⅓ cup cheese sauce over each sandwich. Bake in 325°F. oven for 15 minutes. Yield: 8 servings.

Sister M. Vincentella, O.S.F. Boylan Central
Catholic H.S.
Campus Hills, Rockford, Illinois

CRAB SANDWICHES

1 lge. pkg. cream cheese
Mayonnaise
1 can crab meat
1 med. onion, finely minced
1 t. Worcestershire sauce
Salt to taste
8 Holland Rusks
8 slices tomato
4 slices American cheese

Combine cream cheese, enough mayonnaise to blend, crab, onion, Worcestershire sauce and salt. Spread on rounds of Holland Rusks. Place a tomato slice on top of each open-faced sandwich. Place slices of American cheese on tomato. Place under broiler until cheese is slightly melted and browned. Yield: 4 servings.

Mrs. Martha R. LaCourse, Folsom H.S.
Folsom, California

GRILLED SALMON SANDWICHES

1 c. salmon, flaked
1½ c. cheese, shredded
1 hard-cooked egg, chopped
2 T. pickle relish
2 T. salad dressing
2 T. green pepper (opt.)
¼ t. salt
Dash of pepper
12 slices sandwich bread
Soft butter or margarine

Drain salmon. Combine salmon, cheese, egg, pickle relish, salad dressing, green pepper, salt and pepper. Spread bread with butter or margarine on one side. Spread mixture on buttered side of half of bread slices. Close sandwiches with remaining bread slices. Brush outside surfaces with butter. Toast on lightly greased hot griddle until filling is hot and outside surfaces of sandwiches are golden brown. Yield: 6-8 servings.

Marguerite Holloway, Petersburg Harris H.S.
Petersburg, Illinois

BROILED TUNA SALAD SANDWICHES

1 c. sharp cheese, cubed
1 7-oz. can tuna, drained and flaked
2 T. green pepper, chopped
1 t. salt
1 c. hard-cooked egg, chopped
2 T. onion, chopped
½ c. mayonnaise
6 sandwich buns

Combine all ingredients except buns. Split buns; spread with mixture. Arrange on broiler pan. Broil for 3-4 minutes in hot oven. Yield: 12 servings.

Ruth G. Seitz, North Hills H.S.
Pittsburgh, Pennsylvania

TUNA BAKED SANDWICHES

8 slices bread, trimmed and toasted
1 6½ to 7-oz. can tuna, drained
¼ c. chopped celery
¼ c. chopped green pepper
½ t. dry mustard
2 T. sliced pimento-stuffed olives
2 T. flour
½ t. paprika
1 c. milk
¾ c. grated Cheddar cheese

Place four slices toast on bottom of greased shallow baking dish. Combine tuna, celery, green pepper, mustard and olives; mix well. Spread tuna mixture on top of bread. Mix flour and paprika; slowly stir in milk. Cook over low heat, stirring constantly, until thickened. Remove from heat; stir in cheese. Pour over tuna mixture. Bake at 325°F. for 20 minutes. Top with remaining four slices of toast. Yield: 4 servings.

Photograph for this recipe on page 269

BUN-STEADS

¼ lb. American cheese, cubed
3 hard-cooked eggs, chopped
1 7-oz. can tuna, flaked
2 T. green pepper, chopped
2 T. onion, chopped
2 T. stuffed olives, chopped
2 T. sweet pickle, chopped
½ c. salad dressing
6 coney or wiener buns

Combine all ingredients except buns. Mix lightly. Split buns; fill with mixture. Wrap in foil. Heat in 275°F. oven for 30 minutes. Yield: 6 servings.

Mrs. Mary Wedam, Wray H.S.
Wray, Colorado

TUNA BUNS

¼ lb. grated cheese
3 hard-cooked eggs, chopped
2 T. onions, chopped
1 can tuna
2 T. sweet pickle
Dash of lemon juice
Salad dressing
Buns

Combine all ingredients in a bowl using enough salad dressing to moisten. Fill 1 dozen weiner or hamburger buns generously. Wrap each in Aluminum foil. Bake in 325°F. oven for about 20 minutes. Yield: 12 servings.

Sherry Anderson, Hibbing H.S.
Hibbing, Minnesota

MARINER'S SANDWICH

1 can flaked tuna, drained
2 T. onion, finely minced
½-1 t. lemon juice
Mayonnaise
Salt and pepper
½ c. process cheese, cubed

Mix together all ingredients except cheese. Add cheese; toss well. Spread on 4 slices of toast. Broil until cheese melts. Yield: 4 servings.

Mrs. Elsie Vredenburg, Chesaning H.S.
Chesaning, Michigan

TUNA BURGERS

1 family-size can tuna
½ c. mayonnaise
½ c. chile sauce
1 t. oregano
1 t. grated onion
8 slices American cheese
4 day-old hamburger buns

Flake tuna; add mayonnaise, chili sauce, oregano and grated onion. Mix thoroughly. Open buns; place on cookie sheet. Spread cut sides completely with tuna mixture. Place a slice of cheese on top of each bun. Broil until cheese melts. Yield: 4 servings.

Mrs. Marjorie Carpp, Lawrence H.S.
Lawrence, Michigan

TUNA SANDWICHES

1 7-oz. can tuna
1 c. celery, chopped
⅓ c. onion, minced
½ c. Cheddar cheese, diced
½ c. ripe olives, chopped
¼ c. mayonnaise
Salt and pepper to taste
6 hamburger buns

Mix all ingredients except bread until blended. Divide into 6 parts; spread on buns. Wrap each bun in aluminum foil, sealing ends. Bake in 350°F. oven for 15-20 minutes. Serve hot. Yield: 6 servings.

Mary Carlyn Mitchell, Pelican Rapids H.S.
Pelican Rapids, Minnesota

GOOEY BUNS

1 lb. bologna
¾ lb. sharp cheese
¼ c. prepared mustard
⅓ c. salad dressing
1 onion, minced
4-6 T. sweet pickle
Buns

Grind all ingredients; mix well. Fill weiner buns; wrap each one in foil. Bake in 325°F. oven for 25 minutes. NOTE: These may be frozen after preparation and used for snacks, parties etc. If they are frozen, bake at same temperature, but increase time to 30 minutes. Yield: 12 servings.

This recipe submitted by the following teachers:
Mrs. Kathryn Lotz, Riverdale H.S.
Mount Blanchard, Ohio
Mrs. Margery Heavner, Neponset H.S.
Neponset, Illinois

SURPRISE LUNCHEON SANDWICHES

Butter
16 slices bread
Mayonnaise
2 c. celery, chopped
⅓ c. green pepper, chopped
2 T. onion, chopped
1 sm. can tuna
8 slices Cheddar cheese
4 eggs, beaten
3 c. milk
1 can mushroom soup (opt.)

Butter bread slices on one side; spread other side with mayonnaise. Spread eight slices with filling made of celery, green pepper, onion and tuna. Cover with slice of cheese and second slice of bread. Place in flat baking dish. Cover with mixture of eggs and milk. Refrigerate overnight or for several hours. Bake at 300°F. oven for 1 hour and 30 minutes. Serve with a gravy made of undiluted mushroom soup, if desired. NOTE: These are good also made with chicken, turkey, beef, pork or crab. Yield: 8 servings.

Mrs. Elizabeth Hayton, Huntington Jr. H.S.
Kelso, Washington

WAFFLED SANDWICHES

¼ c. chili sauce
Worcestershire sauce
4 slices American cheese
4 slices lge. bologna or boiled ham
4 thin slices tomato
½ c. butter, melted
8 slices white bread

Blend chili sauce with 1 teaspoon Worcestershire sauce. Spread slices of bread with chili sauce mixture. On 4 slices place slice of American cheese, slice of bologna or ham, and slice of tomato. Cover with remaining bread slices. Melt butter; combine with 1 tablespoon Worcestershire. Brush outsides of sandwiches with butter mixture. Place sandwich on well oiled or greased waffle iron. Press lid down lightly. Grill until sandwich is crisp and brown. Yield: 4 servings.

Jan Nemer, Natrona County H.S.
Casper, Wyoming

QUICK SNACK SANDWICHES

6 slices white or rye bread
6 slices bologna or minced ham
12 slices tomato
6 slices American cheese

On each piece of bread arrange meat, cheese and tomato. Put under broiler; cook until cheese bubbles and browns. Serve immediately. Yield: 6 servings.

Mrs. Betty-Lou Archambault, Merrimack H.S.
Merrimack, New Hampshire

REUBEN SANDWICHES

5-8 slices rye bread
1 can corned beef
1 med. can sauerkraut
4-8 slices American or Swiss cheese

Toast rye bread. Heat corned beef and sauerkraut in separate pans. First add a layer of sauerkraut to toast, then a layer of corned beef. Top with a slice of cheese. Place under broiler until cheese melts. Serve immediately. NOTE: If desired, top cheese with another slice of toasted bread. Yield: 4 servings.

This recipe submitted by the following teachers:
Beverlee Brown, Miller City Schools
Miller, South Dakota
La Donna Snyder, South Central H.S.
Greenwich, Ohio

BROILED SPAMWICHES

1 can Spam
½ bell pepper
⅓ lb. sharp Cheddar cheese
½ onion
½ c. mayonnaise or salad dressing
2 t. prepared mustard
Buns or English muffins

Put all ingredients except mayonnaise, mustard and bread through food grinder. Add mayonnaise and mustard; mixing well. Spread on buns; broil open-faced until mixture begins to bubble. Yield: 8-10 servings.

Doris Mosaly, Emery H.S.
Emeryville, California

LITTLE PARTY PIZZAS

2 c. prepared biscuit mix
½ c. milk
2 T. butter, melted
6 T. tomato paste
½ c. sharp cheese, shredded
Oregano
½ pkg. pepperoni

Combine biscuit mix, milk and butter. Shape into ball; knead a few seconds. Divide into 6 pieces. Roll each piece into ball; place on cookie sheet. Pat each ball to 6-inch circle. Pinch edges to make rim. Spread crust with remaining ingredient Bake in hot oven until brown. Yield: 6 servings.

Mrs. Gary Whiteman, Cando H.S.
Cando, North Dakota

HEARTY SUPPER SANDWICH

Butter
1 egg
Salt and pepper
1 2-inch square cheese
2 slices bread, toasted or 1 bun, toasted

Melt butter in skillet; fry egg. Just before egg would be turned for hard cooked, sprinkle with salt and pepper and place cheese on half of egg. Turn other half of egg over cheese with spatula. Cook until cheese melts. Serve on hot bun or between toast. Yield: 1 serving.

May M. Rorick, The Dalles H.S.
The Dalles, Oregon

TOASTED CHEESE SQUARES

1 loaf unsliced bread
¼ lb. soft butter
1 egg
1 glass Old English sharp cheese

Cut bread into 1¾-inch squares. Remove crust. Cream other ingredients together until smooth. Spread mixture on all sides of bread cubes. Place on greased cookie sheet. Bake in 325°F. oven for 15 minutes or until delicately browned. Serve hot. NOTE: Excellent with salads. May be made ahead of time, wrap and refrigerate. Yield: 8 servings.

Marjorie L. Benesh, Bismarck H.S.
Bismarck, North Dakota

CHEESE DREAMS

6 slices of bread
3 or 4 sl. American process cheese
Butter
2 eggs
2 T. milk
¼ t. salt
Dash of pepper

Make cheese sandwiches as usual with bread, butter and cheese. Beat egg, add milk, salt and pepper. Dip sandwiches into egg mixture; fry in butter, turning to brown both sides. Allow cheese to melt; serve hot from the pan. Yield: 3 servings.

Chloe Bradford, Muskegon Heights Jr. H.S.
Muskegon Heights, Michigan

CHEESE FILLING FOR SANDWICH

4 T. vinegar
2 T. sugar
1 T. flour
1 egg, beaten
½ c. cream
½ lb. American cheese
4 hard-cooked eggs
1 pimento

Combine vinegar, sugar, flour, egg and cream; cook in double boiler until thick. Cool; add cheese, eggs and pimento.

Mrs. Wilda Carr, Holdrege H.S.
Holdrege, Nebraska

SOUFFLE SANDWICH

8 slices bread
American cheese
Butter
2 eggs
1 c. milk
½ T. Worcestershire sauce
1 can mushroom soup
1 can whole mushrooms

Cut crusts from bread. Butter one side; put 4 slices in 8x8 pan, butter-side down. Cover with 4 slices of cheese. Put other 4 slices of bread on cheese, butter-side up. Beat eggs with milk and Worcestershire sauce. Pour over bread and cheese. Cover; refrigerate overnight. Bake uncovered at 325°F. for 45 mniutes. Serve at once with sauce of 1 can mushroom soup and 1 can whole mushrooms and juice from latter. Yield: 4 servings.

Mrs. Rea B. Judd, Medina H.S.
Medina, North Dakota

BEEF AND VEGETABLES

2 c. left-over beef, diced
1 pkg. frozen mixed vegetables or 1½ c. left-over vegetables
1 sm. can mushroom pieces
1 c. left-over gravy
¼ c. Burgundy wine
2 slices sweet onion
Salt and pepper to taste

Combine beef, vegetables and mushrooms in medium casserole. Thin cold beef gravy with Burgundy wine. Pour over meat and vegetable mixture. Separate onion slices into rings; lay on top of mixture. Season to taste. Bake in 325°F. oven until bubbly. Yield: 4 servings.

Mrs. Frank W. Irwin, Meeker H.S.
Meeker, Colorado

CUBED BEEF

1 green pepper, diced
1 onion, chopped
3 stalks celery, diced
Fat
1 to 2 c. left-over meat cubes
1 can tomato soup
½ c. water

Brown green pepper, onion, and celery in fat. Add the meat, soup, and water and simmer. Serve over rice or fried noodles. Yield: 6 servings.

Verda Rex, Fielding H.S.
Paris, Idaho

GRANDMOTHER'S HASH

2 T. fat
1 med. onion, diced
2 c. left-over roast beef, diced
2 c. diced potatoes, cooked
1 c. gravy (opt.)
1 c. water
Any vegetable (opt.)

Lightly brown the onion in fat. Add all other ingredients and simmer slowly for 30 minutes until the flavors have blended and it is piping hot. NOTE: If gravy is omitted, use 2 cups water. Yield: 6 servings.

Mrs. Katherine Potter, Frontenac H.S.
Frontenac, Kansas

HAMBURGER PIE

1 lb. ground beef
1 med. onion, chopped
Salt and pepper
1 can green beans, drained
1 can condensed tomato soup
Left-over corn, peas or other vegetables
6 med. potatoes, cooked
½ c. warm milk
1 egg, beaten

Brown ground beef in its own fat. Add and brown onion before beef is fully cooked. Add salt and pepper to taste. Add beans, soup and any left-over vegetables; pour mixture into a greased 1½-quart casserole. Mash potatoes; add milk and egg. Season to taste. Heap in mounds around top of casserole. Bake at 350°F. for 25 minutes. Yield: 5 servings.

Clare T. Wilson, Bradford H.S.
Bradford, Ohio

LEFT-OVER CASSEROLE

1 c. raw potatoes, sliced
1 c. cooked meat, diced
1 c. left-over gravy
1 sm. onion, minced
½ t. salt
1 c. canned tomatoes

Place potatoes in casserole. Add meat and gravy. Add onion, salt and tomatoes. Bake until potatoes are done at 350°F. Yield: 8 servings.

Myra D. Sorensen, Richfield H.S.
Richfield, Utah

HELEN'S MEAT PIE

6 to 8 slices left-over roast beef, finely diced
1 sm. onion, finely diced
2 T. butter
2 c. left-over gravy
1 med. carrot, diced
1 lge. potato, diced
1 c. cabbage, shredded
Corn or peas, cooked (opt.)
1 sm. recipe baking powder biscuits

Brown meat and onion in butter; add gravy. Add vegetables and simmer for 20 minutes. Prepare biscuit dough. Place meat mixture in bottom of greased casserole. Roll out biscuit dough and place on top. Bake in 400°F. for 15 to 20 minutes or until biscuit is lightly browned. Yield: 4-5 servings.

Pat Van Deest, Alta Community School
Alta, Iowa

HOT TAMALE PIE

2 c. cooked meat, chopped
1 sm. onion, chopped
1 sm. green pepper
2 c. tomato sauce
Salt
Paprika
Tabasco sauce
½ c. corn meal
1½ c. boiling water
½ c. cheese, grated
¼ c. olives, chopped

Put meat, onion and green pepper through food chopper. Mix half the tomato sauce with meat; season highly with salt. Add paprika and Tabasco sauce. Sprinkle corn meal in boiling water with 1 teaspoon salt; stir until thickened. Cook in double boiler for 20 minutes. Line greased pan with corn meal mush; fill with meat mixture and sprinkle with cheese. Add chopped olives and remaining sauce. Cover with mush. Bake at 350°F. for 45 minutes to 1 hour. Yield: 6 servings.

Fernette Honaker, Menaul Presbyterian H.S.
Albuquerque, New Mexico

QUICK BARBECUE

1 c. beef gravy
1 c. catsup
Dash of garlic powder
1 c. water
2 T. A-1 sauce
Tabasco sauce to taste
Left-over roast, thinly sliced

Combine ingredients. Simmer for 1 hour. Serve over French rolls or toasted buns. NOTE: If hot catsup is used, omit Tabasco. Yield: 4 servings.

Mrs. Mary Zinselmeir, Fortuna Union H.S.
Fortuna, California

POTATO CRUST-BEEF CASSEROLE

2 c. roast beef, sliced
1 pt. beef gravy
2 c. flour
½ t. salt
2 t. baking powder
½ c. shortening
1 c. left-over mashed potatoes
¼ c. milk

Place the meat and gravy in a casserole. Sift together the flour, salt and baking powder; working in the shortening and potatoes. Add enough milk to make a soft dough. Turn onto a floured board and pat and roll lightly into shape to cover the dish. Bake at 350°F. until done and lightly browned. Yield: 6 servings.

Janice M. Mountz, Brandywine Heights H.S.
Topton, Pennsylvania

SHEPHERD'S PIE

1 c. gravy
3½ c. ground left-over roast
1 T. instant minced onion
½ c. raisins
1 T. Worcestershire sauce
3½ c. mashed potatoes
1 hard-cooked egg, sliced
Bread crumbs

Mix enough of the gravy with the cooked ground meat to produce a moist, but not soggy, mixture. Add the onion, raisins, Worcestershire sauce and salt. Place the meat and potatoes in layers in a large greased casserole, beginning with meat and ending with potatoes. On the top of each layer of meat place a few slices of egg. Sprinkle bread crumbs over the potatoe top which has been swirled into peaks; place casserole in a 350°F. oven for 40 to 50 minutes until heated through and the top is slightly browned. Yield: 4-6 servings.

Mrs. Ann Ducker, East H.S.
Bremerton, Washington

PORK CASSEROLE

Left-over pork roast, cubed
1 c. onions, chopped
1 c. celery, diced
1 c. water
¾ pkg. noodles, cooked
1 can cream of mushroom soup
1 can cream of tomato soup
Left-over gravy (opt.)
Buttered crumbs

Brown meat. Add onions, celery and water. Cook until tender. Mix with noodles and pour into a greased casserole. Mix soup with any leftover gravy and pour over mixture. Sprinkle top with buttered crumbs. Bake at 350°F. for 1 hour. Yield: 6-8 servings.

Mrs. Mildred Christensen, Boscobel H.S.
Boscobel, Wisconsin

PORK ROAST CASSEROLE

1-2 c. left-over pork roast, cubed
1 10-oz. can cream of celery soup
¼ c. green pepper, chopped
¼ c. onion, chopped
1-2 c. cooked noodles, drained
1 apple, cubed
1 c. canned green beans
Seasonings as desired

Combine all the ingredients and pour into a greased 1½-quart casserole. Bake in 400°F. oven for 20 minutes. Yield: 4-6 servings.

Mrs. Carol Pino, Williamston H.S.
Williamston, Michigan

SWEET AND SOUR NOODLE MEDLEY

1 lb. chop suey meat or left-overs
¼ c. water
2½ c. pineapple tidbits and juice
Flour
3 to 4 T. vinegar
2 t. soy sauce
½ t. salt
½ c. celery, sliced
¼ c. green pepper, cut into 1-inch strips
¼ c. onion, finely chopped
6 oz. med. egg noodles, cooked
2 T. margarine

Brown meat in skillet. Add water; cover and cook gently until tender, about 30 minutes. If using leftovers, just brown and heat. Drain the juice from the pineapple into a large saucepan. There should be about 1 cup of juice. Blend the flour with 3 tablespoons of the juice until smooth. Combine juice, flour mixture, vinegar and soy sauce. Boil until thickened and clear, stirring constantly. Add sauce to the meat; add salt, pineapple and sliced vegetables. Cook until the vegetables are done. Serve medley over egg noodles which have been tossed lightly with the margarine. Yield: 4 servings.

Anna Margaret Holien, Silverton Union H.S.
Silverton, Oregon

BAKED HAM-MACARONI CASSEROLE

¼ lb. uncooked macaroni
2 c. ham, chopped
1 can condensed cream of mushroom soup,
   undiluted
¾ c. water
1 T. onion, minced
¾ c. American cheese, grated

Cook macaroni in boiling, salted water and drain. Combine with ham, soup, water and onion. Place in casserole; sprinkle with cheese. Bake at 350°F. for 45 minutes. Yield: 6-8 servings.

Mrs. Lois Lake, Bazine Rural H.S.
Bazine, Kansas

HASH WITH MACARONI

1 pkg. macaroni
Left-over pork roast or steak
2 lge. onions
1 T. butter
2 T. flour
1½ c. soup stock, or water with cream
Left-over brown gravy (opt.)
Paprika
Salt and pepper to taste
2 T. soy sauce or Kitchen Bouquet
½ t. curry powder (opt.)
Bread crumbs

Cook macaroni until tender; rinse with cold water. Put meat and onions through meat grinder. Melt butter; add the flour and stir until smooth. Add the soup stock and cream, and any leftover brown gravy you may have. Add seasoning. Stir the meat into sauce. Butter a baking dish generously; dust it with bread crumbs. Put one layer of macaroni in casserole; add a layer of meat mixture. Repeat layers, ending with macaroni. Top with bread crumbs; dot with butter. Bake at 350°F. for 45 minutes. Yield: 6-8 servings.

Mrs. Irene Knudsen, Del Norte H.S.
Crescent City, California

CREAMED HAM DELIGHT

2 c. left-over baked ham, cubed
2 c. dried bread, cubed
4 hard-cooked eggs, sliced
2 c. med. cream sauce

Spread a layer of ham on bottom of greased casserole. Cover with layer of bread cubes, then layer of eggs. Pour half the cream sauce on. Repeat layers. Bake in 350°F. oven for 30 minutes. Yield: 4-6 servings.

Mrs. Frances Steube, Groveport Madison H.S.
Groveport, Ohio

HAM AND POTATO CASSEROLE

4 med. potatoes, peeled
½ t. salt
1 c. baked ham, diced
¼ c. instant dry onions
1 can mushroom soup
½ soup can water
½ c. cheese, grated

Slice potatoes into ¼-inch pieces. Salt and boil 15 minutes or until tender. Drain; place a layer of potatoes in a buttered baking dish. Cover with ham; sprinkle with onions. Repeat layers. Mix soup and water; pour over the layers. Sprinkle with cheese. Bake at 350°F. for 20 minutes or until heated through. Yield: 5 servings.

Mrs. Eunice Wood, Glendo H.S.
Glendo, Wyoming

HAM AND NOODLE CASSEROLE

3½ T. butter
2 T. flour
1 c. milk
1 c. cheese, grated
1 t. prepared horseradish
1 t. salt
2 T. tomato catsup
1½ c. cooked noodles
2 c. cooked ham, diced
1 c. cooked peas (opt.)
Bread crumbs

Melt 2 tablespoons butter in sauce pan; blend in flour. Slowly add milk. Cook over medium heat until thickened. Fold in cheese and stir until melted. Add horseradish, salt and catsup. Fold in noodles, ham and peas. Put in buttered casserole. Sprinkle bread crumbs over top and dot with remaining butter. Bake at 350°F. for 20-30 minutes or until bubbly hot. Yield: 4-6 servings.

Mary Frances Armstrong, Lakewood H.S.
Lake Odessa, Michigan

HAM-NOODLE CASSEROLE

4 oz. noodles
1 10-oz. can mushroom soup
1 c. milk
1 t. salt
⅛ t. pepper
1 T. onion, grated
1 c. peas
1 c. ham, diced

Cook noodles in boiling salted water; drain and rinse. Combine mushroom soup, milk, salt and pepper. Add onion, peas and ham. Mix well and combine with noodles. Pour into 2-quart casserole and bake at 375°F. for 30 minutes. Yield: 8 servings.

Lila Wollmann, Armour H.S.
Armour, South Dakota

HAM-NOODLE CASSEROLE

2 c. tomato juice
1 c. water
¼ c. onion, chopped
4-oz. broad noodles
2 c. cooked ham, cubed
¾ c. Cheddar cheese, cubed

Stir tomato juice, water, onion, and noodles together in skillet. Cover and set on medium heat. If electric skillet is used, set temperature for 225°F. Boil until noodles are cooked, 10 to 15 minutes, stirring frequently. Lower heat to simmer; for electric skillet use 175°F. Add ham and stir. Sprinkle cheese over top. Cover and allow cheese to melt before serving, about 5 minutes. Serve hot. Yield: 5-6 servings.

Mrs. Christina Nelson, Pembroke Academy
Suncook, New Hampshire

HAM 'N' EGGS 'N' NOODLES

¼ c. margarine or butter
¼ c. flour
1 T. mustard
⅛ t. white pepper
½ t. salt
2 c. milk
2 t. parsley flakes
1 c. cooked noodles
2 c. leftover ham, cubed
6 hard-cooked eggs, quartered
½ c. Cheddar cheese, grated
½ c. dry fine bread crumbs
Paprika

Melt margarine or butter; stir in flour, mustard, white pepper and salt. Gradually stir in milk. Cook, stirring until sauce comes to a boil. Remove from heat. Add parsley flakes, noodles and ham. Carefully stir in quartered eggs so as not to break them. Pour into lightly greased 2-quart casserole. Sprinkle with cheese, then bread crumbs. Add a generous sprinkling of paprika. Bake at 350°F. about 30 minutes. Yield: 8 servings.

Nancy H. Loose, Oakwood Jr. H.S.
East Detroit, Michigan

AFTER THE HOLIDAY CASSEROLE

3-4 c. cooked left-over vegetables
3-4 c. left-over bread stuffing
Cranberry sauce or relish (opt.)
Sliced turkey
2-3 c. left-over gravy

Place ingredients alternately in greased baking pan. Cover. Freeze for a future meal. When ready to use, remove from freezer 2 hours before meal. Heat at 350°F. for hour before meal. Place cover on baking pan for the last 30 minutes of baking time. Yield: 6-8 servings.

Mrs. F. William Schueler, Masuk H.S.
Monroe, Connecticut

BAKED CHICKEN CASSEROLE

1 pkg. instant chicken noodle soup
3 T. butter, melted
3 T. flour
2 c. green peas, cooked
1 c. sm. white onions, cooked
1 c. cooked chicken, cut-up
1 c. buttered bread crumbs

Make soup according to package directions. Blend butter and flour in a saucepan. Stir in the hot soup; cook until thickened. In a casserole arrange layers of peas, white onions, and chicken. Pour on sauce and top with buttered crumbs. Bake at 450°F. for 15 minutes. Yield: 6 servings.

Mrs. Carol Kauffman, Bloomsburg Area Jr. H.S.
Bloomsburg, Pennsylvania

CHICKEN AND BISCUIT CASSEROLE

1 c. cooked chicken, sliced
1 can condensed cream of chicken soup
2 hard-cooked eggs, sliced
2 T. pimento, chopped
1 c. biscuit mix
¼ t. poultry seasoning
⅓ c. milk

Combine the chicken, soup, eggs and pimento. Place in a greased casserole. Combine remaining ingredients; mix until moistened. Place on top of casserole. Bake at 450°F. for 20-25 minutes. Yield: 4 servings.

Mrs. Jean Hall, Frackville H.S.
Frackville, Pennsylvania

CHICKEN PIE

½ recipe pie pastry
2 T. butter
2 T. flour
1 c. chicken broth or milk
¼ t. salt
⅛ t. pepper
¾ c. cooked chicken, diced
¼ c. cooked potatoes
¼ c. cooked celery or carrots
½ c. cooked or canned peas, drained

Prepare pastry; roll out to ⅛-inch thcik. Melt butter over low heat; add flour and stir well. Add milk all at once and cook stirring constantly until mixture thickens. Add salt and pepper. Add remaining ingredients; mix carefully so as not to break up vegetables. Pour into a casserole or 3 individual casseroles. Cover with pastry. Bake at 425°F. for 12 to 15 minutes. Yield: 2-3 servings.

Mrs. Kathryn Whitten, Hanford H.S.
Hanford, California

CHICKEN SQUARES WITH MUSHROOM SAUCE

3 c. cooked chicken or turkey, diced
1 c. cooked rice
2 c. soft bread crumbs
½ c. celery, diced
4 eggs, beaten
2 t. salt
¼ t. poultry seasoning
2 c. chicken broth or bouillon
1 can mushroom soup
⅓ c. milk

Combine chicken, rice, bread crumbs and celery. Combine eggs, salt, poultry seasoning and broth; mix thoroughly. Stir into chicken mixture. Bake in a greased 9x9x2-inch baking dish at 350°F. for 55 minutes. Cut into squares. Blend soup and milk; heat thoroughly. Serve with chicken squares. Yield: 6-9 servings.

Mrs. Amy E. Day, Elizabeth-Forward H.S.
Elizabeth, Pennsylvania

CHICKEN LICKEN CASSEROLE

2 c. egg noodles
2 T. butter
1-1½ c. cooked chicken, diced
1 8-oz. can peas
½ can cream of chicken soup
½ can cream of celery soup
4 T. Parmesan cheese
Paprika (opt.)

Cook noodles until tender; drain. Coat with butter. Add chicken, peas and soups. Mix gently. Sprinkle with cheese. Paprika can be used for added flavor and color. Bake for 20-25 minutes at 350°F. Yield: 6 servings.

Mrs. Kathleen Cooper, Tintah Public H.S.
Tintah, Minnesota

CHICKEN OR TURKEY CASSEROLE

2 c. left-over chicken or turkey
1 can mushroom soup
1 can cream of vegetable soup or 1 box frozen
   mixed vegetables
4 hard-cooked eggs
Left-over gravy or 1 can chicken gravy
2 slices buttered bread or left-over stuffing

Blend all ingredients except bread and place in casserole. Cover with stuffing or buttered bread. Bake at 350°F. for 30 minutes or until thoroughly heated. Yield: 5-6 servings.

Phyllis Wack, Blue Mountain Jt. H.S.
Schuylkill Haven, Pennsylvania

LEFT-OVER CASSEROLE

2 c. mashed potatoes
1 c. chicken, diced
2 c. cooked noodles
½ c. crushed potato chips
½ c. cheese, grated

Place ingredients in layers in a greased casserole. Bake 30 minutes at 350°F. Yield: 4 servings.

Mrs. Audrey Johnson, Kickapoo H.S.
Viola, Wisconsin

LEFT-OVER CHICKEN CASSEROLE

1½ c. chicken, cut-up
1 c. cooked egg noodles
¼ c. celery, chopped
1 t. dried onions
½ c. fine bread crumbs
1 can cream chicken soup
½ can milk
Cheese, grated

Mix all ingredients except cheese in a casserole; sprinkle cheese over the top. Bake at 325°F. for 25 minutes. Yield: 4 servings.

Nettie Riddering, Melvindale H.S.
Melvindale, Michigan

HOT CHICKEN SALAD

2 c. cooked chicken, cut-up
2 c. celery, thinly sliced
½ c. toasted chopped almonds
½-1 t. salt
2 t. onion, grated
1 c. mayonnaise
2 T. lemon juice
1 c. crushed potato chips
½ c. cheese, grated

Combine all ingredients except cheese and potato chips. Pile lightly in baking dish. Sprinkle with cheese and potato chips. Bake at 400°F. for 25 minutes or at 450°F. for 10-15 minutes. Yield: 6 servings.

This recipe submitted by the following teachers:
Mary Alice Guhin, Simmons Jr. H.S.
Aberdeen, South Dakota
Mrs. L. E. Leete, Deep Creek H.S.
Chesapeake, Virginia

LEFT-OVER CHICKEN AND DRESSING

Roasted chicken or turkey slices
1-2 cans condensed mushroom soup
Left-over stuffing
Sweet onion slices (opt.)
Mushroom pieces (opt.)
Flavored potato chips (opt.)

Arrange ingredients in layers in a buttered casserole. Bake covered for 45-60 minutes at 350°F. Cover may be removed for last 15 minutes to brown the top.

Margaret Molitor, Goodrich H.S.
Goodrich, Michigan

LEFT-OVER TURKEY CASSEROLE

3 T. butter
1 T. flour
1 c. chicken or turkey stock
3 T. Sherry wine
Nutmeg
Salt and pepper
1 c. light cream, scalded
1 c. mushrooms, thinly sliced
Milk
3 egg yolks, beaten
1 t. onion juice
1 T. green pepper, finely chopped
3 c. turkey, diced

Heat butter and stir in the flour until mixture is bubbling, but not brown; gradually add stock and Sherry. Cook for 3 minutes; season with a pinch of nutmeg, salt and pepper to taste. Bring the sauce to a boil; stir in the cream. Stirring occasionally, bring the sauce to a boil again and add the mushrooms cooked in butter. Add a little cold milk to the egg yolks; add to sauce slowly, stirring briskly. Add onion juice, green pepper and the turkey. Taste for seasoning. This mixture may be served on Chinese noodles or rice, or it may be divided in to 6 individual casseroles or

1 large casserole. If served in a casserole, sprinkle top with fine bread crumbs and grated cheese. Dot with butter. Put the casseroles on a baking sheet and brown under the broiler or in a moderate oven. Serve bubbling hot. Yield 6-8 servings.

Mary M. Haines, Vassar H.S.
Vassar, Michigan

TURKEY GOULASH

1 med. green pepper
1 sm. onion
1 T. butter
2 to 1½ c. chicken or turkey broth
2 c. left-over turkey or chicken
1 can mushroom or fresh
Salt and pepper to taste
Cornstarch

Cut onions and green peppers in strips; saute in butter until tender, but not brown. Add broth, mushrooms, chicken, salt and pepper. Simmer for 15 minutes. Thicken with cornstarch. Serve over fluffy rice. Yield: 4-5 servings.

Mrs. Jackelen Merwin, Kingsburg H.S.
Kingsburg, California

POTATOES A LA COMPANY

1 med. onion, chopped
3 T. green pepper
4 T. margarine
1 T. pimento, chopped
2½ T. flour
2 c. milk
Salt and pepper to taste
3 c. cooked potatoes, cubed
¾ c. sharp cheese, grated

Saute onion and green pepper in margarine about 5 minutes. Add pimento and flour; stir. Add milk; stir and cook until thickened. Season. Add potatoes. Pour into greased 1½-quart deep casserole. Top with cheese. Bake at 350°F. about 30 minutes. Yield: 6 servings.

Mrs. Jack W. Wright, Altamont Jr. H.S.
Klamath Falls, Oregon

LAMB AND RICE CASSEROLE

2 c. beef broth, fresh or canned
1 c. canned tomatoes
1 onion, grated
2 c. cooked left-over lamb, diced
1 t. salt
¼ t. pepper
1 T. butter or margarine
½ c. rice
2 T. Worcestershire sauce

Combine broth, tomatoes, onion, lamb, salt and pepper in a casserole. Cook at 350°F. for 10 minutes. Melt butter; add rice, stirring constantly until lightly browned. Add to casserole with Worcestershire sauce. Continue baking for 35 minutes or until rice is tender. Yield: 6 servings.

Mrs. Bernice Anderson, Central Jr. H.S.
Reno, Nevada

BARBECUED BEANS

1 lb. ground beef
½ c. onion, chopped or sliced
½ t. salt
¼ t. pepper
1 1-lb. 2-oz. can pork and beans
½ c. catsup
1 T. Worcestershire sauce
2 T. vinegar
¼ t. Tabasco sauce

Brown beef and onions; pour off fat. Stir in remaining ingredients. Pour into 1½-quart casserole. Bake at 350°F. for 30 minutes. Yield: 6 servings.

Mrs. Jane H. Brown, Enfield Community H.S.
Enfield, Illinois

BEAN BURGERS

½ lb. hamburger
2 med. onions, finely chopped
½ t. salt
2 c. kidney beans, mashed
1 c. chili sauce

Lightly brown hamburger and onions with salt. Add beans and chili sauce. Simmer 10 minutes. Serve on hamburger buns or bread. NOTE: One cup tomato sauce plus ½ teaspoon chili powder may be substituted for chili sauce. Yield: 4-6 servings.

Mrs. R. David Walker, Whiteoak Local H.S.
Mowrystown, Ohio

HAMBURGER BAKED BEANS

1½ lb. hamburger
1 lge. onion, chopped
½ c. catsup
2 T. brown sugar
1 T. Worcestershire sauce
2 lge. cans pork and beans

Brown hamburger with onion. Add remaining ingredients; mix well and simmer for 35 minutes. Yield: 6 servings.

Viola Kanten, Taylors Falls Public School
Taylors Falls, Minnesota

BEEF AND POTATOES

1 lb. ground beef
3 med. potatoes, diced
1 t. salt
1 can cream mushroom soup

Brown the ground beef and pour off any excess fat. Add potatoes, salt and mushroom soup. Simmer over low heat until potatoes are cooked. Serve immediately. Yield: 4-6 servings.

Mrs. Neva Townsend, Ponca H.S.
Ponca, Nebraska

BIG BISCUIT-HAMBURGER BAKE

1 lb. ground beef
½ c. onion, chopped
1 can condensed cream of vegetable soup
½ t. crushed oregano
Dash of freshly ground pepper
½ c. milk
1 c. biscuit mix
½ c. sour cream
½ c. Parmesan cheese, shredded
Snipped parsley

Cook ground beef and onion until meat is brown; drain off excess fat. Stir in soup and seasonings; heat to bubbling. Turn into a round cake dish. Add milk all at once to biscuit mix. Stir with fork into a soft dough; beat 15 strokes. Spread over hot meat mixture. Bake at 450°F. for 15 minutes or until browned. Spread biscuit with sour cream. Sprinkle with Parmesan cheese, then snipped parsley. Bake for 2 minutes. Yield: 6 servings.

Ilona Perala, Delavan-Darian H.S.
Delavan, Wisconsin

CHOW MEIN CASSEROLE

1 lb. hamburger
2 med. onions, chopped
1 can cream of chicken soup
1 can cream of mushroom soup
½ c. rice
¼ t. pepper
1 T. soy sauce
1½ c. warm water
1 can chow mein noodles

Brown meat; drain off fat. Add remaining ingredients except noodles. Pour into 2½-quart casserole. Cover. Bake at 350°F. for 30 minutes. Top with noodles; bake uncovered for 15 minutes. Yield: 4 servings.

Mardeen Christiansen, Nestucca Union H.S.
Cloverdale, Oregon

CHOW MEIN NOODLE CASSEROLE

1½ lb. ground beef
Salt and pepper to taste
¾ c. celery, finely chopped
¼ c. onion, minced
1 can tomato soup
1 can mushroom soup
1 No. 2 can chow mein noodles

Lightly brown ground beef with seasonings, celery and onions. Stir in soups and one-third of noodles. Pour into casserole. Bake 20 minutes at 325°F. Remove from oven and sprinkle top of casserole with remaining chow mein noodles; return to oven for another 15 minutes. Yield: 6 servings.

Mrs. Cleta Salyers, Malvern Community H.S.
Malvern, Iowa

DINNER IN A DISH

1 lb. ground beef
½ c. onion, chopped
1 can green beans
½ t. salt
1 can tomato soup
¼ t. Tabasco sauce
2 c. potatoes, mashed

Brown beef, and onion. Add remaining ingredients except potatoes. Cook to boiling. Pour into greased casserole. Top with potatoes. Bake at 375°F. for 45 minutes. Yield: 5 servings.

Sylvia Saltmarsh, Litchfield Public H.S.
Litchfield, Nebraska

DINNER ON THE DOUBLE

1 slice bread, cubed
⅓ c. milk
1 lb. ground beef
¼ c. onion, chopped
1 T. mustard
2 t. salt
Dash of pepper
¼ c. flour
2 T. fat
4 med. potatoes
6 med. carrots
4 sm. onions
1 c. water
½ t. Kitchen Bouquet

Soak bread cubes in milk. Mix beef, onion, mustard, 1 teaspoon salt, pepper and egg. Add bread cubes and milk; mix. Form in 6 small meat loaves; roll in flour. Brown in hot fat in pressure pan. Add vegetables, water, and remaining seasonings. Cook at 15 pounds pressure for 7 minutes. Reduce pressure under cold running water. Gravy may be thickened with 2 tablespoons flour. Yield: 4 servings.

Mrs. Lois Winkler, Dieterich H.S.
Dieterich, Illinois

DISH DINNER

1 sm. onion, diced
2 sm. green pepper, diced
1 T. shortening
1 lb. hamburger
2 t. salt
¼ t. pepper
2 eggs, beaten
2 c. fresh corn
4 med. tomatoes, sliced
½ c. crumbs, buttered

Fry onion and green peppers in shortening for 3 minutes. Add meat and brown; add salt and pepper. Stir in eggs. Put half of corn in greased baking dish; add half the meat, a layer of tomatoes, and remaining corn. Top with crumbs. Bake 35 minutes at 375°F.

Rebecca Fader, Southwestern H.S.
Shelbyville, Indiana

DOUGIE'S DISH

1 lb. ground beef
1 onion, chopped
½ green pepper, chopped
1 can spaghetti
¼ t. salt
½ t. paprika
1 t. Worcestershire sauce
1 sm. can cream-style corn
1 can tomato soup
½ c. American cheese, shredded
¼ c. corn flakes
1 T. butter

Brown meat and onion; add pepper. Place in greased casserole. Stir in remaining ingredients except corn flakes and butter. Sprinkle with corn flakes; dot with butter. Bake at 350°F. for 30 minutes. Yield: 4-6 servings.

Beverly Frankenfield, Emmaus H.S.
Emmaus, Pennsylvania

EASY CASSEROLE

4 potatoes, sliced
1 can vegetable soup
1 can cream of mushroom soup
1 lb. ground beef

Mix all ingredients; place in greased casserole. Bake at 350°F. until potatoes are done. NOTE: Do not brown meat before mixing. Yield: 8 servings.

Mrs. Shirley Wayne, Rolla Public School
Rolla, North Dakota

EASY TAMALE CASSEROLE

1 lb. ground beef
2 T. olive oil
1 c. onion, chopped
1 clove garlic, minced
1 t. salt
2 t. chili powder
2 8-oz. cans tomato sauce
1 can beef consomme
½ c. parsley, chopped
1 sm. can ripe olives
1 No. 2. can whole-kernel corn
2 3⅓-oz. pkg. corn chips
½ c. cheese, grated

Brown beef in oil. When meat is almost done, add onion and garlic. Add salt, chili powder tomato sauce, consomme, parsley, and olives and corn. Heat to boiling point. Stir in corn chips. Turn into 2-quart baking dish. Sprinkle with grated cheese. Bake at 350°F. for 25-30 minutes. Yield: 8-10 servings.

Mrs. Helen Meyer, Bellflower H.S.
Bellflower, California

FIFTEEN-MINUTE MEAT LOAF

2 eggs, beaten
¾ c. oatmeal, uncooked
1 lb. ground beef
2 T. A1 steak sauce
1 t. salt
¾ c. milk

Combine all ingredients. Divide mixture into 8 equal parts and place in greased muffin tins. Bake for 15 minutes at 375°F.

Bertha A. Achelpohl, Ellinwood H.S.
Ellinwood, Kansas

GOUP

1 lb. ground beef
1 t. salt
1 t. garlic salt
1 can cream of mushroom soup
½ lb. noodles, cooked

Brown meat; add seasonings. Add mushroom soup and noodles. Cook about 15 minutes and serve. Yield: 4 servings.

Nancy Anderson, Hennepin H.S.
Hennepin, Illinois

GROUND BEEF GRAND STYLE

1½ lb. ground beef
1 c. onion, chopped
1 8-oz. pkg. cream cheese, softened
1 can cream of mushroom soup
¼ c. milk
1 t. salt
¼ c. catsup
1 can biscuits

Brown meat and onions; drain. Combine cheese, soup and milk. Add salt, catsup and meat. Pour into 2-quart casserole. Bake at 375°F. for 10 minutes. Place biscuits on the top. Continue baking for 15-20 minutes or until biscuits are golden brown. Yield: 5-6 servings.

Mrs. Judith Wharton, Royalton Jr. H.S.
Royalton, Illinois

HEAVENLY HAMBURGER

1½ lb. hamburger
Salt to taste
6 slices American cheese
1 lb. noodles, uncooked
1 No. 202 can stewed tomatoes

Brown beef; add salt. Place in 2-quart casserole. Cover with cheese and noodles. Add tomatoes. Cover. Bake at 400°F. for 15 minutes. Stir to combine ingredients; continue baking 15 minutes. NOTE: May be cooked in a covered skillet for 30 minutes. Yield: 4 servings.

Mrs. Rafael Martin, Hamilton Union H.S.
Hamilton, California

HAMBURGER FLUFF PIE

1 onion, chopped
Fat
1 lb. ground beef
¾ t. salt
⅛ t. pepper
1 pkg. frozen green beans, cooked
1 can tomato soup
Instant mashed potatoes, prepared
½ c. cheese, shredded

Cook onion in small amount of fat until tender. Add meat and seasonings; brown lightly. Add beans and soup. Pour into greased 1½-quart casserole. Drop mashed potatoes in mounds over meat. Sprinkle cheese over potatoes. Bake at 350°F. for 25-30 minutes. Yield: 6 servings.

This recipe submitted by the following teachers:
Mrs. Gary R. Johnson, Central School
Alexandria, Minnesota
Mrs. Trudy Smith, Hood Jr. H.S.
Odessa, Texas

HAMBURGER HEAVEN

1 lb. ground beef
½ lb. sliced American cheese
1 c. celery, chopped
1 sm. can ripe olives, sliced (opt.)
1 No. 2 can tomatoes
2 c. fine noodles
1¼ c. water
½ t. onion salt
Salt and pepper to taste

Brown meat. Add layers of remaining ingredients. Add seasonings. Rinse tomato can with water; pour over all. Cover. Cook on high heat until steaming. Reduce heat and simmer for 30 minutes. Yield: 6 servings.

This recipe submitted by the following teachers:
Mrs. Irene Struble, Fairview H.S.
Farmer, Ohio
Mrs. Sharon Dunham, Millard Lefler Jr. H.S.
Lincoln, Nebraska

HAMBURGER-MUSHROOM GUMBO

1 can cream of mushroom soup
½ c. milk
1 c. thin onion rings
½ c. celery, chopped
1 T. fat
1½ lb. ground round steak
1½ t. salt
⅛ t. pepper
1½ c. cooked peas
2 c. biscuit mix
½ t. caraway seed

Add milk slowly to soup; stir well and simmer 2 minutes. Cook onions and celery slowly in hot fat in a big frying pan until onions are transparent. Add beef, salt and pepper. Cook until meat is grey, stirring occasionally. Add peas and mushroom sauce; blend and heat mixture thoroughly. Put into a 1½-quart casserole. Place casserole

(Continued on Next Page)

in a 425°F. oven while preparing the biscuits. Prepare drop biscuits using biscuit mix or your own drop biscuit recipe, blending in caraway seed before adding milk. Remove casserole from oven. Drop biscuits over top of meat mixture. Return casserole to oven and bake for 12 minutes or until biscuits are browned. Yield: 6 servings.

Neala R. Yde, John Muir Jr. H.S.
Burbank, California

HOMINY PIE

1½ lb. ground beef
1 T. flour
2 c. canned tomatoes
Salt and pepper to taste
1 t. chili powder
2½ c. hominy
1 med. onion, chopped
¼ lb. American cheese, grated

Brown meat in hot fat; add flour, tomatoes and seasonings. Brown hominy and onion in hot fat; add to meat mixture. Place in greased casserole; sprinkle with cheese. Bake at 350°F. for 30 minutes. Yield: 6 servings.

Katherine Ragsdale, Corning Union H.S.
Corning, California

JESSY'S DISH

1 med. onion, diced
2 T. butter or olive oil
1 med. green pepper, diced
2 lb. ground beef
1 8-oz. pkg. noodles, cooked
1 No. 2 can whole kernel corn
1 No. 2 can stewed tomatoes, quartered
1 can mushroom soup
Salt and pepper to taste
2-oz. Italian cheese, grated

In a large heavy skillet lightly brown onion in oil; add green pepper and beef. Cook until beef is no longer red and pepper is tender. Add cooked noodles, corn, tomatoes and mushroom soup; blend well. Season to taste; simmer for 20 minutes. Sprinkle grated cheese over top and let melt slightly. Serve hot. NOTE: Excess fat may be removed before cheese is added. Yield: 8-12 servings.

Marie Evanoff, Glenrock-Parkerton H.S.
Glenrock, Wyoming

JOHNNY MARZETTI

6 oz. wide egg noodles, cooked
2 lb. hamburger
½ onion, chopped
½ lge. green pepper, diced
Salt and pepper to taste
¼ t. oregano
¾ c. tomato sauce
¾ c. water
6 sl. cheese

Brown hamburger, onion and green pepper in skillet. Add seasonings, tomato sauce and water; simmer until heated. Line a greased casserole with half the drained noodles. Top with half the hamburger mixture and 3 slices of cheese. Repeat layers. Place in 350°F. oven for 30 minutes. NOTE: Mushrooms may be added if desired. Yield: 5-6 servings.

Mrs. Diana Davis, Thomas Jefferson Jr. H.S.
Valparaiso, Indiana

JOHNNY MOSSETTI

2-3 lb. ground beef
Fat
½ lb. green peppers, chopped
½ lb. onions, chopped
½ bunch celery, chopped
1 can tomato soup
1 can tomato paste
1 can mushrooms
Salt and pepper to taste
1 pkg. wide noodles or macaroni
½ lb. American cheese, grated
1 sm. jar stuffed olives

Brown ground beef in a small amount of fat. Add green peppers, onions and celery. Cook until done. Add soup, tomato paste and mushrooms. Season to taste. Cook and drain noodles. Pour into large baking dish. Add meat mixture. Top with cheese and olives. Bake at 350°F. until the cheese is melted and casserole is bubbly hot, about 30 minutes. Yield: 8-10 servings.

Carolyn Houser, Columbia Community H.S.
Columbia, Illinois

OUR FAMILY FAVORITE

¾ lb. ground beef
½ c. onion chopped
½ c. catsup
1½ t. sugar
½ t. oregano
½ t. parsley flakes
½ t. salt
⅛ t. pepper
1 15-oz. can macaroni and cheese
3 T. Parmesan cheese, grated
1 T. butter
Salt and pepper to taste
1 c. bread crumbs
2 T. butter, melted

Saute beef and onion. Drain off excess grease. Add catsup, sugar, oregano, parsley flakes, salt and pepper. Spread in a 1½-quart casserole. Combine ingredients except melted butter and bread in saucepan. Heat until cheese melts. Spread over beef mixture. Combine crumbs and butter; sprinkle over macaroni. Bake at 400°F. for 25 minutes or until bread is toasted. NOTE: As a time saver spread 2 slices of bread with butter and break into crumbs with a fork. Yield: 4 servings.

Patricia C. Harker, Waynesburg H.S.
Waynesburg, Pennsylvania

MACARONI CON CARNE

1 7-oz. pkg. macaroni
1 onion, minced
1 T. butter
1 lb. hamburger
1 can tomato soup
1 c. cheese, grated

Cook macaroni in salted water; drain. Saute onion in butter. Add hamburger; cook three minutes. Stir in soup, cheese and macaroni. Pour into buttered baking dish. Bake at 350°F. for 30 minutes.

Mrs. Zella Weidenbach, Parkston H.S.
Parkston, South Dakota

QUICKIE CASSEROLE WITH MACARONI

1 lb. hamburger
1 med. onion, chopped
½ pkg. shell macaroni
1 No. 2 can tomatoes
Salt and pepper to taste
¼ lb. American cheese, cubed

Brown hamburger and onion. Cook macaroni in boiling salted water until tender. Add macaroni and tomatoes to meat mixture. Season with salt and pepper. Add cheese. Simmer for 15 minutes or until cheese is soft. Yield: 4-6 servings.

Mrs. Eleanor Tedford, Wiggins H.S.
Wiggins, Colorado

TOMATO-BEEF CASSEROLE

1 med. onion, chopped
1 T. shortening
1 10½-oz. can tomato soup
1 c. green beans
½ c. water
1 c. cubed or ground beef
½ c. cooked noodles
½ c. Cheddar cheese, shredded

Lightly brown onion in shortening. Add remaining ingredients except cheese. Pour into a 1-quart casserole. Top with cheese. Bake at 375°F. for 25 minutes or until hot and bubbly. Yield: 4-6 servings.

Mrs. Anna Greeno, Adams-Friendship H.S.
Adams, Wisconsin

POOR MAN'S MOCK STROGANOFF

1 lb. ground beef
½ onion, chopped
Seasoned salt to taste
Seasoned pepper to taste
1 can cream of mushroom soup
1 can milk

Brown meat and onion; add seasonings. Add soup and milk; stir well. Cover and simmer until desired consistency. Serve over hot buttered rice and garnish with parsley. Yield: 3-4 servings.

Lois Engstrom, Hopkins H.S.
Hopkins, Minnesota

QUICK AND HEARTY CASSEROLE

1½ lb. hamburger
2 eggs, beaten
Dash of Worcestershire sauce
1 t. salt
¼ t. garlic salt
Pinch of pepper
2 T. butter
1 16-oz. can mixed vegetables
1 16-oz. can tomato sauce
2 c. mashed potatoes
½ c. cheese, grated
Paprika

Mix meat with eggs, Worcestershire sauce, salt, garlic salt and pepper. Brown lightly with butter. Add vegetables with tomato sauce. Heat, stirring constantly. Put in baking dish; top with potatoes, grated cheese and paprika. Place in 350°F. oven long enough to melt cheese, about 5 minutes. Serve at once. Yield: 6 servings.

Sandra Hatch, Kimball County H.S.
Kimball, Nebraska

QUICKIE CASSEROLE

½ c. onion, chopped
1 T. shortening, melted
1 lb. ground beef
½ t. salt
⅛ t. pepper
1 pkg. frozen green beans, cooked
1 c. white sauce
½ c. cheese, grated
1 c. buttered bread crumbs

Cook onions in shortening until yellow in color. Add ground meat and brown well. Add salt and pepper. Place alternate layers of cooked green beans and beef mixture in greased 1½-quart baking dish. Combine white sauce and cheese; heat until cheese melts. Pour cheese sauce over all and top with crumbs. Bake in 375°F. oven for 25 to 30 minutes. Yield: 6 servings.

Mrs. Anna Mae Gausmann, Wolf Lake H.S.
Wolf Lake, Indiana

QUICK AND SPICY

1 lb. ground beef or chuck
1 T. fat
1 bottle chili sauce
⅓ bottle water
Cooked rice or macaroni

Brown beef in hot fat; stir in chili sauce and water. Simmer for 20 minutes. Spoon over hot rice or macaroni. NOTE: For variety, shape beef into small meat balls. Yield: 3-4 servings.

Sandra J. Gass, East Haven Jr. H.S.
East Haven, Connecticut

QUICK TAMALE BAKE

1 lb. ground beef
¾ c. onion, chopped
2½ t. salt
2 t. chili powder
⅛ t. pepper
1 12-oz. can whole-kernel corn
1 No. 2 can tomatoes
¾ c. corn meal
1½ t. baking powder
1 T. flour
1 T. sugar
1 egg, beaten
⅓ c. milk
1 T. fat, melted

Lightly brown meat and onion together; stir in 2 t. salt, chili powder, pepper, corn and tomatoes. Pour into shallow pan. Mix remaining dry ingredients. Combine egg, milk and fat; stir lightly into dry mixture. Place small spoonfuls of batter on meat mixture. Bake at 400°F. for 20-25 minutes. Yield: 6-7 servings.

Esther M. Williams, Pocatello H.S.
Pocatello, Idaho

QUICK TEXAS HASH

1 med. onion, finely chopped
1 lb. ground beef
2 T. butter or margarine
1 can tomato soup
1 8-oz. can tomato sauce
1 c. instant rice
Salt and pepper to taste

Brown onion and beef in butter; add remaining ingredients. Pour into baking dish; bake at 350°F. for 20-30 minutes. Yield: 6 servings.

Jo M. Klarich, Granger H.S.
Granger, Washington

SEVEN-LAYER CASSEROLE

1 c. rice
1 c. canned whole-kernel corn, drained
1 can tomato sauce
½ can water
½ c. onion, finely chopped
½ c. green pepper, finely chopped
¾ lb. ground beef
Salt and pepper to taste
1 can tomato sauce
¼ can water
4 strips bacon, cut in half

Layer all ingredients in 2-quart baking dish; cover tightly. Bake at 350°F. for 1 hour. Uncover; continue baking for 30 minutes or until bacon is crisp. Yield: 5 servings.

Mrs. Charla Mae Filla, Sterling H.S.
Sterling, Colorado

RICE KRISPIE HOT DISH

1 lb. ground beef
1 med. onion, chopped
½ lge. box Rice Krispies
2 cans chicken and rice soup
1 can cream of chicken soup

Brown meat and onion. Put into baking dish; add all other ingredients and mix. Bake at 375°F. for 50 minutes. Yield: 6-8 servings.

Arlene Lenort, Pine Island H.S.
Pine Island, Minnesota

SAMORE CASSEROLE

½ lb. hamburger
½ onion
1 can tomato sauce
2 cans spaghetti sauce with mushrooms
1 can niblet corn with peppers
Salt and pepper to taste
½ small pkg. noodles, cooked
6 slices cheese

Brown hamburger and onion. Add sauces, corn and seasonings. Add noodles. Cover with cheese slices and bake at 350°F. until cheese melts. Yield: 4 servings.

Janet Malone, Fullerton City Schools
Fullerton, Nebraska

TEN-MINUTE CASSEROLE

1 lb. hamburger
1 sm. onion, minced
3 c. cooked spaghetti
1 can tomato soup

Brown hamburger and onion. Add cooked spaghetti and tomato soup. Mix well and heat thoroughly. Yield: 4 servings.

Mrs. Ramona Flanum, Osceola H.S.
Osceola, Wisconsin

BEEF AND SPAGHETTI CASSEROLE

¾ lb. ground beef or hamburger
½ c. onions, finely cut
1 sm. can tomato sauce
Salt to taste
1 can Italian spaghetti
¼ lb. sharp cheese, grated

Brown meat and onion in skillet. Mix in tomato sauce; add salt. Stir spaghetti into meat mixture and bring to boil. Pour into casserole. Cover with cheese and heat at 350°F. until cheese is melted. NOTE: Parmesan cheese may be sprinkled over casserole if desired. Yield: 6 servings.

Inez Dykstra, Lovington H.S.
Lovington, New Mexico

JIFFY HAMBURGER-SPAGHETTI SKILLET

1 lb. hamburger
1 med. onion, chopped
1 7-oz. pkg. spaghetti, cooked
1 can mushrooms
1 15½-oz. can spaghetti sauce with mushrooms
Salt and pepper to taste

Brown hamburger and onion. Add drained spaghetti, mushrooms and spaghetti sauce; mix well. Cook for 20-30 minutes. Yield: 6 servings.

Anne Weisbrot, Wabeno H.S.
Wabeno, Wisconsin

JIFFY SPAGHETTI

½ lb. ground beef
1 sm. onion, chopped
2 T. fat
⅔ c. chili sauce or catsup
1 t. salt
2 cans tomato paste
½ c. water
¼ t. pepper
Dash of Tabasco sauce
¼ t. garlic salt
1 8-oz. pkg. thin spaghetti, cooked

Lightly brown beef and onion in hot fat. Stir in remaining ingredients except spaghetti and cheese. Simmer, uncovered, for 10 minutes. Serve with cooked spaghetti; sprinkle with cheese. Yield: 4-6 servings.

Mrs. Rose Bryan, Leechburg Union H.S.
Leechburg, Pennsylvania

"PINK" CASSEROLE

1 lb. hamburger
1 sm. onion, chopped
Salt and pepper to taste
1 can cream of mushroom soup
1 can tomato soup
1 can water
1 t. chili powder
½ to ¾ pkg. spaghetti, cooked
Grated cheese

Brown hamburger and onions. Add remaining ingredients except spaghetti and cheese. Simmer 30 minutes. Combine mixture and spaghetti. Pour into casserole; sprinkle with cheese. Cover with foil and bake at 350°F. for 30 minutes. Yield: 8 servings.

Rosalie Hoffman, Valley H.S.
Valley, Nebraska

EASY STROGANOFF CASSEROLE

1½ lb. ground beef
2 T. onions, minced
1-2 T. parsley, minced
¼ t. garlic powder
2 T. butter
½-1 t. salt
½ t. pepper
1 6-oz. can sliced mushrooms, drained
1 can vegetable soup
1 c. sour cream
½ c. milk
Biscuit dough

In deep skillet saute beef, onion, parsley, and garlic powder in butter. Stir in salt, pepper, mushrooms and vegetable soup; simmer for 15 minutes. Blend in sour cream and milk; heat thoroughly. Pour into a 2½-quart casserole. Cover with a baking powder biscuit topping, or serve over baking powder biscuits. Bake at 475°F. until biscuits are browned. Yield: 6 servings.

Sister M. Joelita, O.P. Bethlehem Academy
Faribault, Minnesota

QUICK SPAGHETTI

1 lb. ground beef
1 onion, chopped
1 t. salt
⅛ t. pepper
½ t. chili powder
1 can mushroom soup
1 can tomato soup
Spaghetti

Brown meat and onion, season to taste. Add soups and cook ½ hour. Serve over cooked long spaghetti. Yield: 6 servings.

Katherine McIlquham, Chippewa Falls H.S.
Chippewa Falls, Wisconsin

HAMBURGER STROGANOFF

1 lb. hamburger
Seasonings to taste
1 can cream of mushroom soup
½ soup can milk
1 c. sour cream

Brown hamburger in a large skillet; season to taste. Add mushroom soup, milk and sour cream; stir thoroughly. Simmer about 30 minutes, stirring occasionally. Serve over rice. Yield: 4-6 servings.

Darlene Heilmann, Carpinteria H.S.
Carpinteria, California

QUICK BEEF STROGANOFF

3 minute steaks
2 T. hot fat
1 onion, sliced
1 clove garlic, crushed
1 can cream of mushroom soup
1 c. sour cream
1 3-oz. can mushrooms
2 T. catsup
2 t. Worcestershire sauce

Cut steaks into strips; brown in hot fat. Add onion and garlic; cook 5 minutes. Combine remaining ingredients; add to meat mixture. Heat thoroughly. Yield: 4 servings.

Sharon Klickna, Tularosa H.S.
Tularosa, New Mexico

SPEEDY BARBECUED RIBS

4 lb. spareribs
2 T. fat
2 lge. onions, sliced
½ c. catsup
¼ c. vinegar
2 t. Worcestershire sauce
¼ t. chili powder
½ t. celery seed
2 t. salt
¼ t. pepper
½ t. paprika

Cut ribs in serving pieces; brown in hot fat in pressure pan. Add onion. Combine remaining ingredients. Pour over meat. Cook at 15 pounds pressure for 15 minutes. Allow pressure to go down normally. NOTE: For outdoor flavor, add few drops liquid smoke to sauce before cooking. Yield: 4 servings.

Mrs. Priscilla Watkins, Evans H.S.
Evans, Georgia

BUSY DAY CASSEROLE

1 box dry frying potatoes
1 box frozen green beans
1-2 c. ham, diced
½ c. dried milk
½ c. bread crumbs
¼ c. Parmesan cheese, grated

Cook potatoes as directed on package; do not discard liquid. Add seasonings from potato package, beans, ham and milk. Pour into greased casserole; cover with mixture of crumbs and cheese. Bake at 350°F. for 15 minutes. NOTE: Three to four wieners or 4 slices of bologna may be substituted for ham. If wieners or bologna are used, cut in small pieces and saute in a small amount of butter before adding to mixture. Yield: 6 servings.

Mrs. Annette B. Tramm, Bradley-Bourbonnais
Community H.S.
Bradley, Illinois

HAM AND RICE CASSEROLE

2 c. ham, chopped
2 cans cream of mushroom soup
⅓ c. milk
¼ c. onion, chopped
1 bell pepper, chopped
¼ c. celery, chopped
¼ t. black pepper
2 c. cooked rice
¼ c. almonds, toasted

Brown ham slightly after chopping. Cobine ham, soup, milk, onion, pepper, celery and black pepper. Alternate layers of rice and meat mixture in a casserole. Top with toasted almonds. Bake at 350°F. for 30 minutes. Yield: 6 servings.

Peggy Jean DuBose, Roseville Union H.S.
Roseville, California

QUICK-GEL HAM CASSEROLE

1 envelope unflavored gelatin
1¼ c. milk
1 can frozen cream of potato soup, half thawed
1½ c. diced ham
1 cucumber, peeled and diced
2 T. minced chives
3 radishes, sliced
Chopped parsley (garnish)

Sprinkle gelatin on milk; let stand to soften. Stir over low heat until gelatin is dissolved, 2 or 3 minutes. Remove from heat; spoon in soup. Stir until soup thaws and mixture mounds slightly when dropped from a spoon. Fold in remaining ingredients; chill until firm, about 5 or 10 minutes. Sprinkle with chopped parsley. Serve in casserole. NOTE: Other combinations for frozen soup casseroles: New England style clam chowder with salmon, tuna, cucumber, radishes, celery; green peas with ham soup, with ham or bologna, crisp pepper; cream of shrimp soup with any seafood, sliced olives and slivered almonds. Yield: 4 servings.

This recipe submitted by the following teachers:
Mrs. Bertrice S. Robertson, Collins H.S.
Collins, Mississippi
Dimi Gaitanis, Western Area Joint Schools
Mifflinburg, Pennsylvania

HAM-SPAGHETTI CASSEROLE

1 lge. green pepper, chopped
1 med. onion, chopped
2 T. butter
1 lb. spaghetti, cooked
2 cans cream of mushroom soup
1 c. milk
½ c. Sherry
2 c. sharp cheese, grated
2 c. cooked ham, cut in ½-inch cubes
1 4-oz. can mushrooms
1 4-oz. can pimento, diced
¼ t. pepper
1 t. salt
1 c. buttered bread crumbs

Cook green pepper and onion for 5 minutes in butter. Mix with other ingredients except crumbs. Pour into casserole. Top with crumbs. Bake at 350°F. for 30 minutes. Yield: 10-12 servings.

Mrs. Marilyn Kane, Arlington H.S.
Arlington Heights, Illinois

HAM SUPPER SPECIAL

2 c. cooked ham
¾ c. green pepper, chopped
1 c. onion, chopped
1 T. butter, melted
1 8-oz. pkg. noodles, cooked
2½ c. whole-kernel corn
1 10-oz. can tomato soup
¼ c. olives, diced

(Continued on Next Page)

½ lb. Cheddar cheese, cubed, grated
1 t. salt
¼ t. pepper

Saute ham, green pepper and onion in butter. Add noodles, corn and soup; simmer for 3 minutes. Add remaining ingredients. Pour into greased 3-quart casserole. Bake at 350°F. for 35 minutes. Yield: 8-10 servings.

Virginia Watson, St. Edward H.S.
St. Edward, Nebraska

CHICKEN-CASHEW CASSEROLE

1 can cream of mushroom soup, undiluted
¼ c. water
1 c. cooked chicken, diced
¼ lb. cashew nuts
1 c. celery, finely diced
¼ c. onions, minced
1 3-oz. can chow mein noodles

Combine all ingredients except ½ cup noodles. Place in 1½-quart casserole. Sprinkle with reserved noodles. Bake at 325°F. for 30 minutes. Yield: 4 servings.

Mrs. Harriet Gerou, Beaverton H.S.
Beaverton, Michigan

CHICKEN CACCIATORE

2 lb. chicken legs
½ t. salt
¼ c. salad oil
1 pkg. spaghetti sauce mix
1 lb. canned tomatoes

Sprinkle chicken with salt; brown in salad oil in large skillet. Remove chicken and drain fat. Blend spaghetti sauce mix and tomatoes in skillet. Add chicken. Cover and simmer 30 minutes or until chicken is tender. Yield: 4-6 servings.

Betty Berk, Othello H.S.
Othello, Washington

CHICKEN HOT DISH

2 c. chicken, cubed
½ c. green pepper, finely cut
¼ c. red pepper or pimento, finely cut
4 c. Rice Krispies
1 can chicken-rice soup
1 can cream of chicken or mushroom soup
½ c. cashew nuts

Combine chicken, red and green peppers, and Rice Krispies in a buttered casserole. Combine soups and heat; pour over chicken mixture. Top with nuts. Bake at 350°F. for 40 minutes.

Elva William Schrantz, Flandreau Indian School
Flandreau, South Dakota

CHICKEN QUICKIE

1 6- or 8-oz. can boned chicken
2 hard-cooked eggs, sliced
½ c. cracker crumbs
1 can cream of mushroom soup
2 T. butter

Arrange layers of chicken, egg slices and crumbs in a 1-quart buttered casserole. Cover with undiluted soup; dot with butter. Bake at 350°F. for 20 minutes or until bubbly. Yield: 4 servings.

Dorothy R. Trodahl, Southern Door County H.S.
Brussels, Wisconsin

CHICKEN-RICE QUICKIE

1 8-oz. box instant rice
1 can chicken broth
1 can mushroom soup
1 can boned chicken

Put rice in casserole; add chicken broth and remaining ingredients. Bake at 350°F. until rice is cooked and casserole is browned. Yield: 6 servings.

Mrs. Edith Myers, Lakeview H.S.
Stoneboro, Pennsylvania

CHICKEN ROMANOFF

1 pkg. noodles
2 c. cooked chicken, diced
Parsley flakes

Prepare noodles Romanoff as directed on package. Add chicken; garnish with parsley flakes. Bake at 350°F. for 25 minutes. Yield: 6 servings.

Helena T. Martines, Gompers Jr. H.S.
Los Angeles, California

HOT CHICKEN SALAD CASSEROLE

2 c. chopped chicken
2 c. chopped celery
½ c. blanched almonds
⅓ c. chopped green pepper
2 T. chopped pimento
2 T. chopped onion
½ t. salt
2 T. lemon juice
½ c. mayonnaise
⅓ c. grated Swiss cheese
3 c. potato chips

Mix all ingredients except cheese and potato chips. Turn into casserole and top with cheese and potato chips. Bake 25 minutes at 350°F. Yield: 10 servings.

Rhea Hulse, Bondurant-Farrar Community H.S.
Bondurant, Iowa

CHICKEN SALAD BAKE

¼ c. celery, thinly sliced
½ c. onion, finely chopped
4 T. margarine or butter, melted
¾ c. mayonnaise
¾ c. light cream
1 T. lemon juice
½ t. salt
⅛ t. pepper
3 c. cooked chicken, cubed
1 5-oz. can water chestnuts, drained and sliced
¼ c. Cheddar cheese, shredded
1 can refrigerator biscuits
⅓ c. parsley, chopped

Saute the celery and onions in 2 tablespoons butter in a skillet until tender. Combine in 1-½ quart casserole, the celery mixture, mayonnaise, cream, lemon juice, salt and pepper. Add the chicken, water chestnuts and cheese. Cover. Bake at 425°F. for 15 minutes. Remove the cover. Dip edges of biscuits into 2 tablespoons butter, then into the parsley. Place six biscuits around the edges of the casserole. Bake uncovered for 15 to 20 minutes until the biscuits are a golden brown. The remaining biscuits can be placed on a cookie sheet and baked. Yield: 6-8 servings.

Mrs. Elaine S. Washburn, Mayville H.S.
Mayville, Wisconsin

HOT CHICKEN SALAD

2 c. cooked chicken, diced
2 green peppers, chopped
2 c. celery, thinly sliced
2 t. onion, chopped
2 c. mayonnaise
1 t. salt and pepper
2 T. Worcestershire sauce
Potato chips

Combine chicken with vegetables, mayonnaise and seasoning. Mix lightly and cover with potato chips. Bake 30 minutes at 350°F. Yield: 6 servings.

Mrs. Jeanne Kerker, McKinleyville H.S.
Arcata, California

OVEN CHICKEN SALAD

2 c. cooked chicken, cubed
2 c. celery, thinly sliced
1 c. mayonnaise
½ c. toasted almonds, chopped
2 T. lemon juice
2 t. salt
½ c. onion, grated
½ t. salt
½ c. cheese, grated
2 c. toasted bread cubes

Combine all ingredients except cheese and 1 cup of bread cubes. Spoon lightly into individual baking dishes. Sprinkle with cheese and remaining bread cubes. Bake at 450°F. for 10-15 minutes or until bubbly. Yield: 6 servings.

Jane Wreith, Belvidere H.S.
Belvidere, Illinois

EASY CHICKEN CASSEROLE

2 c. chopped celery
½ c. chopped onion
½ c. water
2 cans chow mein noodles
2 cans mushroom soup
2 c. cooked diced chicken
½ c. cashews
Corn flakes

Combine celery, onion and water; cook 5 minutes. Add all remaining ingredients except corn flakes. Place in a greased casserole. Cover with corn flakes; bake at 325°F. for 45 minutes. Yield: 10 servings.

Mrs. Elenor Rollins, Lowell Jr. H.S.
Lowell, Michigan

EASY CHICKEN CASSEROLE

⅓ c. milk
1 can mushroom soup
1 hard-cooked egg, diced
1 c. cooked chicken, diced
1 T. pimento, diced
1 pkg. corn chips, crushed
½ t. celery salt
Few grains of pepper

Stir milk into soup and blend with other ingredients, saving a few crushed chips for topping. Pour into buttered casserole; top with reserved chips. Bake at 375°F. for 25 minutes. Yield: 3-4 servings.

Helen McGlone, Webber School
Saginaw, Michigan

FIVE-CAN CASSEROLE

1 can chicken-rice soup
1 jar boneless chicken
1 can mushroom soup
1 sm. can evaporated milk
1 lge. can chow mein noodles
Buttered crumbs

Mix all ingredients except crumbs. Pour into casserole; cover with buttered crumbs. Bake at 325° for 45 minutes or until bubbly. Yield: 6-8 servings.

Mrs. Alice Hansberger, Canton H.S.
Canton, Illinois

QUICK CREAMED CHICKEN ON BISCUITS

1-2 cans prepared biscuits
1 can cream of mushroom or celery soup
1 half soup can of water
1 can boned chicken

Bake biscuits according to directions. Warm soup; slowly add water. Add chicken and heat thoroughly. Serve over biscuits. Yield: 6-8 servings.

Ruth Ann Clossman, Centerburg H.S.
Centerburg, Ohio

SCALLOPED CHICKEN

2½ c. cooked chicken, finely cut
2½ c. rich chicken gravy
1 c. fine dry bread crumbs
Salt and pepper to taste
Butter

Place chicken, gravy, and crumbs in alternate layers in a greased baking dish. Season to taste. Dot with butter; bake 350°F. for 20 to 30 minutes. Serve hot. Yield: 6 servings.

This recipe submitted by the following teachers:
Marjetta Hadler, Denton Public School
Denton, Montana
Hilda Rohlf, Tallmadge H.S.
Tallmadge, Ohio

QUICK CHICKEN POT PIE

1 box frozen peas and carrots
1 7-oz. can chicken
1 10-oz. can cream of chicken soup
½ c. milk
1 can refrigerated biscuits

Cook vegetables as directed on package until tender; drain, saving ¼ cup liquid. Combine all ingredients except biscuits. Pour into casserole. Bake at 400°F. until bubbling. Place biscuits on top of mixture; continue baking until biscuits are browned. Yield: 4 servings.

Mrs. Erma Little, Creswell H.S.
Creswell, Oregon

MILDRED WOOD'S FUN RECIPE

1 can mushroom soup
1 can water
1 can cooked chicken or fish, diced
1 can Chinese noodles
1 can celery, chopped
½ can onion, chopped
½ can cashew nuts
Potato chips
Cheese, grated

Use soup can for measuring. Mix all ingredients except potato chips and cheese in a casserole dish. Top with patoto chips and cheese. Bake at 300-325°F. for 1 hour. Cover for first half of cooking time. Yield: 6 servings.

Mrs. Marian E. Henning, Marysville H.S.
Marysville, Washington

NOODLE-CHICKEN CASSEROLE

1 can cream of chicken soup
1 carton sour cream
2 c. cooked noodles
2 c. cooked chicken, diced
¼ c. dried pimento
¼ t. sage
¼ c. buttered crumbs
1 t. poppy seed

Blend soup and sour cream; add noodles, chicken and seasoning. Pour into casserole. Mix crumbs and poppy seed; sprinkle over casserole. Bake at 350°F. for 30 minutes. Yield: 8 servings.

Mrs. Irma B. Mosley, Allegan H.S.
Allegan, Michigan

QUICK HOT CRAB SALAD

1 can crab, shredded
1 can shrimp
1 c. celery, diced
1 sm. onion, minced
1 green pepper, finely cut
1 t. Worcestershire sauce
1 c. mayonnaise
½ t. salt and pepper
1 c. bread crumbs
2 T. butter, melted

Combine all ingredients except crumbs and butter; put into a casserole. Mix crumbs with butter and sprinkle over casserole. Bake in 350°F. oven for 20 minutes. NOTE: To increase the number of servings, use extenders such as boiled eggs, peas, or creamettes. Yield: 4 servings.

Mrs. Opal Brouillard, Barnard H.S.
Barnard, South Dakota

FISH SURPRISE

2 c. cooked fish, boned and flaked
3 hard-cooked eggs
1 c. cooked peas
1 c. cooked potatoes
½ c. cheese, grated
½ c. celery, chopped
¼ c. onion, chopped
1 can undiluted mushroom soup
1 can undiluted tomato soup
1 can water

Mix all the ingredients together well. If slightly dry, add some water to moisten. Put into greased casserole dish. Bake at 350°F. for 30 to 40 minutes. Yield: 6-8 servings.

Mrs. Helen Bell, South Jr. H.S
Grants Pass, Oregon

COMPANY TUNA CASSEROLE

2 sm. cans chunk tuna
2 sm. cans shoe string potatoes
1 sm. can mushrooms, chopped
2 c. canned peas
1 can mushroom soup
3 T. pimento, chopped

Combine all ingredients and place in greased 2-quart baking dish. Bake 30 minutes at 350°F. Yield: 6 servings.

Mrs. Bernadette Schoen, East Troy H.S.
East Troy, Wisconsin

FRIDAY'S HURRY UP CASSEROLE

1 can cream of mushroom soup
1 7-oz. can chunk tuna
1 No. 303 can peas, drained
2½ c. cooked macaroni
Salt and pepper to taste

Mix soup, tuna and peas. Heat until bubbly. Add to macaroni. Season to taste. Pour into buttered casserole and bake for 25-30 minutes at 350°F. NOTE: Milk may be added to thin soup, if desired. Yield: 4-6 servings.

Sandra J. Schrof, Forrest-Strawn-Wing School
Forrest, Illinois

GLORIFIED TUNA

1 4-oz. can mushrooms
½ c. onion, chopped
⅓ clove garlic or ¼ t. garlic salt
¼ c. butter
1 c. condensed mushroom soup
1 T. Worcestershire sauce
2 T. catsup
1 t. paprika
Salt and pepper to taste
1 c. sour cream
2 6½-oz. cans tuna, drained and flaked

Drain mushrooms, saving liquid. Cook onion, clove garlic and mushrooms in butter until tender. Add mushroom liquid, soup, seasonings and sour cream. Stir until blended. Add tuna and stir thoroughly. Serve on a bed of hot rice tossed with butter and parsley. Yield: 6 servings.

Edith Stanley, Peetz H.S.
Peetz, Colorado

MOCK CHICKEN CASSEROLE

1 can mushroom soup
1 c. milk
1 can tuna, flaked
4 hard-cooked eggs, sliced
1 c. potato chips, crushed

Combine all ingredients, pour into casserole. Cover top with additional potato chip crumbs. Bake at 400°F. for 20 minutes. Yield: 4 servings.

Mrs. Pat Coley, Magdalena H.S.
Magdalena, New Mexico

QUICK CASSEROLE

2 cans spaghetti with cheese
1 2-oz. can mushrooms
1 can tuna, drained
1 sm. can pitted ripe olives (opt.)
½ c. salted cashew nuts
3-4 thin slices American cheese

Mix all ingredients except cheese slices in a 1½-quart casserole. Arrange cheese on top. Bake 20 minutes at 350°F. Yield: 4 servings.

Mrs. Hugh M. French, A. C. Davis H.S.
Yakima, Washington

SEVEN-CAN HOT DISH

2 cans tuna fish
1 No. 2 can Chinese noodles
1 can chop suey or Chinese vegetables
1 can cream of mushroom soup
1 can cream of chicken soup
1 soup can milk
1 can water chestnuts, drained and sliced
½-1 c. slivered almonds
Potato chips, crushed

Mix all ingredients except potato chips. Top with potato chips. Bake uncovered at 350°F. for 35 minutes. Yield: 6-8 servings.

Sandra Roadfeldt, Canby H.S.
Canby, Minnesota

SEVEN SEAS CASSEROLE

1 can condensed cream of mushroom or celery soup
¼ to ⅓ c. onion, finely chopped
1⅓ to 1¼ c. water or milk
1 t. lemon juice
¼ t. salt
Dash of pepper (opt.)
1⅓ c. instant rice
1 10-oz. box green peas, partially thawed
1 can tuna, drained and flaked
½ c. Cheddar cheese, grated or cheese slices
Paprika

Combine soup, onion, water, lemon juice, salt and pepper in a saucepan. Bring to a boil over medium heat, stirring occasionally. Pour about half the soup mixture into a greased 1½-quart casserole. In layers add rice, peas, and tuna. Add remaining soup. Sprinkle with cheese and paprika. Cover and bake at 375°F. for 15 to 20 minutes. Cut through mixture with knife or fork after 10 minutes of baking to help distribute soup mixture. NOTE: If desired, any other seafood may be substituted for tuna. Yield: 4 servings.

This recipe submitted by the following teachers:
Mrs. Billie A. McCarroll, Slidell H.S.
Slidell, Texas
Mrs. R. V. Adolphson, Lincoln Southeast H.S.
Lincoln, Nebraska

QUICK TUNA DISH

2 cans cream of mushroom soup
½ lb. cream cheese
1 sm. can tuna
Chow mein noodles

Combine in the top of a double boiler the soup, cream cheese and tuna. Heat over hot water and serve over chow mein noodles. Yield: 6 servings.

Mrs. Bessie Hackett, Danvers H.S.
Danvers, Illinois

TUNA-BROCCOLI CASSEROLE

1 pkg. frozen broccoli
1 7-oz. can tuna
1 10½-oz. can mushroom soup
4-5 oz. milk
½-1 c. potato chips, crushed

Split broccoli stalks. Cook three minutes; drain. Place in 1½-quart baking dish. Cover with tuna. Mix soup and milk; pour over tuna. Sprinkle with potato chip crumbs. Bake at 450°F. for 15 minutes. Yield: 4 servings.

This recipe submitted by the following teachers:

Mrs. Carolyn Updyke, Southern H.S.
Oakland, Maryland

Marlys Wilmer, Henning Public School
Henning, Minnesota

TUNA CASSEROLE SPECIAL

1 7-oz. can tuna, flaked
1 8-oz. can green peas, drained
1 can cream of mushroom soup
Salt and pepper to taste
¼ c. milk (opt.)
Potato chips, crushed

Alternate layers of tuna, peas, and soup in a 1-quart casserole; season to taste. Pour milk over mixture; top with crumbs. Bake at 375°F. for 20-25 minutes or until thoroughly heated. Yield: 4-6 servings.

This recipe submitted by the following teachers:

Mrs. Sue R. McCroskey, South Stanly H.S.
Norwood, North Carolina

Mrs. J. W. Whelan, Tibbetts Jr. H.S.
Farmington, New Mexico

TUNA-NOODLE-ASPARAGUS BAKE

1 can cream of mushroom soup
1 soup can milk
1 7-oz. can tuna, flaked
2 c. wide noodles, cooked
1 box frozen cut asparagus, cooked
Salt and pepper to taste
Buttered crumbs

Heat soup with milk. Add tuna, noodles asparagus and seasoning. Heat thoroughly. Pour into 1-quart or 4 individual casseroles. Top with crumbs. Brown under broiler. Yield: 4 servings.

Mrs. I. T. Wetzel, Bangor H.S.
Bangor, Wisconsin

APPLE-SWEET POTATO BAKE

1 No. 2 can sliced apples
1 can sweet potatoes, halved lengthwise
1 12-oz. luncheon meat, sliced
¼ c. brown sugar
½ t. cinnamon

Alternate layers of apple slices and potato halves in 2-quart baking dish. Cover with meat slices; sprinkle with sugar and cinnamon. Bake at 400°F. for 25 minutes. Yield: 4 servings.

Mrs. Barbara Rawdon, Grants H.S.
Grants, New Mexico

BAKED SAUERKRAUT CASSEROLE

4 slices bacon, diced
¼ c. onion, grated
1 No. 2½ can sauerkraut, drained
1 c. tomato juice
½ c. buttered crumbs

Fry bacon until crisp. Add onion; cook until lightly browned. Add sauerkraut. Place in casserole; cover with tomato juice. Sprinkle with crumbs. Bake at 400°F. for 20 minutes. Yield: 6 servings.

LaVonne L. Wiener, Rock Valley Community H.S.
Rock Valley, Iowa

BROCCOLI CASSEROLE

2 pkg. broccoli
2 T. butter, melted
2 T. flour
1½ c. milk
¾ c. Cheddar cheese, shredded
¾ c. buttered bread crumbs
6 crisp slices bacon, crumbled
½ c. stuffed olives, sliced

Cook broccoli in salted water for 6 minutes. Combine butter and flour. Add milk; cook stirring constantly until thickened. Blend in cheese. Place half of crumbs in greased baking dish; cover with half of broccoli. Sprinkle with bacon and olive slices; pour on half of cheese sauce. Add remaining broccoli, then sauce. Top with remaining crumbs. Bake at 350°F. for 30 minutes. Yield: 6-8 servings.

Mrs. Jane Mosbacher, Dupo H.S.
Dupo, Illinois

CHILI CASSEROLE

2 4-oz. bags corn chips
1 No. 2 can chili con carne
1 c. cheese, grated
1 pkg. frozen corn, cooked
1 onion, finely chopped

Arrange ingredients in layers in greased casserole, reserving enough corn chips to top the casserole. Bake at 350°F. for 30 minutes. Yield: 4-6 servings.

Mrs. Irma Haley, Castleford H.S.
Castleford, Idaho

CHILI PIE CASSEROLE

3 c. corn chips
1 lge. onion, chopped
1 can chili, heated
1 c. grated Cheddar cheese

Place 2 cups of corn chips in a 2-quart baking dish. Arrange onion and half the cheese on top. Pour chili over onion and cheese. Top with remaining corn chips and cheese. Bake at 350°F. for 15 to 20 minutes. NOTE: All of cheese may be used as topping. Yield: 4-6 servings.

This recipe submitted by the following teachers:
Elberta Martin, Marsh Jr. H.S.
Fort Worth, Texas
Wilma Gould, Gorham H.S.
Gorham, Illinois
Mrs. Marshall Byrom, Brenham H.S.
Brenham, Texas
Mrs. Aleta Thompson, McLean H.S.
McLean, Texas

CORN CHIP CASSEROLE

1 lge. bag corn chips
1 can chili con carne
1 4-oz. can taco sauce
1 4-oz. can chopped green chilies
1 med. onion, chopped
2 c. Longhorn cheese, grated

Cover bottom of casserole with corn chips. Combine chili, taco sauce, green chili, onion and 1 cup cheese. Pour mixture over corn chips. Add remaining corn chips and top with remaining cheese. Bake at 375°F. about 25 to 30 minutes until corn chips are slightly browned. Yield: 6-8 servings.

Mrs. Kathryn Fox, Willcox H.S.
Willcox, Arizona

ENCHILADA CASSEROLE

12 corn tortillas, fried and drained
1 can cream of chicken
1 soup can milk
1 sm. can chopped green chili
½ lb. cheese, cut in small pieces

Combine soup, milk, chili, and cheese; heat until cheese melts. Tear tortillas into pieces. Alternate layers of tortillas and sauce in a casserole. Bake 30 minutes in a 350°F. oven. Yield: 6 servings.

Mrs. Louisa M. Krebs, Rapid City H.S.
Rapid City, South Dakota

HOMINY AND TAMALE CASSEROLE

1 No. 2½ can yellow hominy
2 cans beef tamales
1 can tomato sauce
½ c. Cheddar cheese, grated
¼ c. finely chopped green onions, including tops

Into greased casserole place drained hominy. Crumble canned tamales and place over hominy, topping with the tomato sauce. Bake at 400°F. for about 15 minutes. Remove from oven; top with cheese. Return to oven for 3 minutes. Serve piping hot topped with the green onions. Yield: 6 serving

Mrs. Helene Baer Maneval, Sonora Union H.S.
Sonora, California

SATURDAY NIGHT SPECIAL

4 slices bacon, chopped
½ med. onion, chopped
2 c. tomato juice
½ t. salt
¼ t. pepper
Garlic salt (opt.)
1 25-oz. pkg. elbo-roni
½ c. grated cheese

Brown bacon. Saute onion with slightly browned bacon. Add tomato juice and seasoning and simmer. Cook elbo-roni until tender in salted water; drain. Add elbo-roni to simmering sauce. Add cheese and heat until cheese is melted. Yield: 4-6 servings.

Mrs. W. P. Ricketts, Torrington H.S.
Torrington, Wyoming

PENNY SUPPER

6 wieners, thinly sliced
4 med. cooked potatoes, diced
2 T. minced onion
¼ c. butter, softened
1 c. cooked peas
1 t. mustard
1 can cream of mushroom soup
Salt and pepper to taste

Combine wieners, except a few pieces for top, with potatoes, onion and butter. Place in 7x11-inch baking dish. Mix remaining ingredients; toss with wiener mixture. Dot with wiener pieces. Cover tightly with foil. Bake at 350°F. for 25-30 minutes. Yield: 4-6 servings.

Mrs. Ann Hunt, Nampa H.S.
Nampa, Idaho

SPANISH RICE PRONTO

2 T. bacon drippings or butter
¼ c. onion, diced
⅙ c. green pepper, diced
1 c. instant rice
1 c. hot water
1 10½-oz. can tomato sauce
½ t. salt
⅛ t. pepper

Melt fat in saucepan. Add onion, green pepper and uncooked rice. Cook and stir over medium heat until lightly browned. Add remaining ingredients; mix well. Bring to boil; reduce heat. Simmer uncovered for five minutes. NOTE: If desired, 1 1-pound can stewed tomatoes may be substituted for tomato sauce and hot water. Yield: 3 servings.

Jane Wildung, Blue Earth Public School
Blue Earth, Minnesota

Casseroles With A Foreign Flavor

PEANUT BUTTER GRAVY (AFRICA)

1 med. onion, chopped
¼ c. oil
1 can tomato paste
¾ c. peanut butter
3 c. chicken broth or water
Salt to taste
Red pepper to taste

Saute onion in oil. Mix tomato paste and peanut butter; add a little broth. Mix all ingredients and simmer 5 minutes. Serve over hot rice as a main dish. NOTE: Any desired spices may be added.

Selma Sailors, Diller Community Schools
Diller, Nebraska

GREEN MEALIE PUFF (SOUTH AFRICA)

3 c. canned whole-kernel corn
3 T. flour
2½ T. butter
1½ c. milk
1¼ t. salt
¼ t. pepper
3 eggs, separated

Drain corn and finely chop. Make a white sauce of flour, butter and milk. Boil for 1-2 minutes; add corn and seasonings. Remove corn mixture from heat and carefully add well beaten yolks. Allow to stand 2 or 3 minutes. Fold in stiffly beaten egg whites and pour into a buttered baking dish. Bake in hot water at 325-350°F. for 30 minutes or until mixture is puffy and slightly browned. Yield: 6-8 servings.

Dorothy Antey, New Berlin H.S.
New Berlin, Illinois

CARBONADA CRIOLLA—GAUCHO BEEF STEW (ARGENTINA)

½ tripe
1 pig's foot
1 pig's ear
2 whole pig's tails
4 lb. 2 oz. beef chuck
½ t. pepper
Salt to taste
Pinch of Accent
1 T. flour
½ c. oil
1 c. diced onion
1 c. diced green pepper
2 T. diced celery
½ c. minced scallions
½ c. diced carrots
2 apples, diced
1 c. sherry
1 c. red wine
2 qt. brown gravy
1 lb. fresh peeled tomatoes
½ c. kernel corn
2 potatoes, blanched and quartered
1 sweet potato, blanched and quartered
1 c. diced turnips, blanched
½ c. cooked pumpkin
½ c. cooked green beans
½ c. cooked green peas
1 clove garlic, peeled and chopped
4 T. chopped parsley
¼ c. almonds, sauted in butter
1 canned peach half
2 grapefruit sections
20 orange sections

Cook tripe in water for 2 hours. Reserve 2 cups broth. In a separate container cook pigs' foot, ear and tails for 15 minutes. Cut beef into pieces about 2-inches long, 1-inch wide and ½-inch thick. Season and flour beef and saute in oil until almost brown. Add onions, green pepper, celery, scallions, carrots and apple. Stew mixture for 3-4 minutes. Add sherry and red wine and cook 5 minutes longer. Transfer mixture to large casserole. Add brown gravy, tomatoes and corn. Bake at 350°F. about 1 hour or until meat is almost tender. Add cooked tripe, reserved broth, pigs' ear, foot and tails, potatoes and turnips. Bake 45 minutes longer. Remove from oven and add all remaining ingredients except peach half and orange and grapefruit sections. Place mixture in serving dish. Garnish with peach half in center, grapefruit sections alongside and orange sections around rim of casserole pointing to center. Yield: 10 generous servings.

Photograph for this recipe on front cover.

SHEIK MASHI (ASSYRIA)

9 thin shoulder cut lamb chops
2 or 3 lge. onions, sliced
3 T. fat
½ t. salt
⅛ t. pepper
⅛ t. nutmeg
⅛ t. cinnamon
Dash of cloves
Dash of monosodium glutamate
2 lge. eggplants
2-3 c. tomato juice

Cut lamb chops into small pieces; brown with onions in 1 tablespoon fat. Add seasonings. Pare eggplants and cut into 1-inch slices; fry in 2 tablespoons fat until almost tender. Arrange layers of eggplant slices and meat mixture in a casserole. Add tomato juice to cover. Bake uncovered at 325-350°F. until almost dry, about 1 hour. Serve over hot cooked rice. Yield: 6-8 servings.

I. Eugenia Spangler, Big Spring H.S.
Newville, Pennsylvania

HALUSKI—NOODLES WITH COTTAGE CHEESE (AUSTRIA)

¼ lb. butter
½ pkg. noodles or bow ties, cooked
1 t. salt
16 oz. cottage cheese
Fresh dill (opt.)

Melt butter; cook until brown but do not burn butter. Pour butter over cooked noodles and salt to taste. Break up cottage cheese and sprinkle through noodles. Mix well and sprinkle dill on top. Serve at once or keep in warming oven until ready to serve. Yield: 4-6 servings.

Mrs. Mary Mesaris Krasinsky, Exeter H.S.
Exeter, Pennsylvania

SPINACH-RICE (BRAZIL)

¼ c. butter
2 T. onion, chopped
1 pkg. frozen chopped spinach
¼ lb. sharp cheese, cut up
2 t. Worcestershire sauce
2 t. salt
½ t. pepper
1½ t. mixed salad herbs
1 c. milk
2 eggs, beaten
1⅓ c. cooked rice, unsalted

Melt butter in top of double boiler; add onions and cook for a few minutes. Add spinach, cheese, seasonings and milk. Cook over hot water until spinach is thawed and cheese melted. Add beaten eggs to cooked rice and stir in spinach mixture. Put in buttered casserole; place casserole in pan of hot water and bake at 350°F. for 45 minutes or until firm in center like custard. Yield: 6 servings.

Mrs. Leota H. Allen, Grandville H.S.
Grandville, Michigan

PASTEL DE CHOCLO—CORN PIE (CHILE)

1 lb. chuck
1 med. onion, diced
1 T. shortening
1 c. meat stock or bouillon
Salt to taste
Red pepper to taste
Marjoram
Cumin seed
1 T. flour
¼ c. seedless raisins
2 T. ripe olives, diced
2 hard-cooked eggs, sliced
1 No. 303 can whole kernel corn
1 T. butter
⅓ c. dry milk solids
Pinch of sweet basil
Sugar to taste
2 eggs, separated

Chop the meat into 1-inch cubes and brown with the onion in the shortening. Add stock and season-ings. Simmer for 30 minutes. Make gravy in meat mixture by adding 1 tablespoon flour dissolved in a little water. Pieces of chicken may be added, if desired. Place the mixture in a baking dish. Scatter raisins, olives and eggs over it. Heat corn and liquid with butter and dry milk solids, stirring constantly. Add sweet basil, salt and sugar to taste. Add beaten egg yolks, stirring well; fold in stiffly beaten whites. Pour over the meat. Sprinkle with sugar. Bake at 425°F. until browned. Yield: 6-8 servings.

Mrs. Ramona Morgner, Valley H.S.
Albuquerque, New Mexico

BEEF OF THE ORIENT (CHINA)

2 lb. flank steak
1 clove garlic, crushed
Salt to taste
Dash of pepper
¼ t. ground ginger
2 T. salad oil
¼ c. soy sauce
½ t. sugar
2 tomatoes, quartered
2 green peppers, cut in chunks
1 can bean sprouts, drained
1 T. cornstarch
¼ c. water

Cut steak across the grain in thin strips. Fry with garlic, salt, pepper and ginger in oil over high heat until brown. Add soy sauce and sugar; cover tightly and cook slowly for 5 minutes. Add tomatoes, green peppers and bean sprouts; bring to a boil. Cover and cook briskly for 5 minutes. Make a smooth paste of cornstarch and water. Add to beef mixture and cook until sauce thickens, stirring lightly. Yield: 6 servings.

Mrs. Mary E. Burt, West Bloomfield H.S.
Orchard Lake, Michigan

CHICKEN HOT DISH (CHINA)

¼ c. onion, chopped
1 c. celery
Butter
1 can mushroom soup
⅓ c. chicken broth
1 T. soy sauce
3 drops Tabasco sauce
Pepper
2 c. cooked chicken, diced
1 can chow mein noodles
⅓ c. cashews

Fry onion and celery in butter until tender. Add mushroom soup and chicken broth. Season with soy sauce, Tabasco sauce and pepper. Add chicken; simmer. Pour into 1-quart casserole. Sprinkle chow mein noodles and cashews on top. Cover; Bake 20 minutes at 350°F. Yield: 6 servings.

Mrs. Bertha Cruse, Winthrop Community School
Winthrop, Minnesota

CHICKEN CASSEROLE (CHINA)

¼ c. onions, chopped
1 c. celery, diced
1 T. butter
1 can mushroom soup
⅓ c. chicken broth
1 T. soy sauce
3 drops Tabasco sauce
2 c. chicken, diced
1 c. Chinese noodles
½ c. cashew nuts

Saute onions and celery in butter. Combine all ingredients in casserole. Bake at 350°F. for 30 minutes.

Vesta Baker, Paonia H.S.
Paonia, Colorado

CASSEROLE (CHINA)

1 lb. ground beef, browned
1 c. celery, chopped
1 onion, chopped
1½ c. water
Mushrooms (opt.)
Worcestershire sauce (opt.)
1 can cream of celery soup
1 can cream of chicken soup
½ c. raw rice
⅔ T. soy sauce
1 can chow mein noodles

Mix all ingredients except chow mein noodles. Place mixture in casserole. Bake at 350°F. for 1 hour and 30 minutes. Sprinkle with chow mein noodles; bake 10 minutes longer.

Mrs. Mary Ann Bauer, Waupun H.S.
Waupun, Wisconsin

CHICKEN AND LOBSTER CASSEROLE (CHINA)

1 sm. can water chestnuts
1 can bamboo shoots
½ c. raw mushrooms, sliced
1 box frozen peas, slightly thawed
1 cube margarine
1 No. 2 can chicken broth
1 t. salt
¼ c. cold water
¼ c. cornstarch
2 T. soy sauce
1 6½-oz. can lobster
1 chicken breast, cooked
2 hard-cooked eggs, chopped
1 can Chinese noodles

Saute chestnuts, bamboo shoots, mushrooms and peas in margarine for 3 minutes. Add broth and salt; cook for 1 minute. Mix water, cornstarch and soy sauce until smooth; add to vegetables. Cook until thickened, stirring constantly. Pour into a flat casserole; top with pieces of lobster and slices of chicken. Garnish with egg; circle with noodles. Bake at 300°F. for 1 hour, or at 200°F, for longer baking. Yield: 6 servings.

Mrs. Marjorie E. Smith, Red Bluff Union H.S.
Red Bluff, California

CASSEROLE (CHINA)

1½ lb. hamburger
1 med. onion, chopped
2 c. celery, diced
1 can Chinese noodles
1½ c. water
¼ c. soy sauce
1 can cream of mushroom soup
1 can cream of chicken soup
¼ c. rice

Brown hamburger and onion in skillet; add to remaining ingredients, reserving a few noodles for topping. Combine in a 1½-quart casserole. Bake 1½ hours at 350°F. Sprinkle on reserved noodles. Yield: 6-8 servings.

Donna E. Johnson, Crestview H.S.
Convoy, Ohio

CASSEROLE (CHINA)

1 lb. hamburger
1 c. raw rice
1 c. onion, chopped
1 c. celery, chopped
1 c. mushroom soup
2 c. water
2½ T. soy sauce
2 c. bean sprouts

Mix all ingredients and pour into casserole. Bake in 350°F. oven for 1 hour to 1 hour and 30 minutes or until done. Yield: 6-8 servings.

Mary Jane Niboli, Tranquillity Union H.S.
Tranquillity, California

CHICKEN 'N' WALNUTS (CHINA)

1 c. bamboo shoots, cubed
1 c. celery, chopped diagonally
1 c. onions, cut lengthwise
8 water chestnuts, cubed
6 T. oil
½ lb. walnuts
1 lb. uncooked chicken, cubed
¾ t. salt
2 T. cornstarch
3 T. soy sauce
2 T. Sherry wine
1 t. sugar
¼ c. soup stock or bouillon

Lightly saute bamboo shoots, celery, onions and chestnuts in 3 tablespoons oil; remove from pan. Brown walnuts slightly in deep fat. Remove and drain. Dredge chicken in mixture of salt, cornstarch, soy sauce, Sherry and sugar. Saute in remaining 3 tablespoons oil until tender. Add soup stock and heat. Add vegetables and walnuts. Heat thoroughly and serve hot. NOTE: To remove bitter flavor of walnuts, cover with cold water and bring to a boil; boil for three minutes. Drain. Yield: 6 servings.

Mrs. Claudia Finnerud, Wishkah Valley H.S.
Aberdeen, Washington

BAKED CHOP SUEY (CHINA)

1 lb. hamburger
1 c. rice, cooked
1 c. celery, chopped
1 c. onion, chopped
1 can cream of chicken soup
1 can mushroom soup
1 can water
Soy sauce
Salt to taste
1 can Chinese noodles

Brown hamburger. Mix all ingredients except Chinese noodles and place in a baking dish. Bake at 350°F. for 45 minutes. Sprinkle noodles over top. Bake 15 minutes longer. Yield: 8 servings.

Reta Neff, Nappanee H.S.
Nappanee, Indiana

BAKED CHOP SUEY (CHINA)

1½ lb. beef and pork, cubed
1 c. dried celery
1 onion, finely cut
1 can mushroom soup
1 can chicken soup
1 can water
1 c. uncooked rice
2 T. soy sauce

Brown meat; add celery and onion. Simmer slowly for 30 minutes. Add other ingredients carefully. Pour into casserole. Bake for 1 hour and 30 minutes at 350°F. If desired, chow mein noodles may be sprinkled on top. Yield: 6 servings
Mrs. Edith S. Johnston, Milford Township H.S.
Milford, Illinois

HAMBURGER CHOP SUEY (CHINA)

1 lb. ground chuck
2 med. onions, chopped
2 T. shortening
1 can cream of mushroom soup
1 can cream of chicken soup
1½ c. water
½ c. uncooked long grain rice
1 c. celery, chopped
2 T. soya sauce
1 can water chestnuts, chopped (opt.)
1 lge. can Chinese noodles

Brown meat and onions in shortening. Add soups, water, rice, celery, soya sauce, and water chestnuts. Pour into a greased 2-quart casserole; cover tightly with lid or foil. Bake 1 hour and 30 minutes at 350°F. Add noodles to top of casserole and cook 30 minutes uncovered. Yield: 8-10 servings.

Mrs. Joyce Wolfgang Williams, State Executive Secretary, Future Homemakers of America
Tallahassee, Florida

CHOP SUEY (CHINA)

1 lb. hamburger
1 c. celery, diced
2 c. water
1 onion, chopped
3 T. soy sauce
½ c. raw rice
1 can mushroom soup
1 can chicken-rice soup

Brown hamburger. Place all ingredients in a buttered casserole. Bake at 350°F. for 1 hour 30 minutes. Yield: 4 servings.

Sharon Schoeberl, Elkton Public School
Elkton, South Dakota

CHOP SUEY CASSEROLE (CHINA)

1 lb. hamburger
1 c. onion, chopped
1 c. celery, chopped
¼ c. soy sauce
1 can cream of chicken soup
1 can cream of mushroom soup
½ c. instant rice
1 c. water
1 can Chinese noodles

Brown meat; mix with all remaining ingredients except noodles. Bake, covered, for 1 hour in 300°F. oven. Top with noodles and bake uncovered 15 minutes longer. Yield: 6 servings.

Mrs. Nancy Geriets, Northwestern Community Unit School
Palmyra, Illinois

CHOW MEIN (CHINA)

1 lb. pork, cut in thin strips
3 T. salad oil
3 c. celery, thinly sliced
1 c. onion, sliced
1 c. fresh mushrooms, sliced
2½ T. cornstarch
1 can beef broth
¼ c. soy sauce
1 1-lb. can bean sprouts, drained
1 5-oz. can water chestnuts, sliced

Cook pork in 1 tablespoon oil; drain well. Saute celery, onion and mushrooms in 2 tablespoons oil until tender and crisp. Blend cornstarch and ¼ cup water; add broth and soy sauce. Stir into vegetables; add meat, bean sprouts and water chestnuts. Heat until thickened, stirring constantly. Serve over chow mein noodles or rice. Yield: 4-5 servings.

Mrs. Donna Wetter, Dallas Jr. H.S.
Dallas, Oregon

CHICKEN CHOW MEIN (CHINA)

1 lge. can chow mein noodles
2 c. chicken, coarsely chopped
1 can cream of celery soup
1 can cream of mushroom soup
2 c. of chicken broth or rich milk
1 c. sliced almonds
2 c. celery, chopped
1 med. onion, diced

Put half of noodles in bottom of greased casserole. Combine other ingredients; put in casserole. Top with remaining noodles. Bake at 350°F. for 1 hour. Yield: 8-10 servings.

Lila L. Paisley, Mindoro H.S.
Mindoro, Wisconsin

CHICKEN CHOW MEIN SUPREME (CHINA)

⅔-1 c. chow mein noodles
1 c. cooked chicken, chopped
½-⅔ c. slivered almonds
1 can cream of mushroom soup
1 soup can of milk
2 t. green pepper, chopped
2 t. pimento

Spread half of noodles in a greased casserole. Mix chicken, almonds, mushroom soup, milk, green pepper and pimento; pour over noodles in casserole. Sprinkle remaining noodles on top. Bake at 350°F. for 45 minutes. Yield: 6-8 servings.

Mary Jane Rudd, Sheldon H.S.
Sheldon, Iowa

CHOW MEIN–HAMBURGER HOT DISH (CHINA)

1 lb. ground beef
2 sm. onions
1 c. celery, chopped
2 c. water
1 can cream of chicken soup
1 can cream of celery soup
1 8-oz. can chow mein noodles
1 sm. can mushrooms

Combine beef, onions, celery and 1 cup water; cook for 15 minutes. Add remaining water and all ingredients. Pour into casserole; bake, covered, at 350°F. for 30 minutes. Uncover and bake 30 minutes longer. Yield: 6-8 servings.

Mrs. Evelyn Johnson, Bottineau H.S.
Bottineau, North Dakota

CHICKEN OR TURKEY CHOW MEIN (CHINA)

¼ c. oil
1 c. onion, diced
4 c. chicken or turkey
1 c. chicken broth
1½ c. green pepper, chopped
1½ c. celery, chopped
2 T. cornstarch
3 T. soy sauce
1 can chow mein vegetables
1 can water chestnuts, sliced
1 sm. can sauted mushrooms
¼ c. slivered almonds

Combine oil, onion, chicken, broth, green pepper and celery; cook for a few minutes. Add remaining ingredients; heat thoroughly. Serve on chow mein noodles. Yield: 6-8 servings.

Sylvia Benson, Grant Union H.S.
John Day, Oregon

CHOW MEIN HOT DISH (CHINA)

2 lb. hamburger
2 c. celery, cut up
2 c. onion, cut up
1 can tomato soup
1 can mushroom soup
1 can bean sprouts
2 cans chow mein noodles
Salt and pepper to taste

Brown hamburger, celery and onions. Combine with the remaining ingredients; bake in a buttered baking dish at 350°F. for 45 minutes. Yield: 8-10 servings.

Mrs. Mabel L. Hammer, Wolsey H.S.
Wolsey, South Dakota

COMPANY CASSEROLE (CHINA)

1 5-oz. can chow mein noodles
¾ c. celery, finely chopped
1 can mushroom soup
1 3-oz. pkg. cashew nuts, broken
1 T. onion, finely chopped
1 T. Worcestershire sauce
¼ c. hot water, gravy or broth
1 c. cooked fresh pork, chopped

Reserve ¾ cup of chow mein noodles. Combine the rest of the ingredients, mixing only enough to blend. Place into a 1½-quart casserole. Sprinkle reserved chow mein noodles over mixture. Bake uncovered at 325°F. for 45 minutes until celery is still tender-crisp. NOTE: If desired, cooked chicken, 1 can tuna or 1 can shrimp may be substituted for pork. Yield: 4-5 servings.

Kathryn Kangas, Molalla Union H.S.
Molalla, Oregon

HAMBURGER CASSEROLE (CHINA)

1 can cream of mushroom soup
1 can cream of chicken soup
1 lb. ground chuck
¼ c. soy sauce
1 c. celery, chopped
1 c. onions, chopped
1 sm. can water chestnuts
1 c. raw rice
1½ soup cans water
1 can Chinese noodles

Mix all ingredients except the noodles and place in casserole; cook for 1 hour, covered, at 350°F. Remove lid and sprinkle with canned noodles; bake uncovered for 30 minutes.

Mrs. Thelma Moore, Parlier H.S.
Parlier, California

HASH (CHINA)

1 lb. hamburger
1 med. onion, finely chopped
1 c. celery, finely chopped
1 can mushroom soup
1 can cream of chicken soup
½-1 c. uncooked rice
2 c. water
¼ c. soya sauce
1 can bean sprouts (opt.)
1 can chow mein noodles (opt.)

Brown meat; drain off excess fat. Add onion and celery; cook soightly. Add soups, rice, water, soya sauce and bean sprouts. Pour into a casserole; bake at 350°F. for 20 minutes. Sprinkle noodles on top; bake 10 minutes longer. Yield: 8 servings.

This recipe submitted by the following teachers:
Mrs. Thalia Jewel, Klamath Union H.S.
Klamath Falls, Oregon
May Koch, Converse County H.S.
Douglas, Wyoming

ONE-DISH MEAL (CHINA)

1 lb. veal, chopped
2 onions, finely chopped
2 T. fat
½ c. uncooked rice
1 can condensed chicken soup
1 can mushroom soup
1 can peas
4 T. soy sauce
1 t. salt
1 t. pepper
2 c. water

Brown veal and onions in fat. Add browned meat mixture to other ingredients. Bake in greased casserole at 325°F. for 1 hour and 30 minutes. Yield: 8 servings.

Mrs. Eleanore Dahl, Belgrade H.S.
Belgrade, Minnesota

ONE-DISH MEAL (CHINA)

1 lb. veal, cubed
2 med. onions, finely chopped
1 c. celery, finely chopped
2 T. fat
½ c. uncooked rice
1 can condensed cream of mushroom soup
1 can condensed chicken soup
1 c. canned peas
2 c. water
3 T. gravy coloring
1 t. salt
Pepper to taste

Brown veal, onions and celery in fat. Place in 2½-quart buttered casserole. Add remaining ingredients, and mix. Bake at 325°F. for 1 hour and 30 minutes. Yield: 8-10 servings.

Sandra Weidling, Mauston H.S.
Mauston, Wisconsin

ORIENTAL CASSEROLE (CHINA)

1 sm. onion, diced
1 lb. pork shoulder, diced
½ c. brown rice
½ c. long grain white rice
½ t. salt
1 c. celery, diced
3 T. soy sauce
1 can mushroom soup
1 can cream of chicken soup
1 soup can water

Brown onion and pork. Mix all ingredients in well greased baking dish. Bake at 350°F. for 1 hour and 15 minutes, or until rice is tender. NOTE: If desired, leftover roast or chicken may be substitued for pork. Yield: 6 servings.

Cetha Kuske, Britton Public School
Britton, South Dakota

ORIENTAL CASSEROLE (CHINA)

1 can Chinese noodles
1 can mushroom soup
¼ c. light cream or milk
2 T. A-1 sauce
1 can tuna
¼ lb. cashews
1 c. celery, diced
¼ c. onion, chopped
Salt and pepper to taste

Mix half of noodles with remaining ingredients. Pour into a buttered casserole. Top with remaining noodles. Bake at 350°F. for 35 minutes. Yield: 4-6 servings.

This recipe submitted by the following teachers:

Elaine L. Smith, Union City Community H.S.
Union City, Indiana

Mrs. Shirley Moore, Western H.S.
Russiaville, Indiana

ORIENTAL RICE CASSEROLE (CHINA)

½ lb. ground round beef
1 sm. onion, minced
4 T. margarine
¼ c. soy sauce
2 c. celery, diced
1 can mushroom soup
½ soup can water
1 sm. can mushroom pieces
½ c. brown rice
½ c. white rice

Saute meat and onion in margarine; add remaining ingredients. Pour mixture into a lightly greased 3-quart casserole. Bake for 2 hours at 325°F. NOTE: Do not add salt. Yield: 12 servings.

Mrs. Estel Simmons, Norte Vista H.S.
Arlington, California

YUM YUM (CHINA)

1 green pepper, coarsely diced
1 lge. onion, coarsely diced
2 stalks celery, coarsely diced
1 lb. hamburger
1 can condensed mushroom soup
1 No. 2½ can chow mein noodles

Boil green pepper, onion and celery in a small amount of water until tender. Brown meat in skillet, separating into particles. Remove surplus fat as it accumulates. Add mushroom soup and half the chow mein noodles. Add vegetables; mix. Add remaining noodles to top of skillet. Bake in oven at 350°F. for 30 minutes. Yield: 4-6 servings.

Gloria Evernden, Myrtle Point H.S.
Myrlte Point, Oregon

SAUSAGE CASSEROLE OR PARADISE LOAF (CHINA)

1-1½ lb. sausage
1 green pepper, chopped
1 med. or lge. onion, chopped
½ bunch celery, chopped
5 c. water
2 pkg. dry chicken-noodle soup mix
½-1 c. uncooked rice
½ c. sliced almonds
1 4-oz. can sliced mushrooms (opt.)

Brown sausage, pepper, onion and celery. Bring water to boil and add soup mix and rice; simmer 10 minutes or until tender. Add sausage mixture, almonds and mushrooms, if desired. Cover and bake for 30 minutes at 350°F. Remove cover and bake about 30 minutes longer. NOTE: If desired all ingredients except almonds may be combined. Bake at 350°F. for 45 minutes. Sprinkle almonds over top and bake 15 minutes longer. Yield: 8-10 servings.

This recipe submitted by the following teachers:

Elizabeth Thornburg, Montrose H.S.
Montrose, Colorado

Mrs. Virginia Claypool, Marshall H.S.
Marshall, Illinois

Emily Lollis, Thewoka H.S.
Thewoka, Oklahoma

Beverly McCullough, Avalon H.S.
Avalon, Texas

SWEET AND SOUR MEAT BALLS (CHINA)

¼ c. fine dry bread crumbs
1 t. onion, minced
1 t. salt
Dash of pepper
1 lb. ground beef
1 egg
Cooking oil
1 c. celery, sliced
1 red pepper, cut in wedges
1 green pepper, cut in wedges
⅓ c. vinegar
⅓ c. brown sugar
2 T. soy sauce
2 T. cornstarch
4 pineapple slices, halved
Pickled cauliflower pieces

Combine bread crumbs, onion, salt, pepper and ½ cup water; mix well. Add beef and egg; shape into 16 meat balls. Brown slowly in a little oil; remove meat balls. Saute celery and red and green peppers for 5 minutes. Combine 1½ cups water, the vinegar, brown sugar and soy sauce; add cornstarch mixed with a little water. Cook for 3 minutes. Add meat balls, celery mixture, pineapple halves and a few pieces of pickled cauliflower. Heat and serve. Yield: 4 servings.

Judith Hamann, Hibbing H.S.
Hibbing, Minnesota

MANDARIN TUNA SKILLET

3 T. butter or margarine
1 lb. mushrooms, sliced
4 t. cornstarch
1 t. salt
1/8 t. monosodium glutamate
1/8 t. garlic powder
Dash of pepper
1/2 t. soy sauce
1/2 c. orange juice
1 11-oz. can Mandarin orange sections
1 5-oz. can water chestnuts, sliced
2 6½- to 7-oz. cans tuna, drained
3 c. hot cooked rice

Melt butter in large skillet; add mushrooms and cook until tender. Combine cornstarch, salt, monosodium glutamate, garlic powder, pepper and soy sauce in small bowl; blend in orange juice. Drain liquid from Mandarin orange sections and chestnuts; add water to the combined liquids to make 1 cup. Stir into skillet with cornstarch mixture. Add water chestnuts to skillet and cook, stirring constantly, until thickened and clear. Break tuna into large pieces; add to skillet with orange sections. Heat to serving temperature. Serve with hot rice. Yield: 6 servings.

Photograph for this recipe on page 299

ECUADORIAN SEVICHE

2 lb. striped bass
1/2 c. lime juice
1 t. salt
1/8 t. Tabasco
1/2 c. orange juice
1½ t. minced onion
1½ t. minced pepper
1 t. snipped chives or cilantro
1 T. catsup
1 Spanish onion, very thinly sliced
4 scallions
1/2 fresh red pimento
12 orange sections

Cut bass into small, very thin slices. Marinate for 12 hours in lime juice with salt and Tabasco. Add orange juice and minced onion, pepper and chives to marinade. Flavor with catsup. Arrange fish in deep dish with marinade. Place Spanish onion slices in center on top of fish. Finely chop scallions and pimento and sprinkle over entire dish. Garnish with orange sections. Yield: 8 servings.

Photograph for this recipe on back cover.

TOAD IN THE HOLE (ENGLAND)

1½ lb. beef steak or left-over roast
2 eggs
1 c. flour
1/2 t. salt
2 c. milk

Cut beef into 1-inch cubes, leaving a few a little larger. Season cubes well with salt and pepper and place in a shallow greased baking dish. Spread cubes apart so batter will go in between them. Make a batter of eggs, flour, salt and milk; pour over the beef cubes, making sure some of the larger cubes have thin "heads" stuck out of the batter. Bake at 400-425°F. for 30 minutes. Yield: 4-6 servings.

Helen E. Bortz, Osborne Rural H.S.
Osborne, Kansas

LANTTULAATIKKO-TURNIP CASSEROLE (FINLAND)

2½ c. boiled turnips, mashed
4 T. butter
1½ t. salt
1/8 t. pepper
1½ T. sugar
2 eggs, beaten
1¼ c. soft bread crumbs

Combine all ingredients except 1/4 cup bread crumbs. Put into oiled casserole; top with remaining crumbs. Bake at 350°F. for 30 minutes or until brown on top. Yield: 6 servings.

Elma Ranta, Negaunee H.S.
Negaunee, Michigan

LIVER CASSEROLE (FINLAND)

1 c. white rice
1½ c. boiling water
3 t. salt
1 sm. onion, chopped
1 T. margarine
2¼ c. milk
3/4 lb. beef liver, minced
4 T. syrup
1/2 c. raisins
1 t. ginger
1/4 t. white pepper
1 t. marjoram
1 egg, beaten
Bread crumbs

Wash rice and place in boiling water with salt. Boil until rice has absorbed water. Brown onion lightly in margarine. When rice has slightly cooled, add cold milk, liver, onion, syrup, raisins and flavorings. Mix in the egg. Pour into a well greased baking dish. Sprinkle bread crumbs and dabs of butter. Bake at 375°F. for 45 minutes; reduce heat to 350°F. and bake 20 minutes. Serve with cranberries or cranberry jam and melted butter. Yield: 4 servings.

Mrs. Dean Wyler, Garaway H.S.
Sugarcreek, Ohio

FETE DE L'AUTOMNE (FRANCE)

25 slices bread, cubed
1½ lb. cleaned shrimp
1¼ c. green pepper, chopped
1¼ c. sweet onion, chopped
2¼ c. chopped celery
1¼ c. mayonnaise
10 eggs, beaten well
2 qt. milk
2 cans mushroom soup
1 lb. Cheddar cheese, grated
Paprika

Place half the bread in three 2-quart casseroles. Add shrimp, vegetables and mayonnaise. Cover with remaining bread. Cover with eggs and milk. Refrigerate overnight if desired. Before baking, mix in the soup and cheese. Sprinkle top generously with paprika. Bake for 1 hour at 350°F. Yield: 25 servings.

Maxine E. Toynton, Sun Prairie H.S.
Sun Prairie, Wisconsin

PARISIAN CHICKEN (FRANCE)

1 pt. sour cream
1 pkg. dry onion soup mix
2 pkg. frozen broccoli, cooked
2 c. cooked chicken, cut in large pieces
1 c. heavy cream, whipped
2 T. Parmesan cheese

Mix sour cream and dry onion soup. Arrange cooked broccoli in a greased casserole, letting green tops stick up. Spoon half of sauce over broccoli. Arrange chicken pieces over sauce. Add whipped cream to remaining sour cream mixture; spoon over all. Sprinkle Parmesan cheese over top. Bake in 250°F. oven for 20 minutes. Yield: 6-8 servings.

Mrs. Theo Eichler, Whittier Jr. H.S.
Lincoln, Nebraska

QUICHE LORRAINE (FRANCE)

½ lb. bacon
1 9-inch uncooked pastry shell
¼ lb. Swiss or American cheese, shredded
3 eggs
2 c. milk or light cream
1 t. salt
1/16 t. cayenne pepper

Fry bacon until crisp; crumble into pastry-lined pie pan. Arrange cheese over bacon. Beat eggs slightly; add remaining ingredients. Blend and pour over cheese. Bake at 400°F. for 35-45 minutes; do not over bake. Remove from oven while center is still soft. Cool for 5-10 minutes before serving. NOTE: If desired, ¼ lb. diced ham may be used with bacon. Yield: 6 servings.

Patricia L. Kuiper, Naperville Community H.S.
Naperville, Illinois

GOULASH (GERMANY)

1 med. onion, chopped
1 clove garlic, chopped
3 T. cooking oil
1½ lb. stew beef, cubed
2 cans tomato paste
½ t. oregano
½ t. basil
1 bay leaf
1 paste can water

Saute onion and garlic in oil; remove from pan. Brown stew beef in remaining oil in pan. Combine tomato paste, onions, garlic, spices and water; Add beef. Simmer for 4 hours on very low heat. Serve over rice or macaroni.

Mrs. Tranetta McComb, Barrington H.S.
Barrington, Illinois

KALE SUPREME (GERMANY)

1 No. 303 can kale
1 c. cooked cured ham, cubed
⅓ c. oats
⅛ t. salt
Pepper (opt.)

In a buttered casserole, place half of kale, ham, oats and seasonings. Repeat layers. Add all juice from the kale. Cover and bake at 350°F. for 35-40 minutes or until oats are tender. NOTE: uncooked ham may be used; increase baking time to 45 minutes. Yield: 4-6 servings.

Marie S. Reynolds, Twin Valley South H.S.
West Alexandria, Ohio

VEGETABLE STEW (GERMANY)

1 lb. lean hamburger
3 lge. onions, sliced
6 lge. carrots, sliced
4 lge. potatoes, sliced
Salt and pepper to taste
2 bay leaves
1 can tomatoes

Alternate layers of meat, onion, potatoes, and carrots in a heavy sauce pan or casserole. Repeat layers until all is used. Add salt, pepper and bay leaves. Pour tomatoes over all. Simmer for 1 or 2 hours on top of stove or cook in slow oven until tender. Yield: 6-8 servings.

Mrs. Corinne M. Shuff, Saugus H.S.
Saugus, Massachusetts

MOUSSAKA—EGGPLANT CASSEROLE (GREECE)

4 c. eggplant, thinly sliced
½ c. shortening
1 lb. ground beef
2 T. olive oil
½ c. onion, minced
1 c. fresh or canned tomatoes
½ t. salt

(Continued on Next Page)

⅓ c. butter, melted
⅓ c. flour
2 c. milk
3 eggs, beaten

Soak eggplant in salted water for 15 minutes. Drain; press out water in towel. Brown in frying pan with shortening. In second frying pan brown beef in olive oil; add onion, tomatoes and salt. Place layer of browned eggplant in greased casserole; place over it layer of meat mixture; alternate layers until all ingredients are used. Blend butter and flour in saucepan. Add milk, stirring until thickened. Cool slightly. Stir some of mixture into eggs. Combine egg mixture with remaining white sauce and pour into casserole. Bake 40 minutes at 350°F. NOTE: Potatoes, summer squash, zucchini or combinations of any may be used following same procedure. Yield: 4 servings.

Mrs. Marianne Baillos, Waverly Jr. H.S.
Lansing, Michigan

CURRIED CHICKEN (HAWAII)

3-4 c. cooked rice
¼ c. butter
½ c. onion, finely chopped
1 t. curry powder
5 T. flour
1 t. salt
2 c. milk
1 c. chicken broth
1 stewing hen, cooked and cut up

Spread cooked rice into a greased casserole. Melt butter in a skillet; saute onion until limp but not brown. Add curry powder; cook a few minutes. Blend in flour and salt. Add liquids, stirring slowly until thickened. Add chicken. Pour over rice; top with your favorite topping. Bake at 350°F. until top is browned. Yield: 6 servings.

Hazel Lawton, Wendell H.S.
Wendell, Idaho

YAMASTRADI (HAWAII)

2 lb. ground beef
5 med. onions, chopped
2-3 green peppers, chopped
Salt and pepper to taste
1 c. tomatoes or tomato sauce
1 c. creamed corn
½ t. Tabasco
2 t. thyme
2 T. Worcestershire sauce
1 c. green olives, chopped
¾ c. almonds, chopped
½ lb. sharp cheese, grated
1 10-oz. pkg. noodles, cooked

Brown meat, onions and green pepper in small amount of fat or cooking oil. Add remaining ingredients. Turn into greased casserole; cover and bake for 45 minutes at 350°F. NOTE: May be frozen. Yield: 10-12 servings.

Mrs. Mary A. Moore, Texas Education Agency
Stephenville, Texas

ALOHA RIBS (HAWAII)

3 lb. spareribs
½ c. vinegar
1 c. cornstarch
¼ c. dark molasses
¼ c. soy sauce

Cut ribs into serving pieces. Bring 2-quarts water to boil; add vinegar. Add ribs; cover and bring to boil. Uncover and simmer 15 minutes; drain and cool. Mix cornstarch, molasses and soy sauce in large bowl. Add ribs and rub them in mixture until well coated. Fry ribs in hot oil until brown.

GLAZE:

½ c. sugar
¾ c. vinegar
¾ c. water
¾ c. pineapple syrup
½ t. monosodium glutamate
1½ green peppers, cut in strips
1 No. 303 can pineapple chunks, drained

Combine sugar, vinegar, water, pineapple syrup and monosodium glutamate; bring to a boil. Add ribs; cover and simmer 30 minutes. Add green pepper and pineapple last 10 minutes of cooking.

Mrs. Evelyn Meeks, Glenn County Union H.S.
Willows, California

PORK-RICE CASSEROLE (HAWAII)

1 lge. green pepper, finely cut
¼ c. flour
Salt and pepper to taste
2 lb. pork, cut in 1-inch cubes
2 eggs, beaten
Oil
1 med. can pineapple chunks, drained
Pineapple juice
1 can chicken bouillon
2 T. soy sauce
¼ c. cornstarch
¼ c. brown sugar
¼ c. cider vinegar
1 c. rice

Simmer green peppers in water for ten minutes until tender; drain. Combine flour, salt and pepper in shallow dish. Dip cubed pork in beaten eggs; coat in flour mixture. Slowly fry pork cubes in light oil until brown. Pour off excess fat. Add pineapple chunks and green peppers. Mix bouillon, soy sauce, cornstarch, brown sugar, vinegar and pineapple juice; stir well to dissolve sugar and cornstarch. Pour over meat mixture and stir gently to cover all meat particles. Place in casserole and bake at 325°F. until meat is tender, about 45 minutes. Cook rice in boiling salted water and serve with meat. Yield: 8 servings.

Mrs. Lucille Treado, Bishop Baraga Central H.S.
Marquette, Michigan

ESCALLOPED POTATOES (HUNGARY)

½ c. bread crumbs
6 med. potatoes, boiled in skins
6 hard-cooked eggs, sliced
¼ lb. margarine
Salt and pepper to taste
½ pt. sour cream
1½ c. milk

Lightly sprinkle a greased 2-quart casserole with part of bread crumbs. Add in alternate layers sliced potatoes, sliced eggs, dots of margarine, seasonings, sour cream, and bread crumbs. Continue layers to fill casserole. Pour milk over ingredients. Cover; bake at 350°F. for 1 hour. Yield: 4-6 servings.

Mrs. Rosalie Gainer, Midview H.S.
Grafton, Ohio

GOULASH (HUNGARY)

3 lb. top round beef
3 T. flour
1 t. salt
1 t. pepper
2 t. paprika
4 T. butter
1 c. tomato puree
1 c. beef stock

Cut meat into 2-inch cubes. Put flour, salt, pepper and paprika into a paper bag. Add meat cubes and shape to coat evenly. Heat butter and brown meat cubes quickly on all sides. Add tomato puree and stock; cover. Bake at 325°F. for 2 hours and 30 minutes. Yield: 6-8 servings.

Marlene Stagemeyer, Chase County H.S.
Imperial, Nebraska

LEKVAR AND NOODLE CASSEROLE (HUNGARY)

1 c. dry bread crumbs
¼ c. butter
1 6-oz. pkg. thin egg noodles, cooked
1 1-lb. 2-oz. jar lekvar (prune butter)
1 pt. dry cottage cheese
1 egg
3 T. sugar

Lightly brown bread crumbs in butter. Spread a third of the noodles in a buttered casserole. Add all of the lekvar. Cover with half the remaining noodles. Mix cottage cheese, egg and sugar; add to casserole and cover with remaining noodles. Top with bread crumbs. Bake 45 minutes at 325°F. Yield: 6-8 servings.

Mary Louise Vereb Klingensmith
Washington Township H.S.
Apollo, Pennsylvania

CURRY CASSEROLE (INDIA)

1 med. onion, diced
Fat
1 lb. ground beef
1 pkg. frozen peas and carrots, cooked
2 med. potatoes, diced and cooked
1 t. curry
Dash of salt
Dash of chili pepper

Brown onion in fat. Add beef, separating into particles, and brown. Add vegetables; simmer for 2 minutes. Add seasonings. Serve on rice. Yield: 4-6 servings.

Nancy B. Willard, East Haven H.S.
East Haven, Connecticut

CURRY AND RICE (EAST INDIA)

3 med. onions, sliced
1 lump butter or fat
2 lb. round steak, cubed
Salt to taste
4 t. curry powder
1 med. potato, pared and cubed
1 No. 2 can peas
1 c. rice, cooked
4 hard-cooked eggs
Lemon wedges

Cook onions in butter until tender. Brown meat, sprinkling with salt and curry powder. Add potatoes. Cover with water and cook until meat is tender. Add peas and cook until liquid is absorbed. To serve, make a nest of rice on a hot dinner plate. Place half of eggs in nest. Cover generously with curried meat. Squeeze lemon over entire dish. Garnish with remaining egg. NOTE: Curry is best made the day before. Leftover meat may be used. Yield: 6-8 servings.

Mrs. Aleen Hartman, Manderson-Hyattville H.S.
Manderson, Wyoming

KAEDJERE (INDIA)

1 c. hot boiled wild rice, drained
1 c. tuna, flaked
½ c. sliced mushrooms, sauted
2 T. green pepper, minced
2 T. pimento, minced
2 hard-cooked eggs
2 c. curry sauce
Butter, melted
Salted almonds, split

Lightly toss together rice, tuna, mushrooms, green pepper, pimento and diced egg whites. Gently stir in curry sauce. Pour into buttered oblong baking dish; sprinkle with sieved egg yolks. Bake at 350°F. for 30 minutes. Just before serving, dribble butter over top; sprinkle with almonds. Yield: 6 servings.

Mildred Fisher, Florence Township H.S.
Florence, New Jersey

SWEET RICE (IRAN)

½ c. blanched almonds, slivered
¼ c. butter or margarine, melted
½ c. orange marmalade
3 c. cooked rice
2 c. cooked chicken

Brown almonds in butter, stirring often. Add orange marmalade; mix well. Arrange a layer of rice in a buttered 2-quart casserole. Add a layer of chicken and a layer of nut mixture. Repeat, ending with the nut mixture. Cover and bake at 350°F. 35 minutes or until hot and steamy. Remove cover and bake 10 minutes longer. NOTE: This casserole can be prepared ahead of time and frozen. Put into oven without thawing; bake 1 hour at 350°F. Yield: 8-10 servings.

Alice M. Ford, Central H.S.
Cheyenne, Wyoming

MOUSSAKA (ISRAEL)

1 lb. ground lamb, mutton or beef, or mixture
Salt and pepper to taste
1 eggplant
⅔ c. tomato paste
½ c. dry bread crumbs or browned grits

Season meat to taste with salt and pepper; press into the bottom of a greased casserole or baking dish. Slice unpared eggplant into thin rounds and arrange over meat. Top with tomato paste; cover with bread crumbs or grits. Cover tightly and bake at 350°F. for 30 minutes. Remove cover and let bread crumbs brown for about 10 minutes. Yield: 4 servings.

Aida S. Nesselroth, Grover Cleveland Jr. H.S.
Caldwell, New Jersey

EGGPLANT PARMIGIANA (ITALY)

1 clove garlic, finely minced
1 c. onions, chopped
1 c. olive oil
5 c. tomatoes, canned or fresh
½ t. parsley
Salt and pepper to taste
¼ c. flour
4 whole eggs, beaten
2 eggplants, peeled and cut into ⅓-inch slices
1 c. Parmesan cheese, grated
1 c. Mozzarella cheese, sliced

Saute garlic and onions in ¼ cup oil until onion is transparent. Add tomatoes, parsely, salt and pepper; simmer, stirring occasionally, for 30 minutes. Combine flour and ¼ teaspoon salt. Dip eggplant slices in flour, then egg, and fry in remaining oil until lightly browned on both sides. Place alternate layers of eggplant, sauce and cheeses in large casserole. Bake 30 minutes at 350°F. Yield: 6 servings.

Toni Guast, Lackawanna Trail Joint Schools
Factoryville, Pennsylvania

CASSEROLE (ITALY)

1 lge. eggplant
1 egg, beaten
3 T. shortening
3 oz. pepperoni, ¼-inch thick slices
1 lb. ground beef
3 med. onions, chopped
1 No. 303 can tomato puree
⅛ t. basil
⅛ t. oregano
½ c. green pepper, chopped
1 t. salt
Dash of pepper
1 clove garlic, crushed
½ lb. Mozzarella cheese, grated

Peel and slice eggplant in ¼-inch slices; dip in egg and saute in shortening until golden brown. Drain on absorbent paper. In the same pan, saute pepperoni and remove; saute ground beef until crumbly. Add onions and cook over medium heat for 15 minutes. Add tomato puree, basil, oregano, green pepper, salt, pepper and garlic. Arrange one-third of the eggplant in a 3-quart casserole. Top with layers of the meat mixture, pepperoni, and cheese, repeating to make 3 layers of each. Bake uncovered at 350°F. for 1 hour. Yield: 6 servings.

Sarah E. Cooper, Del Mar School
San Jose, California

LASAGNE (ITALY)

1 lb. hamburger
1 onion, sliced
2 T. cooking oil
2 cloves garlic, pressed
Red pepper to taste
1 t. oregano
2 bay leaves
1 t. salt
1 No. 2½ can tomatoes
1 can tomato paste
1 can tomato sauce
1 can mushrooms
4 double or 8 single lasagne noodles
1½ pt. cottage cheese
1 lb. Mozzarella or Cheddar cheese
Parmesan cheese

Brown meat and onion in oil, breaking up meat. Add seasonings, tomatoes, tomato paste and tomato sauce. Rinse cans with water and add to mixture. Add undrained mushrooms. Simmer for 2 hours. Cook lasagne noodles in boiling salted water for 15 minutes until tender. Pour one-fourth the sauce into a 13x9-inch pan. Add a layer of noodles, half the cottage cheese, and Mozzarella; sprinkle with Parmesan cheese. Repeat layers, using half the remaining sauce, and all the noodles and cheese. Pour remaining sauce over top; sprinkle with Parmesan cheese. Bake at 350°F. for 40 minutes. Cool for 15 minutes before cutting into squares. Yield: 16 servings.

Mrs. Mary Beth Houghaboom, Newport H.S.
Newport, Vermont

LASAGNE CASSEROLE (ITALY)

1 lb. ground beef
2 T. salad oil
½ t. garlic salt
¼ c. onion, minced
3 cans tomato sauce
1½ t. salt
½ t. pepper
1½ t. oregano
1 8-oz. pkg. lasagne noodles cooked
½ lb. Mozzarella cheese, thinly sliced
½ c. grated Parmesan cheese

Cook meat, garlic salt and onion in salad oil until meat is well done. Mix ¼ cup tomato sauce with flour; add to meat with remaining tomato sauce, salt, pepper and oregano. Simmer 10-15 minutes or until slightly thickened. Place alternate layers of noodles, cheese and tomato mixture in a greased 3-quart casserole. End with cheese slices; sprinkle with Parmesan cheese. Bake at 375°F. for 20-25 minutes. Yield: 6-8 servings.

Mrs. Norma Martin, El Paso H.S.
El Paso, Illinois

LASAGNE (ITALY)

TOMATO SAUCE:
1 onion, diced
½ sm. green pepper, diced
2 links Italian sausage
2 cans tomato paste
1 qt. canned tomatoes
2 bay leaves
1 T. oregano
Pinch of sugar
1 lb. hamburger

Saute onion, pepper and sausage in oil. Add tomato paste, strained tomatoes, bay leaves, oregano and sugar; stir well. Add hamburger and break up with a fork. Simmer 1 hour to 1 hour 30 minutes.

2 T. butter
1 sm. onion, diced
2 c. milk
3 T. flour
2 egg yolks
¾ c. Parmesan cheese
8-10 lasagne noodles, cooked

Saute onion in butter until golden brown. Add flour and mix well. Add ½ cup milk; stir until smooth. Add egg yolks; stir well. Add remaining milk and cheese. Cool until sauce thickens, stirring constantly. Cut sausage in tomato sauce into small pieces. Place a layer of noodles in a square baking dish; add layers of tomato sauce, sausage pieces and cheese sauce. Repeat layers; top with grated Parmesan c h e e s e. Bake 30 minutes at 325°F. Place under broiler just before serving to melt cheese and brown top. NOTE: Mozzarella cheese may be used instead of cheese sauce. Yield: 8 servings.

Mrs. Winifred W. Langtry, Wallingford H.S.
Wallingford, Vermont

HERMINE'S EGGPLANT PARMESAN (ITALY)

TOMATO SAUCE:
2 T. butter
¼ c. onion, chopped
¼ c. celery, chopped
⅛ t. garlic salt
1½ t. salt
1 t. sugar
¼ t. nutmeg
½ t. oregano
¼ t. pepper
½ t. soda
¼ c. Parmesan cheese
2 6-oz. cans tomato paste

Combine ingredients; cook for 15 minutes.

2 lge. eggplants, peeled
2 eggs, beaten
2 T. milk
1 sm. pkg. Mozzarella cheese, grated
¼ t. salt
¼ t. pepper
¼ c. parsley, chopped
¾ c. Parmesan cheese
3 c. tomato sauce

Slice eggplant ¼-inch thick. Combine eggs and milk. Dip eggplant in egg mixture. Fry in small amount of oil until browned on both sides. Place a layer of eggplant in a buttered 2-quart casserole; top with a spoonful of sauce. Sprinkle with Mozzarella cheese, seasonings, parsley and Parmesan cheese. Repeat layers until all ingredients are used. Bake at 350°F. for 30 minutes. Yield: 8 servings.

Mrs. Janet Iler, Avon H.S.
Avon, Illinois

MOSTACCIOLI (ITALY)

1 lb. box mostaccioli noodles or extra large
    macaroni
½ c. green pepper, chopped
½ c. onion, chopped
1 T. salad oil
1½ lb. ground beef
1 1-lb. can tomatoes
1 6-oz. can tomato paste
½ c. water
1 bay leaf
Salt and pepper to taste
1 lb. Velveeta cheese, sliced
1 sm. can Parmesan cheese, grated

Cook the mostaccioli in boiling salted water. Place a layer of noodles in a deep 9x13 baking dish. Saute the green pepper and onion in oil until tender; add the ground beef and brown. Stir in the tomatoes, tomato paste, water, bay leaf, salt and pepper. Pour some sauce over the layer of noodles. Top with slices of Velveeta and a sprinkle of Parmesan cheese. Repeat layers, ending with Velveeta and all remaining Parmesan cheese. Bake at 350°F. for 30 minutes. Yield: 8 servings.

Mrs. Sara L. Stump, New Paris H.S.
New Paris, Indiana

NOODLE CASSEROLE (ITALY)

1 lb. ground beef
¼ c. onions, chopped
1 med. clove garlic, crushed
1 t. oregano
½ t. salt
1 can tomato soup
⅓ c. water
2 c. cooked wide noodles
1 c. sharp cheese, shredded

Brown ground beef, onion, garlic and seasonings in a skillet. In a 1½-quart casserole combine soup, water and noodles. Add ground beef mixture. Place cheese around edge of casserole. Bake at 350°F. for 30 minutes. Yield: 4-5 servings.

Marilyn Bernd, Washington Jr. H.S.
Rice Lake, Wisconsin

NOODLES ITALIANA (ITALY)

1 garlic clove, minced
1 med. onion, finely chopped
2 T. olive or salad oil
2 lb. ground beef
1 8-oz. can mushrooms
1 8-oz. can tomato sauce
1 can tomato paste
2 t. salt
1 t. oregano
2 eggs
1 8-oz. pkg. wide noodles, cooked and drained
1 pkg. frozen chopped spinach, thawed and drained
1 c. Parmesan cheese
1 c. sm. curd cottage cheese
1 pkg. processed American cheese, sliced

Brown garlic and onion lightly in 1 tablespoon oil; add beef. Cook and stir until brown. Add mushrooms with liquid, tomato sauce and paste, 1 teaspoon salt and oregano; simmer for 15 minutes. Beat 1 egg slightly; pour over cooked noodle mixing well. Beat remaining egg; add spinach, remaining 1 tablespoon oil, 1 teaspoon salt, Parmesan cheese and cottage cheese. Mix well. Pour half of meat mixture into shallow 8x10 baking dish. Place half the noodles on top of mixture. Spread all the spinach mixture over noodles. Add remaining noodles, and top with remaining meat mixture. Cover with foil. Bake at 350°F. for 45 minutes. Remove foil; arrange strips of American cheese on top. Bake for 5 minutes longer. Yield: 8 servings.

Madeline Johnson, Pinehurst Jr. H.S.
Pinehurst, Idaho

NOODLES (ITALY)

2 c. wide noodles
2 qt. boiling water
1 t. salt

Cook noodles in boiling water with salt until tender; drain and rinse.

SAUCE:
1½ lb. lean hamburger
2 T. olive oil
1 c. onions, sliced
½ c. green pepper, minced
1 c. celery, cut
2 c. tomatoes
1 6-oz. can tomato paste
1 6-oz. can water
1 T. sugar
1-2 t. salt
1 c. whole-kernel corn
½ c. pitted ripe olives
¼ t. oregano
¼ t. rosemary
Mozzarella or Romano cheese slices

Brown meat in oil; add onions, green pepper and celery. Simmer, covered, for 10 minutes. Add tomatoes, tomato paste, water, sugar, salt, corn and olives. Stir in noodles. Add seasoning; pour into buttered casserole. Top with cheese slices. Bake at 325°F. for 25-30 minutes. Yield: 8 servings.

Mrs. June Patchett, Young America H.S.
Metcalf, Illinois

PASTA FISOLE—SPAGHETTI AND BEANS (ITALY)

1 c. navy beans
1 sm. onion, chopped
3 T. oil
¼ t. crushed red hot pepper
1 stick pepperoni
1½ c. canned tomatoes
½ lb. No. 9 pasta (spaghetti)

Soak beans overnight in water or soak in baking soda for 30 minutes. Cook until soft, about 2-3 hours, changing water once. Saute onion in oil; add hot pepper and pepperoni. Cook until pepperoni is soft. Add tomatoes and cook slowly for 35 minutes. Cook pasta in salted water until soft, about 18 minutes. Add drained, rinsed pasta to bean mixture. Simmer until ready to serve. A little water may be added to prevent dryness. Yield: 4-6 servings.

Mrs. Betty Jean Flocco, West Allegheny H.S.
Imperial, Pennsylvania

PAVRUNA (ITALY)

1 med. onion, coarsely chopped
¼ c. butter
3 med. extra ripe tomatoes, peeled and cut up
4-6 med. potatoes, diced
3-4 red sweet peppers, diced
½ t. salt

Brown onion in butter in a skillet with tight fitting cover. Add tomatoes; cover and simmer until consistence of puree. Flaten tomatoes to hasten cooking. Add a little water if mixture

(Continued on Next Page)

313

becomes dry. Add potatoes and mix. Cover tightly and simmer until potatoes are nearly tender. Add peppers and continue cooking until both potatoes and peppers are tender; season. Serve hot or warm. Yield: 4 servings.

Martha J. Barocco, Elkland Joint School
Elkland, Pennsylvania

RAVIOLI DELUXE (ITALY)

DOUGH:

6 eggs
3 t. salt
⅔ c. water
2 T. vegetable oil
6 c. flour

Beat eggs until light; add salt, water and oil. Gradually add flour until a stiff dough is formed. Roll dough in an oiled bowl. Cover with a damp cloth and refrigerate overnight. Roll dough on floured board to ⅛-inch thickness. Cut into 2½-inch squares.

FILLING:

4 lb. veal leg roast
2 lb. pork roast
1 onion
Salt and pepper
¼ c. parsley
2 eggs

Roast meat with onions, salt and pepper until thoroughly cooked; cool. Grind meat with parsley; add eggs. If mixture is dry, add drippings from roast. Place a teaspoon of filling on each dough square. Fold into triangular shape and seal edges. Bring corners of folded side together and seal. Let dry several hours. Boil in salted water for 10 minutes.

SAUCE:

1 lb. pork steak, chopped
1 lb. veal steak, chopped
1 c. butter or margarine
½ c. onion, chopped
2 cans tomato paste
Salt and pepper
½ lb. Asiago cheese, grated

Brown meats in butter; add remaining ingredients except cheese. Simmer 2 hours or longer. Add more water if necessary. Stir occasionally. Alternate layers of ravioli with sauce and Asiago cheese. Bake at 350°F. for 20 minutes. Yield: 25 servings.

Odessa L. Carlson, Wakefield H.S.
Wakefield, Michigan

ROME CHOWDER (ITALY)

1 lb. ground beef
2 c. uncooked elbow spaghetti
1 sm. can pimento, chopped
½ t. celery salt
¼ t. paprika
1 lge. can steak sauce with mushrooms

1 t. salt
1 sm. can peas with liquid
1 onion, chopped
½ lb. cheese, cubed
1 1-lb. can tomatoes with juice

Combine all ingredients, including all liquids in cans. Bake in two 1½-quart casseroles in 325°F. oven for 1 hour and 30 minutes.

Patricia Payne, Dale H.S.
Dale, Indiana

SCARPELLI (ITALY)

2 c. flour
1¾ c. milk
1 egg
1 t. salt

Combine ingredients to make a thin batter. Cook 12 pancakes with batter and set aside.

FILLING:

1½ lb. Ricotta cheese, well drained
1 egg
1 t. parsley, minced
2 T. Romano cheese, grated
1 pinch of pepper
Salt to taste

Combine ingredients and mix well. Put several tablespoons of filling on each of the pancakes; turn in edges and roll. Arrange in layers in a buttered casserole, covering each layer with your favorite spaghetti sauc eand grated Romano cheese. Bake 3. minutes in a 350°F. oven. Yield: 4 servings.

Margaret Augustine, Tunkhannock Joint Schools
Tunkhannock, Pennsylvania

TAGLIARINI (ITALY)

2 lb. ground beef
1 lge. onion, finely chopped
1 button garlic, minced
1 green pepper, chopped
1 sm. can mushrooms
2 sm. can tomato puree
1 lge. tomato juice
1 No. 1 can cream-style corn
1 8-oz. pkg. fine noodles
½ lb. cheese, grated

Brown meat in a heavy kettle until well done. Add onion, garlic and green pepper; cook 5-10 minutes. Add mushrooms with juice; cook few minutes. Add puree, tomato juice and corn. Boil hard for 5 minutes. Add noodles; cook until tender. Pour into shallow baking pans. Sprinkle with cheese. Brown 20-30 minutes in 350°F. oven. Yield: 12 servings.

Mrs. W. R. Temple, Fairfield H.S.
Fairfield, Illinois

JAMBOREE (JAMAICA)

2 lb. pork sausage
2 onions, chopped
2 c. celery, chopped
6 c. boiling water
3 pkg. dry chicken-noodle soup mix
1 c. uncooked rice
1 c. green pepper, chopped
1 c. pimento, chopped
1 c. mushrooms, chopped
½ c. slivered almonds

Lightly brown sausage, onions and celery; drain. Combine boiling water, soup mix, rice and vegetables; stir, but do not boil. Add sausage mixture; pour into baking dish. Sprinkle with almonds. Cover and bake at 300°F. uncover and bake 1 hour. NOTE: If desired, mixture may be covered and frozen before adding almonds. Yield: 10-12 servings.

Mary Kay Vog, Brewster H.S.
Brewster, Washington

BEEF SUKIYAKI (JAPAN)

2 med. Spanish onions
2 bunches scallions (opt.)
4 stalks of celery
1 can bamboo shoots or mixed Chinese
    vegetables
1 2-inch sq. beef suet or fat
1 T. gelatin
1 c. beef stock, bouillon or consomme
¼ c. soy sauce
3 t. sugar
1 sq. piece bean curd, cut into ½-inch pieces
1 8-oz. can mushrooms, drained
½ lb. sirloin steak or roast, thinly sliced

Skin and cut onions in half lengthwise; place cut-side down and cut into very thin slices. Remove leafy tops, roots and outside skin from scallions; cut into 3-inch lengths. Remove celery tops; wash and cut stalks diagonally into thin strips. Cut bamboo shoots into thin lengthwise strips. Melt beef suet in a skillet; add all the prepared vegetables. Soften gelatin in half of the stock; add with soy sauce and sugar to the vetgetables. Boil gently for 7 minutes without stirring. Turn the top vegetables to the bottom of the skillet. Reduce heat; add remaining stock and simmer gently for 7 minutes. Push the vegetables to one side of the skillet and add the bean curd. Slice mushrooms lengthwise and sprinkle over top of vegetables. Cook for 3 minutes. Carefully push mixture to one side and drop in the meat. Simmer gently for 30 seconds or until meat has changed color; turn and cook 30 seconds longer. Serve hot. NOTE: If desired, ½ pound spinach or 1½ cups rice may be substituted for the bean curd. Thinly sliced eggplant or asparagus may also be used instead of curd.

Florence L. Tooke, Western Michigan University
Kalamazoo, Michigan

MOCK SUKIYAKI (JAPAN)

1 lb. round steak, thinly sliced
2 T. salad oil
1½ c. celery, sliced
1 med. green pepper, diced
1 lge. onion, thinly sliced
½ c. green onion, sliced
1½ c. sliced mushrooms or 1 6-oz. can, drained
1 10½-oz. can condensed beef broth
1 T. soy sauce
¼ c. water
2 T. cornstarch
4 c. hot cooked rice

Cut meat into bite-size pieces; brown in salad oil. Add celery, green pepper, onions, mushrooms, beef broth and soy sauce. Cover; cook over low heat for 10 minutes or until vegetables are tender. Combine water and cornstarch; add to meat mixture, stirring constantly until thickened. Serve over hot rice. Yield: 4-6 servings.

Emile Rae Fallstrom, Maplewood Jr. H.S.
North St. Paul, Minnesota

SUKIYAKI WITH RICE (JAPAN)

1 onion, thinly sliced
1 bunch scallions, sliced
1 T. cooking oil
1 lb. sirloin, cut into thin strips
¼ c. Sherry
½ c. beef broth
½ T. sugar
¼ c. soy sauce
1 c. bamboo shoots, thinly sliced
2 c. mushrooms, thinly sliced

Saute onions and scallions in oil, stirring frequently. Add meat; stir until seared on both sides. Push meat to one side; add Sherry, broth, sugar, soy sauce, bamboo shoots and mushrooms. Stir and fry 4 minutes. Serve with rice. Yield: 4 servings.

Rosalie Osowski, Buffalo H.S.
Buffalo, Minnesota

CHILI PIE CASSEROLE (MEXICO)

3 c. corn chips
1 lge. onion, chopped
¼ lb. ground beef (opt.)
¼ med. green pepper, chopped (opt.)
1 c. American cheese, grated
1 No. 303 can enchilada and chili sauce
1 banquet can tomato sauce

Place 2 cups of corn chips in a 2-quart baking dish. Add onion. Brown ground beef and green pepper and add to casserole. Add half the cheese. Pour the enchilada sauce and tomato sauce over mixture. Add remaining cheese and top with the remaining corn chips. Bake at 350°F. for 15-20 minutes. Yield: 4 servings.

Janet C. Crocker, South San Francisco H.S.
South San Francisco, California

BAKED CHILI RELLENO (MEXICO)

6 lge. green chilies
½ lb. cheese, grated or cut in strips
2 eggs, separated
¼ t. baking powder
2 T. flour
⅛ t. salt

Peel chilis; remove seeds through a small opening in the side. Fill chilis with cheese. Fasten with a toothpick, handling carefully. Beat egg whites until stiff; beat yolks until thick. Sift together dry ingredients; add to yolks, blending well. Fold in beaten egg whites. Dip chilies in batter; place in greased casserole. Bake at 325°F. until batter is done and lightly browned on top. NOTE: If desired, chilies may be stuffed with well-seasoned cooked meat. Yield: 4-6 servings.

Fern S. Zimmerman, Clayton H.S.
Clayton, New Mexico

CHILI-CHICKEN CASSEROLE (MEXICO)

1 boiled hen
1 c. celery, diced
½ c. onion, diced
1 pkg. condensed chicken soup
1 med. can whole green chilies
1 pkg. tostadoes

Boil chicken; bone. Add celery, onions and condensed chicken soup to chicken broth. Simmer until onions and celery are cooked. Place in a buttered casserole dish in layers of tostadoes, chicken, chilies and broth. Repeat layers. Cook at 375°F. for 30 minutes. Yield: 4-6 servings.

Mrs. Kathryn Williams, Ruidoso H.S.
Ruidoso, New Mexico

CHILI VERDE CON CASO (MEXICO)

4 tortillas
1 lge. can green chilies
1 lb. Longhorn cheese, shredded
2 4-oz. cans tomato sauce
½ 2-oz. can hot sauce

Place 1 tortilla in a large greased casserole. Cover with layer of green chilies and cheese. Add a layer of tomato sauce mixed with hot sauce. Repeat until all tortillas are used, ending with cheese. Bake at 300°F. until mixture bubbles well. Cut in six sections; serve with shredded lettuce. Yield: 6 servings.

Doris C. Dunford, Flagstaff H.S.
Flagstaff, Arizona

GREEN CHILI CASSEROLE (MEXICO)

1½ doz. corn tortillas
Fat
¼ c. milk
1 can cream of mushroom soup
1 sm. can tuna fish
½ can green chili peppers, chopped
⅔ c. cheese, grated

Dice corn tortillas in 1-inch squares. Toast in large skillet with small amount of fat until slightly softened. Dilute soup with milk. Mix tuna, chilies, soup and tortillas. In greased casserole alternate layers of soup mixture and cheese. Sprinkle cheese on top and cover. Bake in 300°F. oven for 30 minutes. Yield: 6 servings.

Ruth L. Davis, Corcoran Union H.S.
Corcoran, California

CASSEROLE (MEXICO)

1 lb. ground beef
1 med. onion, chopped
1 clove garlic
Salad oil
1 can tomatoes
1 can red kidney beans
1 can chili without beans
2 t. salt
¼ t. pepper
1 pkg. tortillas
1 c. Cheddar cheese, grated

Brown the meat, onions and garlic in a small amount of oil. Stir in tomatoes, beans and chili, salt and pepper; bring to a slow boil. Place 3 tortillas in a baking dish. Top with 1 cup sauce; repeat, ending with sauce. Sprinkle cheese on top. Bake 30 minutes at 400°F. Yield: 6 servings.

Joyce Hodges, Yuba City Union H.S.
Yuba City, California

CASSEROLE (MEXICO)

1 lb. ground beef
1 lge. onion, chopped
¼ t. salt
1 1-lb. can chili
1 10-oz. can tomato soup
1 med. pkg. corn chips
1 c. sharp cheese, grated
Dash of hot catsup

Put ground beef in skillet and brown; simmer until done. Add onion and salt. Add chili to tomato soup. Simmer, stirring constantly over low heat. Mixture should be consistency of gravy. If dry, add small amount of water. Line large casserole with half of the corn chips. Pour in meat mixture which has been added to soup and chili; top with remaining corn chips. Sprinkle cheese and hot catsup on top of casserole and bake in 400°F. oven until cheese melts. Serve hot. Yield: 8 servings.

Mrs. Mary Kaye Hancock
Sesser Community Unit School
Sesser, Illinois

CHALUPAS (MEXICO)

1 c. onion, chopped
2 T. butter or salad oil
1 lb. hamburger
2 T. flour
3 T. chili powder
1 c. water
1½ c. tomato soup
1½ c. light cream
Salt to taste
12 tortillas
1½ c. American cheese, grated

Saute half the onions in butter until soft. Add hamburger meat and cook until brown. Add the flour and chili powder and cook five minutes more. Add water. Cover and simmer until thick. Mix soup, cream, remaining raw onion and salt. Cut tortillas in strips and place in a buttered shallow casserole. Alternate with the meat and cheese mixtures until the casserole is filled, ending with cheese mixture on top. Bake at 325°F. until hot and browned. Yield: 6-8 servings.

Mabel Moorhouse, Belen H.S.
Belen, New Mexico

CHILI (MEXICO)

1 lge. onion, finely chopped
1 lb. ground beef
Salt and pepper to taste
1 can pork and beans
1 can kidney beans
2 c. tomato juice
2 T. corn meal
2 t. chili powder

Lightly brown onion with ground beef. Season with salt and pepper. Add remaining ingredients; mix well. Cover and cook slowly 20-30 minutes, stirring occasionally. Yield: 6-8 servings.

Betty Krenik, Goodhue H.S.
Goodhue, Minnesota

ENCHILADA CASSEROLE (MEXICO)

12 tortillas
1 lb. ground beef
1 med. onion, chopped
1 8-oz. can tomato sauce
1 No. 2 can refried beans
Salt
Chili powder to taste
½ lb. Cheddar cheese, grated

Tear tortillas into pieces the size of potato chips or smaller; brown slightly in cooking fat. Brown ground beef slightly; add onions and brown. Combine beef and onions, tomato sauce, refried beans and seasonings. Place a layer of tortillas in casserole dish; add a layer of beef mixture. Repeat layers. Top with cheese. Bake about 30 minutes at 350°F. Yield: 6-8 servings.

Mrs. Evelyn Lewis, Antelope Union H.S.
Wellton, Arizona

ENCHILADAS (MEXICO)

SAUCE:
1 med. onion, chopped
1 clove garlic, chopped
3 T. oil
1 No. 2½ can tomatoes
1 can condensed tomato soup
2 T. chili powder
1 sm. piece stick cinnamon
1 whole clove
3 T. butter
½ t. sugar
½ t. sauce

Saute onion and garlic in oil; add tomatoes, soup, chili powder, stick cinnamon and clove. Simmer until thick, 45 minutes; strain. Add butter, sugar and salt.

MEAT:
1 med. onion, chopped
1 clove garlic
3 T. oil
1 lb. hamburger
2 c. water
1 t. salt
1 t. crushed oregano
Dash of cumin

Saute onion and garlic in oil; add meat and fry until brown. Add remaining ingredients; simmer until almost dry, about 45 minutes.

ENCHILADAS:
Tortillas
Chopped onion
Sharp cheese, grated

Dip tortillas in the hot sauce. Spread each tortilla with 2 tablespoons meat mixture, 2 tablespoons onion, and 2 tablespoons cheese. Roll up; place seam-side down in oblong baking dish. Pour remaining sauce over enchiladas; sprinkle with cheese. Bake at 350°F. for 25 minutes. NOTE: For homemade tortillas, beat together ½ cup yellow corn meal, 1 cup flour, 1 egg and 1½ cups milk. Fry as very thin pancakes, 5 to 6-inches in diameter. Do not dip in sauce before using. Yield: 6 servings.

Mrs. Meredythe B. Olson, Agawam Jr. H.S.
Agawam, Massachusetts

ENCHILADA CASSEROLE (MEXICO)

2 lb. ground beef
1 lge. onion, minced
1 can pork and beans
1 can tomato sauce
1 can solid-pack tomatoes
1 t. salt
Dash of pepper
½ t. hot sauce
½ t. cumin
1 T. Worcestershire sauce
1 T. chili powder
8 corn tortillas
2 c. grated Cheddar cheese
1 can chopped ripe olives

(Continued on Next Page)

Combine meat and onion in large skillet; cook slowly until lightly browned. Combine meat mixture with beans, tomato sauce, tomatoes and seasonings. Heat thoroughly. Place a layer of tortillas in casserole or loaf pan. Cover with layers of meat mixture, cheese and olives. Repeat layers. Top with cheese. Bake 30 minutes at 325°F. Yield: 6-8 servings.

Mrs. Ruth Halstead Thorne, Imperial Jr. H.S.
Ontario, California

ENCHILDAS (MEXICO)

1 lb. ground chuck
1 clove garlic, chopped
2 t. salt
1 T. vinegar
1 T. water
1 T. chili powder
1 med. can kidney beans, undrained

Saute meat and garlic; add remaining ingredients and simmer.

SAUCE:

1 clove garlic, chopped
¼ c. onion, chopped
3 T. salad oil
2 T. flour
2 8-oz. cans tomato sauce
1 T. vinegar
1 beef bouillon cube
1 c. water
2 T. chopped canned green chili peppers
¼ t. cumin seed
½ t. salt
¼ t. pepper
12 tortillas
1 c. Cheddar cheese, grated

Saute garlic and onion in oil; add remaining ingredients except tortillas and cheese. Fill tortillas with meat mixture; roll, putting seam-side down in casserole. Cover with sauce; top with Cheddar cheese. Bake 25 minutes at 350°F.

Mrs. Naomi Wetzel, Courtland H.S.
Courtland, California

ENCHILADA PIE (MEXICO)

1 med. onion, chopped
2 lb. ground beef
1 med. can Mexicorn
Oregano to taste
½ t. salt
2 T. chili powder
2 cans tomato sauce
1 can enchilada sauce
12 corn tortillas
Grated cheese

Saute onion; add meat. Stir occasionally until brown. Add corn and seasonings. Blend tomato sauce and enchilada sauce in a separate container. Pour half of sauce into meat mixture and simmer 15 minutes. In bottom of casserole dish put 4 tortillas, overlapping. Pour half of meat mixture over them. Make another layer of tortillas and meat mixture, ending with 4 tortillas on top. Pour remaining sauce mixture over top. Sprinkle with grated cheese; cover and bake at 375°F. for 20 minutes. Yield: 8-10 servings.

Mrs. D. W. Emery, Patterson H.S.
Patterson, California

ENCHILADA PIE (MEXICO)

1 lb. ground beef
1 med. onion, chopped
1 clove garlic, minced (opt.)
2 T. butter
1 t. salt
¼ t. pepper
1 T. chili powder, or more
1 4½-oz. can ripe olives, chopped
1 8-oz. can tomato sauce
6 tortillas, lightly buttered
2 c. Cheddar cheese, shredded
⅔ c. water

Saute ground beef, onion and garlic in butter. Add seasonings, olives and tomato sauce. In a round 2-quart casserole, alternate layers of buttered tortillas, meat sauce and cheese, ending with tortillas and cheese. Pour water into bottom of casserole. Cover. Bake at 400°F. for 30 minutes. Cut in wedges. Yield: 6 servings.

Mrs. Geraldine Porter, Duarte H.S.
Duarte, California

ENCHILADA PIE (MEXICO)

12 corn tortillas
Cooking oil
1 lb. ground beef
1 clove garlic, finely chopped
1 t. salt
¼ t. black pepper
1 T. chili powder
1 No. 2 can enchilada sauce
½ c. onions, chopped
1 sm. can olives, chopped
1½ c. Cheddar cheese, grated
1 can consomme

Fry each tortilla lightly on each side in 1-inch of cooking oil over medium heat. Fry the beef with garlic, crumbling meat as it cooks. Season with salt, pepper and chili powder; stir in the onion, olives and cheese. Dip enough tortillas in the sauce to cover the bottom of the casserole; spread a thin layer of meat mixture over the tortillas. Repeat layers until all tortillas and the meat mixture are used. Pour consomme over the casserole; top with extra grated cheese. Heat at 350°F. until piping hot. Yield: 8 servings.

Mrs. Ethel Barksdale Teves, East Bakersfield H.S.
Bakersfield, California

ENCHILADA PIE (MEXICO)

1½ lb. ground beef
1 onion, chopped
2 cloves garlic, minced
1 T. vinegar
1 can olives, chopped
2 cans tomato sauce
3 T. chili powder
2 t. salt
½ t. pepper
4⅔ c. water
½ c. cornstarch
2 c. cheese, grated
Crackers or corn chips

Cook beef, onion and garlic. When browned add vinegar, olives, tomato sauce, chili powder, salt, pepper and 4 cups water. Simmer 20 minutes; thicken with ⅔ cup water mixed with cornstarch. Pour one-fourth of mixture over broken crackers or corn chips in a casserole dish; top with cheese. Repeat layers three times. Bake 35 minutes at 350°F. Serve hot. Yield: 8 servings.

Mrs. Normagene Manning, Livingston H.S.
Livingston, California

ENCHILADAS VERDES (MEXICO)

2 T. onions, chopped
1 c. plus
Shortening
2 4-oz. cans green chilies, finely chopped
1 c. canned tomatoes, finely chopped
1 can cream of mushroom soup
Salt to taste
1 doz. corn tortillas
1 c. cheese, grated
Shredded lettuce
Tomato wedges

Saute 2 tablespoons onions in shortening until transparent. Add green chili and tomatoes. Add 1 cup water and simmer for 15 minutes. Add cream of mushroom soup, 1 cup of hot water and salt to the chili sauce. Remove from heat and cover. Fry the corn tortillas one at a time in hot deep fat; drain on paper towles. When cool enough to handle, spread cheese and chopped onion in each tortilla and roll. Place rolled tortillas side by side in an 8x10 casserole dish; pour the chili sauce over the tortillas. Spread remaining onion and cheese over the top. Place in a 350°F. oven for 20 minutes. Serve 3 rolled tortillas per serving and garnish with shredded lettuce and tomato wedges. Yield: 4 servings.

Mrs. Genevieve Johnston, Raton H.S.
Raton, New Mexico

CHICKEN ENCHILADA CASSEROLE (MEXICO)

1 sm. onion, chopped
1 can mushroom soup
1 can chicken soup
1 c. chicken broth
1 lb. Longhorn cheese
½ can green chili peppers, chopped
1 pkg. corn tortillas, uncooked
1 2 to 3-lb. cooked chicken, diced

Brown onions; add soups, chili peppers and broth. Blend well. Place layers of torn tortillas, chopped chicken, soup mixture and grated cheese in a greased baking dish. Repeat layers until all ingredients are used. Bake 30 minutes at 325°F. Yield: 6-8 servings.

Mrs. Barbara Savage, Florence H.S.
Florence, Colorado

GREEN CHILI ENCHILADAS (MEXICO)

1 can cream of chicken soup
1 lge. can evaporated milk
¼ c. onions, chopped
1 sm. can green chilies, chopped
1 t. salt
12 corn tortillas
American cheese, grated

In a saucepan over low heat blend the soup, milk, onions, chilies and salt. Drop the tortillas one at a time into the hot sauce; remove immediately. Place in a baking dish; sprinkle with cheese as you stack them into the baking dish. Pour the remaining sauce over the tortillas; sprinkle generously with cheese and bake at 350° until cheese is melted, about 30 minutes. Yield: 6 servings.

Mrs. Dorothy Riley, Haxtun H.S.
Haxtun, Colorado

GREEN ENCHILADAS

12 corn meal tortillas
½ lb. Tillimook cheese, grated
½ lb. Mozzarella cheese, grated
1 c. onion, finely chopped
1 can cream of chicken soup
½ can water
1 can mild green chilies or 3 green chilies, fried and peeled

Fry tortillas slightly. Fill each with cheeses and 1 tablespoon onion. Fold over and place in buttered casserole, overlapping to prevent spilling. Cover with mixture of soup, water and finely mashed chilies. Bake in 350°F. oven for 30 minutes; or cover and freeze to be baked later. Yield: 6 servings.

Audrey Newman, Los Banos Union H.S.
Los Banos, Caifornia

FIESTA CASSEROLE (MEXICO)

1 c. chopped onion
1 clove garlic, minced
2 T. salad oil
1 lb. ground beef
1 can tomatoes
1 can red kidney beans
1 15-oz. can chili without beans

(Continued on Next Page)

2 t. salt
¼ t. pepper
1 can or pkg. tortillas
1 c. Cheddar cheese, grated

Saute onion and garlic in salad oil until soft; remove from pan. Shape ground beef into a large patty in same frying pan; brown 5 minutes on each side, then break into chunks. Stir in onion mixture, tomatoes, beans, chili con carne, salt and pepper; heat to boiling. Place 3 of the tortillas, overlapping if necessary, in a 12-cup baking dish; top with 1 cup of the sauce. Repeat to make 5 more layers of each, ending with sauce. Sprinkle with cheese. Bake at 400°F. for 30 minutes or until bubbly. Yield: 6 servings.

Esther Darst Minton, Nogales H.S.
Nogales, Arizona

FRIJOLES EN-CASSEROLE (MEXICO)

½ c. onion, finely chopped
1 T. fat
½ lb. ground beef
½ t. sweet basil leaves
¼ t. oregano leaves
1 t. salt
¼ c. green chilies, finely chopped
6 corn meal tortillas
3 c. cooked pinto beans, drained
Cheese, grated

Brown onion in fat; add meat and brown. Add seasonings and green chilies. Brown tortittas in hot fat until crisp. Cover the bottom of casserole with 2 of the crumbled tortillas. Add half of beans. Cover beans with a layer of meat mixture. Sprinkle with a light layer of cheese. Repeat layers, topping with remaining crumbled tortillas. Bake at 350°F. for 30 minutes. NOTE: This may be frozen before baking. Allow longer baking time when frozen. Leftover meats or mushrooms may be substituted for ground meat. Yield: 6 servings.

Lelia Cook Greenwald, Socorro H.S.
Socorro, New Mexico

HIT THE SPOT (MEXICO)

2 c. cooked macaroni
1 can chili con carne with beans
2 cans tomato sauce
3 sm. green Torrido chili peppers
¼ t. salt
¼ t. Tabasco sauce
2 cans diced Vienna sausages
¼ c. Parmesan cheese, grated

Mix cooked macaroni, chili con carne and tomato sauce. Add chopped peppers, salt, Tabasco sauce and Vienna sausages. Place in a casserole dish; sprinkle with cheese. Bake at 325°F. for about 20 minutes, or until casserole bubbles. Serve hot. Yield: 6-8 servings.

Ella W. Adair, Bryce Valley H.S.
Tropic, Utah

LUNCHEON DISH (MEXICO)

1 lb. pork sausage
1 c. onion, chopped
1 c. green pepper, chopped
1 t. salt
1 T. sugar
2 T. chili powder
1 can or 2 c. tomatoes
1 c. milk
1 c. sour cream
2 c. uncooked macaroni

Brown meat; add onion and green pepper. Cook until onion is clear on low heat. Blend in salt, sugar and chili powder. Stir in tomatoes, milk and sour cream. Add the uncooked macaroni. Cover pan; cook for 20 minutes on low heat. Yield: 6-8 servings.

Cherry Courteau, Mountlake Terrace H.S.
Mountlake Terrace, Washington

SQUASH AND CORN CON CARNE (MEXICO)

1 lb. pork, cut in ½-inch cubes
1 lge. onion, chopped
1 clove garlic, minced
1 T. chili powder
Salt and pepper to taste
1 lb. zucchini squash
1 c. tomatoes, chopped
1 8¾-oz. can whole kernel corn, drained
1 c. cheese, grated

Brown pork lightly. Add onion, garlic, chili powder, salt and pepper. Cover and simmer 45 minutes, stirring occasionally. Add a small amount of water if necessary. Cut zucchini into ½-inch diagonal slices. Add to meat with tomatoes and corn. Mix lightly; cover and cook 12-15 minutes or until zucchini is tender. Sprinkle with cheese and serve. Yield: 6 servings.

Margaret Faulkner, Estacada Union H.S.
Estacada, Oregon

TACO CASSEROLE (MEXICO)

1 doz. tortillas
2 lb. hamburger, lightly browned
1 lge. onion, finely chopped
½ lb. cheese, grated
1 can tomato soup
1 can tomato sauce
1 can brown gravy

Fry tortillas lightly in hot grease, about three seconds on each side; drain. Fill tortillas with mixture of browned meat, onion and cheese. Roll up and place in baking dish. Combine remaining ingredients; simmer a few minutes. Pour sauce over tortillas and bake for 30 minutes at 350°F. NOTE: Sprinkle any remaining meat and cheese over tacos in baking dish for a topping before adding sauce. Yield: 12 servings.

Mrs. Jessie Mae McDonald, San Juan H.S.
Blanding, Utah

TACO CASSEROLE (MEXICO)

1 pkg. tortillas
2 can cream of chicken soup
1 T. onion, chopped
1 sm. can green Ortega chilies, chopped
1 can water
Salt and pepper to taste
1½ c. cheese, grated

Cut tortillas in fourths. Fry until crisp; drain. Mix remaining ingredients except cheese. Place a layer of tortillas in a casserole. Pour the mixture over tortillas and put cheese on top. Repeat layers. Bake at 400°F. for 20-25 minutes. Yield: 6-8 servings.

Mrs. Sheila Sigmund, Tucumcari Jr. H.S.
Tucumcari, New Mexico

CHICKEN TACO PIE (MEXICO)

1 1½- to 2-lb. chicken
1 lge. can enchilada sauce
1 can mushroom soup
1 lge. onion, chopped
½ t. garlic salt
Dash of pepper
1 lge. pkg. corn chips
1 c. cheese, grated
1 c. chicken broth

Boil chicken until tender; remove bones and cut into bite size pieces. Combine chicken, enchilada sauce, mushroom soup, onion, garlic salt and pepper. Grease baking dish; line with corn chips. Add chicken mixture. Sprinkle with grated cheese; cover with corn chips. Add chicken broth. Bake at 350°F. for 30 minutes. Yield: 6-8 servings.

This recipe submitted by the following teachers:
Virginia Jones, Carlsbad Mid-H.S.
Carlsbad, New Mexico
Shirley Warren, J. T. Hutchinson Jr. H.S.
Lubbock, Texas

CHICKEN-TACO CASSEROLE (MEXICO)

1 pkg. tortillas
1 can tomato juice or 1 sm. can tomatoes
1 can cream of chicken soup
½ can chopped green chilies
1 med. onion, chopped
1 c. cheese, grated
1 c. thin cream or 1 c. cream of tomato soup

Cut tortillas in fourths and fry. Line bottom of baking dish with the tortillas. Mix tomato juice, chicken soup, and chilies. Add onions; pour a small amount of mixture over tortillas. Sprinkle with cheese. Alternate layers until all ingredients are used. Pour cream over top and bake at 350°F. for 35 to 40 minutes. Yield: 8 servings.

Mrs. Juanita Willis, Carlsbad H.S.
Carlsbad, New Mexico

FESTIVE TAMALE PIE (MEXICO)

1 c. onion, chopped
1 c. or 1 sm. green pepper, chopped
1 T. fat
¾ lb. ground beef
2 8-oz. cans tomato sauce
1 12-oz. can whole kernel corn, drained
½ to 1 c. olives, chopped
1 clove garlic, minced (opt.)
1 T. sugar
1 t. salt
2 to 3 t. chili powder
Dash of pepper
1½ c. American cheese, shredded

Cook onion and pepper in hot fat until tender. Add meat and brown. Add tomato sauce, corn, olives, garlic, sugar and seasonings. Simmer 20 to 25 minutes, or until thick. Add cheese and stir until melted. Pour into greased baking dish.

TOPPING:

¾ c. yellow corn meal
½ t. salt
2 c. cold water
1 T. butter

Stir corn meal and salt into cold water. Cook and stir until thick; add butter. Spoon over meat mixture. Bake at 375°F. for 40 minutes. NOTE: If desired, topping may be spread in strips over mixture. Yield: 6 servings.

This recipe submitted by the following teachers:
Mrs. Wynn Bragg, Manor H.S.
Manor, Georgia
Ruth E. Richmond, Carthage Troy H.S.
Coolville, Ohio

HOT TAMALE PIE (MEXICO)

1 med. green pepper, diced
1 lge. onion, chopped
3 T. salad oil
2 lb. ground beef
2 t. monosodium glutamate
2 t. salt
¼ t. pepper
1 1-lb. can tomatoes
1 T. chili powder
1 12-oz. pkg. corn muffin mix
1 c. evaporated milk
¾ c. sharp Cheddar cheese, grated

Cook green pepper and onion in oil until onion is tender but not brown. Sprinkle beef with monosodium glutamate, salt and pepper; brown in casserole, breaking up meat with fork. Add tomatoes and chili powder; simmer. Follow package directions for preparing corn muffin mix, omitting egg and substituting 1 cup evaporated milk for liquid called for in the directions. Remove casserole from heat; pour corn muffin mixture over top. Sprinkle top with cheese. Bake at 400°F. 20 minutes. Yield: 8 servings.

Karen Lynnes, Central Jr. H.S.
Walpeton, North Dakota

TORTILLA CASSEROLE (MEXICO)

½ lb. hamburger
Fat
9 corn tortillas
1 can cream of mushroom soup
1½ c. milk
¾ c. cheese, grated
1 med. onion, chopped
3-4 canned green chilies, chopped

Brown meat in small amount of fat. Fry tortillas in deep fat; drain. Combine soup and milk. Line greased casserole with layer of tortillas; alternate layers of cheese, onion, meat and chilies with layers of tortillas. Pour soup and milk over tortilla mixture. Bake in 350°F. oven for 45 minutes. Yield: 4-6 servings.

Mrs. Dorothy Archibald, C. C. Snell Jr. H.S.
Bayard, New Mexico

CHICKEN-TORTILLA CASSEROLE (MEXICO)

1 can green chilies, chopped
1 med. onion, finely chopped
2 med. green peppers, chopped
3 T. fat
6 canned tortillas
2 cans tomato paste
1 can water
1 carton sour cream
½ lb. Ricotta cheese
1 egg, beaten (opt.)

Saute chilies, onion and green pepper in fat. Remove from pan; fry tortillas. Dilute tomato paste with water. Break tortillas into fourths; place a layer in a buttered casserole. Add layers of chicken, vegetables, cheese, tomato sauce and sour cream. Repeat layers. Cover top with beaten egg. Bake 20 minutes at 350°F. Yield: 6 servings.

Mrs. Maxine Stelovich, Littleton H.S.
Littleton, Colorado

FRIED RICE CASSEROLE (NEPAL)

2 c. uncooked rice
¼ c. butter
½ c. onion, chopped
1 t. tumeric
2 sm. bay leaves
2 cardamon seeds
2 whole cloves
1 t. salt
2 eggs
Chicken or meat, chopped
½ c. fresh tomatoes, chopped
½ c. fresh or frozen green peas

Cook rice until done. Saute onions, spices, eggs, meat and tomatoes in butter. Add rice; cover with a tight lid and cook for 3 minutes. Add fresh peas and cook covered for 10 minutes or until peas are tender.

Lucile Hunt, Panguitch H.S.
Panguitch, Utah

PERUVIAN SEVICHE

2 lb. striped bass
½ c. lime juice
1 t. salt
⅛ t. Tabasco
½ c. grapefruit juice
1½ T. minced onion
1½ T. minced green pepper
1 t. snipped chives or cilantro
1 Spanish onion, very thinly sliced
2 scallions
½ red pimento
½ green pepper
2 T. kernel corn
Grapefruit sections

Cut the bass into small, very thin slices. Marinate for 12 hours in the lime juice with salt and Tabasco. Add grapefruit juice and minced onion, pepper and chives to marinade. Arrange fish in deep dish with marinade. Place Spanish onion slices in center on top of fish. Finely chop scallions, pimento and green pepper and sprinkle with corn over entire platter. Garnish with grapefruit sections. Yield: 8 servings.

Photograph for this recipe on back cover.

PEARL OF THE ORIENT CASSEROLE (PHILIPPINES)

1½ lb. sweet potatoes
1 t. salt
4 T. butter
⅓ to ½ c. warm milk
3 bananas
12 marshmallows, cut up

Cook, peel and mash sweet potatoes. Add salt and 2 tablespoons butter. Add enough milk to make light and fluffy. Spread on bottom of individual baking dishes. Slice bananas and place on top of potatoes. Dot with marshmallows. Brush with rest of melted butter. Bake at 375°F. for 30 minutes. Yield: 6 servings.

Beverly Parks, Rolfe H.S.
Rolfe, Iowa

HOT DISH (POLAND)

2 c. celery, chopped
1 c. onion, chopped
1 can chicken noodle soup
1 sm. bottle soy sauce
2 c. water
1 lb. raw hamburger, broken up
1 c. raw rice
1 can cream of mushroom soup

Put all ingredients except rice and mushroom soup in a kettle and bring to a boil. Place mixture with rice and mushroom soup in casserole. Bake one hour at 350°F.; stirring occasionally. Yield: 12 servings.

Marlene Lien, Minnesota H.S.
Minnesota, Minnesota

CHOW MEIN (RUSSIA)

1 lb. veal, chopped
2 med. onions, chopped
Fat
2 c. celery, chopped
2 cans chicken with rice soup
1 c. mushrooms, drained
2 cans cream of mushroom soup
2 c. water
1 c. uncooked rice
½ c. uncooked wild rice
½ c. slivered almonds

Brown the meat and onions in a small amount of fat. Add all remaining ingredients except almonds; thoroughly mix. Pour into 2 greased 9-inch casseroles or 1 greased 10x14-inch casserole. Top with slivered almonds. Bake at 350°F. for 1 hour and 30 minutes. NOTE: Leftover chicken, turkey or shrimp may be substituted for the veal. Yield: 10 servings.

Mrs. Janice Erickson, Sunrise Park Jr. H.S.
White Bear Lake, Minnesota

FISH CASSEROLE (RUSSIA)

2 c. cooked fish
2 c. cooked rice
1 lge. sweet onion, sliced and sauted
2 hard-cooked eggs
Bread crumbs
4 T. butter
3 T. flour
2 c. warmed milk
½ t. salt
½ t. nutmeg
Paprika

Use any kind of fish, fresh or canned. If fresh, poach for 5 to 8 minutes and remove all skin and bones. If canned, discard oil, bones and skin. Arrange layers of rice, pieces of fish, sauted onion, sliced egg and a scattering of bread crumbs. Repeat layers 2 or 3 times. Melt butter in a saucepan; stir in flour. Slowly stir in warm milk. Add salt and nutmeg and continue stirring until thick. Pour sauce over the casserole, digging holes with a fork to ensure even distribution. Top with buttered bread crumbs; dust with paprika. Bake 45 minutes at 350°F. Yield: 4-6 servings.

Katherine Langworthy, Three Rivers H.S.
Three Rivers, Michigan

ARROZ CON POLLO—RICE WITH CHICKEN (SPAIN)

1 3-lb. frying chicken
½ c. olive oil
1 med. onion, chopped
3 c. canned tomatoes
1½ t. salt
⅛ t. pepper
1 clove garlic
½ bay leaf
1 c. raw rice

Cut chicken into serving pieces. Heat oil in large, heavy skillet and brown chicken on all sides. Add onion and cook until transparent. Add the tomatoes, 1 teaspoon of salt, the pepper, garlic and bay leaf. Wash rice and sprinkle over tomatoes. Sprinkle in remaining salt. Cook slowly over low heat or in 350°F. oven until the rice is tender and fluffy and the liquid has been absorbed, about 1 hour. Yield: 6 servings.

Mrs. F. E. Dey, Litchfield H.S.
Litchfield, Illinois

CASSEROLE ESPANOL (SPAIN)

1 lb. hamburger
½ t. salt
5 corn tortillas
1 10-oz. can enchilada sauce
1 onion, diced
1 t. crushed oregano
1 sm. can olives, sliced
1½ c. Cheddar cheese, grated

Brown the hamburger and add salt. In a one-quart casserole arrange layers of tortilla covered with enchilada sauce, onion mixed with oregano, hamburger, olives and cheese. Repeat layers using the tortillas as dividers. Top casserole with a generous amount of cheese. Bake in a covered casserole at 300°F. for 1 hour. Yield: 5 servings.

Mrs. Mari Hurley, Central Union H.S.
El Centro, California

PAELLA (SPAIN)

1 sm. onion, diced
1 clove garlic, chopped
½ green pepper, diced
1 tomato, diced
1 lb. shrimp
1½ c. rice
1 T. saffron
Dash of pimento
Salt to taste
Parsley
1 sm. chicken, fried
½ lb. sausage, fried
1 T. lemon juice
1 pkg. frozen peas

Saute onion, garlic, green pepper and tomato Cook shrimp in water. Fry rice in oil used for frying chicken. Add 4 cups of the water that was used to cook shrimp to the rice; season with saffron, pimento, salt and parsley. Add the chicken and sausage to the rice when the water begins to boil. A small amount of lemon juice at this time makes rice loose. After rice has boiled for 5 minutes, add frozen peas and shrimp. Boil for 15 minutes or until rice is almost dry. Let stand for 5 minutes before serving. Yield: 8 servings.

Mrs. Glenellen Woodward, Glenwood H.S.
Chatham, Illinois

BEAN CASSEROLE (SPAIN)

1 lb. pinto beans
1½ lb. ground chuck
Salt and pepper to taste
1 10-oz. can tomatoes and green chili
1 15-oz. can chili without beans
1 T. crushed dried red chili
Corn chips
1 c. Cheddar cheese, grated

Cook pinto beans until tender; reserve juice. Brown meat; season with salt and pepper. Add tomatoes and green chili, chili, juice from cooked beans and the dried red chili. Combine mixture thoroughly. Add the beans; pour into a 3-quart casserole. Sprinkle with corn chips and top with cheese. Bake in 350°F. oven for 10 minutes or until the cheese has melted. NOTE: May be frozen except for corn chips, which will toughen if frozen. Yield: 20 servings.

Alice Maurice, South Mountain H.S.
Phoenix, Arizona

CHILI CON QUESO CASSEROLE (SPAIN)

1 can cream of mushroom or chicken soup
1 soup can milk
½ onion, grated
1 4-oz. can green chilies, diced
12 tortillas
½ lb. American cheese, cubed

Heat together soup, milk, onion, and chilies. Cut tortillas into 1-inch squares. In casserole put a third of soup mixture; sprinkle with a third of tortillas and a third of cheese cubes. Repeat until all ingredients are used. Bake at 375°F. for 35 minutes. Yield: 4-6 servings.

Mrs. Louise J. Strayer, Tempe Union H.S.
Tempe, Arizona

SOPA DA FIDEO (SPAIN)

2 c. fat
1 12-oz. pkg. coiled vermicelli
2 lb. ground beef
4 c. tomato juice
4 c. hot water
1 t. salt
1 T. cumin seed or powder

Heat fat in a 4½-quart saucepan or pot. Crumble vermicelli into fat and brown lightly, stirring to brown evenly. Drain on paper towels. Remove fat from pot and brown beef, stirring to break into bits. Add vermicelli and remaining ingredients. Cover and cook until vermicelli is tender. Add more water as needed to cook. Yield: 12 servings.

Mrs. Josephine M. Jones, Arickaree H.S.
Anton, Colorado

BITIN JANE (SYRIA)

1 lge. eggplant
Oil
3 lb. ground lamb
2 onions, chopped
1 can tomato juice
3 T. flour
½ c. pignola nuts or walnuts, broken up

Peel eggplant and slice lengthwise. Saute each slice in oil in heavy skillet. Saute lamb and onions until meat loses its redness. Add tomato juice; cook 10 minutes. Remove from heat and sprinkle flour on top. Stir to thicken; add nuts. Lay eggplant in pan; alternate layers of sauce and remaining eggplant, ending with sauce. Bake 30-45 minutes 350°F.

TOPPING:

2 eggs
Flour
½ t. baking powder

Beat eggs until lemon colored; add a little flour and the baking powder. Pour over casserole. Continue baking until top is lightly browned and puffed. Yield: 10-12 servings.

Louise Sturgeon, Cody H.S.
Detroit, Michigan

STEW (SWEDEN)

½ lb. ground beef
½ c. uncooked rice
1½ c. raw potato cubes
½ c. onion cubes
1 c. raw carrots, sliced
1 c. canned tomatoes
Salt and pepper to taste

Beginning with ground beef, layer each ingredient in a greased casserole, sprinkling each layer with salt and pepper. The tomatoes should be the last layer. Fill casserole with water so all ingredients are covered. Bake for 2 hours at 350°F. Yield: 6 servings.

Ruth M. Patterson and Catherine D. Snitger
Beaver Area Jr. H.S.
Beaver, Pennsylvania

Breads

The Importance Of Bread In The Diet

Nothing is more tempting than the aroma of bread baking in the kitchen. Bread, the staff of life, is one of man's oldest foods.

Bread, flour and cereals make up one of the basic four food groups which are essential to good nutrition. Four or more servings daily of foods in this group should be included in the diet.

As a rule, protein-rich foods are expensive. Less expensive bread and cereals can be depended upon for part of the daily protein requirements. Bread is not only an inexpensive source of vegetable protein and carbohydrates, but also contains important minerals and B vitamins.

Although bread can be made of flour, salt, water and yeast, it becomes nutritionally more valuable when sugar, shortening and milk are added. The use of yeast also increases the vitamin content of bread.

Too often there is a tendency to eliminate bread completely when one wants to lose weight. Most physicians, however, suggest eliminating all sweets and cutting down on the amount but not eliminating bread.

Know Your Ingredients

To bake really good bread, start with good ingredients. Although the amounts and flavorings in different breads may vary, the basic ways of mixing them will remain the same.

YEAST . . .

Is a living plant which makes batters and doughs rise. Compressed yeast comes in a cake form and must be refrigerated. If compressed yeast is bought fresh, it will keep about two weeks. If stored in a freezer, it will keep for about two months.

Dry yeast comes in a granular form and if stored in a cool, dry place will keep for several months. It needs greater heat and more moisture to activate it than compressed yeast.

Because yeast is a living plant, it likes a warm, even temperature. Too much heat can kill its action and too little can slow it down. To dissolve yeast, rinse the bowl in hot water and dry thoroughly. Dissolve the yeast in the warm bowl in water that is comfortably warm on the inside of your wrist. Check the temperature of the water with a candy thermometer if you wish. It should show a reading of 105-115° F.

FLOUR . . .

Wheat flour is used for making bread because it contains a special substance called gluten. When flour is stirred and kneaded with milk or water, the gluten developes or stretches to form an elastic framework that holds the bubbles of gas produced by the yeast. Without gluten, a satisfactory yeast-raised bread cannot be produced.

White wheat flour is not the only kind of flour which can be successfully used in bread making. Rye flour more nearly resembles wheat flour than any other except that it will not hold the leavening agent. Bread made entirely of rye flour is dark and heavy. Rye breads can be made lighter by making a sponge of wheat flour and letting it rise in order to develop the yeast and mellow the wheat gluten. The rye flour is added to make a dough. The dough will be very sticky and hard to handle, however, if more than half of the flour used is rye.

Whole wheat and graham flours will make a dough that is too sticky to knead if they are used alone without any other kind of flour. These flours are usually combined with at least an equal amount of white flour.

Buckwheat flour is heavier than any other flours, so a smaller amount is used in proportion to the amount of liquids.

Soy flour is milled from soy beans that have been de-hulled and treated. A soya mixture is obtained by using two tablespoons of soy flour in each cup of wheat flour. This can be used in practically any recipe instead of all wheat flour. A little more water and seasoning is usually necessary. Adding soy proteins adds to the nutritional value of the baked product.

LIQUID . . .

water, milk or water in which potatoes have been cooked are the liquids usually used for yeast breads. If fresh liquid milk or reconstituted dry milk is used, it is heated or scalded and then cooled before using. Water makes crusty breads with good wheaty flavor. Milk makes breads with softer crusts and a velvety, creamy white crumb that browns easily in toasting.

Know Your Ingredients (Continued)

SUGAR . . .

furnishes food for the yeast, so that it can form the gas
which makes the dough or batter rise. It adds flavor and
helps the crust to brown as the bread bakes. White sugar
is most often used, but some special breads call for brown
sugar, molasses or honey.

SALT . . .

brings out the flavor. It also controls the action of the
yeast, slowing its rate of gas formation.

FAT . . .

such as margarine, salad or cooking oils, hydrogenated
shortening, lard or butter are called shortening when used
in baked foods. Shortening helps make baked goods tender,
helps keep the baked item soft and in breads gives a soft,
silky crumb.

EGGS . . .

add food value, color and rich flavor to the breads in
which they are used. They also help make the crumb fine
and the crust tender.

OTHER INGREDIENTS . . .

such as spices and herbs give flavor to special breads.
Many festive breads call for fruits, candied or grated fruit
peel or nuts.

Necessary Utensils For Making Breads

A large glass or crockery bowl that holds at least two quarts. When warmed it holds the dough at an even temperature. It also protects the dough from sudden temperature changes or chilling.

A set of measuring cups for measuring dry ingredients.

A measuring cup to measure liquids. This kind of cup has a lip for pouring, like a pitcher, and a little space above the top of the measuring line.

A set of standard measuring spoons.

A small saucepan, about 1 pint in size, for scalding milk and melting shortening.

A large wooden spoon for mixing.

A bread board.

A rubber or plastic bowl scraper.

A large sharp knife or kitchen scissors to cut dough or stiff batter.

A medium size spatula or plain knife.

Baking pans or cookie sheets.

IN ADDITION, THESE EXTRAS
ARE HELPFUL . . .

Wire cooling racks

Pastry cloth

Rolling pin

Egg beater

Pastry brush

Electric mixer

Steps To Successful Bread Making

There are several steps in making bread that are important to the finished product.

1. ADDING OTHER LIQUIDS. Once the yeast is dissolved, other liquids can be added. These must be lukewarm or at room temperature before being added. Liquids that are too warm might kill the action of the yeast. Test the liquid by dropping a small amount on the inside of the wrist. It should feel neither hot nor cold and the thermometer should read 90-95° F.

2. ADDING FLOUR. Measure out the full amount of flour. Stir in half of it or the amount called for in the recipe method and blend it in. Then beat until smooth. Now add enough of the remaining flour to make a rough looking dough that pulls away from the sides of the bowl.

3. KNEADING. This is the important step that makes dough "come alive" and change from a rough, sticky unresponsive mass into a satiny smooth, non-sticky, elastic ball. Turn the dough out onto a lightly floured bread board or pastry cloth. If the dough seems somewhat sticky when you first turn it out, fold the lightly floured cloth over it and press down; then smooth out the cloth and knead, or sprinkle the dough lightly with flour. Flour your hands, too. Kneading is easy. Press the dough into a flat ball with the palms of your hands. Fold it over toward you, then with the heels of your hands, push down and away. Turn it one-quarter of the way around and repeat. Keep folding, pushing and turning until the dough looks very smooth and no longer feels sticky. As you knead, sprinkle extra flour little by little over the dough, until the dough no longer sticks to the board or your hands.

4. RISING. Cover the kneaded dough with a cloth while you wash out the mixing bowl with warm water. Grease the inside of the bowl lightly. Press the top of the ball of dough in the bowl, then turn the dough over. This greases the surface of the dough slightly so it stretches easily as it rises and does not dry out. Cover with a clean towel and set the bowl in a warm place (80-85° F.) free from draft, for the dough to rise until doubled in bulk.

5. TESTING FOR DOUBLED IN BULK. Press the dough with the tip of your fingers, making a dent about ½-inch deep. If the dent disappears, let the dough rise a little longer and test again. If the dent remains, the dough has risen enough and is ready for the next step. If allowed to rise longer, there is danger that the dough will collapse.

6. PUNCHING DOWN. When the dough has doubled, plunge your fist into the center. Then fold the edges of the dough to the center and turn the ball of dough over completely.

7. SHAPING. After punching dough down, divide it into the required number of portions by cutting it with a large knife. Shape each piece into a ball. Cover and let dough "rest" for five minutes. This rest period makes the dough easier to handle and causes the bread to hold its shape better.

8. TESTING FOR LIGHTNESS. After shaping, allow breads to rise until they are doubled in bulk. To tell if they have risen enough, press the bread lightly near the bottom or edge with your little finger. If the small dent remains, the bread has risen enough and is ready for baking.

Baking Temperatures

Baking temperatures for yeast breads vary from moderate (350° F.) to hot (450° F.). The lower temperatures are used for rich doughs to prevent excessive browning. Rolls are usually baked at 400-425° F. while bread may be started at 425° F. then the temperature reduced after 15 minutes to 350° F. If they are baked the entire time at the higher temperature, a browner crust results.

When bread has finished baking, it shrinks slightly from the sides of the pan and sounds hollow when thumped.

Care Of Baked Bread

Remove bread and rolls from their pans immediately. Place loaves, uncovered, on wire cooling racks away from drafts. To prevent drying out of top crusts, brush with melted shortening or cover with a cloth while cooling.

As soon as the bread has cooled thoroughly, wrap carefully in waxed paper and store in closed, dry, ventilated container. The breadbox should be washed, scalded and aired once a week and more often during hot weather.

COMMON CAUSES OF INFERIOR BREAD

INFERIOR FLOUR	The homemaker who thinks she is saving money by buying a less expensive flour for bread making may find that a cheap flour may be an expensive flour when her bread comes from the oven with a poor texture, color, flavor and volume.
INACTIVE YEAST	If it acts at all, old yeast will act very slowly and will not give good results. Yeast plants that are dead cannot leaven bread.
OVER OR UNDER KNEADING	When dough is kneaded too much it becomes sticky and will not rise well in the oven. If dough is kneaded too little, the bread will be streaked and have an inferior texture which sometimes contains lumps.
TOO MUCH FLOUR	Dough that is too stiff results in a coarse-textured bread that is small in volume and has a dry crumb.
OVER AND UNDER RISING	If bread is allowed to rise too long, the loaf will be porous with little flavor and have a pale crust and a bad texture. The bread will crumble badly. The dough may become sour if the rising continues for too long a period. A small flat loaf which browns too quickly in the oven results from too little rising. The crumb will be compact and dull.
INCORRECT OVEN TEMPERATURES	If the oven is too hot, a crust will form on the bread immediately and it cannot continue to rise during the first 10-15 minutes of baking time. The outer surface of the bread browns before the crumb is baked. When the oven is too cool, the bread will continue to rise too long and the bread will be porous in the center and upper part of the loaf. Even before the bread begins to bake, it dries out.

Quick Breads

UPSIDE-DOWN ORANGE BISCUITS

¼ c. butter
½ c. orange juice
¾ c. sugar
2 t. orange rind, grated
2 c. flour
½ t. salt
3 t. baking powder
⅓ c. shortening
¾ c. milk
½ t. cinnamon

Combine butter, orange juice, ½ cup of sugar and orange rind. Cook 2 minutes; pour into 12 muffin tins. Combine flour, salt, baking powder, shortening and milk. Roll out ¼-inch thick. Mix cinnamon and sugar; sprinkle over dough. Roll as for jelly roll. Slice 1-inch thick; place cut side down in muffin pans. Bake at 450°F. for 15-20 minutes. Yield: 12 servings.

Mrs. Ernest Sampson, Huron Jr. H.S.
Huron, South Dakota

SOUTHERN BISCUITS

2-2¼ c. flour
½ t. baking soda
2 t. baking powder
½-1 t. salt
6 T. shortening
⅔-1 c. buttermilk

Sift flour, baking soda, baking powder and salt together. Cut in shortening until it is the size of small peas. Stir in milk to make soft dough. Round up on lightly floured cloth-covered board or wax paper. Knead lightly. Roll out about ½-inch thick. Cut and place on lightly greased baking sheet. Bake at 450°F. for 8-10 minutes. Yield: 20 biscuits.

This recipe submitted by the following teachers:
Helen Barbee, Joliet Township H.S.
Joliet, Illinois
Mrs. Willa Mae Scroggs, Sylva-Webster H.S.
Sylva, North Carolina

ORANGE BISCUITS

2 c. flour
4 t. baking powder
2 T. sugar
1 t. salt
5 T. shortening
1 egg, beaten
½ c. milk

Sift dry ingredients together; cut in shortening. Add beaten egg and milk. Mix until dough can be handled. Turn onto lightly floured board and knead until smooth. Roll dough ¼-inch thick. Brush with melted butter.

FILLING:
Grated rind of 1 lge. orange
1 c. sugar

Sprinkle rind and sugar on rolled dough. Roll as for jelly roll; cut into ¾-inch slices. Place cut-side down on greased cookie sheet. Bake 20 minutes in 425°F. oven. Yield: 16 servings.

Clara Deiter, Dodge City, Jr. H.S.
Dodge City, Kansas

PEANUT-Y TEA RING

10 plain or buttermilk refrigerated biscuits
¼ c. melted butter or margarine
1 c. finely chopped peanuts
½ c. powdered sugar
1 T. water

Separate biscuits. Dip both sides in melted butter, then in peanuts, coating well. Arrange in overlapping circle on greased baking sheet. Bake at 425°F. for 10 or 15 minutes, or until golden brown. Mix powdered sugar and water. Drizzle over hot tea ring. Slide onto serving plate; serve warm. Yield: 6-8 servings.

Photograph for this recipe on page 333

QUICK CINNAMON ROLLS

1 can biscuits
¼ c. butter
½ t. cinnamon
¼ c. granulated sugar
¼ c. raisins (opt.)
¼ c. brown sugar

Flatten biscuits into rectangular shape. Dot with butter; sprinkle with mixture of cinnamon and granulated sugar. Add raisins. Roll up, beginning with wide side, into an oblong roll. Cut in 1 to 1½-inch slices. Place in muffin tins which contain remainder of butter and brown sugar. Bake in 425°F. oven for 10-12 minutes. Yield: 6 servings.

Judith Gress, Moffat County H.S.
Craig, Colorado

SPEEDY MARMALADE COFFEE CAKE

1 pkg. refrigerator biscuits
2 T. butter or margarine, melted
¼ c. sugar
2 T. finely chopped walnuts
2 t. grated orange peel

Dip biscuits in butter. Combine sugar, walnuts and grated orange peel. Dip biscuits in sugar mixture. Overlap biscuits in 9-inch pie plate. Bake in 400°F. oven for 15 minutes or until done. Serve hot.

Jane Spangler, Shippensburg H.S.
Shippensburg, Pennsylvania

BLUEBERRY BUCKLE

½ c. shortening
½ c. sugar
1 egg, well beaten
2 c. sifted enriched flour
2½ t. baking powder
¼ t. salt
½ c. milk
2 c. fresh blueberries

Thoroughly cream shortening and sugar; add egg and mix well. Sift flour, baking powder and salt; add to creamed mixture alternately with milk. Pour into waxed paper lined 8x8x2-inch pan; sprinkle blueberries over batter.

TOPPING:

½ c. sugar
½ c. sifted flour
½ t. cinnamon
¼ c. butter or margarine

Combine sugar, flour, cinnamon and butter until crumbly; sprinkle over blueberries. Bake at 350°F. for 75 minutes. Cut in wedges. Yield: 6-8 servings.

This recipe submitted by the following teachers:
Dorothy Crone, Fayetteville Perry Local
Fayetteville, Ohio
Mrs. Eleanor J. Hayes, Alton H.S.
Alton, New Hampshire

BLUEBERRY BUCKLE

¾ c. sugar
¼ c. soft shortening
1 egg
½ c. milk
2 c. sifted flour
2 t. baking powder
½ t. salt
2 c. blueberries, drained

Combine sugar, shortening and egg; stir in milk. Sift flour, baking powder and salt together; stir into sugar mixture. Carefully blend in blueberries. Spread batter in greased and floured pan.

TOPPING:

½ c. sugar
⅓ c. sifted flour
½ t. cinnamon
¼ c. soft butter

Combine ingredients. Sprinkle over blueberries. Bake 45-50 minutes at 375°F. Yield: 9 3″ sq.

Deborah Mabon, Hughesville H.S.
Hughesville, Pennsylvania

BLUEBERRY STREUSEL

TOPPING:

½ c. brown sugar
1 t. cinnamon
2 T. butter, melted

Combine to sprinkle over dough.

DOUGH:

2 c. sifted flour
⅓ c. sugar

3 t. baking powder
½ t. salt
¼ c. shortening
1 egg, beaten
¾ c. milk
1 c. blueberries, drained
1 T. lemon juice

Sift dry ingredients together. Add all remaining ingredients except blueberries and lemon juice. Pour into greased layer or square pan. Pour lemon juice over blueberries. Toss lightly; scatter over batter. Press in with spoon. Sprinkle brown sugar mixture on top. Bake in 375°F. oven for 30-40 minutes or until done. Yield: 8 servings.

Ardis A. Williams, Yuba City H.S.
Yuba City, California

BONNY BERRY BREAD

½ c. butter
¾ c. sugar
1 egg
⅓ c. milk
2 c. sifted flour
2 t. baking powder
½ t. salt
1 No. 2 can blueberry pie filling

Cream butter and sugar; beat in egg. Blend in milk. Sift together dry ingredients. Add to creamed mixture. Spread half the batter in greased 8x8x2-inch pan; cover with three-fourths can blueberry pie filling. Spread with remaining batter; top with blueberry pie filling. Bake in 375°F. oven 30-40 minutes.

Mrs. Edith Oliveira, Kau H.S.
Pahala, Hawaii

COFFEE CAKE SUPREME

TOPPING:

½ c. brown sugar
2 t. flour
2 t. cinnamon
2 T. melted butter
½ c. chopped nuts

Combine ingredients; mix thoroughly. Set aside.

1½ c. flour
3 t. baking powder
¼ t. salt
¾ c. sugar
¼ c. shortening
1 egg
½ c. milk
1 t. vanilla

Sift flour, baking powder, salt and sugar together. Cut in shortening. Add milk, egg and vanilla. Mix well. Put half of dough in 8x8-inch pan and sprinkle with topping mixture. Add remaining batter and cover with topping. Bake in 375°F. oven for 25-30 minutes. Yield: 8 servings.

Marian P. Wilson, Armijo Joint Union H.S.
Fairfield, California

COFFEE CAKE

TOPPING:

½ c. brown sugar
3 T. flour
1 t. cinnamon
⅛ t. salt
½ c. pecans, chopped
½ c. raisins
3 T. butter, melted

Combine all ingredients. Set aside.

DOUGH:

1½ c. flour
¾ c. sugar
3 t. baking powder
½ t. cinnamon
¼ t. nutmeg
¼ c. shortening
1 egg, beaten
1 c. milk
1 t. vanilla

Sift all dry ingredients together. Cut in shortening. Combine egg, milk and vanilla. Add to dry ingredients. Spread half of batter in a greased square pan. Sprinkle with half of topping. Repeat with batter and topping. Bake in 400°F. oven for about 30 minutes.

Mrs. Mary Kathryn Lands
Amanda-Clearcreek H.S.
Amanda, Ohio

EASY PARTY COFFEE CAKE

TOPPING:

3 T. sugar
2 T. cinnamon

Combine sugar and cinnamon. Set aside.

DOUGH:

1 c. margarine
2 c. sugar
4 eggs
3 c. flour
½ t. salt
3 t. baking powder
1 c. milk
½ c. nuts

Cream margarine and sugar in large bowl. Add eggs one at a time, beating after each addition. Sift flour, baking powder and salt together. Add to sugar mixture alternately with milk. Pour one-third of batter in angel food cake pan. Sprinkle with part of cinnamon and sugar mixture. Repeat, finishing with topping. Sprinkle with nuts. Bake in 350°F. oven for 1 hour. Yield: 12-15 servings.

GLAZE:

2 c. confectioner's sugar
2 T. cream or rich milk
2 t. lemon juice

Combine ingredients. Glaze cake when cool.

Mrs. Nancy W. Anderson, Hanover Horton H.S.
Horton, Michigan

BRAN COFFEE CAKE

1 c. flour
½ t. salt
¼ t. soda
2 t. baking powder
2 c. bran
3 T. shortening, melted
2 eggs, well beaten
1 c. milk
6 T. molasses
¾ c. raisins
Sugar
Cinnamon
Nuts

Sift flour, salt, soda and baking powder. Combine flour with all remaining ingredients except sugar, cinnamon and nuts. Pour in round cake pan. Sprinkle top with cinnamon, sugar and nuts. Bake in 350°F. oven for 30-35 minutes. Yield: 6 servings.

Joyce Titus, New Knoxville H.S.
New Knoxville, Ohio

HAWAIIAN COFFEE CAKE

1 egg, beaten
1 c. crushed pineapple
¼ c. melted shortening
1½ c. flour
2½ t. baking powder
½ t. salt
½ c. sugar
½ c. coconut
½ c. brown sugar
2 T. butter

Combine egg, pineapple and melted shortening. Add mixture of flour, baking powder, salt and sugar; stir only until flour is dampened. Pour into greased 8-inch square pan. Top with mixture of coconut, brown sugar and butter. Bake at 400°F. for 25 minutes. Yield: 9 servings.

Borghild Strom, Pattengill Jr. H.S.
Lansing, Michigan

JIFFY COFFEE CAKE

2 c. flour
½ T. white sugar
¼ t. salt
4 t. baking powder
1 egg
1 c. milk
4 T. butter, melted
3 T. soft butter
⅔ c. brown sugar
1 t. cinnamon

Sift flour, white sugar, salt and baking powder together. Beat egg until thick; add milk and shortening. Blend with rotary beater. Combine egg and flour mixture; stir until just moistened. Put in greased square cake pan. Mix topping of butter, brown sugar and cinnamon. Sprinkle over soft dough. Bake in 350°F. oven for 20 minutes.

Sister Mary Anne, P.B.V.M. Newman H.S.
Mason City, Iowa

MARMALADE COFFEE CAKE

¼ c. shortening
½ c. plus 1 T. sugar
1 egg, beaten
1 T. grated orange rind
1¾ c. sifted flour
2 t. baking powder
½ t. salt
½ c. milk
3 T. butter, melted
1 c. flaked coconut
¾ c. orange marmalade

Cream shortening; add ½ cup sugar and mix well. Add egg and orange rind. Sift together dry ingredients; add alternately with milk to creamed mixture, beating after each addition. Spread dough in greased 9-inch square pan. Brush top with 1 tablespoon butter. Blend coconut with marmalade; add remaining butter. Spread evenly over top of dough. Sprinkle with 1 tablespoon sugar. Bake in 375°F. oven 35-40 minutes. Yield: 9-12 servings.

Mrs. Ruth Schaffner, Cochrane-Fountain City H.S.
Fountain City, Wisconsin

MINCEMEAT COFFEE RING

2 c. sifted flour
2½ t. baking powder
¾ c. sugar
½ t. salt
⅓ c. shortening
1 egg, well beaten
½ c. milk
¾ c. moist mincemeat

Sift dry ingredients into a bowl. Cut in shortening with pastry blender until mixture resembles coarse corn meal. Blend egg, milk and mincemeat; add to flour mixture. Stir until dry ingredients are moistened. Turn batter into well-greased 1½-quart ring mold. Bake in 375°F. oven for 20-25 minutes. Cool about 10 minutes.

GLAZE:

2 T. butter
3 T. hot milk
1 c. confectioner's sugar, sifted
⅛ t. salt

Combine ingredients until butter is melted and glaze is smooth. Frost warm coffee ring. Yield: 15-20 servings.

Margery S. Gibeaut, Cowan H.S.
Cowan, Indiana

ORANGE COFFEE CAKE

3 T. shortening
⅓ c. sugar
1 egg, well beaten
2 t. grated orange rind
⅛ t. almond extract
1¼ c. flour, sifted
2 t. baking powder
½ t. salt
¼ c. orange juice
¼ c. milk

Blend shortening and sugar thoroughly. Add egg; beat well. Stir in grated rind and flavoring. Sift flour, baking powder and salt together. Add to creamed mixture alternately with orange juice and milk. Do not overmix. Spread in greased 8x8-inch baking pan.

TOPPING:

1 c. corn flakes
2 T. sugar
2 t. grated orange rind
⅛ t. allspice
1 T. butter, melted

Combine ingredients. Sprinkle topping over coffee cake. Bake in 375°F. oven for 20 minutes. Yield: 9 servings.

Madge Arlene Humphrey, Weston H.S.
Cazenovia, Wisconsin

STREUSEL COFFEE CAKE

1½ c. sugar
½ c. shortening
2 eggs
1 c. milk
3 c. sifted flour
4 t. baking powder

Mix sugar, shortening and eggs. Stir in milk. Sift flour, baking powder and salt together. Add to sugar and milk mixture. Mix well.

STREUSEL MIXTURE:

1 c. brown sugar
4 T. flour
4 t. cinnamon
4 T. butter

Thoroughly mix ingredients. Spread one-half batter in greased and floured 12x18-inch pan. Sprinkle one-half of streusel mixture on batter. Add remaining batter; sprinkle top with remaining streusel mixture. Bake at 375°F. for 25-35 minutes.

Jeanette Neiss, Sedgwick H.S.
Sedgwick, Colorado

STREUSEL-FILLED COFFEE CAKE

¾ c. sugar
¼ c. soft shortening
1 egg
½ c. milk
1½ c. sifted flour
2 t. baking powder
½ t. salt

Mix sugar, shortening and egg thoroughly. Stir in milk. Sift together dry ingredients; stir into mixture. Spread half of the batter in greased and floured 9-inch square pan.

(Continued on Next Page)

STREUSEL:

½ c. brown sugar
2 T. flour
2 t. cinnamon
2 T. butter, melted
½ c. nuts, chopped

Mix ingredients well. Sprinkle batter with half of streusel mixture. Add remaining batter; sprinkle remaining streusel over the top. Bake at 375°F. for 25 to 35 minutes.

This recipe submitted by the following teachers:

Mrs. Julian Green, Buchholz Jr. H.S.
Gainesville, Florida

Sister Mary Rosario S.C., Marian H.S.
Cincinnati, Ohio

SUGAR LOAF COFFEE CAKE

2½ c. flour
1¼ c. white sugar
3½ t. baking powder
1 t. cinnamon
1 t. nutmeg
2 T. brown sugar
⅓ c. nuts, chopped
½ t. clove
½ t. allspice
¾ c. shortening
1 c. raisins
¾ c. mik
1 egg

Measure sifted flour into bowl. Add all other dry ingredients. Mix well. Cut in shortening until about size of small peas. Set aside 1 cup for topping. Mix milk and egg together; add remaining dry ingredients. Stir just until they are moist. Pour into greased pan. Add floured raisins. Sprinkle reserved mixture over top. Bake in preheated 375°F. oven for 40-45 minutes. Yield: 10 servings.

Sandra Allen, Princeville Community H.S.
Princeville, Illinois

SWEET COFFEE CAKE

TOPPING:

½ t. cinnamon
½ c. pecans, chopped
2 T. light brown sugar
Combine all ingredients.

1 c. butter or margarine
2 c. sugar
2 eggs
1 c. sour cream
½ t. vanilla
2 c. flour
1 t. baking powder
1 t. baking soda
¼ t. salt

Cream shortening, sugar and eggs in mixer. Fold in sour cream and vanilla carefully. Add sifted dry ingredients. Put half of mixture into greased and floured 10-inch tube pan. Sprinkle with half of topping. Repeat. Bake in 350°F. oven for 55-60 minutes. Cool before removing from pan. Sprinkle with sifted powdered sugar.

Wanda Jane Long, Trafalgar H.S.
Trafalgar, Indiana

DUTCH APPLE CAKE

2 c. flour
½ t. salt
3 t. baking powder
¼ c. butter
1 egg, beaten
⅔ c. milk
2 sour apples
2 T. sugar
¼ t. cinnamon

Sift flour, salt and baking powder; cut or rub in butter. Add milk and egg. Spread ½-inch thick in shallow pan. Pare and cut apples in sections lengthwise; set in rows on dough with sharp edges pressed lightly into dough. Sprinkle top with sugar and cinnamon. Bake in 375°F. oven for 25 or 30 minutes. Serve hot with lemon or hard sauce. Cake may also be served with milk or cream.

This recipe submitted by the following teachers:

Mrs. Rosemary K. Harwood, North Stanly H.S.
New Londan, North Carolina

Mrs. C. H. Seeley, Superior H.S.
Superior, Montana

OVEN ALMOND FRENCH TOAST WITH STRAWBERRY BUTTER

2 eggs, slightly beaten
Pinch of salt
2 T. granulated sugar
1 c. milk
½ t. almond extract
12 slices bread
Powdered sugar

Combine eggs, salt, granulated sugar, milk and almond extract in shallow dish. Dip bread into egg mixture; coat each side. Place on well greased cookie sheet. Brown in 450°F. oven for 7 minutes. Turn toast and continue browning. Sift powdered sugar over each piece; serve with strawberry butter. Yield: 6 servings.

STRAWBERRY BUTTER:

½ c. soft butter
⅓ c. powdered sugar
1 10-oz. pkg. frozen strawberries, thawed

Whip butter until creamy; drain juice from thawed berries. Gradually add berries to butter, beating well after each addition. Beat in sugar. Chill until serving time. Yield: 1½ cups strawberry butter.

Mrs. Carolyn Martin, Girard H.S.
Girard, Illinois

PECAN-SOUR CREAM COFFEE CAKE

½ c. margarine
1 c. sugar
3 eggs
2 c. sifted flour
1 t. baking powder
1 t. soda
¼ t. salt
1 c. sour cream
½ c. golden raisins

Cream margarine and sugar. Add eggs, one at a time, beating after each addition. Sift flour with baking powder, soda and salt; add to creamed mixture alternately with sour cream, making three equal additions of each. Blend well after each addition. Sprinkle raisins over top; stir in. Spread mixture in greased 13x9x2-inch baking pan.

PECAN TOPPING:

¾ c. brown sugar
1 T. flour
1 t. cinnamon
2 T. butter
1 c. chopped pecans

Combine brown sugar, flour and cinnamon. Cut in butter, until consistency of corn meal; mix in pecans. Spread over dough. Bake at 350°F. for 30 minutes. Cut in squares. Serve either warm or cold. Yield: 12 servings.

Mrs. Doris G. Kruger, Peotone H.S.
Peotone, Illinois

YUM-YUM COFFEE CAKE

½ c. butter
1 c. sugar
2 eggs
2 c. sifted flour
1 t. baking powder
1 t. baking soda
½ t. salt
1 c. sour cream
1 t. vanilla

Cream butter until soft. Add sugar and cream until light and fluffy. Add eggs; one at a time, beating well after each addition. Sift flour, baking soda, baking powder and salt together. Add dry ingredients alternately with sour cream, beginning and ending with flour mixture. Stir in vanilla. Pour half of batter into a lightly greased 9x9-inch baking pan. Cover with half of nut topping mixture. Pour remaining batter over nut mixture and top with remaining nut mixture. Bake in 325°F. oven for 45 to 50 minutes. Yield: 12 servings.

CINNAMON-NUT TOPPING:

⅓ c. brown sugar
¼ c. white sugar
1 t. cinnamon
1 c. pecans, finely chopped
Combine ingredients. Set aside.

Mrs. Judy Herbig, Timber Township H.S.
Glasford, Illinois

APPLE CORN BREAD

¾ c. sifted flour
¾ c. corn meal
1½ t. baking powder
½ t. salt
1 T. sugar
1 egg, beaten
2 T. oil
¾ c. milk
¾ c. apples, diced

Sift together dry ingredients. Beat egg; add oil and milk. Beat again. Add liquid mixture to dry ingredients along with apples; stir to blend. Pour batter into an oiled 9x9-inch pan. Bake 25 minutes in a 400°F. oven. Yield: 16 servings.

Ellouise Handwerk, Penn Manor Jr. H.S.
Millersville, Pennsylvania

SALMON SOUTHERN CORN BREAD

1 7¾-oz. can salmon
1 c. sifted flour
1 c. corn meal
4 t. baking powder
¼ c. sugar
½ t. salt
1 egg, beaten
1 c. mixed salmon liquid and milk
¼ c. butter or fat, melted

Drain salmon, reserving liquid. Flake salmon. Sift together flour, corn meal, baking powder, sugar and salt. Combine egg, salmon liquid and butter; add to dry ingredients. Mix just enough to moisten. Stir in salmon. Place in a well greased baking dish. Bake at 425°F. for 25-30 minutes. Yield: 6 servings.

Delores Neiwert, Big Piney H.S.
Big Piney, Wyoming

YANKEE CORN BREAD

1 c. flour
1 t. salt
2½ t. baking powder
2-4 T. sugar
¾ c. yellow corn meal
1 egg
1 c. milk
4 T. shortening, melted

Sift flour, salt, baking powder, sugar and corn meal together. Add egg and milk; stir quickly and lightly until mixed. Add shortening. Pour batter into one or two well greased shallow pans. Bake in 400°F. oven for 20-30 minutes. Yield: 9x9 inch sheet.

Mrs. Glenda F. Mooney, Stillwater Jr. H.S.
Stillwater, Minnesota

CORN CRISPS

1 c. yellow corn meal
½ c. sifted flour
¼ t. baking soda
½ t. salt
3 T. salad oil
⅓ c. milk
Parmesan cheese, grated (opt.)
Butter, melted

Sift dry ingredients together. Gradually stir in oil and milk. Knead dough on a lightly floured surface until it holds together. Break off small pieces; roll paper thin. Sprinkle cheese on center, if desired. Place on ungreased cookie sheet. Bake in 375°F. oven for 8-10 minutes. Cool. Before serving brush with melted butter and a sprinkle of salt. Yield: 8 servings.

Marina Economos, Sandstone H.S.
Sandstone, Minnesota

PENNSYLVANIA CORN PONE

1 c. corn meal
½ c. flour
½ c. sugar
½ t. salt
½ t. soda
½ t. baking powder
1 egg, beaten
¼ c. liquid shortening
1 c. thick buttermilk

Sift corn meal and flour; measure. Combine all dry ingredients. Add egg and liquid ingredients to flour mixture. Blend well. Pour into 8x8-inch pan. Bake in 400°F. oven for 20-25 minutes. Yield: 6 servings.

Mrs. George Rearick, Big Spring H.S.
Newville, Pennsylvania

TOMATO-FLAVORED HUSH PUPPIES

1 c. plain corn meal
½ c. flour
½ t. salt
½ t. garlic salt
1 med. onion, finely chopped
½ No. 2 can tomatoes

Sift corn meal, flour, salt and garlic salt together. Add chopped onions. Add cooked tomatoes to make a semi-thin mixture. Drop by spoonfuls into hot shortening, about 375°F. If fat is too hot hush puppies will brown on outside before getting done in middle. Yield: 4-6 servings.

Mrs. Alice H. Harvard, Effingham County H.S.
Springfield, Georgia

SPOON BREAD

1 qt. milk
1 c. corn meal
2 t. salt
4 eggs, separated

Scald milk. Mix meal and salt with enough water to moisten. Add corn meal to milk, stirring constantly. Cook in double boiler until a thick mush is obtained. Remove from heat and quickly stir in beaten egg yolks. Beat egg whites until stiff; fold into first mixture. Turn into greased baking dish. Bake 45 minutes in 300°F. oven. NOTE: If necessary to wait, do not remove from oven.

Ruth Stovall, State Supervisor, Home Economics
Education, State Department of Education
Montgomery, Alabama

SPOON BREAD

2 c. milk
½ c. corn meal
2 T. butter, melted
1 t. salt
1 t. baking powder
3 egg yolks, well beaten
3 egg whites, stiffly beaten

Scald milk in double boiler. Stir corn meal into milk; cook until thick like mush, stirring constantly. Remove from heat; add butter, salt, baking powder and egg yolks. Fold in stiffly beaten egg whites. Bake in 375°F. oven for 30 minutes. Yield: 6 servings.

Mrs. Natalie A. Prentice, Somersworth H.S.
Somersworth, New Hampshire

VIRGINIA BATTER BREAD

1 c. corn meal
2 c. water
1 c. milk
3 eggs, separated
½ c. day-old bread, broken into small pieces
1 t. salt
1 t. sugar
1 t. baking powder
3 egg whites, stiffly beaten
1 T. butter

Cook corn meal in water until it reaches boiling stage, stirring occasionally. Pour milk over bread, add beaten egg yolks, salt, sugar and baking powder. Add to corn meal mixture. Add butter and fold in stiffly beaten egg whites. Pour into greased casserole or baking dish. Bake in a 350°F. oven or 25-30 minutes or until golden brown. Yield: 4 servings.

Virginia O. Savedge, Northampton H.S.
Eastville, Virginia

APPLE MUFFINS

TOPPING:

½ t. cinnamon
½ c. brown sugar
⅓ c. nuts, chopped
Combine ingredients; set aside.

1 egg, slightly beaten
½ c. milk
¼ c. shortening, melted
1 c. apple, grated
1½ c. sifted flour,
½ c. sugar
2 t. baking powder
½ t. salt
½ t. cinnamon

Combine egg, milk, shortening and apples. Sift dry ingredients together; stir into first mixture just until flour is moistened. Batter will be lumpy. Fill greased or paper lined muffin tins two-thirds full. Sprinkle with topping. Bake in 400°F. oven for 25-30 minutes. Yield: 12 muffins

Mrs. Nancy Donaldson, Metamora H.S.
Metamora, Illinois

SPICED APPLE MUFFINS

2 c. sifted pastry flour
½ c. sugar
4 t. baking powder
½ t. salt
½ t. cinnamon
1 c. milk
1 egg, beaten
4 t. butter, melted
1 c. raw apples, finely chopped

Sift together flour, sugar, baking powder, salt and cinnamon. Combine milk, egg and butter; add dry ingredients. Mix just enough to combine; fold in apples. Drop in well greased muffin tins.

TOPPING:

2 T. sugar
½ t. cinnamon
Walnuts, chopped (opt.)

Combine sugar and cinnamon; sprinkle over top of muffins. Bake in 425°F. oven for 15-25 minutes. NOTE: Chopped walnuts may be added to top.

Mrs. Eva Benson, Sweet Home Union H.S.
Sweet Home, Oregon

BLUEBERRY MUFFINS

¼ c. shortening
⅓ c. sugar
2 eggs, beaten
2 c. sifted flour
4 t. baking powder
¾ t. salt
⅔ c. milk
⅔ c. fresh or canned blueberries, well drained

Cream shortening and sugar; add eggs. Mix 1⅔ cups flour, baking powder and salt. Add alternately with milk to sugar mixture. Mix blueberries with remaining flour; stir in lightly. Pour into greased muffin pans. Bake in 400°F. oven for 30 minutes. Yield: 12 muffins

Joyce Fulghum, Howard H.S.
Howard, Kansas

BLUEBERRY MUFFINS

½ c. milk
¼ c. salad oil or melted shortening
1 egg, slightly beaten
1½ c. flour
½ c. sugar
2 t. baking powder
½ t. salt
¾-1 c. fresh or frozen blueberries

Mix milk and shortening with egg. Sift dry ingredients together and add to milk mixture. Blend in blueberries. Bake in greased muffin pans in 400°F. oven for 20-25 minutes. Yield: 12 muffins.

This recipe submitted by the following teachers:
Mrs. Joyce Meek, Yamhill Carlton Union H.S.
Carlton, Oregon

Mrs. Juanita M. Rogers, Paul G. Blazer H.S.
Ashland, Kentucky

BLUEBERRY-ORANGE MUFFINS

3 c. flour
4 t. baking powder
¼ t. soda
½ c. sugar
1½ t. salt
1 c. frozen blueberries, thawed
1 c. nuts, chopped
⅓ c. orange juice
1 egg, slightly beaten
1 c. milk
½ c. butter
1 T. grated orange peel

Sift dry ingredients together. Stir in blueberries and nuts, tossing lightly until coated. Beat remaining ingredients together. Pour into flour mixture; stir just until dry ingredients are moistened. Spoon into greased muffin tins or into loaf pan. Bake muffins in 425°F. for 20 minutes, or golden brown. Bake loaf in 350°F. for 1 hour and 10 minutes or until done. Yield: 20-24 muffins

Vennae Yamada, LaPuente H.S.
LaPuente, California

BRAN MUFFINS

¾ c. milk
1 c. bran shreds
1 c. sifted flour
3 t. baking powder
3 T. sugar
¼ t. salt
1 egg, well beaten
3 T. melted butter or oil

Pour milk over bran in mixing bowl. Sift together dry ingredients. Add egg and butter to bran mixture. Stir in flour mixture, stirring as little as possible. Bake in well greased muffin pans at 425° for 25 minutes. Yield: 10-12 muffins.

Mrs. Mary Jo Clapp, Jamaica Consolidated H.S.
Sidell, Illinois

CARMEL-PECAN OATMEAL MUFFINS

⅓ c. brown sugar
2 T. soft butter
Pecan halves
1 c. sifted flour
¼ c. sugar
3 t. baking powder
½ t. salt
¼ c. shortening
1 c. oatmeal
1 egg, beaten
1 c. milk

Blend brown sugar and butter. Pat evenly in greased muffin cups. Arrange pecan halves in each. Sift together dry ingredients; cut in shortening. Blend in oatmeal. Lightly stir in egg and milk. Fill muffin cups two-thirds full. Bake at 425°F. for 20 minutes. Remove from pans immediately. Yield: 12-15 muffins.

Joyce M. Wingate, Marshall H.S.
Marshall, Michigan

ENGLISH TEA MUFFINS

½ c. butter
⅓ c. sugar
1 egg
2 c. flour
2 t. baking powder
Pinch of salt
¼ t. cinnamon
⅔ c. raisins
1 c. milk
Brown sugar
Pecans, chopped

Cream butter and sugar. Beat in egg. Sift dry ingredients three times; add raisins. Add to sugar mixture alternately with milk. Pour into greased muffin pans. Sprinkle top with brown sugar and pecans. Bake in 350°F. oven for 25-30 minutes. Yield: 15-16 muffins.

Janice Brown, Flagler H.S.
Flagler, Colorado

MARCIE'S MUFFINS

2 c. whole wheat flour
1 t. baking powder
1 t. soda
½ t. salt
2 T. sugar
5 T. shortening, melted
1 egg
1½ c. sour milk

Mix together all dry ingredients. Add shortening, egg and sour milk. Stir until blended but still lumpy. Fill buttered muffin tins two-thirds full. Bake in 400°F. oven for 25 minues. Yield: 12 muffins.

Earlene Miller, Grafton H.S.
Grafton, North Dakota

PARIS PUFFINS

⅓ c. mixed soft shortening and butter
1 c. sugar
1 egg
1½ c. sifted flour
1½ t. baking powder
½ t. salt
¼ t. nutmeg
½ c. milk
6 T. butter, melted
1 t. cinnamon

Mix shortening, ½ cup of sugar and egg thoroughly. Sift all dry ingredients together except remaining sugar and cinnamon. Alternately add dry ingredients with milk to sugar mixture. Fill greased muffin cups two-thirds full. Bake in 350°F. oven 20-25 minutes. Remove from oven; immediately roll in melted butter. Combine remaining sugar and cinnamon; roll puffs in sugar mixture. Yield: 12 muffins.

This recipe submitted by the following teachers:
Mrs. Barbara Paterson, Portland Jr. H.S.
Bloomington, Minnesota
Mrs. Bert Kinzler, New Town H.S.
New Town, North Dakota

SWEET MUFFINS

2¼ c. sifted flour
¼ c. sugar
¾ t. salt
4 t. baking powder
⅓ c. shortening, melted
1 egg, slightly beaten
1 c. milk

Sift together dry ingredients. Make a well in dry ingredients. Combine egg, cooled shortening and milk. Pour liquid mixture into well of flour. Stir 15-25 strokes. Do not overstir. Fill greased muffin tins two-thirds full. Bake in 400°F. preheated oven 20-25 minutes. NOTE: Immediately after mixing, the mixture should be transferred to the pans in order to avoid loss of leavening gas. If the muffins cannot be baked immediately they should be placed in the refrigerator; they should stand no longer than 15-30 minutes after being mixed.

Mrs. Mildred B. Goe, Wy'east H.S.
Hood River, Oregon

WHOLE WHEAT MUFFINS

1½ c. whole wheat flour
½ c. white flour
3 t. baking powder
¼ c. sugar
1 t. salt
1 c. milk
1 egg, beaten
3 t. butter

Mix dry ingredients. Add milk, egg and melted butter. Beat well. Fill greased muffin tins two-thirds full. Bake in 375°F. oven for 20-25 minutes. Yield: 12 muffins.

Clara Mohr, Kyger Creek H.S.
Cheshire, Ohio

POPOVERS

2 eggs
1 c. milk
1 c. sifted flour
½ t. salt
1 T. shortening, melted

Break eggs into mixing bowl; add milk, flour and salt. Beat 1½ minutes with rotary or electric beater. Add melted shortening; beat 30 seconds. Don't overbeat. Fill 8 well greased cups half full. Bake in 475°F. oven for 10 minutes. Reduce heat to 350°F.; continue baking about 25-30 minutes, until browned and firm. A few minutes before removing from oven, prick each popover with sharp prong of fork, to let steam escape. NOTE: If you prefer popovers which are dry inside, turn off oven, let baked popovers stay 30 minutes with oven door ajar. Serve hot with butter. Yield: 8 popovers.

Mrs. Esther M. Hight, Weare H.S.
Weare, New Hampshire

POPOVERS

3 eggs
¼ t. salt
½ t. sugar
1 c. flour
1 c. milk
2 T. shortening, melted

Grease popover or muffin pans. Put in 450°F. oven and heat until sizzling hot. Beat eggs at medium speed until frothy; add salt, sugar, flour and half the milk. Mix again at medium speed until smooth. Add remaining milk and shortening; beat at low speed until blended. Pour into hot pans, filling only half full. Bake at 450°F. for 15 minutes; reduce heat to 400°F. and bake 15 minutes longer. Yield: 12 popovers.

Mrs. Naomi K. Ingwalson, Chinook H.S.
Chinook, Montana

HUNGARIAN STRAWBERRY PANCAKES

1 c. flour
½ t. salt
2 t. sugar
1½ c. cold milk
3 whole eggs
1 lge. sour apple
4 T. lemon juice
4 T. (heaping) strawberry preserves

Sift together flour, salt and sugar. Stir in 1½ cups milk to make smooth paste. Add eggs; beat briskly. Peel and core 1 large apple; cut in fine julienne strips. Marinate in lemon juice. Add strawberry preserves. Fold mixture into batter. Fry in buttered pan. Stack cakes and keep hot.

FILLING:
2 c. sour cream
1 egg yolk
¼ t. salt
4 T. strawberry preserves
Sugar
Cinnamon

Combine sour cream, egg yolk, salt and preserves. Blend well. Put 2 tablespoons filling on each cake; fold in half and serve lightly sprinkled with sugar and cinnamon. Yield: 4 servings.

Jo Collier, Pleasant Hill Community H.S.
Pleasant Hill, Illinois

LIGHT-HEARTED HOT CAKES

1 pkg. active dry yeast
1 c. milk
2 T. peanut oil
¼ c. very warm water
2 eggs, separated
1 c. pancake mix

Dissolve yeast in water. Beat whites until stiff; set aside. Add oil to yolks; beat well. Combine all ingredients, except egg whites; beat with rotary beater until smoth. Fold in egg whites. Brown on a lightly greased griddle. Yield: 6 servings.

Elinor Hagstrom, Central Valley H.S.
Redding, California

NUTTY PANCAKES

1¼ c. sifted flour
3 t. baking powder
1 T. sugar
½ t. salt
1 beaten egg
1 c. milk
2 T. salad oil or shortening, melted
¼ c. nuts, chopped

Sift dry ingredients together. Combine egg and milk. Add to dry ingredients. Stir until flour is moistened. Batter may be lumpy. Add nuts. Pour onto lightly greased pancake griddle. Bake until brown on both sides. Serve with maple syrup or honey. Yield: 8 4-inch cakes.

Mrs. Zaidos Church, Pewamo-Westphalia
Community H.S.
Pewamo, Michigan

OUT DOOR GRIDDLE CAKES

1 c. flour
½ t. salt
2 T. baking powder
2 T. sugar
1 egg, beaten
2 T. shortening, melted
1 c. milk

Combine dry ingredients in bowl. Add remaining ingredients. Beat until smooth. Bake on prepared griddle. Yield: 8 5-inch cakes.

Mrs. Leva Brown, Tecumseh H.S.
Tecumseh, Michigan

CORN MEAL WAFFLES

¾ c. corn meal
¼ c. flour
½ t. salt
2 t. baking powder
1 T. sugar
1 egg, separated
½ c. milk
4 T. butter, melted

Mix dry ingredients by sifting together three times. Add egg yolk to milk and butter; add dry ingredients and mix well. Fold in stiffly beaten egg white. Bake in waffle iron. Yield: 1 serving.

Arva Knight, Bellevue H.S.
Bellevue, Texas

SOUR MILK WAFFLES

3 eggs, separated
2 c. sour milk
2 c. flour
2 t. baking powder
¼ t. salt
1 t. soda
6 T. butter, melted

Beat egg yolks; add 1 cup sour milk. Sift dry ingredients; add to yolks. Add another cup sour milk, and melted butter. Beat egg whites. Fold in beaten whites. Bake on hot waffle iron. Yield: 8 servings.

Mrs. Harriet Mjelde, Three Forks H.S.
Three Forks, Montana

WAFFLES SUPREME

4 eggs, separated
3 T. sugar
1½ c. milk
2 c. sifted flour
2 t. baking powder
½ t. salt
⅓ c. melted butter

Sift flour, baking powder and salt together. Melt butter; cool. Beat egg yolks until thick; add sugar and milk and beat well. Add flour mixture, beating well. Add melted butter. Fold in stiffly beaten egg whites. Bake until golden brown. Serve with favorite syrup. Yield: 3 large servings.

Mary E. Lash, Paramount Sr. H.S.
Paramount, California

MASTER MIX

To be used for biscuits, griddle cakes, muffins, etc.

9 c. sifted all-purpose flour
⅓ c. baking powder
1 T. salt
2 t. cream of tartar
4 T. sugar
1 c. nonfat dry milk powder
2 c. shortening which does not require refrigeration

Sift together dry ingredients three times. Cut in shortening with pastry blender or two knives until mixture looks like coarse corn meal. Store in covered container at room temperature. NOTE: To measure the master mix, pile it lightly into cup and level off with a spatula.

HOW TO USE THE MASTER MIX

Product Number	Temperature Time	master Mix	Sugar	Water	Eggs	Other Ingredients	Amount of Mixing
BISCUITS (15-20)	400°F 10 minutes	3 cups		⅔ to 1 cup			Until blended. Knead 10 times
GRIDDLE-CAKES (18) WAFFLES (6)		3 cups		1½ cups	1		Until blended
MUFFINS (12)	400°F 20 minutes	3 cups	2 T.	1 cup	1		Until ingredients just moistened
GINGER-BREAD (8x8 in.)	350°F 40 minutes	2 cups	4 T.	½ cup	1	½ c. molasses ½ t. cinnamon ½ t. ginger ½ t. cloves	Add half of liquid; beat 2 minutes Add rest of liquid; beat 1 minute.
OATMEAL COOKIES (4 dozen)	350°F 10-12 min.	3 cups	1 cup	⅓ cup	1	1 t. cinnamon 1 c. quick Rolled Oats	Until blended
DROP COOKIES (4 dozen)	350°F 10-12 min.	3 cups	1 cup	⅓ cup	1	1 tsp. vanilla ½ c. nuts or Chocolate Chips	Until blended
COFFEE-CAKE	400°F 25 minutes	3 cups	½ cup	⅔ cup	1	TOPPING ½ c. brown sugar; 3 T. butter; ½ t. cinnamon	Until blended
YELLOW CAKE	350°F 25 minutes	3 cups	1¼ cups	1 cup	2	1 t. vanilla	Add ⅔ of liquid; beat 2 minutes Add rest of liquid; and beat 2 minutes.
CHOCOLATE CAKE	350°F 25 minutes	3 cups	1½ cups	1 cup	2	1 t. vanilla ½ c. cocoa	Add ⅔ of liquid; beat 2 minutes. Add remaining liquid; beat 2 minutes.

Ruth C. Holder, Thorpe Jr. H.S.
Hampton, Virginia

BRUFFINS

1 9-oz. can crushed pineapple
2 bananas
½ c. sugar
1 egg
¼ c. milk
⅔ c. grapenuts
2 c. biscuit mix
1 t. salt
1 c. powdered sugar
2 T. pineapple syrup

Reserve 2 tablespoons syrup from pineapple for glaze. Mash bananas. Combine sugar, egg and milk. Add grapenuts, undrained pineapple, bananas, biscuit mix and salt. Stir mixture until blended, but not smooth. Fill greased muffin pans two-thirds full and bake in 425°F. oven for 20 minutes. Prepare glaze with powdered sugar and pineapple syrup. Dip hot muffins, top-side down, into glaze.

Mrs. Estelle Lair Greene, Yreka H.S.
Yreka, California

TROPICAL BRUFFINS

½ c. sugar
1 egg
¼ c. milk
⅔ c. grapenut flakes or other cereal flakes, crushed
1 9-oz. can crushed pineapple
2 bananas, mashed
2 c. prepared biscuit mix
1 t. salt
1 c. powdered sugar
2 T. pineapple syrup

Combine sugar, egg and milk; mix well. Add cereal, undrained pineapple, bananas, biscuit mix and salt; stir until blended, but not smooth. Spoon into muffin tins almost to top. Bake at 425°F. for 20 minutes. Glaze while hot with powdered sugar blended with pineapple syrup. Yield: 12 muffins.

Helen Janssen, Farmington Community H.S.
Farmington, Illinois

GINGERBREAD MIX

4 c. sifted flour
1 T. soda
1 T. baking powder
1 T. ginger
1 t. salt
¾ c. sugar
¾ c. shortening

Sift dry ingredients together; cut in shortening until mixture resembles corn meal. Cover tightly and refrigerate.

GINGERBREAD:

¼ c. molasses
½ c. sour milk
1½ c. gingerbread mix
1 egg, well beaten

Add molasses and sour milk to mix; blend well. Add egg. Pour into well greased 8x10-inch baking dish. Bake at 400°F. for 25-30 minutes. Yield: 10 servings.

Mrs. Laoma D. Clevenger, Ohio City- Liberty H.S.
Ohio City, Ohio

REFRIGERATOR MUFFINS

2 c. shredded wheat
4 c. All-Bran
2 c. boiling water
3 c. sugar
1 c. (heaping) shortening
4 eggs, beaten
5 c. flour
5 t. soda
1 t. salt
1 qt. buttermilk
Chopped dates or nuts (opt.)

Soak shredded wheat and All-Bran in boiling water. Cream sugar and shortening. Add all ingredients to soaked mixture. Store in covered container in refrigerator. Bake in greased muffin pans in 400°F. oven for 20 minutes. Add chopped dates or nuts if desired. Yield: 6-8 dozen.

Mrs. Richard Sweet, Madison Central H.S.
Madison, South Dakota

ICE BOX BRAN MUFFIN MIX

1 c. shortening
2 c. sugar
4 eggs
1 qt. milk
4 c. All-Bran
2 c. boiling water
2 c. 100% Bran
5 c. flour
5 t. soda
1 t. salt
½ lb. raisins, dates or nuts

Beat shortening, sugar and eggs toegether; add milk and mix well. Pour boiling water over All-Bran. When most of the moisture is absorbed, add to sugar mixture. Add 100% Bran and blend thoroughly. Add remaining ingredients. Mix well. Put into four 1-quart jars. Refrigerate. Bake as needed in greased muffin pans. Bake at 400°F. for 15 minutes; reduce heat and bake at 375°F. for 10 minutes. NOTE: Mixture keeps for a long time. Yield: 4 quarts mix.

Bernice DeLano, Toppenish H.S.
Toppenish, Washington

BUTTER DIPS

⅓ c. butter
2¼ c. sifted flour
1 T. sugar
3½ t. baking powder
1½ t. salt
1 c. milk

Melt butter in pan in oven. Sift together dry ingredients; add milk. Stir slowly with fork until dough clings together. Turn out on floured board. Roll to coat with flour. Knead about 10 times; roll out ½-inch thick into 12x8-inch rectangle. Cut dough in half lengthwise; cut crosswise into 16 strips. Dip each strip into melted butter on both sides. Lay close together in two rows. Bake 15 minutes in 450°F. oven. Serve hot. Yield: 32 butter dips.

Mrs. Karen Courrier, Alden Public School
Alden, Minnesota

NIPPY CHEESE STICKS

2 c. flour
1 T. baking powder
1 t. salt
¼ c. shortening
1 c. milk
1 c. sharp cheese, shredded
Parmesan cheese, grated (opt.)

Sift flour, baking powder and salt together. Cut in shortening until mixture is crumbly. Add milk; stir until flour mixture is well moistened. Fold in sharp cheese. Using two forks, drop mixture on greased baking sheet, stretching batter into long narrow 1x5-inch sticks. Smooth sides. If desired, sprinkle with grated Parmesan cheese. Bake in 450°F. oven for 10-15 minutes. Yield: 12-14 cheese sticks.

Mrs. Frances Fuhrman, Eastern H.S.
Wrightsville, Pennsylvania

MISCELLANEOUS QUICK BREADS, QUICK LOAF BREADS

GARLIC BREAD STICKS

Bread slices
¼ c. butter
Garlic powder or salt to taste
¾-1 c. cereal, crushed

Cut bread slices into 1-inch strips; crusts may be removed. Melt butter; add garlic powder or salt. Dip bread sticks into butter mixture; roll in crushed cereal. Bake in 350°F. oven 5 minutes. Turn to brown both sides. Yield: Varies to individual taste.

Ione Kjos, Wyndmere H.S.
Wyndmere, North Dakota

QUICK SESAME ROLLS

2 c. flour, sifted
3 t. baking powder
1 t. salt
3 T. melted shortening
¾ c. milk
Butter, melted
1 egg white
Sesame seed or poppy seed

Sift dry ingredients together. Add cooled shortening and milk. Mix well. Knead lightly. Roll to ¼-inch thickness. Cut with doughnut cutter. Dip in butter and fold as for pocketbook rolls. Mix egg white with small amount of water. Brush rolls with egg white mixture and sprinkle with sesame seed. Bake in 425°F. oven until brown. Yield: 15 servings.

Mrs. James L. Patton, Bryan Station H.S.
Lexington, Kentucky

APPLE BREAD

½ c. shortening
1 c. sugar
2 eggs, well beaten
1½ T. buttermilk or sour milk
½ c. raw unpeeled apple, grated
¼ c. nuts
½ c. raisins
2 c. sifted flour
1 t. baking soda
¼ t. salt

Cream shortening. Add sugar and eggs. Add milk, apple, nuts and raisins. Sift dry ingredients; add to mixture. Bake in a greased loaf pan for 45 minutes to 1 hour at 350°F. Cool before cutting.

Mrs. Yvonne Lindrum, Montebello Jr. H.S.
Montebello, California

APRICOT BREAD

1 c. dried apricots
1 c. sugar
2 T. soft butter
1 egg
¼ c. water
½ c. orange juice
2 c. flour
2 t. baking powder
¼-½ t. soda
1 t. salt
½ c. chopped nuts

Cover apricots in warm water and soak 30 minutes. Drain and cut with scissors. Cream sugar and butter; add egg. Add water and juice. Sift together dry ingredients and add to other sugar-egg mixture. Blend in nuts and apricots. Pour in greased, waxed paper lined 9x5x2 pan. Let stand 20 minutes. Bake 55-65 minutes at 350°F. NOTE: If desired, water may be omitted and ¼ cup sugar added. Yield: 1 loaf.

This recipe submitted by the following teachers:
Mrs. Alma M. Scott, Marion H.S.
Marion, South Dakota
Mrs. Mary Ada Parks, Anna-Jonesboro H.S.
Anna, Illinois
Mrs. Arthur Deffebach, Ranger H.S.
Ranger, Texas
Mrs. Alice Blakeney, Runge H.S.
Runge, Texas
Ettie Belle Robinson, Dawson H.S.
Dawson, Texas

APRICOT-ALMOND BREAD

1½ c. dried apricots
3 T. soft butter
1½ c. sugar
2 c. sifted flour
2 t. baking powder
½ t. salt
½ t. soda
⅓ c. milk
½ c. almonds, coarsely chopped

Simmer apricots in water to cover for 5 minutes. Drain fruit; reserve juice. Chop apricots. Cream butter with sugar; stir in ½ cup reserved apricot juice. Sift flour with baking powder, salt and soda. Stir dry ingredients into creamed mixture alternately with milk, stirring batter only until blended. Fold in almonds. Pour batter into buttered bread pan; bake in 350°F. oven for 1 hour or until done. NOTE: This bread slices more easily if allowed to stand overnight. Yield: 1 loaf.

Carolyn Ksiazek, Fairbury H.S.
Fairbury, Nebraska

APRICOT-NUT LOAF

2 c. flour
4 t. baking powder
1 t. salt
⅔ c. sugar
½ c. nuts, chopped
¾ c. dried apricots, chopped
1 egg, well beaten
1 c. milk
2 T. shortening, melted

Sift together dry ingredients. Add nuts and apricots. Combine egg, milk and shortening; add to dry ingredients. Stir until just moistened. Bake in 375°F. oven for 1 hour.

Mrs. Betty Hastings, Cloverleaf H.S.
Lodi, Ohio

APRICOT-NUT BREAD

1 c. dried apricots
1½ c. boiling water
3 c. sifted flour
3 t. baking powder
1½ t. salt
¼ t. baking soda
¼ t. nutmeg
1 c. brown sugar
1 egg, beaten
½ c. nuts, chopped

Cut dried apricots into strips. Cover with boiling water. Let stand 15 minutes. Sift flour, baking powder, salt, soda and nutmeg together. Add brown sugar, egg, nuts and fruit mixture. Mix well. Pour into well greased 8x5x3-inch loaf pan. Let stand 15 minutes. Bake in 350°F. oven about 1 hour and 30 minutes. Yield: 12 servings.

Kathleen Allburn, Gregory H.S.
Gregory, South Dakota

BANANA-MOLASSES BREAD

3 ripe bananas
1 egg
⅔ c. sugar
2 T. light molasses
2 T. shortening, melted
2 c. sifted flour
1 t. baking powder
1 t. baking soda
½ t. salt
1 c. walnuts, chopped

Mash bananas until no lumps remain. Add egg; mix well. Beat in sugar, molasses and shortening. Sift together dry ingredients; stir into molasses mixture. Fold in walnuts. Pour into greased 8x5x3-inch loaf pan. Bake in 325°F. oven for about 1 hour. Yield: 24 servings.

Mrs. Fern Garland, McConnellsburg H.S.
McConnellsburg, Pennsylvania

BANANA BREAD

1 c. sugar
½ c. butter or margarine
2 eggs, beaten
1 t. soda
2 c. sifted flour
3 T. sour milk
3 mashed bananas

Cream sugar and butter. Add eggs; beat well. Sift flour and soda together. Add alternately with sour milk. Add mashed bananas; mix well. Pour into greased loaf pan. Bake in 350°F. oven for 1 hour. Cool before slicing. Yield: 16-24 slices.

Mrs. Irma Alice Dixon, Georgetown H.S.
Georgetown, Illinois

BANANA BREAD

1¾ c. sifted flour
2 t. baking powder
¼ t. soda
½ t. salt
⅓ c. shortening
⅔ c. sugar
2 eggs, well beaten
1 c. ripe bananas, mashed
½ c. nuts, chopped (opt.)

Sift together dry ingredients. Cream shortening and sugar. Add eggs; beat well. Add flour mixture alternately with bananas, beating well after each addition. Add nuts. Pour into greased and floured loaf pan. Bake in 350°F. oven for 1 hour and 10 minutes or until well done. NOTE: If desired, dry ingredients can be sifted and combined with all ingredients. Beat with electric mixer. Yield: 1 loaf.

This recipe submitted by the following teachers:
Mrs. Mary Lois Larr, West Ottawa H.S.
Holland, Michigan
Mrs. Estella Hottel, Dimmitt H.S.
Dimmitt, Texas
Sister Mary Michel, S.N.D.
Mary Immaculate School for Exceptional Children
Toledo, Ohio

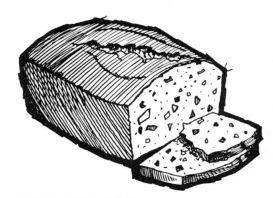

BANANA-NUT BREAD

2 c. flour
3½ t. baking powder
½ t. salt
½ c. sugar
½ c. nuts, finely chopped
1 egg, well beaten
1 c. ripe banana, mashed
¼ c. evaporated milk
⅓ c. oil or shortening, melted

Sift together dry ingredients. Fold in nuts. Combine remaining ingredients; add all at once to dry mixture. Mix quickly, but thoroughly. Pour into large greased loaf pan. Bake in 350°F. oven 50 minutes or until bread shrinks from sides of pan. Let stand in pan 5 minutes before turning out. Cool on wire rack. NOTE: This bread freezes very well.

Mrs. Marjorie Ewers, Lyndon Community H.S.
Lyndon, Illinois

BANANA-NUT LOAF

½ c. shortening
1 c. sugar
2 eggs, well beaten
1 c. mashed bananas
2-2¼ c. sifted flour
1 t. baking soda
Salt to taste
¼-1 c. nuts, coarsely chopped

Cream the shortening until soft; gradually add the sugar, creaming until fluffy. Add eggs and mashed bananas; mix well. Sift flour with baking soda and salt. Stir into creamed mixture. Add chopped nuts; stir. Turn into well greased and floured loaf pan or tube pan. Bake in 350°F. oven for 1 hour to 1 hour and 15 minutes. Place pan on rack. Cool for 10 minutes; then remove from pan.

This recipe submitted by the following teachers:
Mrs. Thordis K. Danielson, New Rockford H.S.
New Rockford, North Dakota
Mrs. Jeanette Nakano, Ewa School
Ewa, Hawaii
Mrs. Pat Vaughan, Fairfield H.S.
Fairfield, Illinois
Marel Bolger, Bentley H.S.
Flint, Michigan

PEANUT-BANANA BREAD

2 c. sifted flour
2 t. baking powder
1 t. salt
¼ t. soda
⅓ c. shortening
½ c. sugar
2 eggs
¾ c. bananas, mashed
½ c. peanuts, chopped

Combine flour, baking powder, salt and soda. Cream shortening and sugar. Add eggs and bananas. Combine mixtures. Add peanuts. Mix thoroughly. Turn into well greased 9x5x5-inch pan. Bake in 350°F. oven 60-70 minutes. Let cool in pan 5 minutes before turning out. Frost while still warm, if desired.

Clinette L. Wolf, West Concord H.S.
West Concord, Minnesota

BANANA-RAISIN BREAD

½ c. shortening
1 c. sugar
2 eggs
2 bananas, mashed
½ c. raisins
2 c. flour
1 t. soda
1 t. salt

Combine shortening, sugar, eggs, bananas and raisins. Sift together dry ingredients; add to first mixture and stir until just moistened. Bake in greased loaf pan at 350°F. for 1 hour.

Mrs. Sally Buys, Lakeshore H.S.
Stevensville, Michigan

BANANA-PUMPKIN-NUT BREAD

½ c. margarine
½ c. granulated sugar
½ c. (firmly packed) brown sugar
1 t. vanilla
2 eggs
½ c. pumpkin, cooked or canned
½ c. ripe banana, mashed
2 c. sifted flour
1¼ t. soda
¼ t. salt
1½ t. pumpkin pie spice
¼ c. wheat germ (opt.)
½ c. pecans or English walnuts, finely chopped

Cream margarine and sugars well. Add vanilla and eggs; beat until light and fluffy. Add pumpkin and banana; mix well. Sift dry ingredients together; add to first mixture. Beat until well blended. Fold in wheat germ and nuts. Pour into greased 9x5x3-inch loaf pan. Bake in 350°F. oven for about 1 hour or until it tests done. Turn out of pan. Cool on rack. Wrap well and store overnight before serving. Yield: 1 loaf.

Mrs. Doris Neill, Palco Rural H.S.
Palco, Kansas

CHEESE-BRAN BREAD

1½ c. sifted flour
1½ t. baking powder
½ t. salt
¼ t. soda
3 slices margarine
1 egg
⅓ c. sugar
1 c. buttermilk
1 c. All-Bran
1 c. Cheddar cheese, grated

Sift flour, soda, salt and baking powder together. Cream margarine, egg and sugar. Add dry ingredients alternately with milk. Fold in bran and cheese; spoon into well oiled loaf pan. Bake in 350°F. oven for 30-45 minutes. Yield: 8 servings.

Blanche Burns, Union H.S.
Strathmore, California

QUICK BRAN BREAD

2 c. All-Bran
2 c. flour
1 c. brown sugar
1 c. raisins
2 c. buttermilk
2 t. baking soda

Combine bran, flour, sugar and raisins. Mix soda and buttermilk; add to dry mixture. Pour into a greased loaf pan. Bake at 350°F. for 30 minutes. Yield: 1 loaf.

Ruth M. Bearup, Silver H.S.
Silver City, New Mexico

BROWN BREAD

1 box raisins or dates or mixed raisins and dates
2 T. butter (opt.)
3 t. baking soda
1 t. salt
2 c. boiling water
1¾-2 c. sugar
4 c. flour
2 eggs, beaten
½ to 1 c. nuts, chopped, (opt.)
1 t. vanilla (opt.)

Place raisins, butter, baking soda and salt in large bowl. Pour boiling water over all; cool. Add sugar, flour, eggs and nuts. Mix well; pour into five greased No. 2 cans, filling half full. Bake in 350°F. oven for 1 hour. Yield: 15-20 servings.

This recipe submitted by the following teachers:

Mrs. Larry Clark, Arkansas City Jr. College
Arkansas City, Kansas

Betty Milling, Greenwood Jr. H.S.
Greenwood, Mississippi

OLD FASHIONED STEAMED BROWN BREAD

2 c. graham flour
1 c. corn meal
½ c. sugar
2 t. soda
½ t. salt
⅔ c. molasses
2 c. sour milk or hot water
½ c. raisins

Combine dry ingredients. Add molasses and milk; stir until mixed. Add raisins. Grease molds or 3-lb. shortening can and covers. Use steamer or deep covered kettle with rack. Have water, to half the depth of mold, boiling rapidly. Keep water boiling; constantly and add more boiling water as needed. Steam 3 hours. If desired, uncover and place in 375°F. oven for 30 minutes to dry top.

Mrs. Carolyn Stone, Whitingham H.S.
Jacksonville, Vermont

BUTTER SWIRL LOAF

½ c. butter
2 eggs
½ c. sugar
2 c. flour
3 t. baking powder
½ t. salt
¾ c. milk

Melt butter; cool. Beat eggs until thick; gradually add ½ cup sugar and ¼ cup butter. Add dry ingredients alternately with milk, blending well after each addition. Turn into greased 9x5x3-inch pan. Sprinkle sugar and cinnamon mixture over batter. Pour remaining butter over top. Cut through the batter several times with a knife. Bake in 375°F. oven for 40 to 45 minutes until golden brown. Cool thoroughly.

TOPPING:

⅓ c. sugar
2 t. cinnamon
Combine for top of batter.

Jo Duncan, Adena H.S.
Adena, Ohio

CARROT BREAD

⅔ c. salad oil
1 c. sugar
2 whole eggs
1½ c. flour
½-1 t. soda
1 t. cinnamon
1 t. nutmeg (opt.)
⅛-½ t. salt
1-½ c. carrots, finely grated
½-1 c. pecans, chopped or walnuts
¾ c. raisins (opt.)

Cream oil and sugar. Add eggs. Sift together dry ingredients; add to creamed mixture. Add carrots, pecans and raisins. Mix thoroughly. Pour mixture into a greased loaf pan and bake in a 350°F. oven for 1 hour. Yield: 12 servings.

This recipe submitted by the following teachers:

Mrs. O. W. Fleming, A & M Consolidated H.S.
College Station, Texas

Mrs. Judy Emert, Sabetha Rural H.S.
Sabetha, Kansas

Geneva Franklin, Powderly H.S.
Paris, Texas

Lucia M. Ober, Exeter Public School
Exeter, Nebraska

CHERRY SWEET BREAD

2½ c. sifted flour
2 t. baking powder
½ t. soda
1 t. salt
½ c. golden raisins
½ c. red and green candied cherries, chopped
1 c. walnuts, chopped
¾ c. butter
1½ c. sugar
2 eggs
1 c. orange juice

Sift together dry ingredients. Sprinkle 1 cup of mixture over combined fruits and nuts. Cream butter and sugar thoroughly. Add eggs; beat until light and fluffy. Add dry ingredients and orange juice, stirring until just blended. Fold in floured nuts and fruit. Spoon batter into well greased 9-inch tube pan. Bake in 350°F. oven for 1 hour or until center tests done. Cool for 5 minutes; remove from pan. Frost; top with nuts, if desired. Yield: 12-14 servings.

Mrs. Anna M. Bryant, Galeton Joint School
Galeton, Pennsylvania

CRANBERRY BREAD

2 c. flour
½-1 t. salt
1½ t. baking powder
½ t. soda
1 c. sugar
1 egg, slightly beaten
3 T. shortening, melted
¾ c. orange juice or juice of 1 orange and
　enough water to make ¾ c. liquid
½ c. nuts
1-2 c. cranberries, cut in halves
Grated orange rind

Sift flour with dry ingredients; add beaten egg, melted shortening and orange juice. Combine only until dry ingredients are moistened. Fold in nuts, cranberries and orange rind. Turn into a greased loaf pan. Bake in 350°F. oven for 1 hour or until done. NOTE: This bread slices better after 24 hours refrigeration. Yield: 1 loaf.

This recipe submitted by the following teachers:
Mary L. Grady, Webb H.S.
Reedsburg, Wisconsin
Pauline Mathews, Fowler Public H.S.
Fowler, Michigan
Eleanor Sturman, Blue Ridge Consolidated H.S.
New Milford, Pennsylvania
Mrs. Gale Damhof, Manton Consolidated H.S.
Manton, Michigan
Mrs. Janelle Stage, C.E. Byrd H.S.
Shreveport, Louisiana
Mrs. Irene Robotham, Bellaire Public H.S.
Bellaire, Michigan
Jane Baker, Paducah H.S.
Paducah, Texas
Mrs. Carol Hawkins, Turlock H.S.
Turlock, California

DATE-NUT BREAD

¾ c. nuts, chopped
1 c. dates, chopped
1½ t. baking soda
½ t. salt
¼ c. shortening
¾ c. boiling water
2 eggs
½ t. vanilla
1 c. sugar
1½ c. sifted flour

Combine nuts, dates, soda and salt in mixing bowl. Add shortening and boiling water. Let mixture stand for 15 minutes; stir. Beat eggs slightly; add vanilla. Stir in sugar and sifted flour. Add to date mixture. Be careful not to overmix. Place in greased 9x5x3-inch loaf pan. Bake in 350°F. oven for 1 hour. Cool in pan before removing. Loosen sides with spatula or knife. NOTE: Allow to cool several hours before slicing. Yield: 10-15 slices.

Mrs. LeRoy Higley, Port Clinton Jr. H.S.
Port Clinton, Ohio

DATE-NUT BREAD

2 c. boiling water
4 c. dates, chopped
4 c. flour
4 t. soda
1 t. baking powder
½ t. salt
½ c. fat
1 c. sugar
2 eggs, beaten
1 t. vanilla
1½ c. pecans, chopped

Add boiling water to dates; cover and cool. Sift flour, soda, baking powder and salt together. Cream fat; add sugar gradually and cream well after each addition. Add eggs, vanilla and date mixture. Add flour mixture gradually; add nuts. Pour into oiled loaf pans. Bake at 350°F. for 1 hour and 30 minutes. Yield: 2 loaves.

Mrs. Karmen Setty, G.L. Dilworth Jr. H.S.
Sparks, Nevada

DATE-NUT BREAD

1 c. dates
1 t. soda
1 t. salt
¾ c. boiling water
¾ c. brown sugar
1 egg, separated
1½ c. flour
1 t. baking powder
1 c. walnuts

Cut dates in large pieces; add soda, salt and boiling water. Let stand while preparing other ingredients. Mix brown sugar and egg yolk; add date mixture. Add flour that has been sifted with baking powder. Fold in coarsely chopped nuts and beaten egg white. Pour into greased and floured 9x5x3-inch loaf pan. Bake in 325°F. oven for 1 hour. Yield: 1 loaf.

Mrs. Margaret K. Shollenberger, Union H.S.
Girard, Pennsylvania

DATE AND NUT LOAF

1½ c. boiling water
1½ c. dates, chopped
½ c. brown sugar
1 T. soft or liquid shortening
1 egg, beaten
2¼ c. flour
1 t. soda
½ t. salt
1 c. nuts, broken

Pour boiling water over dates; let cool. Mix sugar, shortening and egg. Stir in dates and water. Sift together dry ingredients. Add to sugar and date mixture. Blend in nuts. Pour into well greased 9x5x3-inch loaf pan. Let stand 20 minutes before baking. Bake in 350°F. oven for 60-70 minutes. Yield: 10-12 servings.

Mabel D. Beeman, Douglas County H.S.
Castle Rock, Colorado

FRUIT NUT BREAD

½ c. dried apricots
1 lge. orange
Boiling water
½ c. raisins
1 t. soda
1 c. sugar
2 T. butter, melted
1 t. vanilla
1 egg, beaten
2 c. flour
¼ t. salt
2 t. baking powder
½ c. chopped nuts

Soak apricots for 30 minutes. Squeeze juice from orange into cup. Fill cup with boiling water. Put apricots, orange rind, and raisins through food chopper. Add orange juice and water. Stir in soda, sugar, melted butter and vanilla. Add egg and remaining dry ingredients that have been sifted together. Add nuts. Pour into greased loaf pan. Bake in 350°F. oven for 1 hour. Turn out on cake rack to cool. Yield: 1 loaf.

Mrs. LaVera Kraig, Monroe Jr. H.S.
Aberdeen, South Dakota

GRAPENUT BREAD

1 c. sour milk
½ c. evaporated milk
½ c. grapenuts
1 egg
½ t. soda
2 t. baking powder
½ c. sugar
2 c. flour

Mix sour milk, evaporated milk and grapenuts; soak 30 minutes. Add egg and dry ingredients; pour into greased bread pan. Let rise 20 minutes. Bake in 350°F. oven for 45 minutes.

Mrs. Mildred Frazier, Sullivan County H.S.
Laporte, Pennsylvania

GUMDROP BREAD

3 c. sifted flour
¾ c. sugar
3½ t. baking powder
1 t. salt
1 egg, slightly beaten
2 T. salad oil
1½ c. milk
1 c. gumdrops, cut up
½ c. nuts, chopped

Sift dry ingredients. Combine egg, milk and oil. Add dry ingredients and mix. Fold in gumdrops and nuts. Pour into greased loaf pan. Bake in 350°F. oven 1 hour or until done.

Miriam E. Moorman, Mt. Clemens H.S.
Mount Clemens, Michigan

LIGHT NUT BREAD

1 egg, beaten
1 c. sugar
1 c. milk
2½ c. flour
2 t. baking powder
1 t. salt
1 c. chopped nuts

Stir together egg, milk and sugar. Sift together and add flour, baking powder and salt. Mix. Add nuts and pour into greased loaf pan. Let stand 30 minutes. Bake in 350°F. oven for 1 hour. Yield: 1 loaf.

Mrs. Marjorie Nagle, Ashtabula H.S.
Ashtabula, Ohio

OATMEAL BREAD

1 c. uncooked oats
1 c. milk, scalded
½ c. boiling water
⅓ c. shortening
½ c. (firmly packed) brown sugar
2 t. salt
2 pkg. dry yeast
½ c. lukewarm water
5 c. sifted flour

Put oatmeal in large bowl; stir in milk and boiling water. Add shortening, sugar and salt. Cool to lukewarm. Dissolve yeast in warm water. Add to oatmeal mixture with about half the flour; beat until smooth. Add remaining flour, a little at a time. Mix until dough comes away from sides of bowl. Turn onto lightly floured board; knead about 7 minutes; until smooth and elastic. Place dough in greased bowl; turn once to bring greased side up. Cover with a damp cloth; let rise in a warm place until double. Knead down; divide dough into two parts. Shape into loaves. Place in greased 9x4x3-inch loaf pans. Cover; let rise about 45 minutes in a warm place until double in size. Bake in 400°F. oven for 10 minutes reduce heat to 350°F. Continue to bake 40 minutes. Remove from pans immediately; cool on racks. Yield: 2 loaves.

Mrs. J. Dee Cates, Tempe Union H.S.
Tempe, Arizona

OATMEAL-CINNAMON BREAD

2 c. milk, scalded
2 c. rolled oats
½ c. (firmly packed) brown sugar
2 t. salt
2 T. shortening
1 pkg. yeast
¼ c. lukewarm water
4½-5 c. flour

Combine milk, oatmeal, sugar, salt and shortening. Cool to lukewarm. Dissolve yeast in lukewarm water; add to milk mixture. Add 2 cups flour, beating well. Add remaining flour to make a stiff dough. Turn out on floured surface. Knead about 8 minutes. Place in greased bowl.

(Continued on Next Page)

Cover; let rise about 1 hour and 30 minutes. Punch down; turn out on floured surface. Divide dough in half. Round out each portion. Let rise about 10 minutes. Roll into 9x15-inch rectangles.

FILLING:

4 T. sugar
2 t. cinnamon

Sprinkle dough with sugar mixture. Roll up as for cinnamon rolls. Place in greased loaf pans. Cover; let rise until center is well above pan. Bake in 375°F. oven for about 45 minutes.

Mrs. J. A. Myron, Chester H.S.
Chester, Montana

ORANGE BREAD

Rind of 6 oranges
1¾ c. sugar
3 c. flour
3 t. baking powder
½ t. salt
1 egg, beaten
1 c. milk

Cook until tender the peeling from 6 oranges. Grind fine through food chopper. Pack into cup. Add 1 cup sugar. Cook over low heat until thick. Sift together dry ingredients. Add sugar, egg, orange mixture and milk. Pour into greased loaf pan. Bake at 350°F. for 60 minutes. Cool and remove from pan. Wrap bread in foil. Yield: 1 loaf.

Dolores Jean Armstrong, Salem Community H.S.
Salem, Illinois

ORANGE-NUT BREAD

Juice and rind of 1 orange
Boiling water
1 c. sugar
2 T. shortening, melted
1 egg
1 t. vanilla
2 c. flour
¼ t. salt
1 t. soda
1 t. baking powder
Raisins
½ c. nuts, chopped

Add enough water to orange juice to make 1 cup. Grind orange rind. Combine juice with sugar, shortening, egg and vanilla. Add flour, salt, soda and baking powder. Add enough raisins with orange rind to make one cup. Add nuts; mix well. Pour into greased loaf pan. Bake in 350°F. oven for 50 minutes to 1 hour. Yield: 1 loaf.

This recipe submitted by the following teachers:
Mrs. Muriel Olson, Warroad H.S.
Warroad, Minnesota
Margaret N. Chickering, Keene State College
Keene, New Hampshire
Kathleen Gee, Medicine Lodge H.S.
Medicine Lodge, Kansas

ORANGE-CURRANT LOAF

3 c. biscuit mix
¾ c. sugar
1 egg
1¼ c. orange juice
1 T. grated orange rind
¾ c. currants

Combine biscuit mix and sugar; add egg and orange juice and beat well. Batter will be slightly lumpy. Add grated orange rind and currants. Divide batter equally into three well greased 1-pound tin cans, filling slightly more than half full. Bake, uncovered, in 350°F. oven for 45-50 minutes or until done. Cool 10 minutes; remove from cans. Cool thoroughly before slicing. NOTE: Batter may also be baked in greased 9x5x3-inch loaf pan. Yield: 3 loaves.

Marjorie Peterson, Pacific H.S.
San Bernardino, California

ORANGE-DATE LOAF

⅔ c. sugar
⅓ c. soft shortening
2 eggs
Juice and pulp of 1 orange
Water
2 c. sifted flour
1 t. baking powder
½ t. soda
½ t. salt
½ c. nuts, chopped
1 c. dates, cut up

Cream sugar and shortening. Add eggs. Add enough water to orange juice and pulp to make cup. Sift dry ingredients together. Combine with sugar and orange juice mixture. Blend in nuts and dates. Pour into well greased loaf pan. Let stand 20 minutes. Bake in 350°F. oven for 50-55 minutes.

Mildred Snell, Fitch H.S.
Youngstown, Ohio

PUMPKIN BREAD

2 eggs, beaten
1½ c. sugar
1 c. pumpkin
½ c. oil
¼ c. water
¼ t. baking powder
1 t. soda
¾ t. salt
½ t. cloves
½ t. cinnamon
1⅔ c. flour

Combine eggs and sugar; mix well. Add pumpkin, oil, and water. Blend thoroughly. Add all dry ingredients. Bake in soup or vegetable cans, filling them half full. Bake in 350°F. oven for about 1 hour. Yield: 15 servings.

Verlys M. Malme, Erskine H.S.
Erskine, Minnesota

Yeast Breads

MRS. BENELL'S RIZ BISCUIT

1-2 T. sugar
½ t. baking soda
½ cake yeast
1 c. warm buttermilk
3 T. rounded lard
2½ c. flour
½ t. salt
Butter, melted

Dissolve sugar, soda and yeast in buttermilk. Cut lard into flour. Combine salt and flour with buttermilk mixture. Roll dough ⅓-inch thick and cut with a round cutter. Dip each piece in melted butter and place one on top of another, (2 per biscuit). Let rise about 1 hour and 15 minutes. Bake in 425°F. oven for about 10 minutes.

Mrs. Elizabeth S. Caylor
Ball State Teachers College
Muncie, Indiana

ALL-BRAN ROLLS

1 c. shortening
⅔ to ¾ c. sugar
1 c. All-Bran or 100% Bran
1½ to 3 t. salt
1 c. boiling water
2 eggs, well beaten
2 cakes or pkg. yeast
1 c. lukewarm water
6 to 6½ c. flour

Combine shortening, sugar, All-Bran and salt. Add boiling water; stir until shortening melts. Cool to lukewarm; add eggs and yeast that has been softened in lukewarm water. Add 3 cups of flour; beat well. Add remaining flour and beat well. Knead until smooth. Place in greased bowl; cover. Let rise until double in bulk, about 1 hour. Shape into rolls. Allow to rise until double in bulk. Bake at 400-425°F. for 10 to 20 minutes. NOTE: If desired, dough may be refrigerated after kneading. Recipe may be halved. Yield: 36 rolls.

This recipe submitted by the following teachers:
Mrs. Kemper R. Russell, Logansport H.S.
Logansport, Louisiana
Helen Chase, Canby Public School
Canby, Minnesota
Mrs. Inez Calame Bennett, George West H.S.
George West, Texas
Marjorie M. DeSordi, Homer H.S.
Homer, Louisiana
Mrs. Rosemary McCoy, North Jr. H.S.
Waco, Texas
Mrs. Leon White, Jonesboro H.S.
Jonesboro, Texas

BUTTERHORNS

1 c. scalded milk
½ c. shortening
½ c. sugar
½ to 1½ t. salt
1 cake yeast or 1 pkg. dry yeast
2-3 eggs, beaten
4½ to 5 c. flour

Combine milk, shortening, sugar and salt. Cool to lukewarm. Add yeast and stir well. Add eggs and flour; mix to a smooth, soft dough. Knead lightly on floured surface. Place dough in a greased bowl. Cover & let rise until doubled in bulk. Divide dough into thirds; roll each third on lightly floured surface to 9-inch circle. Brush with melted butter; cut into 12 to 16 wedge-shaped pieces. Roll each wedge, starting with wide end. Place end of wedge on bottom to prevent the rolls from unrolling. Let wedges double in size before baking. Bake at 325°F. for 20-25 minutes, or at 400-425°F. for 10-15 minutes. NOTE: To freeze, bake at 275°F. until slightly brown and freeze immediately. Seal and keep sealed until ready for use. Bake at 450°F. for 10 minutes. If desired, rolls may be brushed with beaten egg before baking. Milk may be reduced to ¾ cup, and yeast dissolved in ¼ cup lukewarm water before adding. Yield: 18 servings.

This recipe submitted by the following teachers:
Mrs. Nan Dyer, Mission H.S.
Mission, Texas
Mrs. Jerald Volin, Mead H.S.
Mead, Nebraska
Mrs. Luella Robb, Round Valley H.S.
Covelo, California
Viola Nyhart, Danville H.S.
Danville, Ohio
Mrs. Joyce Unger, Colby H.S.
Colby, Kansas

CORN MEAL BUNS

1 pkg. active dry yeast
¼ c. warm water
2 c. milk, scalded
¼ c. butter or margarine
¼ c. shortening
½ c. sugar
1 T. salt
7½ c. sifted flour
2 eggs, beaten
1½ c. corn meal

Soften yeast in warm water. Set aside. Add butter, shortening, sugar and salt to milk. Cool to luke-warm. Add 3 cups flour, eggs, and yeast mixture. Beat until smooth. Mix in corn meal and 4½ cups flour. Knead 10 minutes. Place in greased bowl, turning once to grease surface. Cover; let rise until double in bulk. Punch down; shape into small balls. Place 2 balls in each cup of greased muffin pans. Brush with melted butter. Cover; let rise until double. Bake in 375°F. oven for 15 minutes. Yield: 3 dozen buns.

Mrs. Harold Poling, Bridgman H.S.
Bridgman, Michigan

CRESCENT ROLLS

1 c. milk
1 t. salt
¾ c. sugar
½ c. shortening, melted
1 cake soft yeast
3 eggs, slightly beaten
6-7 c. flour

Scald milk; add salt, sugar and shortening. Cool to lukewarm. Add crumbled yeast and eggs. Mix well. Gradually add 4 cups flour, beating thoroughly. Cover and let stand in warm place overnight. Beat until no bubbles remain; add enough more flour to make soft dough. Let rise to double in size. Roll in circle ¼-inch thick. Butter and cut in pie wedges. Roll from wide end to point. Let rise. Bake in 400°F. oven for 12-15 minutes or until brown. Yield: 3 dozen.

Mrs. Irene Brown, Wilmington H.S.
Wilmington, Illinois

EASY BUNS

2 pkg. yeast
2 c. warm water
6½ c. flour
2 t. salt
⅓ c. sugar
⅓ c. shortening
1 egg, beaten

Dissolve yeast in water. Stir in 2 cups flour, salt, sugar and shortening. Add egg; beat batter with egg beater. Add remaining flour; mix with spoon. Knead until smooth. Let rise 25 minutes or until doubled in bulk. Shape as desired. Bake in 425°F. oven for 12-20 minutes, depending on size.

Mrs. Don Dubbe, Sturgis H.S.
Sturgis, South Dakota

FANCY YEAST ROLLS

1 pkg. dry yeast
¼ c. water (105°F.)
¼ c. plus ½ t. sugar
2 eggs, beaten
¼ c. soft butter
½ c. evaporated milk
½ c. water
4½ c. flour, sifted
1¼ t. salt

Dissolve yeast in ¼ cup water with ½ teaspoon sugar. Combine eggs with ¼ cup sugar; butter, evaporated milk and ½ cup warm water. Add yeast to egg mixture. Sift flour with salt; combine with egg mixture. Cover and let stand 10 minutes. Knead dough until smooth and elastic. Place bowl of dough in a plastic bag and allow to rise twice. Shape rolls; place on greased pan in a plastic bag. Let rise and bake in 400°F. oven 15 minutes or longer. Yield: 30 average size rolls.

Agnes Van Oosten, Park County H.S.
Livingston, Montana

FAVORITE BUNS

2 cakes yeast
½ c. plus 1 T. sugar
1 c. lukewarm water
3 eggs, beaten
1 c. milk
6 T. shortening
1 t. salt
7 c. sifted flour

Dissolve yeast and 1 tablespoon sugar in warm water. Scald milk and cool to lukewarm. Add shortening, ½ cup sugar and salt. Add eggs and 2 cups of flour. Beat well. Let stand. Add remaining flour very gradually, beating after each addition. When possible put on floured board and knead until all of the flour has been worked into the dough. Do not use additional flour. Place in greased bowl; cover and set in a warm place free from draft. Let rise about 2 hours or until doubled in bulk. Make into rolls and let rise again. Bake in 350°F. oven for 20-25 minutes. Yield: 3 dozen.

Mrs. Wilmuth McBeth, Santa Paula Union H.S.
Santa Paula, California

NEVER-FAIL YEAST DOUGH

1 pkg. cake yeast
1 c. plus 1 t. sugar
1 c. milk, scalded
½ c. butter
3 eggs, beaten
4-5 c. flour, sifted
Butter, melted

Mix yeast and 1 teaspoon sugar. Combine milk, 1 cup sugar and butter; cool. Add yeast to milk mixture. Add eggs, flour and salt. Beat well; dough will be sticky. Place in greased bowl; cover and let rise until doubled in bulk or rrefrigerate overnight. Knead on floured board until bubbles appear. Shape as desired. Brush with butter; let rise until doubled in size. For dinner rolls, bake in 375°F. oven for 12-15 minutes; for pecan rolls, 350°F. 15-18 minutes; for tea rings, 350°F. 30-40 minutes. Yield: 3 dozen rolls, 2 tea rings or 3 dozen pecan rolls.

Rose Ann Bjorkman, Rockridge H.S.
Taylor Ridge, Illinois

ONE-HOUR BUTTERMILK ROLLS

2 cakes yeast
¼ c. warm water
3 T. sugar
½ c. shortening, melted
1½ c. lukewarm buttermilk
4½ c. flour
½ t. baking soda
1 t. salt

Dissolve yeast in warm water. Add sugar and shortening. Add remaining ingredients, beating until smooth. Let rise 10 minutes. Shape into rolls. Let rise 30 minutes. Bake in 400°F. oven for 15-20 minutes.

Mrs. Mary Yost, Warren H.S.
Vincent, Ohio

OLD PLANTATION ROLLS

1 c. scalded milk
¼ c. sugar
½ c. shortening
1 c. cold water
1 egg
1 cake compressed yeast
5½ c. flour
1 t. baking powder
½ t. soda
1½ t. salt

Combine milk, sugar and shortening. Stir until sugar and shortening are dissolved. Cool to lukewarm by adding 1 cup cold water. Add egg and yeast; mix well. Blend in 3 cups flour. Let stand for 20 minutes. Sift together 2½ cups flour, baking powder, soda and salt. Add to soft dough. Knead until dough forms blisters; place in a greased bowl and cover. Let rise for 1 hour. Shape into rolls. Let rise again. Bake in 400°F. oven for 15-20 minutes. Yield: 24 rolls.

Mrs. Loretta Baumbach, Sheyenne H.S.
Sheyenne, North Dakota

POTATO YEAST ROLLS

1 c. scalded milk
¼ c. shortening
½ c. sugar
1 c. mashed potatoes
6 c. bread flour
2 eggs, beaten
1 yeast cake
½ c. lukewarm water
1½ t. salt

Combine hot milk, shortening, sugar and mashed potatoes; cool to lukewarm. Add 1 cup flour; stir and add eggs. Dissolve yeast in lukewarm water. Combine yeast with milk and flour mixture; beat well. Cover; let rise untl mixture is full of bubbles. Add remaining flour to make a stiff dough. Knead unti dough is elastic. Cover; let rise to double in bulk. Shape the dough into rolls. Bake in 400°F. oven for 20-25 minutes.

Helen Hoermann, Jamestown H.S.
Jamestown, North Dakota

RICH DINNER ROLLS

1 c. milk
¼ c. sugar or honey
1 t. salt
¼ c. shortening or margarine
½ c. warm water
2 pkg. or cakes of yeast
2 eggs, beaten
5¼ c. flour

Scald milk; stir in sugar, salt and shortening. Cool to lukewarm. Place warm water in a large bowl. Sprinkle or crumble in yeast; stir until dissolved. Add lukewarm milk mixture, eggs and 2 cups

flour. Beat until smooth. Stir in enough remaining flour to make a soft dough. Turn on lightly floured board; knead until smooth and elastic. Place in a greased bowl. Cover; let rise about 30 minutes in warm place until double in bulk. Punch down. Turn on lightly floured board; shape as desired. Bake at 375-400°F. for 20-25 minutes. Yield: 2 dozen.

This recipe submitted by the following teachers:
Mrs. Minnie Anders, Lena H.S.
Lena, Wisconsin

Margaret Strain, Walnut Twp. Schools
New Ross, Indiana

Anita Mielke, Wild Rose H.S.
Wild Rose, Wisconsin

SPEEDIE ROLL DOUGH

1½ c. warm milk
⅓ c. sugar
⅓ c. shortening
3 t. salt
2 pkg. yeast
½ c. warm water
6½ c. sifted flour
2 eggs

Combine milk, sugar, shortening and salt. Dissolve yeast in warm water. Add to milk with 2 cups flour. Beat with electric mixer; add eggs, beating 1 minute. Work in remaining flour by hand to make stiff dough. Shape as desired. Place in greased pan. Let rise 40 or 45 minutes in warm place. Bake in 375°F. oven for 25-30 minutes. Brush with melted butter. NOTE: Rolls can be frozen.

Betty Ross, Sandwich H.S.
Sandwich, Illinois

THREE-HOUR ROLLS

¾ c. milk
¾ t. salt
¼ c. sugar
¼ c. shortening
2 cakes yeast
¼ c. warm water
1 egg, well beaten
3 c. flour
1 t. baking powder

Combine milk, salt, sugar and shortening in a large saucepan. Heat until milk is scalded and shortening melted. Cool until lukewarm. Crumble yeast into a small bowl; add warm water. Add the yeast and egg to milk mixture. Sift flour and baking powder together; stir in about a third at a time, mixing well after each addition. Add more flour if necessary, so dough will form a ball. Knead dough for about 10 minutes. Place in a greased bowl and let rise until doubled in bulk. Press down and let rise a second time. Press down and form dough into rolls. Let rise. Bake in 425°F. oven about 10 minutes. Yield: 24 rolls.

Mary Osborne, Washington H.S.
Massillon, Ohio

SUPER QUICK BUNS

1 lge. cake compressed yeast or 2 pkg. dry yeast
2 c. warm water
½ c. sugar
2 eggs
3 T. shortening
1 t. salt
7 c. flour

Soften yeast in warm water. Add sugar and eggs to yeast mixture and beat until foamy. Add shortening, salt and flour; mix with electric beater until elastic. Knead enough to mix well. Let rise until double in bulk. Make lightly into buns. Let rise. Bake in 400°F. oven 15-20 minutes. Yield: 36 servings.

Mrs. Charlotte Brainard
Fennimore Community Schools
Fennimore, Wisconsin

YEAST ROLLS OR DOUGHNUTS

1 c. lard
1 c. boiling water
3 eggs
¾ c. sugar
2 t. salt
2 cakes yeast
½ c. lukewarm water
1 c. cold water
8 c. flour

Mix lard and boiling water. Beat eggs; add sugar and salt. Soften yeast in lukewarm water. Add cold water to lard mixture. Stir in yeast, and egg mixture. Stir in flour. Turn on lightly floured board; knead until smooth. May be baked or refrigerated overnight. Form into desired shapes. Let rise. Bake in 375°F. oven for 15 minutes.

Martha Hair, Johnsville-New Lebanon H.S.
New Lebanon, Ohio

REFRIGERATOR ROLLS

¾ c. milk, scalded
6-7 T. sugar
1 T. salt
5 T. shortening
2 pkg. or cakes yeast
½ c. warm water
1 egg, beaten
4-4½ c. sifted flour

Dissolve sugar, salt and shortening in scalded milk. Cool to lukewarm. Dissolve yeast in warm water. Stir in milk mixture. Mix in egg. Add flour, 1 cup at a time, blending until a stiff dough is formed. Place in large bowl; brush top of dough with shortening. Cover with foil or waxed paper. Refrigerate at least 2 hours or overnight. Knead dough until blisters form on surface. Shape as desired. Let rise in warm place for 45 to 60 minutes. Bake at 400°F. for 12-15 minutes. NOTE: Dough will keep in refrigerator for 2 to 4 days. Yield: 2-3 dozen rolls.

This recipe submitted by the following teachers:
Peggy Baker, Monterey H.S.
Monterey, Tennessee
Thelma J. Malone, Crab Orchard H.S.
Marion, Illinois

THE BEST REFRIGERATOR ROLLS

1 c. boiling water
1 c. shortening
1 c. sugar
1½ t. salt
2 eggs, beaten
2 pkg. dry yeast
1 c. lukewarm or cold water
6 c. flour

Combine boiling water, shortening, sugar and salt. Blend and cool. Add eggs. Sprinkle yeast into lukewarm water; stir until dissolved. Combine with egg mixture. Blend in flour; cover and refrigerate for 4 hours. Dough should be in a large mixing bowl as it rises slightly in the refrigerator. This will keep a week to 10 days and may be used as needed. About 3 hours before using rolls, shape, using only enough extra flour to make them easy to handle. Place on greased pan and allow to rise for 3 hours at room temperature or until double in bulk. Bake in 425°F. oven for 12 to 15 minutes.

This recipe submitted by the following teachers:
Joanna C. Klock, Monument Valley H.S.
Kayenta, Arizona
Sara Thompson, Pineville H.S.
Pineville, Kentucky

ICE BOX BUNS

3 T. butter
½ c. sugar
Pinch of salt
2 c. milk, scalded
2 eggs
2 cakes or pkg. yeast
7 c. sifted flour

Combine butter, sugar, salt and hot milk; cool. Beat in eggs and yeast. Beat in 4 cups flour until smooth. Mix in remaining flour. Place in greased bowl; cover. Let stand in a cool place overnight or until doubled in bulk. Shape as desired and let rise until double. Bake for 15 minutes at 400°F. Brush with butter. Yield: 2½ to 3 dozen.

Miriam Erickson, Gibraltar Union H.S.
Fish Creek, Wisconsin

SQUASH ROLLS

½ c. squash
¼ c. sugar
¼ c. shortening
½ t. salt
½ c. scalded milk
½ cake compressed yeast
¼ c. lukewarm water
2½ c. flour

Combine squash, sugar, salt and shortening with milk; heat to lukewarm. Dissolve yeast in lukewarm water. Add to milk. Add flour and mix well. Dough will be soft. Let rise in a warm room until double in bulk. Knead and shape into pan rolls; let rise. Bake in 400°F. oven for 15-20 minutes. NOTE: Good for freezing and rewarming. Yield: 18 rolls.

Dorothy F. Kingsbury, Keene State College
Keene, New Hampshire

BASIC REFRIGERATOR ROLLS

1 cake or pkg. yeast
2 T. warm water
1½ T. margarine or shortening
¼ c. sugar
1 c. boiling water
1 t. salt
1 egg, beaten
3½-4 c. sifted flour

Dissolve yeast in 2 tablespoons warm water. Combine margarine, sugar, boiling water and salt; stir until lukewarm. Add egg, 2 cups flour and yeast mixture; beat thoroughly. Add remaining flour; knead. Place dough in a greased bowl. Grease top of dough. Refrigerate. When ready to use, put dough in a warm place for 1 to 1½ hours; shape into rolls. Let rise until double in bulk. Bake at 400°F. for 20 minutes, or at 425°F. for 12-15 minutes. NOTE: Dough will keep about a week. Dough may be used as a basic recipe for pocketbook rolls, cloverleaf rolls, or any desired roll. Yield: 18 colverleaf rolls.

This recipe submitted by the following teachers:
Sylvia Staudt, St. Anne H.S.
St. Anne, Illinois
Mrs. Helen R. Black, Round Valley H.S.
Eagar, Arizona

BUTTER AND HERB LOAF

2 cakes yeast
¼ c. warm water
⅓ c. shortening
¼ c. sugar
1 T. salt
1 c. scalded milk
2 eggs
4½-5 c. all purpose flour
½ c. soft butter
½ t. caraway seed
½ t. basil
½ t. onion, grated
¼ t. oregano
1 clove garlic, minced
1 t. cayenne

Break yeast into warm water; set aside. Combine shortening, sugar and salt with cooled milk. Blend in eggs and yeast mixture. Gradually add flour to form stiff dough. Knead gently for 2-3 minutes. Place in greased bowl. Cover and let rise 1½ hours. Combine remaining ingredients. Roll out half of dough to ⅛-inch thickness; cut into 5-inch circles using a large can as a cutter. Spread with butter mixture; fold in half. Stand semi-circles side by side on greased cookie sheet, folded side down; press edges together. Sprinkle with sesame or poppy seeds. Let rise 30-45 minutes. Bake in 350°F. oven for 20-25 minutes. Yield: 2 loaves.

Mrs. Judith Hamilton, Westmont H.S.
Campbell, California

BETTE'S BATTER BREAD

2 pkgs. dry yeast
2¾ c. warm water
6½ c. sifted flour
3 T. sugar
1 T. salt
2 T. soft shortening

Dissolve yeast in warm water in large mixing bowl. Add about half the flour, all the sugar, salt and shortening. Beat with mixer on medium speed about 2 minutes or until smooth. Add remaining flour and beat by hand about 1-1½ minutes until flour to blended. Scrape down batter from sides of bowl. Cover. Let rise in warm place about 30 minutes or until doubled in bulk. Beat hard for 30 seconds. This is a thick, somewhat sticky batter. Put into greased bread pans, spreading evenly. Let rise in warm place about 20-30 minutes or until edges of batter reach top of pans. Bake 40 to 50 minutes in preheated 375°F. oven. Remove from pans and cool on racks. Yield: 2 loaves.

Mrs. Bette D. Neal, Platte Valley H.S.
Saratoga, Wyoming

BUBBLE BREAD

1 c. milk, scalded
1 cake yeast
1¼ c. sugar
¼ c. shortening
2 eggs
1 t. salt
Flour
Butter, melted
1 t. cinnamon

Sprinkle yeast on cooled milk. Cream ¼ cup sugar, shortening and salt; add eggs. Combine with milk mixture. Add enough flour to make a soft dough. Place in a greased bowl; let rise until doubled in bulk. Pour dough onto floured board; pat out thin. Combine 1 cup sugar and cinnamon. Cut dough onto rounds with cutter; dip into melted butter, then into cinnamon and sugar mixture. Stand on end in tube pan. Let rise 1 hour and 30 minutes. Bake in 350°F. oven for 25 minutes.

Carol Kamrud, Kerkhoven H.S.
Kerkloven, Minnesota

CARDAMON RAISIN BREAD

1 pkg. yeast
½ c. plus 2 t. sugar
2¼ c. lukewarm water
½ c. sugar
1 T. salt
1 T. (heaping) shortening
6-8 c. flour
1 T. ground cardamon
2 c. raisins

Dissolve yeast with 2 teaspoons sugar and ¼ cup lukewarm water. Combine ½ cups sugar, salt, shortening and 2 cups water. Add yeast mixture;
(Continued on Next Page)

stir. Add flour to form stiff dough. Knead until smooth. Add raisins and cardamon; knead until blended well. Let rise until double in bulk. Work down and let rise until double again. Shape into 2 loaves. Place in greased loaf pans; let rise until double in bulk. Bake in 425°F. oven for 10 minutes; reduce heat to 350°F. and bake 50 minutes. Yield: 2 loaves.

Mrs. Shirley Andersen, Dalton H.S.
Dalton, Nebraska

CHEESE CASSEROLE LOAF

1 c. milk
3 T. sugar
1 T. salt
1 T. shortening
2 pkg. dry yeast
1 c. warm water
1 c. Cheddar cheese, grated
4½ c. sifted flour

Scald milk; add sugar, salt and shortening. Cool to lukewarm. Dissolve yeast in warm water; add to milk mixture. Add cheese and flour; blend well. Cover and let rise 45 minutes or until double in bulk. Stir batter down; beat 30 seconds. Turn into two greased 9x5-inch loaf pans. Bake, uncovered, in 375°F. oven for 1 hour. Yield: 2 loaves.

This recipe submitted by the following teachers:

Mrs. Janice Beck, Ansley Public School
Ansley, Nebraska

Zelma A. Cromer, Lexington H.S.
Lexington, Oklahoma

GRUYERE CHEESE POTATO BREAD

1 pkg. or cake yeast
½ c. scalded milk
3 c. sifted flour
1 t. sugar
1 t. salt
⅔ c. riced potatoes
⅓ c. butter melted
3 oz. Gruyere cheese, shredded
2 eggs

Soften yeast in milk. Sift together flour, sugar and salt. Combine riced potatoes, butter, cheese and eggs. Blend well. Add yeast and milk mixture with dry ingredients. Knead 5-8 minutes. Place in buttered bowl; let rise in warm place until doubled. Punch down. Knead for 2 minutes. Shape into a long roll and place in a well-buttered tube pan or ring mold. Pinch ends together to seal. Let rise in a warm place for 30 minutes. Bake in 375°F. oven for 25-35 minutes. Yield: 1 large loaf.

Catherine D. Magel, Eaton H.S.
Eaton, Ohio

DILLY CASSEROLE BREAD

1 pkg. yeast
¼ c. warm water
1 c. creamed cottage cheese
2 T. sugar
1 T. instant minced onion
1 T. butter
2 t. dill seed
1 t. salt
¼ t. baking soda
1 egg
2¼-2½ c. flour

Dissolve yeast in water. Heat cottage cheese to lukewarm. Combine sugar, onion, butter, dill seed, salt, baking soda and egg in a bowl with cheese and yeast mixture. Add flour to form stiff dough. Cover and let rise until doubled in bulk. Stir down dough. Turn into well greased 1½-quart casserole or 8-inch round pan. Let rise 30-40 minutes or until light. Bake in 350°F. oven 40-50 minutes. Brush with butter and sprinkle with salt. Yield: 1 loaf.

This recipe submitted by the following teachers:
Mrs. Janet Kugler Olmstead, Diamond Jr. H.S.
Lexington, Massachusetts
Mrs. Idy Bramlet, Niobrara County H.S.
Lusk, Wyoming
Mrs. Josephine Kelin, Morgan Public
Morgan, Minnesota
Mrs. Charlotte Tulloch, Elsie H.S.
Elsie, Michigan
Jeanne Mackie, Milwaukie H.S.
Milwaukie, Oregon
Sharron Altmaier, Pleasanton Public School
Pleasanton, Nebraska
Mrs. Carol Biere, Nebraska City H.S.
Nebraska City, Nebraska
Miriam R. Jamieson Frostproof Jr.-Sr. H.S.
Frostproof, Florida
Jeanne Yoxall, Stafford H.S.
Stafford, Kansas
Barbara Farrington, Slayton H.S.
Slayton, Minnesota
Mrs. Frank Anderson, Owosso H.S.
Owosso, Michigan
Faye Sadler, Perryville H.S.
Perryville, Arkansas
Mrs. Rosalie Millar, Edgemont H.S.
Edgemont, South Dakota
Mrs. Mary N. Davis, North Shore H.S.
Houston, Texas
Mrs. Carol Schubert, Hastings H.S.
Hastings, Nebraska
Mrs. Jerry Barton, Matthews Jr. H.S.
Lubbock, Texas
Mrs. Erna E. Peterson, Rush City Public Schools
Rush City, Minnesota

OATMEAL BREAD

2 pkg. dry yeast
½ c. warm water
1½ c. boiling water
1 c. oatmeal

(Continued on Next Page)

½ c. molasses
⅓ c. shortening
1 T. salt
6 c. white flour
2 eggs, beaten

Soften yeast in warm water; set aside. Combine boiling water, oatmeal, molasses, shortening and salt. Cool to lukewarm. Stir in 2 cups flour and eggs; beat well. Add yeast mixture; beat well. Add enough remaining flour to make soft dough. Grease top; cover tightly and refrigerate overnight. Shape into 2 loaves; let rise until doubled. Bake at 375°F. for 45 minutes. Yield: 2 loaves.

Ethel M. Buehl, Detroit Lakes Jr. H.S.
Detroit Lakes, Minnesota

MILK AND WATER BREAD

1 c. scalded milk
1 c. boiling water
2 T. butter
2½ t. salt
3 T. sugar
1 yeast cake
¼ c. lukewarm water
6-7 c. of flour

Combine milk, boiling water, butter, salt and sugar in large bowl. Add yeast dissolved in lukewarm water and 5 cups of flour. Stir until thoroughly mixed. Add remaining flour; mix and turn on floured board. Knead until dough is smooth and bubbles may be seen under the surface. Return to bowl. Cover; let rise 2-3 hours until double in bulk. Punch down; toss on slightly floured board. Knead well. Pour into 2 standard size greased loaf pans, half full. Cover; allow to double in bulk. Bake in 400°F. oven for 35 minutes; reduce heat to 375°F. the last 15 minutes of baking. Yield: 2 loaves.

Irene Kattenhorn, Union Hill H.S.
Union City, New Jersey

HERB BREAD

1 c. lukewarm milk
2 T. sugar
1½ t. salt
1 cake yeast
1 egg
½ t. nutmeg
1 t. dried sage, crumbled
2 t. caraway seeds
2 T. soft shortening
3-3¾ c. sifted flour

Combine milk, sugar and salt; crumble in yeast and stir until dissolved. Add remaining ingredients; knead on floured surface. Let rise and shape into loaf; place in greased 9x5x3-inch pan. Let rise 50-60 minutes until doubled. Bake in 375°F. oven for 45-50 minutes.

This recipe submitted by the following teachers:
Mrs. Ruth F. Gamble, Northern Potter Joint H.S.
Ulysses, Pennsylvania
Mrs. Luella Tupper, Lakeview H.S.
Battle Creek, Michigan

FREDERICKSBURG GRAHAM BREAD

1 pkg. yeast
½ c. warm water
2 T. shortening
½ c. (firmly packed) brown sugar
1 T. salt
¼ c. dark molasses
2 c. milk, scalded
3½ c. graham flour
1 egg, beaten
3 c. white flour

Dissolve yeast in warm water. Thoroughly blend shortening, sugar, salt, molasses, milk and graham flour; cool. Stir in egg and yeast; add white flour to make a stiff dough. Let rise 1 hour or until doubled. Knead well on a lightly floured surface. Place in a greased bowl; turn to grease top. Let rise until doubled. Shape into loaves; place in greased loaf pans. Let rise until doubled. Bake at 350°F. for 1 hour. Remove from pans and cool. NOTE: 2 cups whole wheat flour and 4½ cups white flour may be substituted for the proportions listed above.

This recipe submitted by the following teachers:
Mary Drazer and Martha Sommers, Kouts H.S.
Kouts, Indiana
Margaret Nowatzki, Hazen H.S.
Hazen, North Dakota

SOURDOUGH BREAD

STARTER:
1 pkg. or cake of yeast
2 c. warm water
2 c. flour

Dissolve yeast in water; add flour and mix well. Set in a warm place overnight. Put ½ cup starter in a scalded pint jar; cover tightly. Store in a cool place or in refrigerator for future use.

DOUGH:
4 c. sifted flour
2 T. sugar
1 t. salt
2 T. fat

Sift dry ingredients into a bowl, making a well in the center. Combine remaining starter and fat; pour into the well in flour. Mix well, adding more flour if necessary to make a soft dough. Knead on a floured board for 10-15 minutes. Place in a greased bread pan; let rise in a warm place for 2 hours or until light. Bake at 275°F. for 50-60 minutes. NOTE: To use stored sourdough starter, combine ½ cup starter with 2 cups warm water and 2 cups flour; beat well. Set in a warm place for 6-8 hours or overnight. Reserve ½ cup for future starter. The bread will not be distinctly sour until the starter has been in use for a time. The recipe can be varied by substituting 1 cup whole wheat for 1 cup white flour. Honey, brown sugar or molasses may be used instead of sugar. Yield: 1 loaf.

Patricia Roppel, Ketchikan H.S.
Ketchikan, Alaska

PRUNE BREAD

1 pkg. dry yeast
¼ c. warm water
2 c. milk, scalded
1 t. plus ½ c. sugar
2 t. salt
¼ c. shortening
1 c. cooked prunes, chopped
7 c. flour

Soak yeast in warm water with 1 teaspoon sugar for 10 minutes. Combine ½ cup sugar, salt and shortening with milk. Cool to lukewarm. Add half of flour; beat until smooth. Add yeast and prunes; beat well. Add enough flour to make soft dough. Knead 3 minutes; let rise to double in bulk. Punch down; make into loaves. Let rise. Bake in 350°F. oven for about 40 minutes. Yield: 2 large loaves.

Mrs. Laura Anderson, Sutherlin H.S.
Sutherlin, Oregon

NEVER FAIL SWEET RYE BREAD

⅓ c. molasses
⅓ c. white corn syrup
½ c. brown sugar
2 c. milk
2 T. shortening
1 T. salt
2 pkg. yeast
½ c. warm water
2 c. rye flour
2 c. white flour
Cream

Scald and cool molasses, corn syrup, brown sugar, milk and shortening. Add salt. Dissolve yeast in warm water and add to molasses mixture. Stir in flour to make a stiff dough. Let rise until doubled in bulk. Knead well, using as little flour as possible. Shape into two loaves and place in greased loaf pans. Cover and let rise until doubled in bulk. Bake in 425°F. oven for 30 minutes; reduce heat to 325°F. for 35 minutes. Place on rack to cool. Brush with cream while still warm. Yield: 2 loaves.

Sylvia Quie, Rosemount Jr. H.S.
Rosemount, Minnesota

ROOT BEER-RYE BREAD

½ c. lard
⅔ c. molasses
1 qt. root beer
2 pkg. dry yeast
½ c. lukewarm water
3 c. rye flour
7-8½ c. white flour

Melt lard; add molasses and root beer and heat. Dissolve yeast in warm water; add to mixture. Add rye flour and white flour; mix well and knead. Let rise until doubled in bulk; punch down. Shape into six loaves and let rise. Bake in 325°F. oven for 50-60 minutes. Yield: 6 loaves.

Mrs. Ladonna Nelson, Appleton Public School
Appleton, Minnesota

RICH BREAD

2 pkg. active dry yeast
½ c. warm water
1½ c. lukewarm milk
⅓ c. sugar
1 T. salt
3 eggs
⅓ c. soft shortening
7-7½ c. sifted flour

Dissolve yeast in warm water. Add milk, sugar, salt, eggs, shortening and half of flour. Mix with a spoon until smooth. Add enough remaining flour to handle easily; mix with hand. Turn onto lightly floured board; knead 5 minutes until smooth and elastic. Place in greased bowl; grease top. Cover with damp cloth. Place in warm place until double in bulk. Punch down; let rise again until double in bulk. Shape dough into desired shapes. Bake loaves in 425°F. oven for 25-30 minutes. Bake rolls in 400°F. oven for 15 minutes. Yield: 3 loaves or 2-3 dozen rolls.

Hazel Johnson, Basin H.S.
Basin, Wyoming

SAFFRON BREAD

2 pkg. dry yeast
2½ c. lukewarm milk
½ t. powdered saffron
¼ t. salt
1½ c. sugar
1 egg, beaten
1 c. butter or margarine, melted
8 c. flour
1 c. raisins

Dissolve yeast in ½ cup milk. Mix remaining milk, saffron, salt, sugar, egg and butter. Add small amount of flour; mix. Add dissolved yeast and enough flour to make a smooth batter. Add remaining flour gradually. Knead lightly; add raisins into dough while kneading. Place in greased bowl to rise. Turn out and shape into loaves. Let rise; bake in 350F°. oven for 45-60 minutes. Yield: 2-3 loaves.

Mrs. Janice Portice, West Branch H.S.
West Branch, Michigan

WHITE BREAD

½ c. warm water
2 pkg. dry yeast
3½ c. warm water, milk or potato water
¼ c. sugar
2 T. salt
10½-11½ c. flour
¼ c. shortening

Soak yeast in warm water 5 minutes. Combine liquid with sugar and salt in large bowl; stir to dissolve. Beat in 3-4 cups of flour, softened yeast mixture and shortening until smooth. Add remaining flour, mixing until dough leaves sides of bowl. Turn out on lightly floured board. Knead thoroughly, adding flour as necessary, about 5-10 minutes or until dough becomes smooth and elastic and is no longer sticky. Place in lightly greased bowl.

(Continued on Next Page)

Grease top of dough; cover with waxed paper. Let rise in warm place about 1 hour to 1 hour and 30 minutes or until doubled. Punch down and let rise again until nearly doubled. Divide dough in four equal parts and shape. Let rise in warm place until top and corners of pan is filled. Bake at 400°F. for 45 minutes. Cool on racks. Yield: 4 loaves.

Lois B. Jenkins, Franklin Joint School
Franklin, Pennsylvania

WHOLE WHEAT BREAD

3 pkg. yeast
3 c. lukewarm water
10-12 T. brown sugar
13 c. whole wheat flour
2 c. scalded milk
2 T. salt
6 T. soft shortening

Dissolve yeast in water; add 2 tablespoons sugar and 4 cups flour to make a sponge. Let stand 30 minutes. Mix salt, 10 tablespoons sugar and shortening together. Combine with sponge and add 9 cups flour. Knead well on floured surface. Place in bowl to rise double in bulk. Cover with damp cloth. Punch down and let rise again. Shape into 4 loaves; place in greased pans. Let stand 20 minutes. Bake in 350°F. oven for 1 hour. NOTE: If desired, honey or molasses may be substituted for brown sugar. Yield: 4 loaves.

Mrs. Marion Roy, Dunlap Community H.S.
Dunlap, Iowa

ENGLISH SALLY LUNN

2 pkg. active dry yeast
½ c. very warm water
1½ c. scalded milk, lukewarm
2 T. sugar
1½ t. salt
2 eggs
¼ c. soft shortening
5½ c. flour

Dissolve yeast in very warm water. Stir in cooled milk and remaining ingredients. Beat until smooth. Cover; let rise 1 hour. Beat down; pour into greased 10-inch tube pan. Let rise about 45 minutes to within 1 inch of top of pan. Bake in 450°F. oven 45-50 minutes. Serve hot. Yield: 16 servings.

Mrs. Elizabeth J. Pickel
Farmington Community H.S.
Farmington, Illinois

MY OWN SWEET ROLLS

2 pkg. granulated yeast
⅓ c. plus 1 T. sugar
¼ c. lukewarm water
2 c. milk
¼ c. butter
⅛ c. lard
1 t. salt
3 eggs, beaten
5-6 c. flour

Dissolve yeast and 1 tablespoon sugar in water. Scald milk, butter, lard, ⅓ cup sugar and salt; cool. Combine milk mixture, eggs and yeast. Add flour gradually until a soft dough is formed. Let dough rise twice. Roll out; cut with a round cookie cutter. Bake at 370°F. for 20-25 minutes. Yield: 12 servings.

Mildred McNutt, West Grant Schools
Patch Grove, Wisconsin

SWEET YEAST ROLLS

1 sm. cake yeast, crumbled
2 c. lukewarm water
7 T. melted shortening
⅓ c. sugar
1 T. salt
2 eggs
7 c. sifted flour

Dissolve yeast in 1 cup lukewarm water. Combine remaining ingredients except flour and yeast. Add yeast mixture after it becomes frothy. Gradually add flour; stir mixture until it is ready to knead. Knead it until of desired texture; grease bowl and knead again. Cover bowl with towel; set in warm place. Let rise; knead again. Mold into desired shapes. Let rise again. Bake at 400°F. for 15 minutes. Yield: 4 dozen.

Mrs. Margaret Linder, Mapleton H.S.
Mapleton, Minnesota

CROWN ROLLS

1½ c. warm water
1 pkg. active dry yeast
1⅓ c. sugar
1½ t. salt
⅔ c. soft shortening
2 eggs
1 c. lukewarm potatoes
7-7½ c. sifted flour
2 t. cinnamon
½ c. nuts, finely choped
½ c. butter, melted

Dissolve yeast in warm water. Add ⅔ cup sugar, salt, shortening, eggs and potatoes. Combine yeast and sugar mixture. Add flour until dough is easy to handle. Turn into lightly floured board. Knead until smooth and elastic. Place in ungreased bowl. Grease top; cover with damp cloth. Refrigerate or allow to rise at room temperature. Combine ⅔ cup sugar, cinnamon and nuts. Set aside. If using refrigerator method, about 2 hours before desired baking time, shape into balls. Dip pieces in melted butter, then in sugar and nut mixture, coating well. Arrange in well-greased 10-inch tube pan. Sprinkle remaining sugar and nut mixture over top. Cover. Let rise 30-60 minutes or until doubled in size. Bake in 375°F. oven 30-35 minutes. Yield: 1-10 inch ring and 1½-2 dozen medium rolls.

Mrs. Kathleen F. Kerr, Shippensburg H.S.
Shippensburg, Pennsylvania

WALNUT POTICA

FILLING:

2 eggs, beaten
¾ c. walnuts
½ c. raisins
½ c. honey
2 T. butter
1 t. cinnamon
1 t. vanilla

Combine ingredients. Cook on low heat until thick; cool.

DOUGH:

1 c. milk, scalded
¼ c. butter
½ c. sugar
2 eggs
1 t. salt
1 cake yeast
⅛ c. warm water
4½ c. flour

Combine milk and butter. Cool to lukewarm; add eggs, sugar and salt. Dissolve yeast in warm water. Add yeast and flour to mixture. Knead dough about 10 minutes. Let rise 1 hour until double in bulk. Roll out to a 9-inch circle on floured surface. Roll dough as thin as possible. Spread filling on dough. Roll up as for jelly roll. Let rise 1 hour. Bake in 325°F. oven for 1 hour.

Mrs. Joseph Matanich, Mountain Iron H.S.
Mountain Iron, Minnesota

EXTRA SPECIAL CINNAMON ROLLS

2 pkg. active dry yeast
2½ c. warm water
1 T. plus ½ c. granulated sugar
¼ t. ginger
2 t. salt
2 eggs, well beaten
8 c. flour
2 c. raisins, steamed and cooled
½ c. shortening
Butter, melted
1 lb. plus ⅓ c. brown sugar
9 t. cinnamon
1 c. heavy cream, whipped
½ t. vanilla
Nuts chopped (opt.)

Dissolve yeast in ½ cup water with 1 tablespoon sugar and ginger. Add 2 cups warm water, ½ cup sugar, salt, eggs and 3 cups flour. Beat well; allow to set until light. Add raisins, shortening and enough flour to make a soft dough. Knead until smooth. Let rise until double in bulk. Divide dough into fourths; roll each piece about 22 inches long and ¼-inch thick. Spread with melted butter. Combine 1 pound brown sugar with 8 teaspoons of cinnamon for dough. Sprinkle top of dough with brown sugar mixture. Roll as for jelly roll. Cut into 1-inch pieces. Place in greased pans. Let rise until double in bulk. Combine cream, ⅓ cup brown sugar, 1 teaspoon cin-

namon and vanilla. Spread mixture on rolls. Add nuts, if desired. Bake in 375°F. oven for 25 minutes or until done. Remove from pans immediately.

GLAZE:

1 lb. confectioners' sugar
2½ t. vanilla
Pinch of salt
3 T. butter, melted
hot milk

Combine ingredients for glaze. Frost rolls. Yield: 7 dozen.

Mrs. Ruth Leach, Bird City Rural H.S.
Bird City, Kansas

CHERRY HOT CROSS BUNS

1 13¾-oz. pkg. hot roll mix
¼ c. chopped green glace cherries
¼ c. chopped red glace cherries
1¼ c. sifted confectioner's sugar
5 t. milk
1 8-oz. jar red, stemmed Maraschino cherries

Prepare hot roll mix according to package directions adding chopped glace cherries. After rising, shape into 1½-inch balls and place on greased baking sheets. Let rise in a warm place until doubled in size. Cut deep cross in each bun with scissors. Bake in 400°F. oven for 10-15 minutes or until golden brown. Cool slightly. Combine sugar and milk, mixing until smoth. Pour into crosses. Top with whole Maraschino cherries. Yield: About 18 buns.

Photograph for this recipe on inside back cover

HOT CROSS BUNS

1¼ c. milk
¼ c. shortening, melted
⅓ c. plus 1 t. sugar
½ t. salt
1 cake compressed yeast
2 T. lukewarm water
1 egg, well beaten
½ c. seedless raisins
3½-4 c. sifted flour
1 egg white, slightly beaten

Scald milk; add shortening, ⅓ cup sugar and salt. Cool to lukewarm. Dissolve yeast and 1 teaspoon sugar in lukewarm water. Stir yeast into milk mixture. Add egg, raisins and enough flour to make stiff dough. Place in greased bowl; cover. Let rise until double in bulk. Toss onto floured board and roll to ½-inch thickness. Cut with cookie cutter. Brush each bun with egg white. Cover; let rise again. Bake in 400°F. oven for 15-20 minutes. When cool, make a cross on each bun with powdered sugar icing. Yield: 2 dozen.

Verlys M. Malme, Erskine H.S.
Erskine, Minnesota

RAISED CINNAMON PUFFS

¾ c. scalded milk
¼ c. lukewarm water
1 c. whole bran cereal
¼ c. shortening
¼ c. sugar
1 t. salt
1 pkg. yeast
1 egg, well beaten
2¾ c. sifted flour

Combine milk, bran cereal, shortening, sugar and salt. Stir until shortening is dissolved. Cool to lukewarm. Dissolve yeast in lukewarm water. Ad to bran mixture. Stir egg and flour in thoroughly. Knead until smooth and elastic. Place in a greased bowl; grease top. Cover; let rise until double in bulk. Punch down; let rise 10 minutes. Half fill greased muffin pans with balls of dough. Cover; let rise until double in bulk. Bake in 375°F. oven about 20 minutes or until done.

TOPPING:

½ c. butter or margarine
2 t. cinnamon
⅔ c. sugar

While still hot, roll puffs in melted butter; dip in cinnamon and sugar mixture.

Mrs. Mary Brownell, Orting H.S.
Orting, Washington

GLAZED ORANGE ROLLS

1 c. scalded milk
½ c. shortening
⅓ c. sugar
1 t. salt
1 yeast cake
¼ c. lukewarm water
2 eggs, well beaten
¼ c. orange juice
2 T. orange rind, grated
5 c. sifted flour

Combine milk, shortening, sugar and salt. Soften yeast in warm water; add eggs, orange juice and rind. Combine yeast and milk mixtures; beat well. Add flour and mix to a soft dough. Cover; let stand for 10 minutes. Knead for 5-10 minutes; let rise until double in bulk. Punch down; let stand for 15 minutes, then shape. Cover and let rise. Bake at 400°F. for 12 minutes.

GLAZE:

2 T. orange juice
1 t. orange rind
1 c. sifted confectioner's sugar
Blend ingredients; brush on tops of warm rolls. Yield: 2 dozen.

This recipe submitted by the following teachers:
Mrs. Garnet C. Jackson, Indio H.S.
Indio, California
Mrs. Merry Emme, Chamberlain H.S.
Chamberlain, South Dakota

PETAL COFFEE CAKE

1 pkg. hot roll mix
¾ c. granulated sugar
¼ c. brown sugar
2 t. cinnamon
¾ c. nuts, chopped
½ c. butter, melted
½ c. powdered sugar, sifted
1-2 t. milk

Prepare dough; let rise according to package directions. Combine sugars, cinnamon and nuts. Place a 14-inch sheet of heavy duty aluminum foil on cookie sheet. Grease foil and turn up edges to form a 12-inch round pan. Pinch off a small piece of dough. Roll piece into a 6-inch strip about ½-inch thick. Dip strip in butter, then in sugar-nut mixture. Wind into a flat coil in center of foil pan. Continue making strips, placing them close together to make a round, flat coffee cake. Sprinkle any remaining sugar and nut mixture over top. Cover; let rise about 30 minutes or until double in size. Bake cake in 350°F. preheated oven about 30 minutes or until done. Drizzle top of cake with a glaze made with powdered sugar and milk, if desired. Yield: 24 servings.

Mrs. Verda E. McConnell, Adams City H.S.
Adams City, Colorado

CHRISTMAS STOLLEN

1 yeast cake
¼ c. warm water
1 qt. milk, scalded
2 c. sugar
½ lb. butter
½ lb. shortening
3 eggs
1 t. salt
½ t. nutmeg
1 lemon, juice and grated rind
1 orange, juice and grated rind
5 c. flour
1 lb. white raisins
¼ lb. citron, chopped
1 lb. candied cherries, chopped
1 lb. candied fruits, chopped
1 lb. candied pineapple, chopped
½ lb. Brazil nuts, chopped

Soften yeast in lukewarm water. Stir in warm milk sugar, butter, shortening, eggs, salt, nutmeg, juice and rind of lemon and orange and half of flour. Add fruits and nuts. Add enough remaining flour to stiffen dough. Let rise several hours; shape into loaves and let rise. Bake in 350°F. oven for 1 hour or until done. Yield: 6 loaves.

Mrs. Patricia Jochimsen, Thorp H.S.
Thorp, Wisconsin

CINNAMON RING

⅓ recipe of any sweet dough
¼ lb. butter, melted
Cinnamon
Sugar
Nuts, (optional)

Use any sweet bread dough. After first rising, roll dough out about ½-inch thick on a lightly floured board. Cut with small biscuit cutter. Dip each ring in melted butter, then in cinnamon and sugar mixture. Stand each ring up in a well buttered ring mold. Fill ring mold solidly with rings of dough. Sprinkle a mixture of melted butter, cinnamon and sugar over top of ring. Chopped nuts may be added if desired. Let rise until double. Bake in 375°F. oven for 25-30 minutes.

Idella Reisch, Regent Public School
Regent, North Dakota

RAISED DOUGHNUTS

1 pkg. active dry yeast
¼ c. warm water
¾ c. milk, scalded
½ c. butter
¼ c. sugar
1 t. salt
2 eggs, well beaten
4 c. sifted flour

Soften yeast in water. Combine milk, butter, sugar and salt. Cool to lukewarm. Add eggs and yeast to milk mixture. Mix well. Add half the flour. Beat until smooth. Add remaining flour; beat well. Cover. Chill overnight. Turn onto floured board. Roll ¼ inch thick. Cut for doughnuts, cruellers or bowknots or as desired. Let rise about 35 minutes until almost doubled in bulk. Fry in deep fat at 375°F. until brown. NOTE: Dough will keep up to 4 days. Yield: 2½ to 3 dozen doughnuts.

Mrs. Mina F. Robinson, Perry H.S.
Perry, Kansas

CURRANT BREAD

2 pkg. dry yeast
2 c. warm water
2 c. hot water
3 c. sugar
3 t. salt
1 c. shortening
1 c. butter
18 c. flour
1 t. cinnamon
1 t. nutmeg
3 eggs, beaten
1½ c. mashed potatoes
1 lb. raisins
1 lb. currants
½ lb. citron

Soften yeast in 1 cup warm water. Mix hot water with sugar, salt and shortening. Mix until blended. Add 1 cup of water. Cool to lukewarm. Combine yeast with sugar mixture. Add 9 cups flour, nutmeg and cinnamon; beat for 1 minute. Add 3 eggs; blend thoroughly. Add mashed potatoes. Add remaining flour. Add raisins, currants and citron. Let rise overnight. Place in pans; let rise again. Bake in 400°F. oven for 40-45 minutes. Yield: 5 loaves.

Mrs. Edna L. Ernst, Blue Mountain Joint School
Schuylkill Haven, Pennsylvania

HOLIDAY FRUIT BREAD

½ c. butter
½ c. milk, scalded
1 pkg. or cake yeast
½ c. warm water
¼ c. sugar
1 t. salt
1 c. raisins
½ c. candied fruit
1 egg, slightly beaten
3½ to 4 c. flour

Melt butter in scalded milk; cool to lukewarm. Soften yeast in warm water; add sugar, salt, raisins, candied fruit, all but 1 tablespoon of egg and milk mixture. Mix well. Gradually add flour to form a stiff dough, beating well after each addition. Let rise until doubled in size. Turn out on floured surface; toss lightly until dough is covered with flour, but not sticky. Shape into two round loaves and bake in 8-inch round pans. Cover. Let rise about 1 hour or until double in size. Brush with reserved egg. Bake in 350°F. oven 30-35 minutes. Yield: 2 loaves.

Mrs. Dorothy Johnson, Forest Lake H.S.
Forest Lake, Minnesota

SUGAR PLUM LOAF

2 pkg. dry yeast
¼ c. warm water
1 c. milk, scalded
½ c. sugar
¼ c. shortening
1½ t. salt
4-4½ c. flour
1 t. grated lemon peel
2 eggs, beaten
1 c. candied fruit

Soften yeast in warm water. Combine milk, sugar, shortening and salt. Cool to lukewarm. Add 2 cups flour and lemon peel. Beat until smooth; beat in eggs and yeast. Add fruits. Stir in remaining flour to make soft dough. Cover; let rise 10 minutes. Knead on lightly floured surface until smooth and elastic. Place in greased bowl; cover and let rise until doubled. Punch down. Divide in half; let rise 10 minutes. Place in greased loaf pans. Bake in 350°F. oven for 25-30 minutes. Frost with confectioner's icing. Yield: 2 loaves.

Mrs. Mary Edge, Augusta H.S.
Augusta, Wisconsin

LEMON TWISTS

½ c. boiling water
½ c. sugar
⅔ c. soft margarine
½ c. evaporated milk
2 yeast cakes
½ c. lukewarm water
1½ T. lemon extract
2 eggs, well beaten
3 egg yolks, well beaten
7 c. sifted flour
1 t. salt
Butter, melted

Combine boiling water, sugar and margarine, stirring until margarine is dissolved. Add evaporated milk. Cool. Dissolve yeast in warm water. Mix lemon extract with eggs. Combine all ingredients. Sift flour and salt into liquid mixture. Mix well. Place in greased bowl; cover with damp cloth. Let rise until double in bulk. Roll into rectangle; spread with melted butter. Fold in thirds. Cut into 1-inch strips and twist. Place on greased pan. Let rise 45 minutes. Bake in 425°F. oven for 8-10 minutes.

LEMON ICING:

2 c. confectioner's sugar
2 T. lemon juice
2 T. hot water
1 T. grated lemon rind

Combine ingredients. Beat well until smooth Spread over twists. Yield: 3 dozen.

Mrs. Norman Stewart, New Boston H.S.
New Boston, New Hampshire

ORANGE BREAD

1 pkg. yeast
¼ c. lukewarm water
⅓ frozen Florida orange juice concentrate, thawed, undiluted
¼ c. hot water
¼ c. sugar
3 T. melted shortening
1 t. salt
3 c. sifted flour
1 egg
½ t. grated Florida orange rind

Dissolve yeast in lukewarm water. Combine orange concentrate, hot water, sugar, shortening and salt; stir well. Cool to lukewarm. Stir in 1 cup flour, then yeast. Add egg and orange rind; beat hard. Stir in 1½ cups flour. Sprinkle bread board or pastry cloth with remaining flour. Turn dough out and knead, adding flour as needed. Knead until dough is soft and satiny. Shape into ball; place in lightly oiled bowl. Cover. Let rise in warm, draft-free place about 2 hours, or until doubled in bulk. Punch down; let rest five minutes. Place in lightly greased 9x5x2¾-inch loaf pan. Cover and let rise about 1 hour or until doubled. Bake at 350°F. for 40-45 minutes. Yield: 1 loaf.

Photograph for this recipe on page 325

SWEET ORANGE BREADS

½ c. milk, scalded
¾ c. sugar
1½ t. salt
¾ c. warm water
3 pkg. or cakes Fleischmann's yeast
4¾ c. unsifted flour
¾ c. margarine
3 eggs, beaten
1 T. grated orange rind

Stir ¼ cup sugar and salt into scalded milk; cool to lukewarm. Dissolve yeast in warm water. Stir in milk mixture and 2 cups flour. Beat until smooth. Cover; let rise in warm, draft-free place for about 20 minutes or until light. Cream margarine until light and fluffy. Stir and beat margarine, remaining sugar, eggs and orange rind into yeast mixture with a spoon. Stir in remaining flour; beat hard until smooth and somewhat elastic, about 1 minute. Proceed with one or more variations given below. One-third of batter makes 1 loaf.

ORANGE FROSTING:

1 c. confectioner's sugar
2 T. orange juice
1 t. grated orange rind

Turn one-third of batter into well greased 9x5x3-inch loaf pan. Cover and let rise in warm, draft-free place for about 1 hour. Bake at 375°F. for 25-30 minutes or until done. Cool and frost with combined sugar, orange juice and orange rind.

SPICED FRUIT BREAD:

½ c. seedless raisins
½ c. chopped pecans
½ c. chopped mixed candied fruit
½ t. cinnamon
½ t. ginger
¼ t. nutmeg

Lightly toss together all ingredients. Mix well with one-third of batter. Turn into well greased 1½-quart mold. Cover; let rise in warm, draft-free place about 1½ hours. Bake at 375°F. for 25-30 minutes or until done. Cool. Sprinkle with confectioner's sugar if desired.

DOUBLE-CRUMB COFFEE CAKE:

½ c. sifted flour
⅓ c. (packed) brown sugar
½ c. chopped pecans
¼ c. margarine
1½ t. cinnamon

Rub together with fingers until crumbly the combined ingredients. Sprinkle half of mixture in bottom of greased 8-inch layer cake pan. Turn one-third of batter over crumb mixture. Top with remaining crumb mixture. Cover; let rise in warm draft-free place about 1 hour. Bake in 350°F. oven for 30-35 minutes or until done. Cool. Drizzle with confectioner's icing.

Photograph for this recipe on page 353

Breads From Foreign Lands

CHRISTMAS TWIST HOESKA (BOHEMIA)

1 pkg. yeast
1 c. scalded milk
1 c. sugar
1 c. warm cream
8 c. flour
1 c. butter
5 eggs, well beaten
⅛ t. mace
2 t. salt
1 t. grated lemon rind
1 c. nuts, chopped
1 c. raisins
½ c. candied fruit

Dissolve yeast in cooled milk; add sugar to cream. Blend flour and butter; add eggs and mix well. Add milk and cream to flour mixture. Add mace, salt and lemon rind. Knead well and let rise for 1½ hours. Punch down and work in remaining ingredients; let rise until light. Roll out on a floured board; cut into 9 strips. Braid 4 strips together; braid 3 strips and remaining 2 strips. Place braids on top of each other; bake at 350°F. for 1 hour and 15 minutes. NOTE: If desired, brush top with egg beaten with 1 tablespoon milk and sprinkle with nuts.

Carolyn Mae Horky, Fremont Jr. H.S.
Fremont, Nebraska

HOUSKA (CZECHOSLOVAKIA)

2 pkg. yeast
1½ c. lukewarm water
½ c. butter
½ c. sugar
2 eggs, well beaten
1 c. lukewarm milk
2 t. salt
6 c. flour
1 T. lemon juice
1 T. lemon rind
½ c. nuts
⅓ c. fruits and peels or candied cherries and
    raisins

Dissolve yeast in ½ cup lukewarm water 5 minutes. Crumble butter and sugar together. Add eggs; beat. Add yeast, milk, water, salt and 2 cups flour, mixing thoroughly after each addition. Let dough rise about 15 minutes. Add lemon juice and remaining flour. Mix in thoroughly; knead about 10-15 minutes. Let rise about 1 hour. Add remaining ingredients before last rising. Cut into strips and braid three strips into a loaf. Let rise. Bake in 350°F. for 40 minutes. Frost, if desired. Yield: 2 medium loaves.

Barbara Helt, Williston H.S.
Williston, North Dakota

AEBLESKIVERS (DENMARK)

2 c. buttermilk
2 c. flour
2 t. baking powder
½ t. salt
½ t. soda
2 T. sugar
4 T. butter, melted
2 eggs, separated

Combine all ingredients except egg whites; beat until smooth. Fold in beaten egg whites. Bake in well greased cups of a Danish Aebleskiver pan. Fill each cup about three-fourths full. Bake at 375°F. until golden brown; turn in cup with a fork or knitting needle and brown other side. They will be in shape of a ball. NOTE: A piece of apple, raisins or a nut may be placed in the middle of each skiver just before turning. May be rolled in sugar after baking and served with syrup or honey.

Lucile Haney, Geddes Independent
Geddes, South Dakota

COFFEE KRINGLE (DENMARK)

¼ c. milk
2 c. sifted flour
3 T. plus ¼ c. sugar
½ t. salt
¼ c. margarine
½ c. warm water
2 pkg. or cakes yeast
1 egg, beaten
1½ c. stewed prunes, chopped
3 T. lemon juice
½ t. grated lemon rind

Scald milk; cool to lukewarm. Combine flour, ¼ cup sugar and salt; cut in margarine with pastry cutter. Dissolve yeast in warm water; add milk, egg and flour mixture. Stir until well blended. Place in a greased bowl; turn to grease top. Cover and let rise in a warm place, until doubled in bulk. Combine prunes, 3 tablespoons sugar, lemon juice and lemon rind; set aside. Punch dough down; turn out onto a well floured board. Divide in half; roll each portion to a 16x12-inch rectangle. Place half on a greased 15x10x-1½-inch pan; spread with prune mixture. Cover with second half of dough; seal edges well. Cover; let rise in warm place 30 minutes or until doubled in bulk. Bake in 350°F. oven for 20 minutes. Turn out of pan at once. When cool, ice with confectioner's sugar frosting, if desired. Yield: 8-10 servings.

Faye Arney, Merritt Hutton H.S.
Denver, Colorado

AEBLESKIVER—PANCAKE BALLS (DENMARK)

4 eggs, separated
1 t. salt
2 T. sugar
⅓ c. butter, melted
1 t. nutmeg
1¾ c. rich milk
2 c. sifted flour
3 t. baking powder

Beat egg yolks well; add salt, sugar, shortening, nutmeg and milk. Mix well; add flour and baking powder, sifted together. Fold in beaten egg whites. Fill a greased munk pan two-thirds full; bake at 375°F. until half cooked. Turn with a sharp pointed fork; bake until golden brown. NOTE: Cardamon or lemon flavoring may be added to batter. Currants, seedless raisins or a small piece of apple may be added to Aebleskivers before turning.

Mrs. Beaulah Schroeder, Weed H.S.
Weed, California

PUFFS (DENMARK)

2 c. sifted flour
1 c. butter
1 t. almond flavoring
1 c. sifted flour
3 eggs

Cut ½ cup butter into 1 cup flour. Sprinkle with 2 tablespoons water; mix with a fork. Shape into a ball; divide in half. Pat into two 12-13 inch strips. Place 3 inches apart on an ungreased baking sheet. Mix remaining butter and 1 cup water; bring to boil. Remove from heat; add flavoring. Beat in flour, stirring quickly to prevent lumping. Add eggs, one at a time, beating well after each addition until smooth. Spread evenly over each piece of pastry. Bake in 350°F. oven, 1 hour or until topping is crisp and browned. NOTE: Frost with a confectioner's sugar icing and sprinkle with chopped nuts. Yield: 8-12 servings.

Mrs. Emma Meyer, Florence H.S.
Florence, Wisconsin

ROLLS (DENMARK)

4½ c. flour
1 c. butter
1 c. scalded milk
¼ c. sugar
1 T. dry yeast
¼ t. salt
4 eggs

Mix flour and butter as for pie crust. Combine milk, sugar, yeast, salt and eggs. Add to dry ingredients. Stir well. Refrigerate overnight. Knead on a floured board; shape into rolls or coffee cakes. Place on a greased pan and let rise 1 hour. Bake at 375°F. for 20 minutes. Yield: 30 rolls or 2 big coffee cakes.

Ruth J. Severson, Zion-Benton H.S.
Zion, Illinois

COFFEE TWIST (DENMARK)

1 pkg. dry yeast
¼ c. very warm water
½ c. milk, scalded
¼ c. sugar
1 t. salt
2 T. shortening, melted
1 egg
2¾-3 c. sifted flour

Sprinkle yeast over water; stir until dissolved. Combine milk, sugar, salt and shortening; cool and add yeast, egg and 1 cup flour. Beat vigorously; stir in 1½ cups flour. Knead dough and work in remaining flour. Let rise until doubled in bulk. Punch down; let rest 5-10 minutes. Roll out to a sheet 6 inches wide and ¼ inch thick.

FILLING:
1 T. soft margarine
3 T. sugar
½ t. cinnamon
¼ c. slivered almonds

Spread dough with margarine. Sprinkle with cinnamon and sugar mixture. Roll up and seal edges. Twist roll and form into a circle on a greased baking sheet. Cover and let rise until doubled. Bake at 350°F. for 25-30 minutes. Brush with butter and sprinkle with almonds.

Martha R. Phillips, Kennett H.S.
Conway, New Hampshire

DANISH PASTRY

1 pkg. yeast
¼ c. lukewarm water
1 c. scalded milk
2 T. plus ⅓ c. sugar
1 t. salt
1¼ c. shortening
3 eggs
¼ t. vanilla
½ t. lemon extract
¼ t. mace
3½-4 c. sifted flour

Dissolve yeast in water. Cool milk and add ⅓ cup sugar, salt and ¼ cup shortening. Blend well. Add 2 eggs; beat lightly. Add yeast, flavorings, mace and 3 cups flour; beat until smooth. Add enough remaining flour to make a soft dough. Cover with a damp cloth; let rise until doubled in bulk. Punch down; refrigerate 15 minutes. Roll out to a square ¼ inch thick. Dot with ½ shortening, leaving a 2-inch border. Fold in half; press edges together. Dot with remaining shortening; fold in half and seal edges. Roll dough to ⅓ inch thick; fold in half and in quarters. Repeat folding and rolling 3 times. Refrigerate 15 minutes. Roll out to a 10-inch square ½ inch thick. Cut into strips ¾ inch wide. Shape as desired; let rise until doubled. Beat remaining egg with sugar; brush over dough. Sprinkle with almonds if desired. Bake at 475°F. for 8-10 minutes. Yield: 18-24 servings.

Patricia Joan Fenwick, Cassopolis H.S.
Cassopolis, Michigan

TRADITIONAL AFTERNOON TEA SCONES (ENGLAND)

1 c. flour
Pinch of salt
1 t. cream of tartar
½ t. soda
4 T. butter
2 T. castor sugar
2 T. currants
1 egg
Milk

Sift flour, salt, cream of tartar and soda into a bowl; rub in butter. Stir in sugar and currants; mix to a soft dough with beaten egg and a little milk. Roll out to ½ to ¾-inch thickness; cut into 2-inch rounds. Place on a greased baking tray and bake at 400°F. for 10 minutes. NOTE: Castor sugar is English granulated sugar. Yield: 6 servings.

Mrs. Ann H. Malone, S. Middleton Township H.S.
Boiling Springs, Pennsylvania

GRAHAM BREAD (FINLAND)

2 qt. warm water
1 pkg. yeast
6 c. graham or whole wheat flour
2 T. plus 2 t. salt
18 c. flour, sifted

Combine 1 quart of water, yeast and flour to make a sponge; let set in a warm place 12 hours. Add remaining water, salt and 4 cups flour; blend well. Add enough remaining flour to make a stiff dough. Knead well; let rise 1 hour. Knead down; divide into 8 sections. Shape into balls; let rest 10 minutes. Knead and shape into loaves; place in a greased pan. Let rise 1 hour. Bake 45-60 minutes at 400°F. Yield: 8 loaves

Mrs. Doris Gustafson, Brethren H.S.
Brethren, Michigan

LIMPA—BROWN BREAD (FINLAND)

2 c. boiling potato water
5-6 c. rye flour
4-5 potatoes, mashed
1½ c. molasses, heated
1 cake yeast
3 c. lukewarm water
1 T. salt
1 c. raisins
3 T. shortening

Pour potato water over 3 cups flour until well moistened. Add potatoes and molasses; cover and cool. Combine yeast, water, salt and enough of remaining flour to make a sponge. Knead potato mixture into sponge. Add raisins and shortening. Knead with white flour until stiff enough to handle. Let rise until doubled; punch down. Let rise again. Shape into loaves; let rise 1 hour. Bake at 425°F. for 15 minutes. Reduce heat to 350°F.; continue baking for 50 minutes.

Mrs. Jo Ann Koskela, Virginia H.S.
Virginia, Minnesota

PANNUKKU—PANCAKES (FINLAND)

¼ c. butter
3 eggs, beaten
2 c. milk
½ t. salt
½-¾ c. flour
½ t. vanilla
Sugar

Place butter in a 10- to 12-inch cast iron frying pan; thoroughly heat skillet in a 450°F. oven. Combine remaining ingredients. Pour melted butter into batter; pour batter into heated frying pan. Bake in 450°F. oven 25-30 minutes. Sprinkle top with sugar while hot. Serve with jam. Yield: 6-8 servings.

Mrs. Frances Whited, Toledo H.S.
Toledo, Oregon

BREAKFAST PUFFS (FRANCE)

⅓ c. soft shortening
1 c. sugar
1 egg
1½ c. flour
1½ t. baking powder
½ t. salt
¼ t. nutmeg
½ c. milk
6 T. butter, melted
1 t. cinnamon

Mix shortening, ½ cup sugar and egg. Sift flour, baking powder, salt and nutmeg together. Stir into shortening mixture alternately with milk. Fill greased muffin tins two-thirds full. Bake at 350°F. for 20-25 minutes or until golden brown. Immediately roll in butter then in mixture of ½ cup sugar and cinnamon. Yield: 12 servings.

Mrs. Janet Halvarson, St. Charles H.S.
St. Charles, Minnesota

FRENCH BREAD (FRANCE)

2½ c. warm water
2 pkg. yeast
1 T. salt
1 T. butter or margarine
7 c. flour
Corn meal
1 egg white
1 T. cold water

Dissolve yeast in warm water. Add salt, butter and flour. Stir until well blended; dough will be sticky. Place in a greased bowl, turning to grease top. Cover; let rise in a warm place 1 hour or until doubled in bulk. Turn dough onto lightly floured board; divide into two equal portions. Roll into a 15x10-inch oblong. Beginning at widest side, roll up tightly; pinch edges together. Taper ends by rolling gently back and forth. Place loaves on greased baking sheets sprinkled with corn meal. Cover; let rise in warm place about 1 hour or until doubled in bulk. With a ra-

(Continued on Next Page)

zor, make diagonal cuts on top of each loaf. Bake in 450°F. oven 25 minutes. Remove from oven and brush with egg white mixed with cold water. Return to oven; bake 5 minutes longer. Yield: 21 loaves.

Virginia Everett, Baker H.S.
Baker, Montana

ONION BREAD (FRANCE)

1 pkg. active dry yeast
2¼ c. warm water
1 pkg. dry onion soup mix
2 T. sugar
1 t. salt
2 T. Parmesan cheese, grated
2 T. shortening
6-6½ c. flour, sifted
Corn meal
Egg white

Soften yeast in ¼ cup warm water. Combine soup mix with 2 cups water; cover and simmer 10 minutes. Add sugar, cheese, salt and shortening. Stir and cool to lukewarm. Stir in 2 cups of flour. Beat well; stir in yeast. Stir in enough remaining flour to m a k e a moderately stiff dough. Cover and let rest 10 minutes. Knead until smooth and elastic. Place in a lightly greased bowl; turn to grease top. Cover; let rise 1 hour and 30 minutes. Punch down and divide in half. Cover and let rest 10 minutes. Shape into two loaves tapered at ends. Put in a greased baking dish covered with corn meal. Cut tops ¼-½ inch deep diagonally. Let rise 1 hour. Bake in 375°F. oven for 20 minutes. Brush top with egg white and 1 tablespoon water. Bake 10-15 minutes more or until done. Yield: 2 small loaves.

Mrs. Linda Hale, Wakonda H.S.
Wakonda, South Dakota

DOTCHEN—BERRY CAKE (GERMANY)

½ t. baking powder
1½ c. flour
¼ t. salt
¼ c. sugar
1 c. milk
3 eggs, well beaten
2-3 c. sweetened raspberries, blueberries or blackberries

Combine all dry ingredients. Make a well; add milk and eggs and mix well. Grease a jelly roll pan or cookie sheet that has been lined with foil. Pour in batter. Cover with berries. Bake in 400°F. oven about 25 minutes. Yield: 5-8 servings.

Mrs. Mary Lou Michalewicz, T. F. Riggs H.S.
Pierre, South Dakota

GRANDMA'S COFFEE CAKE (GERMANY)

TOPPING:
¼ c. shortening
1 c. brown sugar
4 T. flour
½ t. cinnamon
⅛ t. salt
½ c. nuts

Combine all ingredients. Set aside.

2 c. flour
¾ c. sugar
¼ t. nutmeg
½ t. cinnamon
1 t. salt
4 t. baking powder
¼ c. shortening
2 eggs
1 c. milk

Sift all dry ingredients together; cut in shortening. Add eggs and milk. Mix well but do not over beat. Pour into a greased 9x13-inch pan; cover with topping. Bake in 350°F. oven for 30 minutes. Yield: 12 servings.

Mrs. Max Mason, Arriba H.S.
Arriba, Colorado

RAFFEE KUCHEN—COFFEE CAKE (GERMANY)

2 c. milk, scalded
1 pkg. dry yeast
½ c. lukewarm water
7 c. flour
¾ c. butter
1 c. sugar
2 eggs
1 t. salt
1 c. raisins

Cool milk. Dissolve yeast in warm water. Combine yeast and milk with enough flour to make a soft batter. Let rise 45 minutes. Add sugar, butter, eggs, salt and raisins. Add remaining flour to make a soft dough. Let rise 2 hours and 30 minutes. Place on floured board; fold, but do not knead. Roll very lightly to 1-inch thickness. Place on greased baking pan. Let rise 1 hour.

TOPPING:
½ c. cream
1 c. brown sugar
2 T. cinnamon

Combine ingredients; sprinkle over batter. Bake in 350°F. oven for 25-30 minutes. Ice with powdered sugar icing. Yield: 6 cakes.

Mrs. Patsy Lenz, Windsor H.S.
Windsor, Illinois

SOUR CREAM TWISTS (GERMANY)

¾ c. margarine
3½ c. flour
1 t. salt
1 pkg. yeast
¼ c. warm water
¾ c. sour cream
2 eggs, well beaten
2 t. vanilla
1 c. sugar
2 t. cinnamon
⅔ c. nuts

Cut margarine into flour and salt. Dissolve yeast in water; stir into flour with sour cream, eggs and vanilla. Mix well. Cover and refrigerate 2 hours or overnight. Divide dough in half; roll each section out on sugar and cinnamon to 8x16 inches. Fold ends in to center; sprinkle with sugar and roll our to 8x16-inches. Repeat, rolling out to ⅓-inch thickness. Press nuts into dough. Cut into 1x4-inch strips. Twist ends in opposite directions, stretching dough slightly. Shape into a crescent; press ends onto baking sheet to retain shape. Let rise 15-20 minutes; bake at 375°F. for 15 minutes or until browned. Yield: 4-5 dozen.

Mrs. Bette Brown, Steamboat Springs H.S.
Steamboat Springs, Colorado

CHRISTMAS BREAD (ITALY)

2 pkg. yeast
1 T. plus ¼ c. water
1 c. milk
⅔ c. sugar
1 t. salt
¾ c. butter
7 c. flour
4 whole eggs
1 egg, separated
1½ t. vanilla
½ c. golden raisins
⅓ c. almonds, finely chopped
⅓ c. candied citron
⅓ c. candied lemon peel

Soften yeast in ¼ cup water. Scald milk; add sugar, salt and butter. Cool to lukewarm. Add 2 cups flour; beat well. Add softened yeast; mix well. Cover; let rise 1 hour until mixture is bubbly. Stir down. Beat 4 eggs and 1 egg yolk; add with vanilla to dough, beating well. Add enough flour to make a soft dough. Turn out on lightly floured board; gradually knead in fruit and nuts. Continue kneading until smooth. Place in greased bowl and cover; let rise until doubled. Punch down; shape into two loaves. Combine egg white and water. Brush tops of bread with part of egg white mixture. Let rise; brush with remaining egg white. Bake in 350°F. oven for 35-40 minutes. Yield: 2 loaves.

Mrs. Dorothy Wynkoop, Greenville H.S.
Greenville, Ohio

ANISE BREAD (ITALY)

1 c. butter
½ c. sugar
6 eggs
4 drops anise oil
1 T. anise seeds
5 c. sifted flour
3 t. baking powder
Pinch of salt

Cream butter, sugar and eggs. Add anise oil and anise seed; stir with wooden spoon until well blended. Sift flour with baking powder and salt. Add dry ingredients to creamed mixture; knead 5 minutes. Shape dough into a 4x9-inch loaf. Place on greased cookie sheet. Bake in 350°F. oven for 20 minutes. Cool slightly; cut loaf into 1-inch slices. Toast in 425°F. oven for 3-4 minutes. Yield: 2 dozen slices.

Mrs. Mildred Christofeno, Jimtown H.S.
Elkhart, Indiana

BREAD STICKS (ITALY)

1 pkg. active dry yeast
⅔ c. warm water
1 t. salt
1 T. sugar
¼ c. soft shortening
2 c. flour
Sesame seeds

Dissolve yeast in water. Add salt, sugar, shortening and half of the flour. Beat vigorously until smooth. Mix in remaining flour. Knead on floured cloth-covered board until smooth. Cover; let rise 1 hour or until doubled in bulk. Divide dough in half. Cut into 24 pieces. Roll into pencil shapes of desired thickness. Place on greased baking sheet 1 inch apart. Brush with egg yolk-water glaze. Sprinkle with sesame seeds. Bake at 400°F. for 20-25 minutes. NOTE: Recipe may be doubled.

This recipe submitted by the following teachers:
Mrs. Arlene Block, Souk-Prairie H.S.
Prairie du Sac, Wisconsin
Clara M. Dayton, Cokeville H.S.
Cokeville, Wyoming

QUICK BREAD STICKS (ITALY)

¾ c. warm water
1 pkg. dry yeast
2½ c. Bisquick
¼ c. butter, melted
Caraway seeds, sesame seeds, poppy seeds, celery seeds or garlic salt

Dissolve yeast in water; beat in Bisquick. Turn onto Bisquick dusted surface; knead about 20 times or until smooth. Divide dough into 16 parts. Roll each piece between hands into 8-inch pencil-like strips. Spread part of butter in jelly roll pan. Place strips of dough in pan ½-inch apart. Brush tops with remaining butter.

(Continued on Next Page)

Sprinkle with caraway seeds, poppy seeds, celery seeds, sesame seeds or garlic salt. Cover with a damp cloth; let rise about 1 hour. Bake in 425°F. oven for 15 minutes or until golden brown. Turn oven off. Allow bread sticks to remain in oven 15 or more minutes to crisp. Yield: 16 servings.

Mrs. Carol Olson, Lincoln Jr. H.S.
Minneapolis, Minnesota

SWEET BREAD (ITALY)

1 c. butter
2 c. sugar
2½ cakes yeast
1 c. warm water
1 t. salt
½ t. nutmeg
1 T. garted lemon rind
½ t. allspice
1 T. vanilla extract
½ t. lemon extract
½ t. cinnamon
8-12 c. flour
1 pkg. white seedless raisins
2 c. nuts, chopped
1 lge. jar plus 1 sm. jar candied fruits
1 c. candied cherries, chopped
½ c. candied pineapple, chopped

Cream butter and sugar. Dissolve yeast in warm water. Combine yeast and creamed mixture with all remaining ingredients. Cover and let rise for 1 hour. Punch down; shape into small loaves or place in greased round cans. Cover with a damp cloth and let rise 1 hour. Bake 1 hour at 350°F. Glaze with favorite glaze and cool. NOTE: May be frozen for 6-8 months.

Louise Hall, Amador County H.S.
Sutter Creek, California

KINUKO'S BREAD (JAPAN)

1 pkg. yeast
1½ T. white sugar
3 c. lukewarm water
⅓ c. (scant) blackstrap or ½ c. Brer Rabbit molasses
2 T. shortening
2 T. salt
4 c. white flour
1 c. (scant) powdered milk
4 c. whole wheat flour
½ c. wheat germ sesame seeds

Soak yeast with sugar in water. Mix all remaining ingredients together except wheat germ and sesame seeds. Add yeast mixture. Knead in wheat germ and enough extra flour to make a workable dough. K n e a d about 10 minutes until smooth. Let rise in greased bowl 3-4 hours, covered with a cloth. Knead again; shape into loaves. Put sesame seeds in greased pans. Place loaves on seeds. Let rise 2 hours. Bake in 400°F. oven for 15 minutes, reduce heat to 350°F. for 15 more minutes. Yield: 6 small or 4 medium loaves.

Mrs. Mary Gorrell Moser,
Mechanicsburg Area H.S.
Mechanicsburg, Pennsylvania

BUNVELOS—PANCAKES (MEXICO)

3 c. sifted flour
1 T. sugar
1 t. baking powder
1 t. salt
4 eggs
1 c. milk
¼ c. butter, melted
½ c. water

Sift all dry ingredients together. Break eggs in dry mixture. Add milk and butter, beating well. Add as much water as needed to make dough easy to handle, without being sticky. Knead well; make into balls the size of walnuts, rubbing each with shortening to prevent sticking. Cover with cloth; let stand 20 minutes. Flour board lightly; roll each ball until very thin. Let stand 5 minutes. Fry in deep hot oil until golden brown. Remove to absorbent paper. Serve with cinnamon and sugar or honey. Yield: 2-3 dozen.

Mrs. Karen Aire, Newman H.S.
Newman, Illinois

JULEKAGE—CHRISTMAS BREAD (NORWAY)

1 cake yeast
¼ c. lukewarm water
½ c. plus 1 t. sugar
1 c. milk
½ c. butter or margarine
½ t. salt
1 t. crushed cardamon seed
3 c. flour, sifted
2 eggs, slightly beaten
½ c. nuts, chopped
1 c. candied orange peel
1 c. lemon peel, chopped
1 c. seeded raisins

Combine yeast, water and 1 teaspoon sugar; let stand. Heat milk to boiling; add remaining sugar, butter, salt and cardamon. Stir until lukewarm. Beat in 1 cup flour. Add yeast mixture, eggs and 1⅔ cups flour. Knead. If necessary, more flour may be added when kneading. Let rise until double in size. Add ⅓ cup flour mixed with fruit and nuts; knead again. Shape into 2 loaves. Place into two buttered loaf pans. Let rise until doubled in size. Bake in 350°F. oven about 50 minutes. Brush top with melted butter or margarine. Cool. Frost top with thin confectioner's sugar and cream glaze. Yield: 2 loaves 9x5x3 inches.

Marjorie Corbin, Holly H.S.
Holly, Colorado

JULE KAGE—CHRISTMAS BREAD (NORWAY)

1 cake yeast
¼ c. water
1½ c. milk
¼ c. butter, melted
6 T. sugar
1 t. salt
1 egg, beaten
¼ c. currants
¼ c. citron, chopped
6 T. raisins
¼ c. blanched almonds, chopped
½ t. powdered cardamom
4½ c. sifted flour

Soften yeast in water. Scald milk; cool. Add butter, softened yeast, sugar and salt. Mix well; stir in egg, currants, citron, raisins and almonds. Sift cardamom with flour; add gradually to make a soft dough. Knead until smooth. Place in greased bowl. Cover; let rise until double in size. Punch down; let rise again. Shape into two loaves; place in pan. Let rise until double. Bake in 350°F. oven for 35-40 minutes. Frost if desired. Yield: 2 loaves.

Mrs. Esther Magill, Kimball H.S.
Kimball, South Dakota

LEFSE (NORWAY)

3 c. potatoes, riced
1 T. sugar
1 t. salt
5 T. shortening, melted
1½ c. flour

Combine riced potatoes, sugar, salt and shortening. Blend well. Add flour gradually. Shape into balls; roll out on lightly floured board to less than ⅛ inch thick. Bake on moderately hot grill. Turn when lefse is full of bubbles. NOTE: May be stored rolled up in a clean towel. Yield: 12 lefse.

Janet Linse, Rice Lake H.S.
Rice Lake, Wisconsin

POTATO LEFSE (NORWAY)

Milk
Butter
Mashed potatoes
Salt
Flour

Add milk and butter to mashed potatoes. Add more salt to potatoes, about 1 teaspoon for every quart. Knead enough flour into potatoes to make a stiff dough. Roll out very thin on well floured board. Cut into pieces. Bake on ungreased griddle, turning to brown both sides. Serve hot with butter. NOTE: Any leftover lefse can be re-heated in a covered pan over low heat.

Mrs. Leonard Klug, Barnesville H.S.
Barnesville, Minnesota

LEFSE (NORWAY)

2 cans evaporated milk
Juice of 2 lemons
1 t. salt
1 c. sugar
1 t. soda
Flour

Combine milk, lemon juice, salt, sugar and soda. Stir in enough flour for dough to handle easily. Roll on a pastry canvas, keeping the dough round. Use a Scandinavian rolling pin; work dough out in all directions. For each lefse, use ball of dough about size of an average hamburger pattie. Use a flat stick to handle and transfer dough to and from lefse grill. Turn; cook on both sides.

TOPPING:
½ c. cream
Sugar

Make paste of cream and sugar. Spread lefse with sugar paste. Place on lefse grill a few seconds. NOTE: These can be kept a long period of time. Soak before using, by dipping in warm water and covering with a towel. Spread with butter and sugar and serve folded and cut.

Ruth M. Dreyer, Circle H.S.
Circle, Montana

LEFSE FOR TEA (NORWAY)

6 T. butter or margarine
1 t. salt
2 T. sugar
1 c. milk
Flour

Add margarine, salt, and sugar to milk; heat to scalding. Immediately add 1½ cups flour. Stir until well mixed. Add more flour to make a dough that can be easily rolled. Roll dough into paper thin circles small enough to bake on a pancake griddle or electric frying pan. Bake until light brown on both sides, turning once. Fold; place between cloths to keep from drying out. NOTE: When cool store in an airtight canister. This is a soft lefse that is delicious with lutefisk or for afternoon coffee. Yield: 8-9 inch circle.

Mrs. Ruth Helman, Sault Ste. Marie Jr. H.S.
Sault Ste. Marie, Michigan

RAISIN BREAD (NORWAY)

2 c. scalded milk
1 cake yeast
½ c. butter
2 eggs
½ c. sugar
2 c. raisins, ground
½ c. nuts, chopped
Flour

(Continued on Next Page)

Cool milk to lukewarm; combine with yeast, butter, eggs, sugar, raisins and nuts. Stir in enough flour to make a soft dough, just enough to handle. Knead until dough is smooth and elastic. Let rise; punch down and let rise again. Divide dough into equal portions; round into bun-like shapes. Place into well greased 1-pound tin cans, filling half full. Let rise until double. Bake in 250°F. oven for 1 hour and 30 minutes. Yield: 4 loaves.

Mary K. Rothe, Welcome Community School
Welcome, Minnesota

KULICH-HOLIDAY BREAD (RUSSIA)

2 pkg. yeast
½ c. lukewarm water
½ c. sugar
2 t. salt
⅔ c. instant nonfat dry milk
2 eggs
½ c. soft shortening
1½ c. water
½ t. yellow food coloring
1 c. raisins
½ c. finely cut toasted almonds
7⅔ c. sifted all-purpose flour

Combine yeast and lukewarm water in 3-quart bowl; stir just to dissolve. Add sugar, salt, instant nonfat dry milk, eggs, shortening, 1½ cups water, food coloring, raisins and almonds. Thoroughly stir in about half of flour. Add remaining flour to make dough easy to handle, mixing by hand. Turn onto lightly floured board; knead until smooth and elastic. Place in greased bowl; turn once so greased side is up. Cover with waxed paper and a towel. Let rise in warm place about 45 minutes or until doubled in bulk. Punch down. Let rise again until almost double. Punch down. Divide dough into four portions. Form into well rounded bun-like shapes. Place in four well greased 1-lb. coffee cans. The cans should be about half full. Let rise until double in bulk. Place cans on cookie sheet. Place in center of oven and bake at 375°F. until well browned, about 40 minutes. Gently cut around sides of cans with a knife. Remove from cans and place on wire rack.

LEMON GLAZE:

3 c. sifted powdered sugar
3 T. water
1 t. lemon juice
1 t. grated lemon rind

Thoroughly blend all ingredients in 1½-quart bowl. Drizzle over tops of kulichs while still warm, allowing glaze to drip over sides. Sprinkle with tiny colored decorettes.

Photograph for this recipe on page 367

CINNAMON-COFFEE ROLLS (SCANDINAVIA)

4 c. sifted flour
1 t. salt
½ c. sugar
1 c. soft margarine or butter
1 pkg. active dry yeast
¼ c. very warm water
3 egg yolks, beaten
1 c. lukewarm milk
¾ t. cinnamon

Combine flour, salt and ¼ cup sugar in large bowl. Cut in margarine with pastry blender until mixture looks like meal. Dissolve yeast in very warm water. Add to flour mixture with egg yolks and cooled milk. Beat well; refrigerate overnight. Roll one-half chilled dough into 12x10-inch rectangle. Brush with melted margarine or butter; sprinkle with mixture of ¼ cup sugar and the cinnamon. Beginning at wide side, roll as for jelly roll. With sharp knife, cut roll into 1-inch slices. Place in greased muffin cups. Roll and cut other half of dough same way. Cover; let rise about 1 hour in warm place. Bake at 375°F. for 20 minutes until golden brown. Remove from pans while hot.

GLAZE:

1½ c. confectioner's sugar, sifted
2 T. soft margarine
1½ t. vanilla
1-2 T. hot water

Combine ingredients to make a medium thick glaze. Frost hot rolls. Yield: 24 servings.

Mrs. Myrne Waldroff
Lakeview Community Schools
Lakeview, Michigan

COFFEE CAKE (SCANDINAVIA)

½ c. milk, scalded
½ c. shortening
½ c. sugar
½ t. salt
1 pkg. active dry yeast
¼ c. warm water
3-3½ c. flour, sifted
2 eggs, beaten
Butter or shortening, melted
⅔ c. brown sugar, firmly packed
2 t. cinnamon
Nuts, chopped

Combine milk, shortening, sugar and salt. Stir until sugar dissolves; cool to lukewarm. Dissolve yeast in water; combine with milk mixture. Stir in half the flour and add eggs; beat well. Add enough remaining flour to make a soft dough. Turn out on lightly floured board; knead until smooth and elastic. Put in greased bowl. Brush with shortening. Cover; let rise about 2 hours until double in bulk in a warm place. Turn out on floured board; spread with butter. Sprinkle with brown sugar and cinnamon. Roll up like jelly roll. Shape into ring on greased

(Continued on Next Page)

baking sheet; pinch ends. Cut almost through the ring toward center in 1-inch slices. Brush with shortening. Cover; let rise 45 minutes. Bake in 375°F. oven for 25-30 minutes. While warm, spread with confectioner's sugar icing; sprinkle with chopped walnuts. Yield: 12 servings.

Lenora Ann Hill, Great Falls H.S.
Great Falls, Montana

PASKA—EASTER BREAD (SLOVAKIA)

¾ c. milk
¾ c. potato water
1 c. butter or margarine
⅔ c. sugar
2 t. salt
2 pkg. dry yeast or 1 lge. cake compressed yeast
½ c. warm water
7 to 8 c. flour
1 c. mashed potatoes (no seasoning)
3 eggs (opt.)
Raisins (opt.)

Scald the milk and potato water; add butter, sugar and salt. Cool to lukewarm. Sprinkle yeast over warm water and let rise for 10 minutes. Sift 4 cups of flour into a bowl; add the lukewarm milk mixture, mashed potatoes, eggs, and yeast. Beat until smooth. Add the remaining flour gradually to form a soft dough. Add raisins if desired. Knead until satin smooth. Let rise for 1 hour in warm place or cover with a damp cloth and refrigerate overnight. This dough can stand in the refrigerator for 3 or 4 days and a portion of the dough may be used as desired. Shape into loaves; place in greased pans. Let rise about 2-3 hours until double in bulk. Bake in 400°F. oven for 10 minutes. Reduce heat and bake in 350°F. oven for 30 minutes or until brown.

Sister M. Daniel, Andrean H.S.
Gary, Indiana

DRESDEN CHRISTMAS FRUIT BREAD (SWEDEN)

2 cakes compressed yeast
4 T. warm water
1 c. shortening or butter
2 c. lukewarm milk
2 eggs
1 c. sugar
1 t. salt
6 c. sifted flour
1½ c. raisins
½ c. candied orange peel, chopped
1 c. blanched almonds, chopped
Grated rind of one lemon
¼ c. butter, melted
Confectioner's sugar

Dissolve yeast in water. Add shortening, milk, eggs, sugar, salt and half of flour. Blend to a smooth batter. Turn onto floured board; knead in remaining flour, except ¼ cup. Knead 5 minutes or until dough is easy to handle. Place dough in greased bowl and cover with damp cloth; let rise until double in bulk. Punch down; let rise again until double in size. Total rising time is about 2 hours. Shake fruit with ¼ cup flour; work into dough. Divide dough into four parts. Form into oval loaves. Brush with melted butter; fold one side over as for parker house rolls. Brush top with butter. Let rise about 30 minutes on greased baking sheet until double. Bake in 375°F. oven for about 30 minutes. Brush with melted butter and sprinkle with sugar. Frost with white icing. Yield: 4 stollen type loaves.

Mrs. James Massa, Winner Public School
Winner, South Dakota

JULE KAGE (SWEDEN)

2 c. scalded milk, cooled
3 eggs, beaten
1½ cakes or pkg. yeast
1 c. candied fruit mix
2 t. salt
¾ c. margarine, melted
1 c. sugar
1 c. raisins
1 c. nuts
¾ t. cardamom
8-9 c. flour
Cream
Sugar
Cinnamon

Make a sponge by mixing milk, eggs, yeast and 2½-3 cups of flour or enough to make a thick batter. Let rise in a warm place, about 1 hour or until light and spongy. Stir sponge down; add fruit mix, cooled margarine, sugar, raisins, nuts, salt and cardamom. Stir in additional flour to make a soft dough. Turn out on lightly floured board; knead until smooth and elastic. Punch down and place in greased bowl; let rise until doubled in bulk. Shape into loaves. Brush lightly with cream and sprinkle with sugar and cinnamon. Bake at 350°F. for 45-60 minutes. Frost top with powdered sugar-butter icing and decorate with candied cherries and citron peel if desired. Yield: 3 loaves.

Hazel Freeman, West Valley H.S.
Yakima, Washington

JULE KAKA (SWEDEN)

3 c. milk
1½ yeast cake
¼ c. lukewarm water
1 t. salt
11 c. flour
1½ c. sugar
2 eggs, well beaten

(Continued on Next Page)

1 c. seedless raisins
1 c. currants
½ c. cut citron or mixed candied fruit
¼ t. nutmeg
¼ t. cinnamon

Heat milk to boiling point; cool. Dissolve yeast in lukewarm water. Combine yeast mixture, salt, 5 cups of flour and milk. Stir well; let rise until very light. Add sugar, eggs, fruit and spices. Mix well; add remaining flour to make a stiff dough. Knead; let rise until doubled in bulk. Mold into loaves; let rise until dough reaches top of pans. Bake in 350°F. oven until brown and loaf sounds hollow when tapped on bottom. Remove from pans; brush with butter. Yield: 3 loaves.

Constance C. Malmsten, Technical H.S.
St. Cloud, Minnesota

LIMPE BREAD (SWEDEN)

2 c. water
½ c. brown sugar
¼ c. molasses
2 t. caraway seeds
1 T. shortening
1 t. grated orange rind
1 t. anise powder
1 cake or pkg. yeast
¼ c. lukewarm water
3 c. white flour
1½ t. salt
2 c. rye flour

Boil water, brown sugar, molasses, caraway seeds, shortening, orange rind and anise powder for 3 minutes. Cool to lukewarm. Add yeast dissolved in lukewarm water. Add white flour to make a soft dough; cover and set in a pan of warm water for 1 hour and 30 minutes. Add salt and rye flour to make a stiff dough. Knead slightly in bowl; let rise 2 hours. Knead; form into 2 round loaves. Dough is sticky and will not be smooth and satiny. Place on greased pan; let rise 30 minutes. Bake at 350°F. for 1 hour. Yield: 2 loaves.

Mrs. Ila Johnson, Stewartville School
Stewartville, Minnesota

LIMPE (SWEDEN)

2 pkg. dry yeast
½ c. warm water
⅓ c. sugar
1 T. salt
2 T. grated orange rind
1 t. caraway seed
½ t. anise seed
2 T. shortening, melted
2½ c. rye flour
2 c. white flour

Dissolve yeast in ½ cup warm water. Combine yeast with remaining ingredients, using enough flour to make dough consistency for kneading. Knead until smooth. Let rise until doubled. Punch down; let rest 10 minutes. Divide and shape into two balls. Place on greased baking sheet to rise until doubled. Shpe into loaves. Place in greased loaf pans. Bake at 375°F. for 30-40 minutes. Yield: 2 loaves.

Mrs. Martha Zimmerman, Taylorsville H.S.
Taylorsville, Illinois

LIMPE (SWEDEN)

¼ c. brown sugar
2 t. caraway seeds
2 t. salt
2 T. shortening
1 pkg. dry yeast
4 c. sifted white flour
2 c. sifted rye flour

Blens sugar, caraway seeds, salt, shortening and ½ cup water. Simmer 5 minutes; add 1 cup water and cool. Dissolve yeast in ½ cup warm water. Add 2 cups white flour to cooled mixture; beat well and stir in yeast. Add remaining white flour; blend thoroughly. Mix in 1½ cups rye flour. Knead bread on a board with remaining rye flour until smooth. Place in a greased bowl; cover and let rise 1 hour and fifteen minutes. Punch down; let rise. Shape dough into 2 balls; place on a greased sheet. Cut 3 or 4 slashes in the top of each loaf. Let rise until doubled in bulk. Bake at 400°F. for 45-50 minutes. For shiny crust, brush with milk or egg white and bake 2 minutes. Yield: 2 loaves.

Mrs. Shirley Newcombe, Vanderbilt Area Schools
Vanderbilt, Michigan

RYE BREAD (SWEDEN)

1 c. plus 2 T. sugar
2 pkg. dry yeast
3½ c. rye flour
2 c. water
2 c. milk
½ c. molasses
2 T. salt
4 T. shortening
8 c. white flour

Combine 2 tablespoons sugar, yeast and ½ cup rye flour. Allow to rise in warm place. Mix 1 cup water, 1 cup milk, molasses, salt, shortening and 1 cup sugar in saucepan; bring to a boil. Cool. Combine with sponge; add 1 cup milk, 1 cup water, white and remaining rye flour. Knead. Let rise until double in bulk. Shape into loaves and place in greased pans. Let rise about 1 hour. Bake in 350°F. oven about 50 minutes or until brown. Yield: 4 loaves.

Mrs. Mary Hallquist, Gibbon H.S.
Gibbon, Minnesota

SWEET ROLLS (SWEDEN)

4 c. sifted flour
1 c. butter
½ c. sugar
2 eggs, beaten
1 pkg. yeast
1 c. warm milk
1 c. flour
Butter, melted
Sugar
Cinnamon

Blend 3 cups of flour, butter and sugar in a mixer until mixture resembles fine crumbs. Add eggs, stirring in with fork. Dissolve yeast in milk. Combine mixtures, adding remaining flour to make a soft dough. Refrigerate dough overnight or until chilled. Roll into two large circles. Spread with butter, sugar and cinnamon. Cut in wedges; roll up from wide edge. Place on cookie sheet. Let rise double in size. Bake in 350°F. oven for 8-10 minutes.

Doris C. Sporleder, Hall H.S.
Spring Valley, Illinois

AWAMAT—SWEET TREAT (SYRIA)

1 cake yeast
¼ c. lukewarm water
7 t. sugar
2 T. shortening
1½ t. salt
2 c. milk, scalded
6 c. flour
Oil for frying

Add yeast to lukewarm water with 1 teaspoon sugar. Let stand for 5 minutes. Add shortening, salt and remaining sugar to milk. Cool to lukewarm. Add softened yeast and 3 cups flour. Beat well. Add enough more flour to make a soft dough. Place remaining flour on board; knead until smooth and elastic. Place in greased bowl; turn over so that greased side is on top. Cover with cloth; let rise until doubled in bulk. Punch down; let rise a second time if desired. Form balls the size of a walnut. Fry dough in hot oil until golden brown.

SYRUP:

2 c. water
2 c. sugar
1 t. rosewater

Combine ingredients. Cook until slightly thick. Dip each piece of fried dough in syrup; place on a rack to drain. Yield: 2 dozen.

Marjorie Shetler, Western Area Joint School
Mifflingburg, Pennsylvania

POTICA (YUGOSLAVIA)

1 cake yeast
1¼ c. milk, scalded
½ c. sugar
1 c. butter or shortening
4 egg yolks, beaten
6 c. sifted flour
1 t. salt
1 t. vanilla
Grated lemon or orange rind

Dissolve yeast in ¼ cup lukewarm milk. Cream sugar and butter; add egg yolks and mix well. Add flour and salt alternately with 1 cup lukewarm milk; beat until bubbly. Add yeast mixture, vanilla and orange or lemon rind. Beat until smooth and dough is not sticky. Place dough in a greased bowl; cover and let rise until doubled in bulk. Roll out on a floured cloth; brush with melted butter.

FILLING:

1 c. honey
1 lb. walnuts, ground
¼ lb. butter
½ c. sugar
¼ c. sweet cream
¼ t. cinnamon
1 t. vanilla
2 egg whites, stiffly beaten
⅔ c. raisins (opt.)

Heat honey; add nuts, butter, sugar and cream. Mix until butter is melted; add cinnamon, vanilla and egg whites. Spread filling over dough; sprinkle with raisins if desired. Roll up dough tightly with hands. Place in a large baking pan; bake at 350°F. for 1 h o u r or u n t i l nicely browned.

Rose Shular, Ottawa H.S.
Ottawa, Kansas

INDEX

Breads, 325-378

Quick Breads, 333

Biscuits, 334
  Orange, 334
  Southern 334
  Upside-Down, 334

Coffee Cake, 334-339
  Almond French Toast, 338
  Blueberry Buckle, 335
  Blueberry Streusel, 335
  Bonny Berry, 335
  Bran, 335
  Easy Party Cake, 336
  Dutch Apple, 338
  Hawaiian, 336
  Jiffy, 336
  Marmalade, 334, 337
  Mincemeat, 337
  Orange, 337
  Rolls, 334
  Sour Cream, 339
  Streusel, 337
  Sugar Loaf, 338
  Sweet, 338
  Yum Yum, 339

Corn Bread, 339-340
  Apple, 339
  Corn Crisps, 340
  Pennsylvania Corn Pone, 340
  Salmon Southern, 339
  Spoon Bread, 340
  Tomato Flavored Hush Puppies, 340
  Virginia Batter, 340
  Yankee, 339

Loafs, 346-352
  Apple, 346
  Apricot, 346
  Banana, 347
  Bran, 348
  Brown Bread, 349
  Butter, 349
  Carrot, 349
  Cherry, 349
  Cranberry, 350
  Date Nut, 350
  Fruit Nut, 351
  Grapenut, 351
  Gumdrop, 351
  Nut, 351
  Oatmeal, 351
  Orange, 352
  Pumpkin, 352

Mixes, 344-346
  Bruffins, 344, 345
  Butter Dips, 345
  Garlic, 346
  Gingerbread, 345
  Ice Box Bran Muffins, 345
  Master Mix, 344
  Nippy Cheese Sticks, 345
  Refrigerator Muffins, 345
  Sesame Rolls, 346

Muffins, 041-343
  Apple, 341
  Blueberry, 341
  Bran, 342
  Carmel Pecan Oatmeal, 342
  English Tea, 342
  Marcie's, 342
  Paris, 342
  Sweet, 342
  Whole Wheat, 343

Pancakes, 343-344

Popovers, 343

Yeast Breads, 354-366

Biscuit, 354

Buns, 354
  Corn Meal, 354
  Easy, 355
  Ice Box, 357
  Super Quick, 357

Butterhorns, 354

Loaf, 358-362
  Butter and Herb, 358
  Bubble, 358
  Cardamon Raisin, 358
  Casserole, 359
  Cheese, 359
  Graham, 360
  Gruyere, 359
  Herb, 360
  Milk and Water, 360

Yeast Breads, continued
  Oatmeal, 359
  Prune, 361
  Root Beer—Rye, 361
  Rich, 361
  Saffron, 361
  Sourdough, 360
  Sweet Rye, 361
  White, 361
  Whole Wheat, 362

Rolls, 354-358
  All-Bran, 354
  Buttermilk, 355
  Crescent, 355
  Fancy, 355
  Ice Box, 357
  Old Plantation, 356
  Potato, 356
  Refrigerator, 357, 358
  Rich Dinner, 356
  Speedie, 356
  Squash, 357
  Three-Hour, 356

Sally Lunn, 362

Sweet Breads, 362-366
  Buns, 363
    Cherry, 363
    Hot Cross, 363
  Christmas Stollen, 364
  Cinnamon, 364, 365
  Coffee Cake, 364
  Current, 365
  Doughnut, 365
  Holiday Fruit, 365
  Lemon Twists, 366
  Orange, 366
  Plum, 365
  Rolls, 362
    Cinnamon, 363
    Crown, 362
    Orange, 364
  Walnut Potico, 363

Cereal Pasta, Egg and Cheese Dishes, 235-268

Barley, 236

Broccoli, 261

Cheese, 261
  Corn, 263
  Carrot, 265
  Fondue, 262
  Loaf, 262
  Pudding, 262
  Rarebit, 263
  Souffle, 264, 265, 266
  Strata, 263
  Tuna, 263

Chicken, 266

Egg, 266-268
  Au Gratin, 268
  Bacon, 266, 267
  Ham, 267
  Omelet, 268
  Souffle, 268, 267

Grits, 236

Macaroni, 236
  Cheese, 236, 237, 238
  Beef, 237
  Ham, 249, 240
  Lenten, 237
  Loaf, 240
  Mousse, 240
  Peanut Accent, 238
  Ravioli, 240
  Souffle, 240
  Tomato, 238, 239

Noodle, 241-246
  Apple Pie, 241
  Bacon, 241
  Baked, 241
  Beef, 241
  Canadian, 242
  Cheese, 243
  Cheeseburger, 241
  Easy, 242
  Gourmet, 242
  Ham, 243, 245
  Hamburger, 242
  Loaf, 244
  Nutty, 245
  Olive, 245
  Romonoff, 245
  Salmon, 246

Cereal Pasta, Egg and Cheese Dishes, continued
  Sausage, 246
  Sour Cream, 246
  Spanish, 246
  Tamale, 246

Lasagna, 247-250
  American, 247
  Clam Sauce, 249
  Homemade Noodles, 247
  Macaroni, 250
  Short Cut, 249
  Sour Cream, 250

Rice, 250-257
  African Chow Mein, 250
  Cashew, 250
  Cheese, 251
  Chicken, 251
  Chop Suey, 251, 252
  Curried, 251
  Green, 251, 252
  Hamburger, 252
  Indian, 253
  Mushroom, 252, 253
  Oriental, 255
  Polynesian, 252
  Pilaf, 253, 254
  Russian, 254
  Salvory, 255
  Spanish, 255
  Turkish, 254
  Wild Rice, 256, 257

Sandwich Omelet, 264

Spaghetti, 257-261

Combination Meat Casseroles, 88-96

African Chop Suey, 88
All In One, 88
American Chop Suey, 88
Applesauce Meat Balls, 88
Buffet, 89
Chop Suey, 89, 90
Chow Mein, 90, 93
City Chicken, 90
Frickadillars, 91
Ham, 89
Ham and Bacon, 89
Ham and Chicken, 91
Lasagna Italina, 92
Marzetti, 92
Macaroni, 93
Meat Balls, 88
Meat Pie, 89
Mushroom, 93
Noodle, 93
Oyster and Ham, 93
Pineapple, 94
Pork and Veal, 94
Sauerkraut and Beef, 94
Sausage Marzetti, 94
Shrimp, 95
Spaghetti, 95
Stew, 92
Stuffed Cabbage. 95
Tamale, 95
Tuna, 89
Turketti, 91
Veal and Beef, 96
Veal and Pork, 90, 96
Vegetable-Giblet, 96
Wild Rice, 96

Convenience Casseroles, 269-298

Freezer, 270-273
  Beef, 270
  Chicken, 271, 272, 273
  Cream Cheese, 270
  Meat Loaf, 270
  Mexican Corn Bread, 273
  Pineapple Ham, 272
  Rice Almond, 272
  Sausage, 272
  Sour Cream, 272
  Spaghetti, 271
  Sweet Potato, 273

Convenience Casseroles, continued
Turkey, 273
  Western, 271
Hot Sandwiches, 273-279
  Cheese, 274, 278, 279
  Chicken, 275
  Crab, 276
  Ham, 275
  Open Faced, 273, 274
  Pizza, 274
  Sausage, 275
  Salmon, 276
  Souffle, 279
  Spam, 278
  Turkey, 275
  Tuna, 276, 277
  Waffled, 277
  Western, 274
Penny-Wise, 279-284
  Cubed Beef, 279
  Barbecue, 280
  Chicken, 282, 283, 284
  Hash, 279, 281
  Ham, 281
    Creamed, 281
    Eggs, 282
    Potato, 281
    Macaroni, 281
    Noodle, 282
  Lamb and Rice, 284
  Pie, 279, 280
  Pork, 280, 281
  Potato, 284
  Shepheard's Pie, 280
  Sweet-Sour Noodle, 281
  Turkey, 284
Quick or Easy Casseroles, 285-298
Apple, 297
Beef, 285-291
  Bean, 285
  Chow Mein, 285
  Macaroni, 289
  Meat Loaf, 287
  Rice Krispie, 290
  Tomato, 289
  Spaghetti, 290, 291
  Stroganoff, 291
Broccoli, 297
Chili, 297, 298
Corn Chip, 298
Enchilada, 298
Pork, 292
Poultry, 293-294
  Chicken, 293
  Cacciator, 293
  Cashew, 293
  Creamed, 294
  Noodle, 295
  Pot Pie, 295
  Rice, 293
  Romanoff, 293
  Salad, 293, 294
  Scalloped, 295
Sauerkraut, 297
Seafood, 294
  Crab, 295
  Tuna, 296, 297
Spanish Rice, 298
Foreign Breads, 367-378
Bohemia, 368
  Christmas Twist Hoeska, 368
Czechoslovakia, 368
  Houska, 368
Denmark, 368
  Aebelskivers, 368
  Aebeleskiver Pancake Balls, 369
  Coffee Kringle, 368
  Coffee Twist, 369
  Danish Pastry, 369
  Puffs, 369
  Rolls, 369
England, 370
  Traditional Afternoon Tea
    Scones, 370
Finland, 370
  Graham Bread, 370
  Limpa Brown Bread, 370
  Pannukku Pancakes, 370
France, 370
  Breakfast Puffs, 370
  French Bread, 370
  Onion Bread, 371
Germany, 371
  Dotchen Berry Cake, 371

Foreign Breads, continued
  Grandmas Coffee Cake, 371
  Raffee Kuchen Coffee Cake, 371
  Sour Cream Twists, 372
Italy, 372
  Anise Bread, 372
  Bread Sticks, 372
  Christmas Bread, 372
  Sweet Bread, 373
Japan, 373
  Kinuko's Bread, 373
Mexico, 373
  Bunelos Pancakes, 373
Norway, 373
  Jule Kage-Christmas Bread, 373, 374
  Lefse, 374
  Potato Lefse, 374
  Raisin Bread, 374
Russia, 375
  Kulich-Holiday Bread, 375
Scandinavia, 375
  Cinnamon-Coffee Rolls, 375
  Coffee Cake, 375
Slovakia, 376
  Paska-Easter Bread, 376
Sweden, 376
  Dresden Christmas Fruit Bread, 376
  Jule Kage, 376
  Limpe Bread, 377
  Rye Bread, 377
  Sweet Rolls, 378
Syria, 378
  Awamat-Sweet Treat, 378
Yugoslavia, 378
  Potica, 378
Foreign Casseroles, 300-324
Africa, 300
  Green Mealic Puff, 300
  Peanut Butter Gravy, 300
Argentina, 300
  Carbonada Criolla-Gaucho Beef
    Stew, 300
Assyria, 300
  Sheik Mashi, 300
Austria, 301
  Haluski, 301
Brazil, 301
  Spinach-Riok, 301
Chile, 301
  Pastel De Choclo-Corn Pie, 301
China, 301
  Baked Chop Suey, 303
  Beef Of The Orient, 301
  Chicken Chow Mein, 304
  Chicken Hot Dish, 301
  Chicken And Lobster, 302
  Chicken 'N' Walnuts, 302
  Chop Suey, 303
  Chow Mein, 303, 304
  Company Casserole, 305
  Hamburger Casserole, 305
  Hamburger Chop Suey, 303
  Hash, 305
  Mandarin Tuna Skillet, 307
  One-Dish-Meal, 305
  Oriental Casserole, 305, 306
  Sausage Casserole or Paradise,
    Loaf, 306
  Sweet and Sour Meat Balls, 306
  Yum Yum, 306
Ecuador, 307
  Ecuadorian, 307
England, 307
  Toad In The Hole, 307
Finland, 307
  Lanttulaatikko-Turnip, 307
  Liver Casserole
France, 308
  Fete De L'Automme, 308
  Parisian Chicken, 308
  Quiche Lorraine, 308
Germany, 308
  Goulash, 308
  Kale Supreme, 308
  Vegetable Stew, 308
Greece, 308
  Moussaka-Eggplant Casserole, 308
Hawaii, 309
  Aloha Ribs, 309
  Curried Chicken, 309
  Pork-Rice, 309
  Yanastradi, 309

Foreign Casseroles, continued
Hungary, 310
  Escalloped Potatoes, 310
  Goulash, 310
  Lekvar and Noodle, 310
India, 310
  Curry Casserole, 310
  Curry And Rice, 310
  Kaedjere, 310
Iran, 311
  Sweet Rice, 311
Israel, 311
  Moussaka, 311
Italy, 311
  Eggplant Parmigiana, 311
  Hermine's Eggplant Parmesan, 312
  Lasagne, 311, 312
  Mostaccioli, 312
  Noodles Italiana, 313
  Pasta Fisole Spaghetti And
    Beans, 313
  Pavruna, 313
  Ravioli Deluxe, 314
  Rome Chowder, 314
  Scarpelli, 314
  Tagliarini, 314
Jamaica, 315
  Jamboree, 315
Japan, 315
  Beef Sukiyaki, 315
  Mock Sukiyaki, 315
  Sukiyaki With Rice, 315
Mexico, 315
  Baked Chili Relleno, 316
  Chalupas, 317
  Chili, 317
  Chili-Chicken, 316
  Chili Pie, 315
  Chili Verde Con Caso, 316
  Enchiladas, 317, 318
  Enchilada Chicken, 319
  Enchiladas Pie, 318, 319
  Enchiladas Verdes, 319
  Fiesta, 319
  Frijoles En-Casserole, 320
  Green Chili, 316
  Green Enchiladas, 319
  Hit The Spot, 320
  Luncheon Dish, 320
  Squash and Corn Con Carne, 320
  Taco Casserole, 320, 321
  Taco Pie, 321
  Tamale Pie, 321
  Tortilla, 322
Nepal, 322
  Fried Rice, 322
Peru, 322
  Peruvian Seviche, 322
Philippines, 322
  Pearl Of The Orient, 322
Poland, 322
  Hot Dish, 322
Russia, 323
  Chow Mein, 323
  Fish, 323
Spain, 323
  Arroz Con Pollo-Rice With
    Chicken, 323
  Bean, 324
  Espanol, 323
  Chili Con Queso, 324
  Paella, 323
  Sopa Da Fideo, 324
Syria, 324
  Bitin Jane, 324
Sweden, 324
  Stew, 324
Ground Meat and Hamburger, 39-58
  Barbeque Burgers, 49
  Cheeseburger, 55
  Chicken, 55
  Chili, 49, 50
    Cheese, 50
    Con Carne, 50
  Chili Corn Pone, 56, 57
  Chinese Goulash, 50
  Chop Suey, 50, 53
  Chow Mein (Mock), 54
  Corn Chips, 51
  Country Pie, 51
  Crust, 49, 50
    Biscuit, 55
  Enchilada, 51, 52

Ground Meat and Hamburger, continued
Hamburger, 51
  Cobbler, 56
  Hot Dish, 52
  Pie, 57, 58
  Potato, 58
Jumbo, 52
Macaroni, 40
  Chop Suey, 40
  Ravioli,, 40
Meat Ball, 52, 53
Meat Loaf, 49, 53
Mexican, 56
Noodle, 41
  Beef-Cheese, 41
  Cashew, 41, 42
  Chop Suey, 53
  Crusty, 42
  Goulash, 42
  Marzette, 43
  Meat Ball, 43
  Nutty, 44, 53
  One-Dish, 44
  Pie, 55
  Pizza, 44
  Sour Cream, 42
  Stroganoff, 44
Potato Pie, 53
Rice, 44
  Almond, 45
  Chili, 44
  Chinese, 46
  Chop Suey, 47
  Chow Mein, 45, 48
  Creole, 46
  Hamburger, 46, 47, 48
  Hash, 48
  Hot Dish, 46, 47
  Porcupine, 45
  Meat Ball, 47
  Stew, 48
  Wild Rice, 45, 46
Stroganoff, 49
String Bean, 58
Stuffed Mat Roll, 54
Tamale, 56, 57
Tortilla, 54
Vegetable, 54, 56

Luncheon Meat, 108-110
Bologna, 108
  Macaroni, 108
  Noodle, 109
Salami, 111
Spam, 109
  Macaroni, 109
  Noodle, 110
  Rice, 110
  Scalloped, 110
  Souffle, 110
  Suey, 110
Sweetbread, 111
Vienna Sausage, 111-112

Meat Casseroles, 19-38
Beef Casseroles, 19-21
  Chuck, 20, 22
  Flank Stak, 21
  Ground Steak, 21
  Macaroni, 20
  Round Steak, 20, 21
  Sirloin Tip, 21
Lamb Casseroles, 37
Pork Casseroles, 22-38
  Apple, 22
  Baked, 22
  Bread Dressing, 22
  Canadian Bacon, 29
  Chicken, 24
  Chow Mein, 29
  Deviled, 23
  Fruited, 24
  Jimsetti,, 29
  Ground, 29
  Kraut, 24
  Lemon, 25
  Noodle, 30
  One-Dish, 23
  Onion, 24
  Potato, 25
  Rice, 22, 23, 25, 26, 30
  Sausage, 30, 31
  Scallop, 25
  Spareribs, 29
  Stuffing, 23
  Sweet and Sour, 30
  Tomato, 24
  Vegetable, 25
Ham Casseroles, 26-28
  Baked, 26

Meat Casseroles, continued
  Canned, 26
  Gourmet, 27
  Pie, 27
  Macaroni, 27
  Noodle, 26, 28
  Oriental, 28
  Sour Cream, 28
  Stuffed, 28
  Tetrazzini, 28
Veal Casseroles, 33-36
  A La King, 34
  Baked, 33
  Butter Crumb Dumplings, 33
  Chop Suey, 33
  Delight, 35
  Goulash, 35
  Green Noodles, 34
  Marengo, 35
  Noodle, 36
  Rice, 36
  Scollapini and Risotto, 35
  Stew, 36
Wild Game Casseroles, 37-38
  Deer, 38
  Dove, 37
  Elk, 38
  Pheasants, 37
    Baked, 37
    Mushroom, 38
    Rice, 38
    Scalloped, 37
    Sour Cream, 38
  Venision, 38

Meat-Vegetable Casseroles, 151-184
Beef, 152-172
  American Sukizake, 152
  Baked Chili, 152
  Bean, 155
  Bean-Burger, 152
  Cabbage, 155
  Carrot, 163
  Cheese Lasagna, 156
  Chili Con Carne, 157
  Chip 'N' Chili, 157
  Chow Mein, 157, 165
  Chinese, 158
  Corn, 153, 157
  Crust, 152
  Eggplant, 153, 158
  Frozen, 159
  Goulash, 159
  Green Bean, 159
  Ground, 156, 160
  Hamburger, 160
  Italian, 162
  Kraut, 162
  Layer, 156
  Loaf-Scalloped Potato, 153
  Lima Bean, 163
  Macroni, 163
  Meat Ball, 163, 164, 171
  Meat Loaf, 164
  Mushroom, 153
  Noodle, 166
  One Dish, 153
  Potato, 153, 159, 165, 167
  Raqout, 155, 159
  Rice, 167
  Seven Layer, 158, 167
  Six Layer, 152, 168
  Shepherd's Pie, 168
  Soup, 170
  Steak In Sauce, 168
  Stew, 159, 167, 169, 172
  Stuffed Peppers, 164, 169
  Tomato, 154
  Tamale, Pie, 170
  Taglarrina, 170
  Veal, 171
  Wild Rice, 172
Pork, 172-174
  Canadian Bacon, 173
  Corn Chowder, 173
  Mushroom 174
  Potato, 173
  Sauerkraut, 174
  Scallop, 174
Ham, 174-177
  Asparagus, 174, 175
  Broccoli, 175
  Corn, 175
  Green Bean, 175
  Noodle, 176
  Lettuce, 177
  Potato, 176, 177
  Scalloped, 177
Sausage, 177-179
  Apple Pork and Beans, 177

Meat-Vegetable Casseroles, continued
  Corn, 178
  Lentil, 178
  Lima, 178
  Potato, 179
  Sweet Potato, 179
  Zucchini, 179
Spareribs, 179
  Lima Bean, 179
Poultry, 180
Chicken, 180-183
  Almond, 180
  Artichoke, 180
  Biscuit, 181
  Buffet, 180
  Cheese, 180
  Corn, 181
  Divan, 181
  Fried, 183
  Green Bean, 183
  Loaf, 182
  Noodle, 182
  Polynesian, 182
  Savory, 182
  Terrazin, 182
  Tetrazzini, 183
Turkey, 184
Seafood, 184

Poultry Casseroles, 59-86
Chicken, 60-83
  A La King, 81
  Almond, 74
  Apple, 75
  Baked, 74
  Barbecued, 74
  Breast, 74, 75
    Wine, 76
  Biscuits, 79
  Cheese, 75, 76
  Crunch, 76
  Creamed, 79
  Curry, 80
  Dressing, 60
  Glorified, 79
  Hawaiian, 80
  Honey, 80
  Hot Chicken Salad, 61
  Hot Dish, 77
  Macaroni, 62
  Noodle, 63
    A La King, 63
    Almond, 63
    Baked, 63
    Cheddar, 64
    Chow Mein, 65
    Creamed, 65
    Finale, 64
    Gravy, 64
    Tetrazzini, 65
  Orange Glazed, 81
  Pimento, 77
  Rice, 65
    Almond, 65
    Baked, 66, 67
    Chow Mein, 66, 69
    Club, 68
    Curry, 67
    Mushrooms, 68
    Oriental, 68
    Piquant, 70
    Scallop, 68, 71
    Sour Cream, 71
    Whole, 71
    Wild Rice, 72, 73
  Scalloped, 78, 81, 82, 83
  Souffle, 80
  Soup, 78
  Spoonbread, 79
  Spaghetti, 73
  Timbale, 78
  Wine, 79
Turkey Casseroles, 83-86
  Chow Mein 85
  Holiday, 85
  Loaf, 85
  Pressed, 83
  Scallop, 84
  Souffle, 85
  Stroganoff, 85
  Tetrazzini, 86

Seafood Casseroles, 113-150
  Clam, 114
  Combination Seafood
    Casseroles 147-150
  Crab, 114-117
    Artichoke, 114
    Chasseur, 115

Seafood Casseroles, continued

    Cheese, 114
    Cornbread, 117
    Deviled, 116
    Lobster, 147
    Mushroom, 115
    Shrimp, 147
    Souffle, 115
Haddock, 117
Halibut, 117
Lobster, 118-119
    Artichoke, 118
    Mushroom, 119
    Pie, 119
    Stuffed, 119
Oysters, 119-121
    Au Gratin, 120
    Corn, 120, 121
    Pudding, 120
    Scalloped, 120, 121
Salmon, 121-125
    Baked, 121
    Creole, 122
    Cheee, 123
    Deviled, 122
    Lasagna, 123
    Loaf, 123
    Macaroni, 122
    Mushroom, 122
    Noodle, 124
    Rice, 121, 124
    Scalloped, 124
    Shell, 124
    Souffle, 124
    Tetrazzini, 124
    Tuna, 148
Scallops, 125
Shrimp, 125-130
    Cheese, 127
    Chinese Fried Rice, 125
    Corn, 125
    Creole, 125, 126
    Deviled, 126
    Macaroni, 126
    Noodle, 130
    Rice, 129
    Sweet and Pungent, 130
    Tomato, 129
    Tuna, 149, 150
    Wild Rice, 127
Sole, 130-131
    Greek, 131
    Rice, 130
    Tapioca Dressing, 150
    Trout, 131
Tuna, 131
    Apple, 144
    AuGratin, 145
    Cashew, 142
    Chip, 141, 145
    Chopstick, 141
    Cheese, 142, 144
    Chinese, 142
    Chow Mein, 145, 146
    Festive, 142
    Green Pepper, 146
    India Curry Sauce, 147
    Lemon, 146
    Macaroni, 131, 133
    Noodles, 133-136
    Olive, 143
    Oriental, 143
    Peas, 141
    Potato Chip, 143
    Rice, 137-138
    Salmon, 148
    Saucy, 143
    Scalloped, 143, 144
    Shrimp, 149, 150

Seafood Casseroles, continued

    Vegetable, 138-140
    Versatile Seafood, 150

Skillet Meals, 218-234

Ala Pilaf, 233
Beef, 218-220
    American Chow Mein, 218
    Austrian, 218
    Bacon, 220
    Bowf A La Mode, 219
    Rice, 219
    Sour Cream, 218
    Stroganoff, 218, 219
    Stew, 220
    Tenderloin, 219
    Veal, 218
Busy Day Supper, 225
Chinaman Pie, 226
Ground-Beef, 220-228
    Bean 'N' Beef, 226
    Beef A Ronie, 220
    Hamburger, 226
    Macaroni, 221
    Meal In One, 227
    Meat Ball, 228
    Mexican, 227
    Noodle, 222
    Rice, 223
        Chop Suey, 223
        Spanish, 223
        Stroganoff, 223
        Vosta Cua, 224
    Spaghetti, 224
        Bean, 225
        Jute, 224
        Italian, 224
        Meat Balls, 225
        Savory Sauce, 225
        Spicy, 225
    Stew, 228
Kidney Bean, 233
    Pork, 228-231
        American Chop Suey, 229
        Asparagus, 230
        Bacon Macaroni, 228
        Dutch, 230
        Rice, 230
        Sausage, 229
        Spanish, 231
        Spanish Rice, 229
        Sweet Sour, 230
        Tomato, 231
        Wine, 231
    Poultry, 231-232
        Chicken, 231
        Tetrazzini, 232
        Turkey, 232
    Rice Dish, 233
        Red Beans and Rice, 233
        Shrimp, 234
        Spaghetti, 234
    Tuna, 234

Variety Meat Casseroles, 97-112

Corned Beef, 98-100
    Asparagus, 98
    Eggs, 98
    Hash, 99, 100
    Lima Bean, 99
    Macaroni, 100
    Mushroom, 100
    Noodle, 98
    Potato, 100

Variety Meat Casseroles, continued

    Peas, 100
    Piminto, 100
Dried Beef, 101-103
    Au Gratin, 101
    Cauliflower, 101
    Corn, 101
    Egg, 102
    Layered, 102
    Noodles, 103
    Peas, 103
    Vegetable, 103
Frankfurter, 103-105
    Barbecued, 103
    Cabbage, 104
    Corn Stuffing, 103
    Hot Dog, 104
    Potato Salad, 104
    Mixed Bean, 105
    Tarter Dogs, 105
Heart, 105
Kidney, 106
Liver, 106-108
    Apple, 107
    Chicken, 106
    Braised, 106
    Potato, 107
    Rice, 107
    Vegetable, 108

Vegetable Casseroles, 185-216

Artichoke, 186-187
Asparagus, 186
Baked Bean, 188-189
    Brown Sugar, 188
    Fiesta, 188
    Old-Fashioned, 189
    Pork and Beans, 189
    Sweet Sour, 188, 216
Beet, 189
Broccoli, 189-190
Brussels Sprouts, 191
    Yams, 191
Cabbage, 191-192
Carrot, 192-193
    Au Gratin, 192
    Buffet Scalloped, 192
    Cheese, 193
    Pinwheel, 214
    Zesty, 193
Cauliflower, 193
Celery, 194
Corn, 194-195
Eggplant, 196-198
Green Bean, 198-202
Green Peas, 202-203
Green Pepper, 203-204
Hominy, 204
Lima Bean, 204-206
Okra, 206
Onion, 206
Potato, 207-209
Sauerkraut, 209
Soybean, 209
Spinach, 209-210
Squash, 210-211
Sweet Potato, 212-213
Tomato, 213-214
Turnip, 214

The cookbooks selected for this special offering have been the five most requested titles from the Favorite Recipes of Home Economic Teachers series.

Favorite Recipes® Press

In 1961, Favorite Recipes Press was created in Montgomery, Alabama, by Millard Fuller and Morris Dees. These two gentlemen created the company to fund their college educations, becoming very successful in the cookbook world. Both sold their interests in the company to Southwestern/Great American and went on to found nationally known organizations—Fuller founded Habitat for Humanity International, and Dees was founder and director of the Southern Poverty Law Center. For more than a decade, Favorite Recipes Press along with the Home Economics Teachers of America published the best-selling cookbook series, Favorite Recipes of Home Economic Teachers—these books were sold nationally by the home economics departments and educators as a fund-raiser for their programs. Almost half a century later these cookbooks are still considered by many as the one set of cookbooks every cook should have.

Favorite Recipes of Home Economic Teachers

.INC

FRP creates successful connections between organizations and individuals through custom books.

 Favorite Recipes® Press

Favorite Recipes Press, an imprint of FRP, Inc., located in Nashville, Tennessee, is one of the nation's best-known and most respected cookbook companies. Favorite Recipes Press began by publishing cookbooks for its parent company, Southwestern/Great American, in 1961. FRP, Inc., is now a wholly owned subsidiary of the Southwestern/Great American family of companies, and under the Favorite Recipes Press imprint has produced hundreds of custom cookbook titles for nonprofit organizations, companies, and individuals.

Other FRP, Inc., imprints include

 BECKON BOOKS    The Booksmith Group
A DIVISION OF FRP   **Community**Classics®

Additional titles published by FRP, Inc., are

Almost Homemade   *Recipes Worth Sharing*   *The Vintner's Table*

Junior Leagues
In the Kitchen
with Kids:
Everyday Recipes
& Activities for
Healthy Living

The Illustrated
Encyclopedia of
American Cooking

Cooking Up a
Classic Christmas

My Favorite Recipes,
A Recipe Journal

To learn more about custom books, visit our Web site, www.frpbooks.com.